ROUTLEDGE LIBRARY EDITIONS: SOCRATES

Volume 2

SOCRATES, MAN AND MYTH

SOCRATES, MAN AND MYTH
The Two Socratic Apologies of Xenophon

ANTON-HERMANN CHROUST

LONDON AND NEW YORK

First published in 1957 by Routledge & Kegan Paul Ltd.

This edition first published in 2019
by Routledge
2 Park Square, Milton Park, Abingdon, Oxon OX14 4RN

and by Routledge
711 Third Avenue, New York, NY 10017

Routledge is an imprint of the Taylor & Francis Group, an informa business

© 1957 Routledge & Kegan Paul Ltd.

All rights reserved. No part of this book may be reprinted or reproduced or utilised in any form or by any electronic, mechanical, or other means, now known or hereafter invented, including photocopying and recording, or in any information storage or retrieval system, without permission in writing from the publishers.

Trademark notice: Product or corporate names may be trademarks or registered trademarks, and are used only for identification and explanation without intent to infringe.

British Library Cataloguing in Publication Data
A catalogue record for this book is available from the British Library

ISBN: 978-1-138-61842-8 (Set)
ISBN: 978-0-429-45011-2 (Set) (ebk)
ISBN: 978-1-138-61852-7 (Volume 2) (hbk)
ISBN: 978-1-138-61857-2 (Volume 2) (pbk)
ISBN: 978-0-429-46116-3 (Volume 2) (ebk)

Publisher's Note
The publisher has gone to great lengths to ensure the quality of this reprint but points out that some imperfections in the original copies may be apparent.

Disclaimer
The publisher has made every effort to trace copyright holders and would welcome correspondence from those they have been unable to trace.

SOCRATES MAN AND MYTH

The Two Socratic Apologies of Xenophon

by
ANTON-HERMANN CHROUST

Routledge & Kegan Paul
LONDON

First published 1957
© by Routledge & Kegan Paul Ltd.
Broadway House, Carter Lane, E.C.4
Printed in Great Britain
by Butler & Tanner Ltd.
Frome and London

TO
R

Contents

	PREFACE	xi
1	THE GENERAL NATURE OF XENOPHON'S SOCRATICA	1
2	XENOPHON'S DEFENCE OF SOCRATES BEFORE HIS JUDGES	17
3	XENOPHON'S MEMORABILIA 1.1.1–1.2.64	44
4	POLYCRATES' Κατηγορία Σωκράτους	69
5	THE ANTISTHENIAN ELEMENTS IN THE TWO APOLOGIES OF XENOPHON	101
6	THE ANTISTHENIAN ELEMENTS IN THE Κατηγορία Σωκράτους OF POLYCRATES	135
7	THE POLITICAL ASPECTS OF THE SOCRATIC PROBLEM	164
8	CONCLUSIONS AND IMPLICATIONS	198
	NOTES	227
	INDEX	325

'If from the proofs I have submitted anyone should be convinced that things were, on the whole, as I have described them, instead of believing what either poets have said of them in terms of exaggeration, or what some storytellers have composed in a language more attractive to the ear than truthful (their subjects admitting of no proof and most of them, through the long passage of time, having come to be regarded as fabulous), and if he should consider that, allowing for their antiquity, these things have been sufficiently ascertained from the most certain data—if he should do all this he would most certainly not be mistaken in his opinion.'

THUCYDIDES 1.21

Preface

THE PURPOSE OF THIS BOOK is to make a critical analysis of the controversial Socratic problem. The Socratic issue owes its paramount difficulty not only to the present status of available source materials, but also to the radical diversity of opinion as to the proper use of these materials. Karl Joël (*Geschichte der antiken Philosophie* 1.731) is fully justified when, referring to present-day Socratic research, he remarked that the famous Socratic dictum, 'I know only that I know nothing', could be applied most appropriately to the problem of the historical Socrates itself. Hence the present author need not apologize either for adding just another work to the existing plethora of Socratic literature, or for having failed to discover the 'definitely historical' Socrates. He believes, nevertheless, that his approach to the problem offers perhaps a few novel suggestions which may deserve some attention and, it is hoped, some further scholarly investigations. The present author, who is not a philosopher, is also fully aware of the possibility that some of his hypothetical theories will meet with strong objections from those who, after having made up their minds about Socrates, have tried to compare the latter to Christ.

That the Socratic problem constitutes a historical issue of the first magnitude and, hence, a source problem in the true sense of the term, is known to all who refuse to submit to uncritical dogmatism or pseudo-authority. The mere fact that Plato, Xenophon, or Aristotle ascribes to Socrates certain sayings or doings, in itself means little to the critical historian who always doubts the historical reliability of ancient philosophers or writers. And this for a very good reason: because it is exactly the testimony of the ancient philosophers and writers which has turned the Socratic problem into an almost futile issue.

The impact which Socrates and the Socratic problem has had upon Western thought is beyond all comprehension. Since it is a lasting and nearly ever-present concern both of philosophers and historians, the problem of the historical Socrates has succeeded in becoming completely buried under an avalanche of *Socratica*, all of which, whether written by a competent scholar or by an incompetent but enthusiastic dilettante, have merely helped to make Socrates a hopelessly elusive if not completely legendary figure.

Preface

We can only point with any real conviction to the facts that Socrates lived; that he was called Socrates; that the name of his father was Sophroniscus while that of his mother was Phaenarete; that he belonged to the *deme* Alopece; that he was an Athenian citizen; that he probably participated in some military campaigns; that he was connected with the trial of the generals in 406; that he was tried and condemned to death; and that he died in 399. Aside from these meagre facts, qualified Socratic scholarship has only succeeded in unearthing more and ever greater difficulties concerning the historical Socrates. What had been accepted only yesterday as a satisfactory scholarly solution of the Socratic problem is being rejected today as fantastic and untenable. And probably today's attempts at a new intelligent answer to this problem will be discarded tomorrow as illusory and without scientific foundation in fact.

It is not the purpose of this book to dissect the Socratic problem in a spirit of destructive pedantry or negative criticism. But neither are we interested merely in recapitulating once more the old Socratic myths, no matter how attractive they may be to an unbound poetic aesthete. In this sense, and in this only, is the present work animated by a spirit of iconoclasm. Still less are we inclined to add just another legend to the already ample store of Socratic legends. The purpose of this book is to penetrate the veil of Socratic fictions and thus reach the level of factual history—if this is at all possible. For if history or historical research has any meaning whatsoever, it signifies the establishment of facts and not myths.

The quest for the historical Socrates, it seems, has shown so far that the closer we adhere to the textual tradition about Socrates, the more it becomes obvious that we know very little about Socrates. This is rather surprising in view of the fact that the historical period in which Socrates lived is fairly well understood, not only as to its general trends, but also as to many detailed events. The particular role, however, which Socrates played in this period is quite indefinite, despite the fact that so much has been written about him. This paradoxical situation permits of only one intelligent interpretation. Whenever we possess an ample literary tradition about a certain historical personality, but are yet unable successfully to reconstruct the historicity of this person, we are compelled to assume that this whole literary tradition never really intended to concern itself with historical reporting of fact. We must surmise, therefore, that this tradition was aimed primarily at creating a legend or fiction. Hence we may also claim that the literary Socrates is essentially a legendary Socrates. He is above all a legend or the product of a legend, created by a host of myth-makers who, like all fiction writers, wove a fabric of myths around some historical facts in which the latter became completely submerged. This should also explain why the many ancient *Socratica*, on the whole, lack truly convincing force, and why there is so much fundamental disagreement among competent Socratic scholars

Preface

over the 'philosophy' of Socrates. In their efforts to resurrect the historical Socrates, these scholars were guided by the highest standards of scholarship and scholarly integrity. But they seem to have overlooked one important fact: barring a few and very meagre data, there exist no reliable reports on Socrates. As a consequence, they confused and identified historical fact with fiction and legend.

Of course, the Socratic legend is not completely devoid of some foundation in history and historical fact. But this in itself does not entitle us to elevate the Socratic legend to the level of historiography, not even under the overt or implied pretext that this legend constitutes a 'superior kind of historiography' which aspires to a 'higher type of truth' in that it employs allegedly 'more beautiful means' in reconstructing the past than the unimaginative methods of the trained historian. Such irrelevant apologies of the myth-makers, with their appeal to 'profounder vision', 'more adequate understanding', 'aesthetic comprehension of fact', or 'synthetic appreciation of a situation', have made the task of the critical historian a difficult and thankless one.

That a man called Socrates lived, will not be disputed; that this man Socrates was a somewhat unusual person may be gathered from the fact that he became the central figure of an important and sporadically brilliant type of ancient literature. But the true reasons or facts which may have impelled the Socratic authors to make him the central figure in many of their most important writings, can no longer be ascertained from this Socratic literature, although we may occasionally gain a glimpse of some of these facts. In a certain way the Socrates of the Socratic tradition is as indefinite and indeterminate as a great event of which we are aware somehow, but which we cannot define properly.

The true historian, upon approaching the Socratic problem, is confronted with the desperately difficult task not only of ascertaining what is fact and what is fiction in this problem, but also of contrasting fact and fancy. By proceeding in this manner he will soon realize that the extant ancient *Socratica* are not historiography or biography, but rather poetry or fabula. Hence these *Socratica* must be understood and interpreted in the light of those principles which apply to poetry rather than history and historiography.

The Socratic source situation confronts us with two major issues: the historical Socrates and the Socratic tradition. No competent contemporary ancient historiographer has really dealt with the historical Socrates from the point of view of the historian. The Socratic tradition, in respect to its volume and literary importance, however, is extremely great. As has already been pointed out, from its very inception this tradition was intended to be fiction and nothing else. We cannot, therefore, claim any reliable ancient text or texts with the help of which we could formulate a definition of the historical Socrates. Nevertheless, throughout these fictions there is at least some historical truth which might

Preface

perhaps be culled from the general flood of legendary *Socratica*. Such an undertaking, it seems, would require that we concentrate on the Socratic reporter or reporters rather than on Socrates himself. These reporters, it must be admitted, are men of a great variety of talents and inclinations who, each in the light of his own temperament or prejudice, have made their characteristic contributions to the general Socratic legend. Hence their different *Socratica* are of a varying quality, often prompted and determined by personal preferences and individual motivations. The result of this particular insight is that, although we are unable to understand Socrates as the 'teacher' of the Socratics, we are in a position to determine that Socrates is the central subject of a great many *Socratica*. And this determination, in turn, provides us with an opportunity to gain at least a glimpse of what the historical Socrates might have been.

For his particular subject the author has chosen some of the *Socratica* ascribed to Xenophon, which he intends to subject to the procedures indicated above. Here, too, he is fully aware of the fact that these Xenophontean *Socratica* are primarily part of the general Socratic legend. They are, on closer analysis, legend in a dual sense: the accounts of Xenophon as regards the sayings and doings of Socrates are in themselves legend; and the materials on which he bases his own brand of Socratic legend are likewise part of an older Socratic legend or legends.

It is well-nigh impossible to measure one's indebtedness to all those scholars whose labours, ideas, hypotheses (and even errors—if this term applies at all to the Socratic problem) have contributed directly or indirectly to the solution of the extremely difficult questions connected with our subject. Hence, citations from the more recent authors of *Socratica* have been kept at a minimum. The present writer hopes, however, that he has not failed to make the proper acknowledgment wherever due. Because of the immense number of works on Socrates and the great variety of their scholarly value, it is a hopeless task to add a special bibliography to this book. Those who wish to check the Socratic literature should consult P. K. Bizoukides, Ἐπιστημονικαὶ πηγαὶ περὶ Σωκράτους (Leipzig, 1921), a work which collates a nearly complete alphabetical list of all *Socratica* published before 1921; and V. de Magalhâes-Vilhena, *Le problème de Socrate: le Socrate historique et le Socrate de Platon* (Paris, 1952), pp. 471–566.

In conclusion the author wishes to thank his many friends both at Harvard and Notre Dame whose constructive criticism, suggestions, and encouragement have enabled him to bring this book to its conclusion. No simple words of acknowledgment, however, could properly express his feelings of gratitude and affection towards the one to whom this book is dedicated.

Notre Dame, Indiana, May 1957

1
The General Nature of Xenophon's Socratica

THE MAIN SOURCES from which we traditionally derive our information about Socrates and 'Socratic philosophy', are the *Socratica* of Xenophon, a few passages from the works of Aristotle, and the dialogues of Plato, particularly the earliest dialogues. To this we may add a host of what for a long time have been considered 'inferior' and, hence, 'less reliable' sources: a few passages from some of the late fifth-century comedians, as well as certain fragmentary reports or allusions which can be credited to a considerable number of allegedly 'minor' Socratic witnesses.

Since the Aristotelian testimony, on the whole, may be discarded as essentially useless,[1] the primary Socratic source problem seems to be reduced to two apparently irreconcilable testimonials: the *Socratica* of Plato and those of Xenophon. In view of the seriously conflicting nature of these two reports, it has become a common, although singularly ineffective, practice of the scholar to turn to Xenophon for additional help or needed correction of Plato's testimony; or to call on Plato for some assistance in reaching the 'proper' understanding of Xenophon's accounts. If he should still be dissatisfied with these two sources, or doubtful about his findings, he could always turn away from both Plato and Xenophon and seek help from every other informant or source of information available: from Aristotle and the Peripatetics; from Antisthenes; from Euclides; from Aeschines; from Aristippus; from the many exponents of those schools which called themselves, or were called, 'Socratic schools'; from biographers; from commentators; from philosophers; and from historians. He may even consult a host of modern critics and authors. But whenever in his quest for the historical Socrates the scholar turns away from Plato and Xenophon (and perhaps even from Aristotle, who for a long time has been credited by some people with having a 'superior' understanding of Socrates), as a rule he does so with the definitely prejudiced feeling of a man who is exchanging what to him appears to be the only creditable sources for something which he considers much less reliable and certain. But this feeling is probably his most serious error. For in so doing he evidences his conviction that Plato and Xenophon—each perhaps corrected by the other—unmistakably contain the historical Socrates; and that the real problem is simply to 'lift' the historical Socrates as well as the 'true' philosophy of Socrates from these two sources.

Schleiermacher, despite the many and at times basic discrepancies which separate the accounts of Plato from those of Xenophon, still believed that Plato and Xenophon were reporting on the historical Socrates. He hoped to solve this conflicting source situation by asking the following question, which to him apparently became fundamental to the whole solution of the Socratic issue: what *could* Socrates have been above and beyond the testimony of Xenophon, provided such a query would not destroy the basic traits of character which Xenophon had definitely declared to be Socratic—and what *must* Socrates really have been so as to inspire and justify a Plato for making him the actual spokesman in the majority of his dialogues?[2] This rather rhetorical question of Schleiermacher, despite the fact that its practical application offers more puzzling and seemingly insoluble difficulties than real solutions, has become something of a canon with many scholars whenever they have tried to deal with the problem of the historical Socrates and his philosophy.[3]

It appears, however, that on account of his artistic temperament and talents, as well as strongly self-revelatory individualism, Plato is further away from the hard facts of historical reality than some of the other Socratic witnesses. In addition, nowhere in the many extant *Socratica* does the intertwining of what may be Socratic ideas and the individuality of the witness seem to be more complete than in the dialogues of Plato. This situation, which must be credited above all to the literary excellence of Plato, resists most stubbornly all scholarly efforts to separate Socrates from Plato. Hence the further question arises, namely, whether the Platonic Socrates is not predominantly a 'literary Socrates' rather than the historical Socrates. In addition, the attempt to solve the Socratic issue solely through reliance on Plato's testimony is tantamount to linking the desperately difficult Socratic problem to the extremely involved general Platonic problem. Needless to say, the uncertainty about some major passages in the Platonic dialogues would seriously affect the solution of the Socratic question. The necessity in this case of submitting the Socratic question to the same philosophical, historical, literary, and philological tests which are essential to the proper interpretation of Plato's works, should further complicate the search after the historical Socrates. And there is no guarantee that despite all these efforts, the Platonic Socrates would prove to be the historical Socrates, or even a remote facsimile of the historical Socrates.[4]

Plato's literary mastery, in its artistic perfection, tends to obliterate the many component elements or motives which are at the basis of his

The General Nature of Xenophon's Socratica

Socratica. Thus it becomes an extremely difficult task also to ascertain the sources as well as the influences which prompted him to create his particular Socrates. In this, Plato, the artist, is somewhat akin to an expert mason who, by polishing down a wall with such perfection that the individual component stones are no longer discernible, succeeds in creating the impression of a single uniform structure. Naturally, in this polishing process the various component stones or elements are also considerably altered, until it becomes nearly impossible to recognize their original size and shape. And the same holds true as regards the various elements that went into the Platonic Socrates.

Xenophon, on the other hand, definitely lacks the literary skill and perfection of a Plato. The many and various component elements of his *Socratica* as well as the background, influences, and motives behind the specifically Xenophontean Socrates, therefore, to some extent can still be recognized because they are frequently left in their original significance or connotations. This, in turn, occasionally permits us to trace them back to their origin and the particular context from which they have been taken. Such being the case, the *Socratica* of Xenophon offer the promise of some definite success in establishing, not what the historical Socrates actually had been—this would be too much to expect —but what he probably might not have been.

Aside from his own rather narrow outlook, Xenophon, it should be borne in mind, never could give, and probably never intended to give the reader a complete and unbiased report on the historical Socrates. His prolonged absence from Athens during some of what may be considered perhaps the most crucial years in the life of Socrates, made it impossible for him to father any first-hand information about Socrates. In consequence, he had to rely on some informant whose historical reliability, however, is likewise open to challenge. Hence all those reports and passages which are introduced with an indefinite λέγεται (it is said)[5] must be used with extreme caution.

The most crucial issue connected with the whole of the Xenophontean *Socratica* concerns the truthfulness and objectivity of Xenophon as a reporter. This particular problem may be briefly stated in the following queries: Did Xenophon really intend to write a historio-biographical report on Socrates? Or did he compose his *Socratica* (*Memorabilia, Defence, Symposium,* and *Economicus*) merely in order to advance, in the name of Socrates, his own ideas and convictions?[6] For the Socratic conversations recorded by Xenophon frequently appear to be nothing other than vehicles of Xenophon's admitted fondness for displaying his literary gifts or for propagating his personal convictions, philosophy of life, and views about a great many things in general. The second question may also be posed in the following manner: To what extent, if at all, does Xenophon, who was definitely a dramatizing witness, consciously or unconsciously impute himself to his 'hero' Socrates?

The General Nature of Xenophon's Socratica

Was he at all aiming at historical truth, or was he primarily interested in devising what strikes us as being a quaint combination of panegyrical and self-revelatory efforts? When answering this particular query, which also touches upon the basic problem of Xenophon's historical reliability, we have also to take into consideration a fact of decisive importance: the strikingly low intellectual level of most of the Socratic discourses. Whenever feasible, Xenophon adopts a frequently unconvincing apologetic tone, creating thereby, among other things, the impression that Socrates must have been a much over-rated individual. The Socrates of Xenophon, to be sure, impresses us as a man prompted by the best of intentions. But, like his author, he appears to be mentally incapable of stating anything more than numerous and boring commonplaces, or even of saying them with any convincing vigour. And finally, we may ask the following question: Did Xenophon, for reasons which are yet to be established, purposely falsify certain facts about Socrates? For this much seems to be certain: as regards much of their content, both the Xenophontean *Socratica* and the other philosophical writings of Xenophon frequently appear to be identical. One has only to compare, for instance, the general characterization of Socrates and that of King Agesilaus,[7] or the Xenophontean explanation for the human greatness of a Socrates and for the distinguished position which Lacedaemon held among the Greek cities.[8] And the same may be said about the character of King Cyrus, which seems to be essentially the same as that ascribed to Socrates, Agesilaus, or Lycurgus.[9] All this would compel us to assume that the characterization or description of Socrates in the Xenophontean *Socratica* is not a truthful description of Socrates but rather an 'ideal' or 'ideal pattern' of a man—ideal from the viewpoint of a Xenophon—which the latter imputes to any person who has caught his fancy or whom he admires.[10]

It appears that the view which holds that the Xenophontean *Socratica* possess, at best, only extremely limited, not to say peculiar, historical source significance or biographical value, is by now generally accepted,[11] notwithstanding some intrepid scholars who still maintain that the Socrates sketched by Xenophon is the historical Socrates.[12] The questionable objectivity of Xenophon as a historiographer or biographer in general becomes manifest, among other things, in the partiality with which he extols Clearchus and Proxenus in his *Anabasis*, and disparages Menon and Neon. His many encomia of Cyrus the Younger purposely fail to record some of the less attractive traits and deeds of Cyrus. Beginning with Book III of the *Anabasis* we are made to believe that Xenophon is the guiding spirit, the one great general of the whole retreat. But Diodorus, who probably uses a more objective source (Sophaenetus ?), never mentions Xenophon even once in connection with this widely known event.[13] Barring a few and what seem to be exceptional instances, the historical veracity and objectivity of the

The General Nature of Xenophon's Socratica

Hellenica has been severely criticized by nearly all competent scholars.[14] Our knowledge and understanding of the events which transpired during this epoch would have to be called deplorable if we had to rely solely on the accounts found in the *Hellenica*. These few examples may suffice to demonstrate beyond all doubt that, on the whole, Xenophon is a most unreliable reporter. Nevertheless, his specific testimony as regards Socrates, particularly on account of his limited artistic and philosophical aptitude, permits us to draw certain important inferences from his *Socratica* which might bring us a little closer to the historical Socrates or to some solution of the many problems connected with Socrates and especially with the Socratic literature.

It will be shown later that *Memorabilia* 1.1.1–1.2.64 originally were published or, at least, intended as an independent Socratic *Apology*. This fact would explain the argumentative nature and form of this particular part of the *Memorabilia*, as contrasted with the remainder of this work which is made up preponderantly of Socratic discourses and 'conversations'. If we accept the theory that *Memorabilia* 1.1.1–1.2.64 originally constituted a separate essay—and there exists no good reason why this should be rejected—then we would still have to refute the contention that the whole of the Xenophontean *Memorabilia* was meant to be historiography and biography. For such a contention could, with some restrictions, apply only to the apologetic part of the *Memorabilia*, but certainly not to the remainder of the work.

With the exception of chapters 1 and 2 of Book I, the *Memorabilia* are, according to their author, partly accounts of what Xenophon prefers to call his personal and intimate recollections, and partly the experiences of other witnesses which he has collated in what appears to be a most haphazard manner. It would perhaps be more appropriate, therefore, to call the second part of this work a 'Collection of λόγοι Σωκρατικοί',[15] rather than 'Memoirs'. As a matter of fact, one of the most striking features of this 'Collection' is the obvious lack of an orderly and articulate arrangement in which this bewildering host of materials of varying significance and value has been assembled. We are left with the impression that the whole *Memorabilia* could neither have been the result of one single uniform draft, nor have been edited by Xenophon himself. For otherwise he would most certainly have noticed himself that *Memorabilia* 1.4.1–9, and *Memorabilia* 4.3.1–18, for instance, are merely two different versions of one and the same topic. Hence we may also surmise that the *Memorabilia*, at least in the form in which they have been handed down, constitute an 'anthology' of notes and literary curios jotted down on different occasions and perhaps intended to serve as materials for a later and more integrated publication.[16]

The form alone in which the 'Socratic conversations' in the second part of the *Memorabilia* have been recorded by Xenophon would suggest that they are to a large degree literary improvisations, if not 'inventions'. No one will seriously deny that some of these discourses may contain an historical element or *residuum*, based perhaps on some genuine reminiscence. But the larger part of the *Memorabilia*, both as regards detail and scope, is not Socratic, but rather 'Xenophontean'. And if Xenophon should have felt free to distort or invent the details and the particular scope of his 'Socratic stories' by adding in a rather wilful manner some of his own ideas, why, then, should he suddenly become scrupulous about some 'basic occurrence' ascribed to Socrates? And there is some probability that this 'basic occurrence' was also invented by Xenophon merely to introduce some 'Xenophontean detail' in the name of Socrates. It appears, therefore, that nearly everywhere Xenophon relies on his inventive powers in order to supplement his obviously defective knowledge about the historical Socrates. Naturally, it could always be argued that the substance of the many Socratic discourses recorded by Xenophon has an historical source, although the latter is overlaid with a host of spurious detail for which we must blame the rather fertile imagination of Xenophon. Such an argument, however, overlooks one important fact: invariably the method of argumentation introduced by the Xenophontean Socrates amounts to nothing other than a rather crude effort of asking leading questions merely for the sake of arriving in a round-about fashion at a cut and dried moral commonplace. This particular 'method', also employed in some of Xenophon's other writings, strikes us as being definitely a Xenophontean procedure. No doubt, Xenophon does not *always* wish to falsify the picture of Socrates, but it is rather mystifying that he should record so many commonplace conversations dealing with such limited and trivial topics. In his philosophical naïveté, Xenophon may very well have believed that Socrates, being a 'sensible man'—sensible from the point of view of Xenophon—would have held these opinions if he had seen fit to discuss them with others.

The Xenophontean *Memorabilia* are one example of that particular literary *genre* called forth by the prolonged and bitter controversy over Socrates, either to defame or to canonize him. In this controversy Xenophon, unlike Plato, chose the form of the narrative memoir. Originally, we must assume, he conceived his work as a rejoinder to the κατηγορία Σωκράτους of Polycrates. Since *Memorabilia* 1.1.1–1.2.64 are primarily determined by this famous anti-Socratic pamphlet, they were composed, as we have already pointed out, in a spirit of rebuttal and apologetic effort rather than portraiture. But as the work grew through the various stages of composition and emendation, Xenophon's original aim shifted gradually from mere refutation to a positive exposition through the use of such literary means as incidents, illustrative dialogues, or anecdotes. Xenophon does not attempt, however, to report the life of Socrates in a systematic manner, but rather to present the reader with a conglomerate of loosely associated glimpses into what he believed to be Socrates' thought on the ideals of human life, illustrated by examples of Socrates' alleged conversations with disciples and friends at what Xenophon considers the height of Socrates' philosophical maturity.[17]

Barring a few exceptions, it seems that in his *Socratica* Xenophon relies on some λόγοι Σωκρατικοί or Socratic *dicta* as they have been recorded or perhaps invented by others. Most likely he was prompted by the desire not only to imitate, but also to improve on some of the earlier *Socratica*.[18] This may be gathered from his own statement (*Memor.* 4.3.2): 'Others who were present on some particular occasions, have recorded the tenor of his [*scil.*, Socrates'] conversation. But I myself was present when he had a particular discussion with Euthydemus.'[19] Such words would also indicate that Xenophon derived the majority of his information from the recollections or, most likely, 'inventions' of others. But since he frequently refers to these 'Socratic conversations' in a manner suggesting that he had attended them personally, he seems to be intent upon creating the impression that he is speaking here of some personal and intimate experience.[20] This alone adds considerably to the difficulty of properly interpreting and accurately evaluating the Xenophontean testimony concerning the historical Socrates.

As a rule Xenophon never quotes his source of information.[21] He either speaks on his own 'authority', claiming that he 'knew' or 'had heard Socrates say', or he merely asserts that 'Socrates maintained'. *Memorabilia* 1.3.8 contain the only instance where Socrates personally addresses Xenophon in a conversation.[22] On two other occasions, namely, in the Xenophontean *Symposium* and on the occasion of a discussion which Socrates had with Euthydemus (*Memor.* 4.3.2), Xenophon insists on having been personally present. But, according to Richter, it is rather obvious that this particular conversation with Euthydemus could not have been held in the manner in which it is recorded by Xenophon and, hence, Xenophon could not possibly have attended it in person.[23] And the Xenophontean *Symposium*, in the opinion of most scholars, cannot be regarded as the authentic report of a participant.[24]

Xenophon introduces five Socratic conversations with the remark: 'I once heard (ἤκουσα δέ ποτε) Socrates state.'[25] Closer analysis should divulge, however, that these five conversations, which Xenophon maintains to have witnessed personally, are probably to a high degree fictitious.[26] In any event, the remark that he allegedly attended these incidents is no guarantee that they actually took place or that they happened in the manner in which Xenophon reports them. Finally, Xenophon prefaces some of his accounts of Socrates' conversations with such indefinite statements as 'I know', 'I heard', or 'I recall'.[27] The accounts thus introduced likewise inspire little confidence as to their authenticity or reliability. The overwhelming majority, if not all of the Socratic discourses recorded by Xenophon in his *Socratica*, it must be conceded, are primarily, though perhaps not completely, fabrications. And if we can attach any credence to Diogenes Laertius (2.65),[28] they would be intentional fictions. It could also be maintained that, aside from being fictitious, Socrates' alleged conversations contain obvious anachronisms. Socrates' discussion on the nature of justice with Aristippus (*Memor.* 2.1.1–34), for instance, could not possibly have taken place until long after the death of Socrates—until the hedonist system of Aristippus had been fully developed.

We would not be amiss if we were to remark that the Xenophontean *Socratica* are not so much the records of some first-hand experience or the accounts of some actual events, but rather the fanciful products of creative writing—his own as well as those of others.[29] In addition, among the many subjects which, according to Xenophon, Socrates allegedly discussed with his friends, there are a number of topics which we know were subjects highly favoured by Xenophon. To cite but a few examples: the lengthy, and seemingly quite competent discourse on the duties and qualifications of a good military commander or cavalry general, as well as the statements on military strategy or tactics in general with which Xenophon credits Socrates,[30] are as fanciful, not to say fictitious, as are the discussions on national economy[31] or politics,[32] likewise attributed to Socrates. Xenophon, the economist, planter, strategist, dog-breeder, historiographer, soldier, hunter—in short, Xenophon, the 'Jack-of-all-trades'—during his long and adventurous life became acquainted with a great variety of tasks connected with practical life. But the particular tasks with which he concerned himself so enthusiastically, in their diversity and detailedness, are really incompatible with the essential one-sidedness of any philosophical theory, and even more so with the one-sidedness of an intellectual theory such as Socrates, according to Xenophon's own testimony, allegedly expounded.[33]

In any event, *Memorabilia* 3.1–6, for instance, contain what must be regarded as typically Xenophontean ideas and views which he also expressed in his *Anabasis, Hellenica, Cyropaedia,* and *De vectigalibus*. Hence we have to admit that Xenophon's reports on Socrates are, in the main, not so much recollections of instances that actually happened as they are inventions.[34] Heinrich Maier states this problem exceedingly well when he insists that 'Xenophon did not hesitate also to incorporate in his characterization of Socrates the most diversified fruits of his acquaintance with the literature of his day'.[35] This is especially true as regards the many detailed and lengthy speeches or harangues which Xenophon imputes to Socrates. But this is not the place to point out in detail the various literary sources on which Xenophon relied for his *Socratica*. The fact that he made ample use of the writings or λόγοι Σωκρατικοί of Antisthenes,[36] Aristippus,[37] Aeschines,[38] Plato,[39] of the

The General Nature of Xenophon's Socratica

δίσσοι λόγοι,[40] as well as of the works of some other authors,[41] is commonly accepted and needs no further elaboration at this point.

It has been suggested that some of the Socratic discourses might have been reported to Xenophon by Lamprocles, Chaerecrates, and others. This suggestion is most unconvincing, unless we should be willing to assume that before leaving for Asia Minor Xenophon went about Athens for the sole purpose of gathering information about Socrates' discourses. But the mere retention of these many and frequently confusing details would have required a truly prodigious memory, not to mention the fact that at the time he allegedly did all this, he could as yet not possibly have had any notion that he would ever write his apologetic *Socratica*. Equally incredible is the assumption that some of the persons who had taken part in these Socratic conversations should have visited Xenophon in Asia Minor or Scillus, or should have sent him lengthy and minute accounts of their experiences with Socrates.[42]

Although Xenophon records a total of forty-nine Socratic conversations, he himself participates actively in only one of these discourses[43] which, it seems, is rather unimportant at that. If Xenophon actually was on intimate terms with Socrates (something which we doubt seriously) and, as would follow, had many opportunities to discuss a variety of philosophical questions with the latter, then it would be difficult to explain exactly why he should report this particular insignificant personal conversation. Is it possible that out of modesty he would have omitted to mention other personal conversations with Socrates? Knowing his pronounced vanity which, as is instanced by the *Anabasis*, often compelled him to exaggerate his own importance or achievements, we may dismiss this argument outright. Or were these 'other conversations' which he might have had with Socrates so insignificant as to warrant their omission?[44] But this too would be incompatible with the conceit of a Xenophon who could always 'retouch' the incident so as to make it appear important. Of the seven other conversations which Xenophon claims to have attended,[45] no less than four [46] and probably all seven are most likely spurious.[47]

With the single exception of *Symposium* 5.5, Xenophon never deigns to describe, comment upon, or characterize the person or persons who participate in his Socratic conversations. Neither does he introduce a large audience which joins in the discussion.[48] As if by pre-arrangement, the conversation always remains strictly a dialogue. In contrast to Plato, the topic of such a dialogue is often tackled without any introductory remarks whatsoever; and the person with whom Socrates converses is frequently not even named, thus remaining a nondescript 'someone'. All these minor 'flaws' in the *Socratica* of Xenophon certainly do not support his ambitious contention that he personally attended all these discussions, the more so, since in some of his other works he displays a certain ability for sketching personalities and their characters. He denies us even a small glimpse of the man Socrates, of his appearance, his mannerisms, and his relations with other people, especially his friends and 'disciples'. Aside from the trial, condemnation, and death of Socrates, Xenophon apparently remembers only the probably legendary clash between Socrates and Critias or Callicles (*Memor.* 1.2.31 ff.), the honourable conduct of Socrates during the trial of the generals (*Memor.* 4.4.2), and the case of Leon of Salamis (*Memor.* 4.4.3). But these 'incidents', if they are at all historical, were probably a matter of common knowledge rather than the prized personal recollections shared only by the close associates of Socrates. This extreme scantiness of concrete data on the life of Socrates might also be submitted as further evidence in support of our insistence that Xenophon's contention of having personally witnessed a number of Socratic conversations is most likely untrue and unfounded.

It may be argued, on the other hand, that the factual setting of, or circumstances surrounding, the various Socratic conversations and discussions are historical, while the specific content of these discourses remains fanciful.[49] But if we can attach any significance to Xenophon's statement contained in *Memorabilia* 1.3.1,[50] we must concede that, on the whole, Xenophon merely tries to demonstrate here as elsewhere how Socrates, through both his example and admonitions, has benefited his friends and associates. This particular passage, as Heinrich Maier has pointed out convincingly, is indicative of the strongly panegyrical nature of the Xenophontean *Socratica*.[51] As a matter of fact, it is quite apparent that these *Socratica* are meant primarily to be unrestrained encomia of Socrates, and nothing else. Throughout the *Memorabilia*, it must be admitted, Xenophon remains too much the apologetic panegyrist to be still regarded as a reliable or convincing historiographer and biographer.[52] For like any professional panegyrist he knows how to distort facts.[53] In consequence, even the few instances, where Xenophon refers to the factual setting in which the alleged Socratic discourses are cited, remain completely subordinate to this dominant eulogistic or apologetic purpose. This may be gathered, among other things, from the wording of the first chapter of the Xenophontean *Defence*: 'Many people have written on this subject [*scil.*, the μεγαληγορία or "high-mindedness" of Socrates] . . . but none of them has brought out clearly the fact that Socrates had come to regard death as something more desirable than life. . . .'[54]

Thus even the different factual settings or circumstances which, according to the accounts of Xenophon, surround the various Socratic discourses cannot be regarded as having much historical source value. And the same holds true as regards the various persons with whom Socrates converses on a number of philosophical or practical issues. The majority of these persons, like the situation in which the discussions occur, seem to have been either invented or, at least, arbitrarily substituted for others, or wantonly connected with the events related by Xenophon. To cite only a few instances: *Memorabilia* 3.7.1–9 contain a discussion between Socrates and a man called Charmides. Among the arguments advanced here by Socrates, we may discern no less than three ideas which apparently have been borrowed from an older Alcibiades dialogue.[55] Hence we may assume that Xenophon substitutes here Charmides for Alcibiades. The same substitution can be detected in Xenophon's *Symposium* (2.14 ff.), where a man called Charmides likewise seems to take the place of Alcibiades.[56] And in *Memorabilia* 4.2.1–40 we find an instance where a man called Euthydemus apparently substitutes for Alcibiades.[57] In *Memorabilia* 3.5.1–28 Socrates holds a political conversation with Pericles the Younger, which must be regarded as an anachronism pure and simple;[58] in *Memorabilia* 4.4.1–25 he discusses the nature of justice with Hippias; in *Memorabilia* 1.4.2–19 he argues with Aristodemus in favour of a more intelligent religion; in *Memorabilia* 1.6.1–15 he debates with Antiphon the propriety of taking any remuneration for teaching; in *Memorabilia* 2.1.1–34 he discusses with Aristippus the necessity of living within a politically organized society in order to achieve true happiness; in *Memorabilia* 2.3.1–19 he converses on brotherly love with the two brothers Chaerephon and Chaerecrates; in *Memorabilia* 2.5.1–5 he debates the nature of friendship with Antisthenes, while in *Memorabilia* 2.6.1–39 he argues the same subject with Critobolus; in *Memorabilia* 2.7.1–14 he discusses with Aristarchus the advantage of remunerative and constructive work, as he does in *Memorabilia* 2.8.1–5, where he addresses Eutherus; in *Memorabilia* 2.9.1–8 he advises the rich Crito; and in *Memorabilia* 2.10.1–4 he counsels the rich Diodorus. But we could go on citing many more instances of this sort.

In some of the instances just cited it is not too difficult to ascertain the ultimate reason or reasons why Xenophon did choose this or that particular partner for Socrates: aside from the ill-concealed fact that Xenophon employs these discussions and dialogues in order to bring out and underline more dramatically the καλοκαγαθία of Socrates,[59] he also essays here, through the medium of what seems to be fictitious Socratic dialogues, to propagate in the name of Socrates his own convictions and views as regards many a philosophical or practical problem. This is more than obvious in the Xenophontean *Oeconomicus*, but no less apparent in the remaining *Socratica* of Xenophon. Hence many, and perhaps all, of the Socratic discussions and discourses incorporated in the Xenophontean *Socratica*, notwithstanding the fact that they are imputed to Socrates, must be considered auto-biographical or self-revelatory statements of Xenophon, rather than reliable reports on the actual 'sayings and doings' of the historical Socrates. In order to pander some of his own practical counsels to his contemporaries and readers, Xenophon converted Socrates into a man of decidedly practical and pragmatic interests who appears not only to be conversant with every problem of life, but also capable of discussing all these problems with apparent competence and self-confidence. In this fashion the Xenophontean Socrates actually is made out to have been at times trivially dull, at times plainly homespun, and occasionally even an obtrusive schoolmaster or moralizing prattler of a very shallow bent of mind.

This does not mean, however, that Xenophon is always deliberately setting out to deceive the reader. Neither can he be accused of having set out to falsify always and intentionally the 'spirit' of Socrates. The problem is much more complex than that: Xenophon the encomiast would naturally portray a different Socrates than Xenophon the apologist, or Xenophon the man of many worldly interests who imputes himself to Socrates, or Xenophon the conceited literary dilettante who in his vanity tries to prove that Socrates is in full accord with his own ideas. Taking also into consideration the peculiar mentality of Xenophon, we must assume that he did not always act in bad faith when he pretended to portray faithfully Socrates and the 'spirit' of Socrates. The error to which Xenophon constantly succumbs is his determined effort of reducing his 'hero' Socrates to a level which is more acceptable and understandable to his rather restricted mentality and outlook on life in general.

Due to his rather adventurous early life, Xenophon, we are forced to assume, had only a vague and, at best, very fragmentary personal acquaintance with the historical Socrates. It is highly doubtful that he ever was a close associate of Socrates,[60] despite his claim to that distinction. The fact that Polycrates, in his κατηγορία Σωκράτους, failed to mention him as another famous example of Socrates' evil influence on his associates and disciples,[61] is certainly not without significance. Xenophon had been condemned for 'high treason' and banished from Athens shortly before the publication of the κατηγορία. Had he actually been one of the close associates of Socrates, as, for instance, Alcibiades and Critias had been, Polycrates surely would not have failed to refer to this most recent political 'outrage' perpetrated by a Socratic disciple or partisan—the treasonable conduct of Xenophon.

One particular occurrence in the life of Xenophon is of special interest to us here, since on this point depends our judgment that Xenophon's acquaintance with the Socratic controversy was sketchy and drawn from the accounts of others. The exact date of Xenophon's banishment from Athens and the true cause or causes of this incident are not fully known. Some hold that he was exiled around the year 399 for having participated in the ill-fated expedition of Cyrus the Younger against his brother and king Artaxerxes, the 'friend' of Athens. These scholars rely for their contention on Dio Chrysostom (*Oratio* 8.1), who states: 'Xenophon was banished owing to his expedition with Cyrus.' The report of Dio is also supported by Pausanias (5.6.5), who maintains

The General Nature of Xenophon's Socratica

that he 'was exiled by the Athenians for having taken part in the expedition against the Great King, their friend, with Cyrus who was the most bitter enemy of democracy'. And Diogenes Laertius (2.58), writing in epigram in honour of Xenophon, alleges: 'The descendants of Cecrops condemned thee, Xenophon, to exile on account of thy friendship for Cyrus.' But the same Diogenes Laertius also records (2.51) that 'about this time he [scil., Xenophon] was banished by the Athenians for siding in with Sparta'.[62] Diogenes Laertius seems to imply here that after the famous Retreat, that is, in the year 399, Xenophon turned over the survivors of the Retreat to the Spartan King Agesilaus. But this is definitely a historical blunder on the part of Diogenes Laertius, since Xenophon turned over part of his troops to Thibron, the Spartan commander in Asia Minor in the year 399, who was replaced the same year by Dercylidas, while Agesilaus assumed command only in the year 396. Hence it is not altogether clear whether by this phrase, 'about this time', Diogenes Laertius means the year 399 or 396. In addition, at this time Athens was a member of the Peloponnesian League and, hence, on friendly terms with Sparta, at least until the year 395 when she broke from Sparta and entered into an alliance with Thebes. It would hardly be correct, therefore, to say that Xenophon could have been accused of *laconism* before the year 395.

Although Diogenes Laertius in his usual fashion seems here to have badly garbled his sources of information, he would on the other hand also lend some support to those views which connect Xenophon's banishment with his participation in the battle of Coronea in the year 394, where he fought on the side of Sparta against Thebes, the ally of Athens. This may be the meaning of Diogenes' statement (2.51) that 'Xenophon sided in with Sparta'. The latter opinion finds additional support in Xenophon's own writings: 'He [scil., Xenophon] left that part of the world [scil., Asia Minor] together with Agesilaus on the march into Boeotia.... After his banishment... Magabazus... restored to him his deposit.'[63] This passage seems to indicate that Xenophon was banished after the year 394, and that the cause of his exile was his campaigning with Agesilaus against Thebes: 'He [scil., Xenophon] was making preparations to return him [scil., to Athens], for as yet the vote of banishment had not yet been passed at Athens.'[64] But we know that Xenophon made no preparations for returning to Europe until Agesilaus was called back to Greece in the year 394 in connection with the outbreak of the First Corinthian War. Hence, provided that this report contains reliable information, we must assume that the sentence of banishment was not passed until Xenophon had left Asia Minor in the year 394 in connection with the outbreak of the First Corinthian War.[65]

Since Xenophon could not possibly have been an eye-witness to the climax of the historical controversy over Socrates, that is, the trial and condemnation of Socrates, he had to rely on the reports extant. And in the relatively short period of time in which he might, if at all, have returned to Athens, he certainly would have been unable to become thoroughly acquainted with the facts as well as the general status of the whole controversy as it stood in the year 394/3. At this time the Polycratean and Antisthenian version of the Socratic problem seems to have been in vogue, and it is this 'vogue' to which he apparently fell victim. Hence the fact of Xenophon's exile and the particular date of this event, as an external circumstance, had probably a decisive influence on his version of the Socratic controversy or issue.

It is quite likely that, aside from Polycrates, the 'friends' as well as some other acquaintance of Socrates may also have refused to regard him as a true Socratic; they might even have looked upon him as an impostor. Hence it seems that, in order to escape this particular charge, Xenophon felt that he had to establish and stress the fact of his having been one of Socrates' close associates, entitled to speak with authority about Socrates. This is apparently the main reason behind his repeated claim that he had personally attended many of Socrates' discourses. But in his effort to prove that he is a fully qualified witness as well as competent authority on the Socratic question, Xenophon goes even further; he insinuates, as may be gathered from *Memorabilia* 1.4.1–2, that he was one of the more intimate friends of Socrates and apparently enjoyed his complete confidence: 'A belief is current, in accordance with views advanced by some about Socrates both in speech and writings—but in either case based on pure conjecture—that Socrates was eminently qualified to stimulate men to virtue as a theorist, but incapable of leading them to virtue himself. This belief considers only the arguments or debates by which he refuted those who considered themselves to be possessed of all knowledge. But what he used to say in his daily conversations with those who spent their time in close association with him, [*this* common belief does not take into consideration]. . . . I shall first mention what I myself once heard him saying in a discussion with Aristodemus. . . .' The meaning of this passage is obvious: while others may think that they know something about Socrates, he, Xenophon, knows Socrates intimately from many close, personal contacts. Hence he is also an eminently qualified Socratic witness.

It is a matter of common knowledge that in several of his works, Xenophon, by the use of direct or indirect means, skilfully manages to bring his own rather insignificant personality on the stage and even into the centre of events in a manner which gives rise to the impression of studied self-glorification and self-exaltation. His *Socratica*, for instance, have thus succeeded in creating the widespread opinion, held both in ancient and modern times, that he was an intimate associate and trusted follower of Socrates—an opinion which he himself brought about purposely by practising that peculiar kind of deception which is apt

The General Nature of Xenophon's Socratica

to produce a false impression without actually making use of too many and too flagrant falsehoods. But the hollowness of these claims and pretensions is fully evidenced by the careless manner in which he manipulates the details. It is here that we can discern in Xenophon a man of manifestly unstable character as well as of many-sided, though undisciplined, interests, all of which he constantly marshals in order to exalt his own rather mediocre self in the eyes of his contemporaries. Perhaps his most noteworthy attribute is his ability to adapt himself to all situations, with the remarkable result that he finds no particular difficulty in championing contradictory views and theses with equal fervor. This 'intellectual flexibility', which was the product not so much of a liberal mind—for Xenophon was anything but a 'liberal'—but rather of a fairly shallow intellect, he combined with what seems to have been a consuming ambition not only to rival—and possibly to exceed—the most renowned authors of his epoch, such as Thucydides, Antisthenes, and Plato, but also to say the final and most authoritative word on the most debated issue of the day: the Socratic issue. But, as Theodor Gomperz has so aptly remarked, 'a borrowed costume is admirably suited to set off the defects of a figure which it does not fit.... A comparison of the copy with the original may be trusted to teach us something about the peculiarities of Xenophon.'[66]

In order to gain or complement his extremely sketchy information about Socrates, Xenophon had to rely heavily on plain 'hearsay', rumours, popular opinion which had been formed during the first decade of the fourth century, and a number of extant λόγοι Σωκρατικοί. What, then, could be more natural for him than to rely upon, and even appropriate some of these older 'sources' which in themselves already were strongly distorted by the fertile imagination or personal bias of their original authors? But in doing so he also gave free rein to his own pedestrian imagination, particularly when he insists that he had personally attended some of the discourses held by Socrates, or when he attributes to Socrates an expert's knowledge of 'economics'[67] or the art of leading mounted troups.[68] Aside from all this, he apparently resorted to a 'reflektierenden Verarbeitung des Erlebten, Gehörten, und Gelesenen zu einem vollständigeren und tiefer eindringenden Verständnis der Persönlichkeit des Meisters'—to a 'speculative elaboration of what he himself had either experienced or heard or read, in order to gain a more penetrating understanding of the personality of the master'.[69] This, then, would bear out our contention that the Xenophontean *Socratica* are not so much historio-biographical reporting of fact, but rather autobiographical or self-revelatory sketches and, therefore, primarily the product of creative writing and unfettered imagination, at least as regards Socrates. They are, needless to say, definitely instances of the larger Socratic legend and as such of extremely limited historical source value. Xenophon himself casts perhaps the fairest verdict about his

The General Nature of Xenophon's Socratica

ability and objectivity as a historical reporter when he says (*Cynegeticus* 13.4–5): 'I am an amateur (ἰδιώτης). . . . I admit that I may not express myself in the language of the expert (οὐ σεσοφισμένως λέγω). But this is really not my intention. . . . My object is rather to give expression to wholesome thought that will meet the needs of readers well versed in virtue.' But then, again, it must also be conceded that the Socratic legend invented or propagated by Xenophon—by no means the only or even the first or perhaps the most important Socratic legend—may contain a nucleus of historical truth around which a complex fabric of fictions has been woven by Xenophon. How skilful, successful, and original he was in his efforts to create his own brand of Socratic legend, remains to be seen.

2
Xenophon's Defence of Socrates before his Judges

THE CORPUS XENOPHONTEUM, to put it briefly, contains what might be called two apologies of Socrates, namely, the so-called *Defence of Socrates before his Judges*,[70] and *Memorabilia* 1.1.–1.2.64.[71] From the fact that the *Defence* in chapter 31 refers to the death of Anytus, we are compelled to assume that it was written after 385/4, since Anytus served in that year as an official 'grain inspector' (σιτοφύλαξ).[72] Certain striking similarities between chapter 20 of the *Defence* and *Memorabilia* 1.2.49–55, and between the general tenor of the *Defence* and *Memorabilia* 4.8.1–11, have been the topic of many scholarly discussions as to the interdependence of these two apologies. It has been suggested that either the *Defence* is an expansion of *Memorabilia* 4.8.1–11, or that *Memorabilia* 4.8.1–11 contain an excerpt from the *Defence*. The better arguments, however, seem to be given by those who regard *Memorabilia* 4.8.1–11 as an excerpt from the *Defence*. Also, it is safe to assume that *Defence* 20 is a summary of *Memorabilia* 1.2.49–55. This bears out our contention that Xenophon first wrote *Memorabilia* 1.1.1–1.2.64 which originally constituted a separate work, then the *Defence*, and, finally, *Memorabilia* 1.3.1–4.8.11. However, some doubts have been entertained on the genuineness of the *Defence*. It has been argued that the *Defence* is written in a manner and style which in its crudeness and exaggerations is 'unworthy' of Xenophon. This argument, it seems, overlooks several important facts: (1) Demetrius Magnes in his canon of Xenophontean writings enumerates the *Defence* among the authentic works of Xenophon; (2) *Memorabilia* 4.8.1–11 in all probability are an excerpt from the *Defence*; (3) there can be little doubt that *Memorabilia* 4.8.1–11 are authentic; (4) that *Defence* 20 is Xenophon's own summary of *Memorabilia* 1.2.49–55; and (5) that *Memorabilia* 1.2.49–55 are authentic.[73]

From the first chapter of the *Defence* we gather that it was primarily written to correct and supplement what others had already said about the trial and death of Socrates: 'For although there are many who have written on this subject, and all without exception concur in stressing the outstanding courage and intrepidity (μεγαληγορία) with which he [*scil.*, Socrates] addressed the assembly . . . yet, that it was his genuine conviction that at his age death was preferable for him to life, they have by no means made fully clear.'[74] It is quite possible that Xenophon might have in mind here the *Apology* of Plato and perhaps other Socratic apologies which are no longer extant.

Since the *Defence* is designed to portray the μεγαληγορία of Socrates, that is, the proud and inflexible conduct which Socrates displayed before his judges, it could not be a simple and detailed account of the events that transpired during the famous trial of 399. For, as Xenophon himself points out (*Defence* 22), it was not his subject 'to mention everything that transpired during the trial'. In harmony with his purpose Xenophon stresses only certain salient incidents or characteristics of Socrates which are intended to bring out and motivate the Socratic μεγαληγορία. In its true significance, therefore, the Xenophontean *Defence* can only be fully understood in its relation to other contemporary apologies. But with the exception of the Platonic *Apology*, all other apologies of Socrates, of which there must have been a considerable number, are completely or nearly completely lost. Plato also presupposes this μεγαληγορία without, however, making a particular issue of this Socratic trait of character. This is especially evident in *Apology* 17A–18A (and *ibid.* at 34C–35D), where the Socratic μεγαληγορία constitutes the basis of Socrates' whole deportment before his judges and the manner in which he conducts his own defence.[75] Hence the question arises whether Xenophon also includes the *Apology* of Plato among those apologies which in his opinion stood in need of correction and improvement. There can be no doubt, in our view, that in the opinion of Xenophon, Plato too had failed to stress and motivate properly the μεγαληγορία of Socrates.[76] Indeed, Plato brings out not only the Socratic μεγαληγορία, but also Socrates' disdain of death; however, he does so by making Socrates engage in some rather lengthy speculations about man's fate after death. It is quite likely that Xenophon considers this motivation of Socrates' fearlessness unsatisfactory and perhaps even un-Socratic. Also, in the *Defence* Xenophon wishes to outline the three forensic speeches delivered by Socrates.[77] In doing so, he tries to demonstrate that Socrates was wholly innocent of the specific charges instituted against him, and that he did not really make any effort at escaping the death penalty. But the various references to Socrates' rejoinders to the specific charges are really of secondary and, we might say, collateral importance: the main purpose of the Xenophontean *Defence* always remains the Socratic μεγαληγορία.

Xenophon's statement that other authors had failed to 'make fully clear' the μεγαληγορία of Socrates induced H. v. Arnim to argue in favour of the priority of the Xenophontean *Defence* to the Platonic *Apology*.[78] If Xenophon had known the Platonic *Apology*, Arnim contends, he would not have asserted, as he does at the outset, that all previous writers on the subject of Socrates' trial had failed to account for the μεγαληγορία of Socrates: 'For as to the nature and the motives of this μεγαληγορία, the Platonic *Apology* gives a far clearer and more satisfactory information than the Xenophontean *Defence*.'[79] Arnim seems to overlook the fact, however, that the *Defence*, which in chapter 31 also refers to the death of Anytus, could not have been written before the year 385/4.[80] If, therefore, Arnim's assumption that the Platonic *Apology* was composed after the Xenophontean *Defence* would be correct, he would also have to concede the highly improbable theory that the Platonic *Apology* was written after 384.

In the *Defence* (chap. 1) Xenophon commences by asserting that 'the loftiness of Socrates' address and the boldness of his speech before his judges' might be interpreted by some as a manifestation of imprudence and impudence. But, according to Xenophon, this was not the case, because the sublimity of Socrates' conduct before his judges, so often interpreted as arrogance, was actually nothing other than an expression of his exalted mind. However, by stating the reasons *why* Socrates assumed such a lofty attitude before his judges, Xenophon attempts to provide us with an improved report on Socrates' deportment during his trial and not merely with a glorified account of the trial and death of Socrates, as other apologists had already done. In all likelihood, the *Defence* is part of that general apologetic literature which became somewhat of a vogue after the publication of Polycrates' κατηγορία Σωκράτους in *c*. 393/2 B.C. Hence it could be maintained that the *Defence*, like *Memorabilia* 1.1.1–1.2.64, is actually a reply to the κατηγορία, although it would be more correct to state that it was motivated by the publication of the Polycratean pamphlet. This in no way alters the fact that the *Defence* is intended to glorify the μεγαληγορία of Socrates. The *Defence*, it must be conceded however, takes only casual issue with Polycrates and his pamphlet.[81] Hence we will have to admit that, although its composition was prompted by the publication of the Polycratean κατηγορία, its main purpose could not have been to rebut Polycrates. Nevertheless the *Defence* seems to be familiar with other 'rebuttals' to Polycrates, such as the *Apology of Socrates* by Lysias.[82]

According to Plato (*Apology* 38DE), Socrates addressed his judges as follows: 'But I had not the boldness or impudence or inclination to address you as you would have liked me to do, weeping and wailing and lamenting....'[83] Furthermore, in *Apology* 17A ff., he asked the same judges for permission to speak in his accustomed manner: 'I am more than seventy years of age, and since this is the first time that I am appearing in a court of law, I am quite a stranger to the language of the court.' Hence the judges must permit him to defend himself in his own fashion.[84]

Xenophon's Defence of Socrates before his Judges

Relying on the report of Hermogenes,[85] an intimate friend of Socrates, Xenophon (*Defence*, chaps. 2–3) states that Socrates, refusing to make special preparations for his impending trial, pointed out that the manner in which he conducted his whole life would be his best defence: 'Throughout my whole life I have steadily persisted in doing nothing unjust. And I consider this to be the best and most honourable preparation [for the impending ordeal].' Essentially the same idea is repeated in *Memorabilia* 4.8.4: 'But when Hermogenes . . . remarked to him [*scil.*, Socrates] that he ought to consider what kind of defence he should make, he said at first, "Do I not appear to have passed my whole life meditating on that subject?" And when Hermogenes asked him, "How so?" he answered that he had gone through life doing nothing but considering what was just and refraining from what was unjust, and this he conceived to be the best meditation for his defence.' For, in the words of Plato (*Apology* 28B), 'a man who is good for anything, ought not to calculate the chance of living or dying. He ought only to consider whether in doing anything he is doing the right or the wrong thing, acting the part of the good man or of the bad man.'[86]

Xenophon's claim that Socrates made no special preparations is somewhat corroborated by Diogenes Laertius (2.40): 'The philosopher [*scil.*, Socrates], then, after Lysias had written a defence speech for him, read it through and said: "A fine speech, Lysias, but it is not suitable to me." For it was plainly more forensic than philosophical.'[87] However, Plato and Xenophon fail to mention the 'Defence' which Lysias allegedly offered Socrates. Since no ancient author apparently has seen this 'Defence', the whole story seems to be spurious. The facts behind this report are probably these: Around 390 B.C. Lysias composed an oration, Ὑπὲρ Σωκράτους πρὸς Πολυκράτην, which was a rebuttal of the κατηγορία Σωκράτους of Polycrates. It is quite possible that Diogenes Laertius (2.40) or his source was of the opinion that the Ὑπὲρ Σωκράτους of Lysias is the 'Defence' which Lysias supposedly offered Socrates before the latter went on trial. The Ὑπὲρ Σωκράτους of Lysias is also mentioned in the *Busiris* (chap. 4) of Isocrates and in the *Scholia ad Aristidem* 1133.16 (Dindorf). Plutarch (*Vita Lysiae*), when enumerating the orations of Lysias, refers to a Σωκράτους ἀπολογία ἐστοχασμένη τῶν δικαστῶν. Plutarch probably took this otherwise unsupported information from Cicero, *De oratore* 1.54.231.[88]

In *Defence* 3, Socrates is said to have refused to prepare his own defence, while in Plato's *Apology* (17A ff.) he asks his judges for permission to address the court in his accustomed manner, claiming that since this was the first time that he had ever appeared in a court of law, he was completely unfamiliar with 'the language of the court'. The forensic speeches of the period, in the main, seem to have followed a definite, not to say platitudinous pattern. The defendant either contended that the accusation, being based on prejudice or personal enmity, is an ἀδικία and a ψεῦδος;[89] or he contrasted his own lack of rhetorical and forensic ability or experience with the skill, acumen, and experience of his adversary. If he should make the latter plea, he then would try to arouse the sympathy of the audience, frequently referring to his advanced age, his physical infirmities, or his total unfamiliarity with legal procedure. Having thus established himself definitely as the pitiful 'under-dog' who properly trembles before his mighty opponent, the defendant then 'courageously' resolved that despite the 'crushing inequality of the odds', he would join the issue, knowing that the 'righteousness of his cause would ultimately triumph', particularly since the 'enlightened' and 'fair' gentlemen of the jury could not possibly fail to see the 'obvious justice of his case'.[90] Socrates' eloquent plea of unfamiliarity with legal proceedings and his alleged lack of rhetorical talent, therefore, may be nothing other than one of these frequently quoted forensic commonplaces. Whether this plea was based upon fact or was merely an instance of subtle irony, cannot be ascertained. In the Platonic *Protagoras* and *Gorgias*, to be sure, Socrates is most emphatic in disclaiming oratorical ability. But during the trial of the generals in the year 406, when he was *epistates* (?) of the *ecclesia*, he seems to have displayed both excellent forensic talent and great oratorical acumen.[91] But then, again, Socrates insists (*Gorgias* 522BC) that if he should ever be brought before a court of law because he had rebuked the Athenians for their conduct, he would be greatly embarrassed and unable to tell the truth to his judges. Hence he has really no way of defending himself successfully. And Callicles bluntly informs Socrates (*Gorgias* 486AB) that if he were ever to be arrested on criminal charges of which he was totally innocent, he would not know how to offer a defence. But Socrates seems to find some solace in the fact that, although he cannot defend himself in the ordinary manner, he still has the only defence which really matters, namely, the support of his own conscience as one who never wronged either man or God. In the opinion of Socrates (*Gorgias* 522D) this does not mean, however, that he should refrain from telling the court the painful truth about Athens or about his 'divine mission', but only that he cannot avail himself of any defence in the sense which Callicles, for instance, might have had in mind. In the eyes of the world, which cannot conceive of a defendant doing anything except devising arguments to procure a favourable verdict, Socrates apparently wishes to appear as a helpless fool who is totally incapable of defending himself against any charge on which he may be arraigned.[92] For a good and just man may not stoop to objectionable forensic tactics merely to secure an acquittal.

Hence Socrates' alleged refusal to appeal to the compassion of his judges also must be understood in the light of the forensic practices employed in the Athenian courts during the fifth and fourth centuries. The very idea underlying the Athenian heliastic courts was bound to give unlimited judicial powers into the hands of incompetence—to permit justice under the law to be destroyed by ignorance of the law. Under such circumstances it was not difficult for cunning pleaders, skilled in arguing beside the point, to cite texts or authorities falsely or to indulge in fallacious interpretation. And there was something still worse and more dangerous: summoning to their aid passionate but irrelevant eloquence, they attempted—and often succeeded—in exciting the blind political, social, or economic prejudices of the heliasts. There were all manner of tested dramatic prescriptions for the performance of a successful act before the tribunal. The defendant could mount the dais clothed in rags and tatters and bearing the staff of the formal suppliant. He could surround himself with his weeping wife and wailing children —the most effective auxiliaries he could possibly muster—in order to influence even the most uncompromising judge.[93] The parade of the prospective widow and the orphans-to-be was uniquely calculated to soften the hearts of the judges.[94] This is what Socrates has in mind when he says (Plato, *Apology* 34CD): 'Perhaps there might be some one who is offended at me, when he remembers how he himself on a similar, or even less serious occasion, pleaded and entreated the judges with many tears, and how he produced his children in court—certainly a moving spectacle—together with a host of relatives and friends. I, who probably am in danger of my life, will do none of these things. . . . I, too, am a man, and like other men, a creature of flesh and blood . . . and I have a family . . . and sons . . . three in number, one almost a man, and two others who are still young. And yet, I will not bring any of them hither in order to plead with you for an acquittal. And why not? . . . I feel that such practices would be discreditable to myself, and to you, and to the whole city. One who has reached my years, and who has a reputation for wisdom, ought not to degrade himself. . . . These things ought not to be done. . . . There seems to be something wrong in asking a favour of a judge and thus procuring an acquittal.'

Also, during the protracted court proceedings reference was frequently made to the defendant's 'patriotism' and to his devotion to the people's welfare. Again, the past of both the prosecutor and defendant was ruthlessly ransacked in order to hurl the vilest calumnies. As soon as the proceedings began to touch upon politics and political party prejudices, the tribunal often became transformed into a political assembly of the people. The judges no longer restrained themselves from yielding to political partisanship which from then on disguised itself as justice. The law, which at Athens was silent in a great many cases where the assessment of penalties was left to the discretion of the judges, remained powerless when pride in irresponsible popular sovereignty completely replaced the feeling of professional responsibility.[95]

Xenophon (*Defence* 4) then maintains that Socrates was compelled by his daemon not to employ the customary forensic oratory, or to appeal to the compassion of the judges in order to secure an acquittal.[96] Following a tradition which differed from the Platonic, he insists that the daemon apparently had commanded Socrates not to interfere with what seems to have been his pre-ordained fate, the more so, since under the circumstances death was more desirable than life: 'When I was proceeding, a while ago, to study my address to the judges, the daemon manifested his disapproval.'[97] In Plato's *Apology* (41D), on the other hand, the Socratic daemon is mentioned only in the last address of Socrates after he had been sentenced to death. Here Socrates maintains that the daemon never gave him any sign during the whole of the trial. This would indicate, according to the Platonic tradition, that the gods were satisfied with the outcome of the trial.

Xenophon (chaps. 5–6 of the *Defence*) insists that Socrates actually believed that this was the best time for him to die: 'Do you not know that up to this moment I will not concede to any man to have lived a better life than I have . . . knowing that my whole life has been spent in holy and just pursuits? And this verdict of self-approval I did find reflected in the opinion which my friends . . . have formed about me.' Having performed his duty both to the gods and to man, he felt that he had achieved the fullness of life, and that by dying now he would be spared the infirmities and unpleasant aspects of old age.[98]

The same idea is restated in *Memorabilia* 4.8.1: 'He [*scil.*, Socrates] was already so advanced in years that he must have ended his life, if not then, at least not long afterwards. . . . He surrendered only the most burdensome part of life, in which all feel their intellectual powers diminish.' For 'should I live any longer', Socrates maintains, 'perhaps I shall be destined to sustain the evils of old age . . . and . . . grow inferior to others in all those qualities in which I was once superior to them. If I should be insensible to this deterioration, life would not be worth retaining. . . .'[99] The idea that under certain circumstances death is something desirable is also found in Plato's *Phaedo* (61C): 'Any man who possesses the spirit of philosophy is willing to die, but he will not take his own life.' For the true philosopher is not fearful of death. Both Xenophon and Plato may have borrowed 'the philosopher's willingness to die' from Antisthenes; or Xenophon (*Memor.* 4.8.1) may have derived it from Plato who, in turn, is probably dependent on some Antisthenian dictum. The Stoics, who in this are admittedly under Cynic influence, made much of this 'readiness to die'.

Furthermore, in Plato (*Apology* 41CD) Socrates likewise expresses the thought that death at his age is nothing to be feared: 'Wherefore, my judges, be of good cheer about death, and know of a certainty that no evil can happen to a good man, either in this life or after death. He and his kind are not forgotten by the gods, nor has my own approaching end happened by mere chance. But I see clearly that the time has arrived when it is better for me to die and to be released from trouble.'[100] For 'no one knows whether death, which men in their fear consider the greatest evil, may not be the greatest good ... and I will never fear or avoid a possible good rather than a certain evil.'[101] Turning on his judges, Socrates wistfully remarks: 'If you had waited only a little time, your desire [to kill me] would have been fulfilled in the course of nature. For I am advanced in years, as you may perceive, and not far from death.'[102]

According to chapter 7 of the *Defence* Socrates continued: 'God out of His goodness has appointed for me not only that my life should end in the ripeness of age, but also that I should have the gentlest of death ... which ... is not only the easiest in itself, but which will cause the least trouble to one's friends, while engendering the deepest longing for the departed.' In this fashion he would be freed from the anxieties and unpleasantness of a lingering death while his mind was still capable of exerting itself 'benevolently' (φιλοφρονεῖσθαι): 'Who can say ... that to die in this way is not most desirable?'

It seems that most people in Athens expected that Socrates, like Anaxagoras and Protagoras before him, would avoid trial by going into voluntary exile.[103] By doing this he would have spared Athens the unpleasantness of such a trial which, after all, might reflect unfavourably on Athens and its well-known reputation for liberalism and toleration.[104] Even the friends of Socrates seem to have expected him to leave Athens voluntarily, a fact which might be inferred from their failure to take seriously the whole proceedings or to make adequate preparations for the trial.[105] Some scholars also maintain that Plato wrote the *Euthyphro* between the announcement of Socrates' prosecution and the actual trial.[106] It is argued that the satirical tone in which the approaching trial of Socrates is discussed here, indicates that neither Plato (nor Socrates) took the whole proceedings seriously.[107] It should also be noted that the closing passage of this dialogue implies that Plato expected that Socrates would escape the trial by going into voluntary exile and leading 'a better life'. Socrates, who had been charged (*Euthyphro* 3A) with being 'a maker of gods', an 'inventor of new gods', and a 'denier of the existence of the old gods', is deeply disappointed because Euthyphro had failed to instruct him on the nature of piety and impiety (*Euthyphro* 15E): 'I was hoping that you would instruct me as to the nature of piety and impiety; and then I would have cleared myself of Meletus and his indictment. I would have told him that I have been enlightened by Euthyphro, that I had given up rash innovations and speculations in which I indulged only through ignorance, and that now I am about to lead a better life.'

In chapters 8-9 of the *Defence* Socrates insinuates that the gods had opposed any plans for his escape, because by his flight he would only have exposed himself to the lingering ills of old age. 'Yet God knows,' Socrates insisted, 'I shall not display an unreasonable desire of death,' by asking for death at their hands: 'On the contrary, if by proclaiming all the blessings which I owe to the gods and to men; if by stating the opinion which I entertain with regard to myself, I shall end up by displeasing my judges, even so I shall choose death rather than cowardly plead for leave to live a little while longer. For thereby I would bring upon myself merely a life impoverished in place of death.'[108]

That Socrates must have been aware of the fact that his very life was in jeopardy, can be gathered from Plato's *Apology* (28AB): 'I know only too well how many are the enmities which I have incurred; and this is what will be my destruction: . . . the envy and detraction of the world which has been the death of many a good man, and will probably be the death of many more. There is no danger of my being the last one.' '. . . the vote of condemnation—I expected it. . . .'[109] Essentially the same idea reappears in *Memorabilia* 4.8.4: 'Hermogenes said again, "Do you not realize, Socrates, that the judges at Athens have already put to death many innocent persons, from being offended at their language, and have permitted many guilty men to escape justice?"' Nevertheless, in the words of Plato and Xenophon he apparently refused to make his escape. For 'wherever a man's place is, whether he himself has chosen this place, or he had been placed there by his commander, he ought to remain in that place even in the hour of danger. He should not think of death or anything, but only of disgrace.'[110] But 'if I am to die unjustly', Socrates pointedly notes, 'my death will be a disgrace to those who kill me unjustly. . . . But what disgrace will it be to me that others could not decide or act justly towards me?'[111] This is what Plato may have had in mind when the Platonic Socrates points out (*Gorgias*) 521E ff.): 'I shall be tried just like a physician would be tried in a court of little boys at the indictment of the cook. Just consider what defence a person like that would make in such an impasse, if someone were to accuse him, saying: "O my boys, many evil things has this man done to you; he is the death of you, especially the younger ones among you. . . ." What do you suppose that the physician would be able to reply when he should find himself in such a predicament? If he told the truth he could only say: "All these evil things, my boys, I did for your health." How great, do you think, would be the outcry from a jury like that? . . . Such, however, would be my own fate, as I well know, if I am brought before the court. . . . It is useless for me to reply, as I truly might: . . . "I do all this for the sake of justice and with a view to your interest . . . and to nothing else." And therefore there is no saying what may happen to me. . . . A man who is thus defenceless, is he in a good position? Yes . . . if he should have that defence and should never have said or done anything wrong, either in respect of the gods or men—this has been repeatedly acknowledged by us to be the best kind of defence. And if anyone could convict me of being unable to defend myself . . . I should blush for shame, whether I was convicted before many, or before a few, or by myself alone. And if I should die from want of ability to do so, this would indeed grieve me. But if I died because I have not the power of flattery or rhetoric, I am very sure that you would not find me deploring death. For no man, unless he be an utter fool and coward, is afraid of death itself, but he is afraid of doing wrong.'[112]

Then Xenophon, still through Hermogenes, recites in chapter 10 of the *Defence* the specific charges levelled against Socrates, and the manner in which Socrates defended himself. He was charged, in the words of Xenophon, with 'not recognizing the gods which are recognized by the city, but as designing to introduce other and new deities; and also of having corrupted youths'. In the *Memorabilia* (1.1.1) Xenophon records the official indictment as follows: 'Socrates offends against the laws by not paying any respect to those gods whom the city worships, and by introducing other and new deities. He also offends against the laws by corrupting youths.' Plato (*Apology* 24B), on the other hand, states: 'Socrates is an evil-doer who corrupts youths and who does not believe in the gods of the city, but has other and new deities of his own.'[113] Diogenes Laertius (2.40), again, reports: 'Socrates does evil in that he refuses to recognize the gods recognized by the city and in that he introduces other and new gods. He is also guilty of corrupting youths.' What this charge of 'corrupting youths' actually meant is most difficult to ascertain. Its formulation is so general that it permits a variety of interpretations. Xenophon and Plato differ considerably on this point. In any event, Xenophon's interpretation that it meant that Socrates had induced his followers or disciples to become dissipated, disobedient, effeminate, greedy, and indolent, is not accepted by Plato. It could be argued that Anytus, a politician prominent in the restoration of Athenian democracy of 403, was annoyed at Socrates' constant denunciation of the incompetence of Athenian democratic statesmen. Such conduct, Anytus might have felt, would undermine the authority of the government in that it produced an attitude of contempt towards the democratic leaders.[114]

In view of the fact that Socrates sought to free man from certain unintelligible religious superstitions, it is not altogether surprising that he should be suspected of being 'anti-religious' or even 'atheistic'.[115] Aristophanes (*Clouds* 830), for instance, calls Socrates a Melian. The inhabitants of the island of Melos, it will be remembered, had stubbornly resisted all efforts on the part of the Athenians to enroll them in the Delian League.[116] In addition, Melos was the home of Diagoras, the notorious 'atheist'. Hence the remark of Aristophanes implies two vicious criticisms: Socrates is a stubborn man who has to be brought to his senses by the use of extreme measures; and Socrates is an 'atheist'.[117] The two religious clauses of the indictment do not mean that Socrates is suspected of holding 'heretical views', or of disbelieving the traditional religious mythologies. The Athenian state religion, being wholly a matter of ritual and worship, had no official theological dogma. Neither was it an offence against religion to disbelieve the mythologies. Hence we must assume that the religious clauses are probably intended to prejudice the court against Socrates by reminding it of the precedents it had established in the case of Anaxagoras or that of Protagoras and Diagoras.[118] In this connection one should compare the deeply religious views of Socrates which the latter professes in the Platonic *Euthyphro* (dealing with the interval between the time when the charges against Socrates were placed before the *archon* and the time of the actual trial), and the purely ritualistic fanaticism of the man Euthyphro who is totally devoid of any profounder understanding of true piety. Euthyphro is the representative of that shallow and decadent formalism to which Greek religion had sunk by the end of the fifth century. The type represented by Euthyphro is also the driving motive behind the religious charges instituted against Socrates.[119]

There seems to have existed a rather curious tradition concerning the charge that Socrates had introduced new deities: allegedly he had insisted that birds, dogs and the like should be worshipped.[120] Xenophon apparently was familiar with a tradition according to which Socrates' frequent exclamation, 'By the Dog', was used by the prosecution to prove that he had introduced 'new deities'.[121] This might also explain why Xenophon (*Memor*. 1.1.14) makes it a point to refer to Socrates' bewilderment over those people 'who worship stones, common stocks, and even beasts'. In any event, the tradition that Socrates worshipped animals or stones should not be scoffed at; it is no more ridiculous than the version, apparently established by Plato and Xenophon, that the Socratic daemon was the cause for the charge that Socrates had introduced new deities. But this does not mean that the Platonic version is the better or older tradition. For what seems to have endowed the 'daemon tradition' with an apparently greater authority is not its superior 'historical truth value', but rather the fact that it has been propagated by Plato and Xenophon.[122]

According to Xenophon (*Defence* 11) Socrates rebutted the charge 'of not recognizing the gods which are recognized by the city' by pointing out that he had always sacrificed at the appointed festivals and common altars, as was evident to all Athenians, 'and might have been evident to Meletus, had Meletus been so minded'. In *Memorabilia* 1.1.2, Xenophon insists that 'he [*scil.*, Socrates] was seen frequently sacrificing at home, and frequently on the public altars of the city'. Furthermore, *Memorabilia* 4.6.2–4, contain the following interesting passages: 'In the first place, then, he discussed piety . . . the most noble of all experiences. . . . Who is a pious man? The man . . . who honours the gods. . . . There are certain laws in conformity with which we must pay our respect. He, then, who knows these laws will know how to pay honour to the gods. . . . He, therefore, who knows how to pay honour to the gods, will he think that he ought to pay this honour otherwise than he knows? Certainly not. . . . He, therefore, who knows what is in agreement with the laws in reference to the gods, will honour the gods in accordance with the laws. . . . Does not he who honours the gods according to the laws honour them as he ought to? . . . And he who knows them as he ought, is he not a pious man? Certainly. He, therefore, who knows what is in accord with the laws regarding the gods may justly be called a pious man.'[123] After having pointed out that no one ever saw Socrates doing or heard him saying anything impious or profane,[124] Xenophon continues (*Memor.* 1.1.20): 'I wonder, therefore, how the Athenians were ever persuaded that Socrates had not the true sentiments concerning the gods—a man who never said or did anything impious towards the gods, but spoke and acted in such a manner as regards the gods that anyone else who would have spoken and acted in the same manner would have been considered eminently pious.'

According to Plato (*Apology* 26c ff.), Meletus accuses Socrates of being a 'radical atheist', who had called 'the sun a stone, and the moon earth'. Obviously, in this instance, Meletus confuses Socrates with Anaxagoras (*Apology* 26d),[125] and Socrates immediately proceeds to show that Meletus had contradicted himself.[126] When Socrates succeeds (Plato, *Apology* 26c ff.) in entrapping Meletus to state that the charge of not worshipping the deities which the city worshipped signifies 'absolute atheism', he can point out the incompatibility of the two parts of the religious indictment. Apparently Meletus was unable or, perhaps, unwilling to reveal the true meaning of the religious charges. But this meaning seems to be indicated in Plato (*Apology* 18a–19d), where Socrates insists that, for want of any specific facts, the prosecution had to resort to the older popular accusations, already recorded by Aristophanes.[127] Here Socrates is looked upon as a blaspheming person because he uses the name 'god' in a non-religious manner in order to designate what he considers to be the 'original substance' or ὕλη.[128]

An observant reader cannot fail to detect that the Platonic *Apology* vindicates Socrates on the score of 'atheism', but remains silent on the charge that he was guilty of some 'religious innovation'. This might be interpreted as an admission of the latter charge. The comic poet Telecleides[129] apparently had tried to relate Socrates and Euripides, who had become suspect on account of the religious views enunciated in his tragedies; and Diogenes Laertius (2.18) maintains, though probably without foundation in fact, that Socrates had helped Euripides in composing some of his tragedies. All these stories may go back to the popular belief that Socrates and Euripides held similar religious views. There exists, however, still another possibility of explaining the significance of this charge of 'atheism'. Although neither Xenophon nor Plato refer to the incident, Meletus might have had in mind the religious 'scandal' of the year 415 in which Alcibiades and other followers of

Xenophon's Defence of Socrates before his Judges

Socrates (Phaedrus, Eryximachus—both 'actors' in Plato's *Symposium* —Andocides, and Acumenus) had been involved.[130]

In chapters 12–13 of the *Defence* Socrates takes issue with the second point of the indictment, namely, that he had conspired to introduce new deities to Athens.[131] He stresses the fact that the Athenians believe that 'the chirping of birds', thunder, or the oracles of the priestess of Delphi are the voice of the deity which thus reveals its will to whomever it pleases.[132] In this he is in complete accord with the religious tradition of Athens, 'with the exception that whereas they say that it is from auguries, omens, signs or soothsayers whence they have their knowledge of the future, I, on the contrary, impute all these premonitions with which I am favoured, to a daemon.[133] And I think that in this I have spoken not only more truly, but also more piously than those who attribute to birds the divine privilege of declaring things to come.' 'And although I have often communicated to my many friends the divine counsels, yet no one has ever found me to be a deceiver or deceived.'

In *Memorabilia* 1.1.9, Xenophon reports that Socrates had maintained that 'it was the duty of men . . . to try to ascertain from the gods by augury whatever was obscure to men. Because the gods always afford information to those towards whom they feel kindly inclined.' 'Most people say that they are diverted from an object, or perhaps directed to it, by birds. . . . Socrates, however, spoke as he thought, for he maintained that the divinity was his monitor . . . [and] that the divinity had forewarned him.'[134] 'Those who inquired of the gods concerning such matters [*scil.*, matters which man may know through the proper exercise of his natural faculties] he considered guilty of impiety and said that it was the duty of man to learn whatever the gods had enabled men to do through learning. But they should try to ascertain from the gods by augury whatever was obscure to men, inasmuch as the gods always give information to those to whom they have been rendered favourable.'[135]

The Socratic daemon of Xenophon[136] differs from the Socratic daemon of Plato in three ways: (1) in Xenophon the daemon appears as a personal or personalized agent; (2) by implication Xenophon identifies this active daemon with the gods, particularly in *Memorabilia* 1.1.2–9; (3) after having identified the Socratic daemon with the gods, Xenophon seems to overlook the fact that between the gods and man there exist always certain intermediaries such as signs, dreams, and the like. Dio Chrysostom (*Oratio* 25.2) speaks of a 'principle [which] is within man himself, a thing which controls the individual and which we call the δαίμων, [which], while being a power outside of man . . . yet rules him and is master of him'. Other writers identify this 'inner power' with τρόπος or ἦθος, as, for instance, Epicharmus, (frag. 258, Kaibel): 'character (τρόπος) is man's good guiding spirit (δαίμων)'; or Heraclitus of Ephesus (frag. 119, Diels): 'character (ἦθος) is the guiding spirit of man (δαίμων)'.[137] The Platonic Socrates also considers dreams divine signs.¹³⁸ The many references to the Socratic daemon in the Socratic literature are probably related to a single original source which, however, can no longer be stated in a univocal manner. The Socratic tradition about the daemon may be subdivided into those versions where the daemon either restrains or compels Socrates to act, and those versions which attempt to interpret the daemon and its meaning. Among these latter interpretations we can distinguish between two traditions, that tradition which reports the way in which it made itself known to Socrates or 'spoke' to him, and that tradition which used the Socratic daemon in order to develop a definite 'demonology'. There also exist a great many stories about people who benefited by listening to Socrates' advice after the latter had been warned by his daemon.¹³⁹

Socrates' references to his daemon, we are told (*Defence* 14–15), caused considerable displeasure among the judges, 'some disbelieving the truth of what Socrates had said, while others simply envied him for being, as they thought, more highly favoured by the gods than they'.¹⁴⁰ But Socrates, rather than assuaging the rising anger of his audience, went on insisting that the Delphic god had said about him that 'he knew no man more free, more just, or more wise than I', and that 'I by far excelled all men'.

Plato, although in a somewhat different manner and different context, likewise records that, by his various statements, Socrates had angered the court: 'I know that the plainness of my speech makes them hate me. . . . Hence the prejudice against me has arisen.'¹⁴¹ The literary tradition seems to imply that Socrates used some inappropriate language which apparently amused and even angered the court. This may be gathered from Plato (*Apology* 17CD), where Socrates begs the court 'not to be surprised or raise a row' over the strangeness of his locution. In the *Theaetetus* (175CD), where Socrates is portrayed as βαρβαριζῶν, we are told that 'his awkwardness is something terrible, making him look like a fool'. It is quite likely that at this point some of the judges started to laugh, something which Plato seems to emphasize in the *Theaetetus*.¹⁴² But soon mere amusement over Socrates' quaint deportment apparently turned into a real disturbance and uproar.¹⁴³

It has been contended that *Defence* 14 does not contain the original story of the Delphic incident,¹⁴⁴ although Diogenes Laertius (2.37–38) seems to corroborate Xenophon's statement when he writes: 'These and the like were his [*scil.*, Socrates'] words and deeds, to which the Pythian priestess bore testimony when she gave Chaerephon the famous reply: Of all men living Socrates is the wisest. For this he was most envied. . . .'¹⁴⁵ Hence it might be well to quote Plato's version of the Delphic incident (*Apology* 20D–21A): 'This reputation of mine has its source in a certain kind of wisdom which I possess. . . . [Concerning this] I will refer you to a witness who is worthy of being believed, and this witness shall be the god of Delphi. . . . Chaerephon, who in early days was a friend of mine ... went to Delphi and boldly asked the oracle ... whether anyone was wiser than I was. And the Pythian prophetess replied that there was no man wiser.' 'By his answer,' Plato continues (*Apology* 23AB), 'he [*scil.*, the Pythian god] intends to show that the wisdom of man is worth little or nothing. ... He ... is the wisest who, like Socrates, knows that his wisdom is worth nothing. And so I go about the world, obedient to the god, searching and inquiring into the wisdom of anyone ... who appears to be wise.'

Of the many problems connected with the Xenophontean *Defence* none deserves more detailed discussion than Socrates' boast that the Delphic Apollo had once declared that 'there was no human being more liberal, or more upright, or more temperate than myself. ... And although he [*scil.*, the god] did not liken me to a god, in excellence he preferred me above all other men.' In Plato's *Apology* (20E ff.), this story in some way is related to the various accounts about Socrates' 'vocation to philosophy',[146] although this connection never becomes fully clear because the oracle, at least in the form in which it has been recorded by both Plato and Xenophon, does not contain a direct command. We must surmise, therefore, that Plato uses and combines[147] here what seems to be two different traditions about the 'calling' of Socrates. One tradition, and probably the older tradition, in a straightforward account apparently mentioned merely the command of the deity which compelled Socrates to 'philosophize' or, to be more exact, to assume the role of the 'missionary evangelist' trying to reform his people.[148] In this, the older account is somewhat on the same level with the 'classical command' of Apollo which made Orestes kill his own mother, irrespective of consequences. In his *Apology* Plato apparently resumes this tradition which from all appearances had been the theme in some older Socratic legend, where it probably played an important, if not central role.[149] But for his own particular purposes Plato could not merely appropriate a story which made Socrates out to be a simple tool of the divine will who acted strictly under compelling orders. Such an over-simplification of the Socratic mission and the reason for Socrates' deportment would have been hardly compatible with the Platonic concept of Socrates' life work. Hence, although he makes reference to this tradition, he tries to de-emphasize the direct divine influence by turning it into a mere side-issue. The manner in which he accomplishes this can be detected in the Chaerephon episode which, for the purpose of "de-emphasis," he relates, although not too convincingly, to Socrates' mission.

Close scrutiny should reveal that in both Plato and Xenophon the Chaerephon episode above all is introduced to explain and justify Socrates' vocation to philosophy, although in itself this story does not seem to contain any direct reference to a 'command' or vocation, except if interpreted in a most liberal, not to say arbitrary manner. For it would be difficult to visualize how one may construe a 'divine command' or a 'divine mission' from the reply of the Delphic oracle that Socrates was 'the wisest of men', or that there was 'no one wiser than Socrates', unless we were to assume that the allegedly unsurpassed excellence of Socrates puts him under obligation to become the saviour of his people.

The story which associates Socrates with the Delphic oracles, we must surmise, is closely related to some ancient Delphic legend. According to some of these legends the oracle had insisted that the happiest man is not the one whom the world at large considers happiest or who regards himself as such, but rather some unknown humble person who lives in total obscurity.[150] In a similar manner the Delphic priestess answers the question as to who might be the wisest man. Here tradition records that the poor and inconspicuous farmer Myson had been designated as 'the wisest man' by Apollo,[151] and not some learned person of renown. This idea seems to be applied also to Socrates, the unassuming Athenian citizen who had never aspired to riches or fame. But the story of the Delphic oracle apparently contains still another element of early Greek mythology or tradition, a story which perhaps is best expressed in the account of 'the tripod found by fishermen and sent by the people of Miletus to all the Wise Men in succession. . . . A dispute arose over the tripod . . . and finally the Milesians referred the matter to Delphi, where the god gave an oracle in this form: . . . Whosoever in wisdom is of all the first, to him I adjudge the tripod. . . . Accordingly they gave it to Thales, and he to another, and so on until it came to Solon who sent it to Delphi with the remark that the god was the most wise.'[152] The idea that God alone is truly wise was also expressed or at least implied by Heraclitus of Ephesus,[153] Theognis,[154] Pythagoras,[155] Plato,[156] and Aristotle,[157] who seem to be aware of the fact that the sublimity of true wisdom makes it impossible for mortal man to acquire a property right in it. The version, which appears in Plato's *Apology* (23AB), that the humblest man is also the wisest man, remains closely related to that other version which concedes that God alone deserves to be called wise. Xenophon, on the other hand, seems to know only of the first version. But the account of the Delphic oracle contains still a further theme. According to Aristotle, Socrates discovered on the temple wall in Delphi the inscription, 'Know thyself.'[158] The meaning of this inscription is difficult to ascertain. In Plato's *Apology* (21B–23B) apparently it assumes the form of a search after a man who is wiser than Socrates, while in the *Phaedrus* (229E–230A) it signifies that it would be ridiculous to concern ourselves about matters which are not really our concern, as long as we are still ignorant about ourselves. Xenophon (*Memor.* 4.2.24–30), on the whole, interprets it to mean a clear understanding of the limitations imposed on one's powers of reasoning and action. In this, the Xenophontean interpretation is closely related to that offered in the Platonic *Phaedrus*.[159] In a certain way the Platonic report in the *Apology* likewise

Xenophon's Defence of Socrates before his Judges

seems to conform to the account of Xenophon insofar as Plato also implies at least the idea of limitation when he points out that most people merely pretend that they know something which they actually do not know.

From all this it would follow that the story of the Delphic oracle or the Chaerephon episode seems to be based on two principal versions or traditions which, in turn, are modified by two additional elements. The first version is the story of Chaerephon, according to which the oracle had declared Socrates the wisest of men, and this because no one had ever considered him as such. The second version is the Delphic inscription, 'Know thyself', which signifies to Socrates that, above all, man should realize his own limitations. The two additional elements are the story, probably taken from the legend of the Seven Wise Men (or from a legend which finds expression in the latter) that no one but God deserves to be called wise; and the axiom, perhaps attributable to Heraclitus of Ephesus, that the prime task of all true philosophy is the unmasking of pseudo-learning.[160]

Socrates then claims (*Defence* 16) that, as the Delphic god had said, he was freer than anyone, because he was not the slave of sensual appetites[161] or indebted to others;[162] that he was more just than anyone, because he had no desire to own what belonged to others;[163] and that he was wiser than anyone, because he never ceased seeking after virtue and the moral good.[164]

This Xenophontean eulogy of Socrates, which, as will be shown later, has a strong Antisthenian-Cynic flavour, is frequently repeated throughout the *Socratica* of Xenophon. Probably the most telling encomium can be found in *Memorabilia* 4.8.11, where Socrates is held up as the man 'most useful to all lovers of virtue in their pursuit of virtue'; as the person who was 'so pious that he did nothing without the sanction of the gods'; as the man 'who was so just that he never wronged anyone'; as the man who was 'so temperate that he never preferred pleasure to virtue'; as the person who was 'so wise that he never erred in distinguishing the better from the worse'; and as the man 'so capable . . . of exhorting people to virtue and honour' that he must be considered the best and happiest of men.

In chapter 17 of the *Defence* Xenophon claims that many people, Athenians and foreigners alike, who made the pursuit of virtue their main task, have found the greatest pleasure in conversing with Socrates:[165] 'Whence was it,' Socrates continues, 'that when every one knew about my inability to return any pecuniary favour, yet so many should be anxious to bestow them on me?[166] Why does no man call me his debtor, yet so many acknowledge that they owe me so much?'[167]

No matter what happens, Socrates continues (*Defence* 18), 'I can always indulge in pleasures . . . by resorting to the reflections in my own mind.¹⁶⁸ . . . If, in whatever I have said about myself no one is able to say that I have been telling falsehoods, who will claim that I do not deserve approbation, and that not only from the gods, but also from men.' The exact wording of chapter 18 reads in part: 'When the city is under siege and everyone bemoans his own loss, how does it happen that I feel in no ways poorer than while the city is in its most prosperous state? And what is the cause that when other people are under a necessity to procure their delicacies from foreign lands at an exorbitant price, I am able to indulge in pleasures far more exquisite by resorting to the reflections of my mind?' In Xenophon's *Symposium* (4.41 ff.) Antisthenes makes similar observations: 'But observe the chief advantage I derive from my poverty: in case the little I have should be taken from me, there is no occupation so mean, no employment in life so lowly as not to support me without the least embarrassment. . . . I can easily and at any time satisfy my appetite by going to the market, not to buy expensive delicacies . . . but the most common food. In this the contentedness of my mind supplies me with delicacies that are wanting in the meat itself.' It will be shown later that both these passages are under the influence of Antisthenian-Cynic traditions.

'Nevertheless, you, Meletus,¹⁶⁹ claim that I corrupt youths,'¹⁷⁰ Socrates continues in *Defence* 19: 'But . . . what pious person have I made impious; what modest person shameless; what frugal person profligate; what temperate person intemperate; what industrious person lazy or effeminate by associating with me?'¹⁷¹ Xenophon takes issue here with the third point of the indictment, namely, that Socrates had corrupted the youth of Athens. Plato's *Apology*, on the other hand, contains no formal rebuttal of this particular charge, although there are several indirect references to it,¹⁷² especially in *Apology* 33D–34A: 'There is Crito . . . and . . . Critobulus . . . [and] Lysanias . . . and . . . Antiphon, and there are the brothers of several who have associated with me. There is Nicostratus . . . and the brother of Theodotus . . . and . . . Paralus . . . and Adeimantus, the son of Ariston whose brother Plato is present, and Aeantodorus, the brother of Apollodorus whom I also see. I might mention a great many others. . . . All these are ready to bear witness in behalf of the corrupter, of the injurer of their kindred. . . .' Plato also insists that, since Socrates had no regular pupils, he could not possibly have corrupted people (*Apology* 33A ff.): '. . . I have never basely yielded to those who are slanderously called my disciples. . . .'¹⁷³ I have no regular pupils. But if anyone likes to come and hear me while I am pursuing my mission, whether he be young or old, he is not excluded. Nor do I converse only with those who pay. But anyone, whether he be rich or poor, may ask or answer me and listen to my words; and whether he turns out to be a bad man or a good man, neither result can in justice be imputed to me. For I never taught or professed to teach him anything. And if anyone says that he has ever learned or heard anything from me in private which all the world has not heard, let me tell you that he is lying.'[174]

Chapter 20 of the *Defence* contains a specification of the charge that Socrates had corrupted youth: Meletus[174a] accuses Socrates of having persuaded many young people that they should heed him more than their fathers. 'And with good reason,' replies Socrates, 'when the point in question has to do with education. . . . For which of you, if sick, would not prefer the advice of a physician to that of his father? Do not the Athenians in the public assembly follow the opinion of whom they consider the most capable and who exhibits the soundest wisdom, although he be not one of their kindred? And in the choice of a general, do you not prefer the man whom you consider the most skilled in military matters to your fathers, brothers, and even to yourselves?'

Chapter 20 of the *Defence* is most likely a summary of *Memorabilia* 1.2.49–55: 'But Socrates, claimed the accuser [Polycrates], taught children to show contempt for their parents, persuading his followers that he rendered them wiser than their fathers . . .' (1.2.49). In this manner he 'not only caused parents, but other relatives to be held in contempt by his followers . . . (1.2.51), persuading young people that he himself was the wisest among all men and most capable of making others wise, and he [*scil.*, Socrates] so disposed his disciples towards himself that other people were of no account with them in comparison with himself' (1.2.52). 'Likewise . . . relatives or kinsmen were of no use to people who were sick, or to people having business in the courts, but that physicians aided the one, and lawyers the other' (1.2.51).[175]

It could be argued that in *Apology* 26B, where Socrates is being accused of corrupting youths, Plato also includes the charge that Socrates had undermined all paternal authority.[176] Since Plato, especially in *Apology* 33A ff., fails to take special issue with this particular charge, it can be surmised that it was never made in court. As will be shown later, the accusations mentioned in *Defence* 20 and *Memorabilia* 1.2.49–55, were contained in the κατηγορία Σωκράτους of Polycrates, from whom Xenophon derived his information. Hence Xenophon rebuts here Polycrates rather than Meletus.

Meletus, apparently compelled by Socrates' argument, concedes (*Defence* 20) that in matters of great importance people should heed the advice of experts rather than that of their parents. Hence Socrates exclaims (*Defence* 21): 'How come, then, that . . . while in every other instance the man who excels . . . is awarded many and very distinguishing marks of honour,[177] I, on the contrary, am persecuted even to death, because I am regarded by many to have excelled in that employment which is the most noble of all, and which has for its aim the greatest good of mankind, namely, the instruction of youths in the knowledge of their duty, and the dissemination of the principle of virtue in the mind of every one'.[178]

Xenophon's Defence of Socrates before his Judges

'Much more than this', Xenophon relates in *Defence* 22, 'was urged in his behalf, either by himself or by friends who pleaded for him. But my subject has not been to mention everything that transpired during the trial.'[179] Xenophon then goes on reiterating that 'the design of Socrates in speaking at this time was no other than to defend himself against anything that might have the least appearance of impiety against the gods or injustice towards men'.[180]

According to Xenophon (*Defence* 22) and Diogenes Laertius (2.41), some of Socrates' friends spoke or testified on his behalf. Plato (*Apology* 21A) also notes the brother of the late Chaerephon being called upon by Socrates to testify in support of Socrates' claims.[181] Diogenes Laertius (2.41) reports that 'during the trial Plato mounted on the platform and began the following address: "Although I am the youngest, O Athenians, of all who ever addressed you"—whereupon the judges called out: "Get down, get down."' Diogenes Laertius relies here on the information of Justus of Tiberias. It should be noted that the dicasts frequently expressed their dissatisfaction with the plea by shouting 'Get down.' Hence the report of Justus of Tiberias does not necessarily mean that Plato was 'shouted down' and thus prevented from making his plea. It appears, however, that the whole story about Plato's intercession in behalf of Socrates is the invention of a later generation of Platonists and as such lacks historical truth.

In Plato's *Apology* Socrates complains that his accusers have hardly uttered a word of truth (17B); that he had many accusers who accused him falsely (18B); and that in his defence he had simply to fight against shadows (18D). He also asserts that he had 'nothing to do with speculations concerning natural philosophy' (19C), and that there is no foundation in the story that he is a teacher (19DE) or that he ever had any disciples (33A ff.). Then Socrates goes on to explain the anger of his three prosecutors (23E–24A): 'Meletus has a quarrel with me on behalf of the poets, Anytus on behalf of the craftsmen and politicians, Lycon on behalf of the rhetoricians.... And I cannot expect to dispose at once of such a mass of calumnies.' This, by the way, is a superb example of Plato's irony. There exists, however, another plausible explanation for the personal enmity of Lycon with Socrates. Originally, Lycon was an acquaintance and perhaps even a friend of Socrates. The wanton killing of Lycon's son Autolycus at the hands of the Spartan garrison during the reign of the Thirty Tyrants caused much indignation throughout Athens. Since public opinion in some way connected Socrates with the Thirty Tyrants (Critias had been a friend and close associate of Socrates), it is quite possible that Lycon wished to avenge the death of his son on Socrates. As regards the enmity of Anytus, Libanius, among other authors, tells an interesting story: Anytus was thoroughly annoyed at Socrates' constant references to cobblers and tanners.[182] According to Xenophon (*Defence* 29–31), this enmity originated when Socrates remarked that Anytus was ruining his son by expecting him to step into his father's tannery business instead of becoming an educated man under the guidance of Socrates. Later, the son of Anytus is said to have turned a rogue.[183] Xenophon seems to imply here that Anytus' prosecution of Socrates had been motivated by this personal enmity. We must assume, however, that this whole story is a fiction, invented probably by some Socratics in order to avenge their 'master'. The fact that Plato in his *Apology* never mentions this incident in itself is some evidence that the story is probably untrue. Antisthenes, on the other hand, probably assailed Anytus in some of his writings, as might be gathered from Diogenes Laertius (6.10): '[Antisthenes] is held responsible for the exile of Anytus.' We have no evidence, however, that Anytus was actually exiled. On the contrary, it seems that all these literary attacks upon Anytus did not prevent him from being elected official 'grain inspector' (σιτοφύλαξ) in 385/4.[184] The after-effects of this slanderous literary persecution of Anytus can still be felt in Aristotle (*Athen. pol.* 27.5), Diodorus (13.64), in the *Scholia ad Plat. Apologiam* (18B), in Libanius (*Apologia Socratis* chap. 10 and *Epist. Socratis* 14.2), Dio Chrysostom (*Oratio* 55.22), and Diogenes Laertius (2.43).[185] The Socratics, it seems, advanced two theories as to the true motive behind the trial and condemnation of Socrates. Both versions try to prove that the prosecution did not proceed from any noble motive.[186] According to the first version, Anytus used the trial in order to avenge himself on Socrates for an alleged personal insult. This version, which probably goes back to a lost Socratic dialogue, is accepted by Xenophon (*Defence* 29 ff.) and can also be detected in Plato's *Meno*. It is nothing other than a poor effort on the part of the Socratics to discredit Anytus. The second version, which is also mentioned in Plato's *Apology* (19B ff.), censures Aristophanes for the prosecution of Socrates.[187]

Since Socrates regarded death so lightly, Xenophon continues in *Defence* 23, he was in no way anxious to importune his judges, as was the custom with others. On the contrary, he thought it the best time for him to die,[188] a fact which becomes even more evident after his condemnation.[189] 'For when he was asked to fix a counter-penalty, he refused to do so . . . saying that to fix a penalty would imply a confession of guilt.' Plato (*Apology* 36B–37C) likewise records Socrates' refusal to fix a counter-penalty: 'What is my due? What shall the man receive who has never had enough sense to be idle during his whole life . . .? What shall be done with such a man? Doubtlessly some good thing . . . if he shall have his just reward. And the good should be of a kind suitable to him. . . . There can be no reward so fitting as maintenance in the *Prytaneum*. . . . And if I propose a fair penalty, I shall maintain that maintenance in the *Prytaneum* is this fair reward. . . . I will not say that I deserve any evil, or propose any penalty. Why should I? . . . Why should I propose imprisonment? And why should I live in prison . . .?'[190]

Xenophon's Defence of Socrates before his Judges

Xenophon reports (*Defence* 24-25) that after his condemnation Socrates rebuked his judges and those who had borne false witness against him for their impiety and injustice: 'But that I in any way should be more perturbed and dejected now than before my condemnation, I cannot see, since I stand here unconvicted of any of the crimes whereof I have been accused.[191] For no one has proven against me that I worshipped any new deity. . . . Neither have they shown once' the means Socrates supposedly used in corrupting youths at the very time he 'was inuring them to a life of manliness and frugality'. As to capital crimes under the existing Athenian laws, Socrates concludes, 'my enemies do not even say that any of these crimes were ever committed by me'.[192]

In Plato's *Apology*, too, Socrates reprehends those who have condemned him (38BC): 'I now depart condemned to suffer the penalty of death. But they, too, go their ways condemned by truth to suffer the penalty of villainy and evil. . . . Athenians . . . [reflect on] the evil name which you will get from the enemies of the city who will say that you killed Socrates, a wise man. . . .' 'I prophesy to you who have murdered me,' Socrates continues (39C), 'that immediately after my death punishment will surely await you. For you have killed me because you wanted to escape the accuser.' But somewhat later Socrates' anger seems to have subsided (41DE): 'I am not angry with those who have condemned me, nor with those who have accused me. They have done me no harm, although they did not mean to do me any good. And for this I gently blame them.'[193]

Since Socrates is of the opinion that he never committed a capital crime, according to *Defence* 26, he marvels at the fact that he should be condemned to death. 'But if I die unjustly, the shame must be theirs who put me to death unjustly[194] . . . and I am persuaded that I too shall have the attestation of time to come . . . that I never wronged any man or made him more depraved;[195] but on the contrary, that I have consistently tried throughout my life to benefit those who conversed with me, teaching them, with all my power and without any reward, whatever could make them wise and happy.'[196]

In the *Memorabilia* (1.2.63) Xenophon adds the following interesting remark: 'Nor was he [*scil.*, Socrates] ever the cause of any war ending disastrously for the city, or of any sedition or treachery;[197] nor did he ever, in his private transactions, either deprive a man of what was for his good, or involve him in evil; nor was he ever under suspicion of having committed any of the crimes which I have just enumerated.' The statement that Socrates was never 'the cause of any war ending disastrously for the city', may contain a thrust at the democratic faction in Athens. In the opinion of the aristocratic or oligarchic party this faction was responsible not only for the outbreak of the Peloponnesian War, but also for preventing this war from coming to an earlier and less disastrous conclusion after the affair of Sphacteria in 425, after the battle of Cyzicus in 410, and after the battle of the Arginusae Islands in 406.

Plato (*Apology* 39CD) likewise suggests that Socrates will have 'the attestation of time to come': 'For I say that there will be more accusers of you than there are now—accusers whom I have restrained so far. And since they are younger they will be less considerate with you, and you will be harder hit by them. If you think that by killing men you can prevent others from censoring your evil lives, you are indeed mistaken.' The anecdotes of Diodorus (14.37) and Diogenes Laertius (2.43) which tell of the repentance of the Athenians for having executed Socrates are historically quite worthless.[198] Plato (*Crito* 48C), however, seems to suggest the possibility of such a change of feeling: '. . . the multitude would be as ready to restore people to life, if they were able to do so, as they are ready to put them to death—and with as little reason'.

The remainder of the Xenophontean *Defence* (chaps. 27-34) recites Socrates' conduct after his trial and condemnation: 'The cheerfulness of his countenance, his demeanour and whole deportment bore testimony to the truth he had just declared.'[199] As such, the concluding chapters of the *Defence* are not really a part of a Socratic apology, but rather belong in the same category as the Platonic *Crito* and *Phaedo*.[200]

A comparison of the Xenophontean *Defence* with the Platonic *Apology* should divulge at once that the former is dependent on the latter in many respects. Essentially both apologies seem to follow the same general plan, to portray Socrates' conduct during the three phases of the trial.[201] As in the Platonic *Apology*, the forensic speeches assigned to Socrates in the *Defence* are distinguished according to the several stages of the trial. The fact that the Xenophontean *Defence*, in its general arrangement as well as in certain details, differs from the Platonic *Apology* would support our contention that in a certain way the *Defence* is also a critique of Plato's *Apology* and the manner in which the latter reports the trial. In *Memorabilia* 4.8.1-11, on the other hand, there is no such 'opposition' to Plato's *Apology*. Also, Xenophon adds to his report a fourth phase, the time immediately before the trial when the inflexible spirit of Socrates becomes particularly manifest (*Defence* 2-9). In Plato, the sequence in which the various charges are disposed of appears to be somewhat arbitrary and not in conformity with the historical events. In addition, Plato never really attempts to rebut directly the official charges, mentioning them only in the most casual manner (*Apology* 24B). And finally, Plato (*Apology* 26C ff.) suddenly introduces the novel charge of 'absolute atheism'. Except for a refutation of the charge that Socrates corrupted youths, Xenophon's *Defence*, however, seems to follow the official indictment in its technical order. The account of the Delphic oracle likewise is treated differently by Xenophon (*Defence* 11) than by Plato (*Apology* 20D-21A). In Xenophon, this account is also more definite and detailed than in Plato. And while

Xenophon's Defence of Socrates before his Judges

Plato merely tells us that the Delphic oracle had called Socrates the wisest among men, Xenophon insists that the oracle had designated him as the wisest, the most just, and the noblest of men.

Perhaps the most serious discrepancy between the Xenophontean *Defence* and the Platonic *Apology* can be detected in the second speech of Socrates, namely, where Socrates suggests what he considers a proper and fair penalty for his conduct. In Plato (*Apology* 36E–37A), as we know, Socrates declares that he had really deserved 'maintenance in the *Prytaneum*'. Then, in a fit of inconsistency, Socrates suggests (*Apology* 38AB) first one *mina*, then thirty *minae*.[202] Xenophon, being more consistent, recounts that Socrates persisted in refusing to fix his own counter-penalty, claiming that to do so would be tantamount to a confession of guilt.[203] Diogenes Laertius (2.41) also reports that Socrates had suggested a fine. According to one version, 'he proposed the sum of 25 *drachmae*', while according to Eubulides, 'he offered the sum of 100 *drachmae*'. Although the report of Diogenes Laertius is not directly based on Plato's *Apology*, the version that Socrates suggested the sum of 100 *drachmae* coincides with the Platonic statement (100 *drachmae* equal one *mina*). Diogenes Laertius (6.20) claims that he derived his information from Eubulides, who, it seems, had composed a book about Diogenes of Sinope. But it is possible that Eubulides may have relied on Plato's *Apology* for his information. In the words of Plato (and Diogenes Laertius 2.42, who in this is probably under the influence of Plato), the first counter-penalty proposed by Socrates—'maintenance in the *Prytaneum*'—apparently was regarded as sheer defiance of the court. Whether any real counter-penalty was ever proposed by Socrates or his friends, remains uncertain. The explicit declaration of Xenophon (*Defence* 23) that Socrates not only refused to name a counter-penalty, but also forbade his friends to do so, is difficult to reconcile with Plato's account. It is possible that in the general uproar which followed Socrates' request for 'maintenance in the *Prytaneum*,'[204] various sums of money were shouted by one person or another, although probably none was officially recorded by the clerk who apparently wrote down only Socrates' demand. This might explain Xenophon's failure to mention a second 'counter-penalty' (proposed, as it seems, by a friend of Socrates). It must be admitted that Socrates' refusal to propose a second counter-penalty is more consistent with the whole characterization of Socrates by Plato and Xenophon.[205]

On the third speech of Socrates,[206] both Plato and Xenophon seem to be in general agreement. In Plato (*Apology* 39C) Socrates commences by prophesying that immediately after his death dire punishment will visit his judges. In Xenophon (*Defence* 30–31), however, Socrates makes the prophecy that the son of Anytus would turn into a disgraceful rogue. In addition, both Plato (*Apology* 41B) and Xenophon (*Defence*

26)²⁰⁷ mention the fate of Palamedes.²⁰⁸ But while in Plato, Socrates hopes to hold conversation with Palamedes in Hades, in Xenophon, the like fate of Palamedes affords Socrates some consolation.²⁰⁹

A general comparison of Xenophon's *Defence* and *Memorabilia*, Book I, chapters 1–2, and Plato's *Apology* should also reveal that Xenophon's characterization of Socrates, in the main, is a laborious and pedantic effort to absolve Socrates from any and all guilt— tactics which Plato, disdaining the pettiness of detailed rebuttal, seems to avoid scrupulously. In so doing Xenophon constantly retouches and alters the portrait of Socrates in order to bring out the fact that the latter always and in every detail of life had conducted himself in a most impeccable manner. Plato, on the other hand, tries to introduce Socrates as a man animated by strong, not to say sacred, convictions and the highest principles. Both Xenophon and Plato, each in his own way, take great pains in showing how Socrates faced death. In the report of Xenophon, Socrates' death, in the final analysis, remains the crowning event of his whole life, an event in which he achieves the full consummation of his conception of 'philosophical happiness'— a philosophical happiness commensurate with the limited outlook of a Xenophon who, after all, would always measure happiness by the standards of worldly success and achievement. In Plato's *Apology* Socrates is made out to be the martyr who dies the death befitting an uncompromising apostle of truth and virtue. The account of the pedestrian Xenophon as well as the particular significance which he attaches to Socrates' deportment in the face of certain death, therefore, is as different from the narrative and interpretation offered by the visionary poet-philosopher Plato as is a somewhat sentimental and essentially conventional elegy from true pathos.

It might also be helpful for a better understanding of the relationship of the Xenophontean *Defence* to the Platonic *Apology* to sketch briefly the different ways in which the apologetic tradition has dealt with the reason why Socrates was condemned to death. Obviously, the official indictment neither justifies nor sufficiently explains the tragic outcome of the trial. Hence, at least in the light of the apologetic tradition, the real cause for this final catastrophe would have to be looked for in Socrates' tacit admission that his case was lost from the beginning, and that an honourable death was for him the only acceptable solution. This seems to become evident not only from the general manner in which, according to the apologetic tradition, he defended himself, but also from the fact that he apparently was intent upon antagonizing his judges. In this the apologetic literature, on the whole, is fully in accord. But as to the explanation of why Socrates regarded his defence as lost, and in particular of why he apparently preferred to antagonize his judges rather than mollify them, the various Socratic sources differ considerably.

Xenophon's Defence of Socrates before his Judges

In a general way these reports can be subdivided into two major groups: those reports which maintain that Socrates acted from an 'inner compulsion' or, akin to the structure of the classical Greek tragedy, from an 'inner necessity' (Plato); and those reports which insist that he never seriously intended to defend himself, because he no longer cared about life (Xenophon). The first group actually contains two distinct versions. According to the first version, Socrates was doomed from the very beginning, because as the only just and virtuous man in Athens he was opposed by the whole of a corrupt and depraved society which could not tolerate him: 'No man who struggles against you ... honestly working against the many lawless and unjust deeds which are done in the city, will save his life.'[210] The second version contends that Socrates had always acted in compliance with a divine command.[211] But now he is faced with the dilemma of choosing between disobedience to God or death: 'Whether you acquit me or not ... I shall never alter my ways, not even if I have to die many times.'[212]

According to the second group of reports, Socrates never seriously intended to defend himself, because he felt that 'death was preferable to life'.[213] Here, too, we encounter two distinct versions of the same theme: one version seems to conform with that resignation or fatalism which was an essential part of the classical Greek view on life in general; and another version definitely endows Socrates' conduct during his trial with a religious or mystical pathos. The first version is the one accepted by Xenophon: should his life be spared, Socrates would only have to face old age with all its infirmities and unpleasantness. So far his life was rich in blessings and happiness, and even should he die now, 'God, in His goodness, has appointed for me not only that I should die at a time which seems to be the most seasonable, but also that the manner in which my life shall be terminated be the most agreeable. For if my death is now resolved upon ... I shall be permitted to choose the means supposed to be the most easy ... and least offending.'[214] The second version, traces of which can be found in Plato's *Crito*, *Phaedo*, and also in the *Apology*, tries to explain the conduct of Socrates in the light of his fervent belief that for him death was merely the gate through which his soul would return to its heavenly home. Hence the last two versions make it appear that Socrates actually desired death—although he claimed that 'the desire of death shall not influence me to go beyond what is reasonable'.[215]

Plato's *Apology*,[216] it may be observed here, cannot possibly contain the actual forensic speech or speeches which Socrates delivered in his own defence. Already during ancient times the historical truth of the Platonic *Apology* had been seriously contested.[217] Without doubt, from the point of view of apologetic oratory, the climax of the Platonic *Apology* is the passage where Socrates proclaims that his whole life's work was nothing other than compliance with a divine mission and that he had dedicated—nay, sacrificed!—the whole of his life to realize this divine ordinance.[218] It is difficult to believe that Socrates ever said such things in open court and in the face of an antagonistic audience, unless he suffered severely from personal vanity and conceit.[219] We may also allege that Socrates' parting remarks to his judges concerning the significance of death and the life thereafter are fictitious.

On the whole we are impressed with the fact that the Platonic Socrates of the *Apology*, unlike the Xenophontean Socrates, never really takes issue with the several points of the official indictment. Neither does the Platonic Socrates directly address his judges. He speaks rather to the Athenian people, to his contemporaries, and perhaps to the whole of mankind. This is definitely a Platonic twist, unknown to Xenophon. In all probability it was not in full accord with the historical events that took place during the actual trial in the year 399. It might be interesting, therefore, to conjecture here that Plato's *Apology* probably was written at a considerable time after the death of Socrates. This may be gathered from the following: Plato's earliest dialogues, namely, the *Laches*, *Charmides*, *Protagoras*, *Lysias*, *Meno* (?), and *Euthyphro*, that is to say, those dialogues which, chronologically, that is, in time of composition, precede the *Apology* and therefore are closest to the trial of 399, do not mention this tragic event.[220] In short, the trial and death of Socrates apparently concerned Plato only after an appreciable time-lapse. This alone would suggest that the Platonic *Apology*, although it deals with the trial of the year 399, probably was stimulated or occasioned not by this trial itself, but rather by the anti-Socratic literature which made its appearance a considerable time after the death of Socrates. In addition, the Platonic *Apology*, on the whole, impresses us as being a studied effort on the part of Plato to avoid as much as possible the methods and arguments employed by the traditional and stereotyped earlier Socratic apologies of which a goodly number must already have existed before Plato conceived his own brand of Socratic apology. For there can be little doubt that the Platonic *Apology*, like the Xenophontean apologies, presupposes the existence of several older Socratic apologies, a fact which should also explain some of the peculiarities of both the Platonic and Xenophontean apologies.[221]

3
Xenophon's Memorabilia 1.1.1–1.2.64

BOOK I, chapters 1 and 2 of the Xenophontean *Memorabilia* is actually an apology of Socrates. Originally it was conceived and carried out independently of *Memorabilia* 1.3.1–4.8.11[222] or the 'Socratic *Memoirs*' (Ἀπομνημονεύματα).[223] Among other things this may be gathered from the introductory passage of Book I, chapter 3, paragraph 1 of the *Memorabilia*, which contains the following remark: '... τὰ δὲ καὶ διαλεγόμενος τούτων δὴ γράψω ὁπόσα ἂν διαμνημονεύσω (I shall write whatever I can remember what he had said about these matters).[224] Whether or not Ἀπομνημονεύματα was the original title which the author gave to his 'collection of recollections' can no longer be ascertained. We may assume, however, that this title was added by a scholiast or scribe at a later date. The scholiast, when 'cataloguing' the writings of the ancients, gave them a title, using as a rule a conspicuous statement or expression usually found in the first sentence of the work. Now the terms ἀπομνημόνευμα (recollection), ἀπομνημονεύω (to remember), or διαμνημονεύω nowhere appear in *Memorabilia* 1.1.1. But *Memorabilia* 1.3.1 contain the word διαμνημονεύω (I remember), which in the form of a statement of purpose indicates the aim of the subsequent narrative. This alone would support our contention that *Memorabilia* 1.3.1 originally constituted the beginning of the Xenophontean *Memoirs* or *Recollections*, while *Memorabilia* 1.1.1–1.2.64 originally seem to have been a separate apologetic essay. The title '*Memorabilia*', as a matter of fact, does not at all fit *Memorabilia* I, chapters 1 and 2. It could be maintained, therefore, that this particular part of the *Memorabilia* was originally an independent short essay, published separately and, we may assume, at a considerable time prior to the writing of the remainder of the *Memorabilia*, that is, *Memorabilia* 1.3.1–4.8.11.

Memorabilia 1.1.1–1.2.64, in all probability, were written between the years 392 and 390, that is, shortly after 393/2, the year in which the κατηγορία Σωκράτους of Polycrates was published.[225] This Xenophontean *Apology of Socrates*, as we might call *Memorabilia* 1.1.1–1.2.64, has an entirely different purpose or motive than the *Defence of Socrates before his Judges*. The *Defence*, it has been noted, was intended to supplement and correct already existing Socratic apologies, namely,

Xenophon's Memorabilia 1.1.1–1.2.64

those apologies which dealt with the trial of the year 399 as well as those rejoinders that had been prompted by the publication of the Polycratean κατηγορία Σωκράτους. It is interesting to observe that the *Defence* not only seems to be acquainted with the κατηγορία of Polycrates, but that it actually makes a short but unmistakable reference to the latter. *Defence* 20, for instance, is nothing other than a short summary of, and reference to, *Memorabilia* 1.2.49–55, and as such is dependent on the latter. *Memorabilia* 4.8.1–11, again, seems to be definitely dependent on the *Defence*. Hence we might establish the following tentative chronology: *Memorabilia* 1.1.1–1.2.64 were published as an independent and separate essay between the years 392 and 390. The *Defence* was written after the year 385/4,[226] and *Memorabilia* 1.3.1–4.8.11 were composed after the *Defence*. On the basis of certain indications we may assume that *Memorabilia* 1.3.1 ff. were written after 370: the conversation between Socrates and the younger Pericles (*Memor.* 3.5.1–28) about the ways by which Athens could recover her ancient spirit, definitely refers to the political situation in Greece as it existed after the battle of Leuctra in 371. This would also support our theory that *Memorabilia* 4.8.1–11 are an excerpt from the *Defence*.[227] All these works, we may surmise, were written at Scillus in Elis where Xenophon took refuge after his banishment from Athens in 393/2.

Although the *Defence* is acquainted with the κατηγορία of Polycrates, it fails to take special issue with the Polycratean pamphlet, and this despite the fact that the *Defence* is also a part of the apologetic literature which was motivated by the Polycratean attack on Socrates in the κατηγορία Σωκράτους. This seems to be a rather puzzling situation, unless we concede that *Memorabilia* 1.1.1–1.2.64 antedate the *Defence*. Since in *Memorabilia* 1.1.1–1.2.64, or at least in *Memorabilia* 1.2.9–61, Xenophon already had thoroughly rebutted the Polycratean κατηγορία, he is of the opinion, we conjecture, that in the *Defence* he can well dispense with the task of making detailed reference to the accusations of Polycrates. Hence we could contend that the *Defence* deals not only with the trial of Socrates, but also with the κατηγορία Σωκράτους of Polycrates, at least in passing.

Memorabilia 1.1.1–1.2.64 actually consist of three distinct parts: The first part, namely, *Memorabilia* 1.1.1–1.2.8, concerns itself with the official indictment of Socrates in 399. In this it is somewhat akin to the *Defence* as well as the Platonic *Apology*. The second part, *Memorabilia* 1.2.9–61, takes issue with the 'accuser', that is, with the charges made by Polycrates in his κατηγορία Σωκράτους. As such it belongs to that type of apologetic literature which came into its own after the publication of the Polycratean pamphlet in 393/2. The third part, *Memorabilia* 1.2.62–64, is once more concerned with the official trial of Socrates in 399. The direct rebuttal of the Polycratean κατηγορία in *Memorabilia* 1.2.9–61, is compressed between two reports on the historical trial of

Xenophon's Memorabilia 1.1.1–1.2.64

Socrates. This does not mean, however, that *Memorabilia* 1.2.9–61 constitute a later insertion, as has been suggested. Since the Polycratean κατηγορία was phrased in the terms of a forensic 'accusation' delivered by Anytus, the chief 'prosecutor' during Socrates' trial, Xenophon apparently felt justified in dealing at one and the same time both with the official indictment of 399 and the charges of Polycrates. In any event, the specific rejoinders to Polycrates are set off from the general *Apology* in that Xenophon introduces his anti-Polycratean arguments with a reference to 'the accuser' (κατήγορος).[228] In short, *Memorabilia* 1.2.9–61 are a rejoinder to a series of arguments prejudicial to Socrates, arguments which apparently had gained credence through the publication of Polycrates' κατηγορία Σωκράτους.

It would be an interesting, but quite fruitless speculation to assume that *Memorabilia* 1.2.9–61 were an original and independent work which had been written prior to *Memorabilia* 1.1.1–1.2.8 and 1.2.62–64, but were later inserted between *Memorabilia* 1.1.1–1.2.8 and 1.2.62–64 by an unknown scholiast or scribe. For this much seems to be certain: *Memorabilia* 1.2.62–64 apparently resume the narrative of *Memorabilia* 1.1.1–1.2.8, interrupted by the inclusion of the rebuttals of the Polycratean κατηγορία in *Memorabilia* 1.2.9–61. If we could accept the theory that *Memorabilia* 1.2.9–61 originally were an independent essay, then we would have to speak of three Socratic apologies of Xenophon, namely, (1) *Memorabilia* 1.1.1–8 and 1.2.62–64; (2) *Memorabilia* 1.2.9–61; and (3) the *Defence*.[229] The relative dates of these alleged three apologies, therefore, would be the following: *Memorabilia* 1.2.9–61 would have to be the first of these three apologies. Xenophon returned from Asia together with King Agesilaus in 394. Probably for this treasonable conduct he was indicted in 394/3 and banished to Scillus. Since the κατηγορία Σωκράτους of Polycrates was published in 393/2, Xenophon had little time between the battle of Coronea and the publication of the κατηγορία to write *Memorabilia* 1.1.1–1.2.8 and 1.2.62–64. Hence we must assume that he composed first the rejoinder to Polycrates, that is, *Memorabilia* 1.2.9–61, if these rebuttals are at all a separate work. In support of the priority of the rebuttals over the remainder of *Memorabilia* 1.1.1–1.2.64 we could also cite the fact that it was the κατηγορία of Polycrates which aroused the apologetic fervour of Xenophon, and that, therefore, a specific reply to the Polycratean charges was the most urgent task confronting Xenophon. The second apology, then, would have been *Memorabilia* 1.1.1–1.2.8 and 1.2.62–64, while the *Defence* would be the third apology which, for reasons already indicated, could not have been written before 385/4. But as has been shown, there exists no particular reason why we should assume that *Memorabilia* 1.1.1–1.2.64 contain two separate apologies, each of which was originally a separate and independent essay. *Memorabilia* 1.2.9–61 fit very well into a general argument and rebuttal of Socrates' alleged corruption of

Xenophon's Memorabilia 1.1.1–1.2.64

Athenian youths. And the Xenophontean rebuttal of this particular charge begins with *Memorabilia* 1.2.1. In addition, it should be kept in mind that Polycrates delivers his tirades against Socrates through Anytus, thus giving the impression that the whole of the κατηγορία is merely a part of Socrates' official prosecution which originally had been engineered by this man Anytus.

Memorabilia 1.1.1–1.2.64, on the whole, also differ considerably from all other known writings of Xenophon in that the general background of this whole account, with the exception perhaps of the specific materials used by Xenophon for his counter-arguments or rejoinders, is apparently to a high degree historical. The usual Xenophontean method of presenting his views in the form of a dialogue plays only a minor role in *Memorabilia* 1.1.1–1.2.64, which, in the main, seem to be a fairly factual and trustworthy report. The apologist, it appears, is quite anxious to avoid flagrant inaccuracies. Apparently he does not dare to digress from the true and probably well known events, realizing that any apology which, save for a few pardonable rhetorical exaggerations, deviates too obviously from the actual truth, is not only fruitless, but in all likelihood more damaging than helpful. Nevertheless, it must be admitted that Xenophon's characterization of Socrates in *Memorabilia* 1.1.1–1.2.64 as well as in the *Defence* is probably exaggerated. It seems that in his apologetic fervour Xenophon tries to portray an essentially idealized and probably Antisthenian Socrates.

In *Memorabilia* 1.1.1 Xenophon lists first the official indictment against Socrates: 'Socrates offends against the law in that he does not recognize (or, worship) the gods whom the city acknowledges (or, worships), and in that he introduces other and new deities. He also offends against the law in that he corrupts youths.'[230] According to Favorinus the bill of indictment began: 'This indictment and affidavit is sworn to by Meletus, the son of Pitthos, against Socrates, the son of Sophroniscus of Alopece.' It ended with the remark, 'the penalty demanded is death'. It may be assumed that the report of Favorinus, recorded by Diogenes Laertius (2.40), is based on historical facts. Xenophon's account is approximately identical with that of Favorinus who allegedly saw the bill of indictment in the public archives of Athens. Xenophon prefaces his report with the following remark: 'The bill of indictment (γραφή) read approximately (τοιάδε τις) as follows.' Since he records merely the 'approximate wording' of this bill, he apparently feels that he can omit both the introductory and concluding passages of Favorinus. There is a simple explanation for the differences that exist between the report of Xenophon and that of Favorinus: the latter might possibly reproduce the official indictment as it had been phrased during the pre-trial examination before the *basileus*, while Xenophon seems to list the charges as they were presented either during the trial itself, or submitted to the *basileus* at the opening of the pre-trial session.[231]

Plato (*Apology* 24B), by recounting the 'theological charge' after the charge of corrupting youth, differs somewhat from Xenophon who presents this matter in the inverse order.[232]

Xenophon proceeds (*Memor.* 1.1.2)[233] to refute the charge that Socrates refused to recognize the gods whom the city worshipped.[234] It should be noted here that Xenophon introduces his defence of Socrates with the term πρῶτον (in the first place). This term seems to indicate an order of presentation proposed by Xenophon. There is, however, never a δεύτερον (in the second place) in the *Memorabilia*, with the possible exception of *Memorabilia* 4.5.1. It is therefore suggested that in Xenophon's *Memorabilia* the term πρῶτον signifies that Xenophon is about to discuss a religious (or 'first') issue. In his rebuttal Xenophon insists that Socrates frequently worshipped at home as well as in public,[235] and that he made use of divination.[236] But because 'Socrates used to say that the deity instructed him personally',[237] people suspected him of introducing new deities into the city.[238] A. E. Taylor (*Varia Socratica* 10–11) suggests that, unlike Plato, Xenophon apparently insinuates here that he knows the exact ground on which this particular accusation is based. In his opinion it was Socrates' claim to possess a 'divine sign' which gave rise to the belief that he had introduced novel deities. But Xenophon's explanation is untenable, something which he himself is naïve enough to point out when he insists (*Memor.* 1.1.3) that Socrates' belief in his 'voice' or 'sign' stands on the same level as the belief of other men in 'supernatural signs'. Hence, if Socrates should have been charged with impiety merely for believing in his 'voice', then practically every Athenian might have been prosecuted on the same charge. Since Meletus in Plato's *Apology* makes no allusion to a 'sign', it may be surmised that it was not referred to in the indictment and, consequently, was not an issue at the trial. It seems, therefore, that Xenophon tries here to defend Socrates against the charge of having introduced 'new deities' by identifying the Socratic daemon with those 'supernatural signs' (σημεῖον) which were commonly accepted as a part of the Greek religious ritual.[239] The interpretation of the Socratic daemon as a mere 'sign' or 'voice' is less dangerous than the affirmation of an active daemon which could be understood as a 'novel deity' introduced by Socrates.

In asserting that the deity instructed him personally, Xenophon continues (*Memor.* 1.1.3), Socrates 'did nothing more novel[240] than those who, when practising divination, consult auguries of all sorts,[241] ... believing that by such means the gods manifest their will. And this was also the tenet of Socrates.' Xenophon seems to stress here that Socrates had always spoken of a sign given by a supernatural being (σημαίνειν), an expression which Heraclitus of Ephesus had already used.[242] In another place (*Defence* 12–13), however, Xenophon refers to a 'voice' (φωνή), an expression which can also be found in some of

Plato's dialogues, although the latter refuses to define more closely this 'voice'.

The religious 'clauses' in the official indictment, it seems, did not refer to Socrates' disbelief in religious mythology which he had so frequently expressed in Plato's dialogues; neither apparently had the charge that Socrates had introduced new deities anything to do with the 'voice' or 'sign' which Socrates allegedly received, at least not according to the report of Plato. This is quite obvious from the fact that no reference was made to this 'voice' during the trial until Socrates himself raised the issue. In Plato (*Apology* 31c), Socrates tells the story about the 'voice', remarking that 'this is presumably what Meletus has ridiculed in his indictment'. Euthyphro (*Euthyphro* 3B ff.), on the other hand, suggests that the 'voice' may be what Meletus had in mind when he called Socrates 'a maker of novel deities'. Xenophon (*Memor.* 1.1.3) seems to repeat the suggestion made by Euthyphro. But he does so only in order to prove that there was nothing in the nature of the 'voice' to support the allegation of blasphemy.[243]

Worship according to the laws of the city was part of the sacred law which also prescribed feast days and festive periods, processions, games, and public sacrifices in which every citizen had a solemn duty to participate in the required form. This sacred law which, among other things, determined the rights and duties of kings, magistrates, clans, and ordinary citizens, was the ultimate foundation of the city itself. It was the true ἴδιος νόμος, the unwritten city constitution (πολιτεία), in other words, the 'proper order' as well as the basic unity and continuity of the city. Hence there always existed a close relationship between religious cult and the city itself, between worship and the basic idea of the common *polis*. One aspect of this ἴδιος νόμος was, therefore, the proper worship of the city gods. Proper worship and regular participation in this worship was the sacred duty of every citizen; it was, as a matter of fact, the common bond of citizenship. Anyone who did not worship as the city worshipped, or who worshipped gods other than those which the city recognized, could either by banished or put to death as one who threatened not only the unity, but the very existence of the city. The close connection between uniformity of worship and unity of the city became manifest in the expression νομίζειν θεοὺς (to worship the gods in accordance with the laws of the city).

The 'religious indictment' of Socrates, it could be argued, was an ingenuous piece of sophistry, drawn up in ambiguous, though apparently carefully chosen, words. We remember that already the seer Diopeithes had condemned the teachers of 'celestial theories' for not believing in 'divine things' (τὰ θεῖα, Plutarch, *Pericles* 32). This statement could mean one of two things: Diopeithes might have objected to a purely scientific explanation of heavenly phenomena, leaving no room for omens and augury; or τὰ θεῖα could refer to religion in general, suggesting that the 'new philosophers' did not believe in the existence of the gods, the senders of these omens. In his *Apology*, Plato seems to imply that the prosecution mainly relied upon, and even fostered, a confusion in the public mind which identified Socrates with such 'new philosophers' as Anaxagoras, Diogenes of Apollonia, Archelaus, Diagoras of Melos, and Protagoras, whose teachings, aside from being opposed to popular Greek religion, were incompatible with the traditional art of augury. This particular confusion can already be detected in the *Clouds* (365) of Aristophanes, where the general theme is being advanced that a man who, like Socrates, studies 'the things in the sky and under the earth', does not believe in the gods.[244] For in the *Clouds* (380 ff.) Dinos not only supersedes Zeus,[245] one of the gods whom the city recognizes under the name of Zeus Polieus; but the cult of Air, Ether, and Clouds takes here the place of the worship of the traditional gods.[246] In addition, the view is being advanced that thunder, lightning, and rain are due to 'metabolic disturbances' in the clouds rather than to divine action. In sum, the Aristophantean Socrates is depicted as denying both the existence of omens and that of Zeus, who is replaced by such 'novel deities' as Air, Ether, and Clouds. These novel deities, no less than their behaviour, are referred to in terms devised by the new physical sciences, something which, according to popular belief, would justify the charge of atheism. Meletus seems to have accepted this popular belief when he charges Socrates with atheism (Plato, *Apology* 26c ff.), without realizing, however, that in doing so he contradicts that part of the indictment which charges Socrates with having introduced novel deities. No wonder that Socrates should come back with the remark that Meletus confuses him with Anaxagoras; that he was never concerned with 'the things in the heavens'; that he never taught anyone in secret (*Apology* 19c); and that there is no truth in Aristophanes' description of his alleged school.[247] All this would also explain why Xenophon should take such great pains to demonstrate that Socrates believed in omens and augury, just as any pious Athenian of old would have done; and that he not only believed in the traditional gods of the city, but also worshipped them in the prescribed manner. Now we can also understand why Xenophon (*Memor.* 1.1.11–12) so vehemently denies that Socrates, in contrast to other philosophers, had ever speculated about such high matters as the cause and nature of the universe. For, as Xenophon puts it, Socrates was surprised that the new philosophers should not realize that these problems were beyond human comprehension.

But while other people merely observed the various manifestations of the divine will, Xenophon continues (*Memor* 1.1.4), 'Socrates insisted that the deity was his personal monitor.'[248] Of these divine manifestations and premonitions he told his friends, who greatly profited thereby.[249] The ever-practical Xenophon apparently wishes to convey here the

Xenophon's Memorabilia 1.1.1–1.2.64

idea that, since advantage attended those who listened to Socrates' premonitions, the signs which Socrates received were definitely sent by the gods.[250] This alone, Xenophon concludes (*Memor.* 1.1.5), should prove that he trusted divine premonitions and hence believed in the gods: 'How could he, who had complete faith in the gods, think that there were no gods.'

In some of their private problems Socrates counselled his friends personally, Xenophon contends (*Memor.* 1.1.6–9), but whenever the solution was doubtful, he advised them to seek auguries.[251] For 'those who would manage families or cities well, he said, needed divination'.[252] But purely technical questions he considered matters of learning and human judgment, although he conceded 'that the gods reserved to themselves the most important problems connected with these technical questions'.[253] And while he called those impious and even insane who held that nothing depended on the gods, he berated those who resorted to divination when dealing with trivial matters. He also insisted 'that it was the duty of men to learn whatever the gods enabled them to do by learning, and to try to ascertain by divination from the gods whatever was obscure to men.[254] For the gods always grant information to those toward whom they are well disposed'.[255]

What Xenophon tries to show here is that those problems which can be reduced to measure (or number) and weight and, hence, are a matter of experience, can be decided without having recourse to divine assistance. The idea that certain questions of practical life can be answered by the use of 'natural reason', is also discussed in Plato (*Euthyphro* 7B–7D). That there exists such a thing as a 'human science of ethics', is one of the problems which Plato attempts to demonstrate. It might be interesting to compare the views advanced here by Xenophon with the ideas championed by some of writers who contributed to the Hippocratic corpus. The author of *On ancient medicine*, in particular, apparently was fully aware of the difference between dogmatic speculation and empirical method. Our author—and it is not impossible that Hippocrates himself wrote this treatise—strongly condemns those 'theoreticians' who, by assuming some dogmatic starting-point, proceed to make certain statements of fact which are manifestly untrue. 'Hence I maintain,' continues our author, 'that [medicine]... has no need of empty postulates such as are inevitable in dealing with insoluble problems beyond the reach of observation, for example, what transpires in the heavens and beneath the earth. If a man pronounces some opinion he has formed on how these things are, it cannot be clear either to himself or to his listeners whether what he says is true or not. For there is no test that can be applied so as to yield certain knowledge.' Our author then goes on to claim that medicine, as an experimental science, needs no remote and abstract assumptions. It rests solely upon competent and methodical discovery. Any other method will lead to utter self-deception. No absolute standards of measure and weight can be fixed: the only acceptable standard for medicine is the way in which the individual patient reacts to a specific cure. The best physician is he who makes the least mistakes.[256] This hostile attitude towards dogmatic *a priori* speculation can easily be explained: medicine, as a 'practical art', had a long and respected history before it ever felt the need of developing anything resembling a scientific basis for its procedure. The physician was a 'healer', a 'worker with his hands', or a 'craftsman in the public service', whose reputation depended on his practical success rather than his theories. Unlike the philosopher speculating on matters beyond the reach of observation and experiment—such as the origin of the universe or the 'things that transpire in the heavens and beneath the earth'—he is compelled to start from accurate observation of individual cases, to note what has gone wrong, and to find out how it can be set right. No wonder that the author of *On ancient medicine* (chap. 13) should also attack the methods and theories of those men who use as their starting-point the postulate that all diseases are due to an excess of dryness or moisture, heat or cold; and that, in consequence, they must be cured by counteracting each of these with its opposite.

Memorabilia 1.1.1–9 deserve some further analysis. After having enumerated the various points of the official indictment, Xenophon (*Memor.* 1.1.2) begins to discuss the charge that 'Socrates ... does not worship the gods which the city worships', and that he had introduced other and new deities'. Proceeding in a somewhat systematic manner, Xenophon proves (I) that Socrates sacrificed frequently to the gods, (*a*) not only at home, (*b*) but also in public; and (II) that he made use of divination. Though the first allegation is not discussed any further by Xenophon,[257] the reference to the use of divination by Socrates becomes the starting-point of a lengthy discussion. In order to prove that Socrates had made use of divination, Xenophon refers to the Socratic daemon with the startling result that this reference, rather than exonerating Socrates of the serious charge of having failed to worship properly the 'accepted gods', may actually substantiate the charge that Socrates had introduced other and new deities. This sudden and unexpected 'twist' then forces Xenophon to explain the Socratic daemon (*Memor.* 1.1.3–5). We may assume, therefore, that *Memorabilia* 1.1.3–5 were a later and somewhat disjointed addition to a general treatment of Socrates' attitude toward worship and divination, necessitated by the possible misunderstanding of the reference to the Socratic daemon. The general discussion of Socrates' attitude toward worship and divination is again resumed in *Memorabilia* 1.1.6

Memorabilia 1.1.6–8 contain what seems to be a coherent presentation of Socrates' religious convictions. *Memorabilia* 1.1.6, in the form of an introductory remark, make the distinction between 'ordinary

Xenophon's Memorabilia 1.1.1–1.2.64

matters of life of necessary consequences' (ἀναγκαῖα) with which every man has to cope by himself through the use of his natural faculties, and the 'darker problems' (ἄδηλα), the issues of which are incalculable and, therefore, require divination. *Memorabilia* 1.1.7, which elaborate this distinction, contain a list of those 'technical arts' (architecture, working of metals, agriculture) which are a matter of human learning and understanding, and those 'political arts' (politics, economics, generalship) which stand in need of divination. This list is somewhat distorted by the addition of the passage, '... ἢ τῶν τοιούτων ἔργων ἐξεταστικόν, ἢ λογιστικὸν ...' (together with the theory of these arts and their logical principles). This passage apparently is meant to connect *Memorabilia* 1.1.6–8 and *Memorabilia* 1.1.9. *Memorabilia* 1.1.9, which seem to take up a somewhat different idea, begin with an antithesis: to hold that nothing is contingent on the gods is as blasphemous as is the opinion that one has to consult the gods on questions, the solution of which could be intelligently arrived at through the natural faculties of man. Thus man is capable of deciding by himself that it is better to proceed intelligently and competently in all his actions and undertakings than to do so without intelligence and competence.[258] All those problems, the answer to which is based upon number, measure, and the like, in the final analysis can be decided competently by man, while those matters which defy mathematical determination stand in need of divination. In this fashion he indicates, as Plato later was to do, that there exists a valid ethical science based on 'natural (mathematical) reason', and that the province of the τέχναι or the ἐπιστήμη must be distinguished from the domain of divination where we also find the answer to the question concerning the last purpose of all human actions.

Although Socrates was constantly subject to public scrutiny,[259] Xenophon continues, (*Memor.* 1.1.10–16), 'no one ever saw him doing or heard him saying anything impious or profane'.[260] Refusing to discuss matters of cosmogony or cosmology, he considered foolish those who engaged in such discussions,[261] particularly since they usually knew nothing about the truly important human affairs. As a matter of fact, he held 'that it was impossible for man to satisfy himself on such points [*scil.*, cosmological questions]',[262] the more so, since on these points there was never any agreement. On the contrary, those who boast that they know something about these matters, go after one another 'like madmen: Some have no fear of what is to be feared, and some fear what is not to be feared; some think it no shame to say or do anything in the presence of others, while some believe that they are not to go among men at all; some pay no respect ... to the gods, and some worship stones, and common stock and beasts. And when speculating on the nature of the universe, some imagine that all that exists is but one, and some that there are worlds infinite in number; some hold that all things are in perpetual motion, and some that nothing is ever moved;

some believe that all things are generated and corrupted, and some that nothing is ever generated or corrupted'.²⁶³ Concerning these philosophers of nature Socrates would inquire whether their speculations were of any practical use 'either to themselves or to anyone else'.²⁶⁴ But he himself would from time to time discuss matters 'concerning mankind,²⁶⁵ considering what was pious and what impious; what becoming (or, beautiful) and what unbecoming (or, ugly); what noble and what base; what just and what unjust; what sane and what insane; what courageous and what cowardly; what a state was and what the character and qualification of a statesman; and what was the nature of government over men. And he also touched on other subjects which to understand he regarded a mark of honour and distinction'.²⁶⁶

The principal effort of Xenophon seems to consist here in absolving Socrates from all suspicion of impiety, blasphemy, or profanity. To this end he makes every effort to contrast Socrates with other philosophers and sophists, particularly the Ionian physicists who since the days of Anaxagoras had been suspected of irreligiousness. *Memorabilia* 1.1.11-16, particularly 1.1.16,²⁶⁷ contain what might be called the educational ideas or ideals of Xenophon. As shall be shown later, he seems to rely here on some Antisthenian-Cynic source. The ideas professed by Xenophon are actually those of a conservative or 'fundamentalist' thinker who perceives in every original thought a covert attack upon religion and tradition. Hence he derides and denounces those who seem to waste their time meditating about the heavens instead of engaging in some practical or lucrative pursuit. *Memorabilia* 1.1.11-16 (and 4.7.1-10), therefore, could also be called an 'autobiographical sketch' of Xenophon. This proclivity for practical and profitable pursuits, this aversion to any innovation or scientific progress, is typically Xenophontean, as his other writings indicate.

Since Socrates 'gave no intimation what his sentiments were in respect to certain matters', Xenophon observes (*Memor.* 1.1.17), 'it is not surprising that the judges should have arrived at a wrong conclusion about him'.²⁶⁸ But this remark probably refers to the 'political views' held by Socrates. Xenophon apparently suggests here that Socrates had never overtly stated his political convictions or participated in the inner-political struggles of Athens. A man, Plato (*Apology* 32A) remarks, 'who will fight for what is right ... must have a private station in life'. Plato seems to suggest here that Socrates did abstain from active participation in politics because he realized that his real gift lay in the power of influencing individuals by conversing with them, and that he had no power of swaying the masses. This is probably the true meaning of Plato, *Apology* 23B, where we are told that to converse with individuals is more valuable than to sway the multitude. Essentially the same idea is repeated by Xenophon (*Memor.* 1.6.15): 'In which of the two ways could I play a more important part in politics,' Socrates says to Antiphon, 'by engaging in them single-handed, or by making it my business to turn out as many good statesmen as possible?'

But Xenophon persists that the judges should have remembered Socrates' honourable and courageous conduct during the trial of the generals in 406 (*Memor.* 1.1.18–20),[269] when, 'in spite of bitter resentment of the people, and the threats uttered against him by influential citizens ... he considered it of higher importance to abide by his oath of office than to gratify the demands of the people in violation of the principle of right and justice, or to safeguard himself from the menaces of the mighty'.[270] 'Unlike many others he thought that the gods were interested in the affairs of man,' holding 'that the gods know all things' and 'give admonitions to men concerning everything human'.[271] Hence Xenophon marvels 'how the Athenians could ever be persuaded that Socrates did not have the right sentiments as regards the gods—a man who never said or did anything impious towards the gods, but spoke and acted in such a manner concerning the gods that had anyone else spoken or acted in the same manner, he would have been ... considered an eminently pious person'.[272] Thus throughout the *Memorabilia*, Xenophon again and again stresses the fact that Socrates had exhorted his listeners to honour the gods which the city honoured.[273]

In chapter 2 of Book I of the *Memorabilia*, Xenophon tries to refute the charge that Socrates had corrupted youths[274] or, as we may gather from the text, that he had undermined the moral and political institutions of democratic Athens with his teachings. Josephus seems to corroborate this statement when he reports: 'On what grounds, then, was Socrates put to death? He never thought to betray his city to the enemy, he robbed no temple. No: because he used to swear strange oaths and maintained ... that he received communications from a daemon, he was condemned to drink the hemlock. His accuser (κατήγορος) brought a further charge against him, namely, the charge of corrupting youths, because he induced them to hold in contempt the constitution and the laws of their city'.[275] It seems that Josephus relied on Xenophon, *Memorabilia* 1.2.9–61 or on Polycrates' κατηγορία Σωκράτους for his source. This may be gathered from his use of the term κατήγορος as well as from the statement that Socrates had induced youths to despise the existing constitution and the established laws of their city.

Xenophon (*Memor.* 1.2.1–3) prefaces his rejoinder with the general observation that Socrates 'was the most rigid of all men in controlling his passions and sensuous appetites'.[276] How, then, could such a man 'render others impious, lawless, luxury loving, incontinent or too effeminate to endure labour?[277] On the contrary, he restrained many from such vices', making them honourable and worthy persons.[278] Although he constantly denied being a teacher, through his personal conduct he induced others to emulate him.[279] K. Joël points out rather convincingly[280] that the Antisthenian pedagogical ideal was to set an example to one's pupils rather than to discuss virtue theoretically. This idea reappears in the Xenophontean *Memorabilia*, especially *Memorabilia* 1.2.2, where we are told that the true influence of Socrates on his disciples consisted in his model conduct.[281] In passing it may be mentioned that according to Plato (*Apology* 39CD), Socrates tells his judges that after his death there 'will be more critics of you, whom I have up to now restrained, though you did not notice. And the younger they are the more troublesome they will be, and the more you will resent them.' This statement involves a contradiction of what has been said in *Apology* 31A. There Socrates, after having described himself as a gadfly, maintains: 'You will not easily find another like me... unless God in His mercy should send you another.' Again, in *Apology* 23C, Socrates refers to certain young men who imitate his ἐξέτασις of the wise. This statement likewise seems to contradict both *Apology* 39CD and 31A: it contradicts 31A in that according to 23C there are followers of Socrates who carry on this ἐξέτασις; and it contradicts 39CD, since according to 23C Socrates seems to be unable to keep in check these young men even during his lifetime. It might be possible to reconcile *Apology* 23C with *Apology* 39CD if we were to assume that the passage, 'whom I have up to now restrained', in *Apology* 39CD signifies merely that Socrates had restrained the *excessive* zeal of his followers without, however, silencing them completely. *Apology* 31A, on the other hand, suggests that Socrates had no associates in his ἐξέτασις whatsoever. *Apology* 33A, again, stresses the fact that Socrates' followers were mere bystanders whenever he engaged in his ἐξέτασις.[282]

Xenophon also informs us (*Memor.* 1.2.4–5) that Socrates 'was not neglectful of the body, nor did he approve of those who neglected theirs'. Denouncing all forms of excess (*Memor.* 1.2.4), he himself favoured moderation because it is 'conducive to physical health without interfering with the cultivation of the mind'. The implication seems to be that Socrates could not possibly have corrupted young people by inducing them to neglect their bodies or their minds. In his moderation he was also averse to any form of ostentatiousness. At the same time 'he did neither tend to make his associates greedy of money',[283] nor would he leave their passions unchecked.[284] And he asked no remuneration from those who desired his company.[285] In *Memorabilia* 1.2.7, Xenophon points out that Socrates 'marvelled that anyone should make money through the teaching of virtue, and should not realize that his highest reward would be the winning of a good friend, as though anyone who had been benefited thus could ever fail to feel profound gratitude for a benefit so great'. This passage actually seems to be directed against Antisthenes who, as Isocrates informs us (*Contra Sophistes* 1–6), was worried that his disciples would not show the proper feeling of gratitude towards their teacher.[286] By refusing to take money from 'those who did seek out his company', Xenophon continues (*Memor.* 1.2.7-8), Socrates believed that, unlike others who accepted pay for teaching virtue, he was retaining the freedom of holding discussion with whomsoever he should choose. He was also of the opinion that those whom he had turned into honourable and worthy persons by his teachings would feel the profoundest gratitude towards him, their greatest benefactor, and would, by accepting his teachings, always be 'good friends to himself and others.'[287] How then, could a man of such character corrupt youths, unless the careful cultivation of virtue be corruption?'[288]

Xenophon then proceeds (*Memor.* 1.2.9) to refute certain charges made by the 'accuser', namely, that Socrates had taught youths 'to despise the established laws by pointing out the foolishness of electing magistrates by beans',[289] particularly since no one would be willing to select a technical expert by the use of the lot.[290] In this fashion, the 'accuser' continues, 'he tended to excite youths to become contemptuous of the established form of government, and thus disposed them to acts of violence'. Beginning with *Memorabilia* 1.2.9., it will be noticed, Xenophon no longer takes issue with the events that took, or may have taken place during the official trial of Socrates in 399, but with the charges contained in the κατηγορία Σωκράτους of Polycrates. 'The accuser' (ὁ κατήγορος) is Polycrates, the author of the κατηγορία Σωκράτους. As a matter of fact, *Memorabilia* 1.2.9-61 contain a detailed refutation of the charges which the Polycratean pamphlet had made against Socrates and the Socratics.[291]

Socrates' contempt for the political leaders of Athens, particularly for the democratic leaders, may be gathered from Plato (*Apology* 21c-22A): 'I went to see a man who had the reputation of being a wise man.... He was a politician.... [But] I found out that the men who had the greatest reputation were all but the greatest fools'.[292] Xenophon's 'political ideal', on the other hand, can be found in *Memorabilia* 3.9.10-11: 'Kings and people in command, he [*scil.*, Socrates] said, were not those who held the sceptre merely, or those elected by and from the multitude, or those who gained authority by the lot, or those who attained it by deceit, or violence, but rather those who knew how to rule. For when some one admitted that it was the part of the ruler to enjoin what another should do, and the part of him who was ruled, to obey, he showed by example that on a ship the skilful person is the commander, and that the owner and all the other people on the ship were obedient to the man who had the knowledge to command.' These ideas are somewhat similar to those expressed in Plato's *Statesman*. We may surmise that Antisthenes, in his dialogue *Archelaus or, Of kingship* (Diogenes Laertius 6.18), already had dealt with the problem of rulership, showing that he is not truly king who merely holds the sceptre, but he who possesses the βασιλικὴ τέχνη. True kingship or rulership is 'government of men with the consent of the governed and in accordance with the laws'. Despotism is 'the government of unwilling subjects, not in accordance with any laws, but forcibly imposed by the arbitrary will of the ruler'.[293] This passage, which impresses us as being Antisthenian, also influenced Plato (*Statesman* 291E) and Aristotle (*Politics* 1295 a 9 ff.).[294] Dio Chrysostom, in his third *Oration* (which is decidedly under Antisthenian-Cynic influence) likewise uses this distinction between the 'good king' and the 'evil tyrant'.

In the form of a rejoinder to the Polycratean allegation that Socrates had disposed people 'to acts of violence' by teaching them 'to despise the established laws', Xenophon points out (*Memor.* 1.2.10–11) that those who have the right understanding of things are opposed to violence, knowing that through gentle persuasion the desired results can always be achieved peacefully:[295] 'The use of violence is not the method of him who cultivates wisdom.' And he 'who ventures to employ violence needs the support of many to fight his battles, while he whose strength lies in persuasiveness triumphs without the assistance of anyone'. Xenophon's rejoinder on the whole is rather feeble and ineffective. This is not altogether surprising since the Socratic literature contains several references to Socrates' display of contempt for the accepted method of electing magistrates by the use of the lot.[296] Hence Xenophon could not very well deny the accusation of Polycrates. To Socrates, the use of the lot in electing magistrates, aside from leaving to chance what deliberate choice should have accomplished, involves the question of whether political office should be granted solely on the strength of political expertness and excellence, or whether it should be granted indiscriminately to all people. But if political office should be bestowed only on those who have this expertness and excellence, then the use of the lot is plain foolishness and contrary to reason or common sense. And this is the view held by Socrates according to the Socratics. In doing this Socrates merely identifies himself with a certain sophistic tradition which had stressed the importance and need of political knowledge and expertness for the qualified ruler. Already the sophists had discussed the merits and demerits of the use of the lot in the election of magistrates.[297] The arguments of the sophists against the use of the lot apparently were taken over by the Socratics, who went to extremes when they insisted that the political *episteme* constituted the sole justification for establishing rulership. Plato's famous philosopher-king (*Republic* 473C, 494B and 501E)[298] essentially is only an elaboration of this conviction.

'But, said the accuser', according to Xenophon (*Memor.* 1.2.12), 'Critias and Alcibiades, the two men who wrought the greatest evils to the city at any time, were both associates of Socrates'.[299] Aeschines (*Contra Timarchum* 173) points out that Socrates' association with Critias was most damaging to the reputation of the former, while

Xenophon's Memorabilia 1.1.1–1.2.64

Isocrates (*Busiris* 5) claims that contrary to the opinion held by Polycrates, Alcibiades was never a pupil of Socrates.[300] In this, however, Isocrates has against him the whole weight of the evidence supplied by Plato, Xenophon, Antisthenes, Aeschines, Lysias and others. The Polycratean charge referred to in *Memorabilia* 1.2.12, as shall be shown later, probably occasioned the whole of the early 'Alcibiades literature', as represented by Aeschines, Euclides of Megara, Antisthenes, and, perhaps, Phaedo of Elis.[301] The unknown author of the *Contra Alcibiadem*, formerly ascribed to Andocides, tries to demonstrate the 'antidemocratic sentiments' of Alcibiades by recounting the latter's conduct towards his brother-in-law Callias and his wife Hipparete (chaps. 13–16),[302] his treatment of the painter Agatharchus (chaps. 17–19) and of the *choregos* Taureas (*chaps.* 20–21) as well as the affair of the Melian woman (*chaps.* 22–23). Then the author proceeds to speak about Alcibiades' scandalous conduct during the Olympic Games (chaps. 25–33) and his contempt for democracy (chap. 27). It is quite possible that the 'accuser' (Polycrates) derived some of his charges from this Pseudo-Andocidean oration, provided that the latter was composed before 393.[303]

By linking Socrates with Critias and Alcibiades (*Memor.* 1.2.12), Polycrates alludes to the theme that a teacher who has evil or corrupt disciples must himself be evil and corrupt. This theme is frequently encountered in ancient literature: 'Wherefore by their fruits you shall know them'.[304] As a rule it was devised in order to discredit the teacher. There exists, for instance, a tradition that Themistocles had been a pupil of Anaxagoras.[305] Aeschines of Sphettus, in his dialogue *Callias* (Diogenes Laertius 2.61), charges Anaxagoras with having been the teacher of Philodemus and Eryxis, two men whose moral depravity was also the target of Aristophanes' ridicule. Plato (*Parmenides* 136E) narrates that among the listeners of Zeno of Elea was a man called Aristoteles who later became one of the ill-famed Thirty Tyrants. The account of Plato probably goes back to an older story which was invented in order to discredit Zeno as an evil teacher and corrupt 'sophist'. Hermippus, on the other hand, reports that Pericles had proved the innocence of his teacher Anaxagoras by referring to his own excellence as a statesman, implying thereby that only good men can have good disciples.

Xenophon, far from apologizing for the deeds of Critias and Alcibiades, shows (*Memor.* 1.2.13–16) that these two men were immoderately ambitious and ruthless, and that they had joined Socrates only to learn how to speak and act in order to promote more successfully their own political schemes. But 'as soon as they considered themselves superior to their associates, they started at once to move away from Socrates and engaged in political life'.[306] In short, Xenophon tries to deny that Critias and Alcibiades could properly be called disciples of Socrates.

Xenophon's Memorabilia 1.1.1–1.2.64

Of these two men, Critias and Alcibiades, the former was thoroughly detested by the vast majority of the Athenians as the chief instigator of the many atrocities and spoliations committed by the Thirty Tyrants. The name of Alcibiades, although he had some admirers not only during his lifetime but also after his death,[307] on the whole was odious both for his private insolence and public acts of treason.[308] That Critias and Alcibiades had at one time been in the company of Socrates is affirmed by the enemies of Socrates and conceded by his friends. While Xenophon insists that this association was merely one of convenience and, hence of short duration, Plato presents the attachment of Socrates to Alcibiades (and Critias) as having been continued and intimate.[309]

'Perhaps someone may observe at this point', Xenophon remarks (*Memor.* 1.2.17), 'that Socrates should not have taught his followers the art of politics before he taught them self-control (σωφρονεῖν)'.[310] Plato (*Republic* 537D–539D) likewise points out the many dangers inherent in the teaching of philosophy (and politics) to the morally unfit. He is aware of the possibility that philosophy may lead to scepticism and lawlessness, and that young people may begin to analyse the first principles of morality and in doing so may cease to respect them: 'Youngsters... often argue for amusement... and rejoice in pulling apart everything.... And they speedily get into a state of not believing anything which they had once believed.... Hence not only they, but also philosophy... are likely to fall into ill repute....'

If all true teachers, Xenophon contends (*Memor.* 1.2.17–18), set themselves up as examples by practising what they teach,[311] then Socrates was certainly an example to his pupils when he discussed virtue and whatever concerns mankind.[312] By his example and persuasion he made them practise self-control,[313] at least as long as they associated with him. In order to exonerate Socrates, Xenophon maintains (*Memor.* 1.2.19) that it is not true 'that a man once good, can never become unjust... and that no one who has once learned any of those things which can be taught, could become ignorant of what he has learned.... Those who do not continually exercise the mind cannot perform what is proper to the mind.' In passing it may be observed that the idea that a man who once knew what justice was would never voluntarily commit an act of injustice, has been ascribed to Socrates by Aristotle.[314] But it is also possible that this Aristotelian report ultimately goes back to Plato[315] or, perhaps, to Antisthenes.[316]

Virtue and intelligence must be continually exercised in order to become a permanent possession. Hence Xenophon observes (*Memor.* 1.2.20–23) that fathers, believing that association with good men is the best training for virtue, but association with bad men the destruction of virtue, make it a rule to keep their sons from associating with bad men.[317] Those who do not maintain the practice and recollection of moral precepts, soon forget the principles of self-control. 'It seems, therefore, that everything noble and good, including to a pre-eminent degree the virtue of self-control (σωφροσύνη), is the result of constant practice and training.' For in one and the same bodily frame sensual desires exist side by side with the soul, exciting the latter to abandon self-restraint for the sake of sensual self-gratification. The idea that virtue is the result of constant practice is probably of Antisthenian origin. Xenophon's own views on the question whether virtue, once acquired, can ever be lost, is contained in *Memorabilia* 1.2.19–23. His general conviction that everything excellent is the result of continuous and intelligent effort, also applies to this question: unless we practise virtue constantly and in the proper manner, we are apt to lose it like any other skill. Xenophon's remarks are definitely directed against Antisthenes, who had maintained that 'virtue can be taught ... and when once acquired, cannot be taken away'.[318]

As long as Critias and Alcibiades remained the associates of Socrates, Xenophon insists (*Memor.* 1.2.24–27), 'they were able, with the assistance of his example, to maintain a mastery over their ignoble inclinations and appetites'. But after they had deserted Socrates (*Memor.* 1.2.24–25), they fell in with bad company; and, giving way to their evil dispositions, they gradually lost the art of self-control[319] and grew headstrong. For this we cannot blame Socrates, who, at least while he was associated with them, kept them well-behaved and modest (*Memor.* 1.2.26).[320] No teacher can be blamed if a formerly competent pupil, after having attached himself to another master, should later deteriorate. 'And no father, if he had a son who in the society of one man remains an honest boy, but after falling into the company of some other person should become vicious, would blame the former associate. Would he not rather ... bestow his sincere praise upon the former?'[321] In the same manner we should judge Socrates, Xenophon maintains (*Memor.* 1.2.28–31): 'If he had committed anything immoral, he would justly be considered to be a bad man. But if he was consistently a good man, how can he reasonably bear the blame of evil which was not in him?'[322] As a matter of fact, he censored Critias for his conduct; and when the latter paid no attention to his remonstrations, he went so far as to compare him to a pig. For this Critias disliked Socrates and as one of the Thirty Tyrants passed a law 'that no one should be permitted to teach the art of disputation, intending thereby to harm Socrates'.[323] While Xenophon seems to insist here that this law was directly aimed at Socrates, it is safe to assume that, if it was at all historical, it was probably directed at the courts and the existing court practices as they had developed since the days of Solon and Cleisthenes. It is also possible that it was aimed at the nefarious practices of the sycophants whom the Thirty Tyrants apparently loathed.[324] Such a law, if enforced for any length of time, would also make impossible the adequate training of young men for the practice of law before the Athenian courts and, hence, gradually destroy the whole court system of democratic Athens. For 'legal training' in ancient Athens was part of general oratory and dialectics.[325] But Socrates, in the words of Xenophon (*Memor.* 1.2.32), was far from being intimidated by the interdict of Critias. On the contary, he observed: 'It would be sufficiently extraordinary if the herdsman of a herd of cattle, who was continually reducing the number of his cattle and rendering it in a worse condition, did not admit himself that he was a sorry sort of herdsman. But that a ruler of a city, who was continually reducing the number of citizens and rendering them in a worse condition, should neither be ashamed nor admit himself to be a sorry sort of ruler, this was more extraordinary still'.[326] Such incidents, we are told (*Memor.* 1.2.33–38), seem to have strained the relationship of Socrates and the Thirty Tyrants.[327] It will be noted that the alleged clash between Socrates and the Thirty Tyrants, described in *Memorabilia* 1.2.31–38, in all likelihood is nothing other than an effort on the part of Xenophon to absolve Socrates from all suspicion of having been an aristocratic-oligarchic partisan.[328] *Memorabilia* 1.2.33–38 also contain an instance of 'Socratic irony' otherwise not to be found in the *Socratica* of Xenophon. This alone would indicate that Xenophon uses here some source which had dramatized this clash very much to the advantage of the witty Socrates who exposes the dull and brutal oligarchic leader.

Xenophon then goes on to claim (*Memor.* 1.2.39) that neither Critias nor Alcibiades ever intended to abide by the teachings of Socrates: 'Where the teacher is not pleasing to the pupil, no real education may be derived from such a teacher. And it cannot be maintained that Critias and Alcibiades associated with Socrates because they found him pleasing to them'.[329] As a matter of fact, from the very beginning of their association with Socrates they were aspiring to the domination of the city.[330] For this end they were eager to meet only men who were most active in the affairs of government. Thus the story is recorded (*Memor.* 1.2.40–46) that at one time young Alcibiades, interested in political discussion and the art of government, had a lengthy conversation with Pericles concerning the nature of just laws.[331] In passing it may be noted that there also exists a report that Pericles had once spent a whole day with Protagoras discussing legal matters.[332] And Heracleides of Pontus, in his *On the laws*, states that Pericles had charged Protagoras with devising the laws for the newly founded city of Thurii.[333] It is not unlikely that the Xenophontean story of the 'political' conversation which allegedly took place between Alcibiades and Pericles, goes back to some of these traditions.

But when Critias and Alcibiades began to consider themselves superior to the people who were charged with the government of the city, Xenophon contends (*Memor.* 1.2.47–48), they ceased to associate with Socrates because he did not agree with their views. There were, however, other young men who did not seek out Socrates' company in order to become crafty politicians, but rather to become honourable and law-abiding citizens. No one of these latter people was ever guilty or accused of any crime.[334]

Xenophon then takes issue (*Memor.* 1.2.49)[335] with the Polycratean allegation that 'Socrates taught children to display contempt for their parents,[336] persuading his followers that he had made them wiser than their fathers,[337] and observing that under the law a son was permitted to confine his father on the charge that the latter was mentally deranged, using as an argument the contention that it was lawful for the more ignorant to be confined by the wiser.' This whole idea may go back to Antisthenes rather than Socrates.[338] The 'accuser', it seems, takes some of the material for his charges against Socrates from Antisthenes, whom he considers perhaps the most important Socratic disciple, probably very much to the chagrin of Plato. On the other hand it should also be borne in mind that the Xenophontean Socrates at times turns out to be an Antisthenian Cynic.[339] But, according to Xenophon (*Memor.* 1.2.50), Socrates merely has said that 'madmen may be confined... while those who did not know what they ought to know, might be expected to learn from those who did know'.[340] It can be gathered from *Memorabilia* 1.2.49–50 and 1.1.16, that the Xenophontean Socrates closely relates μανία (insanity) and ignorance. By implying that insanity is a form of ignorance, he then reaches the conclusion that since it is permissible to imprison an insane person, it is also permissible to dominate an ignorant person. The same idea reappears in *Memorabilia* 3.9.6, where we are told that madness is the opposite of wisdom (σοφία): 'But he [*scil.*, Socrates] did not identify ignorance with madness'. To the ancient Greek, however, μανία usually meant unrestrained passion and excess.[341]

In the words of Xenophon (*Memor.* 1.2.51–52), the 'accuser' had also charged that 'Socrates had not only caused parents but other relatives to be held in contempt by his followers,[342] claiming (*Memor.* 1.2.51) that relatives were of no profit to sick people or persons engaged in forensic litigations, since only a physician could help the former and lawyers the latter'.[343] In addition, the 'accuser' alleged that Socrates had said concerning friends[344] 'that it was of no profit that these friends were well disposed, unless they were also able to assist us in a practical way'.[345] Mere goodness of disposition counts for nothing, for 'only those are worthy of honour who combine with the knowledge of what is right the faculty of expounding it'. In this fashion he succeeded in convincing his pupils, whom he had made to believe that he was the wisest of mankind (*Memor.* 1.2.52), 'that compared to himself all other people were of no account'. As regards these particular charges, which touch upon the fundamental human relations, Xenophon admits (*Memor.* 1.2.53–54) that Socrates had expressed himself concerning parents and other relatives, including friends, in the manner claimed by the accuser: 'I can go further,' Xenophon insists, 'and add some other statements of his', such as 'when the soul has departed, which alone is the seat of intelligence', it is customary among men 'to bury the body of their dearest friend and put it out of sight'; or that even while still alive, 'every man removes from his own body, which he loves above all other things, or allows others to remove from it, everything that is useless and unprofitable . . .' such as his nails, hair, callouses, or saliva, which are likely more harmful than profitable.[346] But by saying all this, Xenophon continues (*Memor.* 1.2.55), Socrates did not intend to teach his followers that they should 'bury their fathers alive, or cut themselves to pieces'. He merely wished to show in this fashion that senseless things are really worthless. On the contrary, this was his method of exhorting every one of his pupils 'to become as intelligent and useful as possible, so that, whether he wished to be honoured by his father, by his brother, or by anyone else, he would not be neglectful of himself through trusting to mere relationship, but strive to be useful to those whose esteem he coveted'.[347]

Xenophon then takes issue (*Memor.* 1.2.56–57) with the charge that Socrates, 'by carefully culling the worst (or, most immoral) passages from the most celebrated poets, and by using them as arguments, had taught his followers to be evil-doers and tyrannical'. Thus he is said to have quoted Hesiod[348] in order to prove to his associates that they should not abstain from any kind of work, even the most dishonourable, as long as it was profitable work. Xenophon points out, however, that Socrates had merely maintained that 'to keep busy is a blessing and a benefit to a man,[349] and to be a lazy do-nothing is disgraceful and evil; that work is good and idleness a curse. . . . But only those who are engaged in doing some good work are really working, while those who play dice or gamble, or are engaged in some base and ruinous activity are truly idle people.' Essentially the same idea is repeated in *Memorabilia* 3.9.9: 'Considering the nature of idleness he [*scil.*, Socrates] said that he found most men doing something. For instance, the dice player, the gambler or the buffoon do something. But he considered these people to be idle, because it was within their power to change their profession and do something better.'

If we can put any reliance on Xenophon (*Memor.* 1.2.58–60), Socrates had also been accused of having quoted a passage from Homer[350] in order to demonstrate that lowly and poor people should be treated with contempt and severity.[351] Isocrates (*Busiris* 5), we know, takes issue with Polycrates for his contention that Socrates had quoted this particular Homeric passage in order to prove Socrates' contempt for the common or lowly people or, to be more exact, the 'people's government' or democracy. Hence we are compelled to assume that *Memorabilia* 1.2.58–59, where Xenophon insists that Socrates never entertained such views, are primarily a rebuttal of Polycrates: 'For he would thus have maintained that he himself ought to be beaten.' He merely observed that people 'who were useful neither in word nor deed: who in time of need were incapable of rendering service to the army or the city or the people, should, especially if, in addition to their incapacity, they were of an insolent spirit, be curbed in every way, be they ever so wealthy'. Contrary to the charge of the accuser, Socrates, always having been a man of a liberal and kindly disposition, 'was evidently a friend of the common people' who never demanded payment from his listeners.[352] The ideas expounded in *Memorabilia* 1.2.60 can also be found in Xenophon's *Symposium* (4.43), where Antisthenes maintains: 'I am niggardly to no one, but . . . share my spiritual wealth with anyone who desires it.' It seems that to give of one's intellectual or spiritual wealth without stinting or remuneration is an Antisthenian-Cynic characteristic which Xenophon attributes here to Socrates. In *Memorabilia* 1.6.3, Antiphon chides Socrates for his refusal to take any money for his teaching, 'the getting of which is a pleasure'. Antiphon seems to imply here that, since Socrates never took any money, he could not have been a competent teacher. Socrates' reply is quite interesting: 'Is it not true that those who take money are bound to carry out the work for which they receive a fee? I, on the other hand, because I refuse to accept any money, am under no obligation to discourse with anyone against my will.' Later in *Memorabilia* 1.6.13 Socrates calls those who sell wisdom to all customers for money σοφίστας or prostitutes: 'But . . . he who . . . teaches another all the possible good, fulfils his duty as a citizen and a good man.' No wonder that 'he [*scil.*, Socrates] also marvelled that anyone should make money through the teaching of virtue, and should not realize that his highest reward would be the gaining of a good friend: as though he who had become a good man could ever fail to feel a deep gratitude for a gift so great'.[353]

According to Xenophon (*Memor.* 1.2.61), in the eyes of many people Socrates had reflected great honour on Athens[354] by imparting freely the knowledge at his command.[355] To Xenophon (*Memor.* 1.2.62), Socrates was a man worthy of honour rather than death.[356] In the *Defence* (chap. 25) Xenophon contends that Socrates never committed any capital crime,[357] and that the prosecution had never charged him with a capital crime during the whole trial. Hence he considers the sentence of death an act of crudest injustice.

Athenian law made a distinction between criminal proceedings where the penalty was not fixed in advance (ἀγῶνες τιμητοί—discretionary crimes), and those proceedings in which the penalty was fixed in advance (ἀγῶνες ἀτίμητοί—non-discretionary crimes). In other words, the penalty was sometimes left to the discretion of the judges or even based on a preliminary agreement between the parties, while sometimes it was determined in advance by law or by some special decree. In proceedings of the first category a special procedure became necessary in order to fix the penalty. The prosecutor and the defendant in turn each proposed a penalty to the tribunal. Both the prosecutor and the defendant were allowed a short time in which to justify their proposal (τίμησις) or counter-proposal (ἀντιτίμησις). Then a second vote was taken in which the judges, in order to preclude any arbitrariness, could only pronounce for one or the other of the two proposals without being able to adopt a middle course or suggest their own penalty.

It seems that the capital crimes which Xenophon enumerates in *Defence* 25 (sacrilege, man-stealing, undermining of walls, betrayal of the city) are 'non-discretionary crimes', that is, crimes which make capital punishment mandatory. This view is supported by the wording of *Memorabilia* 1.2.62, which list the following 'non-discretionary crimes': stealing, stripping people of their clothes, cutting purses, housebreaking, man-stealing. In *Memorabilia* 1.2.63 Xenophon refers to some additional capital crimes, namely, incitement to war, sedition, and treason. The fact that he mentions two distinct sets of capital crimes forces us to assume that the crimes listed in the second set (*Memor.* 1.2.63) are 'discretionary crimes', those for which it is within the discretion of the court to impose capital punishment. If this contention should prove correct, then we would have to charge Xenophon with gross inaccuracy. The crime of theft (κλοπή) was not a 'non-discretionary crime'. In addition, in Xenophon's *Defence* (chap. 25) the crime of high treason (προδοσία πόλεως) is listed among the 'non-discretionary crimes', while in *Memorabilia* 1.2.63 the same crime is found among the 'discretionary crimes'. It should also be noted that the old Athenian law demanding capital punishment for sacrilege (ἀσέβεια) was still in force at the time Socrates was brought to trial. It had been invoked in the case of Anaxagoras and Protagoras, and later was applied to Stilpon, Aristotle, Theodorus, and Theophrastus.[358]

Xenophon becomes very emphatic (*Memor.* 1.2.63-64) when he points out that Socrates 'was never the cause of any evil to the city,— or the perpetrator of treason and sedition'. Obviously, the 'accuser' had also insinuated that Socrates' conduct had been treasonable and seditious. But for some good reason Xenophon prefers outright to deny this most serious charge rather than discuss it at length.[359] In his private life, Xenophon continues (*Memor.* 1.2.64), 'he never deprived any man of what was for his good or involved him in any evil'.[360] 'How, then, could he have been guilty of the charges made against him?—he who was far from disbelieving in the gods . . . and who evidently paid his respects to the gods more than any other man;[361] he who, instead of corrupting youths . . .[362] plainly led such of his associates as had vicious and evil inclinations, to desist from indulging in these inclinations, exhorting them to cherish a love of what is most honourable and most virtuous.[363] . . . Such being his conduct, how is it possible that he was not considered worthy of great honour from the city of Athens?'[364]

Xenophon's Memorabilia 1.1.1–1.2.64

In Plato (*Apology* 36E–37A) Socrates says to his judges: 'If I am to suggest a fair penalty, I should say that maintenance in the *Prytaneum* would be a just reward.'³⁶⁵ This whole story is probably an instance of Plato's irony and hence we cannot attach much credence to this report. Plato (*Apology* 36E–37A) is probably the original source of Diogenes Laertius (2.42)³⁶⁶ who, however, reverses the order of the proceedings recorded by Plato. According to Diogenes Laertius, Socrates first proposes a fine. 'When this caused an uproar, he assessed his penalty at maintenance in the *Prytaneum*.' This claim of 'maintenance in the *Prytaneum*' seems to be Plato's way of demonstrating Socrates' μεγαληγορία,³⁶⁷ of which Xenophon makes such an issue in his *Defence* 1–9. It is also interesting to note that Xenophon does not mention this claim of Socrates in either his *Defence* or his *Memorabilia*, although there were obvious opportunities for doing so in chapter 21 or chapter 23 of the *Defence*. This would suggest that Xenophon did not believe this story which, after all, may very well be the product of Plato's fertile imagination.³⁶⁸

The *narrative* underlying *Memorabilia* 1.1.1–1.2.64 (which differ considerably from all the other Xenophontean *Socratica*), in the main seems to be based on some historical incident. This may be gathered principally from the fact that unlike the other Xenophontean *Socratica*, and *Memorabilia* 1.3.1–4.8.11 in particular, Xenophon resorts here to what appears to be straight reporting. Hence he restricts the use of 'Socratic dialogues' or 'Socratic monologues' to an absolute minimum, something quite unusual in his *Socratica*. At the same time he impresses us with making a special effort at avoiding all the fictions which abound in the other *Socratica* of Xenophon as well as all obvious anachronisms which so often mar his accounts. The characterization of the person of Socrates in its strongly apologetic flavour, however, strikes us as being fictitious, even in *Memorabilia* 1.1.1–1.2.64. One cannot escape the impression, therefore, that this characterization here relies on some model or 'legend' that had already become an established literary tradition.

Xenophon's *Memorabilia* 1.1.1–1.2.64, it should be noted, are definitely unoriginal. When Xenophon wrote this apology, the person or character Socrates had already become a literary figure or legend through the efforts of Antisthenes, Aeschines, and other Socratics.³⁶⁹ All that remained for Xenophon to do was to 'consecrate' this legend and defend it against certain calumnies. Such a design, aside from its pious aspects, is bound to obscure rather than illumine the problem of the historical Socrates because it aims primarily at edification. The real novelty of Xenophon's apologetic effort, aside from its proclivity for the trivial, seems to consist in his extensive rebuttal of the 'accuser' in *Memorabilia* 1.2.9–61.³⁷⁰ Hence we shall have to turn to the problem posed by the Xenophontean 'accuser' who, as has already been suggested,[371] is not Anytus, Meletus, or Lycon, the three official prosecutors of Socrates during the historical trial of 399, but rather the rhetorician and pamphleteer Polycrates who wrote the κατηγορία Σωκράτους around 393/2.

4
Polycrates' Κατηγορία Σωκράτους

BOTH THE XENOPHONTEAN *Defence* and *Memorabilia* 1.2.9–61, (or 64), are to a large extent rejoinders to that type of anti-Socratic literature which, beginning about the middle of the nineties of the fourth century B.C., probably found its most eloquent and notorious expression in the κατηγορία Σωκράτους of Polycrates. The *Defence* makes sense only if we assume that when writing the latter, Xenophon (*a*) was acquainted with the κατηγορία, and (*b*) had already rebutted in *Memorabilia* 1.2.9–61 the specific charges against Socrates contained in the Polycratean pamphlet. The κατηγορία, it will be shown, probably was written in 393/2, while *Memorabilia* 1.1.1–1.2.64, we assume, were composed between 392 and 390, although F. Dümmler (*Akademika* 29) maintains that the κατηγορία was published in the year 382.[372] Aside from Lysias,[373] Theodectes (*D.L.* 2.38) and Demetrius of Phaleron, Isocrates also wrote a rebuttal of the κατηγορία in his *Busiris* (chaps. 4–5),[374] where he insists that the κατηγορία is nothing other than a paradoxical work in which Polycrates attacks a man whom every one else holds in the highest esteem. Careful analysis should also divulge that Plato's *Meno*, *Symposium*, and *Gorgias* already presuppose the κατηγορία Σωκράτους. Hirzel goes so far as to claim that the *Meno* is primarily Plato's reply to this pamphlet.[375] But it would be more correct to say that the *Gorgias* constitutes Plato's reaction against the Late Sophists[376] and the anti-Socratic movement started by them. Consideration of this reaction, it may be added, is very important for an evaluation of the Platonic *Gorgias*.[377]

The loss of the κατηγορία Σωκράτους of Polycrates has seriously impeded our understanding of the many complex problems connected with the trial and death of Socrates. Hence the reconstruction of this pamphlet becomes a necessary pre-requisite for any comprehensive effort at determining and appraising certain aspects of the historical Socrates. That Polycrates was the author of a κατηγορία Σωκράτους is attested by Diogenes Laertius (2.39–40), Themistius (*Oratio* 23), Isocrates (*Busiris* 4), Libanius (*Apologia Socratis*), Aelian (*Var. hist.* 11.10), *Schol. ad Aristidem* (edit. Dindorf) 3.480 and *ibid.* at 3.320, Quintilian (*Instit. orat.* 2.17.4), Suidas (*Polycrates*, where he mentions two λόγοι κατὰ Σωκράτους), and others.[378]

Polycrates' Κατηγορία Σωκράτους

The origin and education of Polycrates, this uncompromising partisan of radical democracy, are obscured by time from the modern scholar.[379] Including the rather scanty information contained in the *Busiris* of Isocrates, the ancient reports on him are extremely meagre and often confusing. We know neither the date of his birth nor that of his death. From the *Busiris* (chap. 50) we may infer that he was an older contemporary of Isocrates who was born in the year 436. Suidas calls him an Athenian, and like Themistius, Hermippus, and Diogenes Laertius, connects him with the official proceedings against Socrates in the year 399. Athenaeus records that Polycrates had forged a 'scandalous treatise on love' in order to discredit Philenis. In addition, the author of the *Deipnosophistae* (8.335CD) maintains that he was 'an Athenian by birth, sly of words, and of an evil tongue'. Dionysius of Halicarnassus (*De Isaeo iudicio* 20), by mentioning him together with such famous orators as Antiphon, Critias, Thrasymachus of Chalcedon, Theodorus of Byzantium, Anaximenes, and Zoilus, seems to have held him in high esteem as a rhetorician, although he deplores his frigidity and vulgarity, as well as his lack of grace and practical oratory. Demetrius (*On style* 120) likewise takes issue with his lack of earnestness: 'Polycrates . . . eulogized . . . with antitheses, metaphors, and every trick of eulogy. He was jesting and not in earnest, and the very inflation of his words is but pleasantry.'

From the *Busiris* (chap. 1) of Isocrates we also gather that fairly early in his career Polycrates, apparently through no fault of his own, had experienced some serious misfortune. We are also told that he had not always been a 'sophist', but that he had been compelled by unfavourable circumstances to seek in sophistry a source of livelihood. Unfortunately, Isocrates does not disclose the exact nature of this 'undeserved misfortune'. Hence we do not know whether he was visited by a personal calamity or whether, as the result of some political event, he was forced to leave Athens and perhaps even to go into exile. The scholiast maintains that 'poverty compelled him to teach rhetoric, and although he was an Athenian, he taught in Cyprus'.[380] The *Busiris* seems to refer to him as a 'beginner' whom Isocrates wishes to help with some practical advice. But neither Plato nor Xenophon make any direct reference to Polycrates, despite the fact that his κατηγορία Σωκράτους made a profound impression on both.

Pausanias (6.17.9) insists that the tyrant Jason of Pherae had rated Gorgias above Polycrates, 'who was a shining light of the Athenian school'. From this remark we would have to infer that at one time Polycrates was at the court of Jason. Since the latter did not become master of Pherae until *c.* 380, Gorgias must still have been alive in 380, when he apparently vied with Polycrates for the favours of the tyrant.[381] We do not know how long Polycrates stayed either in Cyprus or Pherae. In any event, he seems to have returned to Athens, where he apparently followed the career of a 'sophist', as may be gathered from the titles of some of his writings.[382] It is also said that in his works he showed the influence of Gorgias.[383]

Ancient testimony regarding the κατηγορία Σωκράτους of Polycrates is both uncertain and contradictory. The report of Diogenes Laertius (2.38–39) is very confusing since it is based on a variety of conflicting sources which Diogenes, in his usual uncritical manner, has compiled indiscriminately. Quintilian[384] apparently believed that Polycrates delivered the κατηγορία during the official trial of Socrates, while Themistius[385] is of the opinion that it was the 'speech' (κατηγορία) which Polycrates composed and Anytus delivered in court.[386] And the theory that this 'speech' turned the judges against Socrates, is also upheld by the author of the *Hypothesis Busiridis* and by Quintilian (*Inst. orat.* 2.17.4). With the sole exception of Favorinus (D.L. 2.39), all the ancient witnesses seem to hold that the Polycratean κατηγορία Σωκράτους was vitally related to the trial and condemnation of Socrates in the year 399. Favorinus is said to have declared in his *Memorabilia* that the κατηγορία was 'not authentic' (μὴ εἶναι ἀληθῆ), because 'Polycrates mentions here the rebuilding of the Long Walls by Conon, an event which did not take place until six years after the death of Socrates.'[387] By the expression 'not authentic', Favorinus, however, does not wish to deny the authorship of Polycrates, but merely intends to stress the fact that the Polycratean pamphlet played no role during the official trial of Socrates.

The κατηγορία Σωκράτους, which essentially is a fictitious and posthumous 'indictment' of Socrates delivered by Anytus,[388] apparently was a literary sensation. In any event, it unleashed a whole flurry of Socratic apologies,[389] all of which took issue with Polycrates rather than the events that occurred during the official trial of Socrates in 399. Lysias, among others, is said to have written a refutation of Polycrates. This work has been inaccurately identified by Cicero (*De orat.* 1.54.231), as well as by Diogenes Laertius (2.40) who reports that Lysias had prepared a defence speech for Socrates which the latter, however, declined. That the '*Refutation*' of Lysias actually existed may be gathered from Plutarch (*Vit. decem orat.* 836B), who also records that the title of this work was Σωκράτους ἀπολογία ἐστοχασμένη τῶν δικαστῶν. This title in itself would suggest that the '*Refutation*' of Lysias was written in the form of a forensic speech. We may also surmise that Lysias directed his apologetic refutation to Anytus, the fictitious 'spokesman' for Polycrates in his pamphlet. Probably for this reason there arose the story that Lysias wrote his *Apology* for Socrates to be used during the trial of 399.[390]

The following facts arise above all controversy: the 'accuser' (ὁ κατήγορος) in Xenophon's *Memorabilia*[391] is not one of the official prosecutors—Meletus, Anytus, and Lycon—who rendered the indictment

Polycrates' Κατηγορία Σωκράτους

during the trial of Socrates. At the same time we must concede that Xenophon had been acquainted with the κατηγορία Σωκράτους of Polycrates at the time he wrote *Memorabilia* 1.1.1–1.2.64. Also we have sufficient evidence to support our contention that the κατήγορος is Polycrates, the author of the κατηγορία Σωκράτους. Isocrates, in *Busiris* 5, mentions that Polycrates had made Alcibiades a disciple of Socrates. The κατήγορος, in *Memorabilia* 1.2.12, likewise claims that Alcibiades had been a pupil of Socrates, a declaration which is repeated in the *Apologia Socratis* (chap. 61) of Libanius.[392] In addition, the *Scholium ad Aristid. orat.*[393] contains the information that Polycrates had charged Socrates with having praised Odysseus for saying that kings restrain noble people with gentle words, but discipline lowly people with physical blows.[394] In *Memorabilia* 1.2.58, the 'accuser', quoting the identical Homeric passage, also charges Socrates with having displayed the same haughty attitude towards the common people. All this should prove that the 'accuser' of Xenophon's *Memorabilia* is none other than Polycrates.

For the reconstruction of the Polycratean κατηγορία Σωκράτους both the *Apologia Socratis* of Libanius,[395] written c. 350 A.D., and Xenophon's *Memorabilia* 1.2.9–61 must be consulted.[396] It is assumed here that Xenophon and Libanius had read the κατηγορία Σωκράτους of Polycrates. If, on the other hand, as R. Hirzel[397] and others suggest, Xenophon and Libanius relied for their information on the *Apologia Socratis* of Lysias, which was likewise a rebuttal of Polycrates, then any attempt at reconstructing the κατηγορία Σωκράτους of Polycrates would be extremely difficult if not well-nigh impossible. It has been shown, however, that the thesis advanced by Hirzel is untenable.

Judging from Xenophon's *Memorabilia* 1.2.9–61, and Libanius' *Apologia Socratis*, the κατηγορία was primarily a forensic or perhaps 'epideictic' speech, published not earlier than 393/2 B.C. It has also been suggested that the κατηγορία was published during the eighties. This contention is based on the assumption that Gorgias had died around 380,[398] and that Polycrates did not attain to any particular fame until after the death of Gorgias.[399] We base our theory that the κατηγορία was written about 393/2 on the following evidence: at the time of Gorgias' death (presumably in 380) Polycrates had already gained a considerable reputation. Isocrates (*Busiris* 4), for instance, informs us that Polycrates had composed the κατηγορία during the days of his early struggles, that is, before he had gained a considerable reputation. In addition, it is assumed that the *Busiris* of Isocrates, where the κατηγορία Σωκράτους of Polycrates is mentioned by its title, was written not much later than about 390. Also, Polycrates' reference to the rebuilding of the Long Walls by Conon in the year 393 impresses us as being the account of a recent event.

The *Apologia* of Libanius and the rebuttal of Xenophon make it quite

Polycrates' Κατηγορία Σωκράτους

obvious that the κατηγορία was written in the form of a speech, allegedly delivered by Anytus himself.[400] Hence the 'accuser' of Xenophon in one sense is Polycrates, the author of the κατηγορία, and in another sense Anytus, the fictitious spokesman for Polycrates. Diogenes Laertius (2.38–39) seems to have confounded the respective roles of Anytus and Polycrates when he reports: 'The indictment, according to Favorinus in his *Miscellaneous Histories*, was brought by Meletus, and the speech delivered by Polyeuctus. According to Hermippus, the speech was composed by Polycrates. . . . But some say that this was done by Anytus. Favorinus . . . states that the speech of Polycrates . . . is not authentic.' The confusion in this whole report is due to the insertion in the wrong place of two excerpts, one from Favorinus and the other from Hermippus. When these two insertions are removed, the different parts assigned to the three official prosecutors during the trial of 399 become completely clear: 'The indictment was brought by Meletus, the speech was delivered by Anytus, and the necessary preparations were made by Lycon.' The reference to Polyeuctus is definitely due to some error. It must be assumed that instead of Polyeuctus we should read Anytus, and that the name Polyeuctus is merely a bad misspelling of 'Polycrates'. Hence, according to some sources, the κατηγορία Σωκράτους was supposedly delivered by Anytus during the trial of Socrates. Diogenes Laertius (2.39) seems to take notice of this tradition, but contradicts it on the authority of Favorinus.[401]

That the κατηγορία could not possibly have been delivered during the trial of Socrates is obvious. It contains, as we shall see presently, a number of serious 'political charges'. But under the terms of the general amnesty law of 403 no political charges could be brought during the official trial in 399, the more so, since Anytus himself was one of the chief promoters of this amnesty law.[402] In addition, the Polycratean pamphlet contains a reference to the rebuilding of the Long Walls, an event which took place in 393. This fact was also observed by Favorinus.[403] According to Libanius (106.11 ff.), Polycrates praises both Conon and Thrasybulus as the two men who helped to restore (and are expected further to contribute to) the greatness of Athens. Such an obvious, not to say blunt, encomium makes sense only as long as these two men were the leading statesmen at Athens, that is to say, men of influence with favours to bestow. But Conon was captured by the Persians in 392/1, never to return to Athens, and Thrasybulus had lost his popularity and influence before 390. We must assume, therefore, that Polycrates wrote his pamphlet before both Conon and Thrasybulus had been deprived of their political influence and position, that is, before 392/1.[404] It has also been claimed that the κατηγορία was directed at Antisthenes rather than Socrates. This hypothesis contains an element of truth. Antisthenes, to be sure, was a 'Socratic', a fact probably known to Polycrates. In addition, there can be little doubt that Polycrates took much of the material for his anti-Socratic arguments from the writings of Antisthenes, who in many respects had been 'a despiser' of the established institutions of Athens. But the real target of Polycrates is still Socrates.[405]

Xenophon, who refers to four 'accusations', seems to have faithfully recorded the basic charges, which Polycrates instituted against Socrates, in *Memorabilia* 1.2.9, *Memorabilia* 1.2.12, *Memorabilia* 1.2.49, and *Memorabilia* 1.2.56. Schanz, as a matter of fact, claims that Xenophon had listed all the Polycratean charges. He insists also that Libanius, in a spirit of oratorical exaggeration, had added some additional charges, or had raised some minor points of the Polycratean argument to the status of a major and independent charge.[406] Judging from Libanius, however, Xenophon apparently does not take up all the specific issues raised by Polycrates.[407] In this sense the Xenophontean rebuttal must be regarded as being somewhat incomplete. With the exception of some general allusions, Xenophon also fails to record the specific evidence by which Polycrates tried to support his charges.[408] In other words, Xenophon, on the whole, restricts his rejoinders to relatively short refutations of the main Polycratean accusations, instead of dealing in detail with all the points of the κατηγορία.[409] Moreover, the *Apologia Socratis*, obviously a rejoinder to the κατηγορία Σωκράτους of Polycrates, is cast in the form of a forensic speech meant to rebut Anytus,[410] the motivating force behind the prosecution of Socrates in 399. As such, it seems to follow on the whole the anti-Socratic arguments advanced by Polycrates and is, thus, in some respects superior to Xenophon's *Memorabilia* 1.2.9–61 as a historical source for the reconstruction of the Polycratean κατηγορία. In many instances, nevertheless, Libanius seems to rearrange, exaggerate, and perhaps even slightly alter the original meaning and the content of the κατηγορία. But, in general, it can be assumed that the Libanian *Apology* possesses a high degree of historical truth which permits us to reconstruct the general content and basic structure as well as the principal arguments and even some of the detailed statements contained in the pamphlet of Polycrates.

The charges and 'accusations' which Polycrates makes against Socrates, as we shall see presently, are of a type that might be expected of a partisan of the 'extreme' or 'radical' democracy which was once more firmly established in Athens after the overthrow of the Thirty Tyrants in 403. These charges are made by a man who no longer believes that he should abide by the terms of the general political amnesty law of 403 which had made it impossible to indict Socrates for any 'political crimes' during his official trial in 399. For then the provisions of this law apparently were observed in a most scrupulous manner. Thus Polycrates actually charges Socrates with being a μισόδημος[411] or 'hater of the common people', and with being the intellectual leader of oligarchs and vacillating democrats who had planned and perhaps even par-

Polycrates' Κατηγορία Σωκράτους

ticipated in the overthrow of Athenian democracy in 404.[412] Thrasybulus, the friend of Anytus and 'liberator' of Athens, and Conon, the restorer of the Long Walls and, hence, of Athenian might, are extolled as true democrats, patriots, and friends of the Athenian people; both men are pointedly compared with Critias and Alcibiades, the disciples of Socrates,[413] who had been oligarchic partisans, traitors, and despoilers of the city.[414]

T. Humbert[415] reaches the conclusion that the anti-Socratic arguments in the Polycratean pamphlet originally were grouped about, or developed from, the following five basic points: (1) Socrates was the teacher of Critias and Alcibiades; (2) Socrates taught his followers idleness and indifference towards the social life of the city; (3) Socrates taught his followers to despise the established laws and the democratic institutions of Athens; (4) Socrates culled from the ancient poets the most 'immoral' and 'subversive' passages; and (5) Socrates taught his followers to despise their fathers and elders. At least three of the five points listed by Humbert seem to be confirmed by Libanius (20.15–21.5), who states that Socrates 'had never induced anyone of his followers to commit criminal theft, or treachery, or sacrilege, or perjury, or to live in idleness, or to despise the laws, or to bring about the fall of democracy' (δήμου κατάλυσις). Obviously, the reference to 'criminal theft' or 'treachery' points at Critias and his treacherous conduct as the head of the Thirty Tyrants. This may also be gathered from Xenophon, *Memorabilia* 1.2.12, where we are impressed with the fact that Critias was 'the greatest thief' (κλεπτίστατος), the 'most violent, and the most murderous person'. The term 'sacrilegious', to be sure, would apply to both Critias and Alcibiades. The manner in which Critias put people to death without trial, or confiscated their property, was considered sacrilegious by many Athenians. And the affair of the *Hermae* and the Eleusian mysteries with which Alcibiades (and Critias) had been connected in 415 was certainly a sacrilege. The term 'perjury' could refer to the treasonable conduct of Alcibiades in 415, when he went over to the Lacedaemonians, as well as to the regime of Critias. Libanius takes up further the charge that Socrates was the teacher of Critias and Alcibiades and, hence, fully responsible for their conduct, in chapters 109 (74.12), 112 (76.6–8), 136 (90.15–91.1), 148 (99.5), 155 (104.1–3), and 160 (106.11–107.3). The general charges that Socrates was a teacher of idleness and 'subversive' conduct as well as the man who induced people to despise the established laws and the democratic institutions of Athens, in particular, obviously point at Socrates, the teacher, rather than at his pupils. The charge that Socrates taught his followers idleness and 'subversive ways', is further taken up in Libanius, chapters 127 (84.18), 132 (88.10–11), 133 (89.3), and 134 (89.16). And the charge that Socrates induced people to despise the established laws and the democratic institutions of Athens, is expounded in Libanius, chapters 38 (34.13–

Polycrates' Κατηγορία Σωκράτους

35.1), 54 (43.18-20), 80 (58.10-12), and 163 (108.6-7). The testimony of Libanius, therefore, makes reference to three main Polycratean charges, all of which were also recorded by Xenophon, namely, the first three points of our list. Xenophon apparently adds—or elevates to the rank of a main charge—two further indictments, namely, points four and five of our list. That Socrates allegedly culled 'subversive passages' from the old poets is also mentioned in Libanius, chapters 85, 87, 88, and 93; that he taught young people to despise their elders, and children to dishonour their fathers, is mentioned in chapter 102.

H. Markowski,[416] again, insists that the Polycratean indictment contained nine main charges: (1) Socrates undermines the democratic institutions of Athens (*a*) by inducing young men to despise the existing laws, (*b*) by hating the democratic constitution of Athens as well as by seeking to establish a tyranny, (*c*) by doing all possible harm to the city, and (*d*) by abolishing the rule of the people; (2) Socrates teaches the neglect of the gods worshipped by the city; (3) Socrates corrupts the youths of the city; (4) Socrates objects to the most highly respected poets as well as abuses their authoritative sayings (*a*) by criticizing them and (*b*) by quoting them in support of his abominable teachings; (5) Socrates induces people to commit serious crimes such as theft, fraud, sacrilege, acts of violence, and perjury; (6) the vices which Socrates practises in secret are even worse than those he practises openly; (7) Socrates leads the citizens to idleness (*a*) by inducing them to abstain from all sorts of economic pursuits, including the tilling of the land, (*b*) by being not only himself averse to all participation in active public life, but also by preventing others from doing so, and (*c*) by spurning the quest for money and remaining a pauper who gives no consideration to the problem of taxes and public revenues; (8) Socrates is the teacher of Critias and Alcibiades; and (9) Socrates is a dangerous sophist, and in the past the Athenians have punished most severely certain sophists. People who have never been taught by sophists turned out to be the most meritorious citizens. Sophists, on the other hand, are often the perdition of cities and peoples.

According to the *Apologia Socratis* of Libanius, as previously mentioned, Polycrates directed his indictment through Anytus.[417] This Polycratean Anytus, through a 'preamble', apparently attempts first to justify his having prevailed on Meletus to institute legal proceedings against Socrates.[418] He continues to explain the reason for his appearance in behalf of the prosecution, pointing out that his conduct was motivated by his love for Athens and his concern over the well-being of Athenian youths.[419] This well-being, Anytus probably stated, had seriously been threatened by the pernicious activities of Socrates. All this may be inferred from the lengthy and ironical remarks found in Libanius (chaps. 13-43). Here Libanius ridicules what he considers the rather sudden and somewhat perverse 'patriotism' of the Polycratean

Polycrates' Κατηγορία Σωκράτους

Anytus.[420] There can be little doubt that in essence this 'preamble' of the Libanian *Apology* reflects the *prooemium* used by Polycrates in his pamphlet.

Obviously, Socrates' alleged pernicious influence over Athenian youths constitutes a most serious charge in the κατηγορία, as it does in Plato's *Apology*. For it is this influence which made it possible for Socrates to work toward the overthrow of Athenian democracy.[421] All other accusations, it seems, are somehow related to this charge, at least indirectly. A. E. Taylor has pointed out that the suspicion under which Socrates lived is that, although very active and influential in private among 'young oligarchs' such as Critias, Alcibiades, or Charmides, he never came forward and openly placed his talents at the service of democratic Athens. This situation, Taylor continues, 'inevitably creates a suspicion, not only reasonable enough in itself, but apparently so well backed by facts that Plato does not venture to put it between the lines of his reply. The ὑποψία is, in fact, that Socrates is the able and dangerous head of an anti-democratic ἑταιρία. . . .'[422] We may surmise, therefore, that Polycrates, by way of an introductory statement, had set out to justify his attacks upon Socrates by assuring his listeners or readers that he had no personal quarrel with Socrates,[423] and that his action was prompted solely by a strong sense of 'patriotic duty'. This may be gathered from Libanius, chapters 24–30 (27.11–31.4), where Libanius attempts to show that Anytus had a personal grudge against Socrates. Apparently Socrates' constant references to tanners, cobblers, etc., had greatly angered Anytus, the tanner. Libanius also reports (30.8–31.4) that Anytus had promised Socrates that he would withdraw his complaint on the condition that Socrates would desist from referring to tanners. The story that Anytus had made Socrates such an offer is highly improbable, and in all likelihood is based on some unfavourable anecdote about Anytus, invented perhaps by Antisthenes or the Cynics. Xenophon (*Defence* 29), on the other hand, seems to lend some support to this story, when he maintains that Socrates had insisted that 'Anytus . . . [dislikes me] because I told him that I disapproved of his intention of bringing up his son as a tanner.'

Taking his cue from the wording of these introductory remarks, which might have been presented by Polycrates in the form of a 'general bill of indictment', Libanius answers them with the observation that Socrates never induced anyone to commit theft, fraud, sacrilege, or perjury, nor did he ever encourage anyone to live in idleness and sloth,[424] to disdain the existing laws,[425] or to plan the overthrow of the Athenian democracy (δήμου κατάλυσις).[426] In this fashion Libanius also seems to deny the general charge that Socrates had ever endangered the well-being of Athenian youths.[427] Although with some alterations both as to the terms used and the sequence in which these crimes are enumerated, he refutes several times the charge that Socrates had planned or, perhaps, worked for the overthrow of Athenian democracy.[428] It could be argued that the list of crimes enumerated by Libanius in their sequence would suggest that Polycrates climaxed his 'indictment of Socrates' with the allegation that Socrates, by spreading anti-social and anti-democratic ideas, not only was an enemy of the democratic regime at Athens, but actually contributed to its overthrow in 404. This seems to be indicated by the Libanian contention that Socrates did not actively participate either in the revolution of 411 or in that of 404, as well as by Xenophon's statement (*Memor.* 1.2.63) that Socrates 'was never the cause . . . of any sedition or treason. . . .' Some of the charges contained in the Polycratean κατηγορία can also be found in the official 'bill of indictment' or 'bill of particulars' of 399, such as the 'accusation' that Socrates was a sacrilegious person corrupting youths, that he undermined paternal authority,[429] and that he taught his pupils to live in idleness.[430] However, under the Act of Oblivion of 403, promoted by Anytus and other statesmen, the official indictment of 399 could not contain any 'political charges', such as the charge that Socrates was an enemy of the people and a despiser of democracy, and that he had actually worked for the overthrow of Athenian democracy.[431] This does not mean, however, that Socrates was innocent of anti-democratic leanings; for it is not plausible that Polycrates should invent these charges which Libanius tries to refute so vigorously.

Hence it may be inferred that Polycrates, in his effort to elaborate and substantiate his 'accusations', had openly charged Socrates with the anti-social conduct of having taught or induced his followers to commit theft, fraud, sacrilege, perjury, idleness, and to despise the laws of the city. And he probably climaxed his allegations with the gravest and most devastating of all charges, namely, the charge of anti-democratic activities: Socrates was not only a theoretic enemy of Athenian democracy, but he actually had planned as well as actively contributed to the downfall of the city. He thus became the foremost despoiler of Athens itself. All this may be inferred from the rather frantic efforts on the part of Libanius to show that Socrates was not 'a hater of democracy' or μισόδημος.[432] The idea that Socrates was a 'despoiler of democracy', with some reservation can also be found in Plato's *Apology*,[433] where we are told that Socrates had upbraided the incompetence of Athenian politicians. Such words, to be sure, produced a critical and perhaps even hostile attitude of mind towards democracy, its institutions, and its leaders among the younger generation of Athenians.[434]

The Polycratean preamble, it could be argued, was followed by a kind of 'bill of particulars' in which the various charges and incriminations were stated and discussed in detail. But this seems not to have been the case.[435] In Libanius, at least, a lengthy encomium of Socrates and his excellence is added to the *prooemium*.[436] Inasmuch as this encomium is pregnant with hints and allusions concerning a series of unfavourable

Polycrates' Κατηγορία Σωκράτους

views current about Socrates, we may surmise that the Polycratean κατηγορία probably also contained a passage suggesting that the Athenians for a long time had been looking with disfavour upon Socrates and his activities. Libanius (17.1–20.9), in any event, does not mention here any particular 'accuser' such as Anytus or Meletus, but merely refers to 'accusers'. Hence it is quite possible that he meant Aristophanes, Eupolis, or Ameipsias, who, as comic poets, had given expression to some of the unfavourable popular opinions concerning Socrates. It could also be held that the charges mentioned here are of so general a nature that Libanius does not consider it necessary to single out any particular 'accuser'.

Libanius (21.6 ff.) then considers the many blatant misunderstandings and misrepresentations of which the 'noble' Socrates had become the innocent victim.[437] Again and again he stresses the fact (23.2) that Socrates was opposed to the pernicious activities of the sophists;[438] that he was a poor man of simple and frugal tastes (chap. 17);[439] that he did not engage in discussions concerning the nature of the universe, because he considered such discussions senseless and without practical significance (22.9–14);[440] and that, since he had nothing to hide, he had always acted freely in public (24.12 ff.).[441] These lengthy and at times oratorical digressions compel us to assume that the κατηγορία contained a generally unfavourable description of the conduct of Socrates, which conduct not only angered the Athenians, but actually endangered the well-being of the city.[442] If the Libanian *Apology* can at all be regarded as a fairly accurate rebuttal of the Polycratean pamphlet, then we may even surmise that the 'second part' of the κατηγορία also contained lengthy recitations of the general unpopularity of Socrates among his fellow Athenians, and the particular reasons for this unpopularity.

After having sung the praises of Socrates, Libanius proceeds to disprove and rebut the specific charges or allegations made by Polycrates. In the main there can be little doubt that these specific rejoinders follow the general sequence of the original charges made in the κατηγορία. The first point with which Libanius takes issue—a point which, incidentally, was last in the *prooemium*—is the charge that Socrates had not only taught youths to despise the existing laws,[443] but actually had advocated the overthrow of Athenian democracy:[444] ' "Athenians," says he [*scil.*, Polycrates], "Socrates taught young people to defy the established laws. The existence of the city (or constitution) is in peril. They [*scil.*, Socrates and his followers] are ruthless people, advocates of tyranny (τυραννικοί) who are contemptuous of civil equality (τὸ ἴσον)—people we should not tolerate. . . . Should we not rid ourselves of this man before his followers overthrow the authority of the laws?" '[445] Since this particular accusation is refuted both vigorously and at considerable length,[446] we may assume that Libanius considered it the main 'accusation'; and as such it must have taken up a considerable part of the κατηγορία.[447]

Polycrates' Κατηγορία Σωκράτους

Against the Polycratean allegation that Socrates had worked for the overthrow of Athenian democracy, Libanius argues as follows: it is incredible that only as a septuagenarian Socrates, who, since he was not indicted until now, must have been a law-abiding and 'democratic' person all during his life, should suddenly become such a vicious enemy of democratic Athens (chap. 34). Such an assumption is already vitiated by the other Polycratean allegation, namely, that Socrates became an enemy of democracy the moment he began teaching (chap. 35). How, then, is it possible that so great a patriot as Anytus should have tarried so long before indicting Socrates and thereby saving democracy (chaps. 36–40)? Simply because he never had, and still does not have, a case against Socrates (chap. 41). Perhaps some other and more important business had previously prevented the 'patriot' Anytus from saving the city from Socrates. But if this were so, he would be guilty of a serious dereliction of his patriotic duties (chap. 42). And, if Anytus should have been prevented from prosecuting Socrates, why is it that no other citizen had come forward to indict him (chaps. 43–44)? Certainly, no one could have been deterred by a fear of Socrates. No, Anytus proceeds now against Socrates because he suddenly has become a sycophant (chap. 46–47). If Socrates was really an enemy of Athenian democracy and an advocate of tyranny, why did he not make himself a tyrant (chap. 48)? Or, if he worked his pernicious political schemes through his friends, why were these friends not also brought to justice (chaps. 49–52)? You call him an enemy of the people ($μισόδημος$); but has he ever said or written anything against the people or the people's government (chaps. 53–55)? And it is a commonly known fact that he took no part in the two recent oligarchic revolutions (chaps. 57–59).[448]

Xenophon, too, in immediately disposing of the particular charge that Socrates had taught young people to despise the laws, apparently considered it the most important of all accusations that had been directed against Socrates. But he does not say that Socrates had been charged with being 'a hater of democracy' or 'a despiser of the common people' ($μισόδημος$, Libanius 43.18), but merely that he was accused of having ridiculed certain institutions typical of democratic Athens. In *Memorabilia* 1.2.59–60, however, reference is made to the alleged 'antidemocratic' views of Socrates.[449]

In view of the fact that Libanius seems to have somewhat mutilated this particular indictment, we will have to turn to Xenophon in order to reconstruct its probable wording and meaning in the *κατηγορία Σωκράτους*.[450] According to *Memorabilia* 1.2.9, 'Socrates caused his followers to despise the established laws by pointing out how foolish it was to elect the magistrates of the city by the use of beans....'[451] Such remarks excited youths to hold in contempt the established form of government, and disposed them to commit acts of violence.'[452] Libanius, on the other hand, fails to take special issue with Socrates' specific

Polycrates' Κατηγορία Σωκράτους

criticism of the established Athenian legal, constitutional, and political institutions. In a most general manner he mentions (58.10–61.6), however, that Socrates had been indicted for having expressed his displeasure with certain Athenian customs and institutions. This general observation of Libanius is, on the whole, in accord with Xenophon's report (*Memor.* 1.2.9) that Socrates found much fault with the institutions of democratic Athens, particularly the manner in which the magistrates of the city were elected.[453] According to Libanius (58.10–12), Polycrates must have taken exception to Socrates' alleged criticism of Athenian institutions and customs.[454] From Libanius (58.12–59.7) we may also infer that Polycrates had charged Socrates with having preferred the dictatorial rule of one man to a regime under the rule of law, while from another passage (60.19–61.6) we gain the impression that Socrates had actually criticized the legal and political institutions of Athens. Libanius, who fully admits the latter charge, remarks (61.5–6), however, that Socrates did this only because he wished to improve on, and thereby strengthen, the legal and political order of democratic Athens.[455] But it is only Libanius (43.18) who informs us that Socrates had been directly referred to as a 'μισόδημος'.[456]

The Polycratean charge of μισοδημία may be back of *Memorabilia* 4.2.37–39, where Xenophon tries to show that Socrates was friendly towards the 'little people': 'Do you think it possible for some one to know what a democracy is without knowing what the demos is? . . . What do you consider to be the people? The poorer class of citizens, I should say. . . . Which sort of people, then, do you call poor, and which rich? Those who have not sufficient funds to provide for the necessities of life I consider to be poor, but those who have more than sufficient funds I regard to be rich. Have you ever observed that to some who have very small means, those means are not only sufficient, but that they even save from their pittance, while to many people who have very large fortunes, the latter are not large enough? I have, most certainly . . . since I have known some princes who, from poverty, have been compelled to commit acts of injustice like the poorest people. Then, said Socrates, if that is how the matter stands, we must rank these princes among the *demos* (the common people), and those who have but little, but know how to manage this pittance, we must class with the rich.'[457] In order to understand this Socratic encomium of the poor man, we must remember that, according to *Memorabilia* 1.2.59, Polycrates apparently had charged Socrates with having advocated the beating of the poor, the mainstay of Athenian democracy: 'Socrates, however, never said such things,' Xenophon replies, 'for he would thus have suggested that he himself ought to be beaten.'

Despite the fact that Libanius only casually mentions Socrates' alleged contempt for the laws and political institutions of Athens (58.10 ff.), we are nevertheless justified in assuming that Polycrates had actually charged Socrates with having taught his disciples to despise the laws and the constitution of democratic Athens.[458] This seems to follow from Libanius 43.18, where Libanius refers to the Polycratean allegation that Socrates 'hates the people and induces his followers to be contemptuous of democracy (δημοκρατίας καταγελᾶν)'. In Libanius 34.15 ff., we are informed that Polycrates apparently had insisted that the followers and disciples of Socrates were 'advocates of tyranny' (τυραννικοί) and 'despisers of civic equality' (τὸ ἴσον ὑπερῶντας).[459] On the strength of this assumption we are also permitted to conjecture that Socrates' purported contempt for the established legal and political institutions of Athens was used by Polycrates in support of his argument that Socrates had planned and even worked towards the overthrow of Athenian democracy.[460] Hence, at least in the opinion of Polycrates, this disparagement of the established laws, customs, and institutions, as well as of the existing form of government and of the common people in general, was merely a means used by Socrates to achieve this ultimate end. In his argumentation Libanius, however, goes far beyond the report of Xenophon, who merely relates that Polycrates had charged Socrates with having disposed his followers 'to commit acts of violence'.[461] For if we collate Libanius 33.1, 33.14, 38.11, 40.15, 41.2, 41.7, 42.6, 43.1, 43.18, and 45.3, we cannot escape the impression that Polycrates must have accused Socrates of having desired the overthrow of Athenian democracy. In Xenophon, *Memorabilia* 1.2.9, this serious charge is greatly modified and 'played down' by the rather casual observation that Socrates had been accused of 'disposing youths to acts of violence'. It might also be pointed out that according to the report of Libanius, Polycrates apparently had charged Socrates with the *positive* intent of ruining Athenian democracy, something which Xenophon fails to state. Nevertheless, we could maintain that the account of Xenophon and that of Libanius are to some extent mutually complementary. In Libanius 33.1-5, for instance, reference is made to a statement, presumably by Polycrates, that Socrates 'inflicted a great many evils on the city'. The various ways by which he allegedly inflicted these 'great many evils' are listed throughout the Libanian *Apology*. In the words of Xenophon (*Memor.* 1.2.12), Polycrates had accused Critias and Alcibiades, the two disciples of Socrates, rather than Socrates himself of having 'inflicted a great many evils on the city'.

It would be tempting to surmise here that Polycrates followed this particular charge with the other contention which he might also have used in support of his allegation that Socrates had planned the destruction of democratic Athens: the accusation that Socrates had induced his disciples to live in idleness,[462] exhorting them to 'sabotage' the democratic life of Athens by refusing to participate actively in the social, political, and economic activities of the city.[463] This may be gathered from Libanius' remark (21.2) that '[Socrates was never a teacher] ...

Polycrates' Κατηγορία Σωκράτους

of idleness', or from his denial (86.12–15) that by his teachings Socrates not only 'had deprived the soil of its tillers' (86.12–15),[464] but also had prevented people from speaking in public (89.9–10).[465] Libanius (89.16–90.6) concedes that Socrates was not a 'money-changer', that is, one who has made it his purpose in life to accumulate a fortune. Like Plato (*Apology* 31D ff.), he seems to suggest here that some Athenians considered it an inducement to idleness when Socrates maintained that we should be more concerned over our souls than over riches.[466] This could be inferred from Libanius 85.9–14 and *ibid.* at 88.10–89.2, where Polycrates is upbraided for insisting that intellectual labours are nothing other than plain idleness. Apparently in a predominantly commercial city such as Athens, the average burgher regarded this statement of Socrates—if it was at all by Socrates—outright 'heresy'. If the statement that we should care more about our souls than about riches is actually Socratic, then the latter would also have understood the basic importance of leisure (σχόλη) and contemplation for moral and intellectual culture.[467] It will be shown, however, that in all probability the charge that Socrates had induced his followers to live in idleness in order to harm the city was contained in a later part of the κατηγορία.

In chapter 62, Libanius (48.7) asks himself the question: what could have induced the 'accuser' to make such monstrous charges?[468] In his lengthy reply to this query Libanius points first to the allegation that Socrates had quoted from the most celebrated ancient poets in order to give authority and support to those of his teachings which had made his followers unprincipled and tyrannical persons.[469] It should be remembered here that Xenophon, before dealing with the alleged 'abuse of the poets', had mentioned and discussed the 'accusation' that Socrates had educated Alcibiades and Critias,[470] presumably turning them into unprincipled and tyrannical men. But Libanius takes up this charge only in chapters 136–150 (90.15–100.6). Libanius (70.17 and 71.5) also seems to note the Polycratean charge that Socrates by his sayings had undermined all paternal authority[471]—another example of Socrates' alleged efforts at destroying the basic foundations of civilized society in general and filial piety in particular. But Libanius merely observes that Socrates cast such a spell over young people that they began to think of him more highly than of their own fathers or elder brothers. This rather cryptic statement is found amidst the other charge (chaps. 62 ff.) that Socrates had used and abused the venerable poets of old. It is difficult to explain why Libanius failed to take real issue with this particular charge. With Xenophon (*Memor.* 1.2.49 and *Defence* 20) it not only holds the 'rank' of one of the four basic 'accusations', but is also rebutted by him at great length. And finally, Libanius mentions (chaps. 136 ff.) the Polycratean allegation that Socrates had trained and influenced Alcibiades and Critias, the two men who had inflicted a great many evils on the city. It seems, therefore, that Libanius believes that these three charges

Polycrates' Κατηγορία Σωκράτους

or allegations—the 'abuse of the ancient poets', the undermining of filial piety, and the training of Alcibiades and Critias—are merely examples of the more general Polycratean contention that Socrates had rendered youths both unprincipled and tyrannical.[472] This does not mean, however, that Polycrates himself in his κατηγορία had united these three particular charges. In any event, it appears that Polycrates was determined to show, as well as to prove through examples, how disastrous Socrates' teachings had been for the youths of Athens.[473] He succeeded in doing this by collecting several general instances of the many evils Socrates had provoked by his sayings, and by showing in the specific and notorious examples of Alcibiades and Critias the pernicious results of these sayings for Athens.[474]

The whole of Libanius' account seems to support our contention that at this stage of the κατηγορία Polycrates wished to make evident the disastrous effects of Socrates' teachings by citing, perhaps in the form of supporting evidence, a series of incidents the causes of which must be traced back to the activities of Socrates.[475] This might be inferred from the fact that only in 99.15 does Libanius reach the final refutation of Polycrates' charge that Socrates' teachings had pernicious repercussions for the whole of Athenian life;[476] in other words, this final refutation is achieved only after Libanius has dealt with all the individual 'accusations' enumerated in 20.15 ff. And like Xenophon,[477] Libanius takes great pains to absolve Socrates of all the charges presumably made by Polycrates. But since Xenophon does not seem to follow the progress of the argument as it was probably developed in the κατηγορία, it is safer to rely here on the account of Libanius and the manner in which he arranges his rejoinder. For it seems that Xenophon rearranges the Polycratean arguments and allegations according to logical principles rather than oratorical effects. In any event, Xenophon impresses us as joining together a general argument and whatever he regards the particular illustration of this argument. The arrangement of the various arguments in Libanius, on the other hand, strikes us as being more organic and better articulated, and hence of greater oratorical effect than the rather artificial and prosaic line of argument found in Xenophon.[478] And oratorical effect, in the words of Isocrates (*Busiris* 4-5), was certainly one of the strongest motives of Polycrates when he composed the κατηγορία Σωκράτους.

The third Polycratean charge, according to Xenophon (*Memor.* 1.2.49), is that 'Socrates had taught children to show contempt for their parents, persuading his followers that he rendered them wiser than their fathers';[479] that he 'not only caused parents, but also other relatives to be held in contempt by his [followers] . . . saying that relatives were of no profit to people . . .';[480] that he said 'concerning friends that it was of no profit to be well disposed towards them, unless they were capable also of assisting us';[481] and that 'he thus persuaded the younger people

Polycrates' Κατηγορία Σωκράτους

that he was the wisest of all men ... disposing thereby his pupils towards him in a manner that in comparison with himself other people were of little account to them'.[482] Polycrates apparently tried to show here that Socrates had been instrumental in destroying all feelings of filial piety and reverence, as well as all normal and decent human relationships, replacing them with a spirit of calculation and callousness.[483] Libanius casually touches on this charge, remarking (70.17–71.6) that 'those youths who, as you [*scil.*, Polycrates] contend, respected him [*scil.*, Socrates] more than their own fathers; who looked contemptuously down upon their elder brothers; and who were attracted to Socrates as if by a magic force—what else were they seeking but to win the approval of this man?'[484] Libanius mentions here also that in the opinion of Polycrates young people were actually spellbound by Socrates. This would coincide with the report of Xenophon who states (*Memor.* 1.2.49) that, according to Polycrates, Socrates allegedly 'persuaded his followers that he made them wiser than their fathers', and 'that in comparison with himself other people were of little account with them [*scil.*, these young people]'. In Libanius, however, these short references to Socrates' alleged destructive effects on filial reverence are joined with Socrates' alleged 'abuse of the ancient poets' and his ridicule of the existing laws or political institutions.[485] They are, therefore, part of Libanius' rebuttal of the Polycratean accusation that Socrates had used passages from the most celebrated ancient poets to teach his followers disreputable and despotic ways.[486] But despite the obvious seriousness of the Polycratean charges that Socrates had taught his disciples to be contemptuous of their parents, relatives, or friends, and that he ridiculed the existing legal and political institutions of democratic Athens, for some unexplainable reason these charges do not elicit a distinct and effective rebuttal from Libanius. He merely wonders (71.5 ff.) why, if Socrates had actually alienated sons from their fathers or elder brothers, the latter had not long ago taken energetic steps against the 'seducer'.[487] And although Libanius spends considerable time and effort refuting the allegation that Socrates' activities had been a definite threat to democratic Athens (chaps. 34–59 and 61), the particular charge that Socrates had ridiculed the laws of democratic Athens elicits from him only a short remark (59.4–7): 'But if Socrates, even though he believed in democracy, should have denounced some of the existing practices and should have openly stated this, then he merely acted within the spirit of democracy and its laws.' In other words, Libanius seems to maintain that Socrates was within his 'constitutional rights' when he denounced or criticized the constitution. In Xenophon, on the other hand, these two charges and their refutation take up much space.[488] Xenophon's refutation also differs considerably from that advanced by Libanius.

When trying to assign to this Polycratean charge its proper place in

Polycrates' Κατηγορία Σωκράτους

the κατηγορία, we may proceed along the following lines: according to Polycrates, Socrates allegedly had called upon the supporting testimony of 'the most celebrated poets' in order to give his teachings additional authority and weight.[489] In doing so Socrates not only despoiled the venerated bards, but under the disguise of quoting these poets, he also attacked the religious, moral, and legal tradition of the Hellenic world. Thus he undermined not only the foundations of all politically organized society, but also the basis of all human society by destroying the natural bonds which unite parent and child, brother and brother, friend and friend.[490] Hence we may surmise that in the κατηγορία of Polycrates the charge that Socrates' teachings had endangered the most fundamental human relationships, in all probability was followed by, or was part of, the other accusation, namely, that Socrates had quoted from the ancient and most celebrated poets in order to induce his followers to become 'unprincipled and tyrannical'.[491]

Xenophon (*Memor.* 1.2.56) has the 'accuser' state that Socrates 'selected the worst passages from the most celebrated poets of old in order to teach his pupils to be unprincipled and tyrannical'. Libanius, on the other hand, reports (48.8) that the 'accuser' had charged Socrates not only with having rebuked the ancient poets, but also with having pointed out that many of their sayings were objectionable:[492] 'Socrates ... frequently made reference to the poets, but not always in a spirit of disapproval. Wherever they contributed to the moral improvement of the listener, he called them wise, noble, divine. ... But when he realized that they were having evil effects ... then he objected to them ... and would not tolerate that through them the souls of young people might come to perdition.'[493]

Hence there seems to exist a serious conflict between the account of Xenophon and that of Libanius. For according to Xenophon, Socrates apparently made 'positive' use of these ancient poets and, hence, must have approved of their sayings. According to Libanius, however, Socrates was not only critical of their views, but in some instances actually seemed to have rejected them as being in many ways objectionable. M. Schanz agrees with Xenophon by claiming that the 'accuser' had charged Socrates only with frivolous interpretation of the ancient poets.[494] J. Mesk, on the other hand, insists that there is no real conflict between the Xenophontean and the Libanian report.[495] Mesk points out that in the κατηγορία Polycrates probably charged Socrates with having used, abused, and rebuked the ancient poets, thus making it manifest that nothing was sacred to Socrates, not even such venerated and renowned poets as Hesiod, Theognis, Homer, and Pindar.[496]

But the apparently conflicting reports of Libanius and Xenophon respectively can be fully reconciled. In Libanius 61.14–62.6,[497] for instance, we are told that Socrates, by relying on certain passages from the most celebrated poets, had frequently demonstrated to his pupils cer-

Polycrates' Κατηγορία Σωκράτους

tain monstrous consequences which could be drawn from them by indiscriminate reasoning. And in chapter 80 he observes that it had been a common practice in Athens to criticize poets and dramatists. Hence Socrates merely followed a generally accepted custom. Libanius also states that he knows of no law which restrained Socrates from doing so. To forbid anyone to voice his critical disapproval, including a critique of the existing legal or political institutions, would be tantamount to the destruction of democracy by abolishing the freedom of speech.[498] But, Libanius continues (61.7-14), Socrates had done this only to prevent his disciples from practising false reasoning or from incurring irreparable moral damage while relying on the authority of these passages.[499] It seems, therefore, that Polycrates had tried to exploit the elenctic method of Socrates, claiming that although Socrates fully understood these passages, he nevertheless purposely misinterpreted them in order to mislead and corrupt youths. On the strength of such an interpretation of Socrates' action, Polycrates could claim that Socrates both had used and rejected certain sayings of the old poets. For insofar as Socrates allegedly had attributed an immoral or objectionable meaning to these passages, Polycrates could claim that he rejected them—and this is the formula reported by Libanius. But insofar as Socrates is said to have relied on certain misinterpreted or 'perverted' passages from the poets in order to justify and give additional authority to his own teachings, it could be maintained that he made bad use of them: 'But if you [*scil.*, Polycrates] should maintain that he [*scil.*, Socrates] did not have sufficient confidence in himself and therefore relied on the opinion of the poets in order to endow his teachings with authority, then I shall not bother here to point out to you the contradiction in which you involve yourself when you decry Socrates as a person who, at one and the same time, denounces as well as praises one and the same poets.'[500] In other words, Polycrates apparently had also charged Socrates with having referred to the most celebrated poets in order to endow his own teachings with authority and, in doing so, 'made bad use of them'—and this is the formula recorded by Xenophon when he states (*Memor.* 1.2.56) that the 'accuser' had also said that 'Socrates selected the worst passages from the most celebrated poets'.

Obviously, the term 'worst passages' (τὰ πονηρότατα) could not possibly have been contained in the κατηγορία of Polycrates; for otherwise Polycrates would have been in agreement with Socrates. We may conjecture, therefore, that Polycrates had claimed that Socrates dared to designate as evil certain passages taken from the most celebrated poets. This conjecture is based on the presumption that, when formulating his argument, Polycrates proceeds from the hypothesis that the most celebrated poets are above reproach and criticism. Hence the account of Libanius seems to contain an inconsistency, particularly when he reports that Polycrates had charged Socrates with having spoken in a disparaging

Polycrates' Κατηγορία Σωκράτους

manner about the old poets. For if the poets actually contained objectionable sayings, then Socrates would have been justified to reject and speak ill of them. We can hardly imagine, however, that Polycrates would charge Socrates with having belittled the poets and, at the same time, with having quoted passages from the same poets in order to bolster his own teachings. This inconsistency can also be detected in Xenophon's account, namely, where we are told that Socrates allegedly selected 'the worst passages', while he is said also to have adulterated the poets in order to serve his own evil purposes.

A thorough study of the whole context in which, for instance, the Pindaric quotation appears in Libanius (chap. 87), would indicate that Libanius argues here against Polycrates that Socrates had not always reprimanded the old poets for their sayings. On the contrary, he had frequently praised them, provided that they contributed to the moral improvement of people. But if Socrates was of the opinion that their ideas had evil effects upon the listeners, as for instance this βιαιῶν τὸ δικαιότατον which Libanius apparently regards as a genuine Pindaric quotation, then he strongly objected to their teachings; and he did so only in order to protect his followers and disciples. Libanius then illustrates the 'eclectic' method of Socrates with the help of a verse taken from Hesiod that 'work is not something disgraceful, but to be idle is a disgrace'. Continuing his argument in favour of Socrates, Libanius goes on: 'And in the same manner he [*scil.*, Socrates] discussed Pindar, because he was perturbed over Pindar's words that young people, when hearing this "law . . . makes might to be right, doing violence with the greatest of high-handedness", might translate these words into action.'[501]

In chapter 62 (48.8-10) Libanius lists the ancient poets quoted by Socrates as well as the sequence in which these poets had been recited. These 'most celebrated poets' are Hesiod, Theognis, Homer, and Pindar. But when discussing the individual passages from the poets quoted by Socrates, Libanius proceeds in the following sequence: Hesiod, Pindar, Theognis, and Homer.[502] Hesiod's citation is taken up in chapter 86 (61.14-62.8); Pindar's quotation in chapter 87 (62.9-63.3); Theognis' citation in chapters 88-91 (63.4-65.16); and Homer's quotation in chapter 93 (66.6-67.3). The sequence originally recorded by Libanius, we may assume (chap. 62) is merely a kind of listing of the ancient poets allegedly quoted by Socrates. This being the case, Libanius did not have to follow strictly the sequence probably observed by Polycrates. But when Libanius discusses in detail the passages taken from these poets, he probably used the sequence in which they had been cited by Polycrates when the latter built up his argument against Socrates. In any event, it could be claimed that the quotations from Hesiod and Pindar are somewhat related to one another in that they induce people to become 'unprincipled'. The passages taken from Theognis and Homer are likewise related in that they encourage people

Polycrates' Κατηγορία Σωκράτους

to become 'tyrannical'. It must be assumed that a forensic orator as skilled as Polycrates probably observed the rules of consistency when developing his argument. Xenophon (*Memor.* 1.2.56–60), on the other hand, only mentions Hesiod and Homer, that is, one representative from each of the two groups of related quotations.

The κατηγορία, we assume therefore, probably used the following sequence: Hesiod, Pindar, Theognis, and Homer. Polycrates, it seems,[503] quoted first from Hesiod's *Works and Days* 309: 'Work is no disgrace, but idleness is a disgrace.'[504] Polycrates, we may conjecture, went on claiming that Socrates had referred to this passage in order to prove that Hesiod 'bids us to abstain from no kind of work, even if it were dishonest and dishonourable, but to do such work for the sake of profit'.[505] It must be assumed that Polycrates defended the position taken by Hesiod. But from the extant sources we can no longer ascertain the manner in which he did this. Hence we may also surmise that he had alleged that Socrates did 'abuse' Hesiod. Libanius 62.2–4 perhaps contains an answer to this query: 'Hence [referring to the dictum that no kind of work is really dishonourable], if a person breaks through a wall [or, breaks into a house] or into a grave, he can call upon the authority of Hesiod ... for his contention that in doing so he did not commit a wrong.' Polycrates apparently used Hesiod's quotation in order to demonstrate that Socrates had encouraged his followers to ignore the accepted standards of propriety and decorum, particularly as regards the forms of acquisition and employment recognized in a commercial society.

Then, according to Libanius (62.11), the 'accuser' seems to have cited Pindar:[506] 'The law is the king of all, of mortals as well as immortals, doing violence with the greatest of high-handedness.'[507] According to Polycrates, Socrates, it appears, would have made use of this Pindaric statement to demonstrate that crude force is superior to lawfulness and the legal order.[508] If we can put any reliance in the report of Libanius (62.13),[509] then Polycrates must, however, have used a different wording of this Pindaric verse than Libanius. This is clearly suggested by Libanius (62.12–63.3): 'But Socrates' distrust of the poet [*scil.*, Pindar] is so much justified, that the very clever Anytus dared to alter the words of the poet. In doing so he [*scil.*, Anytus] must have thought that he was speaking to barbarians or to people who apparently would not know what is by Pindar and what by Anytus.... But by altering the quotation from the poet, he actually indicted Pindar and praised Socrates.'[510] A. Busse insists that Polycrates apparently had quoted the correct Pindaric passage, 'δικαιῶν τὸ βιαιότατον'.[511] Libanius, on the other hand, being unfamiliar with the original Pindaric verse, relied on the perverted form, 'βιαιῶν τὸ δικαιότατον' ('might makes right'), which he might have found in Plato's *Gorgias* 484B. Polycrates, who apparently quoted the δικαιῶν τὸ βιαιότατον, is accused by Libanius (62.12–

63.3) of having purposely altered the verse to which Socrates justly objected so as to make it sound attractive as well as morally more acceptable, merely in order to demonstrate afterwards that in his evil designs Socrates had rejected also the 'good' sayings of the old poets.[512] Hence Libanius is actually without justification when he reproaches Polycrates for having adulterated the original Pindaric quotation. Furthermore, Polycrates then seems to have proceeded to show that Socrates had quoted and discussed both Hesiod and Pindar in order to substantiate his doctrines of lawlessness and brutal force by which he presumably 'taught his followers to become unprincipled evil-doers'.[513]

While Socrates' alleged misuse of certain passages taken from Hesiod and Pindar was described by Polycrates as having been instrumental in making his followers 'unprincipled evil-doers', Socrates' supposed abuse of some quotations from Theognis and Homer, in the eyes of Polycrates, seemed to prove not only that Socrates was himself a person of 'tyrannical disposition', but also that he had tried to inspire his disciples to become 'tyrannical' themselves.[514] This seems to follow not only from Libanius 63.6–7, where we are told that Socrates had been called an 'advocate of tyranny' (τυραννικός), or from Libanius 34.16, where it is claimed that the followers of Socrates were 'friends of tyranny', but also from Libanius 43.18, where reference is made to the Polycratean allegation that Socrates was 'a hater of the people' (μισόδημος) who 'had induced his followers to ridicule democracy'. The passage from Theognis[515] which, in the report of Libanius, allegedly had been quoted by Socrates in order to achieve this end, reads as follows: 'But a man oppressed by poverty can neither speak up nor do anything, for his tongue is tied.'[516] Libanius, however, merely alludes to these lines. In any event, Theognis (175 ff.) had expressed the idea that poverty, being an evil, must be avoided at all cost. The implication seems to be here that since the poor man is actually powerless, the rich man of necessity must be all-powerful. Hence the poor man has also to submit to the will of the rich man. This is in all probability the implication which Polycrates attributed to Socrates. Libanius (63.8) merely hints at the manner in which Polycrates absolved Theognis from the possible suspicion of having advocated the rule of the rich man over the poor man. This seems to follow from the remark of Libanius: 'The facts which the accuser himself has submitted, would favour our argument. . . .' Libanius (63.18–64.2) then goes on to state at length that it is exactly the poor man who speaks up in the public assembly. The rich often lack proper insight, while the poor frequently admonish people to do what is right: 'Hence Socrates is correct when he maintains that the power of speech is a matter of education, and not of wealth.' Libanius, coming to the defence of Socrates, makes it appear (64.2–11) that Socrates had rejected the ideas of Theognis: 'Since at Athens there are relatively few rich people, but a great many poor people, according to Socrates [*scil.*, according to Socrates' view that the

Polycrates' Κατηγορία Σωκράτους

power of speech is a matter of education rather than of wealth] the majority of you is capable of speaking up, while according to Theognis the great mass of the people is worthy of contempt. Who, then ... of the two [*scil.*, Socrates or Theognis] is the better adviser ...?'

From all this it may be gathered that Polycrates had charged Socrates with having quoted this particular verse for the purpose of ridiculing and deprecating the common or poor man, manifesting thereby his 'tyrannical' or 'anti-democratic' sentiments.[517] In this fashion Polycrates also substantiates his original contention that Socrates had been an enemy of Athenian democracy who for a long time had been planning its ultimate overthrow. The quotation from Theognis, it will be noticed, solicits from Libanius the longest comment, probably for the reason that it could be interpreted as being a manifestation of contempt for 'the little man', the backbone of Athenian democracy, and, hence, for democratic institutions in general. This would also bear out our contention that the Polycratean pamphlet climaxed in the allegation that Socrates was an enemy of democracy, and that he worked towards its overthrow. No wonder, then, that Libanius should spend considerable effort in dealing with the quotation from Theognis.

According to the reports of Libanius (66.6–67.3) and Xenophon (*Memor.* 1.2.58–59), the 'accuser' also claimed that Socrates had often quoted a passage from Homer in order to prove to his listeners that Homer 'had recommended that lowly and poor people should be beaten'. The Homeric episode (*Iliad* 2.188 ff.) to which Polycrates alluded is the incident where Odysseus 'came across a common man who was making a noise. He struck him with his staff and rebuked him, saying: "You churl, hold your peace and listen to better men than yourself." ' By admiring the attitude of Odysseus, Polycrates apparently contended, Socrates again evinced his 'tyrannical' or 'anti-democratic' sentiments: 'Socrates always induced young people to admire Odysseus for such practices, as Polycrates maintains in his work against him [*scil.*, Socrates].'[518] In the defence of Socrates, Libanius (68.13 ff.) requests Anytus (Polycrates) to name one single person to whom Socrates had praised Odysseus for having advocated the beating of the lowly people: 'You [meaning Anytus] too treat gently and with circumspection the rich and the famous people, but use the rod on the poor and lowly.' Libanius discusses as well as rebuts this particular charge by inserting (chaps. 93–95) what seems to be a 'fictitious' speech addressed to the youths of Athens. Lysias likewise takes issue with Polycrates by pointing out that Socrates saw in Odysseus the foremost spokesman of a social order under the rule of law,[519] while Xenophon (*Memor.* 1.2.59–60) claims that Socrates had merely insisted 'that those who did not benefit others either by words or deeds ... especially if they were of an insolent spirit, should be restrained in every way.... But ... Socrates was really a friend of the common people.'[520]

Polycrates' Κατηγορία Σωκράτους

Then Libanius proceeds (71.12 ff.) to defend Socrates against some additional indictments,[521] namely, that he had induced his followers to commit theft, fraud, sacrilege, and perjury.[522] We must surmise, therefore, that also in Polycrates' κατηγορία these particular charges followed the more general allegation that Socrates had taught his disciples to become 'tyrannical' and to despise the established laws and institutions of Athenian democracy by ridiculing the existing form of government. This assumption is based on a remark found in Libanius (71.12), as well as on the account of Xenophon.[523] In chapter 103, Libanius sets out to refute the allegation of Polycrates that Socrates had induced his followers to commit acts of theft, fraud, sacrilege, and perjury.[524] But when he undertakes to rebut these charges in detail, Libanius does not observe the sequence indicated in chapters 20.14 ff. and 71.14. For Libanius (72.8 ff., 73.10) disposes first of the charge of fraud and deception. From the general context we may gather that Socrates allegedly had justified fraud and deception by pointing out that Melanthus, by the use of deception, had defeated King Canthos of Boeotia and thus gained mastery over Attica.[525] Then Libanius (72.10) meets the charge of theft and sacrilege.[526] From his text it might be inferred that Socrates was accused of having justified theft and sacrilege (ἱεροσυλεῖν) by showing that Odysseus had gained much honour for the theft of the Palladion (72,10); that Themistocles had won great glory for deceiving the Greeks into accepting battle at Salamis (72.2);[527] and that Thyestes had defrauded the Athenians very much to their subsequent advantage (73.7).[528] Libanius, who apparently did not clearly distinguish between stealing (κλέπτειν), defrauding (ἀπατᾶν), and committing sacrilege (ἱεροσυλεῖν),[529] opens (73.7) his defence of Socrates by maintaining that Polycrates had conjured up these charges.[530] Polycrates apparently had insisted that Socrates condoned not only the defrauding or deceiving of barbarians—something which some Greeks considered quite permissible—but also that of Greeks by Greeks.[531] Libanius then takes up (74.12) the charge that Socrates supposedly had condoned perjury, pointing out that Polycrates had failed to show one instance where Socrates committed perjury or failed to keep his oath.[532] He omits, however, to mention whether Polycrates had quoted any particular incident justifying this new allegation.[533]

When rebutting the earlier charges made by Polycrates, Libanius and Xenophon resort to denials that Socrates was ever guilty of the acts with which he was charged. But now Libanius and Xenophon seem to change their defence tactics.[534] Xenophon (*Memor.* 1.2.62–63) claims that the worst that could ever be said against Socrates is that he never committed a capital crime. Libanius (71.12 ff.), on the other hand, argues that the acts imputed to Socrates are not always and under all circumstances punishable or even unlawful, but are, particularly in times of war (or civil strife?), permissible. Xenophon's and Libanius' method of dealing

Polycrates' Κατηγορία Σωκράτους

with the Polycratean charges at times strikes us as being an admission of their foundation in fact in each case, while contesting at the same time the malicious twist given to these facts and the inferences drawn from them. It could be argued, therefore, that Xenophon and Libanius would not in essence have admitted these Polycratean statements unless they were true.

If we can place any reliance on chapter 114 of Libanius' *Apologia*, Polycrates must have suddenly shifted his line of attack [535] by alleging that if the public activities of Socrates had been so destructive, how much more pernicious must have been his secret action.[536] Xenophon (*Memor.* 1.1.17) seems to echo this allegation when he states: 'As to those matters on which Socrates gave no intimation what his sentiments were, it is not altogether surprising that the judges should have a wrong opinion about him.' J. Geffken[537] suggests that Polycrates' charge that the secret activities of Socrates must have been even more vicious than his overt actions, may refer to Plato, *Apology* 31c, where Socrates denies that he had ever engaged in politics. But we cannot agree with H. Markowski[538] who claims that Polycrates refers here to 'immoral practices' in which Socrates had allegedly indulged with his pupils. The Socratic *chronique scandaleuse*, it seems, is of a much later date than the Polycratean pamphlet. By distorting the relationship of Socrates and his followers, it seems that Polycrates also had tried to prove that Socrates had excluded older and more mature people from his circle, probably because he found it easier to influence young and inexperienced men.[539] When discussing the 'public conduct' of Socrates, Polycrates apparently had stressed the *direct* and overt damage which Socrates, by corrupting youths, had inflicted on the communal life of the city.[540] Conversely, when listing the 'secret activities' of Socrates, Polycrates seems to allege that Socrates had harmed *indirectly* the communal life of Athens as well as the common good of the city by teaching his disciples to live in idleness and to abstain from all active participation in the social, political, and economic life of Athens.[541] This seems to follow from Libanius' efforts (84.18 ff.) to take issue with Socrates' alleged 'policy' to keep the sons of wealthy families from taking part in the social, economic, and political life of Athens. Libanius also remarks (84.18) that Polycrates had maintained that 'Socrates turned them [*scil.*, young people] into idlers', and that Socrates 'was not a man interested in commerce' (τραπεζίτης).[542] In addition, he makes a rather nasty thrust at Polycrates (Anytus) when he states (88.10) that the latter 'seems to be of the opinion that only sycophants are people engaged in productive activity'. Judging from the many efforts of Libanius and Xenophon to show that Socrates was a very frugal person, inured to hardships, it may also be inferred that Polycrates had charged Socrates with having turned his followers into effeminate fops.[543] Libanius (87.4 ff.) defends Socrates energetically and at great length[544] against the charge of having preached idleness: 'If he [*scil.*, Socrates] ... insisted that it was foolish to spend more effort on the acquisition of money than on the improvement of the soul, maintaining that the most important thing for man was the soul, the second most important the body, and the third most important money—could this perchance be called inducement to idleness? ... He insisted that one should never put in first place what by nature belongs in second place'.[545] Hence we must assume that this particular issue constituted an essential part of the Polycratean κατηγορία.[546]

Attic law knew of a γραφὴ ἀργίας (or, νόμος ἀργίας),[547] which permitted anyone to initiate legal action against persons living in idleness.[548] Since Libanius (chaps. 127 ff.) seems to deny vigorously this particular charge, it is quite possible that Polycrates might have referred to the νόμος (or, γραφὴ) ἀργίας. Pisistratus, in his socio-economic 'reform programme', had issued a law which made idleness a criminal offence. Later Attic historiographers, prompted by their admiration for Solon, whom they considered the father of Athenian democracy, ascribed this particular law to the latter. Apparently this law of Pisistratus was never revoked.[549] On what grounds, then, could Polycrates institute this particular charge against Socrates? Aelian (*Var. hist.* 10.4) perhaps furnishes the answer when he tells us that Socrates had insisted that 'idleness was the sister of freedom', proving his statement with the argument that the Indians and Persians, little concerned with manual labour, were also the most gallant and the most free peoples; while the Phrygians and Lydians, known for their industry, lived in perpetual servitude.[550] In the report of Aelian, Socrates seems to display the same contempt for manual labour and 'the common working people' which we also find in Xenophon (*Memor.* 3.7.3–5) where Socrates in a most contemptuous manner refers to fullers, cobblers, agricultural labourers, carpenters, coppersmiths, merchants, and hucksters. At the same time he extols 'leisure as the best of all possessions'.[551]

In *Memorabilia* 2.7.1–12, however, Xenophon seems to defend Socrates against the charge of having advocated a life of idleness. According to this report, Aristarchus, a scion of a noble family, together with fourteen relatives had fled from Athens to the Piraeus during a political disturbance. There he was left without any means to support properly such a large household. Socrates, on hearing about his plight, counsels him to put the women to some productive work. Aristarchus first rejects this suggestion, insisting that it is impossible to expect freeborn people to work for a living like slaves or lowly artisans. But Socrates dispels his reluctance by showing that idleness is often the cause of misfortune, while honest work frequently becomes the source of wealth and happiness. Aristarchus is persuaded; the women start working and soon every one is happy and contented. Naturally, Socrates points out, all work that is expected to make us wealthy and happy must be honest work.[552] By stressing here the necessity that true work must be honest and useful, Xenophon apparently tries to link the Aristarchus episode to another charge made by Polycrates, namely, that Socrates had taught his followers 'to abstain from no kind of work, even if it were dishonest and dishonourable, but to do such work for the sake of profit'.[553] We know already the manner in which Xenophon (*Memor.* 1.2.57) rebuts this particular charge.[554] The purpose of the Aristarchus story, it seems, is to disprove the allegation that Socrates was a despiser of manual labour and the common labourer, and an advocate of a life of idleness. This story, it should be noted, definitely suggests Xenophon's well known penchant for practical, that is, productive work. Hence it might be the delusion of Xenophon's creative imagination rather than the report of a historical fact.[555]

In chapters 136 ff., Libanius refutes the allegation that Socrates was the teacher of Alcibiades and Critias:[556] '... I shall assume here that Socrates was their [*scil.*, Alcibiades' and Critias'] teacher, although he never admitted to anyone that he was this. You must examine thoroughly the question, whether any person, who wishes to be regarded as a teacher, may be made responsible for the wickedness of those who lack either good will or the ability to learn.'[557] Although Isocrates (*Busiris* 4 ff.) denies any close association between Socrates and Alcibiades, there exists a host of ancient witnesses who testify to the contrary.[558] It seems, however, that prior to Polycrates no one had openly stated that Alcibiades was a typical pupil (and, hence, the product) of Socrates and his teachings.[559] Critias, who is called 'the greatest hater of the common people' ($\mu\iota\sigma o\delta\eta\mu \acute{o}\tau\alpha\tau o\varsigma$),[560] according to weighty testimony was a close associate of Socrates.[561] That this was also a popular opinion at Athens may be gathered from Aeschines (*Contra Timarchum* 173): 'Did you put to death Socrates ... because he was shown to have been the teacher of Critias ...?'[562]

In Xenophon (*Memor.* 1.2.12), we remember, the second charge made by the 'accuser' reads as follows: '... Critias and Alcibiades, after having been associated with Socrates, inflicted a great many evils on the city.' It appears that Polycrates viewed both Critias and Alcibiades as the archetypal results of Socrates' pernicious teachings and activities. If we can place any reliance on the report of Libanius, Polycrates must have asserted that these two men, because of the training they had received from Socrates, had become the great despoilers of Athenian democracy who more than anyone else had caused the downfall of Athens. This seems to follow from Libanius (99.5): 'Critias [so Polycrates alleges] has inflicted great harm upon the democracy' ($\tau \grave{o} \nu \ \delta \acute{\eta} \mu o \nu$).

This particular charge is rebutted less effectively by Libanius than by Xenophon, although it must be conceded that in several instances the account of Libanius (90.15 ff.) supplements the report of Xenophon: 'But he [*scil.*, Polycrates] who has called him [*scil.*, Socrates] the teacher of evil deeds ... has been unable to cite more than two examples:

Polycrates' Κατηγορία Σωκράτους

Alcibiades and Critias.'[563] This statement is interesting because it seems to concede that Socrates had been the teacher of these two evil men. Libanius apparently tries to argue here that of the many followers and disciples of Socrates, only two turned out to be real scoundrels—a fairly good record for any teacher. Libanius also admits (94.4) that Critias purposely had inflicted great harm on the city.[564] Like Xenophon, Libanius (91.2) discusses Alcibiades and Critias separately: 'I would be ashamed if I were to mention Alcibiades ... in the same breath with Critias. The latter with full intent inflicted evils on the city, while Alcibiades also did many good and advantageous deeds for the city, even though he was prevented from being always useful to his city, especially when through certain compelling circumstances he was forced to hurt his city.'[565] Alcibiades, we are told, committed acts of sacrilege,[566] while Critias, by suppressing the freedom of speech,[567] was guilty of deeds against Athenian democracy.[568] If Libanius' as well as Xenophon's many references to the life and activities of Alcibiades and Critias mean anything, then we are forced to assume that the κατηγορία Σωκράτους went into great detail when enumerating all the many political and social evils perpetrated by these two disciples of Socrates. The Libanian references to Alcibiades in particular bear all the earmarks of a strong apologetic effort. As a matter of fact, Libanius, chapters 136-141, may be called an apology of Alcibiades; for he praises here the many political achievements of Alcibiades, as well as his activities which had contributed to the rise of Athenian power, wealth, and fame. This may be Libanius' reply to Polycrates' exaltation of Conon and Thrasybulus.[569]

In order to achieve an effective oratorical contrast to these two 'Socratic scoundrels' (Critias and Alcibiades) Polycrates probably delivered a lengthy encomium of Thrasybulus, the saviour and restorer of Athenian democracy in 403, and Conon, the rebuilder of the Long Walls in 393.[570] During the reign of the Thirty Tyrants (404/3), it will be remembered, Anytus and Thrasybulus were both exiled. Together with Thrasybulus, Anytus organized the revolt against the Thirty Tyrants, an event which centred around the mountain fortress of Phyle. During the difficult and at times desperate struggle Anytus was urged to start a campaign of terror and retaliation. He refused to comply with this request, pointing out that victory had to be won first and democracy once more firmly established in Athens before the question of punishing the guilty could be considered.[571] Acting in this spirit of restraint and conciliation, Anytus became the driving force behind the granting of a general political amnesty in 403, after the Thirty Tyrants had been driven out.[572] When in 399 the democratic regime was once more firmly established, Anytus apparently felt that he could start proceedings against Socrates, whom he probably suspected of having been one of the intellectual leaders of the reactionary forces which had come back into power in 411/10 and again in 404/3.[573]

Polycrates' Κατηγορία Σωκράτους

Then Polycrates apparently proceeded to contrast Alcibiades and Critias with Theseus,[574] the mythological founder of Athens, and with Solon,[575] the great reformer of the early sixth century who in the opinion of many Athenian democrats was the actual founder of democracy in Athens.[576] This is at least the impression we gather from Libanius 101.14, where he makes an extended effort to disprove the validity of Polycrates' attempt at contrasting the 'good democratic statesmen' of Athens with Socrates' two most notorious disciples, who by entering a public career had become the curse of Athens.[577] It is implied, therefore, that Socrates, the teacher of Alcibiades and Critias, is the real culprit because he turned these two into the most mischievous men in the history of Athens. Polycrates, it seems, tries here once more to substantiate his main charge that Socrates during his whole life had been planning and working for the overthrow of Athenian democracy. And this charge is apparently the salient point of the whole κατηγορία to which Polycrates, judging from the rejoinder of Libanius, returns again and again. We may also surmise that in this connection Polycrates insisted as well as attempted to prove that Socrates had fully deserved death.[578]

According to Libanius, it seems that Polycrates did not stop here; for some reason he apparently continued his harangue in favour of capital punishment. Socrates, he must have argued, was a dangerous and mischievous sophist,[579] and as such ought to be treated as other dangerous sophists before him.[580] It was perhaps in reply to the allegation calling Socrates a sophist that in his *Callias* Aeschines should refer to Socrates as a vehement opponent of contemporary sophistry.[581] Since the *Callias* was written some time after the κατηγορία of Polycrates, it might be conjectured that it is part of the Socratic reaction against the Later Sophists in general and against the κατηγορία in particular.[582] Polycrates probably referred here also to the fate that befell Anaxagoras, Protagoras, and Diagoras.[583] Back of this additional Polycratean argument might have been the following consideration: in case the arguments so far presented in favour of capital punishment should prove insufficient and unconvincing, then there would be still another argument in its favour, namely, historical precedent. Hence we may also surmise that this whole second argument constituted a distinct part of the Polycratean pamphlet. In any event, after having touched upon the crime of impiety and sacrilege,[584] Libanius (chaps. 153–160) insists that Socrates had nothing in common with Anaxagoras, Protagoras, and Diagoras. This statement compels us to assume that Polycrates had tried to identify Socrates and some of his teachings with these three men—something which had already been done by Aristophanes in his *Clouds*[585]—and that he had demanded that Socrates share their fate.[586] We remember that both Anaxagoras and Protagoras had been indicted for sacrilege, Anaxagoras for having declared that the sun was nothing other than a molten mass, and Protagoras for his alleged 'atheistic' views. In 431 Anaxagoras escaped punishment by retiring to Lampsacus,[587] and Protagoras did the same by fleeing to Sicily in 411/10.[588] Diagoras of Melos had become notorious for his sacrilegious views about the gods.[589] For having blasphemed the Eleusian mysteries, he was sentenced to death,[590] but apparently he eluded the executioner by taking to flight. The Athenians then put a price on his head.[591] Libanius (chap. 154) approves of the fate that befell Anaxagoras, Protagoras, and Diagoras. But, according to him, this proves nothing, since, in his opinion, Polycrates has failed to demonstrate that Socrates has been guilty of the same crimes for which these three men had been punished.

Then Polycrates, it seems, proceeded by condemning severely the sophistic method of instruction used by Socrates, pointing out that such excellent statesmen as Aristides, Miltiades, and Themistocles had never received any sophistic or philosophical training.[592] We must also assume that Pericles, too, was praised by Polycrates.[593] This seems to follow from the fact that Plato attacks Pericles in his *Gorgias* (515E ff. and *ibid.* at 519A). It has already been mentioned that the *Gorgias* is Plato's reply to the κατηγορία Σωκράτους of Polycrates. Every person who had been exalted by Polycrates apparently is being denounced by Plato in the *Gorgias*.[594] According to Athenaeus (*Deipnosophistae* 5.220), Antisthenes, in his work *Aspasia* (Diogenes Laertius 6.16) and apparently in his πολιτικὸς διάλογος, which is probably identical with the περὶ νόμου ἢ περὶ πολιτείας mentioned by Diogenes Laertius (6.16), also upbraided Pericles. The influence of the *Aspasia* and the πολιτικὸς διάλογος on Plato may possibly be detected in the *Laches* (179A ff.), the *Meno* (93A ff.), and the *Gorgias* (503 ff., 515D ff., 516C, 517B, 519A ff.).[595] Ion of Chios (in his Ἐπιδημία) and Stesimbrotus (in his *On Themistocles, Thucydides, and Pericles*) wrote with a bias for Cimon, the representative of Athenian conservatism, and against Pericles, who was viewed by his political enemies as a dangerous radical.[596] It is also possible that Plato's bias against such men as Themistocles or Pericles was fundamentally influenced by this type of 'anti-modernist' biography.[597]

The eloquent praise which Polycrates bestowed on some of the greatest and most successful of Athenian statesmen who had never been taught by a sophist,[598] was definitely a fine and effective rhetorical point in the whole of the κατηγορία Σωκράτους. Polycrates was thus able to place in a most unfavourable light the disciples of Socrates, particularly Alcibiades and Critias, and, by implication, their teacher Socrates. Libanius (104.11–105.3) counters these assertions with the remark that many people who have not had the benefit of philosophical training did turn out to be great evil-doers, while Pericles, the disciple of Anaxagoras, was held in high esteem by all. According to Libanius (106.5 ff.),

Polycrates' Κατηγορία Σωκράτους

Polycrates might also have suspected some sophists or philosophers, including probably Socrates, of harbouring oligarchic political convictions. And finally, Polycrates might have asserted that philosophers and sophists such as Socrates in the past have frequently been the cause of disunity, defection, and 'treason' among the Greeks. This could be inferred from Libanius' denial (105.13 ff.) that Bias, Melissus, Thales, Pythagoras, and other 'philosophers' of the past had been responsible for the disunity among the Greek cities in Asia Minor, as a consequence of which these cities later became an easy prey to the Persians.[599]

The remainder of Libanius' *Apologia Socratis*, that is, chapters 161 ff., apparently makes only occasional reference to the κατηγορία Σωκράτους of Polycrates, without adding any further information. Hence it is of no particular interest to us.

Although in view of the present status of our source materials some of the minor details in the reconstruction of Polycrates' κατηγορία Σωκράτους may be inaccurate, it is fairly safe to assume that for reasons both of consistent argument and oratorical effect, the Polycratean pamphlet, in the main, proceeded along the following lines:

(I) (*a*) The introductory remarks or preamble in which the 'accuser' justifies and motivates his action, claiming that he was prompted solely by his concern over the city of Athens and its youths.
  (*b*) A lengthy general denunciation of Socrates.
(II) The 'bill of indictment' (κατηγορία): Socrates by his teachings has corrupted the youths of Athens.

In order to substantiate this charge, as well as his contention that Socrates has deserved death, the 'accuser' uses two approaches or lines of reasoning supported by two types of evidence, namely:
  (A) the *direct* approach backed up by direct evidence, and
  (B) the *indirect* approach based on 'circumstantial' evidence.

The *direct* approach (A) uses the argument that Socrates has deserved death because he and his teachings *directly* endangered:
  (1) the democratic institutions of Athens;
  (2) the basic tenets of natural piety and reverence; and
  (3) the very foundations of human society.

The *direct means* by which Socrates did all this were:
  (*a*) He jested with the established laws and institutions, inducing his followers to despise them;
  (*b*) he incited his listeners to place knowledge above everything else; and
  (*c*) he undermined family ties and the bonds of friendship.
  In order to justify his destructive teachings Socrates also called on the authority of the most celebrated poets, using their sayings to:
  (*a*) preach evil and tyrannical conduct;

Polycrates' Κατηγορία Σωκράτους

(β) advocate contempt for the poor and lowly people;
(γ) induce his followers to commit acts of fraud and deception; and
(δ) condone perjury and sacrilege.

The *indirect* approach (B) uses the argument that Socrates has deserved death because he and his teachings *indirectly* endangered:
(1) the social and moral life of Athens;
(2) the political existence of Athenian democracy; and
(3) the economic life of Athens.

The *indirect means* by which Socrates did all this were:
(a) He induced his followers not to take an active part in the social, political, and economic life of Athens; and
(b) he taught his listeners to be effeminate, lazy, and indolent. (The result of his influence can be seen in the conduct of Alcibiades and Critias.)

(III) A presentation of additional reasons why Socrates has deserved death:
(1) He was a sophist, and like all sophists unpopular with the Athenian people;
(2) like all sophists, he was guilty of sacrilege, impiety, and blasphemy;
(3) as with all sophists, nothing good ever came from his teachings (the greatest Athenian statesmen never had any philosophical or sophistic instruction); and
(4) like all sophists, he was opposed to democratic institutions.

On the strength of all these facts and the evidence submitted in their support, Socrates has deserved death, the more so, since the ultimate purpose of all his actions, direct or indirect, was to bring about the downfall of Athenian democracy.

5
The Antisthenian Elements in the Two Apologies of Xenophon

BEFORE INVESTIGATING the Antisthenian-Cynic influences on Xenophon's *Defence* and *Memorabilia* 1.1.1–1.2.64, it should be acknowledged that the Antisthenian-Cynic tradition of the late fourth century is greatly determined by the rather extravagant personality of Diogenes of Sinope. There can be little doubt that Diogenes of Sinope generally continued to propagate the basic doctrines of Antisthenes.[600] However, the tradition, possibly established by Diogenes Laertius (1.14–15; 6.2; 6.21), which makes Antisthenes the founder of Cynicism,[601] has been seriously challenged in both ancient and modern times.[602] It has been contended that a comparison between Antisthenes and Diogenes of Sinope shows more points of divergence than of congruity.[603] While this extreme view may be open to questioning, it could be maintained that Diogenes of Sinope was the founder of *practical* Cynicism in contrast to Antisthenes who seems to have laid its *theoretical* foundations. In this sense, Diogenes of Sinope would have been the 'practical successor' of Antisthenes.[604] But a strong argument against this 'succession theory' could be detected in Diogenes Laertius (6.22), where we are told that Diogenes of Sinope had learned his 'philosophy' from a mouse (and apparently not from Antisthenes): 'By watching a mouse scurrying about, Theophrastus reports, ... not looking for a place to lie down, not afraid of the dark, not seeking any of the things which are considered to be luxuries, he [*scil.*, Diogenes of Sinope] discovered the means of adapting himself to circumstances.' An added argument which points toward the absence of any personal relationships between Antisthenes and Diogenes of Sinope, may be derived from the relative chronology of these two men. The date of Antisthenes' birth is generally set around the year 443. According to Diodorus 15.76, he was still alive in 366. Diogenes of Sinope, it seems, came to Athens around 340, that is, at a time when Antisthenes must have been dead if the date given for his birth is approximately correct.[605]

Whatever may be the outcome of the scholarly controversy over the relationship,[606] it cannot be denied that there exists a remarkable resemblance between some of the fundamental teachings of Diogenes of Sinope and those of Antisthenes. Even should we concede that Diogenes of Sinope and not Antisthenes is the actual founder of the 'Cynic movement', it would be difficult to reject the thesis that Antisthenes supplied Diogenes with many basic ideas. Naturally, this thesis is difficult to prove because, with the exception of a few meagre fragments, all the writings of Antisthenes have been lost. But Dio Chrysostom (*Oratio* 8.1-4) reports: 'It was not long before he [*scil.*, Diogenes of Sinope] despised them all [*scil.*, Plato, Aristippus, Aeschines, and Euclides of Megara[607]] save Antisthenes, whom he cultivated, not so much from approval of the man himself as for his teachings, which he felt to be alone true and best adapted to help mankind. For when he contrasted the man Antisthenes with his teachings, he sometimes would say in a critical mood that the man himself was much weaker. And reproaching him thus, he would compare him to a trumpet because he could not hear himself, no matter how much noise he made. Antisthenes tolerated this banter because he greatly admired the man's character ... [and because] he took delight in the outspokenness of Diogenes. ... Sometimes he used to incite Diogenes, while at other times he tried to relax his tension. ...'[608] If we can rely on this report, the influence of Antisthenes on Diogenes of Sinope must have been considerable. Apart from certain exaggerations, the basic views and the general conduct of Diogenes of Sinope may be accepted as being essentially those of Antisthenes. Therefore, in order to reconstruct the fundamental ideas underlying the philosophy of Antisthenes, with certain reservations we are permitted to make use of the views of Diogenes of Sinope as they have been recorded by later authors and historians.

Aside from Diogenes Laertius, we possess reports on Diogenes of Sinope by Philodemus, Stobaeus, Maximus of Tyre, Epictetus, Aelian, Julian, Athenaeus (who seems to rely on Satyrus), and Plutarch. These authors record a number of apophthegms ascribed to Diogenes of Sinope. As a literary figure he also appears in the works of Lucian and Dio Chrysostom. The *Wiener Diogenes Papyrus*,[609] dating back to the first century B.C., contains nine anecdotes ascribed to Diogenes. The *Papyrus Bouriant* no. 1[610] contains five apophthegms. The *On the Stoics* of Philodemus[611] seems to refer to the *Republic* of Diogenes of Sinope.[612] According to Diogenes Laertius (6.26; 6.80), Sotion of Alexandria, who wrote his *Didache* between 200 and 170 B.C., seems to have discussed Diogenes of Sinope in his fourth and seventh books. The reports of Sosicrates and Satyrus[613] are already under Stoic influence. Diocles of Magnesia, the friend of the Cynic Meleagros of Gadara, likewise wrote on Diogenes.[614] For details regarding the death of Diogenes of Sinope, Diogenes Laertius (6.77; 6.87) most likely used a work on Diogenes by Antisthenes of Rhodes. Of the Early Cynic authors dealing with Diogenes of Sinope perhaps the most important are Crates of

The Antisthenian Elements in the Two Apologies of Xenophon

Thebes,[615] whose works, written *c.* 330, seem to reflect the teachings of Diogenes of Sinope; and Metrocles of Maroneia,[616] who around 300 wrote his *Syngrammata* which were perhaps used by Bion of Borysthenes. The *Sale of Diogenes*, a story probably invented by Menippus,[617] himself a slave, is treated by Eubulus,[618] and also used by Cleomenes in his *On Pedagogues*.[619] It should also be borne in mind that in the course of time the most varied anecdotes became attached to the name of Diogenes of Sinope. Some of these anecdotes are of a strictly rigorous and serious nature, while others have a coarsely hedonistic and burlesque flair.[620]

The sources used by Diogenes Laertius in his 'biography' of Diogenes of Sinope may be classified as follows: chapters 1–24 are a kind of biographical sketch based probably on a single original source which can no longer be determined; chapters 25–69 are a collection of anecdotes based on a multitude of primary and secondary sources; chapters 70–73 contain some of the χρεία of Diogenes of Sinope which might have been taken from the same source as chapters 1–24; and chapters 74–81, in all probability a 'continuation' of chapters 25–69, also contain some additions by Diogenes Laertius. Hence, the whole *Life of Diogenes* by Diogenes Laertius essentially consists of two major parts, a biography and a collection of anecdotes.[621]

The reports of Diogenes Laertius on Antisthenes are extremely meagre, while his accounts of Diogenes of Sinope are both lengthy and sufficiently detailed to give us a somewhat coherent picture of the views held by the latter. According to Diogenes of Sinope (Dio Chrysostom, *Oratio* 8.1–4), Antisthenes probably did not draw from his philosophical maxims all possible practical applications. This seems to have been done by Diogenes of Sinope who, despite all unfavourable anecdotes recorded about him and his personal deportment,[622] must be considered the faithful, though somewhat unorthodox and extravagant, follower of Antisthenes.[623] The Antisthenian problem, then, is simply this: since we are confronted with the nearly complete loss of the works of Antisthenes, it has become a traditional practice to judge him by what Plato and Aristotle—two rather unsympathetic witnesses—had to say about him. To make matters worse, Antisthenes, at least according to a widespread tradition, has been held responsible for the 'clowning' of Diogenes of Sinope who contributed much to the general disregard in which Antisthenes and his teachings were held by later generations.[624] In the light of what has just been said it is reasonable to assume, therefore, that Diogenes of Sinope, even in his exaggerated 'mannerisms',[625] accepted and expanded many of the basic principles of Antisthenian teachings. Hence he may be regarded a fairly reliable, though not always accurate historical source of Cynic philosophy. Impregnating the doctrines of Antisthenes and Diogenes of Sinope is their liking for paradoxes and, as a consequence, their use of radical and frequently shocking ideas or postulates. Paradoxical to the traditional Greek mind, for instance, was the Antisthenian-Cynic idea that toil and lack of fame were a blessing. It is not impossible that the famous Stoic paradoxes, which still preoccupied Cicero, were originally based on Antisthenian-Cynic sayings.

The source situation connected with Diogenes of Sinope presents, nevertheless, many puzzling problems. Aside from possessing an obviously uneven value, the surviving sources, which frequently consist of disjointed references, are of a relatively late date. It is fairly safe to assume that our present-day knowledge of Diogenes of Sinope in the main is based on the remnants of a considerable 'Diogenes literature' which seems to have developed during the first two or three centuries after the death of Diogenes. In a general way the Diogenes literature of this period may perhaps be subdivided into four major groups or types. Theophrastus, in his Περὶ τῶν Διογένους συναγωγή,[626] probably originated a kind of general treatment of Diogenes, although it is possible that he relied on Eubulides, an author who cannot be fully identified, but who might have been a contemporary of Aristotle as well as presumably the father of a Περὶ Διογένους.[627] The second type of Diogenes literature seems to go back to the authors of διαδοχαὶ or *Successions*,[628] while the third group is made up of the compilators of anecdotes, χρεῖα, and apophthegms ascribed to Diogenes.[629] Of the fourth type are those writings, to be credited both to Cynic and early Stoic authors, in which Diogenes of Sinope is presented as the ideal 'wise man' or the 'second Heracles', who could be quoted not only for the purpose of moralizing and edification, but also in order to demonstrate in an eloquent manner how the 'true philosopher', strengthened by his ἐγκράτεια and αὐτάρκεια, deports himself when faced with a concrete and trying situation. But despite the difficulties and complications in the quest of sources, the efforts of many scholars have enabled us to see the main outlines of Diogenes' thought and its reflection of Antisthenian ideas.

At this point a few words should be said about the reason why Heracles, as he was understood by Antisthenes, became the idol and 'patron saint' of the Cynics. Antisthenes, it seems, developed a Heracles type which apparently contained two distinct strains: Heracles, the pupil of Chiron who attained to wisdom and virtue through rigorous moral and physical training; and Heracles, the ἐγκρατής and 'friend of many πόνοι'. This may be gathered from Diogenes Laertius 6.2: 'He [*scil.*, Antisthenes] demonstrated that πόνος is a good thing by referring to Heracles. . . .' But in order to be good, this πόνος must be purposeful work: 'All virtuous life, as Antisthenes says in his work entitled *Heracles*, must be directed to a rational end'.[630] In sum, the many Heracles legends, which were in vogue during the latter part of the fifth century B.C., lent themselves to a number of moralizing interpretations and, hence, were eagerly received by Antisthenes and the Cynics. These legends

The Antisthenian Elements in the Two Apologies of Xenophon

depicted the hero as the undismayed victim of fate who finally overcomes all difficulties by sheer willpower; as the lover of toil and danger who in the end emerges victoriously; and as the often misunderstood benefactor of mankind (εὐεργέτης) who in his φιλανθρωπία wanders throughout the world. As R. Höistad has pointed out, the Heracles theme presented a great many possibilities to any philosophical movement which stresses the emancipation of the individual from all traditionalist notions of collectivism; to a movement which in its social and political discontentment as well as social discrimination demands a radical revision of the whole structure of society; to a movement which in its strongly emotional sense of mission rejects many of the traditional values; to a movement, finally, which puts action above theory, and will power above purely intellectual achievement.[631]

The Heracles figure of earliest Greek literature (Homer and Hesiod) is that of a mighty doer of heroic deeds who lacks any moral or pedagogical purpose. But already in Pindar, Heracles is described as a 'constructive helper' and as a 'giver of strength', in other words, as a 'philanthropist'. It is here that the traditional legends undergo that preliminary ethical refinement and transformation which made it possible for subsequent authors to see in Heracles a παιδεία-ideal. In Euripides, for instance, Heracles seeks the answer to all human sufferings in man himself: a stoic attitude towards the ills of life, a resignation to fate seems to be the only possible solution. Thus Heracles becomes an εὐεργέτης, a 'doer of good deeds'. But this *philanthropia* can be achieved only through suffering, although suffering, the πόνοι, is still an evil which ultimately crushes the hero. It is safe to assume that Antisthenes and the Cynics to some extent were influenced by Euripides who depicts Heracles as the suffering and misunderstood benefactor of mankind. Also, the *Story of Heracles* by Herodorus,[632] probably a contemporary of Socrates, could be cited as one of the possible influences on Antisthenes' conception of Heracles. For Herodorus seems to have suggested that Heracles was a 'philosopher' who entertained notions of an individualistic ethics. In the famous allegory of Prodicus,[633] the πόνος, too, is no longer an evil, but something which the true philanthropist must constantly undergo. Thus in the literary tradition of the waning fifth century the Heracles legend already contains *in nucleo* some of the basic Antisthenian-Cynic elements: the homeless, stateless, and often completely misunderstood hero who undertakes his many laborious wanderings as a benefactor of mankind; the suffering victim of fate who always overcomes fate itself by sheer will power; and the humble man who is in effect the truly kingly person. It is from these elements that Antisthenes and the Cynics moulded their specific Heracles figure. Naturally, by resorting to their own brand of interpretation, they injected their particular preferences and prejudices, especially their notions about παιδεία.[634]

The Antisthenian Elements in the Two Apologies of Xenophon

In order to ascertain whether Xenophon drew on Antisthenian-Cynic speculation, it is worth noting the extent to which Xenophon's 'working habits' disposed him to inaccuracies in attributing statements to Socrates. In *Memorabilia* 1.6.14, Socrates says to Antiphon: 'The treasures also of the wise men of old which they have left written and bequeathed to us in their works, I turn over and peruse in the company of my friends. And should our eye light upon anything we consider good, we make excerpts (ἐκλογαί).' This passage, which might be termed an 'autobiographical note', seems to describe admirably the 'working methods' employed by Xenophon when he composed his *Socratica*.[635] Hence we may surmise that nearly every Xenophontean report on Socrates looks to some prior secondary source. Undoubtedly, Xenophon had some personal contacts with Socrates,[636] but paradoxically enough, these seem to have left little or no visible traces in his writings. This forces us to conclude that the sources employed by Xenophon, that is, the materials from which he apparently took extensive notes, were probably the earliest *Socratica*—antedating the *Socratica* of Plato. Thus the Xenophontean *Socratica* also afford us at least a glimpse of these earliest *Socratica* which, with the exception of a few surviving fragments of Antisthenes and Aeschines, are completely lost. But because of the Xenophontean method of excerpting, collecting, and employing his 'notes', it becomes impossible always to determine what particular earliest Socratic author or authors have been used by Xenophon, although we may surmise that he relied most heavily on Antisthenes.

The very title of Xenophon's *Memorabilia* (Ἀπομνημονεύματα)[637] would lend support to our contention that this work is under Antisthenian-Cynic influence. Ἀπομνημονεύματα, which as a rule is a collection of the sayings or deportment ascribed to a master and collated by his disciples or admirers, constitutes a literary *genre* that probably originated with Antisthenes and the Cynics. Aside from the fact that it was better adapted to the particular audience to which the Cynics addressed themselves, it also suited the purpose of the Cynic who, in the words of Diogenes Laertius (6.27), soon realized that 'when he was gravely discussing (σπουδαιολεγουμένῳ) something, no one would pay any attention to him. So he started to whistle, and as people began to crowd around him, he reproached them with coming in all seriousness to hear nonsense, but slowly and contemptuously when the discourse was of a serious nature.' As a rule, a χρεία (the sayings and actions) of a well-known person is usually at the basis of such ἀπομνημονεύματα, and the χρεία itself is an anecdote with a moral. This description of one of the favourite and typical literary expressions of the Cynics seems to fit fairly well the Xenophontean *Memorabilia*.

One of the instances of what is surely an Antisthenian-Cynic influence on Xenophon can be found in *Defence* (chap. 1). Xenophon writes here about 'the sentiments which Socrates expressed concerning death', claiming that Socrates had insisted that 'death was more desirable for him than life at his age'.⁶³⁸ As a matter of fact, according to Xenophon (*Defence* 6), Socrates seems to have insisted that this would be the best time for him to die happily, thereby avoiding the infirmities and unhappiness of old age.⁶³⁹ This remark reminds us of Antisthenes' reported statement (Diogenes Laertius 6.5) that 'to die happy' was 'the height of human bliss'. Diogenes Laertius (6.68) also informs us that Diogenes of Sinope, 'when asked whether death was an evil thing, replied: "how can it be when in its presence we are not aware of it".'⁶⁴⁰ And Epictetus (*Diss.* 1.24.6) attributes to Diogenes of Sinope the saying that 'death is ... nothing evil or base'.⁶⁴¹ Naturally, this does not prove in any way that the views on death which Xenophon ascribes here to Socrates, are of Antisthenian-Cynic origin. On the strength of Plato's testimony,⁶⁴² which is decidedly not Antisthenian, it appears that they could very well be Socratic, and that in all likelihood the Cynics merely repeated here convictions already held by Socrates. When Xenophon (*Defence* 1ff.) implies, however, that Socrates was deliberately seeking his condemnation and death,⁶⁴³ he probably over-reaches the historical Socrates by crediting the latter with a maxim which seems to have been Antisthenian-Cynic in origin;⁶⁴⁴ at any rate, Plato records no such Socratic view. Too, the thought expressed by the Xenophontean Socrates, that old age is something exceedingly burdensome,⁶⁴⁵ reminds us of certain passages in the dialogue *Axiochus*⁶⁴⁶ which, as K. Joël has pointed out, proclaims what appears to be definitely Antisthenian-Cynic notions.⁶⁴⁷ For had not Diogenes of Sinope insisted that the most wretched thing is 'an old man destitute?'⁶⁴⁸

The remark ascribed to Socrates that, in view of the impending infirmities of old age, this was 'the best time for him to die', seems to have been borrowed from an Antisthenian-Cynic *consolatio mortis*.⁶⁴⁹ Old age, we are told in the *Axiochus* (367B ff.), 'stealthily creeps upon us ... and should one not pay, as a debt, one's life rather quickly, nature, like a usurer ... takes ... from one his eyesight, and from another his hearing. ... And should he still delay, nature brings on paralysis, or mutilation, or distortion of limbs, while those who on the threshold of old age are still physically fit, as regards their mind become twice like children. ... Hence even the gods, who take an interest in human affairs, release from life more quickly those whom they favour most.' Bion of Borysthenes, following the Cynic tradition, recommends suicide as the most expedient method of avoiding the debilities of old age,⁶⁵⁰ while Diogenes of Sinope 'escaped from life by a deliberate act",⁶⁵¹ as did Metrocles, 'who choked himself to death'⁶⁵² probably in order to evade the infirmities of an advanced age. Menippus is also said to have taken his own life (Diogenes Laertius 6.100) when faced with destitution in his last days. All these accounts of 'voluntary escapes' from the unpleasantness of old age, we may surmise, are anecdotes connected with (or perhaps illustrations from) some Antisthenian-Cynic *consolatio mortis* which, in order to dispel fear of death, had also depicted in eloquent words the horrors and miseries of old age.⁶⁵³

It should also be borne in mind that the Cynic 'Socrates,' who in the dialogue *Axiochus* consoles Axiochus and advises him in matters of death, is the same Socrates who in Xenophon's *Defence* (chap. 6)⁶⁵⁴ and *Memorabilia* (4.8.8) comforts himself about his impending death:⁶⁵⁵ 'I am ending my life when only troubles are in view' (*Defence* 27), and thus escape 'the hardest and most unpleasant part of life' (*Defence* 32). In short, there is a similar mood of elation in Xenophon's account of the doomed Socrates and in the definitely Antisthenian-Cynic *Axiochus*. In Plato's *Apology*, on the other hand, Socrates concludes his final address with the remark that only the gods know whether it is better to live or to die. Xenophon, with his Cynic leanings, claims to know without doubt that under the circumstances death would be preferable to life. This difference of opinion may also explain Xenophon's introductory remark in the *Defence*: 'Others, to be sure, have written about this [*scil.*, about the indictment, trial, defence, and death of Socrates] ... but they have not shown clearly that he had come to the conclusion that to him [*scil.*, Socrates] death was more desirable than life [*scil.*, at this late stage of his life].' We may surmise, therefore, that the whole Xenophontean report concerning Socrates' 'happy willingness to die', is probably based on some Antisthenian source or, to be more exact, on some Antisthenian *consolatio mortis* theme in which Socrates and his death were referred to as an illustration and model worthy of imitation.⁶⁵⁶

In *Defence* (chap. 16) Xenophon has this to say about Socrates: 'Have you ever known anyone less enslaved by sensuous desires, one who was more free than the man who refuses to accept gifts? Whom can you deservedly esteem more just than he who can so well accommodate himself to what he already has in his possession as not even to desire what belongs to others?'⁶⁵⁷ The same idea appears in *Memorabilia* 1.2.1, where we are told that 'Socrates ... was the most rigid of all men in controlling his passions and sensuous appetites'.⁶⁵⁸ And in *Memorabilia* 1.2.6–7 Socrates is praised as the one 'who held that those who refrained from demanding a fee retained their freedom', while those 'who took money for their teachings he [*scil.*, Socrates] considered their own enslavers'.⁶⁵⁹ These Xenophontean utterances strike us as being definitely Antisthenian-Cynic.⁶⁶⁰ Of all the virtues which Xenophon ascribes to his subject, Socrates' ἐγκράτεια seems to preponderate. This alone would indicate an Antisthenian-Cynic influence, the more so, since with the Cynics the ἐγκράτεια constitutes the most exalted of all virtues. Also the idea that pleasure enslaves man, while ἐγκράτεια makes him free, is an Antisthenian-Cynic notion.⁶⁶¹ Moral autarchy, as it is commonly known, constitutes the matrix of all Antisthenian-Cynic teachings.⁶⁶² To the Cynics, it appears, Socrates had been a classical example of this autarchy.⁶⁶³ To them he was the noble man who had freed himself from the bondage of all sensuous desires.⁶⁶⁴ For 'only bad men obey their sensuous appetites as slaves obey their masters'.⁶⁶⁵ Following the model established by Antisthenes who in his *Heracles* makes the hero choose between personified virtue and personified vice,⁶⁶⁶ Xenophon in his account of Socrates' moral autarchy likewise personifies evil. Moral autarchy, according to Antisthenes, is closely related to moral autonomy and moral freedom. Hence Diogenes Laertius (6.38) could say about Diogenes of Sinope that 'to fortune he opposed courage; to convention nature; and to passion reason'. With Antisthenes, moral autarchy and moral autonomy signify not merely man's mastery over his own sensuous desires or perhaps the rejection of an all-determining fate. It is this autarchy which distinguishes the free man—the man who is not kept in bondage by ignorance or passion—from the slave—the man who is a captive of his own ignorance and passions. Xenophon seems to have adopted the Antisthenian doctrine of moral autarchy when he enumerates the main virtues of Socrates.⁶⁶⁷

But according to Antisthenes moral autarchy also means man's emancipation from all established laws, mores, and conventions.⁶⁶⁸ Thus, in the words of Diogenes Laertius (6.11), Antisthenes maintained that 'the wise man in all his actions will be guided not by the established laws, but by the principle of virtue'.⁶⁶⁹ The Antisthenian-Cynic concept of freedom, therefore, seems to have been the dominant principle in Cynic philosophy. This concept, which is essentially a negative notion of freedom, is, indeed, nothing other than perpetual freedom *from* something: freedom from all ties which morality, law, tradition, mores, politically organized society, and any form of community existence which life in general imposes on people; freedom from passions, ambitions, and all cultural, social, economic, intellectual, or religious demands; freedom from all care about food, clothing, home, marriage, family, and children; and, finally, freedom from life itself which one can always leave voluntarily if the demand for freedom calls for such a drastic step. Antisthenes, like Antiphon, seems to have rejected the bourgeois code of morality and its codification in the νόμοι. By using the antithesis of φύσις and νόμος, which had been set up earlier by the sophists, he turned it into a political slogan. This is the real meaning of Diogenes Laertius 6.11, where the νόμος τῆς πόλεως is contrasted by the νόμος τῆς ἀρετῆς. It is interesting to note that a *scholion* on Homer, *Iliad* 15.123 (edit. Bachmann), brings out essentially the same idea. It is also fair to assume that Antisthenes creates this antithesis in his polemic against Athenian democracy. This may be gathered from Aristotles *Politics* (1284 a 10 ff.), where we also find the Antisthenian notion, hinted at in Diogenes Laertius (6.12), that the νόμοι τῆς πόλεως primarily are set up for inferior and evil people.

Antisthenes and his followers seem to carry this maxim to its extreme conclusions when they openly decry the existing laws,[670] the established customs, and the traditional institutions of the Greek city.[671] The only 'law' with which they were seriously concerned was 'the law of virtue'.[672] Conversely, they regarded all other moral or legal standards, as well as all instruments of moral and social control, as being completely arbitary, having no compelling force whatever. In this manner the Cynics considered themselves eminently free, enslaved by neither convention nor human dicta. This is also the reason why Diogenes of Sinope could say about himself that 'ever since Antisthenes has made me free, I have ceased to be a slave'.[673] Judged from the standpoint of Antisthenes' maxim of 'autonomous virtue', the established legal order loses all practical significance, as do the accepted mores, customs, and traditions of society. Diogenes of Sinope, we are told, 'allowed convention no authority'.[674] This should also explain why Antisthenes and his disciples discouraged people from participating in the social, political, or economic life of the city.[675] Diogenes Laertius (6.29) seems to have understood the spirit of Antisthenian Cynicism when he reports that Diogenes of Sinope 'would praise those who were about to marry, but refrained from doing so[676] . . . [and] those who were about to enter politics, but decided at the last moment to do no such thing . . .'[677] maintaining that 'intellectual possessions are the sole true possessions'.[678] Antisthenes and the Cynics could claim, therefore, that 'the noble lessons taught . . . by the muses were that wealth amassed is prey to vanity'[679] and, hence, 'harmful'.[680] 'For such is this thing called pleasure . . . that it . . . enslaves the soul'.[681] Hence there is no greater battle to be waged than the struggle against pleasure.[682] And the strongest man is he who can abstain from pleasure as far as possible.[683]

Antisthenes and the Cynics went to extremes in singing the praises of freedom,[684] often declaring that under certain circumstances death was the only practical road to true liberty.[685] They did not only love freedom,[686] but preferred it to everything else, including all the riches or honours of this earth.[687] They maintained that persons attached to wealth were men 'without freedom', while poverty to them meant true liberty.[688] Out of this constant clamouring for freedom, Antisthenes (he himself was the son of a slave woman) and his followers denounced such tyrants as the Macedonian kings,[689] whom they chided because the perennial fear in which they lived turned them into slaves.[690] No wonder that Xenophon (*Defence* 16), who speaks here like a Cynic, should say that Socrates was 'a free man'.

The Antisthenian-Cynic advice to refrain from entering public life and engaging in political activities[691] is not only the practical application of their 'craving for freedom', but also the result of the general Cynic contempt for politicians. In the opinion of the Cynic, politicians enslaved themselves by volunteering to become 'the servants of the people'

—a sure indication of their stupidity and depravity. Antisthenes, for instance, called politicians 'the lackeys of the people',[692] while Diogenes of Sinope referred to Demosthenes as 'the demagogue of Athens'.[693] In addition, the Cynics apparently considered the Athenian generals to be asses[694] and 'the leaders of donkeys'.[695] This Cynic disdain for public officials, at the same time, is also part of their general policy of contrasting the skilled operations of the expert craftsman with the haphazard conduct of political affairs which, as a rule, should matter much more to the intelligent man than more good craftsmanship in a limited trade.[696]

All these Antisthenian-Cynic ideas and maxims, particularly the Cynic concept of the truly virtuous man, seem to constitute the foundation for Xenophon's characterization of Socrates. They furnish the basis for his contention that Socrates was both eminently free and just: far from being himself enslaved by sensuous desires, Socrates kept a most rigid control on his passions and appetites. Thus when Antiphon berates Socrates (Xenophon, *Memor.* 1.6.2-3), he seems to address a Cynic: 'You are living a style of life such as no slave ... would put up with. Your meat and your drink are of the poorest sort. The cloak you wear is most wretched, and you wear it summer and winter. And you never wear shoes or a tunic. Besides, you refuse to take money.... If you intend to make your disciples imitate you, you ought to call yourself a teacher of the art of wretchedness'.

Defence (chap. 16) and *Memorabilia* 1.2.1 (and 1.2.6-7)[697] also seem to refer to the Antisthenian-Cynic doctrine that 'hard toil' ($\pi \acute{o} \nu o \varsigma$) was preferable to pleasure ($\dot{\eta} \delta o \nu \acute{\eta}$): 'I would rather be mad than experience pleasure',[698] is a statement for which Antisthenes later became famous. The Antisthenian-Cynic rejection of pleasure and their high praise of toil has been recorded by Diogenes Laertius (6.71): 'Nothing in life, Diogenes [of Sinope] maintained, has any hope of success without toil'.[699] In the same vein (*Memor.* 1.2.56-57)[700] Xenophon glorifies the $\varphi \iota \lambda o \pi o \nu \acute{\iota} \alpha$ (the love of toil) of Socrates.[701] We know that the concept of $\varphi \iota \lambda o \pi o \nu \acute{\iota} \alpha$ is Antisthenian and that it constitutes one of the basic moral ideals promulgated by the Cynics.[702] By extolling toil,[703] Antisthenes had definitely declared it a moral good: man must face toil and grapple with it.[704] In Xenophon's *Symposium* (4.34 ff.) we are also told that Socrates lived happier than all other people because he was freer than other men who were the slaves of their needs.[705] For 'instead of toiling uselessly,[706] these men should choose such toils as nature recommends, whereby they might live happily'.[707] Obviously, Xenophon ascribes here to Socrates characteristics which are consonant with the Antisthenian-Cynic concept of the ideal man.[708] The early Greek philosopher in his aristocratic bearing had rejected the $\pi \acute{o} \nu o \varsigma$ as something 'burdensome' and hence 'undesirable', befitting a slave rather than a 'gentleman'. We may even assume that Socrates himself did not think too highly of the πόνος. In Plato, for instance, πόνος means intellectual occupation, but never manual toil.[709] The attacks which Isocrates directs against Antisthenes,[710] among other things, also take issue with the Antisthenian πόνος doctrine. And the same may be said about Plato's anti-Antisthenian utterances.[711] Xenophon, we recall, likewise deprecated certain forms of manual labour and manual crafts, because in his opinion they weakened the human body.[712] The πόνος of Antisthenes, however, is not merely stupid toil or slave-like resignation to hardship, but joyous and free submission to the many strenuous tasks of dignified and virtuous life. Hence Antisthenes uses the term πόνος (toil) in preference to ἔργον (work). Ἔργον, it should also be remembered, refers primarily to rural labour and as such had already been praised by Hesiod in his *Works and Days*.[713] Πόνος, on the other hand, signifies toil in general and is often used by Antisthenes to indicate that dignified life as a whole is nothing other than strenuous toil. This is what Diogenes of Sinope has in mind when he states that he was competing against the toughest competitors: ' "Who may they be?" asked the other. "Hardships [πόνους]," he replied," most severe hardships, insuperable for gluttonous and foolish men...." '[714]

In *Memorabilia* 2.1.1–34, to mention only one other instance, Xenophon relates a discussion on the nature of pleasure which allegedly took place between Socrates and Aristippus. In the course of this discussion Socrates, under the uncritical pen of Xenophon, is actually transformed into an Antisthenian Cynic who quotes the famous 'choice of Heracles', so dear to every Cynic. In this fable, which probably goes back to Prodicus, Heracles chooses between pleasure (ἡδονή) and toil (πόνος). Prodicus, we are told, wrote a work entitled ὧραι[715] which apparently made use of some of the ideas on the toiling farmer expressed by Hesiod in his *Works and Days*. Aside from referring to the ancient fable of 'Heracles on the crossroads,' Prodicus turns his pamphlet into an encomium of hard work and incessant toil. The ὧραι are an example of that type of Greek literature which became very popular during the latter part of the fifth century. This *genre* of literature not only dealt in a laudatory manner with the various branches of human activities, but also essayed to prove that certain activities and labours were absolutely necessary to sustain a happy life. Undoubtedly, both Antisthenes and Xenophon were acquainted with this work of Prodicus, although we are inclined to surmise that Xenophon borrowed his ideas directly from Antisthenes rather than from Prodicus.[716] Like Heracles, King Cyrus of Persia,[717] in the Antisthenian-Cynic treatment,[718] also went through a period of arduous labours and perils which, in the end, served a good purpose. King Cyrus rose from his sufferings to become the model king (βασιλεὺς φιλόσοφος) through his many πόνοι, thus turning his sufferings into a decisive asset both for himself and his people. By struggling with his many difficulties he also developed a strongly individualistic ethics, something which Antisthenes and the Cynics tried to accomplish. Antisthenes may possibly have derived some of the materials for his Cyrus ideal from the accounts of Herodotus and the logographic tradition of the fifth century.[719] He might also have made use of Ctesias and the logographic literature (*Persica*) on which Ctesias bases his narrative, particularly his account of the early struggles and sufferings of Cyrus. The Xenophontean *Cyropaedia* to a large extent still reflects the Antisthenian effort to demonstrate the moral development of King Cyrus.[720]

Speaking like a true Antisthenian Cynic, the Socrates of Xenophon repeatedly extols virtue and toil which he calls the only certain road to wisdom:[721] 'He [*scil.*, Antisthenes] demonstrated, by citing the example of Heracles, that toil ($\pi\acute{o}\nu o\varsigma$) is a good thing'.[722] Many of the Antisthenian ideas which Socrates expresses in *Memorabilia* 2.1.1–34, also appear in chapter 16 of the *Defence* and in *Memorabilia* 1.2.1, *et passim*. This may be taken as an indication that definite Antisthenian-Cynic elements are at the basis of these passages. Also definitely Antisthenian-Cynic is the Xenophontean-Socratic praise of toil in *Memorabilia* 1.2.56–57. What Xenophon actually panegyrizes here in the name of Socrates is nothing other than the well-known Antisthenian-Cynic $\varphi\iota\lambda o\pi o\nu\acute{\iota}a$.[723]

Close analysis of *Memorabilia* 1.1.16,[724] 1.2.19,[725] and 1.2.23[726] divulges at once that the views advanced there are actually restatements of the Antisthenian-Cynic concept of the $\dot{\varepsilon}\gamma\varkappa\rho\acute{a}\tau\varepsilon\iota a$ (continence or self-control).[727] Although Xenophon fails to define here the meaning of $\dot{\varepsilon}\gamma\varkappa\rho\acute{a}\tau\varepsilon\iota a$, he nevertheless discusses the various forms and aspects which it assumes in practice. In Xenophon's *Symposium* (4.34–44), Antisthenes expounds rather thoroughly his ideas on the $\dot{\varepsilon}\gamma\varkappa\rho\acute{a}\tau\varepsilon\iota a$ which constitutes one of the central notions in the whole of Antisthenian-Cynic teachings. Essentially the same Antisthenian ideas on the $\dot{\varepsilon}\gamma\varkappa\rho\acute{a}\tau\varepsilon\iota a$ or $\varkappa a\tau\varepsilon\rho\acute{\iota}a$ (hardihood) turn up again in Xenophon's *Memorabilia* 1.1.16, 1.2.19, and 1.2.23, where Socrates is described as the foremost champion of the $\dot{\varepsilon}\gamma\varkappa\rho\acute{a}\tau\varepsilon\iota a$.[728] As a matter of fact, in *Memorabilia*, chapters 5 and 6 of Book I and chapter 1 of Book II, Socrates practically is cast not only in the role of a prophet of the $\dot{\varepsilon}\gamma\varkappa\rho\acute{a}\tau\varepsilon\iota a$, but also in that of a founder of Cynicism. In order to understand the particular attitude displayed here by Xenophon, we must bear in mind that in *Memorabilia* 2.1.1 ff., a 'Socratic' (Xenophon) attacks the views held by another 'Socratic' (Aristippus). Diogenes Laertius (2.65) records that 'Xenophon was not a friend of Aristippus, and for this reason he made Socrates direct a (Antisthenian?) discourse against Aristippus in which the former denounces pleasure.' The 'anti-Aristippian' discourse to which Diogenes Laertius alludes here is undoubtedly *Memorabilia* 2.1.1 ff. Thus it seems that already in ancient times this 'discourse' was considered a literary fiction.[729] In *Memorabilia* 1.1.16, Xenophon also reports that Socrates had mentioned a knowledge which confers 'the patent of nobility on its possessor', and an ignorance which stigmatizes as slaves those affected by it;[730] and in *Memorabilia* 1.2.6, Socrates calls 'slave traders' those who accept money. The use of the term 'slave' in this connection indicates that Xenophon relies on an Antisthenian-Cynic source. Antisthenes, in general, not only revelled in the use of strong and descriptive expressions, but also frequently referred to the antithesis of 'slave' and 'free man' when comparing ignorance and knowledge.[731]

In chapter 18 of the *Defence*[732] the Xenophontean Socrates makes the following interesting observation: 'When the city is under siege[733] and every other person bemoans his loss,[734] why is it that I appear as in no way poorer than while the city remained in its most prosperous state? Why is it that when others are forced to procure their delicacies from foreign lands at an exorbitant price,[735] I can indulge in pleasures far more exquisite by having recourse to the reflections in my mind?'[736] This passage has a familiar ring for those who are acquainted with Xenophon's *Symposium* (4.41–43). Here Antisthenes makes the following typically Cynic remark: 'But observe the advantage I derive from my poverty. In case the little I have should be taken from me . . . I could still maintain myself without the least trouble. . . . Whenever I have the desire to regale myself and indulge in my appetite . . . I have not to purchase expensive delicacies. . . . It is not the excessive price of what we eat that gives us relish. . . . Wealth of my sort will make you liberal'.[737] Identically the same idea can be found in Dio Chrysostom (*Oratio* 6.61–62), who reports the following statement attributed to Diogenes of Sinope: 'If an earthquake destroys all the house as happened once in Sparta, and all the sheep are killed so that not a single man has anything to clothe himself, and want overwhelms not only Attica, but Boeotia as well and the Peloponnesus and Thessaly . . . I shall fare none the worse nor be more destitute than before. For how much more naked shall I be than I am now, how much more homeless? I shall find all the food I need in apples, millet, barley, vetches, the cheapest of lentils, acorns roasted in the ashes and cornel berries . . . on which even the largest animals can subsist.' The same story is also told in Themistius, Περὶ ἀρετῆς or, Περὶ ἀσκήσεως.[738] It is now commonly accepted that the basic tenor of this oration is essentially Antisthenian-Cynic. In chapters 40–41 (pp. 456–457 of the translation) Themistius reports: 'The Ephesians were used to a life of pleasure and luxury. . . . Once they were besieged by an enemy . . . but they continued their mode of living. Soon they were faced with a serious shortage of food. . . . They called a meeting to discuss ways of providing sufficient food, but no one dared to suggest that they should inaugurate a programme of frugality. . . . A man called Heraclitus brought plain gruel and, mixing it with plain water, sat down among them to eat it. And this became a lesson to the whole population'.[739]

The Antisthenian Elements in the Two Apologies of Xenophon

The Cynics, as it is generally known, always held frugality and simple fare in high esteem,[740] preferring, for instance, water to wine.[741] They were not ashamed, as some of their more aristocratic fellow citizens were, to buy their food at the public market and carry it home themselves.[742] They ate and drank when and wherever they felt hungry or thirsty,[743] and often refused even to use eating utensils which they considered superfluous and purely conventional.[744] Xenophon (*Memorabilia* 1.3.5-7) ascribes these Cynic traits and habits also to Socrates: 'So frugal was he [*scil.*, Socrates] that ... he took only so much food as he could eat with relish ... [and] he never drank unless he was thirsty. If he accepted an invitation to dinner he had no difficulty in avoiding over-indulgence—something which is extremely difficult to most men. Those who were unable to do so he advised to be cautious of eating when they were not hungry, and of drinking when they were not thirsty. Such conduct, he said, was ruinous to the constitution in that it was bad for the stomach, brain and soul alike. ... He thought that Circe transformed men into swine by feasting them on so many dainty dishes. Only Odysseus through his continence and the admonitions of Mercury abstained ... and did not turn into a pig'.[745] And Socrates apparently recites a Cynic creed when, in the words of Xenophon (*Memor.* 1.6.4–8), he addresses Antiphon: '... you seem to be under the impression that my life is so miserable that I am convinced that you would prefer death to a life such as mine. Suppose, then, we consider what it is you find so hard in my life. ... Do you think my food despicable on the ground that it is less wholesome or less nourishing than yours? Or because my victuals are more difficult to get than yours, since they are so scarce and so much costlier to procure than yours? Or because your food is more enjoyable than mine? Do you not know that the greater the appetite, the less the need for sauces; the keener the thirst, the less the desire for extravagant drinks? As for cloaks, you know, they are changed on account of cold weather or else on account of hot weather. And shoes are worn as a protection of the feet against injury and inconvenience while walking. Now I ask you, have you ever known me to stay indoors more than others on account of cold weather, or fight with any man for a place in the shade because of the heat, or be prevented from walking to my heart's content on account of sore feet? ... I am always training myself to endure whatever may befall my body ... [thus] avoiding slavery to the belly, or to sleep, or to incontinence. ...'[746] Essentially the same idea is also recorded by Diogenes Laertius (2.27): 'He [*scil.*, Socrates] used to say that he most enjoyed the food which was least in need of seasoning, and the drink which made him feel least hankering after other drink; and that he was nearest to the gods in that he had the fewest wants'.[747]

This contempt for earthly goods can also be found in Diogenes of Sinope. According to the testimony of Epictetus (*Diss.* 1.24.6–7),

The Antisthenian Elements in the Two Apologies of Xenophon

Diogenes had insisted that 'to be naked is better than to wear a purple robe; to sleep upon bare ground better than to have the softest of beds.[748] And he [scil., Diogenes] proves everything he says by his courage, tranquility of mind and freedom....' For had not Antisthenes in his abject poverty[749] insisted that wisdom is the only sure possession—'possession forever'?[750] This is clearly brought out by Epictetus (*Diss.* 3.24.68) when he reports that Diogenes of Sinope had said: 'He [scil., Antisthenes] taught me what was my own and what was not my own. An estate is not my own. Kindred people, domestics, friends, familiar places or manner of life, these all belong to others. What then is your own? The use of appearances of things. And he showed me that I have this. And in having this I am not subject to any restraint or compulsion, and no one can hinder me or force me to use them'. Themistius, who in this speaks like an Antisthenian Cynic, phrases the same idea as follows: 'Only that which is safely man's own [scil., virtue], can be called his true possession. All other things which men may have acquired, are not really his'.[751] What, then, 'is really man's own? Things which others may take away from him, or things over which he has complete control? Do you have complete control over your fields or your slaves...? A tyrant may deprive you of your fields, invaders may lay waste to them, or a cloudburst may wash them away.... And your slave may die or run away....'[752] For there 'is nothing constant in things'.[753] Antisthenes and his followers seem to have concluded, therefore, that 'if you learn and understand merely the things that pertain to physical existence, you remain as ignorant as a wild animal.... For he who concentrates only on the things of this earth...is not a wise man, but akin to an animal wallowing in its own mire'.[754]

The good, according to Antisthenes and the Cynics, is τὸ ἑαυτόν, and τὸ ἑαυτὸν is really the soul; the soul, in turn, is itself when it is rational; and what is rational is good. Only as a rational being, that is, only when acting intelligently, is man himself and, therefore free.[755] Conversely, evil is ἀλλότριον, something which does not pertain to the true self of man as the Cynics understood him. This ἀλλότριον, not being related to the soul, must be material and, hence, irrational. Man, once enmeshed in material and irrational things, or doing whatever is 'not his own', is no longer free, no longer his 'true self', but a slave of something other than himself. No wonder that Antisthenes and the Cynics should insist that 'only intellectual possessions are true possessions'.[756] Wisdom and virtue, we are told, are weapons that can never be lost.[757] 'The god-like man, who is the virtuous man', is in need of but little.[758] 'If some one should maintain that riches or fame are superior to virtue...do not believe him....'[759] The same idea is put into Socrates' mouth by Xenophon (*Memor.* 1.6.10) when he says: 'I believe [said Socrates] that to want nothing is an attribute of the godhead; and to have as few wants as possible the nearest approach to the godhead, that the divine nature is perfection and that to be nearest to the divine nature is to be nearest to perfection.'[760] There exists no good, therefore, that could be called superior to virtue—and virtue is a possession which not even time can challenge. And neither does it desert its owner:[761] 'No one may assume control over man's virtue, because it resides in his reason.'[762]

In Xenophon's *Symposium* (4.34–4.39) we read the following observation ascribed to Antisthenes: 'I hold to the belief... that wealth and poverty lie not in a man's estate, but in the soul of man....[763] But as to me, my riches are so plentiful that I can hardly discover any part of them. Yet for all this I have enough to eat till my hunger is stayed; enough to drink till my thirst is quenched;[764] enough to clothe myself.... When I am at home... the bare walls make my chamber warm, and I have sufficient bedding.... In fact, all these possessions seem to me so enjoyable that I could not wish for greater pleasure from them, but indeed for less. For some of them do seem to me more pleasurable than advisable.' This doctrine which regards asceticism as the surest road to virtue and happiness, actually contains two elements, namely, the principle of moral autarchy and the idea of rigid asceticism. Self-sufficiency is, above all, elimination of all desires ($εὐτέλεια$) of the senses. Plato (*Hippias Minor* 368B ff.) informs us that Hippias had appeared at the Olympic Games showing that everything he wore or used was made by his own hands. It has been said that this type of 'autarchy' influenced Antisthenes' teachings on self-sufficiency. This suggestion seems to overlook the fact that Hippias' 'autarchy' does not signify the elimination of desires ($εὐτέλεια$), as Antisthenes preached it, but is merely $πολυτροπία$, that is, an 'extension' of one's aptitudes till they can fulfil all desires which are not to be eliminated. While the principle of moral autarchy could very well be Socratic,[765] the idea of asceticism and particularly the combination of moral autarchy and asceticism for the sake of man's moral autonomy,[766] impresses us as being definitely Antisthenian-Cynic.[767] This may be gathered from the sixth oration of Dio Chrysostom, who, when writing about Diogenes of Sinope, points out that the rigorous physical regime to which the latter had subjected himself 'had given him better health than those who were gorging themselves... or who stayed indoors and never experienced either cold or heat'.[768] 'Man's ingenuity... at contriving so many implements... has not always been altogether a blessing... since men do not employ their cleverness to promote courage and justice, but rather to procure pleasure. And so, while they are pursuing pleasure at any cost, their lives become constantly less pleasant and more burdensome. And while they appear to be attending their own needs, they perish miserably just because of excessive attention and care.'[769] And Diogenes of Sinope 'used to say that men, owing to their softness, lived more wretchedly than animals'.[770] They are so tender 'because of their mode of life, since, as a rule, they avoid the sun and also the cold'.[771] 'Things, therefore, which were costly or demanded constant attention and worry he [scil., Diogenes of Sinope] rejected by showing that they were injurious to those who used them.'[772] And he, who was 'the only independent man on earth',[773] marvelled 'when he beheld that they did or suffered all this just in order to keep themselves alive. And he also marvelled that their greatest fear was lest their so-called necessities should fail them.'[774] 'But whatever would readily and without effort help the body to withstand the cold of the winter and the pangs of hunger... he would never forgo....'[775] For 'whoever asserts that virtue alone suffices for a happy life, does not say that virtue also generates life. He merely maintains that virtue turns life into a happy one.'[776]

The doctrine which regards asceticism the straightest road to virtue and happiness, has also been ascribed to Socrates. Thus in Plato's *Symposium* (174A), the fact that Socrates for once wore a new cloak and new sandals, is explained as being an exceptional gesture made in honour of the banquet he was attending. In Plato's *Phaedrus* (229A), we are told that Socrates always went barefooted, while in Plato's *Symposium* (219B), Alcibiades extols Socrates' remarkable ability to endure hunger, cold, and fatigue. Aristophanes, in his *Clouds*, not only describes the followers of Socrates as 'barefooted wretches like Socrates himself', but also insists that the followers of Socrates, who are unshaven and unwashed characters, are expected to go hungry and thirsty and to shiver with cold. Socrates himself is depicted as a miserable wretch in dire need of a cloak and sandals. Xenophon, who frequently turns his Socrates into an Antisthenian Cynic, naturally would ascribe to Socrates ascetic leanings. Nevertheless, we insist that the asceticism ascribed to Socrates by his admirers is Antisthenian-Cynic in origin rather than Socratic. The correspondence between Antisthenian-Cynic doctrine and many of the remarks attributed to Socrates in chapter 18 of the *Defence* and *Memorabilia* 1.2.1, are, it would seem, too obvious to admit of any other conclusion than that Xenophon drew directly on the Antisthenian doctrinal corpus.

But the parallels continue. In chapter 19 of the *Defence* Socrates challenges his judges with the question: 'What pious man have I made impious, what modest person immodest, what frugal man a wastrel, what temperate person intemperate, what industrious man idle and effeminate by associating with me?'[777] Essentially the same idea can be found in *Memorabilia* 1.2.2: 'How, then, being such a character himself, could he [scil., Socrates] render others impious or lawless or profligate or incontinent or too effeminate to endure labour and toil.'[778] Needless to say that all these encomia of Socrates suggest Antisthenian-Cynic teachings. From Diogenes Laertius (6.24) we learn that Diogenes of Sinope continually preached that we need either 'reason or a halter' for the proper conduct of life. Therefore we must 'erect walls of defence in our impregnable reasoning'.[779] Since, according to Antisthenes, the most urgent lesson we have to learn is 'how to get rid of having anything to unlearn',[780] we 'must learn from those who know that our faults are to be avoided'.[781] Thus when Xenophon states in *Memorabilia* 1.2.17 that 'all teachers make themselves examples to their pupils as far as they practise what they preach',[782] he is in essence repeating an old Antisthenian-Cynic maxim.[783] Virtue, being something that can be taught,[784] is true education: and education, in the word of Diogenes of Sinope, 'is a controlling grace ... wealth to the poor and an ornament to the rich'.[785] But this 'education for virtue', at least in the opinion of the Cynics, 'is of two kinds, namely, mental and physical'.[786]

These Antisthenian-Cynic maxims might very well be back of chapters 19 and 21 of the *Defence* and *Memorabilia* 1.2.2, 1.2.56–57, and 1.2.64. In chapter 21 of the *Defence*,[787] for instance, it is stated that Socrates 'had excelled in that employment which is the most noble of all, and which has for its aim the greatest good of mankind, the instruction of youths in the knowledge of their duty,[788] and the dissemination of the principle of virtue in the mind of every one'. Naturally, one should compare this statement with the remark credited to Antisthenes: 'He [*scil.*, Antisthenes] would prove that... nobility belongs to no one but the virtuous.'[789] According to the Περὶ εὐγενείας (*On eugenics*),[790] ascribed to Aristotle, Socrates allegedly held that virtuous parents, because of their virtue, give birth to noble children. It is quite possible, therefore, that the ideas expressed here by Xenophon might also be Socratic. But it is probably safer to assume that for his own *Socratica* Xenophon relied on the Antisthenian writings or Antisthenian λόγοι Σωκρατικοί which he apparently considered the true and reliable depository of Socratic teachings.[791]

In chapter 20 of the *Defence* Xenophon records that Meletus[792] had censured Socrates for having persuaded many people to obey him rather than their parents.[793] It has already been pointed out that this particular passage is nothing else than a short summary of *Memorabilia* 1.2.49–51. There we are told that 'the accuser' had charged Socrates not only 'with teaching young people to show contempt for their parents, persuading them that he could render them wiser than their fathers',[794] but also that 'he caused other relatives or kinsmen to be held in contempt by his followers, saying that relatives were of no profit to people who were sick'.[795] And in *Memorabilia* 1.2.52 'the accuser', according to the testimony of Xenophon, is said to have claimed that 'Socrates stated that it was of no profit that friends were well disposed, unless they were also able to give us assistance', implying thereby that 'compared to himself all other people were of no account'.[796] In *Memorabilia* 2.5.1–4, again, Socrates points out that different friends are to be held in different esteem, and that we ought to examine ourselves in order to ascertain whether we deserve the esteem of our friends.[797]

The Antisthenian Elements in the Two Apologies of Xenophon

Here Socrates explains what sort of people we should choose for our friends; how we may ascertain the character of different men before we form a friendship; and how we may win the friendship of other people. Then he continues to explain that friendship can exist only among good and honourable people, even when these men hold different opinions.[798] All these lengthy perorations on friendship could be called an attempt on the part of Xenophon to disprove Polycrates' allegation that Socrates had taught that we should ignore friends unless we are able to derive from them some tangible advantages.[799]

Obviously, Polycrates' charges recorded in *Memorabilia* 1.2.49–52, as well as Xenophon's rebuttals (*Memor.* 1.2.53–55), contain references to the well-known Antisthenian-Cynic rejection and denunciation of all established mores, customs, and traditions, including the 'conventional' and universally accepted forms of filial reverence, kin loyalty, and common bonds of friendship. Thus Diogenes Laertius reports that Antisthenes had exhorted his disciples to 'esteem an honest man above a kinsman',[800] while Epictetus (*Diss.* 3.24.68) quotes Diogenes of Sinope as having said that Antisthenes had taught him 'that kindred people, domestics [and] friends . . . were not my own'. It seems, therefore, that the Antisthenian-Cynic tradition had insisted upon playing down not only the conventional, but even the natural ties which bind together husband and wife,[801] parent and child, brother and brother as well as friend and friend. It is from such and similar Antisthenian-Cynic statements that Polycrates could have gathered the material for his charges that Socrates had undermined the basic foundations of human society through his teachings. In addition, since the Antisthenian-Cynic tradition apparently put 'philosophical considerations' above the duties of filial piety and allegiance,[802] Polycrates could also maintain that Socrates allegedly 'persuaded his followers that he could render them wiser than their fathers'.[803] It should also be borne in mind that because the Cynics were always in search of the 'ideal father', they customarily disapproved of the real father, whom they often blamed for neglecting the proper education of his children.[804] As a matter of fact, they never seem to have agreed with whatever plans a father had for his sons, a situation which Plato satirizes in his *Laches* (179CD).[805] In any event, the Antisthenian doctrine of moral autarchy and moral autonomy, which in its practical implications signifies complete emancipation from all established morals, conventions or laws, could be pointed to by the enemies of the Cynics as the total rejection of everything that had been honoured and respected by man since time immemorial.[806] This, at least, seems to be the conclusion which Polycrates, in his accusations of Socrates, draws from what he believed to be Socratic ideas. But there can be little doubt that these views are Antisthenian-Cynic rather than Socratic.

In chapter 21 of the *Defence*[807] Socrates, referring to his own public rejection, is quoted as having said that 'in every other circumstance the man who excels in any employment is supposed not only to be entitled to common respect, but receives many and very distinguished honours'. Essentially the same idea, although in a somewhat altered manner, appears in *Memorabilia* 1.2.9,[808] where we are told that Socrates had pointed out 'how foolish it was to elect the magistrates of the city by lot, when nobody would be willing to take a pilot elected by beans ... or a person in any other profession which if faultily exercised would cause far less harm than mistakes in the administration of the city'.[809] The Antisthenian aversion to the selection of magistrates by lot is well known: it is closely related to the rejection of τύχη—luck (as contrasted to πράττειν—purposive and intelligent effort): 'They [*scil.*, the Cynics] hold that ... we should nothing entrust to chance.'[810] The Xenophontean justification of Socrates' criticism of certain Athenian political institutions (*Memor.* 1.2.9-11) definitely shows the influence of that Antisthenian-Cynic tradition which had made it a habit to contrast the professional skill of the craftsman with the incompetence of civic officials. We have but to remember what Diogenes of Sinope, 'the observer of mankind and man's folly',[811] said about the expert: 'In the manual crafts and the other arts it can be seen that the craftsmen develop extraordinary manual skill through practice. Take the case of the flute-players and of athletes: what outstanding skill they acquire by their ceaseless toil. If they had transferred their efforts to the training of the mind, their efforts would undoubtedly not have been unprofitable or ineffective. Nothing in life ... has any chance of succeeding without strenuous practice. And this is capable of overcoming any difficulty.'[812]

It has already been pointed out that Antisthenes, as well as his disciples, did not hesitate to express their aversion to all established 'conventional' laws and political institutions[813] by insisting that 'the wise man is self-sufficient ... and will be guided in all his public acts not by the established laws but only by the principle of virtue'.[814] But aside from denouncing and ridiculing the established laws and conventions of society, Antisthenes had also expressed in a most vitriolic manner his keen disapproval of the existing democratic institutions. 'It is strange', he said, 'that we weed our darnel from the corn and unfit people in war, but do not excuse incompetent and evil men from the service of the city.'[815] Diogenes Laertius (6.8) also reports that Antisthenes 'used to recommend to the Athenians to vote that asses are horses. When they considered this suggestion absurd, he replied: but yet generals are found among you who had no training, but are merely elected.'[816] And Crates, probably a pupil of Diogenes of Sinope,[817] 'used to say that we should study philosophy until we are able to realize that generals are nothing other than donkey drivers'.[818] Such statements, to be sure, could be used by Polycrates as materials for his charge that Socrates 'caused his followers to despise the established laws ... and to ridicule the existing form of government, thereby disposing them to acts of violence.'[819] Antisthenes' well-known admiration for Lacedaemon and the Spartan way of life[820] is also strongly reflected in his constant ridicule of, or contempt for, Athenian democracy and its political institutions.[821] This contempt for democracy and the democratic leaders, whom he referred to as 'demagogues', he apparently voiced in his πολιτεία[822] as well as in his *Aspasia*,[823] where he reproaches Pericles, one of the 'democratic demagogues', for having neglected the education of his children.[824] According to Dio Chrysostom (*Oratio* 13.22), Socrates allegedly asked the Athenians whether they really thought 'that the orators are qualified to deliberate, and that their profession is competent to make you good men'. If you do, Socrates continued, 'I am greatly surprised that you have not entrusted the decision in questions of state to them instead of to yourselves. . . . No, for you would be acting just as if you were to appoint ordinary seamen or boatswains to be the helmsmen and captains of your triremes.'[825] 'But as to how you are to learn what is to your own advantage and that of your native city, and to live lawfully and justly and harmoniously in your social and political relations, without wronging or plotting against one another, this you have never learned nor has this problem ever yet given you any concern. . . .'[826]

The Polycratean charges that Socrates had ridiculed the established laws and political institutions of Athens, and that he had insisted that only 'experts' should be the object of respect and honour,[827] seem to suggest an Antisthenian-Cynic source. For if Plato's *Crito* (49E–50A) contains reliable information, Socrates, on the contrary, would have been the most law-abiding citizen, one who forfeited his life rather than disavow the laws of the city. 'If I should escape from prison against the will of the Athenians,' Socrates maintains, 'would I not desert the principles which we have just acknowledged to be just . . .?' 'Do you imagine that a city could exist and not be overthrown, in which the established laws have no power, but are set aside and trampled upon by individuals?'[828] Anyone 'who knows the way in which we [scil., the established laws] administer justice and the city, and still remains, has entered into an implied covenant that he will do as we command him'.[829] Assuming that these statements of Plato actually reflect the attitude of Socrates towards the established laws and legal institutions of Athens, Polycrates would have had no grounds to charge Socrates with having 'caused his followers to despise the established laws', or with 'exciting youths to condemn the existing form of government, thus disposing them to acts of violence'.[830] The Antisthenian-Cynic attitude towards the laws and the institutions of the city, on the other hand, was one of savage scorn. Thus when Polycrates instituted his particular charges against Socrates he must have relied on Antisthenian-Cynic materials. For only in this kind of Socratic literature could he find expressed those views which would lend support to his allegations.

The Antisthenian Elements in the Two Apologies of Xenophon

In *Memorabilia* 1.1.6–9, Xenophon recounts that Socrates had distinguished between those activities which 'needed divination', and those which as predominantly technical arts, were a matter of human knowledge and experience.[831] By the same token, Xenophon continues (*Memor.* 1.1.9), Socrates 'called impious those who instead of exercising their natural reason, resorted to omens when dealing with trivial matters'.[832] These Xenophontean observations remind us of a significant passage recorded by Diogenes Laertius (6.24): 'When he [*scil.*, Diogenes of Sinope] saw interpreters of dreams and those who attended them ... he thought no animal more silly.' Hence 'he would say about those who were excited over their dreams that they cared nothing for what they were doing in their waking hours, but kept their curiosity for the visions called up in their sleep'.[833] And Dio Chrysostom (*Oratio* 10.2) reports that Diogenes of Sinope had chided a man who while pursuing a runaway slave had planned to consult the oracle at Delphi: 'You ridiculous fellow, you are attempting to make use of the god when you are incapable of making use of a slave.'[834] The Xenophontean Socrates, it seems, reflects Antisthenian-Cynic teachings when he cautions his listeners against the use of, or reliance on omens, particularly in the case of trivial matters.

In *Memorabilia* 1.2.4 we read the statement that Socrates 'was not neglectful of the body, nor did he commend those who were'.[835] And in *Memorabilia* 1.2.1 Xenophon observes that Socrates was 'the most able to endure cold, heat and every kind of hardship'.[836] Essentially the same report can be found in the Platonic *Symposium* (219E–220B), where Plato, through Alcibiades, extols the physical hardihood of Socrates: 'I had the opportunity of observing his [*scil.*, Socrates'] extraordinary power of sustaining fatigue. His endurance was simply remarkable. . . . [In this] he was superior . . . to every one. . . . His fortitude in enduring cold was also marvellous. There was a severe frost . . . but Socrates, with his bare feet on the ice and in his ordinary dress, marched better than the other soldiers who had shoes. . . .'[837] Hence it seems that Socrates' unusual ability of sustaining physical hardships was a fact commonly recognized by his disciples and admirers. Nevertheless, we are inclined to hold that Xenophon, with his strong Antisthenian-Cynic leanings, in all probability derived this information from some Antisthenian source.[838] Diogenes Laertius (6.23) recounts that Diogenes of Sinope, in order to inure himself to all kinds of hardships, 'used to roll in his tub over hot sand in the summer, while in the winter he made it a practice to embrace statues covered with snow'.[839] We are also told that he instructed his pupils 'how to ride, shoot with the bow, sling stones, and hurl javelins. Later . . . he would not permit the wrestling instructor to give them full athletic training, but only enough . . . to keep them in good physical condition.'[840]

It seems that already Solon had realized the uselessness of pure athleticism.⁸⁴¹ In Lucian's *Anacharsis*, where Solon and Anacharsis discuss athletics, we also find a strong condemnation of professional athletes.⁸⁴² That Lucian and Dio are influenced by Cynic teachings, needs no comment. The case of Solon, on the other hand, poses some difficulties. According to K. Joël (*op. cit.* at 2.769), the Solon who is opposed to professional athletes is probably taken from an Antisthenian *Symposium*. In the opinion of the Cynics only he is a healthy person 'who engages in a moderate amount of physical work or exercise in order to preserve his health'.⁸⁴³ For 'it behooves the philosopher to exercise his body through physical work. In this manner he acquires a healthy body capable of bearing up hardships. . . . He must be like Crates who habitually exercised.'⁸⁴⁴ Diogenes of Sinope also taught his pupils 'to wait upon themselves, and to be content with plain fare and water to drink. He used to make them crop their hair close . . . and go lightly clad and barefoot . . . [and] he would also take them out hunting'.⁸⁴⁵ It might be somewhat of a surprise that the 'proletarian' Antisthenes extols the art of hunting and declares it a worthy pedagogical device. For hunting, as a rule, was a sport reserved for the Athenian gentleman of means. We must bear in mind, however, that in the Antisthenian-Cynic tradition Heracles, on account of his φιλοπονία and ἀρετή, had become the idol of all Cynics and the model of all true παιδεία.⁸⁴⁶ And an essential part in the education of Heracles was hunting, particularly hunting with dogs (κυνηγεσία). No wonder, then, that this type of physical training should also be held in high esteem by the Cynics.⁸⁴⁷ Diogenes of Sinope, in keeping with the Antisthenian-Cynic tradition, held 'that all training was of two kinds, mental and physical: the latter being that whereby through constant exercise . . . [we] secure the freedom of movement for virtuous actions. . . . Good health and strength . . . are essential both for the body and the soul . . . [because] from physical training we arrive at virtue.'⁸⁴⁸

The 'educational programme' of the Cynics, which appealed so much to Xenophon, actually is a compound of various existing didactic systems interpreted in a Cynic spirit. The ordinary Greek or Athenian elementary education, to be sure, constitutes the backbone of this Cynic educational programme. But it is supplemented by such features as shooting with the bow or riding, features which were derived from the Persian educational system (described by Xenophon in his *Cyropaedia*), as well as hunting, a feature taken from the Spartan educational programme. Naturally, the 'education of Heracles' also influenced the Cynic ideas on education.⁸⁴⁹ While the purpose of the educational programme of the Cynics was to achieve Cynic 'autarchy', they did not intend to train Cynics. Since they considered themselves 'physicians of ailing mankind' rather than philosophers, their efforts were not primarily on behalf of a 'Cynic movement', but rather on behalf of mankind. This is clearly brought out by Dio Chrysostom in some of his discourses.

The Antisthenian Elements in the Two Apologies of Xenophon

The educational notions of Dio Chrysostom, who clearly reflects the pedagogical ideal of the Cynics, is summed up in the following passage (*Oratio* 4.30): '... they have the notion that he who knows much (πλεῖστα γράμματα), such as Persian, Greek, Syrian or Phoenician, and has read the most books, is the wisest and best educated man. But, again, when people find any knaves or cowards or avaricious men among these, they say that this is really insignificant.... The other kind of education men sometimes call simply "education", sometimes "real manhood" or "high-mindedness".... Men of old called those persons "sons of Zeus" who had received the good education and were manly of soul, having been educated after the model of Heracles. Whoever ... possesses this higher education ... has to learn only a few things in a few lessons, namely, the greatest and most important things....'[850]

To the Cynics, physical training and athletic education constituted a vital element in a balanced educational programme.[851] Antisthenes, following the maxim of *mens sana in corpore sano*,[852] placed the training of the body on an equal footing with that of the soul:[853] 'It is necessary that one turn into good men those who are willing that their body be trained through physical exercise, and their mind through learning.'[854] It seems that Antisthenes frequently combined φρόνησις (or, σοφία) and ἰσχύς, something which may already be gathered from the title of his *Heracles*, or *Of wisdom and strength*.[855] Through the efforts of Antisthenes, we must presume, the integration of intellectual and physical training became a Cynic dogma.[856] As a matter of fact, Antisthenes apparently tried to integrate the idea of physical πόνος (toil) with that of the intellectual πόνος (or σοφία). Thus Diogenes of Sinope asserts that all ἄσκησις was of two kinds, namely, training of the mind and training of the body. This training is one by which, through constant exercise, perceptions are formed which, in turn, make possible that type of freedom which leads to virtuous deeds: 'Nothing in life ... has any chance of succeeding without much ἄσκησις, for the latter can overcome any obstacle.' Naturally, such toils must be chosen which are according to nature, that is, reasonable, purposeful, and relevant toils.[857] Since Antisthenes assigned to πόνος and σοφία a central position in his whole doctrine, the Cynic 'good man' is both a φιλόπονος and a φιλόσοφος. We may surmise that the term φιλόπονος originated with the Cynics and probably with Antisthenes. Hence the problem arises whether the term φιλόσοφος did not also originate with Antisthenes.[858]

Perhaps no other philosophical tradition in antiquity stressed more the physical and moral importance of physical exercise. Physical exercise constituted for the Cynic a vital element in the teaching of true virtue as well as in the development of virtuous men.[859] But it should also be borne in mind that in the domain of virtue this Antisthenian ἀσκεῖν denotes the suppression of sensuous desires, the turning of sense appetites into the disciplined practice of self-restraint. In sum, the

The Antisthenian Elements in the Two Apologies of Xenophon

Antisthenian ἄσκησις becomes the determined will to stand up under hardships, the power of self-abnegation through intelligent exercise. Thus with Antisthenes and the Cynics the ἀνδρεία turns into the κατερία and, finally, into the ἐγκράτεια in which the principle of the ἄσκησις, like the πόνος, finds its ultimate moral sanction and justification. It is quite likely, therefore, that Xenophon's allusion to Socrates' alleged concern with proper physical education is based on Antisthenian-Cynic sources and reports, rather than on a Platonic-Academic tradition or doctrine. For the Xenophontean encomium of Socrates' physical prowess as well as interest in physical training and the ability to withstand all sorts of hardships, essentially seems to be a restatement of that Antisthenian-Cynic doctrine which identified ἐγκράτεια and παιδεία, and παιδεία and πόνος.[860]

The Antisthenian-Cynic insistence on rigorous training (ἄσκησις) and hard toil (πόνος) in education was at the time of its introduction definitely a novel idea in Athens. This fact alone should support our contention that Xenophon here ascribes Antisthenian views to Socrates. It is well known that Antisthenes admired the Doric-Spartan παιδονόμος with its strong emphasis on physical training. This may be gathered from the frequent favourable remarks about the Lacedaemonians which have been ascribed to Diogenes of Sinope.[861] Although the young Spartans had been brought up for some time on the principle of strenuous training, the Athenians of the fifth century, on the other hand, frowned on such practices: 'As to our [*scil.*, Athenian] modes of education, they [*scil.*, the Spartans] aim at the development of a manly character by laborious training from their very youth, while we, though living at our ease, advance no less boldly to meet equal dangers. ... And yet if with careless ease rather than laborious practice ... we are willing to face danger, we have the advantage of proving ourselves ... no less bold than those who are always toiling. ... '[862] What Thucydides, through the mouth of Pericles, wishes to convey here is nothing other than the idea that the civilized Athenian was repelled by the vulgar practice of other peoples who prepared themselves for life through stupid toil and brutish training. There can be no doubt that the views uttered by Pericles are the general convictions held by that class of Athenian intellectuals to which in all probability Socrates belonged. Essentially the same idea is repeated by Aristotle (*Politics* 1388 b 8 ff.): 'Of those cities which ... seem to take the greatest care of children, some aim at implanting in them athletic habits. But they succeed only in injuring their physique and in stunting their growth. Although the Lacedaemonians have not fallen into this mistake, yet they brutalize their children by strenuous exercises which they think will make them courageous. ... It is a well-known fact that the Lacedaemonians, while they alone were assiduous in their strenuous drill, were superior to others, but now they are beaten both in war and gymnastic exercises.

The Antisthenian Elements in the Two Apologies of Xenophon

For their superiority of old did not depend on their mode of training their youth, but only on the fact that they did so when their sole rivals did nothing of the kind. Hence we may infer that what is noble, not what is brutal, should have the first place. . . . Parents who devote their children to gymnastics while they neglect their necessary education, actually vulgarize them.' Plato (*Republic* 411c) likewise condemns pure athleticism: 'If a man takes a great deal of exercise and, accordingly, eats much . . . at first the good condition of his body fills him with an attitude of overbearance . . .; [but soon], having no taste of any sort of learning . . . [his mind] will grow feeble . . . and he will end up by becoming a μισόλογος . . . and a person hostile to the Muses. He is like a wild beast, full of violence and fierceness . . . and he lives in complete ignorance . . . devoid of all sense of propriety. . . .'[863]

In *Memorabilia* 1.2.56[864] we are told that Socrates had quoted from 'the most celebrated poets' allegedly in order to bolster and justify his own pernicious teachings.[865] The Cynics, as it is commonly known, made their pupils memorize many passages from the ancient poets.[866] Likewise they wrote copiously on the allegorical interpretation of these poets[867] and also quoted from them frequently, but not always reverently.[868] Like so many other ancient authors, Plato and Xenophon also quote Homer and the 'ancient poets'. But there exists a considerable difference between quoting and interpreting Homer. The allegorical interpretation of Homer and the 'ancient poets' in the light of a definitely moralizing tendency seems to be Antisthenian.[869] The reference to Homer in chapter 30 of the *Defence*,[870] as well as the prophecy (chap. 31) that Anytus would meet with an inglorious end, likewise seem to be under the influence of Antisthenes. This prophecy is probably based on Antisthenes' *On the law* or *On the city* (Diogenes Laertius 6.16). It is believed that in this work Antisthenes attacked the political leaders of Athens during his time, including the politically prominent Anytus.[871] Hence it may be contended that Xenophon is referring to an Antisthenian-Cynic rather than Socratic policy when he discusses Socrates' alleged reliance on ancient poets, or when he rebuts Polycrates' allegation that Socrates had abused these poets.[872]

In *Memorabilia* 1.2.54 Xenophon defends Socrates against the Polycratean charge that the latter had taught his followers 'that a son was permitted under the law to imprison his father for being mentally deranged'.[873] Xenophon's defence is based on the argument that 'every man, while he is alive, by himself removes from his body, or allows to be removed from it, everything that is useless and unprofitable'. This statement, which Xenophon makes also in order to justify Socrates' alleged contention that we should rid ourselves of friends and kinsmen who are no longer of any practical use to us,[874] is definitely of Cynic origin, the general idea being that practically useless persons or things should simply be discarded. In keeping with this basic Cynic maxim is also the advice, volunteered by the Xenophontean Socrates,[875] that as soon as the soul, the seat of the φρόνησις,[876] has left the body, we should bury it at once and without ceremony.[877] This Cynic lack of piety towards the dead is not only the result of their general disregard for everything material,[878] but also an instance of their general rejection of the time-honoured custom of giving the dead a decent burial. For they held that with death the body loses not only its soul, but also its identity and nobility. Cyrus, who in Xenophon's *Cyropaedia* (8.7.25) assumes the role of a Cynic 'preacher', demands that 'when I am dead ... do not enshrine my body ... but remand it to the earth as soon as possible'. This request of Cyrus can also be found in *Memorabilia* 1.2.53, where we are informed that Socrates had insisted that 'as soon as the soul, the seat of all intelligence [φρόνησις, a typically Antisthenian-Cynic term] has left a man, even though he be our nearest and dearest friend, we carry out his body and hide it in a tomb'. We ought to do this, according to the Antisthenian doctrine, because 'that which is without intelligence (ἄφρον) is without any value'.[879] Aristotle (*Eudemian Ethics* 1235 a 36 ff.), quoting *Memorabilia* 1.2.53, which he considers the expression of a genuinely Socratic view, repeats these statements: 'Some, again, maintain that we only regard the useful as a friend ... but the useless ... [we] throw away ...; and that we cast away ... after death our very body, the corpse being useless. ...' Both the *Axiochus* (365A), which is definitely influenced by Antisthenian-Cynic teachings, and the Xenophontean *Cyropaedia* (8.7.20) maintain that the body, after the soul has departed, is without intelligence (ἄφρον) and hence useless. This lack of all sentiment toward the human corpse is strikingly Antisthenian-Cynic: the dying Diogenes of Sinope left instructions that his corpse 'should be thrown out unburied so that the beasts may feed on him, or be thrust into a ditch ...; or that he should be thrown into the Illissus river, in order that he may be of some use to his brethren'.[880] The soul as the seat of the φρόνησις alone constitutes the dignity of man, and hence, his real 'self', while the body from which the soul has departed, is ἄφρον and, therefore, the 'non-self' or ἀλλότριον. It was thus that Antisthenes also could maintain that everything worthwhile he possessed, he possessed in his soul.[881] Because death terminates the 'self' of a person, because it brings to an end his true 'identity' and, hence, terminates the real worth of man, the 'senseless' and 'worthless' human corpse should be disposed of without sentiment and ceremony, like any other worthless thing. The *Axiochus* (365E ff.) expresses most tellingly the Antisthenian-Cynic views on this matter: 'After the union of soul and body has been dissolved ... what is left ... is of the earth (γεῶδες) and devoid of reason (ἄλογον), and, therefore, no longer man.'

This Antisthenian-Cynic contempt for the human corpse, to be sure, is but the practical application of their doctrine that man's most necessary lesson is 'to learn how to get rid of having anything to unlearn'.[882] This doctrine, or at least its practical application, namely, that we should eradicate everything useless, is once more restated by Antisthenes when he exhorts his pupils to 'esteem an honest man above a kinsman'.[883] A repercussion of the latter maxim may be seen in Plato's *Euthyphro* (4A ff.), where Plato apparently satirizes the Antisthenian saying that honesty, virtue, and the pursuit of true knowledge must be placed above all family considerations: a son, who apparently puts 'honesty' above his own kin, has decided to indict his father for homicide. When Socrates hears about the intention of this youth, whom Plato apparently casts in the role of a Cynic, he exclaims: 'By Heracles!'[884] But whenever we encounter this typically Cynic exclamation in Plato's writings, we can be certain that he is paraphrasing or satirizing an Antisthenian maxim by showing its paradoxical consequences.[885]

The connection between the Platonic *Euthyphro* and certain Antisthenian doctrines deserves some attention. According to Diogenes Laertius (6.15), Antisthenes wrote an 'Ὀρέστου ἀπολογία, an *Apology of Orestes*. This work, the authenticity of which we have no reason to question, has a sub-title: *Concerning forensic writers* (δικόγραφοι). The so-called 'forensic writers' are no one else than Antiphon who in his Κατὰ τῆς μητρυιᾶς takes up the 'case' of Orestes. Subsequently the 'Orestes theme' was discussed by a host of philosophers, sophists, and rhetoricians.[886] In the oration of Antiphon, an illegitimate son tries to procure the conviction of the wife of his murdered father on the grounds that the latter had been killed by a slave girl at the instigation of the wife. Antiphon (1.17) cleverly introduces here the name of Clytemnestra in order to relate this affair to the murder of Agamemnon and the subsequent revenge of Orestes. According to a venerable legend, this Orestes had once stood before the Athenian Areopagus to justify the slaying of his mother. We could surmise, therefore, that the Antisthenian *Apology of Orestes* makes reference to the oration of Antiphon, as may be inferred from the sub-title. The main issue, both with Antisthenes and Antiphon, seems to have been the question whether it is proper (εὐσεβὲς) to prosecute one's parent for homicide. In the *Euthyphro* Plato answers this question in the negative. It could be maintained, therefore, that Plato implicitly denounces here the views espoused by Antisthenes in his *Apology of Orestes* which, in turn, was probably stimulated by the oration of Antiphon.[887] And finally, Xenophon's contention (*Memor.* 1.2.55) that Socrates had taught his followers 'to become as intelligent and useful as possible', is as Antisthenian as the remark, ascribed to Socrates by Xenophon (*ibid.*), that 'the senseless or unintelligent is worthless'. Hence the whole of Xenophon's apology of Socrates in *Memorabilia* 1.2.49–55 and *Defence* 20 is based on Cynic ideas, particularly the Cynic maxim that anything which is no longer of any intelligent use to us, including parents, kinsmen, or friends, is worthless in that it impedes rather than promotes our intellectual and moral progress.

In *Memorabilia* 1.1.11–16 we are told that no one ever heard Socrates 'say, or saw him do anything impious or irreverent. In contrast to other sophists, he was opposed to discussions about such matters as the nature of the universe ... or the beginning of the world, or the operation of the heavens. On the contrary he tried to show that those who concentrated on such objects of contemplation were foolish people. ... He then would inquire concerning such philosophers ... whether they expected to apply what they had learned, either for themselves or for anyone else. ... Do the explorers of celestial movements, he asked ... expect that they will create wind and rain and the fruitful seasons? ... These were the remarks he made about those who occupied themselves with such speculations. But he himself never tired of discussing matters which concerned man.' Essentially the same idea can be found in *Memorabilia* 4.7.1–10, where we are told that in all our studies we should concentrate only on the practical aspects of an art or a science. Scientific 'research' was frowned upon.[888] These passages impress us as being a development of the Antisthenian-Cynic doctrine that 'those who had attained to wisdom (σώφρονας γενομένους) had better not study the γράμματα, lest they should be perverted by alien influences'.[889] This should also explain why the Antisthenian Cynics wished to 'dispense with the ordinary subjects of instruction (ἐγκύκλια μαθήματα) ... getting rid of geometry, and music and all such studies'.[890] Of Diogenes of Sinope we hear that 'he would wonder that grammarians should investigate the ills of Odysseus, while they themselves were ignorant of their own ills;[891] or that the musicians should tune the strings of the lyre, while they left the dispositions of their own souls discordant; or that the mathematicians should gaze at the sun and the moon, while they overlooked matters close at hand; or that orators should speak about justice while they themselves refused to practise it. ...'[892] The Antisthenian-Cynic doctrine had maintained that true virtue does not stand in need of any μαθήματα (theoretical learning): 'Virtue is a matter of deeds and does not require a store of words (λόγοι) or much theoretical learning (μαθήματα).'[893] It requires only ἰσχύς,[894] the physical, mental, and moral strength which enables man to exercise the ἐπιμέλεια in connection with πόνος. In its relation to the πόνος, this ἐπιμέλεια becomes the true virtue of man and the guarantee of all success in life: 'Strenuous efforts (ἐπιμέλεια διὰ κατερίας) lead to good and noble deeds.'[895] Ἐπιμέλεια, πόνος (or, κατερία), and ἄσκησις with Antisthenes are three morally interrelated terms which find their practical fulfilment in the 'work well done'—the ἔργον.[896] Hence the Antisthenian virtue of ἰσχὺς is really the ἀρετὴ τῶν καλῶν κ'ἀγαθῶν ἔργων,[897] and as such is nothing other than real εὐπραξία.

The influence of the Antisthenian-Cynic contempt for the theoretical or speculative sciences beyond their immediate practical applicability and usefulness also seems to be strongly reflected in a story found in Plato's *Theaetetus* (174A) where we are told about the witty Thracian handmaid 'who said about Thales, when the latter fell into a well as he was looking at the stars, that he was so eager to know what was going on in the heavens that he could not see what was before his feet'.[898] The Cynic depreciation of scientists is also brought out by Bion of Borysthenes, a follower of the Cynic way of life, who stated that 'astronomers were ridiculous for pretending that they know all about the fish in the sky, though they neglect the fish on the beach'.[899] And Stobaeus, quoting Bion of Borysthenes, tells us the following incident: 'A certain astronomer was exhibiting a map of the heavens. . . . "Here", he said, "are the eccentric stars." "Do not lie," replied Diogenes [of Sinope], "the eccentrics are not there, but here [pointing to the spectators]." '[900] The sayings of Bion, as they have been quoted by Stobaeus, frequently parallel those ascribed to earlier Cynics, particularly to Diogenes of Sinope. Hence one is inclined to assume that Bion made use of a book of 'Cynic sayings and doings' (χρεία) perhaps compiled by Zeno the Stoic. When Plato reports (*Laws* 819D) that 'I, like yourself, late in life have heard with amazement of our ignorance in these matters [*scil.*, the mathematical sciences] and, hence, to me we appear to be more like pigs than men,'[901] he seems to be referring to the general Cynic deprecation of all speculative sciences: 'To the world the philosopher is a fool,' Plato (*Theaetetus* 173E ff.) states regretfully when he apparently thinks of the Cynic attitude toward speculative philosophy, since his mind, 'disdaining the pettiness . . . of human affairs, is flying about . . . measuring earth and heaven'.[902] It was the Cynic who tried to place the 'wise man' (σοφὸς)—'wise' according to the Cynic creed—above the 'scholar' (φιλομαθής), and who rated πρᾶξις above all theory. Theory is the work of the σοφιστῆς, a term which is used here in a distinctly derogatory sense. But it should be borne in mind that the term σοφιστῆς (or, σοφιζόμενος) originally did not have the derogatory connotation it acquired later, probably through the efforts of Antisthenes, Plato (*Phaedrus* 257D), and Isocrates.[903] It could be maintained, therefore, that the kind of 'anti-intellectualism' which Xenophon apparently imputes to Socrates in *Memorabilia* 1.1.11-16, as well as *ibid.* at 4.7.2-10, is essentially of Antisthenian-Cynic origin. It has no parallel in the Platonic *Socratica*.

Xenophon's reliance on Antisthenian-Cynic teachings for his defence of Socrates against the allegations of Polycrates seems to be quite unusual. It is difficult to imagine that Xenophon, a conservative aristocrat, should agree on so many points with Antisthenes, the revolutionary 'proletarian' who in nearly everything was the exact antithesis of Xenophon. Nevertheless, there is one particular aspect of Antisthenian-Cynic philosophy which apparently attracted Xenophon:

the Antisthenian-Cynic doctrine of the ἐγκράτεια (continence or self-discipline). It was this ἐγκράτεια which Xenophon, the former soldier and later plantation owner, could understand and appreciate; it became for him the most outstanding characteristic of Socrates. Under the rather uncritical pen of Xenophon, this Antisthenian-Cynic ἐγκράτεια becomes a Socratic ἐγκράτεια: the Xenophontean Socrates, like an Antisthenian-Cynic, constantly preaches that we should inure ourselves against cold and heat, hunger and thirst, and the many toils of civil and military life. Xenophon, who like the Cynics[904] always was a great admirer of the Spartan way of life,[905] also seems to have shared the Antisthenian-Cynic dislike of the city and its sophisticated ways, preferring the simple, frugal, and toilsome life of the country: 'Life in the city was the beginning of all injustice. It was here that deception and fraud had their origin, so much so that one wonders whether they were not at the basis of founding of all cities.'[906] Xenophon probably also agreed with the Cynic rejection of the ἡδονή and every form of effeminacy (τρυφή). At the same time he was completely in accord with the Cynic exaltation of the πόνος (toil). In addition, the Antisthenian philosophy had a pronounced practical flair which certainly appealed to the ever-practical Xenophon. The very tenor and trend of Antisthenes' ideas, therefore, not only recommended themselves to Xenophon, but probably also induced him to use Antisthenian sources when writing about or defending his idol Socrates.

K. Joël is probably correct when he maintains: 'If the Xenophontean Socrates would actually be the historical Socrates, then the principle of the *Tugendwissen* could not possibly have been the basic principle of Socratic philosophy. The doctrine of the ἐγκράτεια and the κατερία would then have to constitute the foundation of Socratic teachings, and this despite the fact that with the exception of Antisthenes, no Socratic thinker ever reports that this doctrine had been promulgated by Socrates.'[907] The most conspicuous passage in the whole of Book I, chapter 2 of the *Memorabilia* is the Xenophontean remark that of all men Socrates was the ἐγκρατέστατος (the strictest as regards self-control). This statement, or to be more exact, this particular term alone should indicate the high degree to which Xenophon was under the influence of Antisthenian-Cynic doctrines.

To understand Xenophon's long discussion of the alleged Socratic ἐγκράτεια, one must visualize the particular situation which gave rise to this *excursus*. Polycrates, as we have seen, had claimed that Socrates corrupted youths through his wicked socio-political teachings. But he denounced and indicted here what apparently was only a 'literary Socrates', this is to say, a Socrates who had been created by what was probably the first and most zealous Socratic: Antisthenes. Antisthenes, it is presumed here, must have been the literary source from which Polycrates had to derive the basic materials for his κατηγορία Σωκράτους.

The Antisthenian Elements in the Two Apologies of Xenophon

Plato and the other Socratics had not yet come out with their *Socratica* at the time Polycrates composed his indictment of Socrates, not to mention the fact that the materials, charges, and arguments which he used are radically different from those we find recorded, for instance, in Plato's *Apology*. Since Polycrates constructed his whole κατηγορία Σωκράτους in accordance with the particular Socratic tradition which had been initiated by Antisthenes, Xenophon, in Book I, chapter 2 of the *Memorabilia*, was compelled to deliver his defence of Socrates in accordance with the specific formulation in which Polycrates originally had submitted his charges. The amazing result of this peculiar situation is that Antisthenian notions are rebutted by Antisthenian notions. This becomes quite evident in *Memorabilia* 1.2.2, where Xenophon states: 'How can a man such as he [*scil.*, Socrates] possibly have led others into impiety, lawlessness, gluttony, licentiousness, or sloth?' That this passage amounts to a résumé of the Polycratean indictment, needs no comment.[908] Xenophon then proceeds to counter this indictment by enumerating the many instances where Socrates, like a good Cynic, had displayed his inimitable ἐγκράτεια, concluding that it was impossible to imagine how the ἐγκρατέστατος, the most shining light of all ἐγκράτεια, could ever 'corrupt' youths. There can be no doubt that throughout Book I, chapter 2 of the *Memorabilia*, Xenophon, by the constant use of superlatives, advertises Socrates as the perfect incarnation of the Cynic ἐγκράτεια and ἐπιμέλεια.

The tendency of Xenophon to base his whole defence of Socrates on the alleged ἐγκράτεια of the latter, once more becomes evident in the Xenophontean reply to the Polycratean charge that Socrates was responsible for the many crimes committed by Critias and Alcibiades.[909] From the rebuttals offered by Xenophon one would have to infer that Polycrates had made Socrates responsible for the fact that both these men lacked moral ἐγκράτεια because Socrates had failed to teach them how to be ἐγκρατής. But Xenophon makes no reference to their political schemes and treasonable conduct. This would also explain the rather naïve statement made by Xenophon, that Socrates was in no way responsible for the evil deeds of a Critias or Alcibiades: 'It was for learning politics that they had sought out the company of Socrates,'[910] and not for the improvement of their souls, that is to say, for learning how to become ἐγκρατής. Thus for the sake of stressing once more the ἐγκράτεια of Socrates, Xenophon practically concedes the Polycratean allegation that Critias and Alcibiades had learned their evil politics from Socrates.

Xenophon's reliance on Antisthenes and Antisthenian writings for his own Socratica can readily be explained in the light of the fact that the 'catalogue' of Antisthenian works found in Diogenes Laertius (6.15–18), show Antisthenes to have been a very prolific author. In many of his writings, we must assume, Antisthenes not only tried to exalt Socrates by making him a paragon of (Antisthenian) virtue[911] and by converting him into an 'advertisement for Cynicism', but also essayed, in his own fashion, to give the impression that he was closely adhering to the 'teachings' of Socrates.[912] Hence it is not altogether surprising that Xenophon should seek information from Antisthenes on the 'philosophy' of Socrates. But in doing so, Xenophon displayed this type of eclecticism and intellectual bias which lacks sound judgment and true understanding.[913]

There exists what seems to be a final proof in favour of the argument that the characterization of Socrates by Xenophon (and Polycrates) is primarily Antisthenian-Cynic. If the *Socratica* contain any historical truth at all, then Socrates must have been a 'conservative' person both as regards political issues and personal morals. He might have presented an effort not only towards political reaction, but also towards moral reform and a restitution of the *mores patrum*. Like the author of *The Old Oligarch*, he probably thought of his own time as politically and morally decadent. The democratic regime at Athens, it appears, represented to him political decay, which had been brought about by this general moral decline. The subjects to which he dedicated his attention seem to have been the life and the morals of the community, and the men as well as the qualities by which Athens had become a great city. He was probably deploring publicly what he considered the decline of Athens, observing how at first it slowly sank, then slipped down more and more rapidly, and finally began to plunge into headlong ruin, until, in his opinion, it had reached a state of corruption where men could bear no longer either their moral and political diseases or their remedies. That a 'conservative' like Socrates, who probably entertained such views on the moral decline of Athens, could not possibly have uttered statements or used words which in their coarseness and conspicuous absence of the old piety are undoubtedly of Antisthenian-Cynic origin, needs no comment.

6

The Antisthenian Elements in the Κατηγορία Σωκράτους of Polycrates

AN ATTEMPT has been made to reconstruct the *κατηγορία Σωκράτους* of Polycrates with the help of the *Apologia Socratis* of Libanius and the *Memorabilia* (1.2.9–62) of Xenophon. Assuming that this effort has been successful, a comparison of the *κατηγορία* with those extant Socratic apologies which deal, however unreliably, with the official trial of Socrates, furnishes sufficient evidence that the charges made by Polycrates cannot possibly be based upon the actual events which took place during the trial. The *κατηγορία* may never be called a 'trial report' in the strict sense of the term. For the charges enumerated in Xenophon's *Memorabilia* 1.2.9–61, and on the whole repeated in the *Apologia Socratis* of Libanius, could not possibly have been part of the official indictment and proceedings which were instituted against Socrates in 399.

At least two (and possibly all four) of the 'accusations' recorded by Xenophon must definitely be attributed to Polycrates: namely, the charge that Alcibiades and Critias, two men who had 'inflicted a great many evils on the city', had been disciples of Socrates;[914] and the allegation that Socrates had praised Odysseus for his 'anti-democratic' utterances.[915] The two other 'accusations' reported by Xenophon may have been touched upon during the official trial, namely, the charge that Socrates had caused his followers to despise the established laws and political institutions of Athens (*Memor.* 1.2.9), and the allegation that he 'taught children to show contempt for their parents [*Memor.* 1.2.49), their kinspeople [*Memor.* 1.2.51], and their friends [*Memor.* 1.2.52]'. The first charge could have been included in the general indictment that 'Socrates had offended against the laws by corrupting youths'. The second charge might have been the occasion for Socrates' statement (Plato, *Apology* 29B) that 'disobedience to a better . . . is evil'. It may also be back of Socrates' contention (Plato, *Apology* 33C) that no parent, kinsman, or friend stepped forward during the trial in order to testify that he had set child against parent, kinsman against kinsman, or friend against friend. It is our contention, however, that every one of

135

Antisthenian Elements in the Κατηγορία Σωκράτους of Polycrates

these four detailed charges or 'accusations' mentioned by Xenophon must ultimately be attributed to the authorship of Polycrates.

Isocrates (*Busiris* 5) had already disclaimed the Polycratean allegation that Alcibiades was ever a disciple of Socrates, making it quite clear that this particular charge was nothing other than a malicious invention of Polycrates. Socrates' alleged association with Critias, on the other hand, seems to suggest a somewhat different problem. Aeschines (*Adversus Timarchum* 173) points out that Socrates' affiliation with Critias was detrimental in that it became the source of a popular belief that Socrates was in sympathy with the regime of the Thirty Tyrants. It is possible that Xenophon's account (*Memor.* 1.2.29–38) of the clashes between Socrates and Critias may have been merely a literary effort to absolve Socrates from the suspicion of having sympathized with the regime of the Thirty Tyrants.)[916] If this were so, then the report of Xenophon would not differ from the Platonic or Xenophontean 'Alcibiades literature',[917] which primarily sought to prove that Alcibiades was really a good man as long as he remained under the spell of Socrates (*Memor.* 1.2.24): 'Critias and Alcibiades, then, as long as they associated with Socrates, were able, with the assistance of his example, to maintain mastery over their evil inclinations.' In addition, it is not probable that Anytus would have publicly charged Socrates with having associated with Alcibiades, particularly since it is said that Anytus himself had been a former close friend of Alcibiades. And finally, as has already been stated, under the terms of the general amnesty law of 403, of which Anytus was one of the chief promoters, political charges could not be brought against Socrates, at least not during the official trial in 399. Hence neither Socrates' alleged affiliation with Alcibiades or Critias, nor his supposedly 'antidemocratic' leanings could have been litigated in 399.

It must be borne in mind that Xenophon, on account of his prolonged sojourn in Asia Minor,[918] could not possibly have been present at the trial of Socrates. Hence he was unaware of the various incidents which ultimately led to Socrates' condemnation and death. Likewise he was completely ignorant of the evidence adduced by the prosecution in support of the official charges against Socrates. The little he seems to know about these proceedings was probably derived from secondary sources and hearsay.[919] This may be gathered, among other things, from the fact that with one single exception (*Memor.* 1.2.26), which may well be an oversight, Xenophon invariably uses the past tense when referring to the charges made by Polycrates (ὁ κατήγορος ἔφη). Thus it is apparently indicated that he considered these charges historical. It could also be maintained, however, that by using the present in *Memorabilia* 1.2.26 (ὁ κατήγορος αἰτιᾶται) and by observing the anonymity of the 'accuser', Xenophon indicates that he was aware of the fact that the Polycratean κατηγορία Σωκράτους was actually a literary indictment. Yet Xenophon meticulously quotes the allegations and arguments made

Antisthenian Elements in the Κατηγορία Σωκράτους of Polycrates

by the 'accuser'. All this seems to suggest that while he had little personal information about the historical trial, he possessed some excellent and perhaps even first-hand information about the κατηγορία of Polycrates. Surely, then, he must have read or at least heard of the pamphlet of Polycrates. But more than that. It has been claimed that Xenophon possibly considered Polycrates the historical rather than the literary 'accuser', and, like some later authors,[920] interpreted the κατηγορία of Polycrates as part of the official court proceedings against Socrates. Polycrates himself, by voicing his accusations through Anytus, seems to have made such an assumption possible. Whether or not Xenophon was aware that the Polycratean Socrates was probably a fictitious person, becomes a particularly interesting problem when we realize that *Memorabilia* 1.2.9-61 probably portray a literary 'accuser' prosecuting a literary Socrates. The defence of Socrates likewise is undertaken by Xenophon primarily on the strength of a literary fiction rather than on the basis of historical fact. Hence the whole controversy between Xenophon and Polycrates, at least as presented in the *Memorabilia*, seems to be above all a literary controversy or a 'battle of the books'.

Where, then, did Polycrates derive the materials for his κατηγορία Σωκράτους? It is impossible to ascertain whether Polycrates was personally acquainted with the historical Socrates or his authentic teachings, whatever they may have been. The seemingly abundant use of *Socratica* by Polycrates, as well as the chronological date of his life, would indicate, however, that he was compelled to rely extensively on secondary sources and, hence, that he never came in personal contact with the historical Socrates. By *Socratica*, it must be borne in mind, we mean here primarily the philosophical, political, or polemic writings of such men as Antisthenes, Aeschines, Eucleides of Megara, and Phaedo of Elis. These *Socratica*, which made their appearance shortly after the death of Socrates, are distinguished from the *Apologetic Socratica* which, as shall be shown later, were motivated by the anti-Socratic attacks of Polycrates and the late Sophists on the person of Socrates. Polycrates' accusations against Socrates are generally of a kind one would expect to find in a collection of anecdotes, quotations from actual or fictitious speeches, memoirs, or λόγοι Σωκρατικοί. And since Xenophon seems to have consulted the same sources as Polycrates, it became relatively easy for the former not only to understand but also to rebut or contradict the latter. Hence, we must assume that the early λόγοι Σωκρατικοί, especially those of Antisthenes, provided Polycrates with the materials he used when formulating his literary charges against Socrates.[921] It might even be contended that these λόγοι Σωκρατικοί, in their boundless and perhaps even indiscriminate adulation of Socrates, so angered Polycrates that he resolved to stem this tide of Socratic worship by publishing his *Anti-Socratica*. In any event, all this would support the contention that Polycrates not only primarily derived his materials from literary and to a large extent fictitious renditions of Socratic sayings, but also that he directed his charges at what seems to be essentially a literary Socrates. And since Xenophon, in *Memorabilia* 1.2.9–61, likewise appears to rely primarily on some Antisthenian λόγοι Σωκρατικοί for his apologetic efforts, we are entitled to view his rebuttal of Polycrates as a literary apology, and his defence of Socrates as a defence of a literary Socrates.

The correct understanding and evaluation of the so-called λόγοι Σωκρατικοί, as K. Joël has pointed out,[922] compels Socratic scholarship to reconsider many of the claims which in the past have been made about Socrates. These λόγοι, it should be borne in mind, are a literary phenomenon typical of the fourth century before Christ. As a unique form of ancient literature, this literary *genre*, especially its later forms, can be fully appreciated only in the very spirit in which it originated: the 'spirit of competition' with other already existing λόγοι Σωκρατικοί.[923] Obviously, neither Plato nor Xenophon is the only, or even the first, author of such λόγοι.[924] This seems to follow from the remark of Diogenes Laertius (2.64) that 'of all the Socratic dialogues (Σωκρατικοὶ διάλογοι), those of Plato, Xenophon, Antisthenes, and Aeschines are authentic', while 'all the others' must be rejected as spurious.[925] Diogenes' observation suggests that there existed a host of λόγοι Σωκρατικοί. In any event, it must be conceded that soon after his death Socrates became the central figure of a great many λόγοι, some of which mingled fact and fiction, history and legend, in order to create Socratic legends or, at least, to perpetuate some of the older Socratic legends.[926] In keeping with the peculiar spirit of antiquity, the originators of these λόγοι did not yet clearly distinguish between the subject of their work and their own personal convictions. The well-known fact that Plato, for instance, should refer to his writings as παιδεία,[927] merely indicates that philosophy and art, science and poetry were still inseparably fused in one. It may be concluded, therefore, that the authors of the earliest λόγοι Σωκρατικοί were as much writers of fiction as they were reporters of historical events. As Aristotle has already pointed out (*Poetics* 1447 b 11), these λόγοι are μίμησις, which do not intend solely to portray Socrates as he actually was. They remain, on the whole, an idealized and perhaps even nostalgic effort on the part of their authors to recapture some allegedly grandiose aspects of the past. Examination of the literature of this particular period indicates also that the subsequent custom of writing (or speaking) in one's own name or on one's own authority had not yet become the universally accepted literary fashion. At the same time, the acromatic type of literature, the abstract and essentially impersonal way of expressing one's thought or beliefs, was only gradually developing. In this impasse, which was brought on by the forces of tradition, the only feasible literary outlet apparently was to 'hide' behind some historical person of repute, and to turn the latter into the fictitious vehicle of one's message. This is really the μίμησις of the λόγοι Σωκρατικοί.⁹²⁸ Once the peculiar nature and function of these λόγοι have been ascertained, then there can no longer exist any doubt as to their extremely limited value for the reconstruction of the historical Socrates. Even if two or more authors of such λόγοι Σωκρατικοί, including Plato and Xenophon, should be in agreement as to certain aspects of Socrates' life or teachings, we could not consider them reliable evidence. For two fictions, like two lies, do not yet make one truth. Plato, no less than Xenophon, did not write his *Socratica* or λόγοι Σωκρατικοί primarily in order to give a factual report on the historical Socrates, but rather to convey his own convictions through the intermediary of what, under the pen of Plato, has by now been transformed into a legendary Socrates.⁹²⁹ By reflecting primarily the particular mentality as well as the personal convictions of their various authors or originators—some of whom probably had only an extremely vague and highly deficient knowledge of the historical Socrates—these λόγοι Σωκρατικοί of necessity must contain serious distortions of fact, if not outright falsehoods, many of them probably intentional.

The Socrates whom Polycrates indicts so viciously, and whom Xenophon defends so valiantly, seems, as has already been indicated, to have been primarily a product of the earliest Socratic literature. Neither Plato's *Apology*,⁹³⁰ nor other earlier writings, nor Xenophon's *Socratica* could have been the source used by Polycrates. At the time Polycrates composed his κατηγορία Σωκράτους (393/2), Xenophon had not yet started his literary career. Polycrates' only other possible main source of information must have been a Socratic author who by 393/2 had already been a prolific writer. In all likelihood this Socratic author was Antisthenes, who was already a popular author during the late nineties, that is, at a time when Plato and Polycrates had hardly begun their literary careers. Antisthenes and his literary activities in behalf of Socrates and the Socratic tradition must have caught both the attention and the displeasure of the late Sophists, particularly that of Polycrates. There exists some evidence that Antisthenes and Polycrates had previously clashed. Antisthenes, in his praise of Heracles, had probably denounced such voluptuaries as Busiris, about whom, on the contrary, Polycrates had written a *Defence*.⁹³¹ Also, Polycrates, in the form of a paradoxical satire, had sung the praises of Clytemnestra,⁹³² while Antisthenes had applauded Orestes for having avenged his father, Agamemnon.⁹³³

The κατηγορία Σωκράτους, therefore, is quite possibly nothing other than a continuation of the literary feud between Polycrates and Antisthenes; and the κατηγορία may constitute the Polycratean reaction against the Antisthenian encomia of Socrates.⁹³⁴ If this is true, Polycrates' selection of Anytus as his spokesman could be cited as proof that Polycrates directed his pamphlet primarily against Antisthenes and the Antisthenian *Socratica*. Antisthenes apparently disliked Anytus immensely;[935] he was said, in fact, to have brought about the downfall and exile of Anytus.[936] But if the Polycratean κατηγορία is primarily an indictment of the Antisthenian-Cynic Socrates rather than of the historical Socrates, the Xenophontean defence of Socrates is likewise an apology of the Antisthenian-Cynic Socrates. For the Antisthenian-Cynic Socrates is the Socrates whom Xenophon knows and understands.

It should also be kept in mind that in his πόνος and ἐγκράτεια doctrines, Antisthenes seems to have reduced Socrates to a practical and moralizing reformer. Polycrates, again, when he formulated his charges against Socrates, did so as an indignant moralist. When defending Socrates against the allegations made by Polycrates, Xenophon likewise uses arguments pregnant with practical moralizing.[937] Fundamentally, then, the entire literary controversy between Polycrates and Xenophon is to a high degree a form of Antisthenian-Cynic moralizing as regards its basic tenor, quotations, and the particular materials from which the arguments and counter-arguments were derived.

According to Xenophon, *Memorabilia* 1.2.9, 'the accuser' first claimed that Socrates 'caused his followers to despise the established laws', thereby 'exciting them to hold in contempt the existing form of government and disposing them to acts of violence'. He did so, 'the accuser' continues, 'by pointing out how foolish' (ὡς μῶρον) some Athenian laws were.[938] Judging by Libanius' (chaps. 24–59 and 61) vigorous and lengthy rebuttal, this would not have been the first charge instituted by Polycrates, but rather the main one. Libanius, however, badly garbles this particular charge. He also insinuates that Polycrates had called Socrates a μισόδημος, a 'hater of the common people', a term which may also be implied, though not expressly stated in *Memorabilia* 1.2.58–60. From the rejoinder of Libanius it appears that Polycrates had charged Socrates with having planned the overthrow of Athenian democracy.

At this point it may be instructive to review Plato's basic attitude towards democracy, especially towards Athenian democracy. 'Just as a sick body,' Plato maintained (*Republic* 556E), '. . . is something at strife with itself . . . so is this sick city. It . . . makes war upon itself on the slightest of pretexts. . . . And does not this sick city sometimes break into civil war . . .?' This civil war, according to Plato (*Republic* 557A), begets democracy: 'Democracy is born . . . when the poor win the day, killing some . . . banishing others, and sharing with the rest the rights of citizenship and of public offices on the basis of equality. . . .' The Athenian democrats are denounced (*Republic* 560c) as insolent, shameless, and lawless; as profligate and niggardly; as fierce and terrible beasts of prey; as persons who gratify every whim; and as people who live solely for pleasure and for unnecessary as well as objectionable desires. They are accused of calling 'reverence a folly . . . temperance a form of cowardice . . . moderation and orderly expenditure . . . a sort of meanness befitting a boor. . . .' In a democracy, we are told (*Republic*

563A ff.), 'the schoolmaster fears and flatters his pupils . . . and old men defer to the young . . . in order to avoid the appearance of being sour and despotic'.[939] Plato's description of democracy is an intensely acrimonious denunciation of the political life of Athens. Through the use of strong invective he identified political liberty with licence, freedom with lawlessness, and political equality with social disorder. The similarity between Plato's dislike of Athenian democracy and the strongly anti-democratic views held by the author of the *Constitution of Athens* is too obvious to require special comment.

Undoubtedly the historical Socrates found some fault with certain Athenian legal and political institutions; but he never used, at least not according to the testimony of Plato, the unflattering and violent exclamation ὡς μῶρον which is typical of the eternally cavilling and criticizing Cynic. That Antisthenes and his followers openly displayed their contempt for the existing political and legal institutions of the city, is a matter of common knowledge:[940] 'What is Caesar to a Cynic, or what is the pro-consul or, for that matter, anyone else?'[941] For he regards magistrates and honours as being merely 'a shell with nothing inside'.[942] The orations of Dio Chrysostom, the spokesman of the Cynic tradition in this matter, contain some vicious attacks upon Athenian democracy.[943] Stobaeus reports (*Florilegium* 49.47) that Antisthenes and the Cynics had openly declared that through the democratic institutions of Athens the incompetent opinion of the uncouth masses had replaced all virtue and wisdom. For in the eyes of Antisthenes 'no statesman is honest, no general is wise . . . and no populace capable of reason'.[944] Philodemus (*Hercul. Papyr.* no. 339) goes even further when he tells us that 'the Cynics attach no significance to any city (or, any form of government) we know, nor to any law', while Diogenes Laertius (6.11) reports that Antisthenes had insisted that 'the wise man will be guided in all his public acts not by the established laws, but solely by the principle of virtue'. According to Antisthenes, if the wise man does anything, 'he does it in accordance with virtue as a whole'.[945] And 'since Cynicism is the shortest road to virtue, the wise man will play the Cynic'.[946] Dio Chrysostom (*Oratio* 13.18–19), under the influence of some Antisthenian source,[947] maintains that Socrates had insisted that the Athenians may know something about wrestling, poetry, or music, but certainly nothing about the government of cities. For they have never understood the things which were truly to their advantage. As a matter of fact, they have never been concerned with such matters as good government. Neither have they learned how 'to live lawfully, justly, and harmoniously . . . without injuring or plotting against one another'.[948]

The Antisthenian-Cynic idea of φιλανθρωπία, which was frequently symbolized in the conception of the Cynic as the 'watchdog', the 'shepherd', the 'physician', or the 'scout' working in the interest of mankind,[949] leads to the Cynic and subsequently Stoic 'cosmopolitanism'.[950]

Antisthenian Elements in the Κατηγορία Σωκράτους of Polycrates

This idea of φιλανθρωπία or 'cosmopolitanism' eventually became so perverted that it denied the propriety of cherishing particular individuals, including one's wife or children, one's own family, or the city in which one lived. For the love of a particular individual or one's family or one's native city, according to the Cynic, was really nothing other than the manifestation of a kind of 'privileged selfishness', based on silly conventions and shallow sentimentality. Decrying the value and dignity of such 'particularist' institutions as the family or the city, the Cynic proudly referred to himself as ἄκοιος (homeless, clanless, or without family) and ἄπολις (stateless).[951] Hence he could cry out: 'Take notice of me, that I am without a country, without a house, without an estate, without a servant. I lie on the ground. I have no wife, no children, no coat, but only earth and heaven and one sorry cloak. . . . Am I not free?'[952] And he could add this prayer: 'Let my sufficient bed be the whole earth, my house the universe, and the food of my choice the easiest procurable.'[953]

It should always be remembered, however, that the 'cosmopolitanism' of the Cynic was primarily a reaction against every kind of confining influence imposed on the individual by the conventions of politically or morally organized society. This 'conventional compulsion' is eloquently described by Teles: 'The child is hungry and the nurse tries to rock it to sleep; it is thirsty and she washes it; it would like to go to sleep, but she makes a noise with the rattle. Should it escape the nurse, it falls into the hands of the tutor, the trainer, the schoolmaster, the music teacher, or the painter. Advance to the next stage, and there appears the teacher of mathematics, the geometrician, or the riding-master. The boy has to be up at dawn and there is never a moment of spare time. And now he is an ephebus: now he walks in fear of the prefect, the trainer, the drill master, and the master of the gymnasium, by all of whom he is beaten, bullied, and rushed about. . . . Now the youth has come to a man's estate and he is in his prime. He goes on military expeditions and embassies in behalf of the city. He enters political life, becomes a *strategos, choregos*, or *agonothetes*. He praises the days when he was a youth. But time goes on, and he comes to be an old man. Once more an attendant lies in wait for him. . . .'[954] Essentially the same ideas can be found in the dialogue *Axiochus* (366C–367B), which would indicate that the *Axiochus* is under the influence of Antisthenian-Cynic teachings.[955] The 'lamentations' of Teles (or Crates), as well as *Axiochus* 366C–367B, suggest a common source which might have been Antisthenes. In any event, Demetrius[956] ascribes to Antisthenes the following statement: 'Almost always a young man will experience pain from switches.' This statement might have been taken from a lengthy account of the 'sufferings' connected with all stages of life. It is also interesting to note that in the account by Teles (*Axiochus* 366C ff.), and in the general Cynic tradition, the use of the rod is always stressed as a pedagogical tool.[957]

When Diogenes of Sinope insisted that he was a 'citizen of the world',[958] he meant to say that he was not a member of any known or existing Greek political, social or cultural organization. To him 'the only true commonwealth is the one that is as wide as the universe itself'.[959] The Cynic idea of cosmopolitanism, which implies that the true philosopher and the virtuous man can never be a member of any existing political society—that is, of any conventional social organization—also appears in Xenophon's apologetic *Socratica*, although in a somewhat different version. Xenophon (*Memor*. 1.2.31–38) tries to establish the fact that Socrates had been prosecuted both by the 'radical democrats' in 399 and the 'radical oligarchs' in 404/3. The implication seems to be that a person like Socrates, who cannot live either under a democratic government or an oligarchic regime, cannot live under any known form of government and is, therefore, really a κοσμοπολίτης in the Cynic sense of the term. Undoubtedly, Xenophon, who seems to have invented the alleged clash of Socrates with the Thirty Tyrants in 404/3 in order to make his argument in favour of Socrates' cosmopolitanism more plausible, received this inspiration from some Cynic source which probably defined cosmopolitanism as the philosopher's inability to submit to any political organization or civic compulsion.

In his frequent discussions of the established laws or the existing political institutions, the Cynic always deplored the political and moral decadence of the city,[960] demanding a new τέχνη πολιτική which, according to him, only the wise man, the Cynic, possessed.[961] The general outlines of Antisthenes' legal, political, and social τέχνη may be summarized as follows: the wise man (the Cynic philosopher), who lives according to nature and right reason, is above the laws of the state (Diogenes Laertius 6.11; Xenophon, *Memor*. 4.4.13–14). There exists an irreconcilable opposition between the individualistic (Cynic) wise man and the mass of mankind in its strongly conventionalist behaviour. This opposition, which has far-reaching political and social consequences, is nothing other than the eternal conflict between anarchy and blind legalism. The traditional forms of society and their various frameworks are 'collectivist' and, hence, are in sharp contrast to the individualistic ethics which Antisthenes preached. In addition, Antisthenes sharply criticized the leading politicians of his time for their conventionalist policies.

The political views of Diogenes of Sinope are difficult to ascertain. Diogenes Laertius (6.80) lists a *Republic*[962] and a *The people of Athens* by Diogenes of Sinope. But the shorter list of Sotion, quoted by Diogenes Laertius (6.80), omits these two works; and Sosicrates and Satyrus deny that Diogenes of Sinope ever wrote anything (*ibid*.). It may be assumed that Diogenes of Sinope displayed a strong anti-social attitude towards contemporary society, that he vehemently denounced the rigid system of its laws and political institutions, and that he denied its ability to grant men happiness and security. The socio-political views of Crates can be found in his poem *Pera*,[963] which pictures a Cynic utopia, where self-sufficient simplicity, based on moral principles, brings contentment, freedom (especially freedom from enslavement by sensuous pleasures), and eternal peace to its happy inhabitants.

In his perennial search for the 'ideal society' the Cynic vehemently denounced all existing political communities as being based on compulsion and laws rather than freedom and virtue. Wishing to live 'according to nature', he saw in the established political and legal institutions, popular customs, and historical traditions of society a perversion of nature. Small wonder that he should make these 'perversions' the object of his biting ridicule and scathing vituperations.[964] To live according to nature, however, meant to him the discarding of all the accretions of convention and tradition; what remains is 'according to nature', that is, the irreducible minimum necessary to sustain the most simple existence. To live according to nature is to him the only sure road to happiness; to condemn all existing conventions, traditions and institutions with the usual ascetic argument is the greatest of pleasures.[965] This Cynic rejection and ridicule of every norm accepted by convention and society became with the 'extremist' Diogenes of Sinope plain ἀναίδεια (shamelessness),[966] which was primarily used by him to expose the artificiality of convention. And the same explanation may be attached to some of his eccentricities which tradition has recorded.[967] Shamelessness, therefore, is with the Cynic nothing other than the practical counterpart or application of the Cynic 'freespokenness' (παρρησία): 'There are four reasons why the Cynics are so named. First, because of the indifference (ἀδιάφορον) of their way of life. For they make a cult of this indifference (ἀδιαφορία) and, like dogs, eat and make love in public, go barefoot, and sleep in tubs or at crossroads. . . . Secondly, the dog is a shameless animal, and they make a cult of shamelessness (ἀναίδεια), considering the latter not as being inferior to modesty (αἰδώς), but as superior to it. . . . Thirdly, the dog is a good watcher, and they guard the tenets of their philosophy. . . . Fourthly, the dog is a discriminating animal which can distinguish between its friends and enemies. . . . By the same token they recognize as friends those who are suited to philosophy, and treat them kindly, while those who are unfitted for philosophy, they drive away, like dogs, by barking at them.'[968] This 'freespokenness' of the Cynic, this unrestrained criticism and ridicule of all things, which Diogenes of Sinope calls 'the finest thing in the world',[969] is what actually enabled the Cynic to expose not only the pretensions of intellectuals or politicians, but also the defects of society and its institutions.[970]

In their merciless critique of Athenian institutions Antisthenes and his disciples also ridiculed the method of electing magistrates by lot,[971] pointing out that this method was contrary to reason. They frowned upon the Athenian procedure of electing magistrates, since this method relied on chance (τύχη) and thus made it possible for the least qualified person to obtain the most important political positions.[972] The Cynic, who always stressed the εὐπραξία and the πόνος, could only have contempt for the 'passive counterpart' of εὐπραξία and πόνος: the blind workings of mere fortuitous chance (τύχη). To him τύχη and the naïve belief in good fortune was not only the denial of his insistence on the positive value of creative and purposive work, but also a complete frustration of his basic conviction as to the true *ratio essendi* of man. Socrates acts the perfect Cynic when, in the words of Xenophon (*Memor*. 3.9.14–15), he contrasts the εὐτυχία (good fortune) and the εὐπραξία: 'When someone inquired of him what seemed to him the best pursuit for a man, he replied: εὐπραξία. ... I think that τύχη and πρᾶξις are opposites. To hit on something by sheer luck without effort, I call good luck (εὐτυχία), but to do something well after study and practice, I call εὐπραξία. And those who pursue the latter seem to me to do the right things ... and are the best men, dearest to the gods. ... But he who does nothing well [*scil.*, who solely relies on his good fortune] is neither useful in any way, nor dear to the gods.' In the opinion of the Xenophontean Socrates, who speaks here like a Cynic, it is not sufficient that one just does something. One has to do something well, that is to say, expertly and, in consequence, successfully; for practical success depends to a high degree on expertness. This Cynic principle of εὐπραξία, this 'practical and purposive know-how', is definitely opposed to the traditional Greek belief in τύχη,[973] the superstitious assumption that through the display of favours in the form of τύχη the gods manifest their intentions. The Cynic constantly denounced as an abomination that type of human inactivity which relies more on τύχη, that is, on 'divine action' rather than honest, purposive, and intelligent effort.[974] The Cynic deprecation of the τύχη also led them to condemn idleness and loafing (ἀργεῖν). According to the report of Xenophon (*Memor*. 1.2.9), Polycrates had insisted that by ridiculing the established laws and institutions of the city, Socrates had disposed his followers to commit acts of violence (βιαίους). Libanius (58.10) reports that in the eyes of Polycrates the conduct of Socrates had rendered his followers τυραννικούς.[975] This contention of Polycrates seems to have been one of the famous paradoxes by which he tried to distort and ridicule the views of his opponents. As a matter of fact, Antisthenes was strongly opposed to any form of violence (βία) and tyranny.[976] Xenophon (*Memor*. 1.2.10), in a truly Antisthenian-Cynic manner, defends Socrates against this Polycratean allegation by pointing out that he does not believe 'that young men who exercise their intellect (φρόνησιν ἀσκοῦντες) ... could become addicted to violence'. It should be noted that the expression φρόνησιν ἀσκεῖν is definitely an Antisthenian-Cynic concept, closely related to the Cynic notion of the true παιδεία.[977]

It might be useful to quote here Aristotle's views on the τέχνη πολιτική as he stated them in his *Nicomachean Ethics* (1179 a 33 ff.).

Antisthenian Elements in the Κατηγορία Σωκράτους of Polycrates

He concedes that a mere *theory* of happiness does not suffice to make the average individual qualified for happiness. Rather he needs good laws which are first developed theoretically.⁹⁷⁸ At the same time Aristotle stresses the superiority of political theory over mere practical political experience,⁹⁷⁹ because political theory or science can also be taught.⁹⁸⁰ Aristotle goes on to point out that the practising politician cannot teach the science of politics because he relies too much on practical experience. He concedes, however, that practical experience seems to contribute to the practice of the art of politics.⁹⁸¹ In order to elucidate his ideas of 'political expertness', Aristotle uses the example of medicine, pointing out that the mere study of medical books does not alone produce a good physician.⁹⁸² And the same holds true for the politician: a mere acquaintance with the laws or constitutions of other cities does not alone make a good politician. In this fashion Aristotle makes it quite clear that one has to be an expert (theoretical and practical) in the field of politics before one can become a good politician.

If the report of Libanius (58.10)⁹⁸³ is correct in maintaining that Polycrates had charged Socrates with having condemned not only the established laws of the city, but also other Athenian customs and practices, including the constitution, then Socrates, at least in the opinion of Polycrates, must have acted like a typical Cynic.⁹⁸⁴ The Cynic, being frequently a 'foreigner', was less hampered by the ordinary ties of civic life or the influences of national tradition and national pride. In his contempt for wealth and power he remained a person of no attachments, one who considered his fellow men to be fools.⁹⁸⁵ To him, all ordinary standards of value had been completely perverted by these 'fools'. Diogenes of Sinope 'would often vociferate that the gods had given men the means of living comfortably, but that this had been lost sight of because we demand honeyed cakes, unguents, and the like'.⁹⁸⁶ Hence Diogenes could insist that 'things of value are bartered for what is worthless. . . . A statue fetches three thousand drachmas, while a quart of barley flour is sold for two copper coins.'⁹⁸⁷ Themistius, expounding what seems to be Antisthenian-Cynic doctrines, maintains that virtue, which consists in the knowledge of what is within man's powers and what is not,⁹⁸⁸ teaches man how to use things properly: 'But a man without virtue, being also a fool, cannot possibly be without want, even should he wallow in gold and silver.'⁹⁸⁹ Conversely, in itself poverty is no evil.⁹⁹⁰ For 'if wealth were a good, and poverty an evil, why, then, did God not give wealth to good men, and poverty to evil men?'⁹⁹¹

It could be maintained, therefore, that the Polycratean allegation that Socrates 'had caused his followers to despise the established laws', thereby 'exciting youths to condemn the existing form of government and disposing them thus to acts of violence', is nothing other than a restatement of the Antisthenian-Cynic attacks upon the legal and political order of their time.

Antisthenian Elements in the Κατηγορία Σωκράτους of Polycrates

It may be recorded here that *The Old Oligarch*, also referred to as Pseudo-Xenophon, *The polity of the Athenians*,[992] is likewise very critical of the democratic institutions of Athens. This strongly antidemocratic pamphlet, as is now commonly conceded by the majority of scholars, was composed by an unknown author who wrote during the last quarter of the fifth century B.C. It is not impossible that Polycrates may have been familiar with this work, and that he suspected (or perhaps knew) that its author was affiliated with the 'Socratic circle'. Thus, it could be argued that the Polycratean charge which Xenophon records in *Memorabilia* 1.2.9, might refer to the ironical remark found in *The Old Oligarch* 1.2: 'The offices of the city should be thrown open to every one by the ballot or by a show of hands; and the right of speech should belong to anyone without distinction or restriction.'[993] And the charge of μισοδημία, mentioned in *Memorabilia* 1.2.59, could very well have been influenced by *The Old Oligarch* 1.5: 'In the ranks of the common people there will be found the greatest degree of ignorance, disorderliness and rascality—poverty acting as a strong incentive to base conduct, not to mention ignorance and the lack of education.' It seems that certain statements ascribed to Socrates by the Socratics in respect to his views on the common people and their ability to rule, are very much like the utterance made by *The Old Oligarch*: 'A man who, although he himself is not one of the common people, prefers to live in a city governed by a democracy rather than by an oligarchy, may be called one who paves his own way to iniquity. He knows that a bad man has a better chance of slipping through the fingers of justice in a democracy than in a city governed by oligarchs.'[994] This passage reminds us of what Socrates had to say about those who by appealing to the sentimentality of their democratic judges succeed in procuring a favourable verdict.[995]

According to Xenophon (*Memorabilia*, 1.2.12), the second Polycratean charge against Socrates would have recited that Critias and Alcibiades, 'after having associated with Socrates, caused a great many evils to the city'.[996] Isocrates (*Busiris* 5), a contemporary of Polycrates, emphatically denies that Alcibiades had ever been a disciple or follower of Socrates.[997] Athenaeus (*Deipnosophistae* 5.216), on the other hand, insists that Antisthenes had created many stories about Socrates for the purpose of glorifying him, among them the story of his close association with Alcibiades, one of the most notorious personalities of his time. In order to enhance the greatness of Socrates, Antisthenes might have stressed the influence which the former had over the ambitious, strong-willed, and dissipated Alcibiades, an influence which could be recounted under the heading of 'mind over matter', a subject so dear to every Cynic. This story then would be of a similar nature to the account of the alleged meetings between Diogenes of Sinope and Alexander the Great.[998] We also know that Alcibiades plays an important role in the Antisthenian *Protrepticus*.⁹⁹⁹ It is commonly held that together with the *Heracles*, the *Protrepticus* contained Antisthenes' basic teachings. From the reaction which it created we may assume that it must have been a work of considerable importance and influence. Xenophon (*Symposium* 2.26), for instance, refers to the *Protrepticus*, as does Plato (*Symposium* 185c). It is also safe to surmise that Plato, *Republic* 372B, takes issue with some of the statements which could be found in the *Protrepticus*. In the *Protrepticus* Antisthenes introduces Alcibiades in order to prove his argument that reason has full mastery over passion.¹⁰⁰⁰ From all this it may be inferred that the Polycratean charge of Socrates' association with Alcibiades, but not that of his keeping company with Critias, probably goes back to some Antisthenian-Cynic source.

We know that Antisthenes wrote a treatise entitled *Alcibiades*.¹⁰⁰¹ Since Diogenes Laertius lists this treatise as Antisthenes' last work, we may contend at least that it was probably one of his later writings, in all likelihood motivated by the publication of Polycrates' pamphlet.¹⁰⁰² But in some of his other writings Antisthenes also thoroughly discussed Alcibiades and probably his relationship with Socrates. Antisthenes was contemptuous of wealth and physical beauty; he despised the flatterer, and had called love an illness.¹⁰⁰³ Xenophon seems to echo Antisthenes when he maintains that wealth, fame, and physical beauty had brought about the downfall of Alcibiades. If we can rely on Xenophon, *Symposium* 4.3, then Antisthenes would have insisted that at times even σοφία may be detrimental. This is also brought out by Dio Chrysostom (*Oratio* 13.21) who, apparently under the influence of Antisthenes, insists that the σοφία of Palamedes ultimately led to his downfall. Athenaeus (*Deipnosophistae* 5.220) informs us that 'in his second treatise on Cyrus,¹⁰⁰⁴ Antisthenes abuses Alcibiades, claiming that he was perverted in his relations with women as well as in his general conduct'. We may also assume that in his *Aspasia*¹⁰⁰⁵ Antisthenes said many harsh things about Alcibiades which, it seems, are reflected in Athenaeus, *Deipnosophistae* 5.219-220. In addition, it might be claimed that the notorious personality of Alcibiades came under discussion in Antisthenes' *On justice and courage, a hortative work*;¹⁰⁰⁶ *Of law or, Of the commonwealth*;¹⁰⁰⁷ *Of law or, Of goodness and justice*;¹⁰⁰⁸ and *The greater Heracles or, Of strength*.¹⁰⁰⁹ It seems that the five last-mentioned works of Antisthenes, which apparently decry the corruption of the Athenian commonwealth and the incompetence or evil ways of its political leaders or most prominent citizens, were written in rapid succession. They probably belong in that phase of Antisthenes' literary activity during which he denounced the existing legal and political institutions of Athens, including Athenian statesmen. Since in these 'political' works Antisthenes had not only discussed at great length the perverted and evil ways of Alcibiades, but probably also his relations with Socrates, it seems more than likely that Polycrates derived the materials for his charge, as recorded by Xenophon in *Memorabilia* 1.2.12 ff., from the works of Antisthenes.

In *Memorabilia* 1.2.49, Xenophon lists what seems to be the third Polycratean charge: that Socrates had taught 'young people to show contempt for their parents, persuading them that he rendered them wiser than their fathers, [and] observing that under the existing laws a son was permitted to confine his father for mental derangement. In this manner he used . . . to prove that it might be well for the wiser to imprison the more ignorant.'[1010] In order to understand this particular passage more fully, we will have to turn once more to Plato's *Euthyphro* (4A ff.). Here the young Euthyphro informs Socrates of his intention to prosecute his father for murder. Plato's account is definitely a biting satire of Antisthenes' extremist position in matters of 'honourable conduct'. This may be gathered from Socrates' exclamation, 'By Heracles!' (*Euthyphro* 4A), which indicates that Plato is quoting an Antisthenian-Cynic paradox.[1011] The father of Euthyphro had been instrumental in the death of an 'alien day labourer', who himself had previously slain another worker. For this the father had put the murderer in chains. While the father was notifying the officials in Athens of the crime, the chained man died from exposure. The slain person was himself a murderer, while the father was merely careless in preserving the murderer for the authorities. Like Antisthenes, Euthyphro is a fanatic of 'abstract justice'.[1012] His object, as may be gathered from Plato (*Euthyphro* 4C), apparently is to clear himself from the 'religious pollution' incurred by being in any way an accessory to a homicide. He feels that if he files an information against his own father, he has done everything that might be expected of a religiously super-scrupulous man. In order 'to save his soul' he is willing, if necessary, to ignore the most sacred principles of filial piety by handing over his father to the hangman.[1013] This fanatic is much amused over Socrates' effort at making here a distinction between a kinsman and a stranger. For the only thing which matters for Euthyphro (*Euthyphro* 4BC) is 'whether the murdered man was justly slain . . . and if he was unjustly slain, then you have to proceed against the murderer even if he lives under the same roof with you and eats at the same table'. True piety and justice (*Euthyphro* 5D) is 'to prosecute anyone who is guilty of murder . . . whether he be your father or mother. . . .' Stobaeus (*Florilegium* 77.41) tells the story that Pittacus, being called upon to referee a dispute between a father and his son, informed the latter: 'If you bring unfounded charges against your father, then you will be condemned to death; but if your charges are well founded, you deserve being condemned to death.' But Antisthenes, the fanatic of abstract justice who preached the supremacy of the intellectual man over the charitable man, would not permit filial piety—to him a 'conventional absurdity'—to stand in the way of intellectual perfection.[1014] Plato seems to echo this idea (*Crito* 54B) when Socrates insists that one should not think of one's children first and of justice afterwards, but of justice first. From all this it would follow that the charge of Polycrates, as it has been recorded in Xenophon's *Memorabilia* 1.2.49, is based on Antisthenian-Cynic teachings, even though it could be admitted that Socrates, in the light of his own unhappy domestic life, on some occasion might have uttered deprecatory remarks about fathers, kinsmen, and relatives in general.[1015]

But *Memorabilia* 1.2.49–50, aside from deprecating the parent-child relationship in general, also contain the following idea: since it is permissible to imprison a man for insanity, the wiser man should also be permitted to keep the ignorant person in bondage. This seems to be the gist of the story told by Diogenes Laertius (6.29): '... when he [*scil.*, Diogenes of Sinope] was captured and put up for sale, he was asked what he could do. "Govern men," he replied.'[1016] Hence ignorance and madness, at least as regards the manner in which they should be dealt with, are really one and the same things: both the madman and the ignorant person should be restrained by the use of extreme measures. This radical position, which links ignorance and madness, is definitely Antisthenian. Xenophon maintains (*Memor.* 1.2.50) that Socrates had often considered the difference between madness and ignorance. As will be shown presently, Socrates, at least according to Xenophon, did not accept the extreme position which the 'accuser' imputed to him. It is quite likely that Xenophon's denial is influenced by the Polycratean allegation. In any event, we are compelled to surmise that Polycrates is quoting here what seems to be an Antisthenian maxim.[1017] In *Memorabilia* 3.9.6, Xenophon insists that Socrates 'did not identify ignorance with madness'. But when he continues that 'most men ... do not call those mad who err in matters that are beyond the knowledge of ordinary people', he apparently refers to some Antisthenian doctrine which probably held that τοὺς ἄφρονας μαίνεσθαι.[1018] The Antisthenian identification of madness and ignorance seems to have led him to the conclusion that it was permissible not only to imprison a person afflicted with insanity but also to imprison an ignorant person or, at least, to treat him like an insane person by keeping him under strictest control. Furthermore, the same idea reappears in *Memorabilia* 1.2.58, a passage which likewise contains an Antisthenian doctrine, where we are informed that the superior person, that is, the one who possesses true knowledge and wisdom, may (and really should) use any means to gain control over the ignorant person or 'fool'.

Antisthenes had insisted that fathers had frequently failed to give a proper education to their sons. Athenaeus (*Deipnosophistae* 5.220) informs us that Antisthenes had reproached Pericles for having neglected the education of his children, while Plato (*Protagoras* 320A) insists that Pericles gave his sons 'excellent instruction in everything that could be learned from teachers, but in the domain of politics he neither taught them nor gave them teachers'. Hence Paralus and Xanthippus, the sons of Pericles, 'are nothing compared to their father'.[1019] He had taught them to be unrivalled horsemen, but somehow failed to make them virtuous.[1020] And the author of *Alcibiades I* (118E ff.) remarks: 'Did Pericles make anyone wiser? Did he begin by making his sons wise? . . . Did you ever hear of any Athenian or foreigner . . . who was regarded as having grown wiser in the company of Pericles?' Antisthenes, as has been stated, probably had also berated Anytus for his incompetence as a father. Thus, when he exhorted his listeners that they 'should esteem a good man above a kinsman',[1021] he seems also to have had in mind people who in his opinion were incompetent fathers. The story, related by Plato (*Phaedo* 60A), seems to bear out the Antisthenian dictum that we should 'honour a good man above a kinsman': 'When we entered, we found . . . Xanthippe . . . sitting with him, holding his child in her arms. When she saw us she uttered a cry, saying, as women will: "O Socrates, this is the last time that you will hold conversation with your friends, and they with you." Socrates turned to Crito and said: "Crito, let some one take her home." And some of Crito's men, accordingly, led her away while she was crying and beating her breast.' In the hour of death Socrates apparently prefers the company of 'good men' to that of his wife and the mother of his children.[1022] Only good men, Antisthenes insists, can be true friends,[1023] while 'parents and children, lacking wisdom, are mutual enemies'.[1024] And the Cynic certainly did not promote a feeling of filial reverence or piety among his children when he took his son 'to a brothel, telling him that this was the way in which his father married'.[1025] In addition, Antisthenes might have felt that the accepted forms of parent-child relationship were purely conventional and thus deserving of his scathing ridicule. This may also explain the shockingly callous attitude which the Cynics displayed toward the institution of marriage.[1026]

In *Memorabilia* 1.2.51–52,[1027] Xenophon reports that the 'accuser' had insisted that 'Socrates not only caused parents, but also other kinsmen to be held in contempt by his followers, pointing out that relatives were of no profit to people who were sick or to people who were engaged in a law suit, but that physicians aided the former, and lawyers the latter.' Thus, according to Diogenes Laertius (6.30), Diogenes of Sinope, the slave, tells his master Xeniades that he—Xeniades—has to obey him: 'For if a physician . . . were a slave, he would be obeyed.' The idea is that the expert or intellectually more gifted, no matter what his social position, is always superior to the ignorant. Slavery in itself does not make a man an inferior person.[1028] Even friends, the 'accuser' continues (*Memor.* 1.2.52), are of no profit to us in the opinion of Socrates, unless some practical benefit can be derived from them. 'Mere goodness of disposition is without practical significance.'[1029] It is also interesting to note that in the dialogue *Alcibiades I* (105D and 124C), Socrates attempts to convince the young Alcibiades that no relative of his could really be of any assistance to him, and that without his [*scil.*, Socrates'] help he would never realize his ambition.[1030] All these statements attributed to Socrates are definitely part of the Antisthenian-Cynic doctrine that we should honour only those from whom we can derive some practical benefit or advantage.[1031] And this doctrine, as we have already seen, applies to parents, kinsmen, and friends alike.[1032] Therefore, according to the Cynics, we are permitted to treat kinsmen, friends, and even parents, if they are of no practical use to us, like callouses, nails, or saliva which we remove from our body if they should prove themselves worthless encumbrances.[1033] Dio Chrysostom, who in many ways is under the influence of Antisthenian-Cynic teaching, also remarks (*Oratio* 14.7) that useless 'parts' of one's family could be 'removed' in the same manner as we remove useless parts from our body.[1034] The comparison of 'non-profitable' friends or kinsmen to callouses, nails, or saliva in its crudeness as well as naturalistic 'realism' definitely points to a Cynic source who at times seemed to have delighted in saying or doing vulgar things.[1035]

The practical and calculating attitude of Antisthenes and the Cynics towards friendship also seems to be reflected in some of Xenophon's views on this subject (*Memor.* 2.4.6): 'The good friend takes an interest in all the things which are lacking for the well-being of his friends. The promotion of their private affairs and public interests is his concern. Should there be any need that he do a good service to any one of his friends, he will assist him with all his means ... by sharing expenditures with him.' And a friend, after having been helped thus, will certainly return this help (2.10.3). Securing such a grateful supporter would be the equivalent of acquiring dozens of slaves, in that he could become extremely useful to his former benefactor.[1036] In this fashion a man could also ascertain 'of how much value he is to his friends' (2.5.1) and 'how he stands in the estimation of his friends' (2.5.4). 'Good economists tell us that we ought to buy a good article whenever it may be purchased at a low price. Nowadays, when times are troubled, it is possible to obtain good friends at an exceedingly low rate.'[1037] But a man 'who is a spendthrift, incapable of supporting himself and always borrowing from his neighbours, although unable ever to repay them ... is he not a most disagreeable friend?'[1038] Xenophon continues (*Memor.* 2.6.13): 'How did Themistocles make the city love him? ... By conferring upon it some advantage.' For 'when a man wishes to attain to honours in the city in order ... that he may assist his friends ... why should he not ... form friendships with other people? ... How can this be but profitable to him ... particularly since he needs allies. ... But those who are willing to be his allies must be served well by him.'[1039]

The fourth Polycratean charge listed by Xenophon (*Memor.* 1.2.56–59) reads as follows: 'Socrates, by selecting the worst passages from the most celebrated poets and by using them as arguments, taught his disciples to be unprincipled and tyrannical.'[1040] Antisthenes' flair for quoting the ancient poets, as well as his interpretations of their poems is too well known to need any special reference.[1041] It is also a matter of common knowledge that he exploited Greek mythology as treated by the poets in order to illustrate or bolster his own teachings. At the same time he seems to have exhorted his pupils either to follow or reject the example set by the heroes or heroines of ancient mythology and lore. The first[1042] quotation allegedly used by Socrates is taken from Hesiod's praise of toil [1043] and condemnation of idleness.[1044] In the face of the rather widespread contemporary contempt for toil (πόνος), the Cynics with their philosophy of πόνος and ἐγκράτεια admired and often recited this Hesiodic line, which probably held an honoured place in their writings. According to the Cynics, pleasure (ἡδονή), in the conventional sense of the term, is that mortal enemy of the virtuous and wise man which enslaves and debases him. The sole effective remedy against this enslavement is the πόνος,[1045] a term which Antisthenes was perhaps the first Greek author to use in this particular cathartic meaning:[1046] 'He [scil., Antisthenes] demonstrated that toil was a good thing,'[1047] implying thereby that the πόνος was the one thing which prevents us from becoming ensnared by pleasure. And Xenophon (Cynegeticus 12.9) definitely echoes the Cynic tradition when he maintains: 'For those are the best whose πόνοι remove from mind and body whatever is base and insolent, and kindle a desire for virtue in its place. . . .'[1048] Xenophon's frequent use of the term πόνος in connection with his characterization of Socrates clearly indicates that he borrowed this term from some Antisthenian source. We seem to be justified in assuming that Polycrates also found in some Antisthenian writings this particular reference to Hesiod's praise of toil, as well as its more 'radical' interpretation.

It does not become clear from the Xenophontean text, however, why Polycrates thought that any reliance on this Hesiodic passage should make young people 'unprincipled',[1049] unless Polycrates should have contended here that any extravagant praise of toil and strenuous training was contrary to the established tradition of the leading social classes and, hence, was 'revolutionary'.[1050] The answer to this puzzling problem could perhaps be found in Plato's *Charmides* 163BC, where Critias quotes the identical lines from Hesiod—the same Critias, it seems, whom Socrates, according to the second charge of Polycrates,[1051] allegedly had taught to become unprincipled and tyrannical. A careful comparison of Xenophon's *Memorabilia* 1.2.57 and Plato's *Charmides* 163BC will show at once that there exists a certain undeniable similarity between these two passages. In the *Charmides* Critias makes essentially the same artificial distinction between 'work' (πράττειν) and 'doing' (ποιεῖν) that we find suggested in *Memorabilia* 1.2.57. In the *Charmides* (163D) Critias proposes that the term πράττειν (or ἐργάζεσθαι) denotes the 'doing of something good or useful', while the word ποιεῖν merely refers to 'doing something evil or useless'. Socrates ridicules this rather artificial distinction which in his opinion goes back to Prodicus. We can be reasonably certain that this distinction was not made by the historical Socrates, but rather by Antisthenes. Essentially the same idea can be found in Diogenes Laertius (6.46): 'A youth was playing cottabos (κοτταβίζον) in the baths. Diogenes [of Sinope] said to him: "The better you play the worse it is for you."' The implication is here that to gamble is to ποιεῖν, that is, to do something which is evil or useless.[1052] For 'instead of useless toils', Diogenes of Sinope contends, 'men should choose such toils as nature recommends whereby they may live happily'.[1053] Xenophon (*Memor.* 1.2.57) echoes these sentiments when he imputes to Socrates the statement that 'only those who do something good really work (ἐργάζεσθαι) and are useful workers. But those who gamble or do anything pernicious or evil, are called idle (ἀργούς).' In keeping with their profound contempt for εὐτυχία (good fortune) as contrasted by εὐπραξία (intelligent and purposive work),[1054] the Cynics had little use for the dice-player or jester: 'They [*scil.*, the Cynics] hold that ... we should entrust nothing to luck (τύχη).[1055] To be sure, even the dice-player and the jester do something (ποιεῖν τί); but in reality they are idle (σχολάζειν), because they do nothing worthwhile. For what they do actually amounts to nothing—nothing from the point of view of intelligent and purposive effort or pursuit—or, what would be the same from the Cynic point of view, to doing something evil. Hence we may conclude that Antisthenes maintained the following: To do something is good, to do nothing is evil. But to do something actually signifies to do something right, that is, intelligently and with a definite purpose (εὐπραξία). To do nothing (ἀργεῖν) may consist also of gambling (κυβεύειν), an 'activity' which with the Cynics is really something 'passive' in that it relies mainly on τύχη rather than on laborious effort.

But Critias, in Plato's *Charmides* (163D ff.), is not satisfied with maintaining that πράττειν (or ἐργάζεσθαι) means the doing 'of something good or useful', while ποιεῖν merely signifies the 'doing of something evil or useless'. He goes still further in his definition of πράττειν or ἐργάζεσθαι when he identifies it with τὰ ἑαυτοῦ πράττειν (or, οἰκεῖον πράττειν—the 'doing of one's own business', or 'doing what is according to one's nature'). The ποιεῖν, that is, the 'doing of something evil or useless' or, to put it into different words, mere 'activism', on the other hand, is also described as ποιεῖν ἀλλότριον, the 'doing of someone else's business' or 'doing what is not according to one's nature'. In the opinion of Critias, this is the true meaning of the Hesiodic verse which, as he insists, any intelligent person[1056] could easily understand.

Antisthenian Elements in the Κατηγορία Σωκράτους of Polycrates

According to the distinction made by Critias, therefore, the work which one might engage in without disgrace to oneself, is πράττειν or ἐργάζεσθαι, the 'doing of something good or useful', which, in turn, is tantamount to the 'doing of one's own business'. But merely ποιεῖν, the 'doing of something evil or useless', as well as the 'doing of someone else's business', is really idleness, at least morally speaking, and as such is a disgrace. This is, in the final analysis, for Critias the meaning of the Hesiodic passage that 'work (ἔργον) is no disgrace, but idleness is a disgrace'. What Critias discusses here is actually nothing other than a typically Antisthenian-Cynic thesis; it is the Cynic protest against senseless intermeddlers and, by implication, also the Cynic praise of proper, intelligent leisure (σχόλη).[1057] The 'praise of leisure' was probably a major part of Antisthenes' *On justice and courage, a hortative work*, mentioned in Diogenes Laertius (6.16). It is in this book that he probably discussed the concepts of work (ἔργον, πράττειν, ποιεῖν) and leisure (σχόλη). It was this praise of intelligent leisure, it should be noted, which probably furnished Polycrates with his argument that Socrates had induced his followers to live in idleness.[1058] And if Polycrates tries to substantiate his allegation by pointing out that Socrates, when advocating leisure, had exhorted his pupils to care more for their souls than for material things, including their bodies,[1059] then he could have cited the many instances in which the Cynics expressed their contempt for the rich,[1060] the 'busybodies',[1061] and the professional athletes.[1062]

According to the *Apologia Socratis* of Libanius (62.13),[1063] Polycrates apparently charged Socrates with having quoted the Pindaric statement that 'the law is the king of all, of mortals and immortals, doing violence with the greatest of high-handedness'.[1064] It is quite possible that the Cynics recited this verse in order to substantiate their general contention that the established laws, conventions, and customs are nothing other than a form of tyranny of man over man and, hence, have no real compelling force as regards the wise man 'who in all his acts will be guided not by the established laws, but by the principle of virtue', that is, the 'natural law'.[1065] It should be remembered that the contrast between 'nature' and man-made institutions or man-made laws is probably one of the characteristic features of 'sophistic enlightenment'. If anything is at all 'universally valid', it must be 'nature', or, to be more exact, 'human nature' in all its naturalistic implications. Only that could be called 'just' which is determined by 'nature'. But human institutions or man-made laws (νόμοι) go beyond 'nature'. Hence Hippias could say that the man-made laws are man's tyrant in that they compel him to do what is contrary to nature or, at least, contrary to his 'nature'.[1066] In short, since the Cynics believed that the established laws and conventions of society are contrary to nature as the Cynics understood it, and are, therefore, 'tyrannical', they are 'high-handed' and as such, repugnant to the Cynic who strives solely after virtue: 'To convention (νόμῳ) he [scil., Diogenes of Sinope] opposed nature (φύσιν).'[1067]

The constant endeavour of the Cynic to reduce man's wants to 'natural standards', to the absolute and irreducible minimum necessary to sustain the simplest life, brought about this sharp contrast of νόμος —convention—and φύσις—nature. To live according to these 'natural standards' signifies the ideal form of life, for such a life discards the νόμος and the accretions of convention. Hence, the Cynic would ridicule and reject the νόμος, the more so, since complete emancipation from the νόμος became for him the prime prerequisite to happiness, wisdom, and virtue. In this sense Diogenes of Sinope could also refer to himself as a παραχαράκτης τοῦ νομίσματος (debaser of currency).[1068]

The report in Diogenes Laertius (6.20–21) that Diogenes of Sinope had called himself 'a debaser of currency', suggests a rather fascinating interpretation. We are told here that 'Diocles relates that Diogenes went into exile because his father, who was entrusted with the money of the city, adulterated the coinage (παραχαράξαντος τὸ νόμισμα).[1069] Eubulides, however, in his work on Diogenes, states that Diogenes did this.... Moreover, Diogenes, in his work entitled *Pordalus*,[1070] confesses that he adulterated the coinage. It is said that after having been appointed superintendent of the workmen [in the Mint at Sinope], the workers urged him to do this, and that he went to Delphi or to the Delian oracle in his own city, inquiring of Apollo whether he should do what he was urged to do. When the God gave him permission to alter the political currency (συνχωρήσαντος τὸ πολιτικὸν νόμισμα), he failed to understand what this meant and adulterated the state coinage. When he was detected, according to some, he was banished, while according to others he left the city on his own accord.... One version is that his father entrusted him with the money, and that he debased it, in consequence of which the father was imprisoned and died, while the son fled and went to Delphi and inquired not whether he should falsify the currency, but what he should do in order to gain the greatest reputation; and that it was then that he received the oracle [to adulterate the political currency—τὸ πολιτικὸν νόμισμα].'[1071]

C. T. Seltmann, in a paper referred to by D. R. Dudley,[1072] points out that in the period between 362 and c. 310 some of the coins issued by the city of Sinope bore the inscription ΙΚΕΣΙΟ (Hikesias). This would indicate that after 362 a magistrate bearing the same name as that given to the father of Diogenes of Sinope was actually superintendent of the Mint at Sinope. As to the 'debasement of the currency', Seltmann supplies some interesting information. About the middle of the fourth century B.C. a large number of alien and inferior imitations of the Sinopean currency made its appearance, emanating notably from Ariarathes (the satrap of Cappadocia since 351), as the inscription ARIAWRATH (or ABDSSN in Aramaic, using blundered Greek

Antisthenian Elements in the Κατηγορία Σωκράτους of Polycrates

letters) on some of these alien coins would indicate. These counterfeit coins, which seriously threatened the credit of Sinope, were put out of circulation, presumably at Sinope, by being defaced by a large chisel-stamp, apparently on orders of the superintendent of the Mint who wished to protect the credit of the city. This, Seltmann argues, is the παραχάραξις mentioned by Diogenes Laertius. But παραχάραξις, Seltmann insists, cannot mean 'the issuance of adulterated currency', the word for which was παρακοπτειν. In addition, no true Sinopean coin of base metal has ever been found.[1073] If we accept Seltmann's thesis that παραχάραξις means 'defacing' and not 'falsifying' (παρακόπτειν), then the historical facts would bear out the story told by Diogenes Laertius (6.20-21) about Hikesias, the father of Diogenes of Sinope. It is possible that the defacing of a currency bearing the name of Ariarathes was considered an anti-Persian or political crime by the pro-Persian party which might have won control in Sinope after 350. In addition, probably due to negligence on the part of some subaltern official, some of the good Sinopean coins also were defaced (such coins have been found), a carelessness which might have been turned into a serious charge against the superintendent of the Mint. While Hikesias was apparently jailed for this, his son Diogenes, who might have been implicated in the crime of his father, was forced to leave the country. Hence he had ample reason for harbouring a grudge against all society.

While it must be admitted now that the report of Diogenes Laertius is based on historical fact, this account also contains what might be called a symbolic meaning. Aristotle (*Nicomachean Ethics* 1133 a 25 ff.) informs us that νόμισμα (money), like νόμος (positive law), actually signifies 'a standard of convention'.[1074] Thus if Diogenes of Sinope is called an 'adulterer of currency' (παραχαράκτης τοῦ νομίσματος), this might symbolically refer to his efforts at combating and destroying the established and universally accepted conventions (νόμοι) of society. This may also be gathered from Diogenes Laertius (6.71). The play with the two terms νόμος and νόμισμα, therefore, might be a fine allegorical point in the Diogenes tradition. In any event, this allegorical interpretation of the whole story reported by Diogenes Laertius seems to be supported also by the latter in 6.21. After having fled from Sinope where his father had been imprisoned for debasing the currency, Diogenes went to Delphi and inquired, not whether he should falsify the coinage, but what he should do in order to gain the greatest reputation. And then it was that he received the oracle [that he should "alter the currency"].' Since the oracle could not possibly refer to the already accomplished debasing of the Sinopean coinage, it could only mean a παραχαράττειν τὸν νόμον—the debasing of the existing social conventions, institutions, and laws (τὸ πολιτικὸν νόμισμα). But Diogenes of Sinope originally seemed to have failed to understand the true meaning of the god's advice.[1075] All this might also explain why Diogenes of Sinope should declare 'the love of money the mother-city of all evils'.[1076]

The Cynic rejection of the νόμος or convention may be back of their frequent appeals to the habits of animals,[1077] which, in contrast to convention-ridden man, still observe the 'natural standards' and live according to nature (κατὰ φύσιν).[1078] It was 'the way of the mouse' which, according to an anecdote preserved by Theophrastus, converted Diogenes of Sinope to the Cynic way of life and thus made him a wise man.[1079] As a matter of fact, the Cynic παραχάραξις (perversion of convention) seems to have attracted a number of people who wished to stress the gulf which separates the 'wise man' from those ordinary and 'thoughtless' people who still observe the established and accepted standards of conventional life. We may assume, therefore, that Polycrates originally found the Pindaric quotation 'the law is the king of all, . . . doing violence with the greatest of high-handedness', as well as the interpretation which he ascribes to Socrates, in some Antisthenian-Cynic source. The Pindaric citation also appears as a metaphor in Plato's *Symposium* (196C). Agathon, who is influenced by Gorgias,[1080] likewise speaks of the 'kingly law'. And in Plato's *Protagoras* (337D) Hippias calls the law 'the tyrant of men'. Hence it seems that Polycrates could have found this verse both quoted and interpreted by the disciples of Gorgias, including Antisthenes. All this would also explain why Polycrates, at least in the words of Libanius (62.13),[1081] apparently changed the wording of the Pindaric verse. For it is quite likely that the Cynics altered this verse in order to use it more effectively in support of their rejection of all established laws, customs, and traditions which, as pointed out, are but a form of tyranny of man over man.[1082] It is also possible that Polycrates might have had in mind here not so much the original passage from Pindar, as a particular allegorical interpretation of this passage by the Cynics which might have changed its original wording or at least its original meaning.

Polycrates also charged Socrates[1083] with having perverted a quotation taken from Theognis: 'But a man oppressed by poverty can neither speak up or do anything, for his tongue is tied.'[1084] This verse which deplores the misery and helplessness of poverty, was most likely recorded by Antisthenes. As a matter of fact, a statement such as this would certainly elate the Cynics who had announced that 'the term "disabled" (ἀνάπηρος) . . . ought to be applied not to the deaf or blind, but to those who have no wallet'.[1085] For had not Diogenes of Sinope insisted that the most wretched thing is 'an old man destitute'?[1086] Hence it is quite possible that Polycrates could have found this quotation from Theognis as well as its interpretation in the writings of Antisthenes,[1087] who might have made use of it in order to demonstrate that under the existing social conventions and mores 'money makes the man',[1088] while the poor man, were he ever so virtuous, counts for nothing. It is also quite likely that Antisthenes might have refuted the cringing views held by Theognis. The poor but proud Cynic, we may surmise, upbraided the impoverished Theognis for his servile lamentations, pointing out the inherent dignity and nobility of virtuous poverty, which, at least for the Cynic, is no cause for rejection and despondency: 'All things belong to the gods; the wise men are friends of the gods and friends hold things in common. Hence all things belong to the wise.'[1089] And Diogenes of Sinope, who called the ignorant rich 'the sheep with the golden fleece',[1090] would often proclaim loudly 'that the gods had given to men the means of living comfortably, but we have lost sight of this in that we demand honeyed cakes'.[1091] The Cynics insisted that in order to live happily man needed nothing more than virtue, which ought to be the sole object of our attention.[1092] Wealth without virtue is the root of all evil.[1093] Hence virtue and wealth, particularly if the latter is used unwisely, cannot exist side by side.[1094] The Cynic 'way of life', with its total disregard for all established standards and accepted conventions,[1095] is the sole road to wisdom and true happiness.[1096]

In the reports both of Libanius (chap. 62)[1097] and Xenophon (*Memor.* 1.2.58–59),[1098] Polycrates seems to have claimed that Socrates had quoted Homer[1099] in order to give vent to his anti-democratic sentiments. Homer, as it is commonly known, was the favoured ancient poet with Antisthenes.[1100] According to the 'bibliography' listed by Diogenes Laertius (6.15–18), Antisthenes wrote no less than ten works dealing with Homer or Homeric heroes or heroines: 'Antisthenes [held] . . . that some things have been spoken by the poet [*scil.*, Homer] in accord with fancy, and some in accord with reality. Antisthenes, however, did not elaborate the theory, whereas Zeno made it plain. . . .'[1101] Despite his 'religious liberalism', Antisthenes did not reject the traditional mythology of the Greeks. By continuing the allegorical interpretation of these myths which had been initiated by Parmenides, Empedocles, Anaxagoras, Metrodorus, Protagoras, and Prodicus, he constitutes the connecting link between the Pre-Socratic and the Stoic mythological allegory. Odysseus, whose words and deeds are retold by Homer, appears to have been one of the favoured heroes with the Cynics.[1102] Antisthenes is also credited with having composed two fictitious forensic orations, namely, the *Ajax* and the *Odysseus*.[1103] The *Odysseus* is an apology delivered before the assembled host during the Trojan siege. In several respects it is similar to the *Defence of Palamedes* of Gorgias, the teacher of Antisthenes. In the *Odysseus* the hero defends himself against Ajax in their dispute over the armour of Achilles. This dispute brings out the irreconcilable tension between two basic types of men represented by Ajax and Odysseus respectively. Ajax is the simple, straightforward, and honourable man, who does not know the meaning of intrigue and dialectics. Odysseus, on the other hand, is the crafty and clever person who always comes off best because of his imagination, adaptability, and lack of scruples. In this connection it may be noted that Sophocles, in his *Philoctetes*, deals with the same problem. Here Neoptolemus is the straightforward and simple man, while Odysseus is the cunning plotter. As could be expected, Antisthenes sympathizes with his hero Odysseus who symbolizes for him the new or 'progressive trend' over against the old-fashioned conservatism of the clumsy Ajax. In sum, Odysseus is an Antisthenian-Cynic hero because, in the opinion of Antisthenes, he is, despite his outward helplessness, the most effective person; because in all his actions he is a free man, so that not even the most shameless deeds degrade him; because he voluntarily chooses suffering and self-debasement in order to achieve a worthy end; and because he is a clever and intelligent man who always works with a purpose and achieves a worthwhile end.

The many 'labours' (πόνοι) of Odysseus, as well as his superior intelligence and craftiness, impressed the Cynics who took great stock in original intelligence as againt conventional deportment, and in hard toil as against shallow pleasure.[1104] Polycrates makes it appear that Socrates had cited Homer to prove that 'kingly persons should be persuaded with gentle words, while lowly people should be driven with blows', implying thereby that he was an enemy of the common people (μισόδημος) and, hence, an enemy of democracy.[1105] We remember that Xenophon's rebuttal of this particular allegation was rather lame and somewhat ineffective (*Memor.* 1.2.59): 'Socrates, however, said no such thing . . . but what he said was that those who did not benefit others either by words or deeds . . . especially if they are of an insolent spirit, should be curbed in every way, even though they were ever so rich.' To understand the true significance of the whole issue raised by the Polycratean and Xenophontean reference to this Homeric passage, we must keep in mind that this issue actually revolves around the basic Antisthenian-Cynic παιδεία ideal:[1106] Odysseus, the intelligent and rational man, gently persuades other intelligent men through his intelligent approach and rational arguments.[1107] But the stupid or indolent man, the morally and intellectually inferior person, must be persuaded through the use of harsher means. Hence it is not entirely unlikely that Polycrates charged Socrates here with holding what is really an Antisthenian-Cynic doctrine. The Cynics were not only notoriously liberal in the application of the rod, particularly to indolent persons,[1108] but also never disguised their utter contempt for the masses whom they considered indolent and stupid:[1109] 'God has everywhere appointed the superior to care for and rule over the inferior: skill, for instance, over lack of skill; strength over weakness. And for foolish people he has made the wise to have care and thought, to watch and plan. . . .'[1110] For 'he who loves toil (φιλόπονος) and exercises self-control is not only better qualified to be king, but is also able to live a much more pleasant life than those in the opposite case.'[1111] Hesiod (*Works and Days* 293-297) seems to express the same idea when he says: 'Best is the man who sees of himself what must be done, and excellent is he too who follows what is well indicated by others. But he who is suited for neither is useless in all respects.' It is not impossible that the Cynics and Antisthenes in particular borrowed this idea from Hesiod whom they apparently quoted quite frequently. We must also presume that Xenophon's views on παιδεία are under Cynic and, perhaps, ultimately under Hesiodic influence. According to the Aristotelian scholiast, the Cynics are called by that name because, among other reasons, they act like dogs. And 'the dog is a discriminating animal which can distinguish between friends and enemies. . . . By the same token the Cynics recognize as friends those who are suited to philosophy, and treat them kindly; while those who are unfitted for philosophy, they drive away by barking at them like dogs.'[1112] When, therefore, Xenophon tries to rebut the allegation of Polycrates by stating that 'those who did not benefit others either by words or deeds' should be curbed in every conceivable manner, he is repeating only what had been a dogma with Antisthenes and the Cynics.[1113]

Polycrates, according to the words of Libanius (71.12 ff.),[1114] apparently had also charged Socrates with having condoned theft, fraud, sacrilege, and perjury. That at least Diogenes of Sinope saw no impropriety in 'the stealing of anything from a temple or the eating of the flesh of any animal or, indeed, in cannibalism', is attested by Diogenes Laertius (6.73): 'Under the stress of circumstances the wise man will even turn to cannibalism.'[1115] Although this statement is ascribed to the Stoics, it is undoubtedly of Cynic origin.[1116] We may also assume that Diogenes of Sinope defended incest in his tragedy *Oedipus* (Diogenes Laertius 6.80) and in his treatise *Republic* (Diogenes Laertius 6.80);[1117] and cannibalism in his tragedy *Thyestes* (Diogenes Laertius 6.80) and perhaps in his *Medea* (*ibid.*): 'Diogenes has stated that Medea was a σοφή and not a sorceress. For she took over flabby men . . . and by sweat baths made them strong and healthy again. Hence arose the story that she boiled their flesh. . . .'[1118] This remark might refer to the *Medea* of Diogenes of Sinope, who seems to have justified cannibalism in the following manner: 'According to right reason (ὀρθὸς λόγος) . . . all elements are contained in all things and permeate everything: since meat is not only a constituent of bread, but bread a constituent of vegetables; and all other bodies, by way of certain invisible passages and particles, find their way into and unite with all substances in the form of vapour. This he says in the *Thyestes*. . . .'[1119]

Hence it is quite likely that Polycrates found in Antisthenes' writings the material for his charge that Socrates had condoned theft, fraud, sacrilege, and perjury. We remember that Libanius answers this charge with the argument that sacrilege, fraud, theft, and deception were permissible provided that the injured party was a barbarian or an enemy.[1120]

Antisthenian Elements in the Κατηγορία Σωκράτους of Polycrates

We may assume that Antisthenes in his work *On law or, Of goodness and justice*,[1121] had declared that it was not wrongful to steal from or defraud an enemy.[1122] According to Xenophon, (*Memor.* 4.2.17) Antisthenes under certain circumstances permitted the defrauding even of friends; and in the Δίσσοι λόγοι, which express what seem to be Antisthenian-Cynic doctrines, we are told that perjury is right towards enemies (3.6), that temple-robbery may be justified under certain circumstances (3.7–8), and that in certain instances we may deceive our parents or steal from our relatives and friends (3.3–4).[1123] It is commonly held that Antisthenes believed in 'dual morality'. For does not Cyrus—Xenophon's spokesman for Antisthenian maxims—maintain that it was the right of the conqueror to plunder and enslave another city?[1124] The Antisthenian justification of such conduct apparently is closely related to the general Cynic admiration for the crafty deeds of Odysseus,[1125] who, with the full approval of the Cynic, boasts of having looted as well as deceived his enemies,[1126] and even of having stolen the *Palladion*,[1127] thus displaying his virtues as a soldier and military leader, unhampered by artificial conventions and the traditional standards of morality.[1128] Antisthenes' admiration for the 'foxy' Odysseus may have been expressed in his *Odysseus*;[1129] *Cyclops or, Of Odysseus*,[1130] where he probably contrasted the stupid Cyclops and the wily Odysseus; *On the Odyssey* (*ibid.*); *On Odysseus, Penelope and the dog*;[1131] and *Ajax* (?)[1132] which deprecates the clumsy Ajax.

All this would suggest that Antisthenes rather than the historical Socrates, whoever he might have been, supplied Polycrates with the material for the charges he instituted in his κατηγορία Σωκράτους. In doing so, Polycrates, it seems, transformed Socrates into what could be called an Antisthenian Cynic. This, in turn, poses three major problems which, in the light of the present-day source situation, cannot, however, be answered in a completely satisfactory manner. First, it is quite possible that Polycrates earnestly considered Antisthenes a true Socratic and the Antisthenian *dicta* a faithful expression of Socrates' teachings. Secondly, Polycrates, who was probably more interested in rhetorical effects and sensationalism than in historical truth,[1133] might not have been interested in or perhaps not even capable of distinguishing between the historical Socrates and the Antisthenian Socrates. Since the obviously more radical and therefore more sensational sayings of Antisthenes and his followers would supply him with more telling and more damaging anti-Socratic arguments, it is not altogether surprising that he should have relied on Antisthenian *dicta* when framing his κατηγορία Σωκράτους, the more so, since in view of the complete absence of any authentic writings of Socrates he probably considered Antisthenes the faithful disciple and sillographer of Socrates. Thirdly, there always exists the possibility that the authentic Antisthenian teachings were much closer to the original Socratic views than it was

Antisthenian Elements in the Κατηγορία Σωκράτους of Polycrates

commonly conceded, particularly by the extremely unsympathetic Plato (and the Early Academy), who probably contrasted an idealized Socrates with a much maligned Antisthenes.

It is by no means surprising, therefore, that Polycrates should refer to Antisthenian materials for his indictment of Socrates. Antisthenes, much more than Plato, was commonly considered a true Socratic by his contemporaries and, hence, as the one author who could be expected to adhere faithfully to the teachings of Socrates. In addition, Antisthenes was a prolific writer whose *Socratica* soon attracted enough attention to start a definite anti-Socratic, or should we say, anti-Antisthenian literary movement. At the time when Antisthenes had already gained a literary reputation, in all likelihood Plato was still little known and less respected both as a philosopher and author. The Platonic *Gorgias*, as has already been pointed out, is essentially a reply to the κατηγορία Σωκράτους of Polycrates. It is at the same time the first really significant Platonic dialogue, with perhaps the exception of the *Protagoras*. The pre-Gorgian works of Plato, namely, the *Laches, Charmides, Euthyphro, Hippias Minor* (?), *Lysis, Ion* (?), *Apology*, and *Crito*,[1134] which Polycrates might have consulted, are not only some of the least important dialogues of Plato, but as such offer little if any material for Polycrates' particular purpose. Socrates, on the other hand, does not seem to have left behind any writings of his own which might have served Polycrates as source material for his pamphlet. Hence it appears that the closest Polycrates could come to Socrates' teachings at so early a date, aside from the rather vacillating popular traditions and opinions, were the writings of Antisthenes which in all likelihood constituted the first truly significant literary contributions of the Socratics or, at least, the only important and extensive Socratic literature available before 393/2, the year in which Polycrates composed his κατηγορία Σωκράτους. And finally, Antisthenes with his radical critique and deprecation of existing laws, established political institutions, and traditional custom or mores of society, more than anyone else, seemed to furnish Polycrates with the very arguments and materials he was seeking when framing his anti-Socratic charges. The 'anti-social' views of Antisthenes were exactly what Polycrates wished to hurl against Socrates.

7

The Political Aspects of the Socratic Problem

ACCORDING TO LIBANIUS 43.18, Polycrates had charged Socrates with having been a 'despiser of the common people' ($\mu\iota\sigma\delta\delta\eta\mu o\varsigma$)[1135] who taught his followers to ridicule Athenian democracy and its institutions.[1136] This charge recalls to our mind certain discussions of Athenian political life found in *The Old Oligarch* and in Plato's *Gorgias*. Undoubtedly, the discussions in the *Gorgias* in particular are primarily statements of Plato's own views and personal convictions.[1137] But it cannot be doubted that Plato believes himself to be speaking here in the spirit of Socrates. At the same time we should also recall that the lines which Plato has Socrates speak in the *Protagoras* (319B ff.) amount to a vicious denouncement of Athens' democratic institutions. Xenophon, especially in *Memorabilia* 3.7.5–6, also portrays Socrates as 'a despiser of democracy' and the common people,[1138] although it must be conceded that Xenophon does this in a more veiled manner than Plato.[1139]

One of the astonishing features of the Socratic tradition is the paucity of reports on the political activities of Socrates.[1140] This tradition refers to only four public or political incidents in the life of Socrates: his participation in three military campaigns;[1141] the honourable role which he played in the trial of the generals in 406;[1142] his alleged prosecution during the regime of the Thirty Tyrants in 404/3; and his trial, condemnation, and execution in 399 under the restored democracy. The first two reports seem to stress that Socrates' participation in the ordinary political life of Athens did not differ from that of the average Athenian citizen performing his civic duties. The accounts of Socrates' participation in the campaign of Potidaea are of special interest. There existed apparently a report which stressed the fact that he journeyed to Potidaea by ship rather than by land to avoid entering Thessaly.[1143] Thessaly had always been ruled by autocratic princes. We know, for instance, that Pisistratus, the tyrant, had spent considerable time there, forming some friendships which proved very useful when he tried to gain full control over Athens in the year 540/39. Critias, the head of the Thirty Tyrants, 'had fled to Thessaly where he consorted with men who practised lawlessness rather than justice'.[1144] To escape the impression that Socrates ever came in contact with these 'lawless men' and, hence, might have sympathized with their political ideas, the Socratic tradition apparently insisted that he never entered Thessaly. Plato (*Crito* 45C) seems to have been familiar with this tradition; for when Crito suggests that Socrates should flee to Thessaly, where the former has some influential friends, Socrates violently rejects the very idea of going to a place (*Crito* 53D) where there is so much $ἀταξία$ and $ἀκολασία$.[1145] In line with this tradition is also the story that Socrates 'showed his contempt for Archelaus of Thessaly, Scopas of Crannon, and Eurylochus of Larissa by refusing to accept their presents or invitations'.[1146] The reason why Socrates rejected these presents and invitations, according to Aristotle, is that 'one is insulted by being unable to repay favours'.[1147] Socrates is also said to have declined the presents offered to him by Archelaus with the remark that 'in Athens one could buy four measures of grain for one obol. And there are also plenty of drinking fountains.'[1148]

The second report in particular, namely, the account of the honourable role which Socrates played during the trial of the generals, also suggests that Socrates was a man of intrepidity and strong moral conviction who would not surrender his belief in what is right to misguided popular fanaticism and threats. In this, our report, at least by implication, also contains an indictment of Athenian democracy as well as an instance of the general contention, apparently advanced by some Socratics, that, when faced by the 'fierce masses', a man of probity such as Socrates is constantly in danger of losing his life on account of his principles. And finally, the second report is also an instance of the contention, likewise advanced by some Socratics, that a man like Socrates cannot live safely and in accordance with his moral principles or moral convictions under a democratic regime.[1149] The two reports of Socrates' alleged 'clash' with the Thirty Tyrants and of his trial in the year 399, on the other hand, allude more specifically to his conflicts with the existing political regime, namely, with the extreme oligarchs in 404/3 and with the restored extreme democracy in 399. These four scanty reports about the political life of Socrates do not seem to bear out the famous remark attributed to Pericles that Athens was the only city in which a man who held himself aloof from politics was looked upon, not as a peace-loving citizen, but as a useless member of society.[1150]

There can be little doubt that the Socratic tradition wishes to convey the impression that, although some of Socrates' closest friends and associates, besides being partisans of an aristocratic-reactionary movement in Athens, had been among the most active and influential politicians or statesmen of his day (Nicias, Laches, Charmides, Critias, Alcibiades, *et al.*), he himself always preferred either completely to abstain from taking an active part in politics or, at least, to remain in the background. A less favourable view seems to have insisted that,

The Political Aspects of the Socratic Problem

although he remained in the background, he was actually a sinister influence working behind the political scene,[1151] as Polycrates apparently insinuates.[1152] This, then, also would explain why the reports about Socrates' direct political or civic activities are so meagre.[1153] We gather from Xenophon's *Memorabilia* 3.7.1–8 that Socrates had tried to encourage young and talented people to enter a political career, pointing out to them that those who have a gift for politics have also the duty of exercising this gift in the interest of the city.[1154] At the same time he maintains that those who master an art in private need not fear practising it in public.[1155] He then continues by insisting that the popular assembly at Athens is composed of 'fullers, cobblers, farm labourers, carpenters, coppersmiths, shipmerchants or hucksters'. And since these people are held in contempt individually, there is no reason why they should be feared collectively.[1156]

But if Socrates advised others to enter politics, why, then, did he not himself do so,[1157] particularly since he seems to reject the view held by Aristippus, that one could live happily only outside the body politic?[1158] Perhaps Socrates himself provides the best answer to this question when, in the words of Xenophon (*Memor.* 1.6.15), he states: 'Would I better promote the practice of politics if I were to engage in it myself, or if I should devote myself to the training of as many others as possible for the practice of politics?' But there exists also another tradition explaining Socrates' refusal to play an active part in Athenian politics. According to Aelian (*Var. hist.* 2.11),[1159] Socrates is reported to have said to Antisthenes during the days of the Thirty Tyrants, when nearly all the outstanding men of Athens were persecuted: 'Are you still regretting that we two have never achieved any fame or importance?'—implying thereby that since political eminence or notoriety is always fraught with danger, the wise man should live in seclusion.[1160] Plato seems to take up the same theme when he makes Socrates confess: 'Some one may wonder why I go around in private giving advice and concerning myself with the affairs of others, but do not venture to come forward in public and advise the city. . . . This is what restrains me from being a politician:[1161] for I am certain . . . that if I had engaged in politics, I should have perished long ago. . . . No man who antagonizes you or any other multitude, honestly striving against the many lawless and unjust deeds which are committed in a city, can save his life. He who intends to fight for what is right . . . must have a private station and not a public one.'[1162] Socrates implies here that it is impossible for a politician to remain honest and just. Either he gives in sooner or later to the reckless and foolish demands of the many, and thus achieves success at the expense of his peace of mind, or he antagonizes the many by seeking justice at the expense of his life.

Hence it appears that the surviving Socratic literature is not consistent on Socrates' attitude towards active participation in the political life of

The Political Aspects of the Socratic Problem

Athens. On the one hand, he seems to have encouraged others to enter politics, while on the other hand, he defended his own reluctance to do so with the remark that this might cost him his life. In addition—and this is one of the more subtle aspects of the Socratic tradition, difficult to comprehend—he manifests a somewhat conflicting attitude when he counsels discreet retirement from all active political life, while insisting that the true philosopher has a political mission. This becomes especially manifest in Plato's *Apology* (30D-31A), where Socrates compares himself to a 'gadfly sent to the city . . . which requires to be stirred into life. . . . All day long and in all places and at all times I fasten upon you, arousing and persuading and reproaching you.'[1163]

There must have existed for some time a certain anti-Socratic sentiment in Athens, as evinced, for instance, by the *Clouds* of Aristophanes. This sentiment, it seems, prevailed much more among the common people than among the aristocrats—a curious phenomenon which perhaps could be explained by the fact that Socrates may have been a partisan of the aristocratic-oligarchic party at Athens and, hence, a favourite with the latter. It would also shed some light on the question why the common people should have considered him 'anti-democratic'. During the latter part of the fifth century a great many aristocrats probably supported the 'sophists' and the 'sophistic movement' by supplying them with the necessary patronage. This seems to be a most unusual situation, particularly since the Sophists, with their violent criticism of all socio-political institutions and traditions, frequently tended to destroy the principles on which aristocracy rested. For its survival aristocracy necessarily depends upon an instinctive respect for tradition. The aristocrats apparently failed to realize that anything which might undermine this respect seriously menaced their very existence. They seemed to be pleased with a type of training that gave them certain advantages in the law courts or political meetings.[1164] But they did not perceive that these sophistic teachings exercised an influence on the people which could only be detrimental to their own social and political position. The support which the aristocrats offered to the sophists probably led to the popular belief that some of the sophists, among them Socrates and his disciples, were enemies of democracy. This belief found additional support in the fact that several of Socrates' disciples or friends were members of the most aristocratic families in Athens as well as the leaders of the aristocratic-oligarchic forces which constantly vied with the democrats for the political control of Athens. Moreover, Socrates' peculiar manners and mannerisms, his curious appearance and his sometimes offensive candour made him to the common people a haughty aristocrat and a man steeped in sophistry. He was associated with ideas that, in a general way, were indiscriminately attributed to all sophists. Thus, he was sketched as a friend of aristocrats, a despiser of the common people, a corrupter of morals, an atheist, and a dialectician.[1165]

The Political Aspects of the Socratic Problem

It could be maintained that both Plato and Xenophon, being themselves 'aristocrats', attributed 'aristocratic' or 'anti-democratic' sentiments to their idol Socrates. But such an argument casually dismisses the undisputable fact that Antisthenes, by no means a man of aristocratic temperament, also thunders against the democratic institutions of Athens and its democratic leaders in his dialogues *Aspasia* and *Statesman*,[1166] as well as in some of his other writings.[1167] It is fairly safe to assume that Socrates did not completely endorse Athenian democracy, particularly that type of Athenian democracy which degenerated into a 'radical democracy' under the leadership of such men as Cleon, the leather merchant, Eucrates, the rope seller, Hyperbolus, the lamp maker, and Cleophon, the lyre maker: 'As long as Pericles was the leader of the people,' Aristotle maintains (*Pol. Athen.* 28.1 ff.), 'the city was still in a fairly good condition. But after his death everything became much worse. . . . Cleon, the son of Cleaenetus, [became] the leader of the people. This man, more than anyone else, appears to have corrupted the people by his violent methods. He was the first who shouted on the public platform, who used abusive language, and who spoke with his cloak girt up about him, while all others used to speak in proper dress and manner. After this . . . Cleophon, the owner of a lyre factory, [became] the leader of the people. Then Callicrates. . . . Later, however, both of these leaders were condemned to death. For the people, even if they allow themselves to be deceived for some time, later begin to hate those who have induced them to do something improper. After Cleophon there was an unbroken succession of popular leaders who distinguished themselves above all by their brazenness and by their eagerness to cater to the wishes of the masses, having nothing in mind but their immediate interests.' Socrates seems not only to have disliked the forms which the democratic regime at Athens had assumed during the last quarter of the fifth century,[1168] but appears to have been favourably impressed with the aristocratic or oligarchic governments of Crete and Sparta,[1169] or with the pre-Cleisthenean constitution of Athens.[1170] In this manner he gradually acquired the reputation of being a 'reactionary' or perhaps the intellectual leader of the 'anti-democratic reaction' in Athens which in 411 and again in 404 had actually assumed political control for a short period. The popular rumours which circulated on his 'anti-democratic' views did not subside when he began to surround himself with such notoriously 'aristocratic' or 'reactionary' men as Charmides (the uncle of Plato), Adeimantus, Alcibiades, Plato, and others.[1171] It also appears from the writings of Xenophon and Libanius that Socrates had been associated with Critias, the ill-famed leader of the Thirty Tyrants, who with the support of Sparta, had overthrown the Athenian democracy after the conclusion of the Peloponnesian War which ended so catastrophically for Athens in 404.[1172]

Polycrates also seems to have charged Socrates with having planned

The Political Aspects of the Socratic Problem

and contributed to the overthrow of Athenian democracy by ridiculing its laws and political institutions,[1173] and by associating with so evil a man as Critias or Alcibiades.[1174] Polycrates' strictures aside, there can be no doubt that Socrates' efforts to bring about a moral renaissance of the individual man (if this was at all his primary purpose) may also have envisioned a thorough socio-ethical and political reform of Athens as a whole. This becomes quite clear from Plato's *Apology* 30A, where Socrates apparently states his socio-ethical or socio-political programme: 'I shall repeat the same words to every one I meet, be he old or young, citizen or alien, but especially to the citizens, inasmuch as they are my brethren.'[1175] For even if Socrates appears always to address individuals, he nevertheless seems to be fully aware of the far-reaching repercussions his moral teachings had for the whole of the city:[1176] 'For I do nothing but go about persuading you all,' Plato maintains (*Apology* 30AB), '... not to set your heart on your persons or your possessions, but first and above all to care about the greatest possible improvement of the soul. I tell you that virtue is not given by money, but that from virtue comes money as well as every other human good, public as well as private.'[1177] Socrates himself firmly believes (Plato, *Apology* 30A) that 'no greater good has ever happened to the city' than his constant and unremitting work for the moral betterment of its citizens: 'Where I could do the greatest good privately to every one of you, there I went trying to persuade every one of you that he must look to himself and seek virtue and wisdom before he looks at his private interests, and that he must look at the city before he looks at the interests of the city: and that this should be the order which he ought to observe in all his actions.'[1178]

Socrates' concern over the socio-ethical reform of Athens through the moral re-education of its individual citizens also becomes manifest in Plato's *Symposium* 209A, where Socrates calls the ordering of cities 'the highest and fairest form of practical wisdom (φρόνησις) by far'.[1179] And when Polycrates, referring to the dismal human failures of Alcibiades and Critias, apparently reproaches Socrates for having taught 'politics' to his followers before teaching them practical wisdom and restraint (σωφρονεῖν),[1180] Xenophon remarks (*Memor*. 1.2.18) that it has always been Socrates' intention first of all to make virtuous men out of his disciples. In his *Symposium* (216AB) Plato takes up essentially the same issue when he makes Alcibiades confess that Socrates 'forces me to concede that I ought not to live the way I am living, neglecting the needs of my own soul and busying myself with the affairs of the Athenians'. What Plato (or Socrates) tries to suggest here is not, however, that we should refrain from taking an interest in public affairs. In keeping with what he had already said in *Apology* 36c, he merely points out that before becoming involved with public or political problems we should pay attention to our own moral improvement and the needs of our soul.

This idea also seems to be reflected in Xenophon (*Memor*. 1.2.17–18):

'Some people may object at this point that Socrates should have taught his followers self-control (σωφροσύνη) before he instructed them in politics. To this remark I shall make no reply for the present. But I would like to point out that all teachers make themselves examples to their pupils in that they carry out their own precepts by practising what they teach. I know that Socrates made himself an example to his followers by disclosing himself as a man of honourable and excellent character, particularly when he discoursed intelligently on virtue and other matters which concern mankind. And I also know that those two men [scil., Critias and Alcibiades], as long as they kept company with Socrates, were temperate and self-controlled, not from fear of being fined or chastised, but from being persuaded that this was the most excellent way of conduct.'

Of all the surviving evidence only the κατηγορία Σωκράτους of Polycrates directly charged Socrates with a conduct openly inimical to Athenian democracy.[1181] The Platonic *Apology*, on the other hand, omits all references to this grave charge. This rather curious phenomenon can easily be explained. Unlike the Xenophontean *Defence* and *Memorabilia* 1.1.1–1.2.64, the Platonic *Apology* deals with the events which transpired during the official trial in 399. It must be conceded, however, that in many respects Plato's account deviates considerably from the historical proceedings. This trial was held, we must surmise, under the terms of the general political amnesty law which was declared soon after the overthrow of the Thirty Tyrants in May 403.[1182] Thus under the terms of this amnesty, which was apparently strictly observed, no political charges could be instituted openly against Socrates during his trial.[1183] This would explain why, according to Plato's report of the official trial, Anytus seems to have taken great pains not to turn the whole proceedings into a political affair. It would also solve the riddle of Anytus' insistence that Meletus, according to the report of Plato and Diogenes Laertius (2.38 and 2.40), should render the indictment and swear out the affidavit against Socrates. Anytus, however, remains always the principal force behind the whole prosecution of Socrates. The leading role which Anytus played during the trial should also explain why, soon after the condemnation and death of Socrates and again after the publication of the Polycratean κατηγορία which uses Anytus as spokesman, the Socratics singled out Anytus for their most vicious vilifications. In their eagerness to avenge themselves and their master on Anytus, they put into circulation a series of stories about the latter which were meant to discredit him for all time.[1184]

This introduces the involved question of whether the whole trial of Socrates in 399 was not originally a 'political trial', in some way connected with the political events of the years 404/3, even though no overt political charges had been filed or discussed. Out of respect for the terms of the amnesty law or 'Act of Oblivion' of 403, we may assume, the official indictment, as recorded by Xenophon, Plato, and Diogenes Laertius, could contain only 'token charges', the real charges probably being of a political nature. The fact that Anytus was one of the chief promoters of this Act of Oblivion may also explain why the charge of 'impiety' against Socrates was pressed home by Meletus, who must be considered the 'nominal prosecutor'.[1185] This Meletus seems to have been the same man who prosecuted Andocides for the same crime in the same year. If the oration *Contra Andocidem* (which is preserved under the authorship of Lysias) may be regarded as the work of Meletus or as the forensic speech composed by Lysias to be spoken 'in character' by Meletus during the trial of Andocides, then we understand why Anytus should select Meletus as the 'nominal prosecutor' in a proceeding in which the token charge of impiety played a major role. The *Contra Andocidem* is the speech of a sincere but hopelessly fanatical simpleton who would make the ideal tool in a sham trial such as that of Socrates.[1186]

Assuming the political nature of the entire proceedings, we might also explain the unusual conduct which, in the words of Plato, Anytus exhibited during the trial. For he seems suddenly to have realized that Socrates, by eluding the ostensible charges of the indictment, would also elude the true, though unwritten charges underlying the entire proceedings. We must remember that Meletus was not altogether successful in his efforts at substantiating the allegations made in the official indictment. For one moment it appeared that Socrates would be acquitted.[1187] Then Anytus steps in to save the situation for the prosecution. This experienced and shrewd lawyer-politician, who apparently spoke briefly and to the point, must have made a deep impression on the court.[1188] It seems that he refused to go into the technical details of the proceedings. Probably keeping in mind the real, although undivulged nature of the trial, he must have pointed out to the court that since the proceedings had once been started and had been permitted to progress so far, there could be only one possible verdict—a verdict of guilty.[1189] To acquit Socrates, Anytus probably contended, would only make matters worse; for Socrates then could continue with his nefarious activities, claiming that he had the sanction of the law.[1190] In the light of the possible political purpose of the trial, an acquittal would be a real calamity for Anytus and his political followers: it would not only completely defeat this purpose, but actually justify Socrates and his anti-democratic views in the eyes of Athens and the whole world. It would be tantamount, at least in the opinion of Anytus, to a total defeat of the democratic restoration of 403. An acquittal under these circumstances would signify that the Athenian people through their law courts were fully in sympathy with the aristocratic or oligarchic reaction and with its most prominent intellectual leader.

It was a matter of common knowledge in Athens that Socrates had been closely associated with some of the most notorious leaders of the aristocratic or oligarchic reaction against the democratic regime. It could even be argued that he and his friends were to be blamed for the ultimate defeat of Athens in the Peloponnesian War which, aside from the nearly complete loss of the Athenian empire, resulted in the overthrow of democracy at Athens and the temporary restoration of an oligarchic regime. It is certainly not without some significance that after the restoration of the Long Walls in 393, that is, after Athens had once more secured herself against all foreign intervention by other oligarchic cities such as Sparta, the Athenian democrats should recover their courage and institute political charges against Socrates, something which they could not do under the terms of the amnesty law of 403 and which they did not dare to do while the threat of Spartan military intervention still existed.[1191] After 393, apparently it was safe once more to say the things which could not have been said with impunity during the trial in 399. If this hypothesis should prove correct, then it seems that these things were finally said by Polycrates in his κατηγορία Σωκράτους.

It is interesting to observe the many but somewhat unconvincing attempts of the Socratic apologists to absolve Socrates from all suspicion of having been associated with the regime of the Thirty Tyrants. In Plato's *Apology* 32CD, Socrates reports the following incident: 'In the days of the oligarchy the Thirty Tyrants summoned me and four others ... bidding us to bring Leon the Salaminian from Salamis, because they wanted to put him to death.... Then and there I showed not by my words, but by my deeds, that I did not care the least about death, and that my great and only concern was not to commit an unjust and sacrilegious act. For the strong arm of that oppressive power did not frighten me into doing something wrong. Thus ... the other four went to Salamis and fetched Leon, but I went home quietly. For this I might have lost my life....'[1192] Plato cites this incident as a kind of 'counterpart' to Socrates' conduct during the famous trial of the generals of the Arginusae in 406. While in the incident referred to in *Apology* 32CD, Socrates, for the sake of justice, defies a brutal tyrant, during the trial of 406 he defies a frenzied democracy for the same reason, even at the risk of his own life.[1193] These two accounts of Plato convey the idea that a man like Socrates must come into conflict with any form of government, be it a democracy or an oligarchy. Hence there is really no place for the true philosopher in any of the established or historically developed political regimes.[1194]

In *Memorabilia* 1.2.29–38, Xenophon speaks of a serious clash which Socrates allegedly had with Critias and some of the Thirty Tyrants. This clash, with its ensuing enmity, is an incident which is completely unknown to Plato. It originated from a ridiculous and rather sordid incident (*Memor.* 1.2.29): Socrates one day sharply reprimanded Critias for his illicit relationship with Euthydemus.[1195] As a consequence Critias is said to have hated Socrates and 'framed a law that no one should be permitted to teach the art of rhetoric,[1196] intending thereby to harm Socrates.[1197] For he was at a loss to know by what other means he could affect Socrates, except by instituting the common charge made by the people against all philosophers.[1198] In this manner he intended to prejudice him with the people.'[1199] When Socrates realized the despotic ways of the Thirty Tyrants, he observed (*Memor.* 1.2.32) 'that it seemed quite surprising ... that a man, on becoming the ruler over a city, and rendering the people fewer and impoverishing them, should neither be ashamed nor admit that he was a sorry sort of a ruler'.[1200] Naturally, Xenophon continues (*Memor.* 1.2.33), such remarks greatly displeased the Thirty Tyrants, who summoned Socrates, reminding him of the law which made it a criminal offence to engage in rhetoric. The following account is one of the rare instances of 'Socratic irony' which can be found in the *Socratica* of Xenophon (*Memor.* 1.2.33–38):[1201] Socrates, feigning complete ignorance, asked what this interdict against engaging in rhetoric actually meant, proving by his questions that it was impossible to carry out this law, very much to the embarrassment and despair of Charicles.

This whole account contains a definite parallelism to Plato's report (*Apology* 18A ff. and 19A ff.): Socrates realizes the necessity of defending himself against the old disseminators of calumnies. It is quite possible that Xenophon uses here an older text which Plato also might have known. In this text, we may speculate, the clash between Socrates and the Thirty Tyrants was occasioned by the type of rhetoric or dialectics which allegedly was practised by Socrates, while the trial of Socrates in 399 was brought on by Socrates' alleged adherence to natural philosophy. Hence this old text might have attempted to show that under an oligarchic regime Socrates came to grief because of rhetoric and dialectics, while under a democratic regime he met with death because of philosophy. This is essentially only a variation of the theme that a man like Socrates cannot survive either under an oligarchic or a democratic regime, because he does not fit into any known political form.[1202] We may even go so far as to assume that *Memorabilia* 1.2.29–38 is based on two older and different texts, one of which made Charicles, rather than Critias, the chief opponent of Socrates. The substitution of Charicles (who might be identical with the Platonic Callicles) for Critias in this older text could be considered a very subtle twist on the part of a Socratic apologist who did not want to make Critias, a former pupil of Socrates and a 'Socratic' himself, appear in an unfavourable light. Another possible explanation for this substitution would be to assume that the text used here by Xenophon tried to convey the idea that, as a disciple of Socrates and out of respect for his former teacher, Critias did not wish to deal directly with Socrates and, hence, used Charicles. This, then, would be just another 'proof' for the allegation that Socrates was the teacher of Critias and, therefore, fully responsible for the many evil deeds committed by the latter. The dialogue with Charicles also reminds us of the ironical manner in which Socrates disposes of Meletus in Plato's *Apology*. All this seems to indicate that there existed a text which not only contained a report about Socrates' being prosecuted by the Thirty Tyrants for allegedly having engaged in rhetoric and dialectics, but which also gave an account of the manner in which Socrates defended himself against this charge. Naturally, all these stories about Socrates' clashes with the Thirty Tyrants can be dismissed as fiction devised by the Socratic apologists in order to absolve Socrates from any suspicion of having been at any time on friendly terms with these men.

In the κατηγορία Polycrates had charged Socrates with having associated himself with Alcibiades and Critias.[1203] It is interesting to notice that Polycrates seems to have made a distinction between these two men. According to the report of Xenophon (*Memor*, 1.2.12 ff.), Critias was called by Polycrates 'the most avaricious and violent', while Alcibiades was referred to as 'the most intemperate, insolent and turbulent'. Libanius (92.15), on the other hand, refers to the many sacrilegious acts of Alcibiades,[1204] as well as to the 'anti-democratic deeds' of Critias.[1205] But both Xenophon (*Memor*. 1.2.12) and Libanius (chaps. 136 ff.) agree that Polycrates had been justified in claiming that Alcibiades and Critias had inflicted a great many evils on the city. Hence it is not surprising that the Socratics should be most eager to absolve Socrates from all blame for the treasonable and sacrilegious conduct of Alcibiades in particular. This is done by Xenophon in *Memorabilia* 1.2.24–28, 1.2.39, and 1.2.48, as well as by Aeschines,[1206] Antisthenes,[1207] and Plato.[1208] Without doubt, the whole 'Alcibiades literature', of which the Platonic and probably also the Xenophontean *Symposium*[1209] are just two instances, is essentially a literary reaction against the common belief, also manifest in the κατηγορία of Polycrates, that Socrates must be held responsible for the much advertised depravities of Alcibiades. The 'Alcibiades literature', on the whole, far from denying Socrates' close association with Alcibiades, stresses the argument that Alcibiades remained a good man as long as he was under the influence of Socrates: 'I know that [Alcibiades] practised self-control,' Xenophon maintains (*Memor*. 1.2.18), 'as long as [he was] associated with Socrates, and this not from fear of being fined or beaten, but from a persuasion that this was the most excellent manner of conduct.'

In the *Gorgias* (519A) Plato absolves Alcibiades of the charge that he had been the cause of many evils which befell the city of Athens. He points out that these evils were not so much occasioned by the conduct of Alcibiades, but rather were the result of the pernicious policies of Themistocles, Cimon, and Pericles, who 'filled the city full of harbours, docks, walls, revenues and the like, but left no room for justice and temperance'.[1210] Likewise apologetic is the famous passage in Plato's *Symposium* (216A ff.), where Alcibiades openly concedes Socrates' restraining effects upon him: 'But when I leave his presence the love of popularity and sensation always gets the better of me' (*Symposium* 216BC).[1211]

For his apologetic *Socratica* Plato, however, seems to have used the Alcibiades theme less than, for instance, Euclides, Antisthenes, and Aeschines. The two dialogues entitled *Alcibiades* and erroneously ascribed to Plato, on the other hand, are not related to the Polycratean κατηγορία Σωκράτους. *Alcibiades I* and *Alcibiades II* were written considerably later than 393/2 by some unknown author or authors who, while trying to imitate Plato, no longer understood the particular historical circumstances to which the original 'Alcibiades literature' owed its origin.[1212] The Platonic *Symposium*, although it could not have been composed before 385, however, is still part of this 'Alcibiades literature'. When composing his *Symposium*, Plato might have faced the following situation: In order to exonerate Socrates of the charge that he had been responsible for the villainy of Alcibiades, some of the other Socratics possibly painted Alcibiades and his character in the blackest of colours, implying thereby that a man of such vices could never have been under the influence of Socrates.[1213] While he refutes the charges of Polycrates, Plato nevertheless wishes to do justice to Alcibiades. Hence he does not deny Socrates' association with Alcibiades. On the contrary, he shows that Alcibiades was none the worse for this association and that, as long as he was in the company of Socrates and under his influence, he was primarily a tempestuous youth of high-soaring ideas and ideals.

Antisthenes,[1214] Aeschines,[1215] and Euclides[1216] all wrote dialogues entitled *Alcibiades*. Antisthenes' dialogue probably also recounted the many outstanding physical and intellectual traits of Alcibiades and how, despite the efforts of Socrates, he became depraved through bad company and easy success. Of this Antisthenian dialogue we possess five references: one by Satyrus (Athenaeus, *Deipnosophistae* 5.220);[1217] two by Herodicus the Cratetean in his Πρὸς τὸν Φιλοσωκράτην (Athenaeus, *loc. cit.*, *Antisth. frag.* 1); one by Plutarch in his *Alcibiades* (chap. 1); and one each by Proclus (*Comment. in Plat. Alcibiad. I*, edit. Creuzer, 114) and Olympiodorus (*Comment. in Plat. Alcibiad. I*, edit. Creuzer, 28). It is quite possible, as H. Dittmar has pointed out, that Antisthenes discussed the Alcibiades problem also in one of his two dialogues entitled *Cyrus*.[1218] The general tenor of the Antisthenian 'Alcibiades theme', as far as it can be reconstructed from the surviving fragments and the contexts in which these fragments are found, is probably the following: The severe and merciless criticism to which Alcibiades is being subjected by Antisthenes makes it quite clear that Antisthenes wishes to demonstrate that despite Socrates' many efforts, Alcibiades remained a παράνομος (a 'lawless person').[1219] He was devoid of all ἄσκησις and on account of his lawlessness and lack of restraint caused Athens a great many evils. Hence the underlying purpose of the Antisthenian *Alcibiades* is above all to absolve Socrates of the blame of having corrupted Alcibiades and thereby contributing to the downfall of Athens. This apologetic tendency is undoubtedly motivated by the charges made by Polycrates in his κατηγορία Σωκράτους.[1220]

The *Alcibiades* of Aeschines,[1221] it should be remembered, probably constitutes the source for the Pseudo-Platonic *Alcibiades I*,[1222] as well as for some passages in Xenophon's *Memorabilia* 4.2.1–40,[1223] and perhaps *ibid.* at 1.2.24–26. This dialogue of Aeschines characterizes Alcibiades as a young man full of conceit. Conscious of his noble descent, wealth, and good looks, Alcibiades believes that he does not need either ἐπιμέλεια ἑαυτοῦ, or ἐπιστήμη, or ἀρετή. Neither does he recognize any authority. According to Aelius Aristides, who in this is under the influence of Aeschines, Socrates seems to be the only person who can handle Alcibiades.[1224] The characterization of Alcibiades by Xenophon on the whole seems to coincide with that found in the *Alcibiades* of Aeschines. This would suggest that Xenophon relies here on Aeschines. The *Alcibiades* of Aeschines likewise appears to have been occasioned by the pamphlet of Polycrates, who had charged Socrates with having corrupted Alcibiades, the despoiler of Athens. Hence it is primarily an apologetic work, written probably between 392 and 390. A fine point in Aeschines' *Alcibiades* is the fact that Socrates does not denounce here the Athenian statesmen. In this Aeschines differs radically from the author of *Alcibiades I* and from Plato's *Gorgias*. It seems that Aeschines wishes to avoid the impression that Socrates had ever deprecated Athenian democratic institutions or Athenian democratic leaders, as Polycrates had charged him. This alone should lend support to our contention that the *Alcibiades* of Aeschines is an apologetic work occasioned by the κατηγορία Σωκράτους of Polycrates. Thus Aeschines, although he concedes that Themistocles lacked 'political virtue', insists that he possessed the 'art of governing' (ἐπιστήμη πολιτική). This statement might also be an attack on the *Gorgias*, in which Plato denies that politicians possess political virtue and the 'art of governing'. Hence it appears that the Platonic *Gorgias*, which is likewise a rejoinder to the Polycratean pamphlet, was written between 392 and 390, that is, somewhat earlier than the *Alcibiades* of Aeschines. There might also be a close connection between Plato's *Meno* and Aeschines' *Alcibiades* in that both dialogues stress the importance of the θεία μοῖρα.[1225]

It may be surmised, therefore, that the *Alcibiades* dialogues of Euclides, Antisthenes, and Aeschines, which are probably the beginning of the 'Alcibiades literature', were written in an apologetic spirit. They were intended, it seems, to absolve Socrates from the charge that as the teacher and associate of Alcibiades, he was primarily responsible for the evil deeds of his pupil. The dialogue *Alcibiades* of Aeschines,[1226] which, as Diogenes Laertius insists (2.61), is under the influence of the Antisthenian *Alcibiades*, depicts Alcibiades as a youth of burning and ruthless ambition who, by taking advantage of his noble birth, physical beauty, intelligence, and wealth, aspires to be the leader of the whole Hellenic world. Apparently he hopes to excel some day his model, Themistocles.[1227] Socrates shows Alcibiades the vanity and foolishness of his ideas. The political success of Themistocles, Socrates insists, was the result of strict self-discipline, virtue, and diligence.[1228] Originally, to be sure, Themistocles was fond of leading a disorderly and dissipated life. In consequence, his father Neocles disinherited him. But suddenly he became inflamed with the desire to become an outstanding statesman, and, due to his incessant efforts to master himself, he fulfilled his ambition when he became instrumental in turning back the Persian invader at Salamis. Socrates apparently continues his discussion with Alcibiades by asking the latter what particular qualifications he possesses, on the strength of which he could dare to compare himself to Themistocles. Alcibiades, forced to admit that he was lacking in all those virtues which had made Themistocles a great man, tearfully begs Socrates to show him the road to virtue and excellence. Socrates, who seems to be merely reporting this interview with Alcibiades, then goes on assuring his audience that it is not a particular talent of his, but rather divine providence which enables him to exert a momentary influence over Alcibiades. The last lines of this dialogue, which have been preserved read: 'Although I do not possess any special knowledge (μάθημα) which might be useful to anyone . . . I am of the conviction that I could reform Alcibiades through my affection for him (διὰ τὸν ἐρᾶν) and through associating with him constantly.'[1229]

According to Aeschines, Socrates possesses no particular knowledge or art which he could impart. Hence he is not really a philosopher, sophist, or teacher, least of all the teacher of Alcibiades, but rather an 'inspired man' whose notions are prompted by his love for people. In Aeschines (*frag.* 3, Krauss), Socrates states: 'Had I imagined I could benefit him [*scil.*, Alcibiades] by any τέχνη, I should certainly plead guilty of gross folly. But in point of fact, I supposed this advantage over Alcibiades had been given me by Providence (θεία μοῖρα), and there is no reason why one should marvel at this.' In the dialogue *Alcibiades I* (105DE and *ibid.* at 124C), which to some extent is dependent on the *Alcibiades* of Aeschines and, hence, on the *Alcibiades* of Antisthenes, Socrates informs the young Alcibiades that the latter would never attain to his ambitious goal without his aid. And when Socrates insists (105A) that in his opinion Alcibiades, if faced with the alternative of either changing his way of life or dying, would prefer to die, we are strongly reminded of Xenophon (*Memor.* 1.2.16): 'I believe that, had God granted them [*scil.*, Alcibiades and Critias] the choice between a life such as Socrates lived, and death, they would have preferred to die.'

The Political Aspects of the Socratic Problem

It may be assumed, therefore, that both the *Alcibiades I* and *Memorabilia* 1.2.16, rely on some Antisthenian tradition.[1230]

The two dialogues *Alcibiades*, ascribed to Antisthenes and Aeschines respectively, are really a conversation between Alcibiades and Socrates reported by the latter, who wishes to describe the nature of his personal contacts with Alcibiades. In the Antisthenian *Alcibiades* this conversation between Alcibiades and Socrates takes the form of a severe censure of Alcibiades,[1231] while the Aeschinean *Alcibiades* attempts to illustrate Socrates' purpose for associating with Alcibiades as well as the effects he had upon the latter. We encounter here once more the Socratic-apologetic formula that, as long as Alcibiades had listened to the advice of Socrates, he behaved wisely. The apologist seems to conclude that the influence of Socrates over Alcibiades was of short duration, because after awhile the latter apparently avoided the company of Socrates.[1232] But Socrates must not be blamed for this.[1233] Hence the *Alcibiades* or *Symposia* literature of the Socratics is to be primarily understood as a particular aspect of the general apologetic *Socratica*.[1234] Isocrates (*Busiris* 5) seems to offer an explanation for the apologetic trend of the *Alcibiades* literature when he rebukes Polycrates for having made it his purpose to incriminate Socrates: 'You made Alcibiades his pupil who, as far as anyone knows, was never taught by Socrates. But all people would agree that Alcibiades by far excelled his contemporaries. If the dead had the power of judging what has been said about them, Socrates would be grateful to you for your accusation as he would to anyone who has tried to eulogize him. . . .'[1235]

It is most surprising, therefore, that, barring a short and rather unpleasant reference,[1236] the Xenophontean *Memorabilia* do not make a direct reference to the Alcibiades theme, although one would expect this from Xenophon more than from anyone else. Perhaps *Memorabilia* 3.7.1–9 furnish an explanation for this rather unusual omission. This account contains a dialogue between Socrates and Charmides, in which the former encourages the timid but conceited Charmides to enter politics. Among the arguments advanced here by Socrates we find no less than three which probably are taken from some older *Alcibiades* dialogues.[1237] Hence in *Memorabilia* 3.7.1–9, Xenophon seems to be under the influence of what might be the earliest Socratic 'Alcibiades tradition'. The only innovation by Xenophon is his substitution of Charmides for Alcibiades. The reason for this substitution is not very difficult to guess: since Polycrates had charged Socrates with having associated with Alcibiades, Xenophon tries to exonerate Socrates by simply omitting in the *Memorabilia* all overt references to Alcibiades or to a conversation of Socrates with Alcibiades.[1238] In so doing he attempts to create the impression that Socrates never associated with Alcibiades, inferring thereby that the accusation of Polycrates was without foundation. The same may be said about the Xenophontean *Symposium*, where

The Political Aspects of the Socratic Problem

apparently for the identical reason Xenophon substitutes Charmides for Alcibiades.[1239] A third substitution may be detected in *Memorabilia* 4.2.1–40, where Euthydemus takes the place of Alcibiades.[1240] Behind the Euthydemus of *Memorabilia* 4.2.1–10, we may detect not only Alcibiades, but also some other person who defies identification. Why Xenophon should choose Charmides and Euthydemus as substitutes for Alcibiades cannot be explained, unless we concede that these two men had certain character traits in common with Alcibiades.[1241]

In any event, the conspicuous absence of the name Alcibiades in the Xenophontean *Memorabilia* 1.3.1–4.8.11 and the *Symposium* is significant. It can satisfactorily be explained only in the light of Xenophon's effort to avoid mentioning together Socrates and Alcibiades. Hence the Alcibiades issue, which might have been raised first by Polycrates, is treated by Xenophon in the most radical as well as most naïve manner: Alcibiades is simply spirited away.

In *Memorabilia* 1.2.12–39, which, as has been shown, is part of an originally separate and independent Socratic *Apology*, Xenophon concedes, however, that Alcibiades at one time had been seeking the company of Socrates: but he denies most emphatically that there ever existed a real intimacy between the two. According to Xenophon (*Memor.* 1.2.15), Alcibiades associated with Socrates merely in order to 'become without rival in the art of speech and action'. Soon, however, he 'deserted Socrates and engaged in politics, but for which [he] might never have sought his company' (*Memor.* 1.2.16).[1242] As long as he was 'associated with Socrates, [he] was able, through the example of Socrates, to maintain mastery over [his] evil inclinations'; but after departing from him 'he grew neglectful of the duty which he owed himself'.[1243] 'What wonder that [he] became headstrong, particularly since [he was] away from Socrates for so long a time' (*Memor.* 1.2.25). 'And then, if [he] did anything wrong, how can the accuser blame Socrates for it? But for the fact that in early days, when [he was] young ... the same Socrates kept [him] modest and well-behaved, not one word of praise is uttered by the accuser for all this' (*Memor.* 1.2.26). Hence 'it cannot be said of ... Alcibiades that [he] associated with Socrates because [he] found him pleasing. ...' (*Memor.* 1.2.39).[1244]

This Xenophontean reference to an association of Alcibiades with Socrates in the *Memorabilia* is unique. It can be explained only by the fact that *Memorabilia* 1.1.1–1.2.64 were originally a separate essay, distinct from the remainder of the *Memorabilia*. Since *Memorabilia* 1.1.1–1.2.64 took immediate issue with Polycrates, they could not very well ignore Alcibiades or substitute another person for him.

Plato (*Apology* 33A–34C) likewise seems to take issue with the 'Alcibiades problem' when he has Socrates say: '... I have never yielded to any base compliance with those who are slanderously called my disciples or to any other person. I have no regular pupils, but if anyone likes to come and hear me while I am pursuing my mission . . . he is not excluded. . . . Anyone, whether he be rich or poor . . . [is admitted]. And whether he turns out to be a bad man or a good man, the result cannot in justice be imputed to me. For I never taught or professed to teach him anything. And if anyone says that he has ever learned or heard anything from me in private which all the world has not heard, let me tell you that he is lying.'[1245]

Among the works ascribed to Andocides we find a *Contra Alcibiadem*.[1246] Several of the issues which are touched upon in the famous debate between Nicias and Alcibiades,[1247] also appear in this speech.[1248] Thus *Contra Alcibiadem* 21, like Thucydides 6.15, records that in its attitude towards Alcibiades the Athenian populace was animated by a feeling of anger, subservience, and fear. The speech also insists (*Contra Alcibiadem* 16) that Alcibiades is a man who 'refuses to let himself be considered the equal of, or only slightly superior to, his fellow Athenians', while in the account of Thucydides (6.16), Alcibiades is called 'a man proud of his position,' who 'refuses to be on an equality with the rest of his fellow citizens'. And in both the *Contra Alcibiadem* (21–22, 25–32) and in Thucydides (6.16, 6.15, 6.12), Alcibiades boasts of his splendid performances as a *choregos* and as an Olympic victor. And finally, both the author of the *Contra Alcibiadem* (24, 27) and Thucydides (6.16) definitely stress the popular conviction that Alcibiades was aiming at tyranny. Thucydides in particular (6.16) not only maintains that the people of Athens 'were hostile to him [*scil.*, Alcibiades] because they suspected that he aimed at tyranny', but also insists (6.53) that the Athenians thought of him as a second Pisistratus.

The author of the *Contra Alcibiadem* (24), who evidently is not a partisan of radical democracy,[1249] bluntly states about Alcibiades that 'this city will experience the greatest of calamities from this man, and in the future he will be held responsible for such deeds that no one will remember his former villainies'.[1250] One of the most glaring omissions in the *Contra Alcibiadem*, on the other hand, is the complete absence of any reference to the relationship of Socrates and Alcibiades. There are several likely explanations for this astounding situation: The author might have been ignorant of the many episodes in which Alcibiades was linked with Socrates—episodes which are also at the basis of the Socratic 'Alcibiades literature'. If this were so, then we may also surmise that the *Contra Alcibiadem* was composed before this literature had evolved.[1251] Or, like Xenophon and for the same reasons, the author may have made it his purpose in this instance completely to dissociate Socrates from Alcibiades, by omitting all references to the former. This, then, would also explain the curious fact that the author fails to refer to the political activities of Alcibiades which, if he were ever linked with Socrates, would seriously discredit the latter. Here, too, we apparently encounter the tradition, so common among the Socratics, that there never existed a close association of Socrates and Alcibiades, and that Socrates may not be blamed in any way for the many outrages committed by Alcibiades.

The Alcibiades theme, which seems to owe its origin to the allegation that as a teacher of Alcibiades, Socrates is fully responsible for the misdeeds of the former, essentially constitutes a vital aspect of the apologetic *Socratica*. It could even be maintained that this particular allegation was first made in an articulate and definitive manner by Polycrates. This, in turn, would also furnish us with a *tempus post quod* for the origin of the whole 'Alcibiades literature'.

The final and perhaps most difficult question connected with the political implications of the apologetic *Socratica* is this: had everything been said during the trial in 399? We know the wording and content of the official 'writ of indictment'. There is no plausible reason why the correctness of our information regarding this 'writ' should be seriously doubted. We also know that under the general terms of the amnesty law of 403 it was not possible, at least not in 399, to institute political charges against Socrates. Anytus had been one of the chief promoters of this amnesty law, and the same Anytus was also the principal force behind the prosecution of Socrates. It is reasonable to assume, therefore, that Anytus would painstakingly abide by the terms of his own amnesty law. The mere fact that the official 'writ of indictment' does not refer to any 'political crimes' of Socrates in itself means nothing. There is always the possibility that the 'writ of indictment', as it was probably read at the opening of the trial and sworn to by Meletus, was merely a 'token indictment'. This would also explain why Xenophon (*Memor*. 1.2.62–64) could insist that 'the indictment contained no charge making a death sentence mandatory', and why Anytus, according to Plato (*Apology* 29C), brushes aside all legal technicalities or procedural niceties and contends during the trial that Socrates must be punished by death.[1252] But perhaps neither Xenophon nor Plato realized that the only thing to be expected of a brave man defending himself against trumpery charges is just that tone of humorous condescension and irony which Plato apparently reproduced so magnificently, but which probably was not wholly understood in its true significance. This would also shed an entirely novel light upon the so-called Socratic irony which characterizes the Platonic Socrates,[1253] particularly as regards the special circumstances to which it owes its origin.

Neither can we attach too much significance to the fact that Socrates' trial was delayed until the fourth year after the expulsion of the Thirty Tyrants and the restoration of democracy in Athens.[1254] The revolution and counter-revolution of 404/3 had brought the ordinary work of the Athenian law courts into confusion if not to a complete standstill. By the amnesty law or Act of Oblivion of the year 403[1255] all acts committed prior to the summer of 403, that is, prior to the nomination of Euclides to the archonship, were precluded from serving as grounds for criminal prosecution.[1256] The Athenian magistrates had to pledge themselves not to receive any indictment founded on any fact prior to the archonship of Euclides, except charges made against the Thirty Tyrants, the Eleven, the Ten of the Piraeus, and certain individuals expressly excluded from the amnesty.[1257] The heliastic dicasts likewise had to take an annual oath: 'I shall not remember past wrongs, neither shall I abet anyone else who should remember these past wrongs.'[1258] On the proposal of Archinus, one of the close associates of Thrasybulus, a further law was enacted granting every defendant a special motion for dismissal of all proceedings on the grounds that the action was founded on acts committed prior to the archonship of Euclides.[1259]

When democracy was reinstated and the old ordinances or laws of Dracon and Solon were once more restored, the whole body of Attic laws had to be thoroughly revised and codified. The special commission appointed for this purpose did not complete its task, until some time afterwards. It was also soon discovered that some of the old laws would be incompatible with the terms of the general amnesty law which had just been passed. On the proposal of Tisamenus a law was enacted to revise the laws of Dracon and Solon. A body composed of the Five Hundred (or 'Councilmen') and five hundred *Nomothetae* was convened in order to review both the ancient laws and the newly proposed decrees. All the laws thus approved were to be inscribed on the walls of the *Stoa Poikele*. The Areopagus was enjoined to see that they were strictly observed.[1260] Finally, two concluding laws were enacted: the first of these laws forbade the magistrates to act upon, or permit to be acted upon, any law not among those recently published;[1261] the second law provided that all legal transactions which had taken place under the 'old democracy' should be held valid, while all those which had been passed under the Thirty Tyrants were formally annulled.[1262]

In the light of the general amnesty law of 403 and the subsequent legal reforms, it is somewhat surprising that the κατηγορία Σωκράτους of Polycrates should bristle with political charges. Here Socrates is made to appear the vicious despoiler of Athenian democracy who, together with his friends and associates, had not only planned, but brought about the downfall of the Athenian democratic regime in 404. It seems, therefore, that the Late Sophists, since they were not acting in any official capacity, did not consider themselves bound by the amnesty law of 403. Hence they could openly say all the things which the prosecutors could not mention during the official trial. It is safe to assume that Anytus and his associates still remembered the fate of 'one of those who had participated in the restoration [of democracy]. When the latter began to raise complaints in violation of the terms of the amnesty law,' according to Aristotle, 'Archinus summoned him before the Council and persuaded the councilmen to have him put to death without trial.

The Political Aspects of the Socratic Problem

He achieved this by telling the councilmen that now was the moment when they must show whether they were willing to save democracy and to live up to their oaths. For if they were going to let this man off, they would encourage others to do the same thing. But if they executed him, they would set a warning example. This was what actually happened. For when he had been put to death, no one ever dared to violate the amnesty law again.'[1263]

The political charges made by Polycrates were undoubtedly of a very serious nature, the more so, if the materials used by him in the formulation of his charges were of Socratic and not—what they in fact seem to be—of Antisthenian-Cynic origin. It appears that this is the crux of the whole problem arising from the literary controversy between Polycrates and Xenophon. Undoubtedly, some of the Polycratean charges or allegations, as well as certain Xenophontean rebuttals, are based on what seem to be predominantly Antisthenian sources. But in itself this does not prove that the Antisthenian materials used both by Polycrates and Xenophon are in themselves 'un-Socratic', or that they are in conflict with the true teachings of Socrates, whatever they may have been. Antisthenes and his immediate followers might very well have been relatively faithful disciples of Socrates, even should we have to admit that they exaggerated some of the views held by Socrates by carrying them to extreme conclusions or radical applications which go far beyond what Socrates might ever have envisioned. But then again, we must always bear in mind that Antisthenes and probably Socrates were self-appointed social reformers. And social reformers, in their effort to criticize or condemn some of the existing social, moral, political, or legal institutions, are prone to be looked upon by their contemporaries as revolutionaries and, hence, 'despoilers' of the established social order.

If the political charges made by Polycrates were true—and history seems to support them to some extent—then we would have to concede that the trial and particularly the literary controversy over Socrates was not so much a *Philosophenstreit*, but above all an incident in the long and bitter struggle between the aristocratic-oligarchic partisans and the democratic party at Athens. The idea that Socrates' trial of 399 was a political trial also seems to find some support in the hint given by Anytus (Plato, *Meno* 95A) that Socrates will suffer one day for 'speaking ill of the people'.[1264] It might be conjectured that this remark refers to Socrates' contempt for the democratic institutions of Athens. The evidence of Plato's *Apology*, on the other hand, seems to be against the assumption that the trial of Socrates was a political trial. Here Socrates is made repeatedly to state that he is being prosecuted because of a long-standing popular prejudice against him as a philosopher or sophist. It could be argued, therefore, that if the real offence had been $\mu\iota\sigma o\delta\eta\mu\acute{\iota}\alpha$, Socrates would not have insisted that impiety was the real ground of his prosecution. Like Anytus, Meletus, and Lycon, who were restrained

The Political Aspects of the Socratic Problem

from turning the trial of Socrates into a political affair by the Act of Oblivion of 403, so also Plato might have had reasons of his own for avoiding all references to the political nature of Socrates' prosecution.[1265]

When the aristocratic-oligarchic party lost out to the democratic forces in May of 403, Socrates, who was probably considered one of the most influential intellectual leaders of the aristocrats, was hopelessly doomed. Perhaps the questions connected with the accusations of Polycrates could best be solved in the following manner: the general Polycratean charge that Socrates had planned and (perhaps through the instrumentality of his friends, disciples, followers, or partisans) actually brought about the fall of the Athenian democracy in 404, on the whole could very well have been based on historical fact.[1266] Plutarch (*Cato* 23) might possibly reflect the political implications of the whole Socratic controversy when he reports that Cato the Elder had maintained that 'Socrates was a mighty prattler who attempted, to the best of his ability, to become the tyrant [oligarchic leader?] of his city by abolishing its [democratic?] customs and by inducing his fellow citizens to hold opinions which were contrary to the established laws.'[1267] But the various instances of particular substantiation of this general charge by Polycrates, as well as the special instances which Polycrates cites in support of his 'bill of particulars', are most likely of Antisthenian origin.

Even assuming that this general Polycratean charge against Socrates is historically correct, and that the materials used by Polycrates are actually Socratic, it would be naïve to attach to Socrates the epithet of 'traitor'. From the seventh century to the Roman conquest, Greek history is largely a chain of political massacres, banishments, confiscations, plottings, and counter-plottings. The 'democratic' elements in the city—the small artisans and shop-keepers, workmen and tradesmen, sailors and fishermen, in short, the humblest of craftsmen or *demiourgoi* and the whole mass of hired men who are referred to simply as *thetes* or 'doers'—suddenly had found capable leaders and organizers. Thanks to the great economic changes which Greece had undergone during the eighth and seventh centuries, these 'democratic' elements had come to realize both their social significance and their political power. From that time on the city was split into two camps or parties, the old aristocrats or oligarchs and the new 'democrats'. The oligarchs or aristocrats, who in certain Greek cities had to swear at the altar a solemn vow of eternal hatred and ferocity against the people and the popular movement, fiercely resisted the rise to power of the 'democrats' to whom the privileges of birth or wealth meant little or nothing. These party strifes and party hatreds at times assumed the form of veritable vendettas. In the midst of all these revolutions and counter-revolutions one could hear the blood-curdling cries of savage joy and merciless fury. To understand to what inhuman extremes human passions could rise in these political upheavals, one has only to read Thucydides' many accounts of

The Political Aspects of the Socratic Problem

shocking civil conflicts aggravated by foreign wars. Beginning with the latter part of the sixth century it had become the practice of Athenian aristocrats and oligarchs to seek Spartan intervention in order to gain political control or maintain themselves in power against the 'democrats'. Such conduct, at least in the eyes of antiquity, was not regarded as 'treason' in the ordinary, or should we say, modern and odious sense of the term. It was a commonly accepted and frequently applied practice in the many and bitter inner-political struggles which characterize the history of the various Hellenic city-states. Naturally, if these methods met with failure, the perpetrators of such a *coup d'état* were often ruthlessly removed by the victorious opposition, not so much as 'traitors' but as the partisans of a defeated political cause or faction upon whom all victorious opposition wreaked its deadly revenge.

A study of Athenian history and Athenian political developments should make it obvious that the city was not the only institution which made demands on the allegiance of the Athenian citizen.[1268] Long before he became a member of the city, the Athenian citizen, as a rule, had been a member of such kin organizations as the *phratria*,[1269] *genos*, *phyle*, *oikos*, or perhaps one of the many religious groups.[1270] Aside from these various and more tangible 'groupings', we also find in Attica—as elsewhere—groups, based on friendship,[1271] in which the members, on a purely voluntary basis, were held together by congeniality, similarity of interest, identity of social status, and frequently by closeness of age.[1272] The loyalty and attachment which these 'friendship groups' elicited were extremely strong.[1273] Hence it is not surprising that membership in such friendship associations was often prized above citizenship, since a man's attachment to his city was fundamentally connected with his belonging to one or several of these lesser associations.[1274] These different lesser groups to a varying degree competed not only with the city, but also with one another for the allegiance of the Athenian. At times they even exacted a loyalty from their members which was incompatible with allegiance to the city.[1275]

In the domain of concrete existence such lesser groupings, which could also be called 'clubs' or *hetaireiai*,[1276] gave definite expression to the differences of interest, conviction, education, and social, political, or economic status which separated the urban element from the rural population; the educated people from the uneducated; the enlightened man from the superstitious; the conservative thinker from the progressive or radical; the land owner from the 'lack land'; and the aristocrat from the 'democrat'.[1277] Since its earliest history there had always existed in Greece a large variety of private societies or free associations, usually of a religious, utilitarian or sentimental character. In Homeric times the most illustrious warriors, united into *hetairoi* by a special bond, considered it their duty to have the same friends and the same enemies. Later the well born and the rich banded together in *hetaireiai* or 'clubs',

The Political Aspects of the Socratic Problem

where the members not only gave each other mutual support in all difficulties, law suits, or political schemes,[1278] but also met for regular festive banquets. Aside from these 'clubs', we also find certain confraternities which originally were called *thiasoi*. They went back to pre-Homeric and perhaps even pre-Hellenic times when some people had united in order to maintain the worship of those deities which had been excluded from the official pantheon.

Some of these *hetaireiai* gradually degenerated into associations to satisfy the desire for purely material pleasures.[1279] Others, especially in ports, commercial centres, or industrial suburbs, progressively acquired an important commercial significance in the economic life of Greece, becoming what might be called forerunners of 'business-associations'. In addition, men of the same nationality, profession, or religion formed special clubs which had their own officers, 'by-laws', and regular meetings. Foreign merchants and their servants or slaves, often dressed in outlandish costumes, regularly assembled in chapels to perform their native religious cults. Philosophers followed the fashion and soon began to become 'heads of schools'; together with congenial friends or 'disciples' they segregated themselves from society, preferring the privacy of a secluded place to the *agora*, the palaestra, or the shop.

In the long and turbulent course of Athenian constitutional history some of these lesser organizations or 'clubs', particularly when they joined together for common political action, became the basis of a fundamental political division within the city of Athens, namely, the oligarchic or aristocratic faction and democratic faction.[1280] This situation, which should clearly indicate the passionate attachment of the Athenian 'party man' to his 'club' and to his political faction rather than to the city itself, is perfectly portrayed by Thucydides [3.82]: 'Throughout the whole of Greece, ... we witness political convulsions. Everywhere the democratic leaders made efforts to call in the Athenians, while the oligarchs invited the Lacedaemonians.... Particularly during war time ... occasions for calling upon them were easily supplied by those who wished to engineer a revolution. And many dreadful things befell the cities through this kind of sedition.... The cities were thus torn asunder ... by the clever cunning of their [leaders'] designs and the monstrous cruelty of their vengeance.... Reckless daring was regarded as courage and loyalty to one's friends.... Anyone who counselled avoidance of brutal measures was looked upon as a person who destroyed his party.... Kindred ties became less of a bond than a party or a club. But such associations ... are founded in opposition to the laws. The mutual basis of confidence [among these 'club members'] ... was ... by the fellowship in some act of lawlessness.... Oaths held good only as long as there was no recourse to any other action.... The cause of all these happenings was the lust for power pursued for the gratification of covetousness and ambition, and the violence of the parties contending with each other. The leaders in the cities . . . by putting forward either the political equality of the people or a moderate form of aristocracy, merely paid lip service to the common interest, while in truth they made the people their victims. And while striving by every means to obtain [their goal] . . . they . . . carried out the most dreadful deeds . . . [doing] what was pleasing to . . . their party. . . . Piety was alien to either party. Those who succeeded in effecting some vile purpose under some fair pretext were the more highly spoken of. . . . In this manner all kinds of villainy resulted from these seditions throughout Greece.'

The words of Thucydides should make it sufficiently clear that at Athens, as elsewhere, intense party loyalty was incompatible with 'patriotism'.[1281] Despite grave and even deadly dangers from without, civil dispute and party strife did not cease within the city. On the contrary, whenever an hostile attack upon a city is recorded by the historians, there is nearly always some allusion to a faction within the city walls which is preparing to betray the city to the enemy in order to gain political control over the city, if necessary with the assistance of the invader.[1282] Even men who had no political injury or grudge to avenge, armed themselves against their native city simply from sympathy with the institutions of another city; and political factions would rather see the loss of national independence than the triumph of the opposing faction. For did not Brasides contend that submission to the opposite political party 'is more grievous than foreign domination'?[1283] In the light of these bitter factional disputes and the subsequent recriminations, the notion of the city or the concept of patriotism necessarily must have had a particular meaning for any politically interested or politically ambitious Athenian. The leaders no less than the partisans of either the democratic or oligarchic party seem to have been animated by fanatical partisanship rather than by patriotic loyalty or attachment to the established laws or existing constitution.[1284]

It has become an obsession with some modern historians to identify Athens with the cause of Athenian democrats. At the same time the oligarchs are denounced as philo-Laconians, anti-Athenians, or 'traitors'. If this were true, then the cause of the democrats would have to coincide with the concept of the city. Unfortunately, the evidence does not support such an assumption. The democrats, like the oligarchs, bore Athens only one kind of love—the desire to dominate it completely. When this dominion was threatened, both the democrats and the oligarchs were willing to do anything to maintain their own ascendancy: to kill or exile arbitrarily a large number of their fellow citizens who did not agree with them, or, as in the particular case of the oligarchs who were mostly in the minority, to surrender the Athenian empire and betray the city to Sparta or any foreign power that might assist them in the realization of their political ambitions. But the record of the 'democrats' is equally disconcerting. Cleisthenes, who is frequently identified with the founding of Athenian democracy, apparently was willing to surrender Athens to the Persians merely in order to maintain his political position.[1285] Phaidon, who on account of his opposition to Critias was made one of the Ten appointed to effect the reconciliation with the democrats in 403, abused his position of trust by trying to incite Sparta anew against Athens. When he failed in his plot, he attempted to hire mercenaries against his own city.[1286] It would also be difficult to maintain that such 'democrats' as Callixenus, the instigator in the condemnation of the generals of the Arginusae; Archedemus, who was likewise connected with these infamous proceedings; Cleigenes (Cleisthenes); Epigenes; or Demophantus (Demophanes)—all of which in their democratic fervour equalled the perfidy of the Thirty Tyrants— were Athenian patriots.[1287]

Thus it could be maintained that the period of Socrates' political activities—open or clandestine—on the whole was one of far-reaching internal disturbances, when partisanship frequently amounted to nothing less than betrayal of the city. Thucydides (2.65) seems to support this view when he records that the Athenians 'thought of their private gain and private ambitions and, hence, adopted evil measures towards themselves and their allies. These measures, if successful, led to honour and benefit of individuals, but if they failed, proved detrimental to the city. . . .' Each party, ignoring the needs and interests of the city, exploited its political power for its own ends and tried to crush ruthlessly all opposition, thereby working towards the ruin of the city. It is, indeed, rather difficult to find a prominent Athenian politician of this period whose political actions were not motivated by partisanship or loyalty to some faction within the city. Few, indeed, were those men whose political conduct is consistent with our notion of patriotism and patriotic loyalty; and few men would have hesitated to collaborate with a foreign enemy if this promised political domination over the city and defeat of their political opponents. Apparently they did not let any kind of patriotic attachment to the city get in the way of their partisan ambitions. To them the city was primarily a place of social, cultural, political, or economic opportunity, but not an object of a deeply felt loyalty or devotion. Political parties, like 'clubs', on the other hand, held for the Greek a different meaning. Believing that his private interests could be successfully pursued only with other people of similar social, cultural, political, or economic conviction, he identified, at least during the time of Socrates, his personal ambitions and outlook with the cause espoused by either the democrats or oligarchs. Hence it came about that his most abiding loyalties belonged to one of these two factions[1288] which, in turn, flourished on mutual and unbounded hatred of each other. And it was exactly this hatred of the rival party that enabled each faction to exercise and maintain a profound and abiding hold over its members.

The Political Aspects of the Socratic Problem

In the light of what has just been said about the fanatical party politics which constantly kept Athens in a state of political convulsion, the trial and condemnation of Socrates could very well have been engineered by Socrates' political enemies—the democrats—who in this merely wished to avenge themselves on a detested oligarch for what they had to suffer under the regime of the Thirty Tyrants. Hence the trial of Socrates might be regarded as a 'political trial',[1289] or to be more precise, a 'partisan trial', although the partisans of the restored democracy apparently succeeded in veiling the true purpose or nature of these proceedings by resorting to some innocuous looking charges. We have but to remember the abominable conduct of such 'democrats' as Callixenus or Archedemus, who, during the trial of the generals of the Arginusae, under the pretext of punishing alleged acts 'in dereliction of a humanitarian duty', gave vent to their fierce partisan hatreds by putting to death these generals in what seems to be a complete disregard for the established laws.[1290] No wonder that Socrates should object to such methods, probably not so much because they were in violation of the laws, but perhaps because as a partisan of the same political group to which these generals belonged,[1291] he felt that their cause was also his own.[1292] Socrates had been at the time 'president' of the popular assembly, or at least a member of the Council. He actually attempted at the last minute to snatch a political victim from the fanatical democrats. In his extreme intractability he incurred the displeasure of the 'sovereign people'—the democratic faction then in power. The people, enraged against him, demanded that anyone who stood out against the declared 'will of the people' should be dealt with as a traitor. They probably felt that by trying to set himself above the will of the people, he displayed his utter contempt for the people ($\mu\iota\sigma o\delta\eta\mu i\alpha$) and for the democratic institutions of Athens.[1293] No wonder that subsequently he should be suspected of $\mu\iota\sigma o\delta\eta\mu i\alpha$ and of harbouring anti-democratic or oligarchic sentiments. For his protest in 406 might have been more a manifestation of partisan loyalty than the profession of his attachment to strict legality. It might not be too far-fetched to suspect, therefore, that the same democratic partisan motives were also behind the proceedings against Socrates in 399, which would then have to be considered merely another instance of the many acts of monstrous and cruel revenge which, whenever possible, the political party in power constantly tried to wreak upon the other party or parties and their individual members.[1294] Obviously, the tactics employed in such practices completely ignored all those considerations which are commonly referred to as law, justice, and plain fairness. Such 'technicalities' had to give way before a fanatical attachment to 'partisan politics' and abject party loyalty which seemed to thrive on unreasonable hatred and merciless persecution of the dissenter.

Under the circumstances we can only deplore that so little may be

The Political Aspects of the Socratic Problem

regarded as established fact about the historical trial of Socrates. Recently two scholars of eminence, by adducing rather weighty evidence, have contended that Socrates never defended himself at all[1295]—a gesture which would lend some support to the theory that the whole trial was a 'partisan affair'. For in the face of partisan prejudice and partisan fury it is useless, if not undignified, to make a spectacle of oneself[1296] by putting up a defence when the outcome of the trial is a foregone conclusion. The argument has been made that in Plato's *Gorgias* (486AB), Callicles, in a prophetic mood, draws a merciless, if imaginary, portrait of Socrates' utter helplessness when, one day, he will be summoned into court: he will become dazed and stand there with his mouth wide open, not knowing what to say—and so be condemned.[1297] Somewhat later, in the same dialogue (526E–527A), Socrates, after repeating phrase after phrase the former argument of Callicles, responds by depicting the helplessness of Callicles before the Judges of the Dead.[1298] In the light of this evidence it has been claimed that it would be difficult to maintain the historicity of Plato's *Apology*. But more than that, by way of direct evidence, there is also the explicit statement of Maximus of Tyre that Socrates did not defend himself, and 'kept silent without faltering'.[1299] Perhaps the account of Maximus is true; knowing that his implacable political opponents and enemies were in full control of the situation, and that he could expect neither justice nor mercy in this bitter political strife, Socrates, in a spirit of defiance, preferred to remain silent rather than to humble himself by pleading in his own behalf, only to be shouted down or ridiculed.[1300]

In support of the contention that Socrates did not defend himself in court, we may also adduce the astonishingly large number of widely different 'speeches' and 'apologies' credited to Socrates or devised by others for Socrates at the time of his trial, or composed in his behalf at a later date. This might indicate that there was never a real speech by Socrates. The 'Apology of Socrates' finally became a universal school theme for fledgling rhetoricians, and even special rules were set up as to how it should be conducted properly.[1301] Xenophon (*Defence* 1) implies that at the time he wrote his *Defence* there existed already several apologies of Socrates; and Maximus of Tyre reports that in his time a great many apologies of Socrates were still being written (*Oratio* 1.1). The continued appearance of a host of Socratic apologies in itself would suggest that there never existed a defence offered by Socrates himself during his official trial in the year 399. The striking diversity, not only of manner, but also of content, in the surviving apologies of Socrates would be difficult to explain if Socrates had actually made a sustained speech in his own defence.

A detailed discussion of the political background of the Socratic controversy would require a separate historical study and is, therefore, outside the particular scope of this book. This much, however, may

The Political Aspects of the Socratic Problem

be suggested here: the *historical* Socrates could very well have been primarily a *political* rather than a *philosophical* figure in the cultural and political life of Athens.[1302] For does not Socrates himself admit (Plato, *Gorgias* 521D): 'I think that I am the only or almost the only Athenian living who practises the true art of politics. I am the only politician of my time. . . . But when I speak my words are not uttered with any view of gaining favour. . . . I look to what is best and not to what is most pleasant. . . .' In the opinion of his contemporaries Socrates might have been above all a partisan, if not actually one of the intellectual leaders of the aristocratic-oligarchic reaction or party[1303] which since the days of Isagoras (508/7) had been struggling against the democratic reforms of Cleisthenes and their subsequent development under Ephialtes, Pericles, Cleon, Eucrates, Hyperbolus, Peisander, Callicrates, and Cleophon. In this struggle the oligarchs sought the armed intervention of Sparta several times in order to gain or retain the political control in Athens. Socrates, it seems, sympathized with the aristocratic-oligarchic party where he also found the majority of his friends and followers.[1304] The report of Diogenes Laertius (2.106 and 3.6), therefore, contains some interesting information: 'Hermodorus tells us that after the death of Socrates, Plato and the other philosophers [probably the 'Socratics'], being alarmed over the cruelty of the tyrants, came to him [*scil.*, Euclides of Megara].' The 'tyrants' could be the leaders of the restored 'radical democracy' who apparently assumed a threatening attitude toward the Socratics, whom they considered partisans of the oligarchic reaction. The account of Hermodorus would indicate, therefore, that the Socratics left Athens as 'political refugees', and that at the basis of the whole Socratic problem was a serious political issue which had all the ugly features of a bitter partisan struggle.

After the famous trial of 399, which might have been a political trial, the partisans of the aristocratic-oligarchic party and those of the democratic party opened what could be called a literary campaign over Socrates. The 'oligarchs' apparently started this literary controversy with a flood of political pamphlets which soon turned into a flood of Socratic apologies; while the democratic partisans, represented by the Late Sophists and Polycrates in particular, replied by apparently calling Socrates a 'traitor' who had planned and heavily contributed to the ultimate defeat of Athens, as well as to the establishment of an oligarchic regime under the rule of the Thirty Tyrants, who were protected and supported by a Spartan army garrisoned at Athens. The aristocratic-oligarchic partisans, among them Plato,[1305] Xenophon, Aeschines, and perhaps even Antisthenes,[1306] came to the literary defence of Socrates. Being probably unable to refute the political charges made by the democrats, they based their apologetics on the allegation that personally Socrates had been the most excellent and most virtuous man who in the interest of his fellow citizens had spent his whole life searching after

The Political Aspects of the Socratic Problem

philosophical truths and the just and good life. But the thesis which sees in Socrates primarily a political rather than a philosophical figure does not preclude the possibility that, like so many of his prominent contemporaries, he was also interested in philosophical theories and issues. We have only to remember Pericles, who, although he was an eminent statesman or 'politician', also displayed a deep concern with philosophy and philosophical speculation, as evidenced by the fact that he kept company with such men as Anaxagoras, Damonides of Oa, and possibly Protagoras.

The inability of the Socratic apologists to refute the political charges made by the democrats becomes especially noticeable with Xenophon whose method of dealing with the Polycratean 'accusations', in particular, often strikes the reader as being an admission of their foundation in fact in each case. Close analysis will divulge that he merely contests the malicious twist given to these facts and the inferences drawn from them, but never really denies the facts as such. Xenophon would not have admitted these things, we may surmise, unless they were actual facts too commonly known to be denied outright.

By acting primarily as Socrates' 'character witnesses',[1307] these apologists might gradually have turned the 'politician' Socrates into a lofty and idealistic philosopher. To consider Socrates primarily a politician, however, seems to ignore the 'testimony' of the comic poets of the latter half of the fifth century.[1308] The *Clouds* of Aristophanes was written about 424/3, but the version which has come down to us is apparently a later revision of the original play which Plato knew and took issue with in his *Apology* (19B). We may assume that, in the place of the lengthy quasi-philosophical discussion between the δίκαιος λόγος and the ἄδικος λόγος (*Clouds* 889-1104), there stood originally a passage in which Socrates, in the best demagogical tradition, tried to make the worse cause appear to be the better.[1309] Also in 424/3, Ameipsias composed his *Konnos*, in which Socrates is called the most outstanding man by a few (perhaps by the partisans of the aristocratic-oligarchic party?) and the greatest living fool by many people (perhaps by the partisans of the democratic party?). Two years later (421), Eupolis, in his *Flatterers*, introduces Socrates as a beggarly prattler who concerns himself about everyone and everything except his own affairs (a characteristic trait of the Cynics and of all idealistic social or political reformers). Unlike Aristophanes, Ameipsias and Eupolis do not seem to have considered Socrates a sophist or a philosopher of nature, but rather what might be called a political or social agitator. Hence it may be assumed that the general traits of Socrates' personality, as well as his activities described in the *Konnos* or the *Flatterers* and supported by the evidence found in Plato's *Apology* 32AB, were common knowledge in Athens around 420 B.C. The testimony of Ameipsias and Eupolis, if it may at all be taken seriously, would therefore not contradict our

The Political Aspects of the Socratic Problem

contention that Socrates was primarily a political figure. In his efforts to convince people of the evils and mistakes of democracy, he possibly went about the streets of Athens, worrying more over the political happenings in Athens and their effects upon the citizens, than over his own personal affairs. In this fashion he might have become a 'public character' applauded by a few and ridiculed by the many.

This still leaves unanswered the particular problem posed by the *Clouds* of Aristophanes. We know that the physical speculations which Aristophanes ascribed to Socrates are actually those of Diogenes of Apolonia,[1310] while the discussions about the gender of words or the maxim of turning the worse argument into the better are of Protagorean origin. Hence no philosophical or speculative utterance which Aristophanes claims for Socrates is really Socratic, but originated with some other philosopher or sophist. This, in turn, would indicate that Aristophanes could not find a single philosophical statement directly attributable to Socrates; as a consequence, he had to credit him with views actually held by other thinkers. This fact in itself would to some extent likewise lend support to our thesis that Socrates was not primarily a philosopher, but rather a well known 'public character' and politician or political agitator who, as a partisan of the aristocratic-oligarchic opposition, attempted to persuade the Athenian people of the errors and alleged evils of their democratic regime. It is quite possible that Socrates, when haranguing the 'democrats', also discussed certain theoretical issues connected with the problem of 'the good life', or the life within society—problems which were also debated by contemporary philosophers and sophists. But such discussions probably were only incidental to his political activities. Thus it came about that Socrates may have acquired in the eyes of the Athenian populace the reputation of being a 'philosopher' or sophist who argued and discussed everything. And Aristophanes, in his *Clouds*, merely repeats what had become a popular, although probably unfounded belief. This would also explain why he could not attribute to Socrates any authentic philosophical teachings and, hence, had to credit him with the sayings of other philosophers. In any event, the testimony of Aristophanes, if it could be called such, by no means would disprove our contention that the historical Socrates was primarily a 'politician' rather than a 'philosopher'. The fact that in the original version of the *Clouds* of 424/3 Socrates is depicted as a haranguing demagogue or 'lawyer' engaged in making the worse cause appear to be the better, seems to be of decisive importance here. Only in a later version, which might be under the influence of the literary Socratic tradition, is he credited with being a 'philosopher' discussing the δίκαιος λόγος and the ἄδικος λόγος.[1311]

But there is another possibility of interpreting the presentation of Socrates in the *Clouds* of Aristophanes. The *phrontisterion* or 'thinking-shop' of Socrates could very well be a witty parody on a 'club' to which

Socrates belonged. This club, like so many Athenian *hetaireiai*, might have engaged in what was considered irreligious, impious, agnostic, or 'modernistic' practices. We recall that the club of the Triballi held sacrilegious feasts;[1312] and that the club of Cineas celebrated feasts on forbidden days, where the members ridiculed the traditional gods of the city and made sport of the laws of the state.[1313] The profanation of the Eleusian Mysteries,[1314] perpetrated by the club of Alcibiades (to which Socrates might have belonged), in all likelihood is also an instance of this practice of ridiculing certain accepted beliefs, standards of conduct, or institutions.[1315] The irreverent, impious, agnostic, and 'revolutionary'[1316] practices of some of these clubs, of which the *phrontisterion* is possibly only a parody, were generally known and widely discussed in Athens. The theory which sees in the Aristophantean *phrontisterion* merely a 'club' to which Socrates belonged, finds additional support in the 'rites of initiation' mentioned in *Clouds* 258 ff., where the theory is expounded that Socrates was a member of a club.

It is also interesting to note here that the Socratic tradition tries to establish the fact that Socrates was persecuted not only by the 'radical democrats' or the extreme political 'left', but also by the oligarchs or extreme political 'right'.[1317] The implication is that a man of the type of Socrates, being unable to live in harmony with either of the two extreme forms of government, cannot live under any intermediary or moderate constitution. Hence he has actually no place in any known political society. Conversely, since no existing form of political organization apparently has any use for a Socrates, Socrates should not have any use for any constitution and, hence, has the right to ignore it. This, then, the Socratics, and particularly Antisthenes might have argued, would absolve Socrates from all obligation towards the city and its laws, and by implication also absolve him from the crime of treason. Plato's *Crito*, therefore, could also be interpreted as being a rejection of this kind of 'apology' which would admit the lawlessness or 'treason' of Socrates, but would justify it under the circumstances by insisting that Socrates had no obligations whatsoever towards the existing laws or the constitution and, hence, could not infringe upon them since they were not really existing for a Socrates.

Socrates' unbending respect for the laws of the city, portrayed in the Platonic *Crito*, accords badly with the undisguised contempt for the 'administration of the laws' which he displays in the *Apology*. Here all pretence of modesty and respect is soon cast aside when he begins to address his judges in a tone of unmistakable disdain. As in the *Gorgias* (521D ff.), he is at no pains to conceal his profound contempt for them personally and for the institutions which they represent. Actually on trial for his life before a jury representing the laws of Athens—the same laws he so piously respects in the *Crito*—his demeanour would suggest that these laws or institutions are on trial before him. This is at least

The Political Aspects of the Socratic Problem

the particular twist which Plato seems to give the conduct of Socrates during the trial.

At times Plato seems to contradict the thesis that Socrates might have been primarily a 'politician' rather than a philosopher: '... I do not venture, [maintains Socrates,] to come forward in public and give political advice.... I am convinced ... that if I had engaged in politics, I would have perished long ago.... No one who opposes you and any other multitude by decrying the many deeds of lawlessness and injustice committed in the city, can save his life. He who intends to fight for what is right, if he wishes to live even for a short while, must have a private station in life and not a public one.'[1318] This passage, which might very well be an instance of Plato's irony, implies that under a democratic regime such as Athens had known after the death of Pericles, good and honest men were either excluded from active participation in government, or, if they tried to take an active part in it, were running the risk of losing their lives:[1319] '... some lofty soul born in a mean city whose policies he condemns ... has tasted how sweet and blessed a possession philosophy is, and has also seen enough of the madness of the multitude. He knows that no politician is honest. Such a philosopher may be compared to some one who has fallen among wild beasts: he will not join the wickedness of his fellow men, but neither is he able singly to resist all their fierce natures. Realizing that he would be of no use to the city or to his friends and partisans, and knowing that he would throw away his life without doing any good either to himself or to others, he holds his peace and goes his own ways. He is like one who in the driving storm ... retires under the shelter of a wall. And seeing the rest of mankind full of wickedness, he is content if only he can live his own life and be free from evil and wickedness....' The same idea reappears in Plato's (?) *Epistle* 7.330E-331A: 'When men are travelling altogether outside the path of right government and flatly refuse to move in the right path, and start giving notice to their adviser that he must leave the government alone and make no change in it under penalty of death—if such men should ever order their counsellors to pander to their wishes and desires, and to advise them in what way their object may most readily and easily be accomplished once for all, I should consider as unmanly one who accepts the duty of giving such kind of advice, and one who refuses to do so a true man.' And then Plato continues (*Epist.* 7.331CD): 'The wise man should go through life with the same attitude of mind toward his city. If the latter should appear to him to be following a policy which is not a good one, he should say so, provided that his words are not likely either to fall on deaf ears or to lead to the loss of his own life.'[1320]

Xenophon (*Memor.* 1.6.15), reporting on an alleged conversation between Socrates and Antiphon, likewise insists that Socrates was wholly averse to any active participation in politics, as may be gathered

The Political Aspects of the Socratic Problem

from Antiphon's remark that Socrates 'did not take an active part in the affairs of the city'.[1321] Moreover, Xenophon (*Memor.* 1.1.17) maintains that 'it is not altogether surprising that his [*scil.*, Socrates'] judges should arrive at wrong conclusions concerning Socrates, particularly as regards those matters on which he gave no intimation what his personal convictions were'. This significant remark might possibly allude to the 'political views' held by Socrates. Xenophon apparently suggests here that Socrates had never stated his political convictions, nor ever participated openly in the many inner-political struggles which were so prominent in the history of Athens during the fifth century. Naturally, it is quite possible that, contrary to the facts, both Plato and Xenophon wish to create here the impression that Socrates had never actively engaged in politics. This, then, would be part of the Socratic legend. But even the statements of Plato and Xenophon do not wholly eliminate the possibility that Socrates might have influenced the political life of Athens at least indirectly. For if Libanius' *Apologia Socratis* contains reliable information, then Polycrates would have alleged that Socrates' secret activities must have been even more pernicious and more destructive to the Athenian commonweal than his public conduct.[1322]

By turning Socrates into an excellent man and idealistic philosopher, the Socratics made over the 'politician' Socrates, who might have been the historical Socrates, into a philosophical legend or, to be more precise, a literary legend. The traditional treatment of the Socratic problem, by following the example set by Aristotle, has always tried to emphasize in a most one-sided manner the alleged 'philosophy' of Socrates. Conversely, it has failed completely to understand Socrates and the Socratic issue in the light of the political and social history of Athens during the latter part of the fifth century.[1323] In this fashion Socrates was gradually turned into a 'professional philosopher', something he most likely was not. As a matter of fact, nearly every Socratic has modelled his 'Socratic legend' after his own image: Antisthenes made him out to be a Cynic; Aristotle a 'conceptualist'; Plato a 'philosopher of ethics'; and Xenophon, the plantation owner, even tried to turn Socrates into an 'agricultural expert'. In this sense the 'philosopher' Socrates was 'all things to all men', or, to be more exact, 'all philosophies to all philosophers'. Hence it may safely be concluded that historically speaking he was no philosopher at all, at least no 'philosopher' who held a definite system of ideas. Heinrich Maier seems to have grasped in part this problem when he writes: 'The alleged "philosophy" to which Socrates dedicated his life was not metaphysics... or ethics or rhetoric. It was not at all science (*Wissenschaft*) in the ordinary sense of the term... but a quest of the good moral life.'[1324] It is also significant that the Socratics, or at least the earliest of them, depicted him neither as a scientist, nor as a metaphysician, nor as a prophet of religion. And there is also no attempt to turn him into a 'genius'. He is made out to be simply a 'philosopher' in the original and homely sense of the term—a 'wise man'.[1325]

This would explain to a certain degree our difficulty in establishing the 'philosophical teachings' of the historical Socrates. It would also explain, among other things, why in their arguments and counter-arguments Polycrates and Xenophon had to resort to what seems to be *Antisthenica*; why, to mention just one other instance, Aristophanes, Eupolis, or Ameipsias imputed to Socrates statements and actions which popular opinion had attributed indiscriminately to all Sophists.[1326] In the absence of any distinct 'philosophical teachings' of Socrates they had no choice but to rely for their materials on vague prejudices and public opinion which was probably as indefinite as it was inaccurate.

8
Conclusions and Implications

THE APOLOGETIC FERVOUR of the early Socratics during the first decade of the fourth century must have caused much consternation, as well as deep resentment, among the so-called Late, or Rhetorical, Sophists,[1327] who probably considered themselves the spokesmen of the restored democracy at Athens. The latter apparently saw in the energetic and eloquent efforts of the Socratics to rehabilitate their master a serious threat to the recently restored democratic regime, particularly since the Socratics probably combined their praise of Socrates and their insistence on his complete innocence with a defence of the oligarchic-aristocratic form of government. Also, in all likelihood, the Socratics once more subjected the restored democracy to vitriolic attacks. It could be maintained, therefore, that in their apologies of Socrates the Socratics tried, at least on a literary plane, to carry on the old and bitter struggle between oligarchs and democrats long after history had decided this struggle in favour of the democrats. Hence this 'literary battle' could also be regarded as just one particular aspect of, or incident in, the general controversy which had been raging between the partisans of oligarchy or aristocracy and the partisans of democracy.[1328] In addition, the Late Sophists might also have considered the apologetic efforts of the Socratics a serious professional competition with their own activities. Should these efforts of the Socratics remain unchallenged, they might prove as dangerous to the Late Sophists and their political or professional aspirations as Socrates possibly had been to the sophistic movement of his day. Perhaps a belated oligarchic victory, after all, might even lead to their banishment or, at least, to a serious restriction of their activities, as had been the case during the reign of the Thirty Tyrants.[1329] Obviously, these Late Sophists did not propose to surrender to this new threat or concede victory without a desperate struggle. As a matter of fact, it seems that they soon engaged in a series of sharp literary counter-attacks which left little if anything unsaid. One of these counter-attacks is the κατηγορία Σωκράτους of Polycrates.[1330] Polycrates probably had no personal quarrel with Socrates in particular.[1331] It may be conceded therefore, that the κατηγορία, aside from its political implications, was primarily occasioned by the professional ambition of

Conclusions and Implications

Polycrates,[1332] who during his lifetime succeeded in becoming one of the more notorious rhetoricians. In this sense it could also be claimed that the Polycratean κατηγορία was what might be called the 'masterpiece' in the polemical exchange of ideas between the earliest Socratics and the Late Sophists. It could even be argued that the κατηγορία had been occasioned by Anytus, who, through the intermediary of Polycrates' rhetorical talents, might have wished to counter any dissatisfaction with Socrates' condemnation and death in 399 (Diogenes Laertius 2.43) by proving once more that Socrates had justly deserved death. This dissatisfaction, if it existed at all outside the Socratic circle, had probably been instigated and promoted by the Socratics.

It should be remembered that the Socratics in their λόγοι Σωκρατικοί or *Socratica* had apparently made Socrates their inimitable idol as well as their spokesman. Therefore, in order to discredit more effectively the Socratics, the anti-Socratic Late Sophists had only to direct their attacks against the possible 'founder' of the Socratic movement. These attacks took the form of an even more vicious bill of indictment than had been presented during the official trial of Socrates in the year 399. And this is exactly what Polycrates proposed to do in his κατηγορία Σωκράτους. By composing a pamphlet in the form of a rather lengthy literary indictment of Socrates delivered in the name of Anytus, and hence backed by the authority of one of the most outstanding leaders in the restoration of Athenian democracy in the year 403, as well as the most renowned official prosecutor of Socrates during the historical trial, Polycrates apparently caused more than a mere sensation.[1333] He also embarrassed the Socratics to no mean degree in that he tried to discredit politically both Socrates and the Socratics by calling them, as it seems, the 'despoilers of Athenian democracy'. Such charges, unless refuted successfully, could have dangerous, if not fatal, effects since they might lead to the expulsion of all Socratics from Athens.[1334] Hence the Socratics, among them Xenophon, saw themselves compelled to reply to the accusations made by Polycrates. This seems to be the most likely explanation for the origin of *Memorabilia* 1.1.1–1.2.64 and the *Defence*.

At the time Xenophon started his literary career, that is, after his exile to Scillus for high treason in 394/3, the anti-Socratic literary movement, of which the Polycratean κατηγορία is only one instance, was not the sole problem besetting some of the Socratics; serious danger also presented itself in the person and writings of Antisthenes. This danger was by no means negligible, particularly since it originated within the ranks of the Socratics themselves and thus internally threatened the unity of the 'Socratic tradition'. The feud between the 'Platonic Socratics' and the 'Antisthenian Socratics'—the latter were later re-enforced by Aristippus and his followers—lasted for nearly half a century. It was really a struggle over the question of 'orthodoxy' and,

Conclusions and Implications

hence, over the intellectual leadership among the 'heirs' of Socrates. It culminated in the issue of whether Plato or Antisthenes had a better right to consider himself the true successor of Socrates and his intellectual legacy.[1335]

Memorabilia 1.1.1–1.2.64 are not so much concerned with the official trial of Socrates in 399, but rather with the Polycratean κατηγορία Σωκράτους of 393/2. Those parts of the *Memorabilia* which deal with this trial, namely *Memorabilia* 1.1.1–1.2.9 and perhaps *ibid.* at 1.2.62–64, are merely an incidental and, in comparison with Plato's *Apology*, an abbreviated observation meant to furnish a kind of exalted background for the rebuttals of the Polycratean allegations. Xenophon's *Defence*, on the other hand, is a comprehensive though belated reply to the anti-Socratic literary movement which probably started shortly after the death of Socrates in 399. In the *Defence* Xenophon takes issue both with the official trial and the pamphlet of Polycrates. It seems, however, that the composition of the *Defence* had been occasioned primarily by the publication of the Polycratean κατηγορία and the appearance of other anti-Socratic writings which originated with the Late Sophists during the first half of the fourth century. All this forces us to conclude once more that there are two types of Socratic apologies which must be clearly distinguished: those apologies which were occasioned by the trial, condemnation, and death of Socrates in 399, and therefore, take issue with the proceedings during this trial; and those apologies which were occasioned by the appearance of a certain type of anti-Socratic literature and, hence, are primarily literary rebuttals of the renewed attacks on Socrates. Plato's *Apology*, it seems, is the only extant contemporary apology dealing exclusively with the trial of Socrates. All other extant contemporary apologies, including the two Xenophontean apologies, primarily take issue with the anti-Socratic writings which made their appearance after the death of Socrates. This does not mean, however, that the latter kind of apologetic *Socratica* omits all reference to the Socratic trial. From a purely literary point of view and in order to establish the proper dramatic setting, it appeared fitting to preface all these literary apologies with a discussion of the historical trial, the more so, since this sensational event was still fairly fresh in the mind of nearly every Athenian. But the main purpose of this latter type of apology was a refutation of such pamphleteers as Polycrates and the Late Sophists.

The Late Sophists, to be sure, were also fully aware of the anti-sophistic tendencies of the Platonic *Protagoras*. Hence there is a possibility that the κατηγορία Σωκράτους of Polycrates was their reply to the *Protagoras*. This assumption, if it could be maintained, would also fit the general chronology of Plato's earliest dialogues. But on closer scrutiny it must be conceded that the Platonic *Gorgias*, and not the *Protagoras*, contains Plato's final reckoning with the Late Sophists.

Conclusions and Implications

The *Gorgias*, strictly speaking, is no longer a 'Socratic' or 'early' Platonic dialogue. It marks the beginning of Plato's mature and independent philosophical views, the transition from 'Socratic' dependence to Platonic independence. Hence it is of great importance to date the *Gorgias* correctly as well as to point out the particular incident which occasioned its composition. We hold that the *Gorgias* should be dated between 392 and 390, shortly after the publication of the Polycratean κατηγορία Σωκράτους. Some scholars have suggested that the κατηγορία is Polycrates' reply to Plato's *Gorgias*. It is safer to assume, however, that the *Gorgias* constitutes Plato's rebuttal of Polycrates and the Late Sophists in general. Among other things, the *Gorgias* marks Plato's complete and irreparable break with the Late Sophists. This break is so complete that only the publication of so vicious and anti-Socratic an attack as that contained in the Polycratean κατηγορία could have occasioned it. While in the *Protagoras* Plato's hostility towards the sophists is still relatively moderate, it becomes actually venomous in the *Gorgias*. This alone would indicate that the *Gorgias* was written some time after the *Protagoras*, and that a particularly irritating incident must have induced Plato to assume this new and completely intransigent attitude towards the sophists. A further proof for the 'dependence' of the *Gorgias* on the Polycratean κατηγορία might be seen in the fact that Plato here rejects exactly those statesmen whom Polycrates had extolled in his pamphlet.[1336]

In the *Gorgias* Plato abandons the apologetic standpoint he had maintained so far in order to launch his most violent attacks upon the sophists of Polycrates' type, a type which is also well defined and characterized by Isocrates.[1337] Here Plato denounces and condemns with all his eloquence the very spirit of the sophistic tradition, that cheap and shallow demagoguery which, in the final analysis, was responsible not only for the destruction of Socrates, but also, at least in the eyes of Plato, for the moral and political decline of Athens.[1338] In the *Gorgias* (462E)[1339] Socrates identifies rhetoric (the Late, or Rhetorical Sophists) and cookery. Hence it may be assumed that the 'cook' who indicts the 'physician' (Socrates) in a court of little boys (the Athenian court of the *heliaea* which sentenced Socrates to death), is none other than these Late Sophists. This would also support the theory which maintains that the trial and condemnation of Socrates were engineered by these sophists, the spokesmen of the restored democracy. For this reason the *Gorgias* must be considered Plato's attempt at settling accounts with the Late Sophists, and with Polycrates in particular. This unqualified condemnation of Polycrates and his clique in the *Gorgias* is, on the one hand, the result of Plato's determination to expose the vicious and dangerous teachings of the Late Sophists. Thus Polus, the disciple of Gorgias,[1340] becomes in the *Gorgias* the prototype of the Late Sophist. Polus is characterized by Plato as the most destructive

Conclusions and Implications

representative of that generation of sophists to which Polycrates also belonged.[1341] In addition, it could be maintained that the *Gorgias* is, on the other hand, Plato's rebuttal of Polycrates' κατηγορία Σωκράτους in particular. It is, therefore, occasioned immediately by the publication of the κατηγορία, and as such is primarily an incident in the literary controversy over Socrates and the events connected with his later life. This controversy was carried on between the Socratics and the Late Sophists during the nineties of the fourth century. It was the more bitter and merciless since the Late Sophists, probably through the pen of Polycrates, had hit at Plato and the Socratics where the harm would be greatest: they had seriously slandered Socrates,[1342] the venerated and idolized 'teacher'.

It is somewhat surprising, therefore, that in the *Meno* Plato should come to the rescue of Anytus, who was the most formidable actor in the official prosecution of Socrates as well as the person whom Polycrates had selected as his spokesman when hurling his accusations against Socrates. This novel twist in the Platonic literature seems to be rather puzzling, to say the least, particularly since the *Meno* was apparently composed after the *Gorgias*. In order to understand this unusual attitude of Plato towards Anytus in the *Meno*, we shall have to review once more the whole situation brought on by the literary battles which started soon after the death of Socrates. The Late Sophists had launched their malicious attacks upon Socrates through the man who seems to have been their main representative, Polycrates, who, in turn used Anytus as his fictitious spokesman. Hence the Socratics, particularly Antisthenes, felt that they had to retaliate by heaping on Anytus the most vicious vituperations. It is quite possible that the followers of Antisthenes, never loath to resort to outrageous charges, excelled in the 'smear campaign' against Polycrates and Anytus. The mere fact that Antisthenes and the Antisthenians led this campaign might explain why Plato, who never had much use for the person or ideas of Antisthenes, should assume a more restrained attitude towards Anytus.[1343]

Plato, who was perhaps aware of the fact that Anytus merely served as the fictitious spokesman of Polycrates, apparently did not approve of the conduct of the Antisthenian Socratics (*Meno* 95A): 'I think that Anytus is outraged. And he may well be, for he thinks ... that I am insulting these people and ... that I am of the opinion that he is one of these people. But some day he will know the meaning of defamation, and, if he ever does, he will forgive me.' There is but one satisfactory explanation for this rather surprising attitude of Plato: aside from taking issue with some of Antisthenes' teachings, he wished to show that Anytus is not really the vicious person the Socratics made him out to be, but is merely a narrow-minded person of little understanding, unworthy of much attention. In other words, the man who seems to join Polycrates in his denunciation of Socrates is contemptible and insignifi-

Conclusions and Implications

cant,[1344] as is, by implication, Polycrates. Perhaps Plato felt indebted to Anytus for abiding by the terms of the amnesty law of 403, that is, for not mentioning any political charges during the official trial of Socrates. This conduct of Anytus, it might be contended, made it possible for Plato to devise his own particular brand of *Socratica*. Since he did not have to take issue directly with any embarrassing political charges, and since he felt that, unlike Xenophon, he could completely ignore the allegations made by Polycrates, Plato more than anyone else was free to frame his particular accounts of the 'philosopher' Socrates. This would also account for the fact that the Platonic Socrates is the most exalted Socrates ever created by a Socratic.[1345]

It has been suggested[1346] that the κατηγορία of Polycrates was not so much directed against Socrates himself, as against a particular group of Socratics, namely, Antisthenes and his followers. This suggestion, which in principle must be rejected as rather fantastic, contains, however, an element of truth: much of the material which Polycrates used when formulating his anti-Socratic charges was probably taken from the numerous writings of Antisthenes. If our hypothesis should prove correct that Polycrates did not aim his pamphlet directly at Antisthenes but rather at Socrates, then we must also assume that the manner in which Polycrates employs Antisthenian materials in his attacks upon Socrates would indicate that he regarded Antisthenes not only as the faithful disciple of Socrates, but also considered him the most outstanding person among the Socratics. This opinion of Polycrates, we may conjecture, was probably not uncommon during the early part of the fourth century.[1347] It has already been pointed out that, according to the report of Xenophon (*Memor*. 1.2.9),[1348] Polycrates had charged Socrates with having taught youths to ridicule the established laws and despise the existing political institutions of the city.[1349] Libanius seems to go even further than that when he implies in his rebuttal that Polycrates had accused Socrates of having not only desired but actually brought about the downfall of Athenian democracy. Xenophon's (and Libanius') reply to this Polycratean charge, we know, is rather feeble.[1350] He does not deny that Socrates ever made derogatory remarks about the laws and political institutions of Athens. Here, as elsewhere, Xenophon's and, for that matter, Polycrates' immediate source seems to have been Antisthenes, although we would also be justified in assuming that Xenophon might speak here from some personal experience. Antisthenes, it appears, had preached 'the supremacy of an intellectual and moral aristocracy', meaning thereby himself and those who accepted his teachings. From the standpoint of this beggarly 'aristocracy of the intellect' he proceeded to criticize most relentlessly the existing legal, social, and political institutions of Athens.[1351] Naturally, it could be surmised that the Antisthenian attitude toward the institutions of democratic Athens might ultimately go back to Socrates,

Conclusions and Implications

and that hence there was some foundation in the charge of Polycrates that Socrates had not only derided, but actually helped to bring about the downfall of Athenian democracy. Plato, it should be remembered, likewise reports that Socrates had uttered many rather severe criticisms of the political institutions of Athens.[1352]

The influence of Antisthenes on the Polycratean κατηγορία may also be detected in the allegation that Socrates selected certain passages from the ancient poets and by using them as arguments had taught his followers evil ways.[1353] Where, then, did Polycrates find the evidence on which he could base this particular charge, except in the writings of Antisthenes? Aside from some works of Antisthenes, the very titles of which suggest discussions and interpretations of the ancient poets,[1354] we may assume that in his κατηγορία Polycrates also made ample use of the many λόγοι Σωκρατικοί which had come into their own shortly after the death of Socrates. Antisthenes and his followers were not only the first but also probably the most prolific authors of such λόγοι Σωκρατικοί or 'Socratic anecdotes'. Undoubtedly, these Antisthenian λόγοι frequently made Socrates out to be a Cynic 'philosopher', the originator of many a 'diatribe' or 'apophthegm'.[1355] They could also be called a collection of allegedly Socratic χρεία, and the χρεία was one of the preferred literary forms employed by the Cynics. This being so, we ought not to be surprised that Socrates should be credited with having indulged in one of the favourite pastimes of Antisthenes and the Cynics—the quoting from, and the liberal interpretation of, the 'most celebrated poets of old'. Hence the original source for Polycrates' charge that Socrates had abused the ancient poets in order to lend support and authority to his evil teachings, in all likelihood must likewise be looked for in the works of Antisthenes, who, as it is commonly realized, wrote rather extensively on Homer,[1356] Pindar, Theognis,[1357] and Hesiod.[1358]

In Plato's *Charmides* (161A ff.) Critias, by using what seems to be an Antisthenian definition, calls σωφροσύνη outright τὰ ἑαυτοῦ πράττειν (doing of one's own business). He also quotes here the verse from Hesiod's *Works and Days* 309, that 'work is no disgrace'. This quotation, according to Xenophon (*Memor.* 1.2.56) and Libanius (61.17), had likewise been attributed to Socrates by Polycrates, who wished to prove thereby that Socrates had insisted that Hesiod 'bids us to refrain from no kind of work, even if it were dishonest and dishonourable, but to do such work for the sake of profit'.[1359] It is not improbable that this Polycratean allegation originally goes back to some Antisthenian interpretation of Hesiod. This may be gathered not only from some of the general Cynic remarks that the decent man should support himself by honest work,[1360] but also from Plato's *Charmides* 163BC. Here the Antisthenian 'doing one's own business' is further explained by the statement that 'only things nobly and usefully made' are called 'works'

Conclusions and Implications

(τὰ γὰρ καλῶς τε καὶ ὠφελίμως ποιούμενα ἔργα).[1361] In essence this Antisthenian idea can also be found in the *Memorabilia* (1.2.56), although it must be admitted that the manner in which it seems to have been used by Polycrates amounts to a rather serious distortion of what apparently had been its original meaning.[1362] Xenophon (*Memor.* 1.2.57), who likewise interprets this Antisthenian notion in his own fashion, counters the Polycratean allegation with the remark that Socrates had merely insisted that 'to be busy was beneficial and good for man (τὸ μὲν ἐργάτην... ὠφελιμόν τε... καὶ ἀγαθόν), and to be without work was obnoxious and evil for man; that to work was a (moral) good (ἐργάζεσθαι ἀγαθὸν) and to be idle an evil. At the same time he said that only those who do something good are really working (τοὺς μὲν ἀγαθόν τι ποιοῦντας ἐργάζεσθαι)....'

Combining the information contained in Plato's *Charmides* 163BC and Xenophon's *Memorabilia* 1.2.56–57, we are permitted to conclude that the Antisthenian position as regards 'work' was probably this: no kind of work is dishonourable,[1363] provided it be beneficial to man. And 'beneficial' (ὠφέλιμος) signifies here, as we may gather from *Charmides* 163BC and *Memorabilia* 1.2.57, something which promotes man morally or something that is done out of a sense of moral duty and thus enhances man's dignity. In the light of this realization, the τὰ ἑαυτοῦ πράττειν of the Platonic *Charmides* acquires an entirely novel meaning. Plato insists here that mere craftsmen and 'technicians' can also possess 'practical wisdom' (σωφρονεῖν), because they not only know their own business (τὰ ἑαυτοῦ πράττειν), but also the business of others (τὰ τῶν ἄλλων πράττοντας).[1364] Critias (*Charmides* 163A) counters this argument by distinguishing between ποιεῖν and πράττειν, and between ποιεῖν and ἐργάζεσθαι. This distinction, in turn, induces him to quote the verse from Hesiod's *Works and Days* 309, claiming that Hesiod did not have in mind mere craftsmen: 'I understand him to have distinguished between "the making of something" (πρᾶξις) and "the doing of something" (ἐργασία).' It is also admitted (*Charmides* 163BC) that 'the making of something' (ποίημα) at times can be disgraceful, particularly when it is not related to something good, 'while work (ἔργον) is never disgraceful', because 'work (ἔργον) refers to things nobly and usefully made'. There can be little doubt that this whole discussion in the *Charmides*, as well as the particular interpretation of Hesiod presented there, goes back to some Antisthenian source.[1365]

The 'things nobly and usefully made' (τὰ γὰρ καλῶς καὶ ὠφελίμως ποιούμενα) of the *Charmides* (163C), in *Memorabilia* 1.2.56—that is, in Xenophon's report of the words of Polycrates—turn into 'doing of work for the sake of profit' (ποιεῖν ἐπὶ τῷ κέρδει). *Memorabilia* 1.2.56–57 also seem to indicate that Polycrates and Xenophon derived the material for their charges or counter-charges respectively from a passage in some Antisthenian work where τὰ ἑαυτοῦ πράττειν had been

Conclusions and Implications

interpreted by Antisthenes in the spirit of Hesiod, who had insisted that no work carried out from a sense of moral duty could be called undignified or dishonourable, because only idleness is disgraceful. This assumption is also supported by *Memorabilia* 3.9.14–15, a passage which likewise seems to be under the influence of Antisthenes. Here Xenophon contrasts εὐτυχία (good fortune or luck) and εὐπραξία (good conduct).[1366] Good conduct is defined as 'achieving anything successfully through proper learning and practice' (τὸ δὲ μαθόντα τε καὶ μελετήσαντα τι εὖ ποιεῖν). This definition, in turn, reminds us of Plato, *Charmides* 163BC, and Xenophon, *Memorabilia* 1.2.56–57. In *Memorabilia* 3.9.15, Xenophon adds the following interesting observation in the form of an illustration: 'Those are the best as well as the most favoured in the sight of the gods who,[1367] for instance, in husbandry perform well the things of farming, or in the art of healing do well all that which pertains to healing, or in statecraft do well the affairs of state. But the man who does nothing well and is no good at anything, is neither useful for any purpose nor acceptable in the eyes of the gods.'[1368] From all this we may infer that *Memorabilia* 3.9.14–15 and *ibid*. at 1.2.56–57, are definitely influenced by the Antisthenian τὰ ἑαυτοῦ πράττειν which, it may be surmised, meant originally that everyone should be 'doing his own business' and doing it well.[1369] In Plato's *Charmides* 163BC, as we have already observed, this 'doing one's business' is further explained as the 'doing something which is both noble and good (or useful).'[1370] In other words, this τὰ ἑαυτοῦ πράττειν[1371] is something exceedingly proper in that it is related to some kind of good. And everything that is related to some good is, by its very definition, in accord with man's nature and, hence, truly 'man's own (οἰκεῖον)'. That, however, which is 'related to something evil' (πονηρός) is contrary to man's nature, and, therefore, 'not man's own' (ἀλλότριον).[1372] Thus it might be maintained that this Antisthenian τὰ ἑαυτοῦ πράττειν signifies, in the final analysis, man's acting in conformity with his own nature, or, what would be essentially the same thing for the Cynics, acting virtuously.

The apologetic remarks with which Xenophon tries to counter the Polycratean allegation that Socrates had declared any and every kind of work honourable, even the most disgraceful as long as it profited the actor, seems to contain some historical truth. In *Memorabilia* 2, chapters 7–8, Socrates is said to have rebuked some of his followers for holding that it is unworthy of a free citizen to engage in labours usually performed by slaves and the lowliest of people.[1373] We may suggest, therefore, that Polycrates, who apparently relies on Antisthenian doctrines which he possibly mistakes for Socratic dicta, tries here to discredit Socrates in the eyes of the average Athenian by pointing to Socrates' alleged contempt for certain commonly established standards of conduct accepted by the burghers of Athens. In this, Polycrates could be

Conclusions and Implications

called the spokesman of the typically urban middle class of Athenian burghers who looked down upon anyone who, like Antisthenes, would extol the dignity of manual labour. The idea that the Athenian burgher had certain definitely conservative notions about propriety and the things that were beneath his dignity, seems to be at the bottom of the story related by Diogenes Laertius (6.35): 'Someone dropped a loaf of bread and was ashamed to pick it up. Whereupon Diogenes [scil., Diogenes of Sinope], wishing to teach him a lesson, tied a rope to the neck of a jar and dragged it across the Ceramicus.' Essentially the same story is repeated ibid. at 6.36: 'Someone wanted to study philosophy under him [scil., under Diogenes of Sinope]. Diogenes gave him a salted fish to carry and told him to follow him [making him appear to be Diogenes' servant]. And when he refused to do this and, throwing away the fish, left him ... [Diogenes] said: "The friendship between you and me came to an end over a salted fish." '[1374]

Polycrates apparently also charged Socrates of having taught or induced his followers to live in idleness, and that he did so in a spirit of 'anti-social' and 'anti-democratic' resentment.[1375] This charge may be based on the Socratic (or perhaps Antisthenian) insistence that we should be more concerned with our souls than with our material well-being.[1376] Xenophon apparently fails to refute specifically this particular allegation, which he disposes of in a general manner in *Memorabilia* 1.2.1–2, 1.2.57, and 1.2.62.[1377] Libanius seems to suggest that this Polycratean charge actually contained two particular indictments, namely, that Socrates made his disciples neglectful of all practical earthly pursuits (*Libanius* 88.14), and that Socrates persuaded his followers to abstain from all participation in the social, economic, and political life of Athens (Libanius 84.18), thus inflicting great evils on the city. It must be conceded that these allegations of Polycrates, but not his inferences, are amply supported by the whole of Socratic literature.[1378]

Xenophon (*Memor.* 1.2.51) also reports that Polycrates had charged Socrates with having 'not only caused parents, but other relatives to be held in contempt by his followers'.[1379] Friends, too, unless they were of assistance, were disparaged (*Memor.* 1.2.52), because 'it was of no profit that they [scil., Socrates' followers] were well disposed towards people unless the latter were able also to give some practical assistance'. *Memorabilia* 2, chapters 4–6 and 10, in which Xenophon discusses the alleged teachings of Socrates on friendship, seem to supplement the statements contained in *Memorabilia* 1.2.52. Here, too, the Xenophontean Socrates displays a definitely utilitarian point of view as regards friendship and human relationships in general. Hence, it could be maintained that both *Memorabilia* 1.2.52 and *ibid.* 2, chapters 4–6 and 10, as has already been shown, are under the spell of Antisthenian-Cynic doctrines[1380] which declare that the real significance of friendship is closely related to the gain which we may derive from our friends.[1381] This would

Conclusions and Implications

again bear out our contention that Polycrates borrowed much of the material he used against Socrates immediately from the writings and sayings of Antisthenes, and that for his counter-arguments and rebuttals, as well as for much of what he incorporated into his *Memorabilia*, Xenophon likewise relied on Antisthenian teachings.

We may assume, therefore, that some of the Antisthenian λόγοι Σωκρατικοί, though probably falsely, had credited Socrates with something very characteristic of the Cynic—with having originated a number of diatribes and 'apophthegms'.[1382] In this manner Socrates was made out to be a genuine Cynic, not only as regards certain ideas which he allegedly expounded, but also as to the form in which he had stated them.

The same may be said about *Memorabilia* 1.2.49–55. Here Xenophon lists those Polycratean charges and allegations which could make Socrates the despoiler of the basic ties of filial reverence, kinship, loyalty, and social solidarity. It has already been suggested that Antisthenian ideas may have supplied Polycrates with his arguments. It is a well known fact that Antisthenes and his followers, on the whole, assumed a radically negative attitude towards all established institutions, traditions, customs, and civilities.[1383] Wealth[1384] and refinement,[1385] honour[1386] and fame[1387] meant to them as little as family [1388] or native land,[1389] or the arts and sciences.[1390] Refusing to recognize the laws[1391] and standards of civilized society,[1392] they went so far as to scoff openly at the most elementary demands of morals and the accepted forms of decency.[1393] At the same time they did not hesitate to deride the religious convictions of the day.[1394] But we could also concede that some of the Polycratean charges, in a certain sense at least, might have been based on some Socratic dictum which was later enlarged upon and 'radically exaggerated' by Antisthenes and the Cynics in their λόγοι Σωκρατικοί. By using the rather crude literary forms of the Cynic χρεία or διατριβή, these *Socratica* were apt to make Socrates appear in a very unfavourable light. But it should also be remembered that Xenophon does not deny outright the truth of some of the Polycratean allegations listed in *Memorabilia* 1.2.49–55. We can no longer fully ascertain, however, whether this attitude of Xenophon is determined by the fact that he actually believed these Antisthenian χρεία or diatribes to be true Socratic statements, or whether he knew through some other sources that Socrates himself had held such 'unorthodox' views.

In the light of the justifiable assumption that on the whole Socrates was a man of 'conservative' ideas both as regards politics and personal conduct, we are inclined, however, to credit Antisthenes with having originated the supposed 'radicalism' of Socrates. But then, again, it seems that Xenophon acknowledges the fact that there is an element of truth in the contentions of Polycrates (*Memor.* 1.2.53): 'I am aware, indeed, that he [*scil.*, Socrates] expressed himself concerning parents and other relatives as well as friends in such manner as this.' Xenophon's words here, practically amounting to an admission, probably do not lack factual foundation. When the younger followers of Socrates gathered around him, he probably drew sharp criticism from mothers and fathers. This, in turn, may have forced Socrates to present his pupils with the alternative of either abiding by the wishes of their fathers and thus remaining 'uneducated', or forsaking their parents for the sake of their intellectual, political, and moral improvement.[1395] Perhaps he tried to recruit a group of young Athenians for his political programme which, as may be gathered from circumstantial evidence, probably aimed at a restoration of the oligarchic regime. Naturally, he expected that his followers would forsake everything in order to dedicate all their energies and loyalties to this programme, since, as he proudly proclaims in Plato's *Apology* (30D ff., and 33A ff.), he himself attempted to carry out his 'divine mission' with a fanatical zeal, paying no heed to the ordinary demands of life, including his wife and family. Such a situation could well be at the basis of Polycrates' charge that 'by thus persuading youths that he himself was the wisest of men and most capable of making others wise, he [*scil.*, Socrates] so disposed his followers towards him that other people were of no account with them in comparison with himself'.[1396]

The *Socratica* of the fourth century might be subdivided into the following main stages: Immediately after the death of Socrates in 399, the Socratics, we may assume, in their predominantly aristocratic or oligarchic leanings released a flood of political tracts, perhaps from the relative safety of voluntary political exile. These tracts, possibly under the pretence of protesting the innocence of Socrates, attacked the restored democracy at Athens. All these pamphlets, it seems, are completely lost, although their repercussions can still be felt during the later stages of the literary controversy over Socrates. The spokesmen of the restored Athenian democracy, often referred to as the Late, or Rhetorical, Sophists, at once rose to the defence of Athenian democracy. The rejoinders of the Late Sophists would constitute the second stage of the Socratic controversy. Hence it could be maintained that the first two stages of this controversy, which could also be called the two 'political stages', were primarily a literary continuation of the old and bitter political struggles between the partisans of oligarchy or aristocracy and those of democracy. During this literary struggle, at least in its earlier stages, the Socratic issue as such was probably a mere 'side-issue' which, however, to an eminent degree lent itself to the formulation of political charges and counter-charges, particularly since the trial of Socrates seems to have been connected with a great deal of public notoriety. Approximately at the same time, we must assume, the first or panegyric λόγοι Σωκρατικοί, especially those of Antisthenes, may have made their appearance, although in all likelihood these particular

Conclusions and Implications

λόγοι originally were not directly connected with or, at least, not immediately occasioned by, the general 'political controversy'. Hence it is vital to distinguish clearly between the 'occasional references' to Socrates during the literary struggle carried on by the democrats and the oligarchs, and the first λόγοι Σωκρατικοί. It could also be maintained that the first λόγοι Σωκρατικοί were not of a primarily apologetic nature, but were rather a sort of Socratic χρεία or διατριβή, in which Antisthenes, in keeping with a well-established tradition, expounded some of his own views and convictions in the name of Socrates, thereby creating the impression that these *Antisthenica* actually were true *Socratica*. The existence of these first or panegyric Socratic χρεία or λόγοι Σωκρατικοί also explains the main source or sources from which Polycrates subsequently derived the materials for his 'anti-Socrates' arguments.

The Late Sophists in their counterblasts seemed to have gradually concentrated their attacks upon the person of Socrates, whom they probably considered the 'founder' and intellectual leader of the oligarchic-aristocratic movement during the later part of the fifth century, or a key-member in some politically prominent 'oligarchic club'. In order more effectively to discredit the Socratics, the Late Sophists apparently felt that they had only to draw up a more vicious and more detailed 'bill of indictment' of Socrates than had been presented during the official trial in 399. This was done, among others, by Polycrates, who in his pamphlet tried to make it quite clear that Socrates was the true cause for the downfall of Athens and the abolishment of Athenian democracy in 404. It is also quite possible that the defenders of aristocracy or oligarchy—in short, the Socratics themselves—may have injected the Socratic issue into the original political controversy. In order to denounce the democratic regime more effectively by reciting some of the 'depravities' committed by the latter, they may have referred to the 'case of Socrates' as just one instance of the many democratic 'outrages'. No wonder that the defenders of democracy should insist that the condemnation of Socrates was fully justified by the facts which they now began to divulge, and not, as the aristocrats probably insinuated, an instance of 'judicial murder'.

The more general anti-aristocratic or anti-oligarchic tracts of the Late Sophists thus were suddenly replaced by specifically 'anti-Socrates' treatises which made Socrates the chief target of their incriminations. This change of emphasis as well as object in the anti-Socratic literature is particularly noticeable in the κατηγορία Σωκράτους of Polycrates. This rhetorician, it will be remembered, skilfully combined the 'political controversy' of the first stage with a 'personal indictment' of Socrates in his κατηγορία which, judged by the reaction which it created, must be considered the most important literary document of the second stage. With its pointed and particularized attacks upon Socrates, this

Conclusions and Implications

work, published in 393/2, may be regarded not only as the concluding event in the second stage of the Socratic controversy in that it probably constituted the transition from the 'political argument' to the 'personal argument,' but also as the literary event which ushered in the third stage of the Socratic controversy. Being predominantly a personal denunciation of Socrates as the intellectual leader of the oligarchic-aristocratic reaction rather than a political tract defending democracy against the partisans of aristocracy, the κατηγορία could also be called that incident which gave birth to the 'Socratic legend' or, to be more exact, to the many 'Socratic legends' which, as has been shown, are primarily of an apologetic nature. The Socratic rejoinders to this novel anti-Socratic literature, which is actually an 'anti-Socrates' literature, constitute the third or 'personal' stage in the Socratic controversy. This 'anti-Socrates' literature forced the Socratics to come to the personal defence of Socrates himself, not only in the interest of their own cause, but also in that of the man with whom by now they were fully identified. Faced with a series of detailed and serious charges which cast a most unfavourable light not only upon their 'teacher', but also upon their political convictions, the Socratics had to resort to detailed rebuttals, many of them based on fiction or, at least, gross distortions. In our opinion these detailed rejoinders, or λόγοι Σωκρατικοί, which must be dated after 393/2, mark the beginning of the 'Socratic legend' or 'Socratic Apologies'.[1397]

As far as it can still be determined, the most prominent apologists for Socrates during the third or 'personal' stage were probably Antisthenes, Aeschines of Sphettos, Euclides of Magara, and Phaedo of Elis. We must clearly distinguish, however, between the early Antisthenian λόγοι Σωκρατικοί which furnished Polycrates with much of the material he used in his 'indictment of Socrates', and the later or apologetic λόγοι Σωκρατικοί of Antisthenes which were occasioned by the publication of the Polycratean κατηγορία Σωκράτους. There exists no particular reason why we should not assume that Aeschines, Euclides, Phaedo, and other Socratics likewise wrote 'pre-Polycratean' or panegyric λόγοι Σωκρατικοί as well as 'post-Polycratean' or apologetic λόγοι Σωκρατικοί. Obviously, the motive, tenor, and content of these 'post-Polycratean' or apologetic λόγοι are somewhat different from those of the pre-Polycratean λόγοι, although it must probably be conceded that this difference is primarily one of emphasis. Unless the distinction between pre-Polycratean and post-Polycratean *Socratica* is fully understood, the whole problem connected with the κατηγορία Σωκράτους of Polycrates, and the far-reaching effects it had upon the subsequent development of the Socratic legend, cannot be properly understood.

During the fourth stage of this controversy, which is likewise a 'personal stage', the most prominent Socratic apologists were Xenophon

Conclusions and Implications

and Plato, who apparently developed further the apologetic efforts and tactics peculiar to the third stage. In so doing they also promoted greatly the 'Socratic legend', which by now assumes rather large proportions and considerable eminence. In their apologetic *Socratica* both Xenophon and Plato reflect the influences and trends of the preceding stages, especially those of the third stage. Xenophon in particular seems dependent on this third stage from which he apparently derived many of his apologetic arguments and materials. Plato to some extent makes a studied effort to avoid the apologetic methods employed by his predecessors, although in many instances he too remains under their influence.

The difference in the treatment of the Socratic problem by either Xenophon or Plato, aside from their basically different talents and 'philosophies', may go back to their literary rivalry. Thus Diogenes Laertius (3.34) reports: 'It seems that Xenophon was not on good terms with him [*scil.*, Plato]. In any event, they have written similar narratives as if out of a spirit of rivalry to each other. . . .'[1398] But despite the statements of Diogenes Laertius, we cannot detect any instances of overt anti-Platonic sentiment in the *Memorabilia*. Xenophon mentions Plato only once (*Memor.* 3.6.1), and then only in passing. There seems to be a peculiar design behind this policy of Xenophon: Plato, who is introduced in *Memorabilia* 3.6.1 as one of Socrates' intimate associates, is not being criticized by Xenophon, and this despite the fact that Xenophon often does not seem to be in agreement with Plato and his views on Socrates.[1399] Why, then, should Xenophon neither praise nor condemn Plato in the *Memorabilia*? Simply because he probably knew that Plato was opposed to Antisthenes and the Antisthenian tradition about Socrates, and that by criticizing or condemning Plato he would, indirectly at least, strengthen the position of Antisthenes as regards the latter's views on Socrates. But he does not praise Plato either, because he disagrees with him on the Socratic issue.[1400]

We have already pointed out the rather startling fact of Xenophon's frequent recourse to Antisthenian-Cynic sources or Antisthenian λόγοι Σωκρατικοί for his defence as well as eulogy of Socrates. This reliance is most surprising in view of the fundamental differences in their basic outlooks on life in general. More than that, it poses a final problem which should indicate the complexity of the many problems connected with the Xenophontean *Socratica*. In *Memorabilia* 1.4.1, Xenophon states: 'A belief is current among certain people (τινές), in accordance with views advanced by some (ἔνιοι) about Socrates both in speech and writings—but in either case based on pure conjecture—that Socrates was eminently qualified to stimulate men to virtue as a theorist, but incapable of leading them to virtue himself. It would be well for those who accept this view to weigh carefully not only what Socrates achieved by way of eristic debate when he cross-examined (ἐρωτῶν ἤλεγχεν)

Conclusions and Implications

those who considered themselves possessed of all knowledge, but also his every day conversations with those who spent their time in close association with him.'

One thing becomes quite obvious from this highly significant passage: Xenophon wishes to discredit here that type of Socratic traditon which sees in Socrates nothing other than a representative of the technique of protreptic or eristic argument.[1401] Who then, in the opinion of Xenophon, are the 'certain people' (τινὲς) who originated this tradition which, according to Xenophon, definitely constituted the wrong or, at best, extremely one-sided and inaccurate view on Socrates? It would be safe to assume that these 'certain people' (τινὲς) are Antisthenes and his followers.[1402] But Xenophon does not merely single out these τινὲς for his polemics; he also attacks 'some people' (ἔνιοι) who by their 'speech and writings' seem to have furnished the τινὲς with their materials and arguments.[1403] Who are these 'some people' (ἔνιοι) who are definitely distinguished from the 'certain people' (τινές)? The answer to this question perhaps can be found in the dialogue *Cleitophon* (410B ff.) —erroneously incorporated in the *corpus Platonicum*—where a person called Cleitophon concedes that Socrates was undoubtedly a master of protreptics, but certainly unable to tell us how we could actually become virtuous persons.[1404] It is well known that the *Cleitophon* contains a viciously polemic attack upon the Antisthenian-Cynic tradition about Socrates.[1405] We may infer, therefore, that the ἔνιοι likewise are Antisthenes and the Antisthenians who are credited here with having 'written down' the discourses of Socrates.[1406] This information is of particular interest to us in that it declares Antisthenes and his followers, at least according to the testimony of Xenophon, the originators of the first λόγοι Σωκρατικοί.

The real meaning of *Memorabilia* 1.4.1, therefore, must be recognized in Xenophon's rejection of certain aspects of the Antisthenian tradition about Socrates. In order to endow his own 'anti-Antisthenian' position with proper authority, Xenophon also tries to impress the reader with the fact—however fanciful—that he had been one of the closest associates of Socrates and, hence, extremely well qualified to rebuke Antisthenes.[1407] But despite his disagreements with the Antisthenian tradition about Socrates, Xenophon, who fully realized that he had to rely on extant λόγοι Σωκρατικοί for his own *Socratica*, made use of the *Socratica* of a man whose views on Socrates he is apparently not always willing to share.[1408]

The distinguishing feature of the two Xenophontean apologies is detected in the fact that in connection with his refutation of Polycrates, Xenophon also refers to the historical trial of Socrates. But these references, which with Xenophon seem to be of minor instance, apparently constitute only a dramatic background for his detailed rejoinders to Polycrates. Plato, however, impresses us as having preferred to deal exclusively with the historical trial as such, ignoring in his *Apology* the allegations made by Polycrates and the Late Sophists.[1409]

In this, Plato seems to resume the apologetic tenor predominant during the earlier stages of the controversy over Socrates. For he not only protests against the guilt of Socrates, but uses his *Apology* to decry the evils of the restored Athenian democracy. Xenophon, on the other hand, seems to continue that type of apologetic tradition which apparently was motivated by the publication of the λόγοι Σωκρατικοί, and which became established during the third stage of the Socratic controversy. This later apologetic tradition, we may assume on the strength of its pronouncedly Antisthenian flair, probably goes back to Antisthenes who might be called its originator. Hence it could be contended that there existed not only two distinct types of Socratic indictments, the official forensic indictment of the year 399 and the literary indictment made subsequently by the Late Sophists and Polycrates in particular, but also two distinct apologetic traditions, namely, the 'Platonic tradition' and the 'Antisthenian tradition' of which Xenophon seems to be a belated spokesman.

While Plato apparently protests against the guilt of Socrates in the light of the events which supposedly transpired during the historical trial and, hence, takes issue with the official indictment, trial, and condemnation of Socrates, Xenophon, in keeping with the policy followed by the 'Antisthenian tradition' of dealing with the literary charges, primarily concerns himself with the allegations made by Polycrates. This obvious difference which exists between Plato and Xenophon in their respective treatment of the Socratic issue, in itself, is of great significance. Unlike Xenophon, Plato might have been aware of the possibility that Antisthenes and Antisthenian teachings, and not Socrates, were actually the main target of the belated and detailed charges made by the Late Sophists and Polycrates; hence he refused to enter this particular controversy which, at least in his opinion, had nothing to do with the actual facts as they had been presented during the official trial. Another possibility for explaining the attitude of Plato might be detected in his refusal to be counted among the Antisthenian Socratics of whom he heartily disapproved. Since the particular Polycratean charges in their possibly Antisthenian origin, as well as the rebuttals of these charges, seem to have been the foremost concern of the Antisthenian Socratics, he omitted all references to the Socratic-Polycratean controversy, manifesting thereby his disassociation from the Antisthenian group on this whole issue. A third possibility of explaining Plato's efforts to ignore the Polycratean charges could be detected in the fact that Plato, unlike Antisthenes and Xenophon, might have felt that the allegations made by Polycrates were unworthy of a rejoinder, and that a distinct rebuttal of these charges would only give the Polycratean pamphlet an importance which it never possessed

Conclusions and Implications

in the eyes of Plato. And finally, Plato might have realized the essential truth of the Polycratean allegations. Unable to refute them successfully he might have argued that it would be better to ignore them rather than make matters worse by a feeble and unconvincing effort to challenge them.

In the final analysis, the problem of the two Socratic apologies of Xenophon consists in this: both the *Defence* and *Memorabilia* 1.1.1–1.2.64 were occasioned or stimulated by the publication of the Polycratean κατηγορία Σωκράτους after 392. Unlike Plato's *Apology*, the Xenophontean apologies are primarily rebuttals of Polycrates' allegations and charges; only incidentally do they deal with the official trial of 399. When formulating his accusations against Socrates, Polycrates to a large extent seems to have made use of materials which he found in the writings or λόγοι Σωκρατικοί of Antisthenes and the Antisthenians. Antisthenes, to be sure, was a Socratic, although it is impossible to ascertain with any degree of definiteness whether he represented faithfully the teachings of the historical Socrates—provided, naturally, that it is at all permissible to speak of 'the teachings of Socrates'. As a matter of fact, we would be inclined to surmise that on certain important points Antisthenes probably deviates rather considerably from the views which Socrates might have held. Hence it must also be conceded that in many of his anti-Socratic allegations Polycrates most likely missed the mark in that he seems to have had in mind an Antisthenian Socrates rather than the historical Socrates.

In his rebuttals of Polycrates, Xenophon likewise appears to rely on Antisthenian materials, something which can easily be verified from his general treatment of the Socratic question. For this much appears to be certain: Xenophon, who was both a poor historian and an indiscriminately eclectic author, frequently transforms Socrates into a fervent spokesman for Cynicism; at times the Xenophontean Socrates actually impresses us as being an Antisthenian Cynic. Consequently, the literary battle between Polycrates and Xenophon is frequently fought over Antisthenes rather than Socrates himself. This, in turn, would force us to concede that both the Polycratean charges and the Xenophontean rebuttals, at least as regards their literary expression as well as their various details, might well be without foundation in fact. But in the face of the present status of available source materials it is impossible to ascertain with any degree of certainty the extent to which these accusations and rebuttals would apply to the historical Socrates. The crux of the whole controversy between Polycrates and Xenophon seems to rest on the fact that we are faced not only with the nearly complete loss of all the writings of Antisthenes, but also with the total absence of any authentic works by Socrates.

The historical period in which Socrates lived is fairly well known. The particular role which Socrates played in this period, however, is rather nebulous and incomprehensible, and this despite the fact that we possess an abundance of ancient *Socratica*. Such an unusual situation admits of only one intelligent interpretation: these *Socratica* were never intended to deal with the historical Socrates.[1410] We must assume, therefore, that these *Socratica* were primarily motivated with the purpose of establishing a legend.[1411] The ultimate reason for such a policy seems to be quite obvious. The Socratics, in their apologetic fervour, could not possibly recount the historical facts. This, in turn, forced them to embark upon fiction, unless they wished to admit some ugly truths or remain silent and thus concede by default the charges which had been made against Socrates. Hence it may also be contended that the literary Socrates as he was presented by the Socratics is basically a legendary Socrates and as such hardly the historical Socrates. This would also explain why the many ancient *Socratica*, on the whole, lack truly convincing force. It would also explain why such divergent and often incompatible philosophies as Plato's 'idealism', Aristippus' 'hedonism', or Antisthenes' 'cynicism' should claim to be Socratic in origin.[1412] This does not mean, however, that the Socratic legend is completely devoid of all historicity. For nearly every legend, no matter what its particular features may be, has an historical core which is often completely obscured or perverted by a fabric of myths woven around it.

While nearly all legends, as a rule, have some vague foundation in historical fact, so late a legend as the Socratic myth devised by the Socratic apologists usually relies upon some earlier legend for both its source and model. It may not be altogether fantastic to conjecture that the mythological *Defence of Palamedes*,[1413] in the form in which it has been recorded by Gorgias of Leontini,[1414] or at least the general theme underlying the trial of Palamedes, could very well be at the basis of some of the later Socratic apologies, particularly the *Apology* of Plato and the two apologies of Xenophon.[1415]

The Gorgian *Defence* contains the following interesting passages which might have influenced Plato and Xenophon: (1) 'the indictment and the defence is not primarily an issue of life or death. . . . Death comes to all men. . . .'[1416] The issue is really one of honour or dishonour: whether I am to die justly or unjustly and under a cloud of disgrace.'[1417] (2) 'You have the power to decide. Right is on my side, but the power over life and death is on yours. . . . You can kill me.'[1418] (3) 'If . . . the accuser were prosecuting me because he knew or honestly believed that I was betraying Greece . . . he would be the best of men. For in this case he would be ensuring the safety of his country, his parents, and all of Greece. . . .'[1419] (4) 'Where shall I begin with my defence? An argument unsupported by proof engenders fear, and fear makes speech difficult, . . . unless truth and compulsion guide me. . . .'[1420] (5) 'The accuser cannot know for certain that I committed the crime [of which I am

Conclusions and Implications

accused] ... for I know for certain that I did not commit it. ...'[1421] (11) '... If any free man has some information about my alleged crime, let him step forward. ...'[1422] (15) '... Nor was the love of wealth or the desire for possessions my motive. I have moderate means, and I need but little. Wealth is ... not needed by those who are able to control their desire for pleasure, but by those who are enslaved by their desires. ...'[1423] (24) '... You have no real knowledge of the facts of which you accuse me. ... You are the most despicable of men, to bring capital charges against me merely on the strength of conjecture. ...'[1424] 'You are accusing me of opposites. ... How can we believe a man who in the same speech, addressed to the same audience, says opposites about the same things?'[1425] (27) '... I prefer to seek acquittal through my virtues or good deeds, rather than through your vices.'[1426]

(28) 'I must speak now of myself to you men [*scil.*, the judges][1427] ... and do so in a manner unbefitting anyone but a person accused of a crime. I shall submit to your scrutiny my past life, and I shall mention my good deeds. I pray that no one will resent this. For I am compelled to do this in order that I may refute serious charges. ...'[1428] (29) '... My whole past has been blameless. ...'[1429] (30) '... I claim to be the benefactor of Greece, nay, of the whole of mankind. ...'[1430] (31) '... I mention these things ... in order to show that by devoting myself [to the welfare of Greece] I am bound to abstain from committing wicked deeds.'[1431] (32) 'I deserve to suffer no evil. ...[1432] I have been considerate to the old and helpful to the young; I was never envious of the rich, but merciful to the distressed. ... I did not despise poverty, neither have I ever given preference to wealth over virtue. I was useful in counsel, active in war, carrying out commands and obeying my superiors. But it is not for me to exalt myself. I do so merely under the compulsion of self-defence.'[1433] (33) 'Finally, I shall speak of you to you. Lamentations, prayers, and the pleas of friends are useful when the final decision rests with the masses. But before you, the foremost among the Greeks, I do not need to resort to such devices. ...'[1434] (34) 'You must pay heed not to words but to facts. ... Good men avoid wrong-doing. ...'[1435] (35) '... you run a great risk of acquiring a reputation for injustice. To good men, death is preferable to dishonour ...'[1436] (36) 'If you put me to death unjustly, ... you will bear the blame in the eyes of every Greek. ...[1437] The blame will be yours, not that of my accuser, because the final decision rests solely with you. ... There could be no greater crime than if you as Greeks were to put to death a Greek [who has been] ... a benefactor of the whole of Greece. ...'[1438]

The striking similarity as regards both thought and expression, between the Gorgian *Defence of Palamedes* and certain passages from Xenophon's *Defence* or *Memorabilia* 1.1.1–1.2.64, as well as Plato's *Apology*, is obvious, not to say suggestive.[1439] This similarity cannot possibly be accidental. The manner, for instance, in which the Platonic Socrates (*Apology* 25E) twice proves Meletus the liar, undoubtedly goes back to chapter 26 of the Gorgian *Palamedes*. And like Palamedes (*Palamedes* 28 ff.), who recites his εὐεργεσία, so also Socrates (*Apology* 20D ff.) reminds his listeners that he does not really defend himself for his own sake, but merely attempts to prevent his judges and fellow-citizens from committing an act of injustice—another instance of his εὐεργεσία towards Athens. Socrates' concern over the possibility that his judges may commit an act of injustice (*Apology* 30C), itself may be based on *Palamedes* 35. And when he refuses to yield to convention or submit to the νόμος, whenever the latter is opposed to the δίκαιον, he seems to echo Palamedes (*Palamedes* 33). Also important is the fact that both Palamedes (*Palamedes* 33) and the Platonic Socrates (*Apology* 34BC) reject the idea of appealing to sympathy and compassion. Socrates' 'cross-examination' of Meletus, which leads him to the conclusion that Meletus does not really know or understand what the charges against him actually mean (*Apology* 26A), has an interesting and suggestive parallel in chapters 23–25 of the *Palamedes*. From these examples it may be inferred that in his defence the Socrates of Plato's *Apology* follows what appears to be an established literary pattern: the 'tragic defence' made by the innocent benefactor of mankind who, on account of his εὐεργεσία, is being prosecuted by some vile and jealous person.

The earliest known literary formulation of this tragic theme is probably by Aeschylus, of whose *Palamedes* we possess one and perhaps even two fragments.[1440] In Aeschylus, we may surmise, the Palamedes tragedy essentially centres around the ἔλεγξις τοῦ βίου. But, like the justification of Prometheus, so also the *Palamedes* was apparently an ἀπόδειξις τῶν εὐεργεσιῶν.[1441] With Euripides, who likewise wrote a *Palamedes*, as with Gorgias, the justification of Palamedes also went into the accusations as well as their refutation. In this sense both Euripides and Gorgias apparently inject a somewhat novel aspect into the Palamedes theme. Plato, in his *Apology*, seems to resume the theme as it had been treated by Aeschylus. This may be gathered from the fact that in both Plato and Aeschylus the 'defendant' insists that he has only followed 'the dictate of the deity'. It could therefore be maintained that in many respects Xenophon and Plato may have made the mythological *Defence of Palamedes* their model when they composed their legendary *Defence of Socrates*. Another possibility would be that the *Defence of Palamedes* and the Xenophontean or Platonic *Defence of Socrates* make use of a still earlier common model which can no longer be identified.

At this point we might speculate on the attitude which Antisthenes would have taken toward the Palamedes theme. The tradition, fully established by Aeschylus, Euripides, and Gorgias, apparently had Palamedes made out to be a σοφός, the inventor of many a science,[1442]

Conclusions and Implications

the enemy of the sly Odysseus, and the opponent of Agamemnon. We remember that Antisthenes was contemptuous of the type of σοφός which Palamedes represented, as well as of the scientific achievements in general. On the other hand, he greatly admired the craftiness of Odysseus and the τέχνη βασιλική of the 'shepherd king' Agamemnon. The aversion of Antisthenes to Palamedes may be gathered from Dio Chrysostom (*Oratio* 13.21), a work which, as Dümmler has shown, is based on some Antisthenian writing opposed to the 'new παιδεία' introduced by Palamedes. It seems that Antisthenes had felt that by teaching the Greeks 'the new way', Palamedes had brought upon himself his own misfortunes and, hence, had no one to blame but himself. In any event, this is the impression we get from Dio Chrysostom.[1443]

Xenophon likewise seems to have used the 'Palamedes theme'. The similarity particularly between certain passages in Xenophon's *Defence* and some ideas found in Gorgias' *Defence of Palamedes*, as regards both expression and content, is quite apparent. Thus Xenophon (*Defence* 27) makes Socrates state: οὐ γὰρ πάλαι ἴστε ὅτι ἐξ ὅτουπερ ἐγενόμην εατεψηφισμένος ἦν μου ὑπὸ τῆς φύσεως ὁ θάνατος. This reminds us of Gorgias, *Palamedes* 1: θάνατον μὲν γὰρ ἡ φύσις φανερᾷ τῇ ψήφῳ πάντων κατεψηφίσατο τῶν θνητῶν ᾗπερ ἡμέραι ἐγένετο. The fact that Gorgias speaks here in general terms as well as in the active voice, while Xenophon uses the passive voice as well as reports a particular instance, would indicate that Xenophon is the borrower. It could even be argued that *Defence* 27 contains a 'quotation' from the Gorgian *Palamedes*. This view seems to find additional support in *Defence* 26, where Socrates says: 'I find a certain consolation in the case of Palamedes who suffered a fate not unlike my own.' O. Frick insists, however, that the *Palamedes* of Euripides may be at the basis of the Xenophontean reference to the fate of Palamedes.[1444] But the case for Euripides is not very strong. Nowhere in his numerous writings does Xenophon ever mention Euripides. Neither can we detect in these writings the influence of any of the great Greek tragedians. On the other hand, he refers to Gorgias several times and always in a flattering manner.[1445] The thesis that Xenophon is under the influence of the Gorgian *Palamedes* is further supported by *Memorabilia* 4.2.33: 'Have you not heard of the woes of Palamedes... [and] how for the sake of his wisdom Odysseus envied him and slew him?' From the Gorgian *Defence of Palamedes* 33, we gather that envy (φθόνος) was the reason why Palamedes was prosecuted by Odysseus, who was jealous of Palamedes on account of his wisdom.[1446] It is extremely unlikely, on the other hand, that Euripides in his tragedy should have made the envy of Odysseus the cause of Palamedes' tragic misfortune.[1447]

Aside from Xenophon and Plato,[1448] the 'Palamedes myth' also seems to have been used by Satyrus in his (perhaps fictitious) account of the trial and death of Anaxagoras. According to Diogenes Laertius

Conclusions and Implications

(2.12–13), 'Satyrus, in his *Lives* (*Bίοι*),[1449] states that the accuser [of Anaxagoras] was Thucydides, [the son of Melesias and] the political opponent of Pericles; and that the charge was one of impiety as well as treasonable correspondence with Persia [medism].'[1450]

This would also bring up the further question, whether the many reports on the trial and death of Anaxagoras did not supply the later Socratic apologists with some of the materials which they wove into their probably fictitious accounts of the trial and death of Socrates. Perhaps the exclamation, 'Friend Meletus, you think that you are prosecuting Anaxagoras,'[1451] is indicative of Plato's dependence on his original model or source. As a matter of fact, the 'Anaxagoras myth' displays certain suggestive similarities with the 'Socrates myth' which cannot be taken too lightly. Naturally, it could also be maintained that the various accounts of the trial and death of Anaxagoras were modelled after the Socratic reports on the trial and death of Socrates.

There exist no less than six known reports of versions of the trial and death of Anaxagoras. According to the report of Hieronymus of Rhodes, preserved by Diogenes Laertius (2.14), 'Pericles accompanied [Anaxagoras] into Court. He [*scil.*, Anaxagoras] was so weak and wasted by illness that he owed his acquittal not so much to the merits of his case, but rather to sympathy.'[1452] The general idea underlying this particular report may be at the basis of the statements which Xenophon puts into the mouth of Socrates, that at his age he could expect only the 'torments of illness' and the 'painful decay which is incident to old age'.[1453] It may even be back of the Platonic statement (*Apology* 29D): 'If you had waited only a little, your desire [to kill me] would have been fulfilled in the course of nature. For I am far advanced in years ... and not far from death.'

In his *Lives*,[1454] Hermippus, the disciple of Callimachus, records what seems to be a very ancient version of the trial of Anaxagoras when, in the words of Diogenes Laertius (2.13), he states that Anaxagoras 'was imprisoned pending his execution. But Pericles went before the people asking them whether they could find any fault with him and the manner in which he was conducting the affairs of state. And when they replied in the negative, he continued: "Well, I am his [*scil.*, Anaxagoras'] pupil. Do not be carried away by gossip and put the man to death. Let me prevail upon you and release him." And so he was released. But he could not brook the indignity he had suffered and committed suicide.' The story told by Hermippus that Pericles had proven the innocence of Anaxagoras by referring to his own excellence, is merely an aspect of the theme, also employed by Polycrates, Xenophon, and Plato, that the excellence or evil of a teacher can be determined by the excellence or evil of his pupil.[1455]

Ephorus, who recounts what might possibly be the earliest known account of the trial and death of Anaxagoras, records that at the out-

Conclusions and Implications

break of the Peloponnesian War the seer Diopeithes, an implacable enemy of all 'modernism' and 'foreign ideas' or 'foreign influences', and a political opponent of Pericles, introduced a law making it a criminal offence to deny the gods which the city worshipped or to discuss matters of astronomy and meteorology. Pericles, being aware of the fact that this law was directed against Anaxagoras no less than against himself for having associated with the latter, became greatly perturbed and persuaded Anaxagoras to avoid trial under this new law by going into voluntary exile.[1456] Here we find the story, also contained in the Platonic and Xenophontean reports, that the defendant was indicted under a law which made it a specific crime not to recognize the gods which the city worshipped.

In his *Succession of philosophers*, Sotion, according to Diogenes Laertius (2.12), maintained that Anaxagoras 'was indicted by Cleon for impiety,[1457] because he had insisted that the sun was a red-hot mass. His pupil Pericles defended him, and he was fined five talents and banished.' Alcidamas, who is probably the source for Diogenes Laertius (2.14,) insists that Anaxagoras went into voluntary exile.[1458] And Sotion, as has already been noted, reports that Anaxagoras was not only accused of impiety, but also of *medism*. Then Sotion goes on to assert that 'a sentence of death was passed [on Anaxagoras] by default. When the latter was told that he had been condemned to death, and that his sons had died, he commented on the death sentence: "Long ago nature condemned to death both my judges and myself." And as regards his sons he said: "I know that my children were born to die." '[1459] It is interesting to note here that similar views on death have been ascribed to Socrates by Plato and Xenophon.

In sum, the tradition about the indictment, prosecutor, motives of the prosecution, and defence of Anaxagoras in its many variations could very well have furnished the model or models for the Platonic and Xenophontean *Apologies*, not only as regards the general theme, but also with respect to some detailed accounts. But more than that. Tradition also has it that at one time Anaxagoras had been an extremely wealthy man, but that he neglected his patrimony.[1460] In addition, it is said that he never troubled himself about public affairs: 'When some one asked him, "Have you no concern in your native land?" he replied, "Oh yes, indeed," pointing to the heavens.'[1461] For in his own words, he was born 'to study the sun and the moon and the heavens'.[1462] It may be maintained, therefore, that Anaxagoras anticipated also the cosmopolitanism of the Cynics which Xenophon occasionally wishes on Socrates, and the political indifferentism which some Socratic apologists have ascribed to Socrates. And when Anaxagoras remarks that the truly happy man is most likely a person no one has ever heard of,[1463] he seems to be touching upon the theme which reappears in the 'Chairophon episode'.[1464]

Conclusions and Implications

The Socratic story, particularly the accounts of his anti-democratic sentiments, his unpopularity, and his ultimate fate, also bears close resemblance to the life and fate of Antiphon of Rhamnus. Of Antiphon it was said that he was second to none in virtue, and that he was most able in expressing his views as well as in persuading people—characteristics which were also ascribed to Socrates. He was credited with having had a vast, though 'subterranean' political influence among oligarchic circles in Athens. Although he seldom, if ever, came into the open, Antiphon ceaselessly tried to undermine the democratic regime of Athens and its institutions. He seems to have been an uncompromising foe of Athenian democracy, a relentless despiser of the common people. This anti-democratic attitude of Antiphon, in many respects reminiscent of certain passages found in *The Old Oligarch*, became manifest, among other things, in his *Choreutes*, where he gave prominence to the many corruptions and evil deeds perpetrated by the officials of democratic Athens. Whenever possible, he seems to have put his cleverness and oratorical genius at the service of those who opposed Athenian democracy and the policies advocated by the Athenian democrats. Tradition also has it that he was the teacher of Alcibiades. Presumably he was most influential with the extremely powerful oligarchic *heteirai* or 'clubs' which combined in the year 411 and engineered the overthrow of the democratic regime. Antiphon apparently played a key role in this revolution. When after a few months this whole movement collapsed, he was charged with 'treason' and put on trial for his life. In his defence he is said to have delivered the greatest speech ever made within living memory by a man tried under similar circumstances. In spite of his efforts, however, he was sentenced to death and executed.[1465]

It could therefore be argued that in certain respects Socrates might have been the 'political successor' of Antiphon or, at least, a person who held political convictions very similar to those professed by Antiphon. The testimony of Polycrates, if it can be accepted as reliable evidence, would amply support such an argument. Of special interest is the fact that both Antiphon and Socrates did their political work 'behind the scenes'; that both seemed to have been despisers of Athenian democracy and the common people; that both criticized and belittled the institutions of Athenian democracy, thereby giving expression to their anti-democratic feelings; and that both apparently were viewed with suspicion by the people. In the case of Antiphon we know for a fact that he was tried and sentenced to death for the decisive role which he played in the oligarchic revolution of 411, while in the case of Socrates we can only surmise that his trial and death might have been connected with the oligarchic revolution of 404/3.

The problem connected with Socrates apparently also rests on the fact that at least for his partisans and followers he died the death of a

Conclusions and Implications

'martyr'—perhaps that of a 'political martyr'. And martyrdom, whether based on fact or fiction, in itself has always been one of the strongest incentives for starting an ever expanding and ever more 'miraculous' legend. It is possible that Socrates' alleged 'martyrdom' earned him, at least in the *Socratica* of his followers and admirers, a posthumous legendary nimbus which scholarly historical research can no longer hope to penetrate successfully. Socrates' disciples and admirers, in the diversity of their literary and artistic talents as well as in the variety of their philosophical inclinations, have tried to erect a literary legend of manifold forms, all of which are as intangible as they are elusive.[1466] We need not doubt that the Socratics portrayed Socrates as each of them wished to see him. In consequence, every Socratic, barring those instances where they borrowed from one another or from a common source, created his own brand of Socrates or 'Socratic martyr'. In the course of time this practice necessarily led to a diversity of 'Socratic schools', each claiming to give an accurate account of Socrates. Hence, we may conclude that whatever each of these Socratics offers as the 'true philosophy of Socrates', probably is nothing other than the peculiar kind of philosophy advanced by this particular Socratic himself.[1467] Or, as Karl Joël has so aptly put it: 'For Plato [Socrates] was a sublime ideal; for Antisthenes a model which called for imitation; and for Xenophon a pedagogical pattern.'[1468] The dramatists, too, have depicted this Socrates, sometimes as a madcap who, when invited to a party, would make off with the wine jug; sometimes as a pathetic simpleton who worried about the welfare of every one else while he himself remained oblivious of whether he had enough to eat; sometimes as a confused (and confusing) blend of Diogenes of Apollonia, the nebulous 'philosopher of nature', and the aggressive sophist Protagoras. But let it be repeated here once more: the suggestion that Socrates might have been primarily a political rather than a philosophical figure in the history of Athens, is merely an hypothesis;[1469] it does not exclude or even refute the possibility that he might also have been a man of personal probity and integrity, prompted in all his actions by sincere convictions, or that, like so many 'politicians' of his day, he might have been interested in discussions concerning the nature of virtue, both individual and social.

Socrates, we are convinced, never wrote down any of his convictions, whatever they may have been;[1470] apparently, for reasons of his own, he was completely devoid of the urge, so common among many of his more outstanding contemporaries, to put down and thus stabilize in some literary form his thoughts and ideas. This alone should be considered ample proof for the allegation that he was not a 'philosopher' or, to be more exact, a systematic or dogmatic thinker. A thinker, however, who fails to confine to writing some of his thoughts, always runs the risk of becoming something like an uncharted ocean: he may be

Conclusions and Implications

profound, but his profundity will remain beyond measure and, hence, both intangible and without real meaning. Only by committing himself to something tangibly definite, to something that may withstand the flux to which all things intangible must fall victim—in sum, only by writing and composing—can the thinker achieve the stability of intelligent articulation and intelligible discipline. Admittedly, in the final outcome such a commitment always leads to a sort of 'dogmatism', even in the case of the most volatile sceptic. Thought, despite (and probably also on acount of) its original flexibility, whenever stabilized, must somehow become 'dogma' in order to achieve intelligibility—when, in other words, it is expressed in and through a definite and stable 'thought content' which, in turn, must be manipulated in accordance with the principles of unity, identity, and continuity of subject and method. The written word, more than anything else, is the stable and therefore lasting and reliable monument of fleeting thought. And only as a stable monument may it serve as the secure stepping-stone to further articulate and disciplined thought. Socrates, it seems, has remained that measureless, inscrutable, and perhaps even profound ocean which by now may defy all navigation and sounding. But as such an unchartered expanse he was to an eminent degree destined to become that inexhaustible fountain-head which forever could feed the streams of many a legend and myth.

We are compelled to arrive at the following conclusions: the two Socratic apologies of Xenophon apparently were occasioned not by the historical trial of Socrates in 399, but by the anti-Socratic literary campaign launched by the Late Sophists, particularly by the κατηγορία Σωκράτους of Polycrates which was published in 393/2. Although both the Xenophontean *Defence* and *Memorabilia* 1.1.1–2.64 contain references to the historical trial of Socrates, these references are incidental to the real purpose of Xenophon which was to refute the Late Sophists and especially Polycrates. The κατηγορία of Polycrates, like the other anti-Socratic writings of the Late Sophists, is no longer extant. But it is possible to reconstruct the essential features of the κατηγορία with the help of Libanius' *Apologia Socratis* and Xenophon's *Memorabilia* 1.2.9–61. There are no known authentic works of the historical Socrates. The secondary Socratic sources—namely, the early dialogues of Plato, the *Socratica* of Xenophon, the few references to Socrates found in the writings of Aristotle,[1471] and the utterances made by the comic poets of the late fifth century—on the other hand, supply only unsatisfactory and at times seriously conflicting reports about Socrates and his teachings. Since these secondary sources might be, and probably are part of the 'Socratic legend', we are unable to ascertain with any degree of certainty the philosophical views held by the historical Socrates—provided that he ever dealt with philosophy. But despite the lack of a reliable account of the historical Socrates, the reconstructed κατηγορία

Conclusions and Implications

Σωκράτους of Polycrates impresses us as being based on Antisthenian-Cynic rather than historical, that is, Socratic materials. The Xenophontean rejoinders to the κατηγορία Σωκράτους, it seems, are likewise based on Antisthenian-Cynic teachings. Thus the whole Socratic controversy between Xenophon and Polycrates is primarily a literary battle fought over Antisthenes or *Antisthenica* rather than over Socrates.[1472] To make matters even more involved, barring a few fragments and some not altogether reliable secondary sources, the works of Antisthenes which apparently supplied both Polycrates and Xenophon with their information, are completely lost. Hence it is also impossible to establish the extent to which Antisthenes could be called the faithful disciple and expounder of Socrates and his teachings, if—we repeat—it is permissible to speak of 'the teachings of Socrates'.

The path which may lead to the discovery of the historical Socrates, needless to say, is both an extremely difficult and painful one. It is a difficult journey because it carries us through a maze of fragmentary, grotesquely distorted, and seriously conflicting reports. It is a painful journey in that it compels us constantly to discard certain notions which in the course of time have become very dear to the Western mind. And the unmasking of attractive legends, like the loss of the fairy tales of our childhood, is always a saddening experience.

This difficult and painful journey, it should be borne in mind, must be concluded in what could be styled three distinct stages. Of necessity, the first stage is one of ruthlessly negative criticisms carried out in a spirit of dissecting pedantry. Since Socrates did not leave behind any authentic works of his own, we are compelled to fall back on the accounts of others in order to gain some information about the historical Socrates. But no ancient author, it seems, really intended to take up the issues connected with the historical Socrates. As a matter of fact, we are inclined to believe that the whole of the ancient literary tradition about Socrates primarily was meant to create a legend rather than to report historical facts: it was never intended to be historiography or biography. Aristotle had already insisted that the λόγοι Σωκρατικοί[1473] were part of poetry (μίμησις).[1474] And Plato seems to have had a true understanding of the nature of these λόγοι when he states that 'the mere fragments...of your [*scil.*, Socrates'] words (λόγοι), *even if repeated at second hand and incorrectly reported*, amaze and take hold of the souls of every man, woman, and child who should hear about Socrates'.[1475] The few possible historical facts which might have become incorporated into this legend probably did so as the result of mere accident rather than design on the part of its author or authors. And nearly every legend contains a kernel of historical truth. Since the whole of the ancient Socratic literature seems to be primarily intentional legend, the only thing we may confidently assert about the historical Socrates is that we know practically nothing about him.

Conclusions and Implications

The second stage of our journey is obviously determined by the methods employed during the first stage. It may be called that phase of Socratic research which necessarily must concentrate on the Socratics —the various authors of the many Socratic legends. These Socratic legends, it should be remembered, are definitely 'auto-biographical' or 'self-revelatory' sketches reflecting the philosophical and literary talents of their authors. Such an insight, although it adds little or nothing to our direct and factual knowledge about the historical Socrates, enables us better to understand the Socratics in their characteristic contributions, as well as the different personal motives behind their *Socratica*. This, in turn, should give us at least a hint of what Socrates might probably *not* have been. Hence the second stage is actually a destructive-construction journey in that it throws some light on the differences which probably exist between the historical Socrates and the fictitious *Socratica* of the strongly individualistic Socratics.

The third stage of our quest for the historical Socrates consists perhaps in the following realization: it is most unlikely that an ordinary person of no real historical significance should become the subject of a brilliant and voluminous type of ancient literature which succeeded in transforming its 'hero' into one of the truly great philosophers of the Western world. Such happenings are not the result of mere accident. For no insignificant person, to be sure, could have been honoured so much by so many brilliant writers as has Socrates. But we can no longer ascertain the factual and detailed reasons why this man Socrates should have been exalted as no other mortal man has ever been exalted—why, in other words, a historical personality named Socrates should fall heir to a most distinguished literary tradition. Neither can we fully explain the reasons why even Socrates' contemporaries would refer to him only '*in der Indirektheit der Dichtung*'—in the irreducible indirectness common to all fictions.[1476]

Notes

NOTES TO CHAPTER I—PAGES 1-16

[1] Cf. A.-H. Chroust, 'Socrates in the light of Aristotle's testimony', in *The New Scholasticism* 26, no. 3 (1952) 327-365; Th. Deman, *Le témoignage d'Aristote sur Socrate, Collection d'études anciennes*, Assoc. Budé (Paris, 1942).

[2] F. Schleiermacher, *Sämtliche Werke* (1838) vol. 8, part 2, 297 ff.

[3] Cf. E. Zeller, *Die Philosophie der Griechen* vol. 2, part 1 (4th edit., 1889) 92.

[4] Cf. A.-H. Chroust, 'Socrates—a source problem', in *The New Scholasticism* 19, no. 1 (1945) 52 ff. and *ibid.* at 57 ff.; J. Stenzel, 'Über den Zusammenhang des Dichterischen und Religiösen bei Platon', in *Schlesische Jahrbücher*, philos.—histor. Klasse, Abt. 2 (1924) 143 ff.

[5] Cf. *Memor.* 1.2.30 and *ibid.* at 1.2.40; *et passim*.

[6] It has been claimed that the *Socratica* of Xenophon to a large extent are under the influence of Cynic teachings. Cf. A. Krohn, *Sokrates und Xenophon* (Halle, 1874); K. Lincke, *De Xenophontis libris Socraticis* (Jena, 1890); K. Joël, *Der echte und der xenophontische Sokrates*, 2 vols. (Berlin, 1893-1901); F. Dümmler, *Antisthenica* (1882); F. Dümmler, *Akademika* (1889).

[7] Cf. E. Richter, 'Xenophon-Studien', in *Jahrbücher für classische Philologie* 19, Supplement (1893) 101-104. Both the apologetic *Socratica* of Xenophon and his *Agesilaus* are primarily encomia.

[8] Cf. E. Richter, *op. cit.* at 104-107.

[9] Cf. E. Richter, *op. cit.* at 112-118.

[10] As to certain similarities between the various writings of Xenophon, cf. the remarks found in E. Richter, *op. cit.* at 118-123.

[11] Cf. U. v. Wilamowitz-Moellendorff, 'Phaidon von Elis', in *Hermes* 14 (1879) 187-193; L. Robin, 'Les mémorables de Xénophon et nôtre connaissance de la philosophie de Socrate', in *L'année philosophique* 21 (Paris, 1910) 1 ff.; John P. Mahaffy, *History of classical Greek literature* (3rd edit., 1890) vol. 2, 60 ff. and *ibid.* at 79; J. P. Mahaffy, *Problems in Greek history* (1892) 104 ff.; H. Maier, *Sokrates* (Tübingen, 1913) 13-77; E. Richter, *op. cit.* at 59-154. Ancient authors who deprecated the

Notes to Chapter I

historical value of Xenophon's works were Sextus Empiricus, *Adversus mathematicos* 7.8 ff., and Cicero, *Acad.* 1.4.

[12] Cf. A. Döring, *Die Lehre des Sokrates als soziales Reformsystem* (München, 1895); E. Zeller, *op. cit.* 2, part 1 (1889) 44–232.

[13] Cf. K. Sittl, *Geschichte der griechischen Literatur* 2 (1886) 437 ff.

[14] Cf. K. Sittl, *op. cit.* at 2.437 and *ibid.* at 2.440: '[The *Hellenica*] ... is not a purely historical work, but rather a piece of propaganda. ... It casts an unfavourable light on the character and ability of Xenophon as a historiographer.' *Ibid.* at 2.442: 'In his *Hellenica* Xenophon manifests his complete lack of historical understanding.' *Ibid.* at 2.441 and 2.443. The views expressed by Sittl are now generally accepted.

[15] The *Memorabilia*, at least Book I, chaps. 3 ff., were collected or written primarily for the purpose of glorifying Socrates. This may be gathered from *Memor.* 1.3.1: 'It may serve a good purpose to show how he [*scil.*, Socrates] benefited those who associated with him . . . if I were to set down my various recollections (γράψω ὁπόσα ἂν διαμνημονεύσω).'

[16] Cf. A.-H. Chroust, 'Socrates—a source problem', in *The New Scholasticism* 19, no. 1 (1945) 60.

[17] D. R. Stuart, *Epochs in Greek and Roman biography* (Berkeley, 1928) 34.

[18] Cf. K. Joël, *op. cit.* 1.21.

[19] Cf. *The Defence of Socrates before his Judges*, (subsequently referred to as *Defence*) 22: 'Undoubtedly, there were many other things said during the trial . . . but I have not been careful enough to collect all that was said.'

[20] Cf. *Memor.* 1.4.2. and *ibid.* at 2.4.1; 2.7.1; 4.8.4; *Defence* 2 and *ibid.* at 10; 29.

[21] The one notable exception is Hermogenes. Cf. *Defence* 2. *Memor.* 4.8.4.–10 contain a conversation which Hermogenes is said to have had with Socrates. Hermogenes, in the words of Xenophon, later reports this conversation to Xenophon. One wonders, however, how Hermogenes could have done this. Was it by letter, or during a visit to Scillus or perhaps to Asia Minor, or after Xenophon had returned to Athens after a long exile? Cf. E. Richter, *op. cit.* at 124.

[22] Compared with other Socratic discourses, the topic of this particular conversation, which also appears in the Xenophontean *Symposium* (4.10 ff.), is of very little significance.

[23] Cf. E. Richter, *op. cit.* at 126 and *ibid.* at 93.

[24] Cf. *ibid.* at 126.

[25] *Memor.* 1.6.11–14, where this remark appears at the end of the report. Cf. *Memor.* 2.4.1 and *ibid.* at 2.5.1; 1.4.2; *Oeconomicus* 1.1.

[26] Cf. E. Richter, *op. cit.* at 126–7.

[27] *Memor.* 2.7.1: 'I shall state what I know about him [*scil.*, Socrates].' *Memor.* 2.9.1: 'I recall that he [*scil.*, Socrates] once heard Crito say.'

Notes to Chapter I

Memor. 2.10.1: 'I remember, as known to myself, the following conversation between him [*scil.*, Socrates] and Diodorus.' *Memor.* 3.3.1: 'When someone was elected hipparch, I recall that he [*scil.*, Socrates] conversed with him as follows.' *Memor.* 4.4.5: 'I recall a conversation he [*scil.*, Socrates] had with Hippias.' *Memor.* 4.5.2: 'I recall . . . a conversation he [*scil.*, Socrates] once had with Euthydemus.' *Memor.* 1.2.53: 'But I recall that he [*scil.*, Socrates] said this.'

[28] 'Xenophon was no friend of Aristippus. For this reason he made Socrates direct against Aristippus the discourse in which he denounces pleasure.' The 'discourse' which Diogenes Laertius mentions here is *Memor.* 2.1.1–34. It is interesting to note that already Diogenes Laertius seems to be aware of the fictitious nature of this 'discourse'.

[29] Cf. A.-H. Chroust, 'Socrates—a source problem' 61 ff.

[30] *Memor.* 3.1.1–3.3.14. The whole of these accounts reminds us of Xenophon's *Hipparchus* and *Cyropaedia* 1.6.12 ff., as well as *ibid.* at 8.5.15. The *Hipparchus*, the authorship of which has remained unassailed on the whole, was written *c.* 365. Cf. H. Roquette, *De vita Xenophontis* (1884) 2.24, pp. 95–96. It is singularly full of Xenophon's idiosyncrasies to the point of being an auto-biographical sketch. Cf. J. Hartman, *Analecta Xenophontea* (1887) 320.

[31] *Memor.* 3.6.1–18. A similarity of subject and tone can be found between these passages and Xenophon's *De vectigalibus*, which apparently was written around 355. The *De vectigalibus* deals with the social, political, and economic situation that prevailed in Greece just after the conclusion of the so-called Social War. The authorship of the *De vectigalibus*—the ancient original title seems to have been πόροι ἢ περὶ προσόδων—is still hotly debated. Cf. G. Sauppe, *Liber de vectigalibus*, praef. 194; A. Zurborg, *De Xenophontis libro qui πόροι inscribitur* 17; A. Wilhelm, 'Untersuchungen zu Xenophons πόροι', in *Wiener Studien* 52 (1934) 18–56.

[32] *Memor.* 3.5.1–28, where Socrates holds a political conversation with Pericles the Younger. The literary setting of this conversation would suggest that it took place in 407/6, the year Pericles the Younger was *strategos*. (He was executed in the year 406 as one of the generals commanding in the battle of the Arginusae islands.) But the political situation which is at the basis of this conversation indicates that it was held after the battle of Leuctra (371), when Thebes had obtained hegemony in Greece by defeating Sparta; or perhaps even after 369, the probable year in which the decree of exile against Xenophon was rescinded. Cf. Diogenes Laertius (subsequently referred to as D.L.) 2.59.

[33] Cf. K. Joël, *op. cit.* at 1.13.

[34] Cf. Fr. Leo, *Die griechisch-römische Biographie* (Leipzig, 1901) 90.

[35] H. Maier, *Sokrates*, 39, note 1.

[36] The Antisthenian sources used by Xenophon will be discussed later in great detail.

Notes to Chapter I

37 Cf. *Memor.* 2.1.1–34 and *ibid.* at 3.8.1–10, as well as the whole of the Xenophontean *Symposium*. This would indicate that Xenophon made use of some of Aristippus' writings.

38 The connection between *Oeconomicus* 3.14 and the *Aspasia* of Aeschines (frag. 9, edit. Krauss) has already been pointed out by U. v. Wilamowitz-Moellendorff, *Aristoteles und Athen* 2.99. Cf. H. Dittmar, *Aischinos von Sphettos* (Berlin, 1912) 34 ff. For the connections between Xenophon's *Symposium* and the *Callias* of Aeschines, see H. Dittmar, *op. cit.* at 209 ff.; for the connection between *Memor.* 2.6.36 and the *Aspasia* of Aeschines, cf. H. Dittmar, *op. cit.* at 35; and for the connection between *Memor.* 4.2.2 or *ibid.* at 4.8.6 and the *Alcibiades* of Aeschines, see H. Dittmar, *op. cit.* at 124 ff.

39 There exist a great many suggestive similarities between the *Socratica* of Xenophon and a vast number of passages in the dialogues of Plato. Cf., among others, *Memor.* 4.4.5–25, and *Gorgias* 490E–491B; *Memor.* 4.2.1–40, and the whole tenor of the *Hippias Minor*; *Memor.* 3.9.14–15, or *Memor.* 4.2.31–35, and *Euthydemus* 278E ff., *Memor.* 1.4.8, and *Philebus* 29A ff.; *Memor.* 4.4.3–4, and *Apology* 32C as well as *ibid.* at 34C ff.; *Memor.* 2.1.17, and *Euthydemus* 291B as well as *Statesman* 300E; *Memor.* 3.9.1, and *Meno* 70A as well as *ibid.* at 92E; *Memor.* 4.2.31 ff., and *Meno* 87E ff.; *Memor.* 4 4.5–6, and *Symposium* 221E; *Memor.* 4.5.12 and *ibid.* at 4.6.1, and *Sophist* 253D; *Memor.* 4.6.2, and the whole tenor of the *Euthyphro*; *Memor.* 4.8.1, and *Apology* 38C; *Memor.* 4.8.8, and *Apology* 38A; *Anabasis* 2.5.7, and *Laws* 905A; *Defence* 28, and *Phaedo* 59A; *Memor.* 4.6.10–11, and the tenor of the whole *Laches*; *Memor.* 4.2.2–6, and *Meno* 90C ff.; *Memor.* 4.2.11–12, and *Republic* 331C ff. as well as *ibid.* at 382C and 389B; *Memor.* 4.6.2–4, and the tenor of the *Euthyphro*; *Memor.* 4.2.24–26, and *Phaedrus* 229E ff.; *Memor.* 4.6.1, and *Phaedrus* 262AB as well as *Charmides* 166D; *Memor.* 4.5.11, and *Sophist* 253CD; *Memor.* 4.5.12, and *Statesman* 285D–287A; *Memor.* 4.6.1, and *Statesman* 285D–287A; *Memor.* 4.6.13–15, and *Phaedo* 101D as well as *ibid* at 100A; *Memor.* 4.6.13–15, and *Republic* 532A ff. as well as *ibid.* at 511B, 510B, and 437A.

40 *Memor.* 4.2.13–19 seem to be closely related to δίσσοι λόγοι (or διαλέξεις), chap. 3 (in Diels-Kranz, *Die Fragmente der Vorsokratiker*, 5th edit. (Berlin, 1935), vol. 2, 410–411). The same may be maintained about some passages in *Memor.* 4.4.1–25, in which Socrates discusses the nature of justice with Hippias. M. Pohlenz, *Aus Platons Werdezeit* (Berlin, 1913) 72 ff., points out that the δίσσοι λόγοι are an excerpt from a lecture by Hippias.

41 In his *Anaximenes von Lampsakos* (Berlin, 1905) 65 ff., P. Wendland has shown that *Memor.* 3.6.1–18 are based on an old text on rhetoric.

42 Cf. E. Richter, *op. cit.*, at 128 ff.

43 *Memor.* 1.3.8 ff. The ideas advanced in this conversation not only

Notes to Chapter I

reappear in the Xenophontean *Symposium* (4.10 ff.), but are also expressed there in nearly identical words.

[44] If this were true, then Socrates himself would already have realized the insignificance and low mentality of Xenophon.

[45] *Symposium, Memor.* 1.4.2–18, *Memor.* 1.6.11–14, *Memor.* 2.4.1–7, *Memor.* 2.5.1–5, *Memor.* 4.3.2–17, and *Oeconomicus*. The *Memorabilia* and the *Oeconomicus* are both *Socratica* and, hence, are really closely related to each other as regards their form and the spirit in which they were composed. Cf. K. Joël, *op. cit.*, at 1.36; K. Lincke, *Xenophon's Dialog περὶ οἰκονομίας* (Leipzig, 1879) 49 ff. Lincke deprecates the historical reliability and value of the *Oeconomicus*. About Lincke's views, cf. K. Joël, *op. cit.* at 1.34 ff.

[46] *Symposium, Oeconomicus, Memor.* 1.4.1–7, and *Memor.* 4.3.2–17.

[47] Cf. E. Richter, *op. cit.* at 134 and *ibid.* at 125–127.

[48] The 'audience', whenever mentioned, remains mute or, at best, joins in with a sedate laughter. Cf. *Memor.* 1.3.8 and *ibid.* at 1.6.1; 1.6.14; 2.5.1; 3.1.4; 3.1.5; 3.8.1; 3.11.2; 4.2.3; 4.4.5; *et passim*.

[49] Such 'factual settings' are particularly important for Books I and IV of the *Memorabilia*. But otherwise these factual settings are frequently only cryptic statements and, therefore, of little help in establishing historical truth in that they give us merely a general hint as to the particular occasion for a lengthy discourse.

[50] 'But in order to illustrate the claim that he [*scil.*, Socrates] improved those who associated with him—partly by the display of his own virtue, partly by indulging in discussion and argument—I shall set down whatever I remember of him as regards these matters.'

[51] H. Maier, *Sokrates* 35–36.

[52] Cf. K. Joël, *op. cit.* at 1.12 and *ibid.* at 1.27.

[53] Cf. K. Sittl, *Geschichte der griechischen Literatur* 2 (1886) 447.

[54] Cf. *Memor.* 1.4.1 and *ibid.* at 4.3.2.

[55] Cf. note 1237, *infra*.

[56] Cf. *ibid.* at 3.9; 4.8; 4.27; 4.29 ff.; 4.52; 8.35–41.

[57] Cf. notes 1223, and 1240, *infra*.

[58] See note 32, *supra*.

[59] We shall show later the particular reason why Xenophon should make such an effort to stress (and perhaps even over-stress) the unrivalled moral and intellectual eminence of Socrates.

[60] The story, retold in *Anabasis* 3.1.4 ff., if it is at all to be believed, would not indicate that a close personal relationship ever existed between the two men. Cf. D.L. 2.49–50, a passage which seems to rely on the report of the *Anabasis*.

[61] *Memor.* 1.2.12–39; Libanius, *Apologia Socratis* (edit. Foerster) vol. 5, 90 ff.

[62] If this report is correct, then the true cause of Xenophon's banishment would have been his *laconism*.

Notes to Chapter II

[63] Xenophon, *Anabasis* 5.3.7. Cf. D.L. 2.51.

[64] Xenophon, *Anabasis* 7.7.57.

[65] In view of the fact that the evidence for dating Xenophon's banishment around the year 399 is supplied by ancient authors who wrote some time after the event took place, we shall hold here with those scholars who consider Xenophon's participation in the battle of Coronea (394) the true cause of his exile.

[66] Theodor Gomperz, *Griechische Denker* 2 (2nd edit., Leipzig, 1912) 102.

[67] In the Xenophontean *Oeconomicus*.

[68] *Memor.* 3.3.1 ff., which is really an excerpt from the *Hipparchus*.

[69] H. Maier (*Sokrates* 39), in our opinion, over-rates Xenophon's 'personal contacts' with Socrates. On the whole, Maier, although quite in doubt as to the general reliability of the Xenophontean testimony, seems to give too much credence to Xenophon as a Socratic witness.

NOTES TO CHAPTER II—PAGES 17–43

[70] For the title of this work, cf. G. Grote, *History of Greece* 8.641; L. Schmitz, 'On the Apology of Socrates commonly attributed to Xenophon', in *Class. Mus.* 5.222 ff.; J. Hartman, *Analecta Xenophontea* (1887) 111 ff.; E. Richter, 'Xenophonstudien', 61–96.

[71] Some scholars insist that *Memor.* 1.2.62–64 are not a part of this second *Apology*. J. Mesk, 'Die Anklagerede des Polykrates gegen Sokrates', in *Wiener Studien* 32 (1911) 57, note 1. E. Richter, *op. cit.*, 59–155, suggests that Xenophon actually wrote four apologies of Socrates. *Apology I*, according to Richter, consists of *Memor.* 1.1.1–9 (or 1.1.19), 1.3.1–4, 1.1.10 (or 1.1.20)–1.2.5, 1.3.5–15 and 1.2.62–64; *Apology II* consists of *Memor.* 1.4.1–19 and 4.3.1–4.6.15; *Apology III* consists of *Memor.* 1.5.1–2.1.34 and 3.8.1–3.9.15; and *Apology IV* is the *Defence of Socrates before his Judges*. Cf. the review of Richter's theory by F. Dümmler, in *Kleine Schriften* (1901) 1.301. While the theory proposed by Richter is plausible, it fails to take account of Polycrates' κατηγορία Σωκράτους, which had a definite influence on the apologetic writings of Xenophon.

[72] Lysias, *Oratio* 22.7. The story told in D.L. (Diogenes Laertius) 2.43 that Anytus was exiled soon after the death of Socrates is probably an invention of some Socratic. Later authors also took revenge on Anytus by insisting that he died miserably. According to Themistius (5.20, p. 293, edit. Dindorf), he was banished from Athens and later stoned to death in Heraclea, where he sought refuge. In the words of Diogenes Laertius (2.43, 6.10), he tried to find asylum in Heraclea,

Notes to Chapter II

but was immediately driven from this town. Xenophon, *Defence* 31, reports that he was much abused after Socrates' death.

⁷³ As to the authenticity of the Xenophontean *Defence*, see the following authorities: U. v. Wilamowitz-Moellendorff, 'Die xenophontische Apologie', in *Hermes* 32 (1897) 99 ff., and K. v. Fritz, 'Zur Frage der Echtheit der xenophontischen Apologie', in *Rheinisches Museum* 80 (1931) 36–68, call it a spurious work, though in his *Platon* (1920) 2.50, Wilamowitz allows the Xenophontean authorship to be conceivable. M. Schanz, in *Apologia Socratis* (1893) 83; O. Immisch, in *Neue Jahrbücher für das klassische Altertum* (1900) 389 ff.; O. Frick, in *Dissertationes philolog. Halenses* 19 (1911); H. v. Arnim, in *Xenophons Memorabilien und die Apologie des Sokrates* (Copenhagen, 1923); H. Gomperz, in *Neue Jahrbücher für das klassische Altertum* (1924) 129–173; and A. Busse, 'Xenophons Schutzschrift und die Apologie', in *Rheinisches Museum* 79 (1930) 215 ff., strongly defend Xenophon's authorship.

⁷⁴ Cf. *Memor.* 4.4.4 and *ibid* at 4.8.5 ff.; 4.3.2; 1.4.1: 'Some people seem to hold, in accordance with certain views maintained concerning Socrates. . . .' Obviously Xenophon attempts here to make it clear not only that his views or recollections concerning Socrates differ from the reports of other men, but that he considers these other reports unsatisfactory.

⁷⁵ Cf. also Plato, *Phaedo* 58E.

⁷⁶ Cf. M. Schanz, *Apologia Socratis* 79.

⁷⁷ It might be assumed here that in his *Defence* Xenophon made use of the Platonic *Apology*. Cf. R. Hackforth, *The Composition of Plato's Apology* (1933) 12–46.

⁷⁸ *Xenophons Memorabilien und die Apologie des Sokrates* (Copenhagen, 1923) 12 ff.

⁷⁹ *Ibid.* at 19.

⁸⁰ U. v. Wilamowitz-Moellendorff, *Aristoteles und Athen* 2.374; A. Menzel, *Hellenika* (1938) 44 ff.

⁸¹ Cf. *Defence* 20–21.

⁸² Isocrates (*Busiris* 6) insinuates that a number of apologetic *Socratica* existed around 390, the probable date of the *Busiris*.

⁸³ Cf. notes 89–95, *infra*, and the text thereto.

⁸⁴ Cf. Plato, *Apology* 34CD; *Gorgias* 486AB and *ibid.* at 522BC; 522D; Xenophon *Memor.* 4.8.1–2.

⁸⁵ About this Hermogenes, cf. Xenophon, *Memor.* 4.8.4 ff.; Pauly-Wissowa, *Realencyclopädie der classischen Altertumswissenschaften* (1912) 15th Halbband, col. 865, no. 21. Hermogenes is the only source which Xenophon quotes by name in his *Socratica*. See note 21, *supra*. Hermogenes seems to have been a follower or friend of Antisthenes. A. W. Winckelmann, *Fragmenta Antisthenis* (1842), index. Antisthenes' reference to the disinherited brother who lives in abject poverty (Xenophon, *Symposium* 4.35), or to an impoverished friend (Xenophon,

Notes to Chapter II

Memor. 2.5.3–4), may also allude to this Hermogenes. Cf. the sympathetic reference to Hermogenes in Xenophon, *Memor.* 2.10.3–6, which parallels those made in the Xenophontean *Symposium.*

[86] Cf. Xenophon, *Memor.* 4.4.10: 'A man who does the just thing cannot himself be unjust.' Plato, *Apology* 41D: 'No evil can occur to a good man, either in life or after death.' Plato, *Gorgias* 526D: 'Renouncing the honours to which this world aspires, I desire only to know the truth, and to live as well as I can; and when I die, to die as well as I can. And to the utmost of my powers I shall exhort all other men to do the same.' Plato, *Crito* 43BC: 'When a man has reached my age he should not wince at the approach of death.' *Gorgias* 522DE; Libanius, *Apologia Socratis*, chap. 3 (15.7–11, edit. Foerster).

[87] Cf. Xenophon, *Memor.* 4.8.1 and *ibid.* at 4.8.5; Cicero, *De oratore* 1.54.231; Quintilian, *Institutiones orat.* 2.15.30 and *ibid.* at 11.1.11; Valerius Maximus 6.4.2; Stobaeus, *Florilegium* 5.76.

[88] Cf. F. Blass, *Attische Beredsamkeit* (2nd edit., 1887) 1.351 and *ibid.* at 1.357; 1.365–370; 1.247–249; R. C. Jebb, *Attic Orators* 1.153 ff.; R. Hirzel, 'Polycrates' Anklage und Lysias' Verteidigung des Sokrates', in *Rheinisches Museum* 42 (1887) 239 ff. There exists a tradition which attempts to distinguish between two Socratic apologies by Lysias. One apology, it is said, is the one which Lysias offered Socrates before the latter went on trial in 399 (D.L. 2.40–41; H. Sauppe, *Oratores Attici* 2.203 ff.). The other apology constitutes Lysias' rejoinder to Polycrates' pamphlet and hence was written after 393/2 (R. Hirzel, *op. cit.* at 249; F. Blass, *op. cit.* at 1.342). Hirzel (*loc. cit.*) rightly denies the validity of such a distinction. For the *Apologia Socratis* of Lysias, cf. also Stobaeus, *Florilegium* 7.56; Plutarch, *Vit. decem orator.* 836; and the fragments of Lysias' *Apology*, in H. Sauppe, *op. cit.* 2.204.

[89] Demosthenes 27.1; Isaeus 10.1; Antiphon, *On the murder of Herodes* 1–7.

[90] Demosthenes 27.2; 57.2; Isaeus 8.4–5; Lysias 19.11; 30.6; Andocides, *De mysteriis* 2. Cf. A.-H. Chroust, 'The legal profession in ancient Athens', in *Notre Dame Lawyer* 29, no. 3 (1954) 374.

[91] Xenophon, *Hellenica* 1.7.15; *Memor.* 1.1.18 and *ibid.* at 4.4.2; Plato *Apology* 32B.

[92] The same theme—the helplessness and frustration of the philosopher in a court of law—appears also in Plato, *Theaetetus* 172C–175D. Cf. Plato, *Republic* 517A and *ibid.* at 517D; *Laches* 196B; Libanius, *Apologia Socratis*, chap. 46 (39.10–12, edit. Foerster, vol. 5, Leipzig, 1919). H. Gomperz, 'Sokrates Haltung vor seinen Richtern', in *Wiener Studien* 54 (1936) 32–42, and W. A. Oldfather, 'Socrates in court', in *Classical Weekly* 31, no. 21 (1938) 203–211, insist that Socrates never made a formal defence at all. See A. D. Winspear, *Who was Socrates?* (1939) 72. This latter view would find some support in Maximus of Tyre, *Oratio* 3 (edit. Hobein). Diogenes Laertius (2.41–42) likewise fails

Notes to Chapter II

to refer to a formal defence made by Socrates. Cf. H. Gomperz, *op. cit.* at 35.

⁹³ Cf. Plato, *Apology* 37A ff.; Xenophon, *Defence* 32; *Memor.* 4.8.5: 'The judges at Athens have already put to death many an innocent man, because they were offended at his language. . . .' *Ibid.* at 4.4.4: '. . . to speak so as to gain the favour of the judges, and to supplicate them . . . he [*scil.*, Socrates] refused to do . . . although he might easily have been acquitted . . . had he only in a slight degree adopted any of these practices.' Libanius, *Apologia Socratis* chap. 3 (15.11–16, Foerster): 'As regards certain methods, employed by not a few men (whose guilt is beyond all doubt) in order to procure an acquittal, namely, to arouse sympathy by shedding tears and the wailing of their children—as regards such methods he [*scil.*, Socrates] refused to make use of them. In this his contempt for such practices went so far as to cause some among you [*scil.*, the judges) a mounting feeling of anger against him. . . .' See Aristophanes, *Wasps* 568 ff.; A.-H. Chroust, 'The legal profession in ancient Athens', in *Notre Dame Lawyer* 29, no. 3 (1954) 379 ff. As to the sons of Socrates (Lamprocles, Sophroniscus, and Menexenus), see Plato, *Apology* 34D and *ibid.* at 41E; *Crito* 45CD; *Phaedo* 60A and *ibid.* at 116B; *Gorgias* 486A ff. and *ibid.* at 508CD; Aristotle, *Rhetoric* 1390 b 30.

⁹⁴ Cf. G. Glotz, *La solidarité de la famille dans le droit criminelle en Grèce* (Paris, 1904) 552 ff.

⁹⁵ See the general tenor of Aristophanes' *Wasps*.

⁹⁶ Cf. Xenophon, *Memor.* 4.8.5 and *ibid.* at 4.8.1–3. An interesting analysis of the Xenophontean treatment of the Socratic daemon can be found in K. Joël, *op. cit.* at 1.70–89, especially at 1.71–72.

⁹⁷ *Memor.* 4.8.5.

⁹⁸ Cf. Plato, *Apology* 35A: '. . . they seemed to fancy that they were going to suffer something dreadful if they died; and that they could become immortal if you only allowed them to live.' *Phaedo* 116E–117A; *Gorgias* 474BC and *ibid.* at 489AB; 508C ff.

⁹⁹ Cf. *Memor.* 4.8.8; Plato, *Apology* 17A ff. and *ibid.* at 19A; 29AB; 30C; 34C ff.; *Crito* 43D; Dio Chrysostom, *Oratio* 28.7.

¹⁰⁰ Cf. Xenophon, *Anabasis* 6.5.14; Sophocles, *Oedipus Rex* 465.

¹⁰¹ Plato, *Apology* 29AB. Cf. *ibid.* 42A.

¹⁰² Plato, *Apology* 38C. Cf. Plato, *Phaedo* 66A ff.; Xenophon, *Memor.* 4.8.1; Libanius, *Apologia Socratis* chap. (15.18–16.1, Foerster).

¹⁰³ Plato, *Apology* 29C.

¹⁰⁴ Plato, *Gorgias* 461E.

¹⁰⁵ Plato, *Crito* 45E.

¹⁰⁶ Cf. C. Ritter, *Platon* 1 (1910) 368.

¹⁰⁷ *Euthyphro* 3A ff.

¹⁰⁸ The idea that under certain circumstances death is something desirable can also be found in Plato, *Phaedo* 61C: 'Any man who

possesses the spirit of philosophy is willing to die, but he will not take his own life. . . .' Cf. *ibid.* at 64c; 67c ff.; 64E ff.; *Republic* 486A ff., where Plato insists that the true philosopher is not fearful of death. *Gorgias* 522DE; Libanius, *Apologia Socratis*, chap. 6 (17.1–8, Foerster). Both Xenophon and Plato may have derived this idea from Antisthenes, or Xenophon may have borrowed it from Plato who, in turn, was dependent on some Antisthenian dictum. The Stoics, who in this are admittedly under Cynic influence, made much of this 'readiness to die'.

[109] *Apology* 36A. Cf. Xenophon, *Memor.* 4.8.6 ff.; *Defence* 33.

[110] Plato, *Apology* 28D.

[111] Xenophon, *Memor.* 4.8.9 and *ibid.* at 4.8.4; Plato, *Gorgias* 511B: 'The bad man will kill the good and true man.'

[112] Cf. *ibid.* at 464D.

[113] Cf. Plato, *Apology* 26B.

[114] Cf. Plato, *Apology* 19D–20C and *ibid.* at 23C–23E; 24C–26B; *Gorgias* 517A: 'In the city of Athens no one has ever shown himself to be a good statesman. . . .' *Ibid.* at 521D: 'I think that I am the only or almost the only Athenian living who practises the true art of politics. I am the only statesman of my time.' *Meno* 95A, where Anytus predicts that Socrates will one day suffer for 'speaking ill of the people', that is to say, for ridiculing the democratic regime of Athens.

[115] Cf. Aeschines, *Alcibiades*, frag. 1.55–65, edit. Krauss.

[116] Thucydides 5.84 ff.

[117] As to the 'impiety' of Socrates, cf. the interesting remarks by A. E. Taylor, *Varia Socratica* (First series, 1911) 1–39, and A. S. Ferguson, 'The impiety of Socrates', in *Classical Quarterly* 7 (1913) 157–175.

[118] Cf. notes 583–591, *infra*, and the text thereto.

[119] U. v. Wilamowitz-Moellendorff, *Platon* 1 (1919) 158, maintains that Plato (*Apology* 24B ff.) indicates that Socrates treated the gods as non-existent. This might imply, in turn, either theoretical disbelief (cf. *Apology* 26C and *ibid.* at 29A; 35D) or neglect of ceremonial duties. But, technically speaking, theoretical disbelief does not constitute ἀσέβεια and, hence, could not have come under the jurisdiction of the *king archon*. The charge, therefore, must have been one of non-conformity in religious practice, a fact which is clearly brought out by Xenophon's rebuttals in *Defence* 11–13 and *Memor.* 1.1.2–20.

[120] *Anonym. Hypothesis Busiridis*, in *Isocrate* 1 (Paris, 1928) 186 (edit. G. Mathieu et É. Brémond).

[121] *Defence* 24; *Scholia ad Plat. Apol.* 21E. Cf. Josephus, *Contra Apionem* 2.263: '. . . Socrates was put to death . . . because he used to swear strange oaths. . . .' Undoubtedly, Josephus refers here to Socrates' practice of swearing 'By the Dog', apparently his favourite oath. Other references to Socrates' use of unorthodox oaths can be found in Plato, *Gorgias* 461A and *ibid.* at 466c; 482B; *Republic* 399E; Libanius, *Apologia Socratis* 74.13–16 (edit. Foerster); Aristophanes, *Clouds* 627 and *ibid.*

Notes to Chapter II

at 814; Lucian, *Vit. auct.* 16. Even some of the early Christian authors denounced Socrates for his 'swearing'. Theopilus, *Ad Autolycum* 3.2; Tertullian, *Apologia* 14; Lactantius, *Instit. div.* 3.20.15.

[122] Cf. Josephus, *Contra Apionem* 2.263: '. . . Socrates was put to death . . . because he maintained as some say . . . that he received communications from a daemon. . . .'

[123] Cf. *Memor.* 1.3.1–4 and *ibid.* at 4.3.3–9; 4.3.13–18; Plato, *Euthyphro* 12E.

[124] *Memor.* 1.1.11.

[125] 'Friend Meletus, you think that you are prosecuting Anaxagoras.'

[126] *Ibid.* at 27A ff. See also Aristotle, *Rhetoric* 1395 a 15 ff., where the same argument is restated. Plato, *Apology* 35D: 'I do believe that there are gods and this in a sense higher than that in which any of my accusers believe in them.'

[127] *Clouds* 247 and *ibid.* at 252; 380; *et passim.*

[128] Cf. A. E. Taylor, *Varia Socratica* (First Series, 1911) 1.39; A. S. Ferguson, 'The impiety of Socrates', in *Classical Quarterly* 7 (1913) 157–175.

[129] D.L. 2.18 mistakenly writes Aristophanes. Cf. M. Meinecke, *Comicorum graec. poet. frag.* 2.371 ff.

[130] Cf. Andocides, *De mysteriis* (edit. Blass); Lysias, *Oratio* 6.

[131] Cf. Plato, *Apology* 26B ff.; Xenophon, *Memor.* 1.1.3: 'He introduced nothing newer than those who, when practising divination, consult auguries, voices, omens and sacrifices.' *Ibid.* at 1.6.2–3.

[132] Cf. Plato, *Apology* 27BC: 'Can a man believe in spiritual agencies and not in spirits and demigods? . . . I teach people to believe in divine or spiritual agencies. . . .' *Memor.* 1.1.3: 'The gods, by their own means, signify what will be advantageous: and this was the opinion Socrates entertained.' Xenophon, *Anabasis* 3.2.11; Aristophanes, *Birds* 720.

[133] It is seemingly implied here that the Athenians had considered Socrates' references to his daemon tantamount to an 'introduction of new deities'. This is the second charge against Socrates. *Memor.* 1.1.2. Cf., however, notes 115–122, *supra*, and notes 243–247, *infra*, and the text thereto.

[134] *Memor.* 1.1.4. Cf. Plato, *Apology* 31CD: 'You have heard me speak oftentimes . . . of an oracle or sign which comes to me. And this is the divinity which Meletus ridicules in the indictment. This sign, which is a kind of voice, began to come to me when I was a child.' *Ibid.* at 40AB: '. . . the divine faculty, of which the internal oracle is a source . . . made no sign of opposition. . . . This is an intimation that what has happened to me is good. . . .' *Ibid.* at 41D: '. . . it was better for me to die . . . and therefore the oracle gave no sign.' For additional references to the Socratic 'daemon', see Plato *Phaedrus* 242BC; *Republic* 496C; *Euthydemus* 272E; *Theaetetus* 151A; *Euthyphro* 3BC; and Pseudo-Platonic *Theages* 128D; *Alcibiades I* 195AB; Xenophon, *Memor.* 4.8.4–5 and *ibid.*

at 1.4.14; 4.3.17; 1.4.2; 1.4.10; 1.1.2–5; 4.3.12–14; 4.8.1; *et passim*; *Symposium* 8.5; *Defence* 4 and *ibid.* at 5; 12; 13.

[135] *Ibid.* at 1.1.9. Cf. *ibid.* at 1.1.19: 'He [*scil.*, Socrates] held that the gods paid regard to men . . . and gave admonitions to men concerning everything human.' *Ibid.* at 1.1.6: 'Concerning those things of which it was doubtful how they should be determined, he [*scil.*, Socrates] sent people to consult auguries. . . .' *Ibid.* at 4.8.1; 1.1.2: 'It was common knowledge that Socrates used to say that the deity instructed him.' *Ibid.* at 1.1.4: 'He also told many of his friends to do certain things, and not to do others, intimating that the deity had forewarned him. And advantage attended those who did abide by his suggestions, and repentance those who disregarded them.' *Ibid.* at 1.1.5: 'But he would have seemed to be both [a fool or a boaster] if, after saying that intimations were given him by a god, he would have been proven guilty of falsehood . . . he would have uttered no predictions, if he had not believed that they have held true. But who in such matters would trust anyone but a god? And how could he, who trusted the gods, think that there were no gods?'

[136] Aside from *Defence* 12–14, Xenophon mentions the Socratic daemon also in *Memor.* 1.3.4 and *ibid.* at 1.4.3; 1.4.15; 1.4.18; 2.6.8; 4.3.12; 4.8.1; 4.8.5; 4.8.6; 4.8.11; *et passim*. Cicero, in *De divinatione* 1.54.122, translates the Greek δαιμόνιον with *divinum quoddam*, and not with *genius*. He probably borrowed this translation from Antipater whom he also quotes. The late Hellenistic and early Christian tradition held that Socrates had intercourse with a demon. Cf. Plutarch, *De genio Socratis* 20 ff.; Maximus of Tyre 14.3 ff. and *ibid.* at 14.6; Apuleius of Madaura, *De deo Socratis*; etc.

[137] Cf. Menander, *Epitrepontes* 479 ff.

[138] Cf. *Phaedrus* 60E and *ibid.* at 61A; *Apology* 33C; *Crito* 44AB.

[139] Cf. H. Düring, *Herodicus the Cratetean* 44 ff.; Plutarch, *De genio Socratis* 580D; Pseudo-Plato, *Theages* 129D.

[140] Cf. Plato, *Apology* 21B ff.: 'I am going to explain to you why I have such an evil name.' Then Socrates goes to tell the court that he went about searching after a man wiser than himself. He finally comes to the conclusion that the Delphic message calling Socrates the wisest among men did not really apply to himself, but to all men who realize that human wisdom 'is worth little or nothing'. *Ibid.* at 23B. Cf. *Memor.* 4.3.12, where we are told that Socrates is the favourite of the gods. Dio Chrysostom, *Oratio* 23.8.

[141] *Apology* 24A. Cf. *ibid.* at 28A; 36A; 37A.

[142] Cf. *Theaetetus* 172C ('They appear to be comical speakers') and *ibid.* at 174C ('makes them laugh'); 174C ('appears comical'); 175B ('is laughed down'); 175D ('makes them laugh again'); *Republic* 517A ('would he not make them laugh'); *Gorgias* 484D ('become utterly ridiculous').

Notes to Chapter II

[143] This inference may be drawn from the many allusions found in Plato, *Apology* 17D ('pray, not to raise a row'); *ibid.* at 20E ('pray, not to raise a row'); 21A ('not to raise a row'); 30C ('not to raise a row'); 27B ('not to raise a row'); *Gorgias* 522A; Xenophon, *Defence* 14–15; D.L. 2.41–42.

[144] Cf. W. Nestle, 'Sokrates und Delphi', in *Württemberger Korrespondenzblatt* (1910) 87; Dio Chrysostom, *Oratio* 55.8; Athenaeus, *Deipnosophistae* 5.218.

[145] D.L. might be here under the influence of Xenophon. Cf. Aristotle, frag. 3 (1474 b 10–12); Plato, *Phaedrus* 230A; Xenophon, *Memor.* 4.2.24–30.

[146] Plato, *Apology* 23B and *ibid.* at 28E; 29E; 30A; 30E; 31AB; 37E.

[147] This 'combination' is indicated in Plato, *Apology* 33C, where Socrates maintains that 'the duty of ἐξέτασις has been imposed upon me . . . by oracles, visions, and every other way in which the divine will ever manifests itself. . . .'

[148] This tradition seems to be reflected in Plato, *Phaedo* 60E ff., where Socrates relates certain persistent dreams which commanded him to 'cultivate and make music'.

[149] The story that Socrates acted under direct divine command must not be confounded with the 'workings' of the Socratic daemon.

[150] Cf. Herodotus 1.30; Valerius Maximus 7.1.2.

[151] D.L. 1.30. Cf. *ibid.* at 1.13; 1.106.

[152] D.L. 1.28. Diogenes Laertius (*ibid.* at 1.28–29) also records a different version of the same story which is said to go back to Callimachus.

[153] In H. Diels, *Die Fragmente der Vorsokratiker* (5th edit.) 22 B 32.

[154] 141 ff.

[155] In Cicero, *Tuscul. disp.* 4.3–4; Jamblichus, *Vita Pythag.* 58 ff.; D.L. 1.12.

[156] Plato, *Phaedrus* 278D; *Apology* 23AB. Cf. *Symposium* 203D ff.; *Lysis* 218A ff.

[157] Aristotle, *Metaphysics* 982 b 17 ff.

[158] Frags. 3–4 (1474 b 10–1475 a 5). These fragments, it should be remembered, originally were part of the περὶ φιλοσοφίας. The Aristotelian passage probably goes back to Plato's *Phaedrus* (229E ff.) or to Xenophon's *Memorabilia* 4.2.24–30, which seem to be based on the *Phaedrus*. Cf. Dio Chrysostom, *Oratio* 4.57 and *ibid.* at 10.22; Plutarch, *Adversus Coloten* 20.

[159] Cf. A.-H. Chroust, 'Socrates in the light of Aristotle's testimony', in *The New Scholasticism* 26 no. 3 (1952) 364.

[160] In H. Diels, *op. cit.* at 22 B 46. Cf. O. Gigon, *Sokrates* (1947) 93–105.

[161] Cf. Xenophon, *Memor.* 1.2.1: 'Socrates . . . was . . . the most rigid of all men in controlling his passions and appetites. . . .' *Ibid.* at 1.5.3

Notes to Chapter II

and 1.5.4; 1.5.6; 1.6.2–3; 2.1.1 ff.; 4.5.9; 3.9.4; 1.6.5; 1.6.9 ff.; 1.3.14; Plato, *Phaedo* 66D.

[162] Cf. Xenophon, *Memor.* 1.2.6–7: 'He [*scil.*, Socrates] held that those who refrained from demanding a fee retained their freedom, and called those who took money for their teaching their own enslavers. . . . He expressed wonder, too, that anyone professing to teach virtue, should demand money. . . .' Plato, *Apology* 19DE: 'Little foundation is there in the report that I am a teacher, and take money.' *Ibid.* at 33AB: 'Nor do I converse only with those who pay. . . .' Xenophon, *Memor.* 1.6.1–5 and *ibid.* at 1.6.11–14; 1.2.61; D.L. 2.31, where we are told that Socrates declined Charmides' offer of some slaves. *Ibid.* at 2.25; 2.24; 2.27; Dio Chrysostom, *Oratio* 55.9.

[163] Cf. Xenophon, *Memor.* 4.8.11.

[164] Cf. Plato, *Apology* 30AB and *ibid.* at 29DE: 'I shall never cease from . . . exhorting anyone whom I meet. . . .' *Ibid.* at 30E–31B: 'I am that gadfly which God has sent to the city . . . exhorting you to pay heed to virtue. . . .' Xenophon, *Memor.* 1.1.16: 'He [*scil.* Socrates] would hold discourse . . . considering what was pious and what impious; what becoming (or, beautiful) and what unbecoming (or, ugly); what noble and what base; what just and what unjust; what sane and what insane; what constituted fortitude and what cowardice. . . .' *Ibid.* at 1.2.1–11; 1.2.64: '[Socrates] plainly led such of his followers as had vicious inclinations, to cease indulging in them and exhorted them to cherish the love of that most excellent and honourable virtue by which men govern successfully families and cities.' *Ibid.* at 1.3.5–15; 1.4.1; 1.5.1–6; 3.9.1–15; 4.4.1–4; 4.5.1–12; 4.6.2–11; 4.8.1–11.

[165] Cf. Xenophon, *Memor.* 1.2.60–61: 'But Socrates . . . conferred glory upon the city . . . by freely imparting whatever he had to bestow. . . .' Cf. also Thucydides 1.120.

[166] Cf. D.L. 2.24 and *ibid.* at 2.25 and notes 1146–1148, *infra*, and the text thereto.

[167] Cf. Plato, *Apology* 23C: 'Young men of the richer classes . . . come to me on their own accord. Like pretenders they also examine and they often imitate me. . . .' Libanius, *Apologia Socratis* 3.39; D.L. 2.31 and *ibid.* at 2.65; 2.74.

[168] Cf. Plato, *Apology* 37E–38A: '. . . to discuss virtue daily and those other things about which you hear me examining myself and others, is the greatest good of man. . . .'

[169] Every time Plato refers to Meletus, he uses some word of disparagement. Cf. *Euthyphro* 2B, where Meletus is called an 'unknown individual (a man of no account), with long hair, wispy beard, and hooked nose'. *Gorgias* 521C, where Meletus is called an 'utterly bad and worthless creature'. *Apology* 26B and *ibid.* at 26E.

[170] Cf. Xenophon, *Memor.* 1.1.1 and *ibid.* at 1.2.12: '. . . Critias and Alcibiades, after having been associated with Socrates, inflicted a great

many evils on the city. . . .' *Ibid.* at 1.2.1: 'It also seems fanciful that anyone could believe that Socrates corrupted youths.' D.L. 2.40; Xenophon, *Memor.* 1.2.9: 'He [*scil.*, Socrates] caused, said the accuser, those who conversed with him to hold in contempt the established laws. . . .' *Ibid.* at 1.2.49; 1.2.51; 1.2.56; 1.2.64.

[171] Cf. Xenophon, *Memor.* 1.2.2: 'How, then, being of such a character himself, could he [*scil.*, Socrates] render others impious or lawless or profligate or incontinent or too effeminate to endure labour?' *Ibid.* at 1.2.56–57; 1.2.64; 1.2.3: '. . . association with a good man is an exercise in virtue. . . .' Plato, *Apology* 37E–38A.

[172] *Apology* 24C: 'Socrates is an evil-doer who corrupts youth. . . .' *Ibid.* at 33C: '. . . if I am or have been corrupting youth. . . .' *Ibid.* at 26B: 'Still I would like to know . . . on the strength of what facts am I accused of corrupting youth?' *Ibid.* at 34A ff.; 30B; 23CD.

[173] Socrates might be referring to Alcibiades and Critias. Cf. Xenophon, *Memor.* 1.2.12 ff.

[174] Cf. Xenophon, *Memor.* 1.2.3: 'Not that he [*scil.*, Socrates] ever professed to be an instructor of this kind. . . .' Aeschines, *Alcibiades,* in *Aeschinis reliquiae* frag. 4 (edit. Krauss). This passage in Aeschines is taken from Aristides, *Oratio* 45. Libanius, *op. cit.* chaps. 22–23 (26.5–27.11, Foerster) and chap. 37 (34.5–11). Cf., however, Plato, *Laches* 200C ff., where we are told that Socrates was the best of teachers, something that is even conceded by Nicias; Plato, *Protagoras* 318D ff., where the Socratic method of teaching is favourably compared to that employed by Hippias; Xenophon, *Memor.* 1.2.31–37, where we are told that Critias and Charicles (Callicles?) ordered Socrates to desist from teaching. *Ibid.* at 4.7.1–10; 1.1.11–16; 1.6.14; Plato, *Meno* 89A ff.; *Laches* 180D and *ibid.* at 200D; 197D; 200A; *Apology* 20A ff.; *Republic* 400B and *ibid.* at 424C; *Theaetetus* 151B.

[174a] Xenophon confounds here Meletus with Polycrates. Cf. *infra.*

[175] Cf. *Memor.* 2.2.1–14; Plato, *Gorgias* 522BC; *Memor.* 1.2.9: '[Socrates] said how foolish it is to elect the magistrates of the city by beans when no one is willing to take a pilot elected by beans . . . or a person in any other profession. . . . A man should inquire whether it would be better to take for the driver of his chariot one who knows how to drive, or one who does not know; or whether it would be better to place over his ship one who knows how to steer it, or one who does not know. . . .' Aristotle, *Rhetoric* 1393 b 3–8, where the argument, found in Xenophon, *Memor.* 1.2.9, is repeated. Aristotle undoubtedly relies here on Xenophon (or Polycrates) or perhaps on Antisthenes, the possible source of Xenophon (or Polycrates). Xenophon (*Memor.* 1.2.52) seems willing to concede the truth of this particular charge: 'I am aware . . . that he made such statements concerning parents and other relatives or kinsmen as well as friends. . . . But Socrates made such remarks, not to teach any one of his followers to bury his father

Notes to Chapter II

alive . . . but in order to become as intelligent and useful as possible, so that if he wished to be honoured by his father or brother or by anyone else, he might not be neglectful of himself by trusting his relatives.' Cf. *ibid.* at 4.1.1–4 and 4.2.1–40.

[176] This argument could be based on the Pseudo-Aristotelian *On virtues and vices* (1251 a 31 ff.), where the concept of *aseby* also includes the denial of all paternal authority. This passage from *On virtues*, however, is essentially Xenophontean or, to be more exact, Antisthenian. Cf. D.L. 6.12.

[177] Xenophon may possibly allude here to 'maintenance in the Prytaneum'. Plato, *Apology* 36c ff.

[178] Cf. Xenophon, *Memor.* 1.2.2: '. . . he [*scil.*, Socrates] restrained many of his followers from such vices, inducing them to love virtue. . . .' *Ibid.* at 1.2.55; 1.2.64; 1.1.6–9; 1.1.16; 1.2.1; 1.2.4–8; 1.2.29; 1.2.57; 1.2.64; *et passim.*

[179] Cf. *Memor.* 1.1.17.

[180] See *Apology* 24B: 'Against these [*scil.*, the specific charges] I must make a defence.' *Ibid.* at 26D and 27A–28A, where Socrates stresses the fact that a man who believes in divine agencies must also believe in the deity. *Ibid.* at 28D–30C, where Socrates tells his judges that he shall go on being a preacher: 'For this is the command of God' (30A). *Ibid.* at 30D: 'I am not going to argue for my own sake, as you may think, but for your sake, that you may not sin against God by condemning me, who am His gift to you.' *Ibid.* at 32A: 'I have never yielded to injustice from any fear of death. . . .' *Ibid.* at 35BC and 35D: 'Do not require me to do something which I consider dishonourable and impious and wrong. . . . I do believe that there are gods . . . and to you and to God I commit my cause. . . .' *Ibid.* at 37AB: 'I am convinced that I never intentionally wronged anyone, although I cannot convince you. . . . But I will assuredly not wrong myself. . . .'

[181] Cf. Plato, *Apology* 33D–34B, where a number of people are mentioned who failed to support the allegation of Meletus that Socrates had corrupted the youth of Athens, and who probably testified in favour of Socrates.

[182] Libanius, *Apologia Socratis* chap. 26 (28.14.–29.9, Foerster). Libanius also insists that Anytus had been willing to withdraw his complaint if Socrates would desist from referring constantly to his tannery business. *Ibid.* at chap. 30 (30.9–31.4, Foerster).

[183] Plato, *Meno* 95A.

[184] Cf. Lysias, *Oratio* 22.7 ff.; U. v. Wilamowitz-Moellendorff, *Aristoteles und Athen* 2.374.

[185] Cf. Pauly-Wissowa, *op. cit.* (1894 edit.) 1, col. 2656.

[186] Cf. Plato, *Apology* 24C.

[187] Cf. O. Gigon, *Sokrates* (Bern, 1947) 74–78. *Schol. ad Plat. Apol.* 18B, contains a 'life of Anytus' which might go back to Antisthenes.

Notes to Chapter II

Cf. Libanius, *Apologia Socratis* chap. 24 and *ibid.* at 29; *Epist. Socratis* XIV; Plato, *Meno* 94E ff.; Athenaeus, *Deipnosophistae* 7.329.

[188] Cf. Xenophon, *Defence* 5; Plato, *Apology* 28B: 'A man . . . ought not to calculate the chance of living or dying.' *Ibid.* at 28E–29A: 'It would indeed be strange if I were to desert my post through fear of death. . . .' *Ibid.* at 30BC: '. . . but whatever you shall do, I will never alter my ways. . . .' *Ibid.* at 30CD: 'Nothing will injure me, not Meletus nor yet Anytus . . . because a bad man is not permitted to injure a man better than himself.' *Ibid.* at 34CD and 34E: 'One who has reached my age, and who has a name for wisdom, ought not to degrade himself. . . .' *Ibid.* at 39C: 'I suppose that these things may be regarded as being ordained by fate, and I think that they are well.' *Ibid.* at 42A: 'I go to die, and you to live: which is the better God alone knows.' *Gorgias* 474BC ff. and *ibid.* at 478E; 508C; 522DE. Essentially the same idea can be found in Libanius, *Apologia Socratis* chap. 32 (31.10–16, Foerster) and *ibid.* at chap. 33 (31.17–32.12, Foerster).

[189] Xenophon repeats here statements already made in *Defence* 1–9. See *Memor.* 4.8.1–10; Plato, *Apology* 37A and *ibid.* at 37E–38A.

[190] Cf. *ibid.* at 38A: ' I have never been accustomed to think that I deserve to suffer any penalty.' Cicero, *De oratore* 1.54.232. As to the meaning of this 'maintenance in the *Prytaneum*', which is also mentioned in D.L. 2.42, cf. R. Schöll, 'Die Speisung im Prytaneion', in *Hermes* 6 (1872) 14–54; E. Preuner, 'Zum attischen Gesetz über die Speisung in Prytaneion', in *Hermes* 61 (1926) 470–474. The story that Socrates had suggested 'maintenance in the *Prytaneum*', is undoubtedly fictitious. On this point, it seems, Plato does not simply report, but rather relies on a theme which had already been employed by Aeschylus (*Sept.* 592) and Xenophanes. It would be interesting to compare here Plato, *Apology* 36B or *ibid.* at 36D, and Xenophanes, *Elegy* 2, quoted in Athenaeus, *Deipnosophistae* 10.413F ff.; H. Diels, *Die Fragmente der Vorsokratiker* (1st edit.) 50–51; J. Morr, 'Die Entstehung der platonischen Apologie', in *Schriften der deutschen wissenschaftlichen Gesellschaft Reichenberg*, Heft 5 (1929) 26–27.

[191] Cf. Plato, *Apology* 37A: '. . . I am convinced that I never wronged intentionally anyone.' Xenophon, *Memor.* 1.1.2: 'What proof did they submit?' *Ibid.* at 1.1.11: 'No one ever either saw Socrates doing, or heard him saying anything impious or profane.' *Ibid.* at 1.1.17; 1.1.20; 1.2.1–2; 1.2.2–11; 1.2.64; 4.8.2–3.

[192] The capital crimes under existing Athenian law which Xenophon enumerates here are sacrilege, kidnapping, destruction of the city walls (or housebreaking), and betrayal of the city. In *Memor.* 1.2.62, Xenophon mentions the following capital crimes: '. . . stealing, stripping people of their clothes, cutting purses, housebreaking, kidnapping, or sacrilege'. Cf. Aristotle, *Pol. Athen.* 52.1. As to temple robbery or sacrilege, see Plato, *Republic* 413A.

Notes to Chapter II

[193] Cf. *ibid.* at 19A; Xenophon, *Memor.* 1.1.17: 'It is unusual that in this case the judges should have come to a wrong decision.' Plato, *Gorgias* 521B.

[194] Cf. Plato, *Apology* 38BC and *ibid.* at 39C; 41D; 30CD; Xenophon, *Memor.* 1.1.17 and *ibid.* at 1.1.20; 1.2.1; 1.2.62; 1.2.64.

[195] Cf. Xenophon, *Memor.* 4.8.10: 'I have never wronged any man or rendered him less virtuous . . . but I have always tried to make those better who conversed with me.'

[196] Cf. Plato, *Apology* 25D and 37A; Xenophon, *Memor.* 1.2.1–2 and *ibid.* at 1.2.8; 1.2.9–11; 1.2.15; 1.2.18; 1.2.48; 1.2.57; 1.2.60; 1.2.61; 1.2.62–63; 1.2.64. Cf. also *ibid.* at 1.3.1–15; 1.4.1–19; 1.5.1–6; 4.8.10; Plato, *Gorgias* 526D.

[197] Cf. Josephus, *Contra Apionem* 2.263: 'He [*scil.*, Socrates] never sought to betray his city to the enemy; he robbed no temple. . . .'

[198] G. Ritter, *Platon* 1 (1910) 77.

[199] Cf. *Memor.* 4.8.4–10.

[200] *Defence* (chaps. 27–34) is not, as some scholars have tried to suggest, based on Plato's *Crito*. Cf. *Memor.* 4.8.2–3.

[201] This is not the place to discuss the interesting theory, advanced by K. Joël, that the Platonic *Apology* was directed against the *Clouds* of Aristophanes. K. Joël, *Der echte und der xenophontische Sokrates* 2.811 ff.

[202] Cf. *ibid.* at 37B.

[203] From *Defence* 23 we gain the impression that Xenophon deliberately contradicts here the account of Plato.

[204] Xenophon, *Defence* 14; D.L. 2.40.

[205] The suggestion has also been made that the story of the 'counter-penalty' proposed by Socrates has been invented by Plato. A. Geissler, 'Der Strafantrag in der platonischen Apologie', in *Blätter für das Gymnasial-Schulwesen* 42 (1906) 381–391, and the literature cited there. R. J. Bonner, 'The legal setting of Plato's Apology', in *Classical Philology* 3 (1908) 177. Geissler's theory would find some support in Xenophon, *Defence* 23.

[206] *Defence* 24–26; *Apology* 38C–42A.

[207] Cf. *Memor.* 4.8.10. In Xenophon (*Defence* 26) the death of Palamedes furnishes a far nobler theme of praise than the conduct of Odysseus who slew him. *Memor.* 4.2.33, recounts the woes of Palamedes, 'that most renowned theme of songs, [and] how for his wisdom's sake Odysseus envied him and slew him'. These two Xenophontean passages strongly recall Euripides' *Palamedes*: 'You have slain, you have slain, Danaoi, the all-wise and innocent, the nightingale of the Muses.' A. Nauck, *Trag. Graec. Frag.* (2d edit.), *Eurip.* 588. The anonymous author of the *Hypothesis Busiridis* (in *Isocrate* 1.187 ff., Paris 1928, edit. G. Mathieu and É. Brémond) states that 'it is said that Euripides wished to speak of Socrates. But he became frightened and hence

Notes to Chapter II

invented his *Palamedes* in order to allude to Socrates and the Athenians: "You have killed the best of the Greeks." And the audience understood his allusion and began to cry.' D.L. 2.44 also seems to indicate that the lines from the *Palamedes* of Euripides had been 'dedicated' to Socrates. But he adds that Philochorus, probably in his *Life of Euripides*, 'asserts that Euripides died before Socrates'. Hence the story told in the *Hypothesis Busiridis* contains a serious anachronism in that Euripides already had died in 406. U. v. Wilamowitz-Moellendorff, 'Die xenophontische Apologie', in *Hermes* 32 (1897) 103 ff. It will later be shown that not the *Palamedes* of Euripides, but rather the *Defence of Palamedes* by Gorgias served as a model for Xenophon (and Plato).

[208] About Palamedes, cf. Ovid, *Metamorph.* 13.5.

[209] M. Schanz, *Apologia* 80–81, holds that Xenophon's digressions from the Platonic *Apology* are sufficient evidence to prove that Xenophon considered Plato's *Apology* more fiction than historical account. R. Hackforth, *The composition of Plato's Apology* (Cambridge, 1933) 15 ff., denies, however, that Xenophon's *Defence* contains any allusion to Plato's *Apology* or *Phaedo*. U. v. Wilamowitz-Moellendorff, *op. cit.* at 104 ff., on the other hand, insists that essential parts of the Xenophontean *Defence* are under the influence of Plato's *Apology* (the Palamedes reference goes back to *Apology* 41B; *Defence* 29 to *Apology* 39B; etc.) and the *Phaedo* (*Defence* 28 goes back to *Phaedo* 89B and *ibid.* at 117D). The problem of the historicity of Plato's *Apology* is discussed by H. Gomperz, 'Sokrates Haltung vor seinen Richtern', in *Wiener Studien* 54 (1936) 32–43, and by W. A. Oldfather, 'Socrates in court', in *Classical Weekly* 31, no. 21 (1938) 203–211. Cf. the literature quoted there.

[210] Plato, *Apology* 31E–32A.

[211] Plato, *Apology* 30A ff.

[212] Plato, *Apology* 30AB. The similarity of this Socratic dilemma with the *Antigone* issue is obvious.

[213] Xenophon, *Defence* 1. Cf. *ibid.* at 6–9.

[214] Xenophon, *Defence* 7. This passage reminds us of Diogenes Laertius' comments upon the death of Chilon (1.73) and Bias (1.84). This version, which is accepted by Xenophon and which might go back to Antisthenes, seems to presage a Stoic viewpoint. And, as Diogenes Laertius (6.104) points out, the Antisthenian-Cynic tradition influenced some of the Stoic teachings.

[215] Xenophon, *Defence* 9. Cf. E. Meyer, *Geschichte des Altertums* 5 (3d edit., 1921) 227.

[216] For a detailed discussion of Plato's *Apology*, cf. the important work of R. Hackforth, *The composition of Plato's Apology* (Cambridge, 1933).

[217] Cf. Aelius Aristides, *Oratio* 49 (vol. 2, p. 518, lines 13–16, edit. Dindorf; vol. 2, p. 168, lines 7–10, edit. Keil).

Notes to Chapter III

[218] Plato, *Apology* 31AB.

[219] Cf. I. Bruns, *Das literarische Porträt der Griechen* (1896) 210; M. Schanz, *Apologia* (1893) 74.

[220] The *Euthyphro* refers to events immediately preceding the trial of Socrates and, in a certain way, alludes to this event by way of anticipation.

[221] Cf. O. Gigon, *Sokrates* (1947) 30–31.

NOTES TO CHAPTER III—PAGES 44–68

[222] Some scholars deny that *Memor.* 1.1.1–1.2.64 originally were an independent Socratic apology. Cf. O. Gigon, *Sokrates* (1947) 50.

[223] With the exception of some minor passages, the genuineness of the *Memorabilia* cannot be questioned. In their literary form the *Memorabilia* could also be called a panegyric work. Cf. Dionysius of Halicarnassus, *Ar. rhet.* 9.12; L. Dindorf, *Xen. Memor.*, praef. XIV.

[224] Cf. D.L. (Diogenes Laertius) 2.48. '[Xenophon] . . . Ἀπομνημονεύματα ἐπιγράψας. . . .' Dionysius of Helicarnassus, *Ar. rhet.* 9.12.

[225] Cf. Christ-Schmid, *Geschichte der griechischen Literatur* (6th edit.) 1.508: 'The first two chapters [of the *Memorabilia*] probably constitute the earliest work of Xenophon.'

[226] Anytus was still alive in 385/4, even though *Defence* 31 seems to refer to his death.

[227] Cf. E. Richter, *op. cit.* 129 ff.; R. Hackforth, *op. cit.* 22 ff.; H. v. Arnim, *Xenophons Memorabilien und die Apologie des Sokrates* (Copenhagen, 1923).

[228] Cf. *Memor.* 1.2.9 and *ibid.* at 1.2.12; 1.2.26; 1.2.49; 1.2.51; 1.2.52; 1.2.56; 1.2.58; 1.2.60. The 'accuser' is naturally Polycrates.

[229] As to Richter's theory of four Xenophontean *Apologies*, cf. note 71 *supra*.

[230] Cf. Plato, *Apology* 24B and *ibid.* at 26B; Xenophon, *Defence* 10; D.L. 2.40.

[231] Cf. notes 113–114, *supra*, and the text thereto.

[232] Plato (*Euthyphro* 3B) reports an episode which took place during the preliminary proceedings against Socrates. It seems that originally Meletus had charged Socrates with being 'a poet and a maker of gods, and that [he invents] new gods and [denies] the existence of the old gods'. In the actual indictment, however, this particular charge was changed. Presumably, either the βασιλεύς declined to accept the charge in the form stated in *Euthyphro* 3B, or Anytus later induced Meletus to alter it so as to make it more general and vague.

[233] J. Hartman, *Analecta Xenophontea* (1887), claims that the following passages from Xenophon's *Memorabilia* are spurious: 1.1.2–9;

Notes to Chapter III

1.2.17–18; 1.2.29–38; 1.2.62–64. This view of Hartman, however, is rejected by most scholars.

[234] Cf. *Defence* 10–15 and *ibid.* at 24; notes 115–130, *supra*.

[235] Cf. *Defence* 10–11; *Memor.* 1.3.1–2.

[236] Cf. *Defence* 12–13 and notes 132–135, *supra*.

[237] Cf. *Defence* 13 and note 134, *supra*.

[238] Cf. *Defence* 11–12 and note 131, *supra*; Plato, *Euthydemus* 302BC; *Phaedo* 118A.

[239] Cf. *Memor.* 1.1.3 and *ibid.* at 1.1.9; *Defence* 12–13, where Socrates speaks of a θεοῦ φωνή.

[240] Cf. *Defence* 13; 24; note 191, *supra*.

[241] Cf. *Defence* 12–13 and note 131, *supra*; Aristophanes, *Birds* 721; *Frogs* 196; *Ecclesiazusae* 792.

[242] Cf. H. Diels, *Die Fragmente der Vorsokratiker* (5th edit.) 22 B 93.

[243] Cf. notes 117, 125–130 and 135, *supra*; R. Hackforth, *The composition of Plato's Apology* (1923) 58 ff.

[244] Cf. Plato, *Apology* 18B.

[245] Cf. *ibid.* at 828; 1472.

[246] *Clouds* 263 ff.

[247] Cf. F. M. Cornford, *Principium sapientiae: The origins of Greek philosophic thought* (1952) 133 ff. and *ibid.* at 140; C. Phillipson, *The trial of Socrates* (1928) chap. 13.

[248] Cf. *Defence* 13 and notes 134 and 135, *supra*; *Defence* 14 and notes 136–140, *supra*.

[249] Cf. *Defence* 13; notes 135 and 139, *supra*; Xenophon, *Anabasis* 3.1.4; *Symposium* 4.48.

[250] Cf. *Defence* 13 and notes, 131–133, *supra*; Plato, *Apology* 35D.

[251] Cf. *Defence* 12 and notes 131–135, *supra*.

[252] Cf. *Memor.* 4.7.10.

[253] Cf. *Defence* 12–13.

[254] Cf. *Memor.* 1.3.4 and *ibid.* at 1.4.15; 4.3.13–14. Xenophon's own belief in the decisive importance of omens is fully brought out in his *Anabasis*. Cf. *ibid.* at 5.5.2–3; 6.4.13–16; 6.5.3; 5.2.9; 7.2.14–17; 5.6.16; *et passim*; *Oeconomicus* 5.19 and *ibid.* at 5.20; 6.1; 7.7 ff.; 11.8; *De vectigalibus* 6.2 and *ibid.* at 6.3; *Hipparchus* 5.14 and *ibid.* at 6.1; 1.1; 3.1; 9.8; 9.9.

[255] Cf. *Defence* 13 and notes 132 and 135, *supra*; *Memor.* 1.4.18–19 and *ibid.* at 4.3.3–9; 4.7.10.

[256] *On ancient medicine*, chaps. 1–12.

[257] This issue is treated in *Memor.* 1.3.1–5 and *ibid.* at 4.3.15–17.

[258] The same idea is also at the basis of *Memor.* 1.1.7.

[259] Cf. *Defence* 11; *Memor.* 1.1.2; Dio Chrysostom, *Oratio* 13.14 and *ibid.* at 13.16. Dio Chrysostom, *Oratio* 13.14–28, contains a résumé of alleged Socratic teachings. J. Wegehaupt, *De Dione Chrysostomo Xenophontis sectatore* (Gotha, 1896) 56 ff., maintains that this résumé was

taken from the dialogue *Cleitophon*, erroneously ascribed to Plato. F. Dümmler, *Akademika* (1889) 1–17, on the other hand, claims that the *Archelaus* (or, *On kingship*), ascribed to Antisthenes (D.L. 6.18), is the common source used both by Dio Chrysostom and the author of the *Cleitophon*. H. v. Arnim, *Leben und Werke des Dion von Prusa* (1898), again, insists that one of the four λόγοι προτρεπτικοί ascribed to Antisthenes is this common source.

²⁶⁰ Cf. *Defence* 24 and notes 117, 133 and 191, *supra*. As to Xenophon's accounts of Socrates' 'piety', cf. *Memor.* 1.1.16 and *ibid.* at 4.6.2–4; 1.3.1–3; 4.3.1–18. For some interesting details of this question, see K. Joël, *op. cit.* at 1.89–170. Compliance with the prescribed religious rituals and avoidance of ἀσέβεια seem to have been the basic characteristics of Xenophon's piety. Plato, *Euthyphro* 14B.

²⁶¹ D.L. 2.45: 'In my opinion Socrates discoursed on physics. . . .' See A.-H. Chroust, 'Socrates and Pre-Socratic philosophy', in *The Modern Schoolman* 29, no. 2 (1952) 119–135; Plato, *Phaedo* 98A ff. Cf., however, Plato, *Apology* 19CD. Libanius, *op. cit.* chap. 16 (22.9 ff., Foerster) possibly relies on Xenophon, *Memor.* 1.1.11 ff.

²⁶² Cf. Plato, *Apology* 19CD; Aristophanes, *Clouds* 101. Plato, *Apology* 19CD, is also referred to in D.L. 2.45.

²⁶³ *Memor.* 1.1.14. This passage contains a strong condemnation of 'pre-Socratic' natural speculations.

²⁶⁴ Cf. *Defence* 13; Plato, *Apology* 26c ff.; Xenophon, *Memor.* 4.7.1–10 and *ibid.* at 4.6.2–4; Plato, *Laches* 199D; *Protagoras* 330B ff.; *Gorgias* 507A.

²⁶⁵ Cf. *Defence* 16–17 and *ibid.* at 21. See note 178, *supra*.

²⁶⁶ Cf. *Defence* 19 and note 171, *supra*; *Defence* 21 and note 178, *supra*; Libanius, *op. cit.* at chap. 13 (21.3–5, Foerster).

²⁶⁷ Cf. *Memor.* 4.7.1–10.

²⁶⁸ Cf. *Defence* 11 and *ibid.* at 26; notes 180, 181, 191, 192 and 194, *supra*.

²⁶⁹ Cf. *Memor.* 4.4.2. Xenophon, in *Memor.* 1.1.18, mentions nine generals, while in *Hellenica* 1.7.1 ff. he refers to eight generals. *Ibid.* at 1.6.29 and 1.7.33; 1.6.16; Plato, *Apology* 32BC. Aristotle, *Pol. Athen.* 34.1, speaks of ten generals. The Platonic report seems to be inaccurate, provided Xenophon, *Hellenica*, contains the true historical events. L. Breitenbach, 'Xenophon's Hellenica', in *Rheinisches Museum* 27 (1872) 514 ff. *Memor.* 4.4.1–4, are actually excerpts from an earlier Xenophontean report. Thus *Memor.* 4.4.2 have their source in *Memor.* 1.1.18; *Memor.* 4.4.3 in *Memor.* 1.2.33–38 and perhaps in Plato, *Apology* 32CD; and *Memor.* 4.4.4 perhaps in Plato, *Apology* 34C ff. In addition, *Memor.* 4.8.3–10 seem to be based on Xenophon's *Defence*.

²⁷⁰ The reference to the fact that Socrates remained faithful to his oath to observe the established laws of Athens (*Memor.* 1.1.18) is for Xenophon an indication of Socrates' true piety. Plato (*Apology* 32BC) like-

Notes to Chapter III

wise refers to this incident, but he uses it in an entirely different sense. See Plato, *Gorgias* 473E and the general tenor of the *Crito*.

[271] Cf. *Defence* 13 and notes 132 and 134–135, *supra*; *Defence* 21; *Memor.* 1.2.2 and *ibid.* at 1.2.55; 1.2.64; Plato, *Apology* 41CD; *ibid.* at 35D; 42A; *Crito* 43D and *ibid.* at 54E. Cf. notes 251–255, *supra*.

[272] Cf. *Defence* 11 and *ibid.* at 21; note 178, *supra*.

[273] Cf. *Memor.* 1.3.1 and *ibid.* at 4.3.16–18; 1.4.10; 4.6.2–4; 4.8.1–11.

[274] Cf. *Defence* 19 and note 172, *supra*; *Defence* 25 and notes 164, 171, 173 and 191, *supra*, and the text thereto; *Memor.* 1.2.17–18 and *ibid.* at 1.2.64.

[275] Josephus, *Contra Apionem* 2.263–264.

[276] Cf. *Defence* 26 and notes 161 and 162, *supra*; Pseudo-Plato, *Erastes* 132C; Xenophon, *Memor.* 1.3.5–15 and *ibid.* at 1.5.1–6; 1.6.1–10; Libanius, *op. cit.* at chap. 16 (22.4–9, Foerster) and *ibid.* chap. 24 (27.12–28.7, Foerster).

[277] Cf. *Defence* 19 and notes 164, 171, 174 and 191, *supra*; *Memor.* 1.6.1–10 and *ibid.* at 1.2.3; 3.14.1–7; 4.3.1–2. *Memor.* 1.6.1–10 seem to be of Cynic-Antisthenian origin, although Plato, *Gorgias* 492E, also praises frugality. Other passages which are probably of Cynic origin can be found in *Memor.* 2.1.1–34 and *ibid.* at 4.5.1–12; 1.3.5–7; 1.4.1; 4.4.3–12; 3.9.9; 2.1.17–34; Xenophon, *Symposium* 4.37 ff. See D.L. 2.27 and *ibid.* at 2.25; 2.31.

[278] Cf. *Defence* 21 and note 178, *supra*; *Defence* 24 and note 188, *supra*. Cf. *Memor.* 1.1.16 and *ibid.* at 1.6.1–10; 2.1.1–20; Libanius, *op. cit.* chap. 13 (21.3–5, Foerster).

[279] Cf. *Defence* 18 and note 174, *supra*; *Defence* 26. See, however, *Memor.* 1.4.1.

[280] *Der echte und der Xenophontische Socrates* 1.505 ff. and *ibid.* at 1.514 ff.

[281] Cf. *Memor.* 1.2.8 and *ibid.* at 1.2.17; 1.2.64; 1.4.19; *et passim*.

[282] Cf. note 174, *supra*.

[283] As to Socrates' poverty, cf. Plato, *Apology* 31C; Dio Chrysostom, *Oratio* 55.9.

[284] Cf. *Defence* 16–19 and notes 165–168, *supra*.

[285] Cf. *Defence* 17 and notes 162, 167 and 168–174, *supra*; Plato, *Protagoras* 313C and *ibid.* at 328B; Xenophon, *Memor.* 1.6.13–14.

[286] Similar ideas can also be found in Plato, *Gorgias* 519CD.

[287] Cf. *Defence* 17 and notes 162, 167 and 168–174, *supra*; *Memor.* 1.6.13–14.

[288] Cf. *Defence* 19 and notes 164 and 168–174, *supra*; *Memor.* 1.2.64.

[289] Cf. *Memor.* 3.9.10–11; Aristotle, *Athen. pol.* 8.1; *Politics* 1273 b 40 and *ibid.* at 1274 a 16; *Rhetoric* 1393 b 3–8; Δίσσοι λόγοι, in H. Diels, *Die Fragmente der Vorsokratiker* 636, lines 21 ff.

[290] Cf. *Defence* 20–21; *Memor.* 3.5.14–28 and *ibid.* at 3.6.1–18.

[291] Cf. Christ-Schmid, *Geschichte der griechischen Literatur* (6th edit.)

Notes to Chapter III

1.508, note 3. In essence Plato's *Gorgias* is likewise a refutation of Polycrates.

[292] Cf. Plato, *Gorgias* 517A and *ibid.* at 521D; *Meno* 95A; *Apology* 19D–20C and *ibid.* at 22A ff.; *Euthyphro* 2B; *Gorgias* 521C; *Apology* 26B and *ibid.* at 26E.

[293] Xenophon, *Memor.* 4.6.12.

[294] Cf. Xenophon, *Cyropaedia* 1.2.2 ff. and *ibid.* at 1.3.18; 8.5.24 ff.

[295] Cf. *Defence* 19 and *ibid.* at 21; notes 164, 168–174 and 178 *supra*; *Memor.* 1.2.64.

[296] Cf. Aristotle, *Rhetoric* 1393 b 3 ff.

[297] Cf. *Dialexis* (Δίσσοι λόγοι) 7.

[298] Cf. [Plato?] *Epist.* 7.326AB.

[299] Cf. Xenophon, *Hellenica*, Books I and II.

[300] Cf. F. Blass, *Attische Beredsamkeit* (2nd edit.) 2.248, note 8.

[301] Cf. notes 1212–1235, *infra*; Pseudo-Andocides, *Contra Alcibiadem* (edit. Blass), which allegedly was delivered in 415. F. Blass, *Attische Beredsamkeit* 1.280 ff., and especially *ibid.* at 1.298 and 1.332–339.

[302] Cf. Thucydides 6.89.

[303] Plutarch's *Alcibiades* likewise seems to rely on the *Contra Alcibiadem*.

[304] St. Matthew 7.20 and *ibid.* at 7.16.

[305] Cf. C. Müller, *Fragmenta historicorum graecorum* 107, frag. 1 (Stesimbrotus).

[306] Cf. note 167, *supra*.

[307] Cf. Isocrates, *Oratio* 16.

[308] Cf. Pseudo-Andocides, *Contra Alcibiadem*.

[309] As regards the association of Socrates and Alcibiades, the following dates should be kept in mind: beginning with the year 420, in which Alcibiades entered the political life of Athens, it seems unlikely that he should have seen much of Socrates. In 415 Alcibiades, after having sailed for Sicily on the ill-fated 'Sicilian Expedition', became a permanent exile with the exception of three or four months in 407. At the time of the trial of Socrates, Alcibiades was dead, having died in 404.

[310] Cf. *Memor.* 2.1.1–10.

[311] Cf. *Memor.* 1.2.3 and notes 279–282, *supra*.

[312] Cf. *Memor.* 1.1.16.

[313] Cf. notes 171, 174 and 178, *supra*.

[314] Aristotle, *Nicomachean Ethics* 1145 b 21–27 and *ibid.* at 1113 b 14–17.

[315] Cf. Plato, *Protagoras* 352BC and *ibid.* at 357C–357E.

[316] Cf. D.L. 6.12 and *ibid.* at 6.13; 6.105; Plato, *Protagoras* 340D and *ibid.* at 344D. See note 757, *infra*.

[317] Xenophon quotes here Theognis 35–36, as well as another unidentified poet. Cf. Xenophon, *Symposium* 2.4; Plato, *Meno* 95D; note 317, *supra*. A similar idea is expressed by Plato, *Apology* 33E–34B.

Notes to Chapter III

³¹⁸ D.L. 6.105 and *ibid.* at 6.12. It seems, therefore, that although Xenophon owes many of his ideas to Antisthenes, he does not always concur with his views.

³¹⁹ Cf. Xenophon, *Hellenica* 2.3.36; Pseudo-Plato, *Theages* 130A.

³²⁰ Cf. note 164, *supra*.

³²¹ Cf. *Memor.* 1.2.20.

³²² Cf. Xenophon, *Defence* 16 and *ibid.* at 24; notes 164 and 191, *supra*.

³²³ Cf. D.L. 2.19–20 and *ibid.* at 2.24; Xenophon, *Memor.* 4.4.3.

³²⁴ Cf. Xenophon, *Hellenica* 2.3.12; Aristotle, *Pol. Athen* 35.3; Diodorus 14.4; Lysias 25.27.

³²⁵ Cf. A.-H. Chroust, 'The legal profession in ancient Athens', in *Notre Dame Lawyer* 29 (1954) 385 ff.

³²⁶ Cf. Plato, *Gorgias* 516E.

³²⁷ Cf. *Memor.* 4.4.3; Plato, *Apology* 32CD; (Plato?) *Epist.* 7.324E–325A. In *Memor.* 1.2.37, Critias says to Socrates: 'It will be necessary for you to abstain from speaking of shoemakers, carpenters, and blacksmiths.' Cf. *ibid.* at 3.7.6. The idea that Socrates always discusses the same topics with the 'common people' also appears in Plato, *Gorgias* 490E–491B, Xenophon, *Memor.* 4.4.5 ff., and Plato, *Charmides* 163B. Cf. Dio Chrysostom, *Oratio* 55.22.

³²⁸ Cf. Aeschines, *Contra Timarchum* 173.

³²⁹ Cf. *Memor.* 1.2.16: 'For if a god had given them [*scil.*, Critias and Alcibiades] their choice whether to live such a life as they saw Socrates living, or to die, they would have chosen rather to die.'

³³⁰ Cf. Thucydides 6.92.

³³¹ *Memor.* 1.2.40–48, it will be noticed, show a certain affinity with Plato, *Republic* 338C.

³³² C. Müller, *Fragm. histor. graec.* 107, frag. 11 (Stresimbrotus).

³³³ Cf. O. Voss, *De Heracleit. Pont. vita et scriptis* (Rostock, 1896), frag. 21.

³³⁴ Cf. *Defence* 19 and notes 171 and 178, *supra*. As to the meaning of 'the other young men' in *Memor.* 1.2.48, cf. Plato, *Crito*, *Apology*, and *Phaedo*.

³³⁵ If we compare *Memor.* 1.2.49–55 and *Defence* 20, we cannot escape the following conclusions: first, *Memor.* 1.2.49 ff., like the whole of *Memor.* 1.2.9–61, is a rebuttal of the charges made by Polycrates in his κατηγορία Σωκράτους; secondly, *Defence* 20 is definitely dependent on *Memor.* 1.2.49–55: *Defence* 20 is nothing other than a short summary of *Memor.* 1.2.49–55. This alone should indicate beyond all doubt that the *Defence* was written at a later date than the whole of *Memor.* 1.1.1–1.2.64.

³³⁶ Cf. *Defence* 20 and notes 175–176, *supra*; Aristophanes, *Clouds* 1407.

³³⁷ Cf. Plato, *Apology* 29B: '. . . disobedience to a better, whether God or man, is evil and dishonourable. . . .'

Notes to Chapter III

[338] Cf. D.L. 6.12.
[339] Cf. Xenophon, *Memor.* 2.2.1-14.
[340] Cf. *Defence* 20 and notes 175-178, *supra*.
[341] Cf. K. Joël, *op. cit.* at 1.337 ff.
[342] Cf. *Memor.* 2.3.1-19.
[343] Cf. *Defence* 20 and note 175, *supra*; D.L. 6.12 (Antisthenes); *Memor.* 2.9.1-18.
[344] Cf. *Memor.* 2.4.1-7.
[345] Cf. D.L. 6.12 (Antisthenes); Xenophon, *Memor.* 2.5.1-5 and *ibid.* at 2.6.1-39; Plato, *Protagoras* 338C ff.
[346] Cf. Aristotle, *Eudemian Ethics* 1235 a 35-1235 b 1.
[347] Cf. *Defence* 21 and notes 175-178, *supra*; *Memor.* 4.7.1.
[348] Hesiod, *Works and Days* 309. Cf. Plato, *Charmides* 163B.
[349] Cf. *Defence* 19; *Memor.* 2.8.1-16.
[350] Homer, *Iliad* 2.188 ff.
[351] Cf. Plato, *Symposium* 220B; Xenophon, *Memor.* 3.7.5-6.
[352] Cf. *Defence* 26 and note 334, *supra*; *Defence* 16 and notes 162-164, *supra*; D.L. 2.65. Plato, in *Apology* 31AB and *Euthyphro* 3D, speaks of the φιλανθρωπία of Socrates.
[353] Xenophon, *Memor.* 1.2.7.
[354] Cf. Libanius, *Apologia Socratis*, chap. 14 (21.9-10, Foerster) and *ibid.* chap. 22 (26.14-15, Foerster).
[355] Cf. *Defence* 18 and note 165, *supra*; *Defence* 17 and note 167, *supra*; *Defence* 26 and notes 194-196, *supra*.
[356] This passage seems to refer to Socrates' suggestion that 'maintenance in the *Prytaneum*' would be a just reward for his merits. Plato, *Apology* 36E-37A. Cf. notes 365-368, *infra*, and the text thereto; note 190, *supra*; *Memor.* 1.7.1-5.
[357] Cf. *Defence* 26 and notes 192 and 193, *supra*; Xenophon, *Symposium* 4.36; Plato, *Republic* 575B; *Gorgias* 508E.
[358] Cf. Xenophon, *Hellenica* 1.7.20 ff.
[359] Cf. chapters IV and VII, *infra*.
[360] Cf. *Defence* 25; *Memor.* 1.2.63 and notes 171 and 191, *supra*.
[361] Cf. *Defence* 24.
[362] Cf. *Defence* 25 and notes 171-172, *supra*.
[363] Cf. *Defence* 16 and note 164, *supra*; *Defence* 25 and notes 191 and 195, *supra*.
[364] Cf. *Defence* 18; Xenophon, *Anabasis* 3.1.5 ff., where the fact is stressed that Socrates always acted the perfect citizen.
[365] Cf. D.L. 2.42: 'I assess the penalty at maintenance in the *Prytaneum*.' *Memor.* 1.2.62. See also note 204, *supra*, and the text thereto.
[366] Cf. note 190, *supra*.
[367] Cf. notes 75-79, *supra*, and the text thereto.
[368] Cf. notes 202-205, *supra*, and the text thereto.
[369] Cf. J. Geffken, *Griechische Literaturgeschichte* 2 (1934) 11-12.

Notes to Chapter IV

³⁷⁰ It should be noted that in *Memor*. 1.2.9–61, Xenophon refers to the κατήγορος, while in *Memor*. 1.2.62–64, which constitutes the summation of his apology, he uses again the terms γραψόμενος or γραφή.

³⁷¹ Cf. note 228, *supra*.

NOTES TO CHAPTER IV—PAGES 69–100

³⁷² Cf. D.L. (Diogenes Laertius) 2.38.

³⁷³ Cf. notes 87 and 88, *supra*, and the text thereto.

³⁷⁴ Composed *c*. 390. Cf. R. C. Jebb, *Attic orators* 2.91; F. Blass, *Attische Beredsamkeit* 2.248; G. Mathieu et É. Brémond, *Isocrate* 1.184.

³⁷⁵ R. Hirzel, 'Polycrates' Anklage und Lysias' Verteidigung des Sokrates', in *Rheinisches Museum* 42 (1887) 249; F. Dümmler, *Akademika* (1889) 28.

³⁷⁶ Cf. C. Ritter, 'Bericht über die in den letzten Jahrzehnten über Platon erschienenen Arbeiten', in *Jahresbericht über die Fortschritte der klassischen Altertumswissenschaft* 191 (48. Jahrgang, 1922/3) 209 ff., and the literature cited there; J. Humbert, 'Le pamphlet de Polycrates et le Gorgias de Platon', in *Revue de Philologie* 5 (1931) 20 ff.

³⁷⁷ Cf. A.-H. Chroust, 'Socrates—a source problem', in *The New Scholasticism* 19 (1945) 50, note 21.

³⁷⁸ Cf. Christ-Schmid. *Geschichte der griechischen Literatur* (6th edit.) 1. 508, note 3; A. Gercke, in Sauppe's edition of the Platonic *Gorgias* (1897), pp. XLIII ff.; Th. Gomperz, *Griechische Denker* (3d edit.) 2.279 ff.; H. Raeder, *Platons philosophische Entwicklung* (1905) 123 and *ibid*. at 136; R. Foerster, *Libanii opera* (1909) 5.4 ff.; M. Schanz, *Apologia Socratis* (1893) 22–45; J. Mesk, 'Die Anklagerede des Polykrates gegen Sokrates', in *Wiener Studien* 32 (1911) 56–84; J. Mesk, in *Berliner philologische Wochenschrift* (1911) 1151 ff.; H. Maier, *Sokrates* (1913) 22–24 and *ibid*. at 132 ff.; 379 ff.; M. Pohlenz, *Aus Platons Werdezeit* (1913) 164 ff.; C. Ritter, in *Jahresbericht über die Fortschritte der klassischen Altertumswissenschaft* 191 (1923) 209 ff.; J. Geffken, 'Studien zu Platons Gorgias', in *Hermes* 65 (1930) 17 ff.; H. Markowski, 'De Libanio Socratis defensore', in *Breslauer Philologische Abhandlungen*, Heft 40 (1910); K. Meiser: 'Zu den Deklamationen des Libanius über Sokrates', *Sonderabdruck aus den Sitzungsberichten der kgl. bayr. Akademie der Wissenschaften*, phil.-hist. Klasse, no. 16 (1910); J. Humbert, 'Le pamphlet de Polycrates et le Gorgias de Platon', in *Revue de Philologie* 5 (1931) 20 ff.; C. G. Cobet, *Novae lectiones* (1858) 662–682; K. Praechter, *Die Philosophie des Altertums*, in Ueberweg-Heinze, *Grundriss der Geschichte der Philosophie*, vol. 1 (1926) 149; L. Dindorf, in his edition of the works of Xenophon, praef. XXIII; G.

Notes to Chapter IV

Sauppe in his edition of the works of Xenophon, praef. XI. L. Breitenbach insists, however, that the κατήγορος is none other than Meletus. 'Wer ist der κατήγορος in Xenophons Commentarien?' in *Jahrbücher für classische Philologie* 15 (1869), or, *Neue Jahrbücher für Philologie und Paedagogik* 39, 801–815. The opinion advanced by Breitenbach can no longer be upheld.

[379] Cf. Pauly-Wissowa, *Realencyclopädie der classischen Altertumswissen-schaften*, Neue Bearbeitung (Stuttgart, 1952) 42, 1736–1752.

[380] *Anonym. Hypothesis Busiridis* 1.

[381] If the account of Pausanias is correct, then Gorgias must have been about 100 years old at the time he met Polycrates in Pherae. Pausanias makes Gorgias about 105 years old at the time of his death, which took place in the year 376 (?).

[382] Polycrates is credited with having composed the following works: *Helena, Clytemnestra, Alexandros* (?), *The defence of Bursiris, Censure of the Lacedaemonians, The indictment of Socrates, The praise of mice* (Aristotle, *Rhetoric* 1401 a 13 and *ibid.* at 1401 b 15), *Praise of poets* (?), *The Praise of counterpebbles* (ψῆροι, Alexander, Περὶ ῥητόρ. ἀφόρμ., in L. Spengel, *Rhetores Graeci* 3 [1856].3), *Praise of salt* (cf. Plato, *Symposium* 177B), *Praise of pouring vessels* (βομβύλιοι, Isocrates, *Helena* 12), *Praise of beggars* (Isocrates, *Helena* 8), *Praise of exiles* (Isocrates, *Helena* 8), and an epideictic speech (perhaps the *Agamemnon*, mentioned by Demetrius, *On style* 120). Cf. also F. Blass, *Attische Beredsamkeit* (2d edit., 1892) 2.370–372; R. C. Jebb, *Attic orators* 2 (1893) 90–92.

[383] Cf. Baiter-Sauppe, *Oratores attici* 2.132; H. Markowski, *De Libanio Socratis defensore* 42; E. Scheel, *De Gorgianae disciplinae vestigiis* (1890); J. Humbert, 'Le pamphlet de Polycrates et le Gorgias de Platon', in *Revue de Philologie* 5 (1931) 22.

[384] *Instit. orator.* 2.17.4: '... [Polycrates] ... composuisse orationem quae est habita contra Socratem dicitur'. The '*dicitur*' would indicate that Quintilian was not altogether certain about the authorship of Polycrates, and whether this oration was delivered against Socrates 'personally', that is, during the trial.

[385] *Oratio* 23 (p. 357, edit. Dindorf).

[386] This tradition is recorded by Hermippus. D.L. 2.39.

[387] D.L. 2.39.

[388] Cf. R. Hirzel, 'Polycrates' Anklage und Lysias' Verteidigung des Sokrates', in *Rheinisches Museum* 42 (1887) 239–241.

[389] A. Bentley, *Dissertatio de epistola Socratis* 6; M. Schanz, *op. cit.* at 22 ff.

[390] R. Hirzel, *op. cit.* at 239 ff. As to the tradition that Lysias wrote two Socratic *Apologies*, see notes 87–88, *supra*.

[391] Cf. *Memor.* 1.2.9 and *ibid.* at 1.2.12; 1.2.26; 1.2.49; 1.2.51; 1.2.52; 1.2.56; 1.2.58; 1.2.59; 1.2.60.

[392] Subsequently quoted as Libanius, chap. 61.

Notes to Chapter IV

[393] In vol. 3, p. 480, edit. Dindorf.

[394] Homer, *Iliad* 2.188 ff.

[395] *Libanii opera*, edit. R. Foerster (Leipzig, 1909) vol. 5, pp. 13–121. Wherever feasible, page and line of the Foerster edition will be quoted.

[396] Attempts at reconstructing the κατηγορία Σωκράτους of Polycrates have been made, among others, by J. Mesk, 'Die Anklagerede des Polykrates gegen Sokrates', in *Wiener Studien* 32 (1911) 57–84; A.-H. Chroust, 'Xenophon, Polycrates and "The Indictment of Socrates" ', in *Classica et Mediaevalia* 16 (1955) 1–77; and M. Schanz, *Apologia Socratis* (1893) 22–45. Cf. R. Hirzel, 'Polykrates' Anklage und Lysias' Verteidigung des Sokrates', in *Rheinisches Museum* 42 (1887) 239 ff. While M. Schanz sees in Xenophon's *Memorabilia* 1.2.9–61 the more reliable source, J. Mesk relies mostly on the *Apologia Socratis* of Libanius. As to the sources used by Libanius, cf. H. Markowski, 'De Libanio Socratis defensore', in *Breslauer Philologische Abhandlungen* 40 (1910).

[397] R. Hirzel, *op. cit.* at 246 and *ibid.* at 249.

[398] Cf. Pausanias 6.17.9.

[399] As to the extreme difficulty in establishing the biographical data of Gorgias, cf. F. Blass, *op. cit.* at 1.47.

[400] Meletus, according to Plato, seems to have been the main *actor* in the prosecution of Socrates, while Anytus remained the main *architect* of the trial. Plato, *Apology* 18AB and *ibid.* at 28A; 29C; 30B; 31A; 36A; *Epist.* 7.325B; Xenophon, *Memor.* 1.1.1; *Defence* 29 ff. R. Hackforth, *The composition of Plato's Apology* (1933) 78. *Schol ad Plat. Apolog.* 18B tells the story that Anytus allegedly bribed Meletus to charge Socrates with impiety. See D.L. 2.38, a passage which is very confusing in that it contains insertions from Hermippus and Favorinus. Meletus, who was not very successful in his speech for the prosecution (Plato, *Apology* 36AB), was rescued by Anytus, an experienced forensic orator, who pointed out that since the issue had reached the stage of a public trial, only a verdict of guilty could save the sovereignty of the Athenian people. The consequences of an acquittal, according to Anytus, would be disastrous for Athens in that it would actually amount to an official sanction of Socrates' activities. Cf. Plato, *Apology* 29C and *ibid.* at 36AB; 30B; 31A.

[401] Cf. C. Cobet, *Novae lectiones* (1858) 662 ff.; *Hypothesis Busiridis*, in *Isocrate* (edit. G. Mathieu and É. Brémond) 1.186.

[402] Aristotle, *Athen. Pol.* 39.6.

[403] D.L. 2.39.

[404] Cf. M. Pohlenz, *Aus Platons Werdezeit* (1913) 164–165.

[405] Cf. K. Joël, *Der echte und der xenophontische Sokrates* 2.112 ff.

[406] *Op. cit.* at 37. Cf. K. Rogge, *Libanii Apologia* (1891) 8.

[407] Xenophon, for instance, does not specifically mention the charge, found in Libanius 84.18, that Socrates had been leading youths to

Notes to Chapter IV

idleness and sloth. But this omission could be explained by the fact that Xenophon had already dealt with this point in *Memor.* 1.2.2.

408 This is done in a rather thorough fashion by Libanius.

409 The four 'accusations' recorded by Xenophon are also found in Libanius, with the difference that for some unknown reason Libanius deals exhaustively only with the charges listed by Xenophon in *Memor.* 1.2.49–55 and *ibid.* at 1.2.56–61.

410 This fact in itself forces us to assume that the *Apologia* of Libanius constitutes a refutation of Polycrates, who rendered his charges through Anytus. Cf. M. Schanz, *op. cit.* 27.

411 Xenophon, *Memor.* 1.2.59.

412 Cf. Xenophon, *Memor.* 1.2.63: 'He [*scil.*, Socrates] was never the cause . . . of any sedition or treason. . . .'

413 This is denied by Isocrates, *Busiris* 5. Cf., however, Xenophon, *Memor.* 1.2.12 ff. As to the quotations from ancient poets (Xenophon, *Memor.* 1.2.56–58) in connection with the alleged corruption of youths by Socrates (*Memor.* 1.2.9 ff.), the *Apologia* of Libanius and the *Memorabilia* to Xenophon seem to coincide to a remarkable degree.

414 Xenophon, *Memor.* 1.2.9.

415 'Le pamphlet de Polycrates et le Gorgias de Platon', in *Revue de Philologie* 5.28–31.

416 'De Libanio Socratis defensore', in *Breslauer Philologische Abhandlungen* 40 (1910) 5–20.

417 It appears from Libanius 14.10 that Meletus had spoken first for the prosecution, and that Lycon was expected to 'relieve' Anytus after the latter had completed his arguments. *Ibid.* at 14.12; Plato, *Apology* 23E ff. and *ibid.* at 36A; Libanius 115.19 ff.; D.L. 2.38–39. This 'pattern' of sequence in the delivery of the three speeches for the prosecution seems to follow that indicated in Plato's *Apology*.

418 Libanius, chaps. 31–43. Cf. D.L. 2.38: 'Anytus . . . helped to persuade Meletus to indict him [scil., Socrates]. . . .'

419 Libanius 20.11 and *ibid.* at 29.15; 31.17; 30.4; 34.12; Plato, *Apology* 24C and *ibid.* at 25C; 26A.

420 Cf. note 448, *infra* and the text thereto.

421 Cf. Libanius 79.1 and *ibid.* at 79.6; 79.12; 79.18; 80.17.

422 A. E. Taylor, *Varia Socratica* 12. Cf. *ibid.* at 30.

423 Cf. Xenophon, *Defence* 30; Plato, *Apology* 23E.

424 Cf. Xenophon, *Memor.* 1.2.2 and *ibid.* at 1.2.62. *Defence* 19 and *ibid.* at 25.

425 Cf. Xenophon, *Memor.* 1.2.9 and *ibid.* at 1.2.2; 1.2.63; *Defence* 20–21.

426 Libanius 20.14 ff.

427 Libanius 20.14 ff. Xenophon, *Memor.* 1.2.59–60.

428 Libanius 30.2 and *ibid.* at 38.1; 78.15; 36.13; *et passim*; Xenophon, *Memor.* 1.2.63.

Notes to Chapter IV

[429] Plato, *Apology* 23C; Xenophon, *Memor.* 1.2.49–55; *Defence* 20–21.
[430] Plato, *Apology* 29E.
[431] Cf. Isocrates 18.23; Aristotle, *Pol. Athen.* 39.6; Xenophon, *Hellenica* 2.4.43.
[432] Libanius 20.14 ff.; Xenophon, *Memor.* 1.2.59–60 and *ibid.* at 1.2.63.
[433] *Apology* 19D–20C and *ibid.* at 21B–22A; 23CD; 24C–26D.
[434] Cf. Plato, *Meno* 95A.
[435] Cf. J. Mesk, *op. cit.* 60 ff.
[436] Libanius chaps. 14 ff. This is also true of Xenophon. Cf. *Memor.* 1.2.1–8 and *ibid.* at 1.2.62–64; Plato, *Apology* 30B; *Phaedrus* 241C; *Laws* 726A and *ibid.* at 731C.
[437] Cf. Xenophon, *Memor.* 1.1.1 ff. and *ibid.* at 1.2.64; *et passim*.
[438] Cf. Xenophon, *Memor.* 1.1.11; Plato, *Apology* 19CD. This Libanian rebuttal may indicate that Polycrates had accused Socrates of being a sophist or a 'physicist' of the type of Anaxagoras.
[439] Cf. Xenophon, *Memor.* 1.2.1–2 and notes 274–281, *supra*; *Memor.* 1.2.14 and *ibid.* at 1.2.5. This could mean that Polycrates had charged Socrates with having indulged in vices and luxurious idleness. See Plato, *Apology* 23B and *ibid.* at 38B ff.; Plutarch, *Aristides* 1.9; Libanius 87.5 ff.
[440] Cf. notes 261–264, *supra*. It seems that Libanius relies here on the testimony of Xenophon. In any event, Libanius chap. 16 and Xenophon, *Memor.* 1.1.11–16 are strikingly similar. See *Memor.* 4.7.1–10; Plato, *Apology* 19C.
[441] Cf. Xenophon, *Memor.* 1.1.10. See note 259, *supra*; *Defence* 11; Plato, *Apology* 18D; Libanius 113.3.
[442] We shall see later what particular aspects of Socrates' general conduct Polycrates considered dangerous to Athens and Athenian democratic institutions.
[443] This is the first charge listed by Xenophon. Cf. *Memor.* 1.2.9 and *ibid.* at 1.2.63. The passages where Libanius refers to this particular charge are found in 21.2; 58.11–12; 38.11–14; 41.9–11; 42.5–6; 59.4–5; 78.15–17; 109.9–10.
[444] The specific passages where Libanius mentions this charge are 21.3; 33.4–5; 43.1–2; 43.18–20; 45.2–4. Cf. *ibid.* at 108.6; 41.2–4; 41.7–8; 46.2–8; 47.7–14; 48.2–4; 60.17–18. If the general tradition about Socrates contains reliable information, he apparently found much to criticize in the democratic institutions of his native city. He seems to have had little esteem for a city governed by an assembly composed of 'fullers, cobblers, masons, metal-smiths, labourers, peddlers, and hucksters'. Xenophon, *Memor.* 3.7.6.
[445] Libanius 34.15 ff. Cf. *ibid.* at 108.6 ff.: '. . . you [*scil.*, Polycrates] have the audacity to call Socrates a friend [or, advocate] of tyranny'. *Ibid.* at 58.10, where Libanius takes up the accusation that Socrates had criticized certain Athenian legal or constitutional practices. *Ibid.* at

Notes to Chapter IV

43.18 ff., where Libanius takes issue with the Polycratean contention that Socrates 'hates the people (μισόδημος) and induces his followers to ridicule democracy' (δημακρατίας καταγελᾶν).

[446] Libanius chaps. 34–59 (32.13–47.7) and *ibid.* at chap. 61 (47.14–48.6).

[447] In Xenophon, *Memor.* 1.2.9–11, this rebuttal is a relatively short one.

[448] Libanius refers here to the 'oligarchic revolution' of the year 411 and that of the year 404, which is commonly called the regime of the Thirty Tyrants.

[449] Xenophon (*Memor.* 1.2.60) rebuts these allegations by pointing out that 'Socrates was evidently a friend of the common people'.

[450] The passages where Libanius cites some of these particular charges are: 33.1; 34.14; 38.11; 40.15; 41.2; 41.7; 42.6; 43.1; 43.18; 45.3.

[451] Cf. notes 289 and 295–298, *supra*, and the text thereto.

[452] This latter account may very well be Xenophon's personal version of Polycrates' charge that Socrates advocated the overthrow of Athenian democracy.

[453] Cf. Plato, *Apology* 19D–20C and *ibid.* at 21B–22A; 23CD; 24C–26D.

[454] Cf. *ibid.* at 59.4–7, where Libanius contends that criticism of existing laws, customs, or institutions is fully within the spirit of a democracy. *Ibid.* at 59.7–60.18.

[455] Libanius (61.5–6) concludes his statements with the remark that such a conscientious critic as Socrates is really 'a lover of the city'.

[456] Cf. Libanius 43.19–20: '[Socrates] induces his followers to ridicule democracy.' *Ibid.* at 45.2–4: '[Socrates] persuaded young people to work towards the enslavement of the city.' *Ibid.* at 108.6: 'Socrates ... [was] a friend of tyrants.' *Ibid.* at 33.5: '[Socrates is supposed] ... to cause harm to the city.' *Ibid.* at 41.2–4: 'Socrates was a hater of democracy.' *Ibid.* at 47.8: '[Socrates is a] teacher of tyrants.' *Ibid.* at 48.3, where Libanius contends that Polycrates had failed to demonstrate Socrates' alleged 'love of tyrants'. *Ibid.* at 60.17–18, where we find another reference to Socrates' alleged 'hatred for the people'. *Ibid.* at 20.15–21.3: 'Socrates was never an advocate ... of the destruction of democracy (δήμου κατάλυσις).' *Ibid.* at 44.1–3: 'Does Socrates write against the existing constitution ...? Does he preach its overthrow?' *Ibid.* at 36.13–15: '... Socrates allegedly undermines democracy and trains citizens who will be a threat [to democracy].' *Ibid.* at 43.1–2: 'The whole youth [of Athens] has been corrupted by his teachings, and desires nothing more than the overthrow of the existing constitution.' See Plutarch, *Cato* 23: '[Cato] says that Socrates was a mighty prattler who attempted, the best he could, to become the tyrant of his city, by abolishing its customs and institutions, and by inciting his fellow citizens to hold opinions which were contrary to the established laws.'

[457] See Plato, *Gorgias* 513A. In Xenophon, *Hellenica* 2.3.47, Thera-

Notes to Chapter IV

menes calls Critias the 'greatest hater of the common people' (or, of democracy—μισοδημότατος).

⁴⁵⁸ We must assume, therefore, that Xenophon's report, in *Memor.* 1.2.9 and perhaps *ibid.* at 1.2.59-60, is both accurate and reliable. See *Memor.* 1.2.63. Thucydides (6.89) recounts that Alcibiades, the disciple of Socrates, had called democracy 'an acknowledged absurdity'; and the author of the *Contra Alcibiadem* (chap. 27), formerly ascribed to Andocides, maintains that Alcibiades had demonstrated that 'democracy is nothing other than a sham'.

⁴⁵⁹ Cf. *ibid.* at 108.6-7, where we find another reference to Socrates' alleged 'advocacy of tyranny' (τυραννικός). *Ibid.* at 58.12-15. In the *Wasps* (474-476) of Aristophanes, Bdelycleon is called a μισόδημος, a μοναρχίας ἐραστής, and a philo-Laconian.

⁴⁶⁰ Libanius chaps. 34-59 and 61. Libanius in his rebuttal charges Anytus with serious dereliction of duty for having failed to proceed against Socrates any sooner. Cf. note 448, *supra*, and the text thereto. This failure of Anytus seems to indicate that Anytus is himself a traitor, or that he knew all along that he had no case against Socrates. The same idea can be found in Plato, *Apology* 24c.

⁴⁶¹ *Memor.* 1.2.9.

⁴⁶² Libanius 84.18: 'But Socrates, he [*scil.*, Polycrates] contended, induced people to be idle.'

⁴⁶³ Cf. Plato, *Gorgias* 515E ff.

⁴⁶⁴ Cf. *ibid.* at 43.13, where we are told that Polycrates had charged Socrates with 'not being a tax-payer', and, hence, a person who from sheer laziness failed to make a financial contribution to the commonwealth.

⁴⁶⁵ Cf. Plato, *Statesman* 268B. Libanius 89.9-10 seems to find some support in the many reports about Socrates' efforts to persuade certain people to refrain from entering political life because of insufficient ability and training. Xenophon, *Memor.* 3.1.1-11 and *ibid.* at 3.6.1-18. To offset this charge, Xenophon might have written *Memor.* 2.1.1 ff. and *ibid.* at 3.7.1-9; 1.2.1-2. Cf. notes 276 and 277, *supra*; *Defence* 19 and *ibid.* at 25.

⁴⁶⁶ Cf. also Aristophanes, *Clouds* 316 and *ibid.* at 334; 1498.

⁴⁶⁷ In this connection we cannot recommend highly enough the splendid book of J. Pieper, *Leisure the basis of culture*, transl. by A. Dru (London 1951).

⁴⁶⁸ Cf. Xenophon, *Memor.* 1.2.1-2 and *ibid.* at 1.1.20; 1.2.62-64.

⁴⁶⁹ Cf. Xenophon, *Memor.* 1.2.56-61 and notes 348-353, *supra*. It is interesting to note that this argument is used in the last place by Xenophon, while Libanius seems to make use of it in the first place.

⁴⁷⁰ Cf. Xenophon, *Memor.* 1.2.12. This is in essence the second Polycratean charge listed by Xenophon. See A. E. Taylor, *Plato, the man and his work*, 6th edit. (London, 1949) 165, note 2.

Notes to Chapter IV

⁴⁷¹ Cf. Xenophon, *Memor.* 1.2.49.

⁴⁷² Libanius, chap. 61 (47.14–48.6), where this becomes quite obvious. Xenophon, *Memor.* 1.2.9: '... he disposed them to acts of violence.' Libanius 20.15.

⁴⁷³ The same could be inferred from Xenophon, *Memor.* 1.2.12 ff.

⁴⁷⁴ According to Xenophon (*Memor.* 1.2.12), the Polycratean charge would have been that 'Critias and Alcibiades, after having been associated with Socrates, inflicted a great many evils on the city'. Cf. Libanius chaps. 136 ff.

⁴⁷⁵ This also seems to follow from the account of Xenophon, *Memor.* 1.2.12 ff.

⁴⁷⁶ There is a short allusion to this final refutation in Libanius 33.9.

⁴⁷⁷ Cf. *Memor.* 1.2.12–30 and *ibid.* at 1.2.53–55.

⁴⁷⁸ Cf. J. Mesk, *op. cit.* at 63 ff.

⁴⁷⁹ See *Defence* 20. The same theme appears in Xenophon, *Cyropaedia* 3.1.38–40, where we are told that the King of Armemia had killed a 'sophist' because the latter had so influenced the King's son that he held the 'sophist' in higher esteem than his own father. The parallel between *Memor.* 1.2.49 and *Cyropaedia* 3.1.38–40 is obvious. The 'sophist' of the *Cyropaedia* is Socrates, who, according to Xenophon, was likewise put to death for having, among other things, induced his followers to think of him more highly than of their fathers. In the *Cyropaedia* Xenophon apparently has undergone a change of attitude. For here he condones the killing of the 'sophist'. Cf. F. Beyschlag, 'Ein literarischer Rückzug Xenophons', in *Blätter für das Gymnasial-Schulwesen* 37 (1901) 49–59.

⁴⁸⁰ Xenophon, *Memor.* 1.2.51. See note 479, *supra*.

⁴⁸¹ Xenophon, *Memor.* 1.2.52. See note 345, *supra*.

⁴⁸² Xenophon, *Memor.* 1.2.52.

⁴⁸³ This is in essence the third charge listed by Xenophon. Xenophon reiterates this charge in *Defence* 20.

⁴⁸⁴ According to Xenophon (*Memor.* 1.2.55), these youths were seeking 'to be esteemed' by every one.

⁴⁸⁵ Libanius, chaps. 85–101. Cf. *ibid.* at 48.8–14.

⁴⁸⁶ Cf. Xenophon, *Memor.* 12.56.

⁴⁸⁷ Plato's remark in *Apology* 33D ff., namely, where Socrates marvels at the failure of fathers and brothers to step forward to indict him for having corrupted the younger people, is probably related to this Polycratean charge.

⁴⁸⁸ Xenophon, *Memor.* 1.2.9–11. Cf. *ibid.* at 1.2.49–55 and 1.2.56–60.

⁴⁸⁹ Cf. Xenophon, *Memor.* 1.2.56–60; Libanius 48.8–14 and *ibid.* at 68. 19–21. The Libanian rebuttal of this charge is found in chaps. 63–79. According to Xenophon's arrangement this would be the fourth 'accusation'.

⁴⁹⁰ Libanius 70.17–71.6. This charge constitutes the third 'accusation' in the report of Xenophon. *Memor.* 1.2.49–55. In Xenophon it is sub-

Notes to Chapter IV

divided into three distinct parts or three particular 'accusations'. This subdivision, although not expressly mentioned by Libanius, might actually go back to Polycrates.

[491] Xenophon, *Memor.* 1.2.56. See also J. Mesk, *op. cit.* at 65.

[492] Cf. *ibid.* at 48.12-14.

[493] *Ibid.* at 61.7-14. Instances where, in the opinion of Libanius, Socrates was justified in objecting to the sayings of the old poets, are cited in Libanius 62.2-4 (Hesiod), *ibid.* at 62.10-13 (Pindar), *ibid.* at 63.4-8 and 64.2-7 (Theognis), and *ibid.* at 66.6-67.16 (Homer).

[494] *Op. cit.* at 41.

[495] *Op. cit.* at 66.

[496] Cf. Libanius 48.12 ff.

[497] Cf. Libanius 62.7 ff. and *ibid.* at 63.4 ff; 67.17 ff.

[498] Cf. Libanius, chaps. 73-77. Diogenes Laertius (6.69) reports that Diogenes of Sinope had called freedom of speech the most beautiful thing. Plato, *Gorgias* 461E: '. . . Athens . . . is the most free-spoken city in the whole of Greece. . . .'

[499] Cf. *ibid.* at 82.10 ff. In Plato's *Protagoras* Socrates frequently refers to the ancient poets in a rather unflattering manner. It could be claimed that the practice of slandering the ancient poets goes back to the tradition established by Antisthenes and his interpretation or interpolation of the ancient poets.

[500] Libanius 68.19 ff.

[501] Cf. notes 507-512, *infra*, and the text thereto.

[502] Xenophon, in *Memor.* 1.2.20, quotes Theognis; in *Memor.* 1.2.56, Hesiod; in *Memor.* 1.2.58, Homer; and, in *Memor.* 1.2.57, once more Hesiod. In *Memor.* 1.2.56-60, he observes the following order: Hesiod and Homer. Pindar, on the other hand, is completely omitted, and Theognis seems to be mentioned 'out of order' in *Memor.* 1.2.20.

[503] Libanius, chap. 86 (61.14-62.4).

[504] Xenophon, *Memor.* 1.2.56-57; Libanius 61.17. Plato, *Charmides* 163BC and notes 348-349, *supra*.

[505] Libanius 61.17. Cf. Xenophon, *Memor.* 1.2.56.

[506] Libanius, chap. 87 (62.11-12). This quotation from Pindar is omitted by Xenophon. See note 502, *supra*.

[507] Frag. 169 (edit. Bergk), or frag. 151 (edit. Böckh). This quotation, although probably in a 'corrupted form', can also be found in Plato, *Gorgias* 484B (cf. U. v. Wilamowitz-Moellendorff, *Platon* 2.98 ff.) and *ibid.* at 488B; *Laws* 714D and *ibid.* at 690BC; *Protagoras* 337D, where we find the proper interpretation of this Pindaric passage. Wilamowitz, *loc. cit.*, as well as in *Sitzungsbericht der Berliner Akademie* (1899) 78, assumes that the Pindaric quotation in Plato, *Gorgias* 484B—βιαῶν (or, βιαίων) τὸ δικαιότατον—is an 'intentional forgery' committed by Plato, and that Polycrates had used the correct wording, the δίκαιον τὸ βιαιότατον. Cf. J. Geffken, 'Studien zu Platons *Gorgias*', in *Hermes*

65 (1930) 14 ff.; A. E. Taylor, *Plato, the man and his work* (6th edit., London, 1949) 117, note 2 and *ibid.* at 103, note 1; A. Busse, 'Zum Pindarzitat in Platons Gorgias', in *Hermes* 66 (1931) 126–128 and *ibid.* at 367–368. The version, βιαιῶν τὸ δικαιότατον, in *Gorgias* 484B, could be Plato's invention; he might have devised it intentionally in order to characterize the sophist Callicles. J. Geffken, *op. cit.* at 19. It is also possible that Plato has been the victim of an error. This is the view held by Wilamowitz-Moellendorff. In any event, the Platonic version of the Pindaric passage was still known to Libanius (62.12 ff.). That Plato might have been familiar with the correct version may be inferred from *Laws* 715A and *ibid.* at 690C: τὸ βιαιότατον τὸν νόμον. The 'perverted' version, aside from the *Gorgias* 484B, can also be found in the *Protagoras* 337D, where this ὁ δὲ νόμος τύραννος ὢν τῶν ἀνθρώπων πολλὰ παρὰ τὴν φύσιν βιάζεται is nothing other than a paraphrase on the βιαιῶν τὸ δικαιότατον of *Gorgias* 484B. Cf. Plato, *Laws* 890A: εἶναι τὸ δικαιότατον ὅτι τὶς ἂν νικᾷ βιαζόμενος. In Herodotus 3.38 we can likewise detect the influence of this 'perversion' of the Pindaric quotation. The relationship of the Platonic *Gorgias* to the Polycratean κατηγορία Σωκράτους has been determined by some scholars on the basis of this Pindaric quotation. Cf. note 516, *infra*.

[508] In Plato's *Gorgias, Protagoras*, and the first book of the *Republic*, the same argument is being made by certain sophists who are rebuked by Socrates for their viewpoint. Cf. note 507, *supra*.

[509] Cf. *ibid.* at 63.1.

[510] Cf. J. Geffken, 'Studien zu Platons Gorgias', in *Hermes* 65 (1930) 19; J. Humbert, 'Le pamphlet de Polycrates et le Gorgias de Platon', in *Revue de Philologie* 5 (1931) 37 ff. and *ibid.* at 44 ff.; note 507, *supra*.

[511] 'Zum Pindarzitat in Platons Gorgias', in *Hermes* 66 (1931) 126 ff. and *ibid.* at 367 ff. Cf. U. v. Wilamowitz-Moellendorff, *Platon* 2.99.

[512] Cf. J. Geffken, 'Studien zu Platons Gorgias', in *Hermes* 65 (1930) 19.

[513] Cf. Xenophon, *Memor.* 1.2.56.

[514] Libanius 63.4; Xenophon, *Memor.* 1.2.58–60. About the allegation that Socrates rendered his disciples 'tyrannical', see also Xenophon, *Memor.* 1.2.56.

[515] Libanius, chap. 88 (63.4–63.8).

[516] Theognis 177 ff. Xenophon does not refer to the lines assigned to Theognis. Cf. note 502, *supra*.

[517] Libanius chaps. 88–92 (64.3–66.5).

[518] Aelius Aristides, *Schol.* ad Ὑπὲρ τῶν τεττάρων 133.16 (vol. 3, p. 480, edit. Dindorf).

[519] Lysias, *Apologia Socratis*, in *Schol. ad Aristidis orat.*, vol. 3, p. 480, edit. Dindorf.

[520] Xenophon's and Libanius' failure to mention and use as an effec-

Notes to Chapter IV

tive defence against the charge of μισοδημία the story (Aristotle, *Rhetoric* 1398 a 24; D.L. 2.25, who also names Scopas and Eurylochus) that Socrates once had turned down an invitation of the 'tyrant' Archelaus of Thessaly, suggests that this story as well as the reasons for which Socrates refused the invitation, probably were invented by Antisthenes in his dialogue *Archelaus*. Cf. Plato, *Gorgias* 470D, a passage which indicates that there never existed any relations betwen Socrates and Archelaus.

[521] Libanius refutes here the charges stated in Libanius 20.14 ff.

[522] Cf. Libanius 20.14 ff. and *ibid*. at 76.6 ff.; Xenophon, *Memor*. 1.2.63.

[523] Xenophon (*Memor*. 1.2.62–63) absolves Socrates from the charge of having committed (or condoned) theft, sacrilege, and the like.

[524] Xenophon, *Defence* 21.

[525] Libanius 72.10. In Xenophon there is no reference to the Melanthus episode.

[526] Cf. *ibid*. at 73.7 and 74.8. D.L. 6.73.

[527] Cf. Herodotus 8.75.

[528] About Thyestes, see Pauly-Wissowa, *Real-Encyl.*, Zweite Reihe (R-Z), 11. Halbband (1936) 662 ff. M. Schanz, *op. cit.* at 43, holds that Polycrates had charged Socrates with having justified theft and perjury by using a quotation from Homer, *Odyssey* 19.395 ff. He bases his view on the possibility that Libanius may be alluding here to this Homeric passage. Lysias, *Schol. ad Aristidis orat.* 3.320, edit. Dindorf, likewise mentions the theft of the *Palladion*.

[529] Cf. Libanius 75.4 ff. and *ibid*. at 83.1 ff. (ἱεροσυλεῖν); Antisthenes (?), *Odysseus* 3 ff.; *Schol. ad Platon. Apologiam* 20E, edit. Baiter-Orelli-Winckelmann, p. 893b 14–23; Xenophon, *Cyropaedia* 1.6.27; *Memor*. 4.2.14–18; Plato, *Republic* 382C and *ibid*. at 389B; Thucydides 5.9.3; Δίσσοι λόγοι (H. Diels, *Fragm. d. Vorsokr.* 641.4–643.16).

[530] Cf. *ibid*. at 74.8. Cf., however, M. Schanz *op. cit.* at 44.

[531] Xenophon (*Memor*. 4.2.16–18) under certain circumstances condones also the deception of friends and relatives.

[532] Cf. Xenophon, *Memor*. 1.2.28; Libanius 75.4–6 and *ibid*. at 76.7–8; 74.18 ff.

[533] Libanius (81.14) makes a general reference to the perfidious conduct of Pandaron, who treacherously broke the solemn pledge to observe the terms of an armistice between the Achaeans and the Trojans. Homer, *Iliad* 4.81 ff. See Plato, *Republic* 377A and *ibid*. at 379E.

[534] Cf. J. Mesk, *op. cit.* at 70.

[535] The transitory or antithetical remark in Libanius 77.13 (chap. 114) probably indicates that in the κατηγορία this new general charge or allegation must have followed the preceding charges.

[536] Libanius 77.13. Cf. *ibid*. at 33.20; 34.7 ff.; 79.6–7; Plato, *Gorgias* 485D; A. Gercke, in Sauppe's edition of Plato's *Gorgias* (1897) XLV ff.;

Notes to Chapter IV

Xenophon, *Memor.* 1.1.10 and *ibid.* at 1.1.11; *Defence* 11. Cf., however, Plato, *Apology* 32E ff.

[537] *Op. cit.* at 20.

[538] 'De Libanio Socratis defensore', in *Breslauer philologische Abhandlungen* 52.

[539] This may be gathered from Libanius 79.1 and *ibid.* at 79.6; 79.12; 79.18; 80.17. Cf., however, Plato, *Apology* 29DE; and *ibid.* at 30A; *Apology* 23C; Xenophon, *Memor.* 1.2.60 and *ibid.* at 1.2.5–7; 1.2.48 and note 334, *supra*; Xenophon, *Defence* 19 and *ibid.* at 17.

[540] Libanius 19.18; and *ibid.* at 28.1 ff.; 30.3; 35.3; 75.3; 103.7 ff.; *et passim*.

[541] Cf. Libanius 84.18 and *ibid.* at 86.12; 87.4; 89.3; 89.10; 89.16; 90.1; 90.5; Plato, *Apology* 29D ff. and *ibid.* at 23B; 31CD; 36BC; *Gorgias* 486D; Isocrates, *Oratio* 10.5; Lysias (?), *Oratio* 33.3.

[542] Libanius 89.16.

[543] The charges that Socrates taught his followers to live in idleness, or the allegation that he turned them into fops, could easily have arisen from Socrates' exhortation that we should care more for our soul than for material things. Libanius 88.14; Plato, *Apology* 29DE; *Gorgias* 515E, Xenophon, *Memor.* 1.2.1–2, and notes 276–277, *supra*; *Memor.* 1.2.62 and *ibid.* at 1.2.6–7; *Defence* 16.

[544] Chaps. 127–135 (84.18–90.14).

[545] Libanius 85.6–16.

[546] Cf. M. Schanz, *op. cit.* at 37, who believes that this point was merely a side issue used by Polycrates in order to demonstrate that Socrates' conduct was detrimental to the common welfare of the city.

[547] Cf. Demosthenes, *Contra Eubul.* 32.

[548] Cf. Meier-Schoemann-Lipsius, *Der attische Prozess* (1883) 1.364.

[549] Cf. Plutarch, *Moral.* 221C, where we are told that the Spartan Herondas witnessed the sentencing of a man for idleness.

[550] Cf. Xenophon, *Memor.* 2.1.13.

[551] D.L. 2.31.

[552] *Memor.* 2.7.10.

[553] *Memor.* 1.2.56. Cf. notes 504 and 505, *supra*, and the text thereto.

[554] Cf. *ibid.* at 3.9.9; note 349, *supra*, and the text thereto.

[555] Plato and Aristotle, who are also interested in the problem of 'idleness', treat it in a fashion quite different from that proposed by Xenophon. In Plato, where 'idleness' assumes the form of 'philosophical leisure', Socrates is always ready to discuss philosophy. But whenever he feels that the discussion leads nowhere, he breaks it off under the pretext that he has to attend to some work. That this 'work' is merely a pretext to rid himself of a dullard becomes obvious from the fact that in Plato Socrates has no definite 'profession', no definite work he might have to attend. To be a philosopher means with Plato to have leisure, that is to say, to be actually idle as regards the ordinary tasks of average

Notes to Chapter IV

life. In Aristotle leisure signifies the complete absence of any ordinary 'work duties'. Leisure is one of the prerequisites of perfect—philosophical—happiness. Work exists solely for the sake of leisure. Hence Aristotle calls the intellectual life the most perfect life because it is 'work in leisure'. Cf. J. Pieper, *Leisure the basis of culture*, transl. A. Dru (London 1951).

556 The refutation of this allegation by Libanius takes up chaps. 136–152 (90.15–102.12). The length of this refutation should be an indication that Libanius must have considered this allegation a very serious matter.

557 Libanius 95.12.

558 Cf. Plato, *Symposium* 215A–223A; Aristippus (D.L. 2.23); *et al.*

559 K. Joël, *op. cit.* at 2.1126 ff., maintains that Polycrates had derived the materials underlying this particular accusation from Antisthenes.

560 Xenophon, *Hellenica* 2.3.47. Cf. Libanius 43.18, where Socrates is called μισόδημος.

561 Cf. Plato (*Critias, Charmides, Protagoras, Timaeus, et passim*) and Xenophon (*Memor.* 1.2.14 ff. and *ibid.* at 1.2.26; 1.2.29–30; *et passim*).

562 That Alcibiades and Critias at one time had been close friends may be gathered from the latter's *Elegy on Alcibiades*. Cf. Diels-Kranz, *Die Fragm. d. Vorsokr.* (6th. edit., 1952) 2.377–78; Hephaestion, *Enchiridion*, edit. Consbruch (Leipzig, 1906) 9; Plutarch, *Alcibiades* 33. Like Alcibiades, Critias also seems to have been involved in the scandal of the *Hermae*. Andocides, *De mysteriis* 1.47. This would suggest that they both belonged to the same 'club'. Critias is said to have hated Phrynichus, the leader of the oligarchic reaction of the year 411, because of the latter's hostility to Alcibiades. Thucydides 8.48.4 and *ibid.* at 8.50 ff.; 8.54.3; Lycurgus, *Leocr.* 113. Later Critias proposed several times the recall of Alcibiades from exile. Thucydides 8.97.3. And both Critias and Alcibiades were banished in the year 407. Xenophon, *Hellenica* 2.3.15 and *ibid.* at 2.3.18; 2.3.36.

563 Cf. *ibid.* at 100.6–101.2; 33.9.

564 Cf. *ibid.* at 91.2.

565 Cf. *ibid.* at 95.11–12. Libanius seems to condone here the 'treason' of Alcibiades, when, compelled to flee on account of the affair of the *Hermae*, he went over to the Spartan side. Thucydides 6.61 and *ibid.* at 6.89–92.

566 Cf. Libanius 92.15 and *ibid.* at 94.10; 95.8; Xenophon, *Memor.* 1.2.12: 'Alcibiades was the most intemperate, insolent, and highhanded....' Thucydides 6.27. Throughout his *Apology*, Libanius wishes to convey the impression that Alcibiades, although an unruly person, never was guilty of a deliberate act against the welfare of the city. Cf. chap. 136, where Libanius insists that Alcibiades was forced through circumstances not of his making to betray his city, implying thereby that he really did so against his will.

Notes to Chapter IV

[567] Cf. Xenophon, *Memor.* 1.2.31. The Cynics, in particular, were much in favour of freedom of speech. D.L. 6.69; Libanius, chap. 80.

[568] Libanius 99.5. Cf. Xenophon, *Memor.* 1.2.12 and *ibid.* at 1.2.24–38; Libanius, *De Socratis silentio*, in *Libanii Opera* (edit. R. Foerster) vol. 5., p. 135, line 2.

[569] Cf. Libanius 106.10–107.2.

[570] Libanius 106.12 ff.

[571] Lysias, *Oratio* 13.78. Cf. Isocrates. *Oratio* 18.23.

[572] Xenophon, *Hellenica* 2.4.43; Aristotle, *Pol. Athen.* 39.6.

[573] Cf. Aristotle, *Rhetoric* 1401 a 34: 'There is Polycrates' saying that Thrasybulus put down the Thirty Tyrants.' Xenophon, *Hellenica* 2.4.2–26.

[574] Libanius 101.16 and *ibid.* at 102.8 ff.

[575] Libanius 93.3 and *ibid.* at 101.7; 102.9.

[576] By mentioning Solon (98.3 and 101.17; 102.4), Polycrates may have alluded to an interesting incident in Athenian history. In 411 Athenian democracy had been replaced for a while by an aristocratic-oligarchic reaction under the leadership of Theramenes. The watchword of Theramenes and his followers was 'the old constitution of our fathers', that is, the so-called constitution of Dracon. In this they actually refuted the constitution of Solon, the great reformer of the early sixth century. Aristotle, *Pol. Athen.* 29.3. As a matter of fact, they condemned Solon as the author of democracy, calling him the first one of a long line of mischievous demagogues.

[577] In *Memor.* 1.2.48, Xenophon cites many former disciples of Socrates who sought his company in order to become 'honourable and good men.... And no one of all these men, whether in his youth or in his old age, either was guilty, or was ever accused of any crimes.' Cf. Plato, *Apology* 33B–34B.

[578] Xenophon (*Memor.* 1.2.62–64) emphatically denies that Socrates had deserved death. In chap. 152 (101.14–102.12) Libanius mocks Polycrates with the remark that it would not have been necessary to put to death a man solely because he has failed to measure up to the immemorial achievements of a Theseus or Solon. The decree of Demophantus of 410, mentioned in Andocides, *De mysteriis* 1.96 ff., provided that anyone who in the future should participate in any way in the overthrow of the Athenian democratic institutions was to be declared a public enemy, to slay whom (καὶ λόγῳ καὶ ἔργῳ καὶ ψήφῳ καὶ τῇ ἐμαυτοῦ χειρί) each and every citizen bound himself by an oath. This was not an ordinary decree but the adopted report of a legislative commissioner, as the words τάδε Δημόφαντος συνέγραψεν indicate.

[579] The evil connotation which the title 'sophist' must have had in Athens during the early part of the fourth century may be gathered from Plato, *Meno* 91C and *Protagoras* 314D.

[580] Libanius 102.13.

Notes to Chapter IV

[581] In *Aeschinis fragmenta*, edit. Krauss, frag. 16 and *ibid.* at pp. 90 ff.

[582] The report in Xenophon (*Memor.* 1.2.31–38) concerning Socrates' alleged clash with Critias and Charicles (or Callicles), is probably based on the popular assumption that Socrates himself was one of the sophists who had been 'silenced' by a decree of Critias. This popular assumption was perhaps shared by Polycrates and his circle. Cf. our interpretation of this story in the next to the last chapter.

[583] Libanius 103.7 ff. (chap. 154).

[584] Libanius 103.2 ff.

[585] Cf. Plato, *Apology* 19BC.

[586] This seems to follow from Libanius 103.7, where he insists that Socrates should never have shared the fate of Anaxagoras, Protagoras, and Diagoras.

[587] D.L. 2.9 and *ibid.* at 2.12–14.

[588] D.L. 9.51 and *ibid.* at 5.55.

[589] Cicero, *De natura deorum* 1.2.63 and *ibid.* at 1.2.117; Aetius, *Placita philos.* 1.7.1; Aelian, *Var. hist.* 2.31, frag. 33; Sextus Empiricus, *Pyrrh. hypoth.* 3.15; *Adv. math.* 9.51. See Aristophanes, *Frogs* 320; *Clouds* 830, where Socrates is called a Melian, the implication being here that Socrates was as sacrilegious and atheistic a man as Diagoras of Melos.

[590] In 415, according to Diodorus 13.6.

[591] Cf. Aristophanes, *Birds* 1073; Josephus, *Contra Apionem* 2.37 ff.; Libanius 104.10–12. As to the fate of Diagoras, cf. Libanius 105.4–12.

[592] Libanius 104.1 ff.

[593] Cf. Libanius 101.6.

[594] Compare Libanius 104.3 and 104.5 (Themistocles) with Plato, *Gorgias* 516C and 519A; Libanius 104.2 and 104.4 (Miltiades) with Plato, *Gorgias* 516E.

[595] Cf. J. Geffken, 'Studien zu Platons Gorgias', in *Hermes* 65 (1930) 14–37.

[596] E. Heuer, *De Stesimbroto Thasio eiusque reliquiae* (Münster, 1863); C. Müller, *Fragmenta histor. graec.* 2.46.

[597] Cf. D. H. Stuart, *Epochs of Greek and Roman biography* (Berkeley, 1928) 44 ff. M. Pohlenz, *Aus Platons Werdezeit* (1913) 164 ff., and U. v. Wilamowitz-Moellendorff, *Platon* (1919) 2.98 ff. and *ibid.* at 1.221 and 1.260, maintain that the κατηγορία Σωκράτους was Polycrates' reply to Plato's *Gorgias*. This reopens once more the problem whether or not the Polycratean pamphlet antedates the Platonic *Gorgias*, a problem which has been the subject of many a learned debate. The majority of earlier scholars (Cobet, Dindorf, Hirzel, Wilamowitz-Moellendorff, Schanz, and others) held that the *Gorgias* precedes the κατηγορία. Cf. U. v. Wilamowitz-Moellendorff, *Sitzungsbericht der Berliner Akademie* (1899) 78, and *Platon* 2.97 ff., where the famous Pindar quotation (cf. notes 506–513, *supra,* and the text thereto) is used in order to

Notes to Chapter V

establish the priority of the Platonic *Gorgias*. M. Pohlenz, (*loc. cit.*) bases the priority of the Platonic *Gorgias* on the argument that only after Plato had made the distinction between the true and the false statesman (*Gorgias* 522D), could Polycrates have developed his theory of the pernicious activities of the 'philosophical statesmen'. Libanius 104.1ff.; Xenophon, *Memor.* 1.2.17; J. Humbert, 'Le pamphlet de Polycrates et le Gorgias de Platon', in *Revue de Philologie* 5 (1931) 20–77, especially at 37 ff. A. Gerke, in his revised edition of Sauppe's *Platons ausgewählte Dialoge* 3 (1897) XLIII ff., however, insists that the *Gorgias* is later than the κατηγορία. His view found gradual acceptance by most scholars. Cf. Th. Gomperz, *Griechische Denker* 2 (3rd edit.) 279 and *ibid.* at 571 ff.; H. Raeder, *Platons philosophische Entwicklung* (1905) 123 and *ibid.* at 136; E. Mesk, *op. cit.* at 56 ff.; H. Maier, *Sokrates* (1913) 22–24 and *ibid.* at 132 ff. and 379 ff.; O. Apelt, *Platonische Aufsätze* (1912) 10 ff.; J. Humbert, *op. cit* at 37 ff.; J. Geffken, *Griechische Literaturgeschichte* 2 (1934) 76, note 6. The relationship of Plato's *Gorgias* to the κατηγορία of Polycrates is also basic for the exact dating of the *Gorgias*. M. Schanz, in the commentary to his edition of the Platonic *Crito* (1880) 15, suggests that the *Gorgias* was written immediately after the death of Socrates in 399; U. v. Wilamowitz-Moellendorff, *Platon*, 1.208 ff., dates it shortly before Plato's first Sicilian voyage (*c.* 388/7); M. Pohlenz, *op. cit.* at 67, dates it between 394 and 391; K. Praechter, *Die Philosophie des Altertums, Friederich Ueberwegs Grundriss der Geschichte der Philosophie, Erster Teil* (Berlin, 1926) 12th edit., 1.208, dates it close to the Polycratean pamphlet; H. Maier, *op. cit.* at 123, note 1, dates it between 393 and 388; O. Apelt, *op. cit.* at 11, proposes the year 390 as the *tempus post quod* for its dating. K. F. Hermann, *Geschichte und System der platonischen Philosophie* (1839) 635 and *ibid.* at 391, following Schleiermacher and Socher, however, dates the *Gorgias* after the first Sicilian voyage, as do E. Frank, *Platon und die sogenannten Pythagoreer* (1923) 90, J. Stenzel, *Platon der Erzieher* (1928) 92, and H. Raeder, *op. cit.* 122 ff. See A.-H. Chroust, 'Socrates—a source problem', in *The New Scholasticism* 19, no. 1 (1945) 50, note 21.

[598] Cf. Athenaeus, *Deipnosophistae* 5.220D: 'The dialogue, entitled *Statesman*, by Antisthenes, denounces all the demagogues at Athens.'

[599] Cf. Libanius, chap. 158.

[600] This is rather obvious from Xenophon's *Symposium*. Cf. *ibid.* at 3.8 and 4.2 ff.; 4.34 ff.; 4.61 ff.; 6.5; 8.4 ff.; *et passim*.

[601] This tradition may go back to Sotion of Alexandria, Heracleides

Notes to Chapter V

Lembos, and Sosicrates of Rhodes. It was also accepted by Diocles and Favorinus.

[602] Cf. D. R. Dudley, *A history of Cynicism* (London, 1937) 1 ff.

[603] For examples of divergences, see D. Dudley, *loc. cit.*

[604] Cf. Th. Gomperz, *Griechische Denker* 2 (3d edit.) 126 ff. Gomperz, who apparently accepts the 'succession theory', bases his view primarily on Dio Chrysostom (Dio of Prusa), *Oratio* 8.1-2, and Stobaeus, *Florilegium* 13.19, where Diogenes of Sinope reproaches Antisthenes for not practising what he preaches.

[605] Cf. notes 1068-1076, *infra*.

[606] K. Joël, *Der echte und der xenophontische Sokrates* 2.950-952, discusses also the possible oriental and particularly the Persian influences (Avesta and Zendavesta) on Cynicism. Cf. W. Geiger, *Ostiranische Kultur im Altertum* (Erlangen, 1882); R. Höistad, *Cynic hero and Cynic king* (Uppsala, 1948) 7 ff.

[607] Cf. D.L. (Diogenes Laertius) 6.24.

[608] Cf. D. L. 6.21.

[609] Cf. W. Crönert, *Kolotes und Menedemos* 49.

[610] Cf. W. Crönert, *op. cit.* at 157.

[611] In *Hercul. Papyri* nos. 155 and 339; cf. W. Crönert, *op cit.* at 53-67.

[612] Cf. D.L. 6.80; Plutarch, *Lycurgos* 31.

[613] D.L. 6.80.

[614] D.L. 6.20 and *ibid.* at 6.56.

[615] D.L. 6.85-93.

[616] D.L. 6.94-95.

[617] D.L. 6.99.

[618] D.L. 6.30.

[619] D.L. 6.75.

[620] Cf. K. v. Fritz, 'Quellenuntersuchungen zum Leben und Philosophie des Diogenes von Sinope', in *Philologus*, Supplement 18, no. 2 (Leipzig, 1926); F. Sayre, *Diogenes of Sinope: a study of Greek Cynicism* (Baltimore, 1938); G. A. Gerhard, 'Zur Legende vom Kyniker Diogenes', in *Archiv für Religionswissenschaft* 15 (Leipzig, 1912).

[621] Cf. K. v. Fritz, 'Quellenuntersuchungen zum Leben und Philosophie des Diogenes von Sinope' (1926); D. R. Dudley, *op. cit.* 1-58.

[622] Cf. D.L. 6.20-81.

[623] Cf. D.L. 6.21.

[624] The preserved fragments from the works of Antisthenes were collected by A. W. Winckelmann, *Antisthenis fragmenta* (1842), subsequently quoted as *Antisth. frag.*

[625] Cf. Dio Chrysostom, *Oratio* 8.3: 'Antisthenes ... used to say that Diogenes was like a wasp, the buzz of whose wings is slight but the sting very sharp.' Cf. what Emperor Julian had to say about contemporary Cynicism in his sixth and seventh *Orations*.

Notes to Chapter V

⁶²⁶ D.L. 6.20. Theophrastus (D.L. 5.44 and 6.22) also discusses Diogenes of Sinope in his *Megarian dialogue* (Μεγαρικός).

⁶²⁷ D.L. 6.20. It is impossible to determine whether this Eubulides is identical with the contemporary and opponent of Aristotle, or whether the name 'Eubulides' is here merely a misspelling of the otherwise unknown Eubulus who is credited with having authored *The sale of Diogenes*. D.L. 6.30.

⁶²⁸ Cf. D.L. 6.87.

⁶²⁹ The originators of this literary type are probably Crates of Thebes and his contemporary Metrocles of Maroneia. D.L. 6.33.

⁶³⁰ Cf. D.L. 6.104.

⁶³¹ R. Höistad, *Cynic hero and Cynic king* 34.

⁶³² Cf. F. Jacoby, *Fragm. histor. graec.* 1.125 ff. and *ibid.* at 502 ff.; F. Jacoby, in Pauly-Wissowa 8.981.

⁶³³ Cf. Xenophon, *Memor.* 2.1.21 ff.

⁶³⁴ H. Dittmar, in his 'Aischines von Sphettos' (Berlin, 1912) 300 ff., has collected the scanty references to Antithenes' preoccupation with Heracles. But it is impossible to reconstruct from this meagre and fragmentary evidence the manner or the extent to which Antisthenes in particular used and re-interpreted the materials of the traditional Heracles legend. Cf. R. Höistad, *op. cit.* at 33 ff.

⁶³⁵ Cf. A.-H. Chroust, 'Socrates and pre-Socratic philosophy', in *The Modern Schoolman* 29 (1952) 126 ff.

⁶³⁶ Christ-Schmid, *Geschichte der griechischen Literatur* (6th edit.) 1.494, suggests that Xenophon became acquainted with Socrates in 404. But soon thereafter he left Greece to join the ill-fated expedition of Cyrus the Younger.

⁶³⁷ Cf. note 224, *supra*, and the text thereto.

⁶³⁸ Cf. *Defence* 5 and *ibid.* at 6; 7; 8; 9; 23 and notes 86, 98–102 and 108, *supra*.

⁶³⁹ Cf. *ibid.* at 7–8. 'The desire of death', which Xenophon ascribes to Socrates, seems to have a definitely Antisthenian-Cynic flair. In *Defence* 9 Socrates states that 'the desire of death shall not influence me beyond what is reasonable'. For a Cynic even 'the desire of death' had to be 'reasonable'.

⁶⁴⁰ Cf. Cicero, *Tuscul. disp.* 1.43.104.

⁶⁴¹ Cf. *ibid.* at 1.9.13; 4.1.30.

⁶⁴² Cf. notes 98–102, *supra*.

⁶⁴³ Cf. *ibid.* at 9; *Memor.* 4.8.8.

⁶⁴⁴ Cf. D.L. 6.18–19: 'Once Diogenes, when he came to see him [*scil.*, Antisthenes], brought a dagger. When Antisthenes cried out, "Who will release me from my pains?" Diogenes replied: "This," showing the dagger.' Metrocles (D.L. 6.95), Menippus (D.L. 6.100), and even Diogenes of Sinope (D.L. 6.76) are said to have committed suicide. Aelian 10.11. The Stoic view on suicide probably is under the influence of

Notes to Chapter V

Cynic tradition. Cf. D.L. 6.104, where we are told that in many respects the Cynic teachings became the model for Stoic thought. As to the Stoic notion on suicide, see Seneca, *De brevitate vitae* 19.2; *De benificiis* 7.1; *Epistola* 101.10; *Natural. quaest.* 5.32.

[645] Xenophon, *Defence* 1. Cf. *ibid.* at 5–8; *Memor.* 4.4.8.

[646] Cf. Plato, *Laws* 646A; Aristophanes, *Clouds* 1417. The date of the *Axiochus* is uncertain. O. Immisch (*Philogische Studien zu Platon*, Erstes Heft, *Axiochus*, Leipzig, 1896) suggests the years 305/300 as a probable date. J. Chevalier (*Étude critique du dialogue pseudo-platonicien l'Axiochos sur la mort et sur l'immortalité*, Paris, 1924) believes that this dialogue is of Neo-Pythagorean origin, written during the first century B.C. Since Bion of Borysthenes might have influenced the *Axiochus*, it is also held that this dialogue was composed during the end of the second century B.C. Cf. O. Hense, *Teletis reliquiae* 10.14. This *Axiochus* is not identical with the *Axiochus* ascribed to Aeschines. Cf. note 1206, *infra*.

[647] *Op. cit.* at 2.184 ff. and *ibid.* at 2.172 ff. Antisthenes is credited (D.L. 6.5) with having maintained that 'to die happily is the height of bliss'. This statement reminds us of *Axiochus* 372A: 'The soul is immortal ... after a life of bliss. ...' Cf. *ibid.* at 372B:' ... I am so far from fearing death that I already begin to love death.' *Ibid.* at 366D ff.; Stobaeus, *Florilegium* 98.72 (Crates).

[648] D.L. 6.51. Cf. *ibid.* at 4.48 (Bion of Borysthenes).

[649] Cf. notes 644–647, *supra*, and notes 955–957, *infra*. Tradition ascribes to Antisthenes a Περὶ ζωῆς καὶ θανάτου and a Περὶ τῶν ἐν ᾅδου (D.L. 6.17), and to Diogenes of Sinope a Περὶ τοῦ ἀποθανεῖν (D.L. 6.80). These works may have been the *consolationes mortis* on which also the *Axiochus* is based.

[650] Stobaeus, *Florilegium* 5.67. Cf. D.L. 4.48: 'Old age is the harbour of all ills.'

[651] D.L. 6.77. Cf. what D.L. 6.92 records about the death of Crates 'who went to the house of Hades, bent by old age'.

[652] D.L. 6.95.

[653] In this sense it might be maintained that the Cynics were actually the first systematic πεισιθάνατοι.

[654] *Ibid.* at 27; 32 ff.

[655] Like the *Axiochus*, so also the Xenophontean *Defence* mentions the loss of eye-sight, hearing, and reasoning power.

[656] Both the *Axiochus* (367BC ff.) and Xenophon (*Defence* 7) insist that for the aged man death was actually a gift bestowed upon him by the gods as a special favour.

[657] Cf. notes 161–164 and 276, *supra*; Xenophon, *Memor.* 1.6.6–7.

[658] Cf. notes 161 and 352, *supra*; *Memor.* 1.2.14: 'Socrates lived most contentedly on very small means, [and] abstained from every kind of pleasure.' *Ibid.* at 4.5.1–12 and 1.5.6; D.L. 2.25 and *ibid.* at 2.27; Dio

Notes to Chapter V

Chrysostom, *Oratio* 8.21 ff. and *ibid.* at 6.8 ff. As to the Antisthenian doctrine of freedom and continence (ἐγκράτεια), see K. Joël, *op. cit.* at 2.561–628, especially 2.609 ff.

[659] Cf. note 162, *supra*; D.L. 2.27: 'He [*scil.*, Socrates] prided himself of his plain living, and never asked a fee from anyone.'

[660] Cf. *Antisth. frag.* 20; *Defence* 25, where it is said that Socrates was 'inuring youths to a life of patience and frugality'. This statement contains the essence of the Antisthenian-Cynic educational ideal. Cf. Xenophon, *Memor.* 1.3.5 and *ibid.* at 1.6.1–5; 1.6.8–10; 1.7.1–5; 1.5.1–4; 2.1.1–7; 3.13.1–2; 3.14.1–7; 4.3.1; 4.5.1–12; 1.6.6–7; *Pol. Lac.* 2.1–3.6.

[661] Cf. notes 630, *supra*, and 727–728, 904 and 937, *infra*.

[662] Cf. D.L. 6.11: 'The wise man is self-sufficient.'

[663] Cf. D.L. 6.11: 'Virtue ... needs nothing else except the strength of a Socrates.'

[664] Cf. Epictetus, *Diss.* 3.22.2.

[665] D.L. 6.66.

[666] The Antisthenian-Cynic antithesis of personified virtue and personified vice can also be found in Antisthenes' *Of Helen and Penelope* (D.L. 6.17) and *Hercules or Midas* (D.L. 6.18). Helen and Midas are the representatives of vice and dissipation. And vice, besides being an evil, is also the enslaver of man. Penelope and Heracles, on the other hand, personify virtue, ἐγκράτεια, as well as glorious toil. Virtue, especially the ἐγκράτεια, as well as toil which also implies the notion of duty, is good in that it makes man free.

[667] Cf. *Memor.* 4.8.11. Antisthenes prefers the term φρόνιμος to that of σοφός. Aristotle, *Nicomachean Ethics* 1141 b 3. This might be the reason why Antisthenes entitled one of his works Ἡρακλῆς ἢ περὶ φρονήσεως. D.L. 6.18.

[668] *Antisth. frag.* 47.

[669] Cf. *Schol. Lips.* ad. *Iliad.* 15. 123: 'Antisthenes states that if the wise man does anything, he does it in accordance with virtue as a whole.'

[670] This attitude towards the laws and political institutions of the city in all likelihood provided Polycrates with the materials for his charge that 'Socrates caused his followers to despise the established laws ... and to condemn the existing form of government.' Xenophon, *Memor.* 1.2.9.

[671] Cf. D.L. 6.72–73.

[672] Cf. D.L. 6.104: 'Life according to virtue is the end to be sought.'

[673] Epictetus, *Diss.* 3.24.67. Cf., in this connection, *St. John* 8.32: 'And you shall know the truth, and the truth shall make you free.'

[674] Cf. D.L. 6.71.

[675] *Antisth. frag.* 59. This was, according to Libanius, one of the allegations of Polycrates by which he tried to prove that Socrates had planned the overthrow of Athenian democracy. See note 541, *supra*.

Notes to Chapter V

[676] Cf. *ibid.* at 6.54 and 2.33, where the same idea is ascribed to Socrates. Epictetus, *Diss.* 3.22.8: '[The Cynic insists that he should] not be burdened by vulgar duties or entangled in relations. . . . There are some duties due to one's father-in-law, some to other relations of one's wife, some to one's wife herself. In addition, one is confined to the care of one's family. . . . What, then, will become of the King [the Cynic], whose duty it is to be the overseer of all those men who have married and are the fathers of children . . . and who treat their wives well . . .? Where shall he find the leisure for all this overseeing if he were tied down by such vulgar duties [as marriage]? . . . Do you see to what we would reduce our Cynic and how we would deprive him of his kingdom [if we would make him comply with convention]?' The problem of whether one should marry a fair wife or a woman belonging to a family of wealth and influence, is discussed at great length in Xenophon, *Hiero* 1.27 ff.

[677] Cf. *ibid.* at 2.29, where we are told that Socrates dissuaded Glaucon from entering politics. Plato, *Gorgias* 522B. The degree to which Xenophon is dependent on Antisthenian-Cynic teachings can be gathered from a comparison of D.L. 6.29 and *Memor.* 1.1.8: 'For neither can a politician foresee whether his leadership of the city would turn to good or evil; nor can a man who weds a fair wife in hopes of happiness, know whether through her he shall not reap sorrow. Neither can he who has built up powerful political connections in the city know whether he might be banished on account of his political connections.' Aelian, *Var. hist.* 2.11, reports that during the reign of the Thirty Tyrants Socrates allegedly had said to Antisthenes: 'Are you still regretting that we two have never achieved any fame or position of importance?' Socrates, speaking like a true Cynic, implied that since political eminence is always fraught with danger, the wise man should live in seclusion. Cf. A.-H. Chroust, 'The philosophy of law of the Epicureans', in *The Thomist* 16 (1953) 80 ff. See also Bion of Borysthenes (D.L. 4.48 and *ibid.* at 6.3); Dio Chrysostom, *Oratio* 13, where Dio speaks about his political banishment on account of his reputed friendship with a politically influential man. This man was probably T. Flavius Sabinus, who was executed under Emperor Domitian in A.D. 82. Suetonius, *The Life of Domitian* 10.22; Philostratus, *Apollonius of Tyana* 7.7.

[678] Xenophon, *Symposium* 4.34; *Memor.* 2.3.2–3 and *ibid.* at 2.4.1–5; 4.1.5.

[679] D.L. 6.86 (Crates). Cf. Epictetus, *Diss.* 3.24.68; Theodorus, *Curatio graecorum affectionum* 12.49.

[680] D.L. 6.95 (*Metrocles*). Cf. note 678, *supra*; Dio Chrysostom, *Oratio* 10.14: 'Men have suffered many more injuries and many more evils from money than from poverty, particularly if they lacked sense.'

[681] Dio Chrysostom, *Oratio* 8.21–22.

[682] Dio Chrysostom, *Oratio* 8.20.

Notes to Chapter V

[683] Dio Chrysostom, *Oratio* 8.23–24.

[684] Antisthenes wrote a work on *Freedom and slavery* (D.L. 6.16). Cf. Epictetus, *Diss.* 3.22.84.

[685] Epictetus, *Diss.* 4.1.30 ff. See notes 649–656, *supra*, and the text thereto.

[686] Clement of Alexandria, *Stromat.* 2.413A; Julian, *Oratio* 6.199E and *ibid.* at 6.202A.

[687] D.L. 6.71.

[688] Clement of Alexandria, *Stromat.* 2.413A; Epiphanius 1089C; Stobaeus, *Florilegium* 97.31.

[689] D.L. 6.43 ff. and *ibid.* at 6.50; 6.60; 6.63; 6.68; Epictetus, *Diss.* 3.22.92.

[690] Xenophon, *Symposium* 4.36; Stobaeus, *Florilegium* 49.47; D.L. 6.50; Dio Chrysostom, *Oratio* 6.38; Julian, *Oratio* 6.198.

[691] *Antisth. frag.* 59.

[692] D.L. 6.24. Cf. *ibid.* at 6.41. Anecdotes show Diogenes of Sinope in constant conflict with politicians such as Demosthenes (D.L. 6.34) and rulers or 'tyrants' such as Philip of Macedonia (D.L. 6.43), Alexander the Great (D.L. 6.38; 6.60; 6.63; Dio Chrysostom, *Oratio* 4.16 ff.), Perdiccas (D.L. 6.44), and Craterus (D.L. 6.57). The theme that the true philosopher is always at odds with a tyrant, may go back to the *Archelaus* of Antisthenes. Cf. F. Dümmler, *Akademika* (1889) 1–18; Xenophon, *Symposium* 4.34 ff.

[693] D.L. 6.34. Cf. *ibid.* at 6.8; Athenaeus, *Deipnosophistae* 5.220D.

[694] D.L. 6.8. Cf. Xenophon, *Memor.* 3.4.2, where we are told that merchants are able to collect money, but incapable of leading an army. *Ibid.* at 3.9.10–13.

[695] D.L. 6.92.

[696] Cf. D.L. 6.70 and *ibid.* at 6.5; 6.8; Xenophon, *Memor.* 4.6.14 and *ibid.* at 4.7.1.

[697] Cf. Xenophon, *Memor.* 1.2.62–64 and *ibid.* at 1.2.18; 1.2.14; 1.2.2; *Defence* 25 and notes 161–164, 178, 276, 313, 362 and 363, *supra*.

[698] D.L. 6.3. Cf. *ibid.* at 9.101; Gellius, *Attic nights* 9.5.3; Theodorus, *Curatio graec. affectionum* 12.47; Epictetus, *Diss.* 3.22.2; Clement of Alex., *Stromat.* 2.412; Sextus Empiricus, *Adv.* mathematicos 11.74; Dio Chrysostom, *Oratio* 8.20–21 and *ibid.* at 8.29; 3.123; Eusebius, *Praeparatio evangelica* 15.13.7. Plato, *Philebus* 44C, seems to take issue with this Antisthenian statement.

[699] Cf. *ibid.* at 6.2: 'He [*scil.*, Antisthenes] demonstrated that toil was a good thing.' Dio Chrysostom, *Oratio* 8.11 ff. and *ibid.* at 9.11 ff.; Xenophon, *Memor.* 2.1.17–20; Stobaeus, *Florilegium* 29.65.

[700] Cf. Xenophon, *Defence* 19 and note 349, *supra*.

[701] Cf. Xenophon, *Memor.* 2.7.1–14, where Socrates calls work something honourable and becoming.

[702] Cf. Dio Chrysostom, *Oratio* 3.85.

Notes to Chapter V

[703] Cf. D.L. 6.2, quoted in note 699, *supra*.

[704] Dio Chrysostom, *Oratio* 8.23.

[705] Cf. *Memor.* 2.1.17-20 and the references cited in note 660, *supra*.

[706] Cf. D.L. 6.27 and *ibid.* at 6.70; Epictetus, *Diss*. 3.15.4.

[707] D.L. 6.71; Xenophon, *Memor.* 2.1.17-20. Cf. also the sixth and seventh *Orations* of Dio Chrysostom.

[708] Cf. Xenophon, *Memor*. 2.1.19-20. See also the seventh (or, *Euboean*) *Oration* of Dio Chrysostom, which is actually a Cynic praise of the simple life.

[709] *Republic* 486C and *ibid.* at 526C; 531A-531D; 535BC; 536D; *et passim*. Cf. note 541, *supra*, and notes 860-861, *infra*, and the text thereto.

[710] *To Neocles* 39; *Helena* 8.

[711] Cf. *Republic* 372B or *Symposium* 177B, which contain subtly antagonistic allusions to Antisthenes' πόνος doctrine.

[712] Cf. *Oeconomicus* 4.2; *Pol. Lacedaem.* 1.2-4, where Xenophon agrees with Lycurgus who had decreed that the Spartan women should engage in athletic competition rather than spin wool, because the latter was unhealthy. The idea of φιλοπονία (cf. Dio Chrysostom, *Oratio* 3.85) was later adopted by the Stoics who related it to their conception of moral duty. Through Stoic influence this idea was subsequently accepted by the early Christians. This is perhaps the greatest and most important historical contribution of the otherwise much maligned Cynics: that they exalted the dignity and worth of honest toil by endowing it with a high moral significance. See the Pauline exhortations that the Christians had the moral duty to work and toil. Cf. *1 Thessal*, 4.11; *2 Thessal.* 3.10; *1 Corinth.* 4.12; *Ephes.* 4.28.

[713] Cf. *ibid.* at 287-292, where Hesiod points out that 'the road which leads to virtue is rough at first and hard to travel and full of abundant sweat and toil, and steep withal'.

[714] Dio Chrysostom, *Oratio* 8.11-13. Cf. *ibid.* at 8.18 and 8.26-27; 9.11-12.

[715] *Scholia ad Aristoph. Nub.* 361.

[716] Cf. Dio Chrysostom, *Oratio* 1.65; 8.29 ff.; W. Nestle, 'Die Horen des Prodikos', in *Hermes* 71 (1936) 167 ff.; K. Joël, *op. cit.* at 2.125 ff.

[717] As to the Antisthenian-Cynic glorification of King Cyrus, cf. R. Höistad, *Cynic hero and Cynic king* 73 ff.

[718] D.L. 6.16 and 6.18 mentions a *Cyrus*; a *Cyrus, or Of sovereignty*; a *Cyrus, or The beloved*; and a *Cyrus, or The scout*.

[719] It is not impossible that Plato, too, might have borrowed from Herodotus. Cf. *Laws* 694C ff. and *Menexenus* 239D. It is even possible the famous 'philosopher king' of Plato is influenced by this Cyrus tradition.

[720] Cf. Xenophon, *Memor*. 1.1.16 and *ibid*. 1.2.39 ff.; 2.1.1 ff.; 2.6.1 ff.; 3.2.1 ff.; 3.5.1 ff.; 3.9.10 ff. and 4.6.12, although Xenophon seems to suppress the δοῦλος motif.

Notes to Chapter V

[721] Cf. D.L. 6.71: 'The manner in which he [*scil.*, Diogenes of Sinope] lived was the same as that of Heracles when he preferred freedom to everything.' This statement contains the highest praise that could be bestowed upon a Cynic.

[722] D.L. 6.2.

[723] Antisthenes is said to have written at least two works dealing with the φιλοπονία of Heracles. Cf. D.L. 6.18; Eusebius, *Praeparatio evangelica* 15.3.7; Lucian, *Vit. auct.* 8; Julian, *Oratio* 6.

[724] Cf. *Defence* 16–17 and *ibid.* at 19 and 21; notes 178, 265 and 266, *supra*, and the text thereto.

[725] Cf. notes 314–316, *supra*, and the text thereto.

[726] Cf. note 318, *supra*.

[727] Cf. Xenophon, *Memor.* 1.5.1–4 and *ibid.* at 1.6.8–10; 3.13.2; 4.3.1.

[728] How much Xenophon was impressed by the Antisthenian-Cynic idea of the ἐγκράτεια and by Antisthenes himself may be gathered from D.L. 6.15, where we are told that Xenophon had called Antisthenes 'the most temperate of all men (ἐγκρατέστατον)'. Cf. Cicero, *De oratore* 3.17.62.

[729] Cf. F. Dümmler, *Akademika* (1889) 169 ff.

[730] Cf. *Memor.* 4.2.22.

[731] Cf. Antisthenes' work entitled *On freedom and slavery*, cited in D.L. 6.16.

[732] Cf. Xenophon, *Symposium* 4.41 ff.

[733] Cf. Xenophon, *Hellenica* 2.2.10.

[734] Cf. Xenophon, *Memor.* 2.7.1–14.

[735] Cf. Plato, *Republic* 404D.

[736] See Aelian, *Var. hist.* 9.7, where we are told that in the midst of the many vagaries of life, including the trying experiences of the Peloponnesian War, Socrates always remained serene and even tempered.

[737] The same idea appears in Xenophon, *Memor.* 1.5.1 and *ibid.* at 4.2.38; Dio Chrysostom, *Oratio* 6.61–62; Libanius 23.17–24.6. Hermogenes, who so often is quoted as Xenophon's source of information (cf. *Defence* 2–10), is probably a follower of Antisthenes. Cf. note 85, *supra*.

[738] A translation of this oration by J. Gildemeister and F. Büchler can be found in *Rheinisches Museum* 27 (1872) 438–462.

[739] Cf. Plutarch, *De garrulitate* 17.

[740] Cf. *Antisth. frag.* 63; Diogenes Laertius 6.25 and *ibid.* at 6.35; 6.48; 6.50; 6.58; 6.61; 6.105.

[741] Cf. D.L. 6.31 and *ibid.* at 6.90; Xenophon, *Memor.* 3.13.2–3.

[742] Cf. *Antisth. frag.* 64; D.L. 6.36.

[743] Cf. D.L. 6.34 and *ibid.* at 6.58; 6.61; 6.64; 6.67; 6.69.

[744] Cf. D.L. 6.34; Dio Chrysostom, *Oratio* 6.8–15; Seneca, *Epist.* 90.11. Hence Plato, when referring to the manners of the Cynics, calls their 'social ideal' a 'city of pigs'. *Republic* 372A ff. H. v. Arnim, *Leben*

und Werke des Dion von Prusa (1898) 263, is of the opinion that the sixth *Oration* of Dio Chrysostom had been compiled from four different sources: (1) a *Vita Diogenis*; (2) a collection of the 'Sayings and Doings', ascribed to Diogenes; (3) a Cynic diatribe extolling the advantages of 'natural life' as lived by animals over the artificiality of conventional life; and (4) a Cynic diatribe on the misery of tyrants, of which we have a reflection in Xenophon's *Hiero*. The Cynic diatribe on the misery of tyrants might possibly be the *Archelaus* of Antisthenes (D.L. 6.18), or a Cynic work which is under the influence of the *Archelaus*.

[745] Xenophon refers here to Homer, *Odyssey* 10.233 ff. Cf. Aelian 8.9; Clement of Alexandria, *Stromat.* 2.492.24; *Paedagogus* 2.173.33; Plutarch, *Moralia* 128D; Xenophon, *Memor.* 3.13.2–3 and *ibid.* at 3.14.1–7; Dio Chrysostom, *Oratio* 6.12: 'Diogenes [of Sinope] always waited until he was hungry or thirsty before he took nourishment.'

[746] Cf. *ibid.* at 2.1.30 ff.; Pseudo-Lucian, *The Cynic* 2 and *ibid.* at 4; 9. Socrates' remark that Antiphon probably would prefer death to a life such as his, can also be found in *Memor.* 1.2.16, where it refers to Critias and Alcibiades: '... had God granted them the choice beween the life they saw Socrates leading, and death, they would have chosen rather to die.' The same idea reappears again in the dialogue *Alcibiades I* 105A.

[747] Cf. also *ibid.* at 2.25: 'Often when he [*scil.*, Socrates] looked at the many goods offered for sale, he would say to himself, "How many things are there I can do without." '

[748] Cf. Xenophon, *Memor.* 1.2.5: 'He [*scil.*, Socrates] was not, however, ostentatious in his clothes or sandals, or in any of his habits.' Epictetus, *Diss.* 3.22.2; D.L. 2.27–28.

[749] *Antisth. frag.* 57. See D.L. 6.68 and *ibid.* at 6.105; 6.87; 6.50.

[750] D.L. 6.13. Cf. Xenophon, *Memor.* 2.3.2–3 and *ibid.* at 2.4.1–5; 4.1.5.

[751] Themistius, Περὶ ἀρετῆς 28 (p. 447). Cf. Plato, *Symposium* 205E; *Charmides* 163C.

[752] Themistius, *op. cit.* at 29–30 (p. 447). Cf. D.L. 6.93: 'When Alexander asked him [*scil.*, Crates, the Cynic] whether he liked to have his native city [Thebes] rebuilt, he replied: "What for? Perhaps another Alexander will come and destroy it again." Ignominy and poverty he called his country, which fate could never conquer.'

[753] Themistius, *op. cit.* at 25 (p. 444).

[754] Themistius, *op cit.* at 33 (p. 451).

[755] Cf. Philoponus, *Schol. ad Arist.* 35 (edit. Brandis).

[756] Xenophon, *Symposium* 4.34.

[757] D.L. 6.12. Cf. *ibid.* at 6.13: 'Wisdom is a most secure stronghold which never crumbles away.' Themistius, Περὶ ἀρετῆς 29 (p. 448). Xenophon disagrees with those views. *Memor.* 1.2.19: 'Perhaps many of those who profess to be philosophers [the Cynics?] may say that

Notes to Chapter V

a man once just can never become unjust..., and that one who has once learned any of the things that can be taught, can never become ignorant of them. But regarding this I am of a different opinion.' The doctrine that 'virtue once acquired cannot be lost', is perhaps Socratic. Cf. Aristotle, *Nicomachean Ethics* 1145 b 21–27; *ibid.* at 1147 b 3–15 and 1113 b 14–17. Similar ideas are to be found in the Pseudo-Platonic dialogue *On justice* 374A, and in Epicharmus, *frag.* 78 (edit. Kaibel), in *Comic. graec. frag.* 1.1.104; *Magna Moralia* 1200 b 25 ff. *Nicomachean Ethics* 1145 b 21–27 in all likelihood goes back to Plato, *Protagoras* 352BC, 357C, and 358BC, while *Nicomachean Ethics* 1113 b 14–17 has a parallel in Plato, *Protagoras* 345D and probably *ibid* at 358 BC. K. F. Hermann, in *Geschichte und System der platonischen Philosophie* (1839) 330, note 328, has collated the many passages where Plato (Socrates?) insists that 'no one does wrong of his own free will'. There exists a view, however, that Antisthenes was opposed to this Platonic notion.

[758] D.L. 6.104. Cf. *ibid.* at 6.44.

[759] Themistius, *op. cit.* at 31 (p. 449).

[760] Similar notions can be found in Plato, *Theaetetus* 176B; Pseudo-Lucian, *The Cynic* 12 (vol. 3, p. 398, edit. Jacobitz): 'If you think that, because I need and use but few things, I live the life of a beast, such an argument would lead you to the conclusion that the gods are yet lower than beasts. For they have no needs whatever. But to get a better understanding of the comparative merits of great and little needs, you have only to remember that children have more needs than adults, women more than men, the sick more than the healthy, and generally the inferior more than the superior. Accordingly, then, the gods have no needs and those men who have the fewest needs are nearest to the gods.'

[761] Themistius, *op. cit.* at 31 (p. 449).

[762] Themistius, *op. cit.* at 32 (p. 450). Cf. *ibid.* at 30 (p. 448), where Themistius reports that Stilpon had denied that anything which ever was really his had been taken from him; for no one, Stilpon insists, could possibly rob him of his wisdom and virtue.

[763] Cf. Plato, *Apology* 29D–30B.

[764] Cf. Xenophon, *Memor.* 1.2.1; Dio Chrysostom, *Oratio* 6.12; D.L. 2.27.

[765] Socrates, as we may gather from the Platonic *Symposium*, enjoys good living if it comes his way. Antisthenes, however, according to Xenophon, *Symposium* 4.41–42, drinks wine but informs his listeners that he enjoys costly wine less than he would a far simpler drink if he were really thirsty. Cf. Dio Chrysostom, *Oratio* 6.8 ff.

[766] With Diogenes of Sinope, it will be noted, asceticism becomes an end in itself.

[767] Dio Chrysostom, *Oratio* 6.8 ff.

[768] *Ibid.* at 6.8. Cf. *ibid.* at 8.16.

Notes to Chapter V

⁷⁶⁹ *Ibid.* at 6.27.–28.
⁷⁷⁰ *Ibid.* at 6.21–22. Cf. *ibid.* at 6.27 ff.
⁷⁷¹ *Ibid.* at 6.27.
⁷⁷² *Ibid.* at 6.30. Cf. *Oratio* 10.7–11 and *ibid.* at 10.15 ff; D.L. 2.25.
⁷⁷³ *Oratio* 6.34.
⁷⁷⁴ *Ibid.* at 6.34. Cf. *Oratio* 8.6–7.
⁷⁷⁵ *Oratio* 6.30.
⁷⁷⁶ Themistius, Περὶ ἀρετῆς 39 (p. 455). Cf. also *ibid.* at 38 (p. 455).
⁷⁷⁷ Cf. notes 172–174, *supra*.
⁷⁷⁸ Cf. *Memor.* 1.2.56–57; *ibid.* at 3.3.9 and notes 277, 278, 348 and 349, *supra*, and the text thereto.
⁷⁷⁹ D.L. 6.13.
⁷⁸⁰ D.L. 6.7.
⁷⁸¹ D.L. 6.8.
⁷⁸² Cf. Xenophon, *Memor.* 1.4.1, where we are told that Socrates not only exhorted men to practise virtue, but actually led them to the practice of virtue.
⁷⁸³ At least for the Cynics, these ideal teachers who 'practise what they preach', are the Cynics themselves.
⁷⁸⁴ D.L. 6.10. Cf. *ibid.* at 6.105; Xenophon, *Memor.* 1.2.9.
⁷⁸⁵ D.L. 6.7–8.
⁷⁸⁶ D.L. 6.70.
⁷⁸⁷ Cf. note 178, *supra*.
⁷⁸⁸ Cf. Xenophon, *Memor.* 1.6.15 and *ibid.* at 4.2.6–7; 4.5.1.
⁷⁸⁹ D.L. 6.10–11.
⁷⁹⁰ The fragments of this work are found in *Opera Aristotelis* (edit. Bekker) 1490 a 1–1491 a 23.
⁷⁹¹ Socrates, if we are correctly informed, was averse to any kind of literary activity. Cf. Dio Chrysostom, *Oratio* 55.8. Plato (*Phaedo* 60D) and D.L. 2.42, mention Socrates as the author of a poetical version of one of Aesop's fables as well as of a hymn to Apollo. But little reliance can be based on these reports. The so-called *Letters of Socrates* (*Epistolographi graec.*, edit. R. Hercher 609 ff.), an allegedly Socratic dialogue *On the soul*, preserved in Syriac, (V. Ryssel, in *Rhein. Mus.* 48 [1903] 75), the γνωμικὰ ὁμοιώματα (A. Elter, *Gnomika homoiomata*, [1900]), and the hymn mentioned by Athenaeus (*Deipnosophistae* 14.628 ff.) are all spurious. Cf. E. Diehl, *Antologia lyrica graeca* 1.85 ff.
⁷⁹² Xenophon confounds here Meletus and Polycrates.
⁷⁹³ Cf. notes 175–176 and 336–343, *supra*; Xenophon, *Memor.* 2.2.1–14, where Socrates discusses the duties of children to their parents. These exhortations might be an effort to disprove the Polycratean contention that Socrates had taught his followers to despise their parents.
⁷⁹⁴ *Memor.* 1.2.49.
⁷⁹⁵ *Memor.* 1.2.51. Cf. note 343, *supra*.

Notes to Chapter V

[796] The particular implication here seems to be that Socrates allegedly had insisted that since he alone could effectively assist or be useful to his friends and followers, no one else really mattered.

[797] *Memor.* 2.6.1–39.

[798] *Memor.* 2.7.1–2.10.6, where Socrates recounts the several manifestations of friendship.

[799] Antisthenes and the Cynics had stated that poverty was a great evil. Hence Polycrates probably concluded that Socrates had looked on friendship only in the light of the material advantages we might derive from it. Cf. D.L. 6.33: 'He [*scil.*, Diogenes of Sinope] said that the term "crippled" (ἀνάπηρος) ought to be applied not to those who are deaf or blind, but to those who have no wallet (πήρα).' *Ibid.* at 6.51: 'To the question what is wretchedness . . . he [*scil.*, Diogenes of Sinope] replied: "An old man destitute." '

[800] D.L. 6.12. Cf. *ibid.* at 6.105: 'The wise man . . . is a friend of the like.' Themistius, Περὶ ἀρετῆς 31 (p. 448). This idea can also be found in Xenophon, *Memor.* 2.6.14–23. Plato, in *Lysis* 214B ff., treats this problem differently.

[801] D.L. 6.11. Cf. *ibid.* at 6.72 and 6.3; 6.88; Xenophon, *Symposium* 4.40; *Memor.* 1.3.14.

[802] Cf., however, D.L. 6.65.

[803] Xenophon, *Memor.* 1.2.49.

[804] Cf. *Antisth. frag.* 65. Plato's *Laches*, *Protagoras*, and *Meno* also touch upon the problem of why the sons of famous men seem to have a proclivity for turning out to be complete failures. The story told about Anytus, who, contrary to the advice of Socrates, did not wish his son to study philosophy, and thus contributed to the moral degeneration of the latter (Plato, *Gorgias* 522B; Xenophon, *Defence* 31), presumably is nothing else than a malicious invention which most likely originated with the Cynics.

[805] Dio Chrysostom, *Oratio* 55.22, observes that Socrates, 'when conversing with Anytus, would refer to tanners and cobblers'. This statement, which is probably of Antisthenian origin, expresses the Cynic contempt for men of the type of Anytus. *Ibid.* at 3.26 ff. Demetrius of Byzantium (D.L. 2.21) reports that 'frequently, owing to the vehemence with which he [*scil.*, Socrates] advanced his arguments, men set upon him with their fists and tore out his hair'. These men might possibly have been the fathers of those young people whom Socrates tried to 'lure away' from parental authority.

[806] D.L. 6.71: '. . . he [*scil.*, Diogenes of Sinope] allowed convention no authority. . . .'

[807] Cf. note 178, *supra*.

[808] According to Xenophon, this would have been the first charge made by Polycrates.

[809] Cf. notes 289 and 290, *supra*; Themistius, Περὶ ἀρετῆς 28 (p. 447):

Notes to Chapter V

'Those who wish to sail safely upon the oceans, above all need competent helmsmen and sailors.' Δίσσοι λόγοι 8.2 ff.

⁸¹⁰ D.L. 6.105. Cf. notes 973–975 and 1052–1055, *infra*, and the text thereto.

⁸¹¹ Dio Chrysostom, *Oratio* 9.1.

⁸¹² D.L. 6.70–71. Cf. Xenophon, *Memor.* 4.6.14 and *ibid.* at 4.7.1.; Δίσσοι λόγοι 8.2 ff.

⁸¹³ Cf. the Cynic criticism of Athenian political institutions as recorded by Dio Chrysostom, *Oratio* 13 (*In Athens or, About banishment*); Stobaeus, *Florilegium* 49.47. It is believed that the thirteenth oration of Dio Chrysostom is based on the *Archelaus*, ascribed to Antisthenes. F. Dümmler, *Akademika* (1889) 1–18.

⁸¹⁴ D.L. 6.11. The Cynic idea of good rulership is expressed in the four *Dialogues on Kingship* (*Orations* 1–4) by Dio Chrysostom. Cf. Xenophon, *Memor.* 3.2.1 ff.

⁸¹⁵ D.L. 6.6. Cf. Xenophon, *Memor.* 3.1.1–3.3.14.

⁸¹⁶ Cf. Xenophon, *Memor.* 3.4.2.

⁸¹⁷ D.L. 6.85.

⁸¹⁸ D.L. 6.92.

⁸¹⁹ Xenophon, *Memor.* 1.2.9.

⁸²⁰ Cf. *Antisth. frag.* 66 and *ibid.* at 53; 65; Xenophon, *Memor.* 3.4.14.

⁸²¹ *Antisth. frag.* 59 and *ibid.* at 52. See Stobaeus, *Florilegium* 49.47; Plato, *Republic* 558C; Aristotle, *Politics* 1284 a 15; D.L. 6.5 and *ibid.* at 6.8.

⁸²² Athenaeus, *Deipnosophistae* 5.220. The πολιτικὸς διάλογος mentioned by Athenaeus is probably identical with the Περὶ νόμου ἢ περὶ πολιτείας quoted in D.L. 6.16.

⁸²³ Cf. Athenaeus, *op. cit.* at 5.220; D.L. 6.16.

⁸²⁴ The Antisthenian denunciation of Pericles and the democratic leaders for their inability to educate their children properly is perhaps reflected in Plato, *Laches* 179A ff.; *Meno* 93A ff.; *Gorgias* 503C ff. and *ibid.* at 515DE; 516C; 517B; 519A ff. But Plato's antagonism to Pericles and some other outstanding Athenian statesmen of the post-Cleisthenian period might also have been motivated by the fact that Polycrates had made it a point to extol these men. Cf. note 1305, *infra*.

⁸²⁵ The thirteenth *Oration* of Dio, chaps, 14–28, contains a résumé of the alleged teachings of Socrates. Cf. note 259, *supra*.

⁸²⁶ Dio Chrysostom, *Oratio* 13.19.

⁸²⁷ Cf. notes 972 and 1028–1032, *infra*.

⁸²⁸ Plato, *Crito* 50AB.

⁸²⁹ Plato, *Crito* 51DE.

⁸³⁰ Xenophon, *Memor.* 1.2.9. It is possible that Plato's *Crito* was primarily an apologetic work, composed from a desire of Plato to defend Socrates against the Polycratean charge that he was a despiser

Notes to Chapter V

of the laws. Thus the Platonic evidence showing that Socrates was a law-abiding citizen would be worthless. But perhaps the *Crito* is much too restrained to be considered a rebuttal of Polycrates.

[831] Cf. notes 251-253, *supra*; *Defence* 12-13, and notes 131-133, *supra*.

[832] Cf. note 255, *supra*.

[833] D.L. 6.43.

[834] Cf. *ibid.* at 10.17.

[835] Cf. *Memor.* 4.7.9: 'He [*scil.*, Socrates] recommended to his followers to take care of their health....' *Ibid.* at 3.12.1-8. Dio Chrysostom, *Oratio* 6.8: 'Diogenes [of Sinope] was not neglectful of the body....' See notes 740-747 and 765-767, *supra*. The interesting and apparently Antisthenian theory that ἐγκράτεια in matters of eating (the ἐγκράτεια γαστρός, Xenophon, *Hellenica* 5.3.21) constitutes an essential part of the Cynic παιδεία, is discussed by K. Joël. *op. cit.* at 2.58 ff.

[836] Cf. note 276, *supra*; D.L. 6.104 and *ibid.* at 2.27-28: Aristophanes, *Clouds* 412-417. Aelian, *Var. hist.* 13.27, records that because of his rigorous and sensible way of life Socrates was the only Athenian who did not become affected by the 'great pestilence' of 430/29.

[837] As to Plato's insistence that endurance must be inculcated in the young people, see *Republic* 390c. Cf. D.L. 2.22: 'He [*scil.*, Socrates] took care to exercise the body and kept in good physical condition.'

[838] Cf. note 791, *supra*, and the text thereto. It has already been stated that Xenophon regarded the *Socratica* of Antisthenes as the true and reliable depository of Socratic sayings and doings. See also the sixth and eighth *Orations* of Dio Chrysostom.

[839] *Ibid.*: 'He [*scil.*, Diogenes of Sinope] would walk upon snow barefoot....' *Ibid.* at 6.104 and 6.34. See the description of Diogenes' hardihood in Dio Chrysostom, *Oratio* 6.8-12; Xenophon, *Pol. Lac.* 2.3.

[840] D.L. 6.30. Cf. *ibid.* at 6.91-92, where we are told that Crates the Cynic regularly performed his gymnastic exercises. Diogenes' reluctance to let his pupils have 'full athletic training' might be closely related to his general disdain of 'professional athletes'. *Antisth. frag.* 56; D.L. 6.28 and *ibid.* at 6.44; 6.47; 6.49; 6.51; 6.57; 6.86; Dio Chrysostom, *Oratio* 9.14-22; *Oratio* 8.11 ff. and *ibid.* at 8.15 ff.; 8.20 ff.

[841] D.L. 1.55-56.

[842] Cf. also Dio Chrysostom, *Oratio* 32.14 and *ibid.* at 8.26 ff.

[843] Themistius, Περὶ ἀρετῆς 28 (p. 447).

[844] Themistius, *op. cit.* 41 (p. 457). The reference to Crates, the Cynic (cf. D.L. 6.91-92), in itself would indicate that Themistius thinks here of Antisthenian or Cynic views.

[845] D.L. 6.31. Cf. the description of the *paidonomos* in Xenophon, *Pol. Lac.* 2.1-3.6.

[846] Cf. *Antisth. frag.* 16.

[847] These ideas were probably expressed by Antisthenes in his works on *Heracles*, of which Diogenes Laertius (6.16 and *ibid.* at 6.18)

Notes to Chapter V

enumerates no less than three. The Cynic views on hunting are still reflected in Xenophon, *Cynegeticus* 1.2, and *ibid.* at 12.18; *et passim*; *Cyropaedia* 2.3.7–15. See G. Kaibel, 'Xenophons Kynegetikos', in *Hermes* 25 (1890) 581–597, especially at 589; F. Dümmler, 'Zum Herakles des Antisthenes', in *Philologus* 50 (1891) 288–296; K. Joël, *op. cit.* 2.53 ff.

[848] D.L. 6.70. Cf. the remarks of R. Höistad, *Cynic hero and Cynic king* 41 ff.

[849] Cf. notes 846 and 847, *supra*, and the text thereto.

[850] Cf. *ibid.* at 1.61.

[851] D.L. 6.30.

[852] Cf., however, Stobaeus, *Florilegium* 2.13.88: 'Monimus stated that it was better to lack sight than education.'

[853] *Antisth. frag.* 48; D.L. 6.70. Cf. also *Cleitophon* 407E.

[854] *Antisth. frag.* 65.

[855] D.L. 6.18. See here also the statement of Protagoras, recorded in Plato, *Protagoras* 326BC: 'Then they send them [the children] to the master of gymnastics, in order that their bodies may serve well the virtuous mind, and that they may not be compelled through physical weakness to assume a role of the coward in war or on any other occasion.' This passage may be Antisthenian. Similar ideas can be found in Xenophon, *Memor.* 3.12.1–18, especially *ibid.* at 3.12.2 and 3.12.4.

[856] Cf. Dio Chrysostom, *Oratio* 9.14–22; D.L. 6.30–31; *Antisth. frag.* 48.

[857] D.L. 6.71. The ταύτην in D.L. 6.70 is definitely related to ἄσκησιν in general, and not merely to τὴν δὲ σωματικὴν [ἄσκησιν], as some people have suggested. The relation becomes obvious if one realizes that the whole gist of D.L. 6.70–71 is (*a*) the psycho-physical nature of the ἄσκησις; (*b*) the necessity of a psycho-physical ἄσκησις; and (*c*) the superiority of the mental over the physical ἄσκησις. Similar ideas can be found in Xenophon, *Memor.* 2.1.1 ff., a passage which is definitely under Antisthenian-Cynic influence. Cf. R. Höistad, *op. cit.* at 41. ff. Xenophon, *Memor.* 4.7.9, probably expresses the Cynic views on physical hygiene. Cf. also Dio Chrysostom, *Oratio* 8.29 ff.

[858] U. v. Wilamowitz-Moellendorff, 'Von des attischen Reiches Herrlichkeit', (Nachträge) in *Philologische Untersuchungen* 1 (1880) 214–215, maintains that the term φιλοσοφία was an Attic word which probably originated with the Socratics. K. Joël, *op. cit.* at 2.365, insists that it originated with Antisthenes.

[859] This may be gathered from Plato, *Protagoras* 342D and *Euthydemus* 283A, where we find what appears to be a reference to the Antisthenian ἀρετὴν (or, σοφίαν) ἀσκεῖν.

[860] Cf. *Antisth. frag.* 59. See *ibid.* at 39; 42; 43; 65; D.L. 6.51 and *ibid.* at 6.70–71; R. Höistad, *op. cit.* at 41 ff.

[861] D.L. 6.27 and *ibid.* at 6.59; 6.41. Cf. also K. Joël, *op. cit.* 2.48 ff.

Notes to Chapter V

[862] Thucydides 2.39.

[863] Cf. *ibid.* at 410c ff.: '[Our youth] will not, like common athletes, exercise . . . merely to develop his muscles. . . . The mere athlete becomes too much of a brute; . . . he is liable to become hard and brutish.'

[864] This passage, according to Xenophon's listing, contains the fourth 'accusation' of Polycrates.

[865] Cf. notes 348–351 and 486–489, *supra; Memor.* 1.2.58–59 and notes 351, 497–501 *et passim, supra.*

[866] D.L. 6.31.

[867] Cf. D.L. 6.15–18. See *ibid.* at 6.80 and notes 1356–1358, *infra*.

[868] Cf. D.L. 6.36 (Euripides, *Medea* 410); *ibid.* at 6.52 (*Iliad* 10.343 and 10.387); *ibid.* at 6.53 (*Iliad* 5.10 and 18.95); *ibid.* at 6.55 (*Iliad* 5.366 and 8.45); *ibid.* at 6.55 (Euripides, *Phoenicians* 40); *ibid.* at 6.57 (*Iliad* 5.83); *ibid.* at 6.63 (*Iliad* 16.82a (?), transl. Barnes. There is no such passage in the extant MSS of Homer's *Iliad*); *ibid.* at 6.66 (*Iliad* 3.65); *ibid.* at 6.104 (Euripides, *Antiope, frag.* 205, edit. Dindorf); *ibid.* at 6.90 (*Iliad* 1.59); *ibid.* at 6.98 (Euripides, *Bacch.* 1236); *ibid.* at 6.103 (*Odyssey* 4.392).

[869] Cf. Plutarch, *De audiendis poetis* 12; *Antisth. frag.* 26 and *ibid.* at 27 ff. and 72. In their interpretation of the 'ancient poets' the Cynics actually continued a tradition which had been established by Xenophanes, Parmenides, Empedocles, and Protagoras. The Stoics inherited this tradition from the Cynics and passed it on to the Neo-pythagoreans, Neo-platonists, and, above all, to Philo of Alexandria. Through Philo the method or practice of interpreting in an allegorical manner certain authoritative texts entered the Christian orbit.

[870] Cf. *Iliad* 16.851 ff., where the dying Patroclus prophesies the approaching death of Hector who had slain him; or *Iliad* 23.358 ff., where the dying Hector prophesies the imminent death of his slayer Achilles. See Cicero, *De divinatione* 1.30; Plato, *Apology* 39c.

[871] D.L. 6.10 probably contains a reference to this work.

[872] The Homeric quotations and interpretations found in the Xenophontean *Memorabilia*, it should be borne in mind, all seem to be of Antisthenian-Cynic origin or at least dependent on a specific Antisthenian-Cynic topic, such as, for instance, the characterization of the 'good King Agamemnon' (*Memor.* 3.2.2 and *ibid.* at 3.1.4 ff.; Homer, *Iliad* 3.179), the 'shepherd of the people' (*Memor.* 3.2.1; Homer, *Iliad* 2.243), the 'crafty' or 'logical' Odysseus (*Memor.* 4.6.15; Homer, *Odyssey* 8.171; cf. also Stobaeus, *Florilegium* 4.407), and the 'wily' sorceress Circe who by feasting men to excess, 'turned them into swine' (*Memor.* 1.3.7; Homer, *Odyssey* 10.281 ff.; see also Dio Chrysostom, *Oratio* 8.21–22).

[873] *Memor.* 1.2.49. Cf. Plato, *Laws* 929D: 'If disease or age or ill temper, or all these together, should make a man lose his mind . . . (but this is not apparent except to those who live with him); and if this man

should become the ruin of his household . . . and if his son should be in doubt as to whether he would have to indict his father for insanity; let the law provide that the son shall go first to the eldest guardians of the laws. . . . And they shall duly look into the matter and decide as to whether the son should indict him or not. And if they advise him to proceed . . . and if the father is adjudicated *non compos mentis*, he shall henceforth be declared incapable of taking care of even the smallest details of his own life . . . and he shall be as a child. . . .'

[874] Xenophon, *Memor.* 1.2.51–52. Cf. also *ibid.* at 2.5.1–4 and notes 342–347, *supra*.

[875] Xenophon, *Memor.* 1.2.53.

[876] The expression that the soul is the seat of the φρόνησις, is probably Antisthenian.

[877] Cf. *Antisth. frag.* 60 and 63; D.L. 6.52 and *ibid.* at 6.79; the dialogue *Axiochus* 305A–305E; Aristotle, *Eudemian Ethics* 1235 a 37; Xenophon, *Symposium* 4.34 and *ibid.* at 4.41; 4.43.

[878] Antisthenes and Diogenes of Sinope stressed the care of the soul at the expense of material things (but not at the expense of the living body). D.L. 6.27 and *ibid.* at 6.58; 6.65; 6.67. Epictetus, *Diss.* 3.22.21 and *ibid.* at 3.22.60, two passages which are definitely under the influence of Antisthenian teachings.

[879] Xenophon, *Memor.* 1.2.55.

[880] D.L. 6.79. Cf. *ibid.* at 6.52.

[881] Cf. *Antisth. frag.* 60 and 63; Xenophon, *Symposium* 4.34 and *ibid.* at 4.41; 4.43; 4.64; D.L. 6.27 and *ibid.* at 6.58; 6.65; 6.67.

[882] D.L. 6.7.

[883] D.L. 6.12. Cf. Epictetus, *Diss.* 1.7.31. Even the most enthusiastic apologist of Socrates could not claim that the latter was the ideal 'family man', or that his domestic life was a happy one. Cf. Xenophon, *Symposium* 2.10, *Memor.* 2.2.1–4; Plato, *Republic* 549A; *Phaedo* 60A ff.; *Apology* 23A ff.; *et passim*. This could have been a plausible reason why Socrates might perhaps have thought not too highly of family ties and domestic relations in general. It would also explain why Xenophon seems to be unable to rebut successfully the Polycratean charge that Socrates had undermined the bonds of filial and domestic duties. In any event, Xenophon tries to justify the actions of Socrates rather than to deny the allegations of Polycrates.

[884] Plato, *Euthyphro* 4A.

[885] Cf. Cicero, *Paradox.* 3.24; *De finibus* 4.76. See K. Joël, *op. cit.* at 2.317 and *ibid.* at 2.508–510.

[886] Cf. U. v. Wilamowitz-Moellendorff, 'Die erste Rede des Antiphon', in *Hermes* 22 (1887) 198 ff.; Aristotle (?), *Magna Moralia* 1188 b 31. We know also that Polycrates composed a *Defence of Clytemnestra*. Cf. Quintilian 2.17.4.

[887] Aristophanes (*Clouds* 903 ff.) refers to the legend about Zeus

Notes to Chapter V

having clapped into irons his own father. K. Joël, *op. cit.* at 2.817, insists that this passage, like those of Plato (*Euthyphro* 4A ff.; 5E; *et passim*; *Republic* 378B; *Symposium* 195C), is really a parody of Antisthenes' doctrine that everything, including filial piety, must be sacrificed to 'justice'. Cf. *Clouds* 1332 and *ibid.* at 1377; 1379, where Pheidippides stresses the fact that he was justified in beating his father; 1437 ff., where the father Strepsiades concedes that a father who does wrong may justly be punished by his son; 1446 ff., where Pheidippides maintains that with the help of 'the worse reason' he might prove that it is right for him to beat his father. There may exist some connection between Aristophanes and Xenophon, *Memor.* 2.2.1 ff., Aeschylus, *Eumenides* 657 ff., Euripides, *Orest.* 555 ff., and perhaps even the *Apology of Orestes* of Antisthenes.

[888] See D.L. 2.21: '... he [*scil.*, Socrates] was convinced that the study of nature was of no concern to us'. A.-H Chroust, 'Socrates and pre-Socratic philosophy', in *The Modern Schoolman* 29, no. 2 (1952) 119–135.

[889] D.L. 6.103.

[890] D.L. 6.103–104.

[891] Cf. Stobaeus, *Florilegium* 5.4.53: 'Bion [of Borysthenes] said that grammarians who busy themselves with the wanderings of Odysseus are heedless of their own, nor do they realize that they are astray on this very point, i.e., that they are wasting their time on worthless pursuits.'

[892] D.L. 6.27–28. Cf. *ibid.* at 6.39; Xenophon, *Memor.* 4.4.4–11; Dio Chrysostom, *Oratio* 8.9.

[893] D.L. 6.11.

[894] D.L. 6.11: '[True happiness] ... needs nothing other than the strength of a Socrates.' The original passage may have read 'Heracles' instead of 'Socrates'.

[895] Cf. Xenophon, *Memor.* 2.1.20, who speaks here like a professional Cynic. The κατερία is here synonymous with πόνος.

[896] This becomes quite clear from Xenophon, *Memor.* 2.1.20.

[897] Xenophon, *Memor.* 2.1.20.

[898] The mother of Antisthenes is said to have been a Thracian handmaid. Cf. D.L. 6.1. Hence the whole story is probably a reference to some statement made by Antisthenes.

[899] Stobaeus, *Florilegium* 11.20.7. Cf. D.L. 6.7 and *ibid.* at 6.28; 6.39. For other examples of Bion's denunciation of astronomy and grammar, see Stobaeus, *Florilegium* 2.1.30 and *ibid.* at 3.4.32; D.L. 4.53.

[900] Stobaeus, *Florilegium* 2.22. Cf. D.L. 6.28 and *ibid.* at 6.39.

[901] Cf. Plato, *Republic* 372C, where the social ideals of the Cynics are compared to a 'state of pigs'. Aristotle, *Nicomachean Ethics* 1141 b 3 ff.: '... philosophical wisdom is scientific knowledge.... This is why we say that Anaxagoras and Thales ... have philosophic ... but no practical wisdom, when we see that they do not know what is to their

advantage, and why we say that they know things . . . which are practically useless.' Seneca's contempt for the purely speculative sciences (*Epist.* 88. 7-9) might likewise be based on Antisthenian-Cynic sources.

[902] Cf. Plato, *Phaedrus* 249c; *Republic* 498E and *ibid.* at 500A; 489D.

[903] Cf. Herodotus 1.29 and *ibid.* at 2.49; 4.9; Simplicius, *Comment. in Arist. Phys.* (edit. Diels) 151; K. Joël, *op. cit.* at 2.630 ff.; A.-H. Chroust, 'Philosophy: its essence and meaning in the ancient world', in *Philosophical Review* 56, no. 1 (1947) 19-58; *Antisth. frag.* 65; D.L. 6.56 and *ibid.* at 6.86; 6.88; Stobaeus, *Florilegium* 33.14.

[904] Diogenes of Sinope is said to have insisted that he saw nowhere good men, 'but good boys at Lacedaemon'. D.L. 6.27. *Ibid.* at 6.59: 'He [*scil.*, Diogenes of Sinope] was returning from Lacedaemon to Athens, when some one asked him: "Whither and whence are you going?" And he replied: "From a man's apartment to that of a woman." ' The same idea underlies the story that he went about in broad daylight with a lamp, looking for a man. D.L. 6.41. What Diogenes of Sinope admired about the Spartans was their education of youth which consisted in a combination of rigorous training (ἄσκησις) and hard toil (πόνος). See notes 861-863, *supra*, and the text thereto.

[905] Xenophon, *Memor.* 3.4.14; *Pol. Lacedaem.* 1.1 and *ibid.* at 10.1 ff.; *et passim*.

[906] Dio Chrysostom, *Oratio* 6.25. Cf. *ibid.* at 6.34. The sixth *Oration* of Dio is nothing other than a compilation of Cynic ideas. See also *Oratio* 7, the *Euboean Discourse*, which is a eulogy of the simple rural life. Crates, *frag.* 6, (H. Diels, *Poet. philos. frag.*, vol. 1): 'Luxury and extravagance are not the least of the causes which produce civil unrest and tyranny.'

[907] K. Joël, *op. cit.* at 2.629.

[908] In any event, it differs considerably from the 'official indictment' of the year 399.

[909] Xenophon, *Memor.* 1.2.12 ff.

[910] Xenophon, *Memor.* 1.2.16.

[911] D.L. 6.2. See *ibid.* at 6.11. Socrates, as far as we can ascertain, had defined virtue as rational insight, by which he meant the knowledge of the good. But he had failed to endow this concept of the good with a definite and concrete meaning. This deficiency made it possible for the Cynics to superimpose on this vague Socratic concept of the good their particular ideas concerning the meaning of virtue and goodness.

[912] Xenophon must have been aware of this when in his *Symposium* he identifies Antisthenian views with Socratic ideas.

[913] A classical example of Xenophon's eclecticism and lack of good judgment in his attempt at reconciling in his Socrates the hedonistic concept of pleasure (ἡδονή), which Xenophon seems to approve, although with some reservations, and the Cynic idea of hard toil (πόνος), which also appealed to him. Cf. *Memor.* 4.5.1-12 and *ibid.* at 2.1.1-34.

Notes to Chapter VI

NOTES TO CHAPTER VI—PAGES 135–163

[914] *Memor.* 1.2.12 ff.

[915] *Memor.* 1.2.58–59. Cf. the charge mentioned in *Memor.* 1.2.56.

[916] Cf. note 1317, *infra*, and the text thereto.

[917] Cf. notes 1203–1251, *infra*, and the text thereto.

[918] Xenophon stayed in Asia from 403/2 to 394, when he returned to Greece in the company of the Spartan King Agesilaus. D.L. 2.49–50. Cf. notes 60–65, *supra*, and the text thereto.

[919] Cf. M. Schanz, *op. cit.* at 24.

[920] Cf. D.L. 2.38 and notes 384–387, *supra*, and the text thereto.

[921] Cf. K. Joël, *Geschichte der antiken Philosophie* 1 (Tübingen, 1921) 752; *Der echte und der xenophontische Sokrates* 1.481 and *ibid.* at 2.1123 ff.

[922] K. Joël, 'Der λόγος Σωκρατικός', in *Archiv für Geschichte der Philosophie* 8 (1895) Heft 4, 466–483.

[923] Aristotle, *Rhetoric* 1417 a 20; *Poetics* 1447 b 11; *frag.* 61 (1486 a 12); *Politics* 1265 a 12.

[924] Cf. Aristotle, *frag.* 61 (1486 a 12); Xenophon, *Defence* 1; *Memor.* 1.4.1 and *ibid.* at 4.3.2. E. Zeller, *Archiv für Geschichte der Philosophie* 7 (1894) 102, maintains that Aristotle's references to λόγοι Σωκρατικοί have in mind the *Socratica* of Plato. Zeller apparently overlooks the fact that in *frag.* 61 Aristotle quotes the 'dialogues' of Alexamenus. Cf. K. Joël, 'Der λόγος Σωκρατικός', 468, note 2.

[925] Diogenes Laertius quotes from Panaetius.

[926] This was done, among other authors, by Xenophon and Lysias.

[927] Plato, *Phaedrus* 276B and *ibid.* at 276D; *Timaeus* 59B.

[928] K. Joël, 'Der λόγος Σωκρατικός', 476.

[929] It goes without saying that the earlier λόγοι Σωκρατικοί decisively influenced the later λόγοι Σωκρατικοί.

[930] Plato's *Apology* does not supply Polycrates with any material for his charges against Socrates. But the Platonic *Apology* (29B and 33C ff.) could reflect the influence of the κατηγορία Σωκράτους. This could be adduced as evidence for the contention that the Platonic *Apology* had been occasioned by the κατηγορία although it does not take direct issue with the κατηγορία.

[931] Isocrates, *Busiris* 4. Cf. F. Blass, *op. cit*, 2.367.

[932] Cf. Quintilian, *Institutiones rhetor.* 2.17.4. See F. Blass, *op. cit.* 2.370.

[933] Cf. D.L. 6.15, where a *Defence of Orestes* by Antisthenes is recorded.

[934] Cf. K. Joël, *Der echte und der xenophontische Sokrates* 2.1124.

[935] Cf. *Antisth. frag.* 63.

[936] D.L. 6.10. That this account is not supported by historical facts has already been pointed out.

Notes to Chapter VI

[937] In this the Platonic *Apology* radically differs from the apologetic *Socratica* of Xenophon.

[938] Cf. notes 289–291 and 449–455, *supra*.

[939] Cf. Karl A. Popper, *The open society and its enemies*, vol. I: *The spell of Plato* (London, 1945).

[940] *Antisth. frag.* 47. Cf. Aristotle, *Politics* 1284 a 15 ff.; D.L. 6.5 and *ibid.* at 6.6.

[941] Epictetus, *Diss.* 3.22.6.

[942] Epictetus, *Diss.* 3.22.14.

[943] Dio Chrysostom, *Oratio* 13.14 and *ibid.* at 13.14–20; 13.23; 13.25.

[944] Athenaeus, *Deipnosophistae* 5.220.

[945] *Schol. Lips. ad Iliad.* 15.123.

[946] D.L. 7.121.

[947] H. v. Arnim, *Leben und Werke des Dion von Prusa*, insists that *Oratio* 13.14–28 is based on one of the four λόγοι προτρεπτικοί of Antisthenes. See notes 259 and 825, *supra*.

[948] Dio Chrysostom, *Oratio* 13.19–20. Cf. Δισσοὶ λόγοι 7.1–6; Pseudo-Lucian, *The Cynic* 15 (vol. 3. pp. 399–400, edit. Jacobitz): 'All human evils spring from the desire for these [*scil.*, gold and silver], seditions and wars, conspiracies and murders. The cause of all these is the desire for more.'

[949] Cf. D.L. 6.33 and *ibid.* at 6.40; 6.46; 6.56; 6.60; 6.61 ff.; *et passim*; Epictetus, *Diss.* 3.22.3 and *ibid.* at 3.22.8; 3.22.6; 3.22.13; Themistius, Περὶ ἀρετῆς 43 (p. 457).

[950] Many of Dio Chrysostom's orations also manifest this cosmopolitanism. In this Dio is definitely under Antisthenian-Cynic (and Stoic) influence.

[951] Cf. D.L. 6.38. *Ibid.* at 6.63, where Diogenes of Sinope refers to himself as a 'citizen of the world' (κοσμοπολίτης). *Ibid.* at 6.72; 6.12; 6.93; Epictetus, *Diss.* 3.22.66; Plutarch, *De adulat.* 28; Dio Chrysostom, *Oratio* 4.13: 'He [*scil.*, Diogenes of Sinope] took the whole wide world for his hearth-stone.' Plato (*Theaetetus* 173C) makes a wry comment on Cynic cosmopolitanism: '. . . only his body is in the city. . . .'

[952] Epictetus, *Diss.* 3.22.5. Cf. D.L. 6.93.

[953] Pseudo-Lucian, *The Cynic* 15 (vol. 3. p. 399, edit. Jacobitz).

[954] O. Hense, *Teletis reliquiae* (1909) 38.3.

[955] Cf. notes 646, 647 and 649–656, *supra*, and the text thereto; Plato (?), *Epinomis* 973D, which seems to contain a reference to this subject; Plato, *Protagoras* 325C ff.; Aristotle, *Nicomachean Ethics* 1102 b 5; F. Dümmler, *Akademika* (1889) 169 ff.; K. Joël, *Der echte und der xenophontische Sokrates* 2.184 ff.; U. v. Wilamowitz-Moellendorff, 'Antigonos von Karystos', in *Philologische Untersuchungen*, Heft 4, (1881) 295, note 6.

[956] Demetrius, *De elecutione* (edit. Roberts) 249.

Notes to Chapter VI

⁹⁵⁷ F. Dümmler, *Akademika* 170–171, believes that the original source of all these statements is Prodicus.

⁹⁵⁸ D.L. 6.63.

⁹⁵⁹ D.L. 6.72.

⁹⁶⁰ Cf. D.L. 6.8 and *ibid.* at 6.11; 6.38; 6.5; 6.6; Athenaeus, *Deipnosophistae* 5.220; Dio Chrysostom, *Oratio* 13.19 and *ibid.* at 13.22.

⁹⁶¹ The list of Diogenes Laertius (6.15 ff.) which enumerates the works of Antisthenes, contains the following 'political' titles: *Concerning law, or Concerning the Commonwealth* (6.16); *Concerning law, or Concerning goodness and justice* (6.16); *Cyrus, or Concerning sovereignty* (6.16— perhaps all the works entitled *Cyrus* contain some of Antisthenes' political ideas); *Menexenus, or Concerning rulership* (6.18); and *Archelaus, or Concerning kingship* (6.18). A work entitled Πολιτικός is mentioned in Athenaeus, *Deipnosophistae* 5.220D. We may assume that Antisthenes discussed problems of law, state, and society in some of his other writings, such as the *Aspasia* (D.L. 6.16; Athenaeus, *op. cit.* at 5.220D and perhaps *ibid.* at 13.589E, where he denounces the immorality of Cimon). It seems that the *Aspasia* contained Antisthenes' criticism of Athens' leading statesmen and politicians. Some of Antisthenes' political views can also be gleaned from Xenophon, *Symposium* 4.34 ff., and from a number of passages in the *Memorabilia*.

⁹⁶² The *Republic* is also mentioned by Philodemus (*Hercul. papyr.* 339; cf. K. v. Fritz, 'Quellenuntersuchungen zum Leben und Philosophie des Diogenes von Sinope', in *Philologus*, Suppl. 18, no. 2 (Leipzig, 1926) 55 ff.

⁹⁶³ D.L. 6.85. Cf. E. Diehl, *Anthologia lyr. graec.* 1.1.122 ff.

⁹⁶⁴ Themistius, Περὶ ἀρετῆς 43–44 (pp. 458–459).

⁹⁶⁵ Cf. D.L. 6.3: 'I would rather be mad than feel pleasure.' Dio Chrysostom, *Oratio* 8.21 ff.

⁹⁶⁶ The Cynics distinguished between a 'good ἀναίδεια' and a 'bad ἀναίδεια'. Cf. *Antisth. frag.* 9; Philoponus, *Schol. ad Arist.* 23 (Brandis). This distinction is clearly illustrated in Xenophon, *Cyropaedia* 8.1.30, a passage which seems to be under Antisthenian-Cynic influence.

⁹⁶⁷ Cf. D.L. 6.35 and *ibid.* at 6.63; 6.32; 6.41; *et passim*. Dio Chrysostom, *Oratio* 8.36.

⁹⁶⁸ Cf. *Schol. ad Arist.* 23 (edit. Brandis).

⁹⁶⁹ D.L. 6.69.

⁹⁷⁰ The views of the Early Stoics on the state and on cosmopolitanism may very well be under the influence of Antisthenian-Cynic teachings. Cf. D.L. 6.104. *Ibid.* at 6.15: 'Antisthenes . . . laid the foundation of their [*scil.*, Stoic] conception of the state.' *Ibid.* at 7.4: 'For awhile he [*scil.*, Zeno] was instructed by Crates [the Cynic; cf. D.L. 6.85–93]. At that time he had written his πολιτεία [*ibid.* at 7.33–34; 7.131] which, as some have said jestingly, was written on the dog's tail.' This last remark may refer to the influence which Antisthenian-Cynic teachings had on the πολιτεία of Zeno. For other examples of this influence, see D.L.

Notes to Chapter VI

7.131 and *ibid.* at 7.188; Sextus Empiricus, *Pyrrh. Hypoth.* 3.246 and *ibid.* at 3.205; *Adv. math.* 11.192; Dio Chrysostom, *Oratio* 10.

[971] Cf. Δίσσοι λόγοι 8.2 ff.

[972] Cf. D.L. 6.8 and *ibid.* at 6.6; 6.5; 6.12 ff.; 6.63; 6.105; Aristotle, *Athen. Polit.* 8.2; *Rhetoric* 1393 b 3–8; Stobaeus, *Eclogues* 2.348; *Florilegium* 108.71; Epiphanius, *Expositio fidei* 1089C; notes 289, 809–826 and 905, *supra*, and 993, *infra*.

[973] The 'orthodox Greek', it should be remembered, was a worshipper of the τύχη which meant to him release from undesirable πόνος and πρᾶξις. Cf. note 809, *supra*, and notes 1052–1055, *infra*.

[974] When Xenophon insists (*Memor.* 1.1.3 and *ibid.* at 1.1.9) that the gods favour certain people, he means that they 'help only those who help themselves'. Cf. *Memor.* 1.1.7–9, which should bring this out clearly; Plato, *Euthydemus* 279A ff.

[975] Cf. *ibid.* at 64.4 and the whole of chapter 61; notes 459, 469, 472, 513 and 514, *supra*; Xenophon, *Memor.* 1.2.59.

[976] See Xenophon, *Symposium* 4.36; Dio Chrysostom *Oratio* 6.50; D.L. 6.50

[977] Cf. Xenophon, *Symposium* 4.64; *Memor.* 1.2.60.

[978] There can be no doubt that Aristotle refers here to the 'political science' established by Plato. Cf. *Nic. Eth.* 1180 a 5 ff., where Aristotle speaks of the necessity for 'preambles to laws', an idea we also find in Plato, *Laws* 719E ff.

[979] Cf. *Nic. Eth.* 1180 b 7–28 and *ibid.* at 1181 b 13 ff.

[980] Cf. *Nic. Eth.* 1180 b 35; *Metaphysics* 981 b 7–9.

[981] *Nic. Eth.* 1181 a 9–12. Aristotle refers here to Isocrates, whom he apparently considers the 'archtype' of a 'sophist'. Isocrates (*Oratio* 15.79 ff.) had remarked that originally the art of legislating well was a difficult task. But after a great many laws had been introduced, the later legislators no longer needed any creative ability or ingenuity. They had merely to select from the already existing laws those which had worked well in other cities.

[982] *Nic. Eth.* 1180 b 13 ff.

[983] Cf. notes 443–461, *supra*.

[984] Cf. *Antisth. frag.* 53 and *ibid.* at 66. Antisthenes and his followers vehemently criticized the manners and mores of the 'modern' Athenians, comparing them most unfavourably with those of the Spartans. See D.L. 6.10 and *ibid.* at 6.9; 6.8; 6.25; 6.27; 6.31; 6.33; 6.41; 6.44; 6.46; 6.47; 6.48; 6.51; 6.54; 6.58; 6.59; 6.60; 6.61; 6.62; 6.65; 6.66; *et passim*; Xenophon, *Memor.* 3.4.14.

[985] Themistius, Περὶ ἀρετῆς 42–43 (p. 457).

[986] D.L. 6.44. Cf. Epictetus, *Diss.* 3.22.3–4.

[987] D.L. 6.35. Cf. *ibid.* at 6.86 (Crates): '. . . for a flatterer five talents . . . for a philosopher three obols.'

[988] Themistius, *op. cit.* at 35 (p. 452).

Notes to Chapter VI

⁹⁸⁹ Themistius, *op. cit.* at 40 (p. 456).

⁹⁹⁰ Themistius, *op. cit.* at 47 (p. 462). Cf. *ibid.* at 36 (p. 453), where we are informed that wealth generates only conceit.

⁹⁹¹ Themistius, *op. cit.* at 36 (p. 453).

⁹⁹² Cf. A. Kirchhoff, *Xenophontis qui fertur libellus de republica Atheniensium* (1874).

⁹⁹³ Cf. *The Old Oligarch* 1.6.

⁹⁹⁴ Cf. *The Old Oligarch* 2.20.

⁹⁹⁵ Cf. Plato, *Apology* 34CD and *ibid.* at 37A; Xenophon, *Memor.* 4.4.4.

⁹⁹⁶ Libanius (chap. 62) also mentions the allegation that Socrates had educated Critias and Alcibiades. Cf. note 470, *supra*. In chaps. 136–152, Libanius presents his refutation of the Polycratean charge that Socrates had been the teacher of Critias and Alcibiades. The refutation of this allegation by Libanius is less effective than that offered by Xenophon. Cf. notes 556–578, *supra*, and the text thereto.

⁹⁹⁷ Even Xenophon seems to insinuate that Alcibiades was never a 'real' follower of Socrates. Cf. *Memor.* 1.2.14–16 and *ibid.* at 1.2.18; 1.2.24–27. Cf. note 1244, *infra*, and the text thereto. Pseudo-Andocides, *Contra Alcibiadem*, never mentions any association between Socrates and Alcibiades.

⁹⁹⁸ Cf. D.L. 6.32 and *ibid.* at 6.60; 6.68. Here, too, the Cynic philosopher vanquishes the indomitable conqueror.

⁹⁹⁹ The full title of the work (D.L. 6.16) was *On justice and courage: a hortative* (προτρεπτικὸς) *work in three books*.

¹⁰⁰⁰ For his information that Critias had been one of Socrates' associates, Polycrates might have relied here on some popular tradition which, in turn, could have been based on historical fact. Aeschines (*Adversus Timarchum* 173) points out that Socrates' association with Critias discredited him in the eyes of the Athenians.

¹⁰⁰¹ Cf. D.L. 6.18.

¹⁰⁰² Cf. notes 1214, 1217–1220, 1226 and 1231, *infra*, and the text thereto.

¹⁰⁰³ Cf. Xenophon, *Symposium* 4.34 ff.; *Antisth. frag.* 29 and *ibid.* at 45; 56–59; *et passim*.

¹⁰⁰⁴ D.L. 6.16 mentions a work on *Cyrus* as well as a treatise on *Cyrus, or Of sovereignty*, while in 6.18 he refers to a *Cyrus, or The beloved*, and to a *Cyrus, or The scout*. We must assume that Athenaeus alludes here to *Cyrus, or Of sovereignty*.

¹⁰⁰⁵ D.L. 6.16.

¹⁰⁰⁶ D.L. 6.16.

¹⁰⁰⁷ D.L. 6.16.

¹⁰⁰⁸ D.L. 6.16.

¹⁰⁰⁹ D.L. 6.16.

¹⁰¹⁰ Cf. *Memor.* 1.2.59: 'Socrates . . . said . . . that those who did not benefit others either by word or deed . . . if the necessity should arise

Notes to Chapter VI

... could be curbed in every way. . . .' *Memor.* 1.2.51; *Defence* 20, and notes 873, 335, 336, 340 and 341, *supra*. Libanius (chap. 62) implies that Polycrates had charged Socrates with abusing the ancient poets in order to undermine paternal authority. See notes 471, 483, 484 and 490, *supra*. Libanius (70.17 and 71.5), however, mentions this particular charge only in passing. Cf. Δίσσοι λόγοι 3.3, where we are told that under certain circumstances it is permissible to deceive one's parents.

[1011] Cf. Plato, *Euthydemus* 303A; *Phaedo* 89C; *Crito* 54A: 'Think not of life and children first, and of justice afterwards, but of justice first. . . .'

[1012] D.L. 6.12: 'Esteem an honest man above a kinsman.'

[1013] Cf. A. E. Taylor, *Plato, the man and his work*, 6th edit. (London, 1949) 147.

[1014] Cf. Aristophanes, *Clouds* 1407, where Pheidippides 'drags his father Strepsiades through the mire'. Cf. notes 873–887, *supra*, and the text thereto.

[1015] Cf. note 883, *supra*.

[1016] See *ibid.* at 6.36: 'To Xeniades, who had purchased him, he said: "Come, see that you obey orders." '

[1017] Cf. *Memor.* 1.1.16, where σωφροσύνη and μανία are sharply contrasted.

[1018] Cf. Xenophon, *Memor.* 3.9.6 ff., a passage which seems to be directed against Antisthenes; F. Dümmler, *Akademika* (1889) 257, note 1; K. Joël, *Der echte und der xenophontische Sokrates* 1.344 ff.; note 341, *supra*.

[1019] Plato, *Protagoras* 328C. Cf. *ibid.* at 314E and *Meno* 94B.

[1020] Plato, *Meno* 94B.

[1021] D.L. 6.12.

[1022] Cf., however, *ibid.* at 116A, where we are told that in his last hour 'his children were brought to him, and the women of his family also came. He talked to them and gave them a few directions.'

[1023] D.L. 6.12. Cf. *ibid.* 7.33; Xenophon, *Memor.* 2.6.16 and *ibid.* at 2.6.19–20; 2.6.22.

[1024] D.L. 7.33. Although this statement is ascribed to the Early Stoics, there can be little doubt that Zeno is here under the influence of Cynic tradition. Cf. note 970, *supra*.

[1025] D.L. 6.89.

[1026] Cf. D.L. 6.3 and *ibid.* at 6.29; 6.54; 6.72 (the same idea is voiced by some early Stoics; D.L. 7.33); *Antisth. frag.* 60; Aristotle, *Politics* 1266 a 34; Plato, *Republic* 449E ff. and *ibid.* at 457C ff.; 461E ff.; 543A; *Statesman* 272A; *Laws* 807B and *ibid.* at 739C; *Timaeus* 18D; D.L. 4.48 (Bion of Borysthenes); Lucian, *Vit. auct.* 9; Epictetus, *Diss.* 3.22.8; Xenophon, *Memor.* 1.1.8; Philodemus, in *Hercul. Papyr.* no. 339; Dio Chrysostom, *Oratio* 10.29 ff. Antisthenes probably expresses most of these views in his *On the procreation of children, or On marriage.* D.L. 6.16.

[1027] Cf. notes 342–347, *supra*; *Defence* 20 and note 175, *supra*. As to

Notes to Chapter VI

Libanius' efforts to rebut this charge (Libanius 70.17 and *ibid.* at 71.5), see note 1010, *supra*. Libanius touches on this issue only in a most casual manner. Cf. note 484, *supra*.

[1028] Cf. *Antisth. frag.* 56; note 1016, *supra* and the text thereto.

[1029] Cf. *Memor.* 1.2.59, where essentially the same idea is expressed by Xenophon in the name of Socrates. Themistius (Περὶ ἀρετῆς 44, p. 459) informs us that the true philosopher is able to distinguish between friend and foe.

[1030] This should be considered sufficient evidence to prove that the *Alcibiades I* is under Antisthenian influence.

[1031] Cf. Δίσσοι λόγοι 3.3–4, where we are told that under certain circumstances it is permissible not only to deceive one's parents, but also to commit acts of violence towards, and theft from, one's relatives or friends.

[1032] Cf. *Antisth. frag.* 55 and *ibid.* at 47; D.L. 6.30 and *ibid.* at 6.88; Xenophon, *Symposium* 4.64; Stobaeus, *Florilegium* 79.51; 6.3; Xenophon, *Oeconomicus* 2.15 and *ibid.* at 11.1; Aelian 9.28; Dio Chrysostom, *Oratio* 14.21.

[1033] Cf. *Memor.* 1.2.54. See *Antisth. frag.* 55.

[1034] Cf. notes 879–881, *supra*.

[1035] Cf. D.L. 6.26 and *ibid.* at 6.32; 6.46; 6.69; Dio Chrysostom, *Oratio* 8.36; *et passim*.

[1036] Cf. Xenophon, *Memor.* 2.10.3.

[1037] Xenophon, *Memor.* 2.10.4. Xenophon, *ibid.* at 2.10.5, also informs us that 'Diodorus . . . at no great expense to himself, secured a friend who . . . both profited and pleased him by his services.'

[1038] Xenophon, *Memor.* 2.6.2. Cf., however, *ibid.* at 2.6.7: 'A man who is known to have served well his former friends, will undoubtedly treat well also his future friends.'

[1039] Xenophon, *Memor.* 2.6.25. Cf. *Defence* 19.

[1040] Libanius (chap. 62) refers to the Polycratean allegation that Socrates had quoted from the most celebrated ancient poets in order to substantiate his own mischievous teachings by which he rendered his followers unprincipled and tyrannical. Cf. notes 469, 486–491 and 500–520, *supra*, and the text thereto. According to Libanius (48.12), Polycrates would have charged Socrates not only with having rebuked or criticized the most celebrated ancient poets, but also with having declared that many of their sayings were objectionable. See *ibid.* at 61.14; 62.7; 63.4; 67.17; notes 492 and 497–501, *supra*.

[1041] Cf. notes 868–869, *supra*. F. Dümmler (*Antisthenica* 31 ff.), has made it quite clear that in his *Hippias Minor* Plato ridicules the *Homerica* of Antisthenes. See also F. Dümmler, *Akademika* 56.

[1042] According to Libanius (chap. 62) Polycrates would have Socrates quote Hesiod, Pindar, Theognis, and Homer, in that order. Cf. notes 502–503, *supra*.

Notes to Chapter VI

[1043] Hesiod, *Works and Days* 309.

[1044] *Memor.* 1.2.56. Cf. Libanius 61.17, and notes 348, 349, 504 and 505, *supra*.

[1045] D.L. 6.2. Πόνος is also the only sure antidote for λύπη (grief).

[1046] The term πόνος is never used by Plato in the sense of a prophylactic against sensual pleasure.

[1047] D.L. 6.2.

[1048] Xenophon, following an Antisthenian tradition, uses here the πόνος in a cathartic sense. Cf. *ibid.* at 12.15; 12.22.

[1049] Cf. Xenophon, *Memor.* 1.2.56–57, and notes 504–505, *supra*.

[1050] Cf. notes 861–863, *supra*, and the text thereto.

[1051] *Memor.* 1.2.12. Libanius, chaps. 62 and 136. See notes 469–474 and 556–569, *supra*.

[1052] Cf. *ibid.* at 3.38 (Plato); 6.66: 'To a man who was pressing hard his suit to a courtesan, he [*scil.*, Diogenes of Sinope] said: "Why, hapless man, are you at such pains to gain your suit when it would be better for you to lose it?"'

[1053] D.L. 6.71. Cf. also *ibid.* at 6.27; Xenophon, *Memor.* 3.9.9, where Xenophon makes Socrates speak like a Cynic.

[1054] Cf. notes 973 and 974, *supra*, and the text thereto.

[1055] D.L. 6.105.

[1056] The term φρόνιμος used here by Critias is a typically Cynic term.

[1057] As to the Antisthenian concept of leisure, cf. K. Joël, *op. cit.* at 2.769.

[1058] Libanius 19.18 and *ibid.* at 19.28; 30.3; 35.3; 75.3; 103.7 ff.; notes 541–543, *supra*; D.L. 2.31: 'He [*scil.*, Socrates] would extol leisure as the best of possessions.'

[1059] Libanius 84.18 and *ibid.* at 86.12; 87.4; 89.3; 89.10; 89.16; 90.1; 90.5; Plato, *Apology* 29E; Xenophon, *Defence* 16; *Memor.* 1.2.6–7 and *ibid.* at 1.2.62; note 543, *supra*.

[1060] Cf. D.L. 6.8 and *ibid.* at 6.10; 6.11; 6.12; 6.28; 6.32; 6.34; 6.35; 6.45; 6.47; 6.50; 6.54; 6.57; 6.62; 6.74; 6.86; 6.88; 6.95; *et passim*.

[1061] Cf. D.L. 6.27–28 and *ibid.* at 6.42; Plato, *Republic* 351A ff. and *ibid.* at 433D; *Gorgias* 470B; *Laws* 716A ff.

[1062] Cf. D.L. 6.33 and *ibid.* at 6.49; 6.60; 6.61–62.

[1063] Cf. *ibid.* at 63.1. The quotation from Pindar is not to be found in Xenophon's *Memorabilia*. Cf. notes 502 and 506, *supra*.

[1064] Pindar, *frag.* 169 (edit. Bergk). Cf. note 507, *supra*.

[1065] D.L. 6.11.

[1066] Plato, *Protagoras* 337C.

[1067] D.L. 6.38.

[1068] D.L. 6.20–21.

[1069] Cf. D.L. 6.56.

[1070] Cf. D.L. 6.80.

[1071] Cf. D.L. 6.49 and *ibid.* at 6.56; 6.71.

Notes to Chapter VI

[1072] *A history of Cynicism* 24 and *ibid.* at 54. The views advanced by Seltmann are open to serious challenge. Cf. W. H. Waddington, E. Babelon and Th. Reinach, *Recueil général des monaies grecques d'Asie Mineure*, vol. 1, fasc. 1 (Paris, 1925) 192 ff.; E. S. G. Robinson, 'A find of coins of Sinope', in *The Numismatic Chronicle* 20 (1920) 1 ff.; D. M. Robinson, 'Ancient Sinope', in *American Journal of Philology* 27 (1906) 246 ff.; R. Höistad, *Cynic hero and Cynic king* 10 ff. The paper of C. T. Seltmann is now published under the title 'Diogenes of Sinope, son of the banker Hikesias', in *Transactions of the International Numismatic Congress* 1936, edit. by J. A. H. Mattingly and E. S. G. Robinson (London, 1938).

[1073] Cf. W. H. Waddington, *Recueil* (2nd edit.) 202/44, 203/46–48; 204/51–52.

[1074] Cf. Aristotle, *Nicomachean Ethics* 1133 b 12 and *ibid.* at 1135 a 1; 1135 a 21 ff.; *Politics* 1280 b 11.

[1075] Cf. I. Bywater and J. G. Milne, '$Παραχάραξις$', in *Classical Review* 54, no. 1 (1940) 10–12. The idea of $παραχαράττειν\ τὸν\ νόμον$ is also contained in the report found in D.L. 6.36: 'To Xeniades, who purchased him [*scil*. Diogenes of Sinope], he said: "Come, see that you obey orders." When Xeniades quoted the verse, "Backward the rivers flow to their source" [Euripides, *Medea* 410], Diogenes asked: "If you had been ill and had engaged a physician, would you then, instead of obeying him, have quoted, Backward the rivers flow to their source"?'

[1076] D.L. 6.50.

[1077] Cf. Dio Chrysostom, *Oratio* 6.21–22, who through Diogenes of Sinope appeals to the example of animals and primitive men.

[1078] Cf. D.L. 6.71.

[1079] D.L. 6.22.

[1080] Gorgias was the first teacher of Antisthenes. D.L. 6.1.

[1081] Cf. *ibid.* at 63.1.

[1082] Polycrates, in the account of Libanius, then goes on to show that Socrates had quoted this adulterated passage from Pindar in order to substantiate his doctrine of lawlessness. But such an inference would apply to a Cynic rather than to Socrates, whose aversion to any form of lawlessness and violence has been pointed out eloquently in Plato's *Crito*, provided the *Crito* contains reliable information. Cf. note 507, *supra*.

[1083] Libanius 63.8.

[1084] Theognis 177 ff. Cf. note 516, *supra*. Xenophon alludes to this passage from Theognis in *Memor*. 1.2.20.

[1085] D.L. 6.33.

[1086] D.L. 6.51.

[1087] Diogenes Laertius (6.16) lists a work *On Theognis* by Antisthenes in which he may have quoted and discussed the passage taken from Theognis.

Notes to Chapter VI

[1088] Cf. D.L. 6.8: 'When someone extolled luxury, he [*scil.*, Antisthenes] replied: "May the sons of your enemies live in luxury." ' *Ibid.* at 6.50; 6.28: 'And he [*scil.*, Diogenes of Sinope] would wonder that the avaricious should cry out against money, while being inordinately fond of it.'

[1089] D.L. 6.37 and *ibid.* at 6.72. Cf. Dio Chrysostom, *Oratio* 3.110.

[1090] D.L. 6.47.

[1091] D.L. 6.44.

[1092] D.L. 6.12 ff. and *ibid.* at 6.63; 6.105; Stobaeus, *Eclogues* 2.348; Stobaeus, *Florilegium* 108.71; Epictetus, *Diss.* 1.24.6 ff.

[1093] Stobaeus, *Florilegium* 1.30 and *ibid.* at 10.42; 97.27; 15.10; Xenophon, *Symposium* 4.35 ff.; D.L. 6.47 and *ibid.* at 6.50; 6.60; 6.95.

[1094] Stobaeus, *Florilegium* 93.35.

[1095] Cf. Epictetus, *Diss.* 1.24.6; D.L. 6.11 and *ibid.* at 6.72; 6.92; 6.26; 6.83; 6.86.

[1096] Cf. D.L. 6.104; Stobaeus, *Florilegium* 95.11 and *ibid.* at 95.19; Lucian, *Vita auctor.* 11; Epiphanius, *Expositio fidei* 1089c.

[1097] Cf. notes 502 and 518–520, *supra*.

[1098] With Xenophon this is the second quotation from the ancient poets, while with Libanius it is the fourth.

[1099] *Iliad* 2.188 ff.

[1100] D.L. 6.84: 'Among the disciples of Diogenes [of Sinope] . . . [was] Menander . . . a great admirer of Homer. . . .'

[1101] Dio Chrysostom, *Oratio* 53.5.

[1102] Antisthenes is said to have written the following works about Odysseus or the *Odyssey*; *Odysseus, or On Odysseus* (D.L. 6.15); *On the Odyssey* (D.L. 6.17); *Cyclops, or On Odysseus* (*ibid.*); *Of Odysseus, Penelope and the dog* (*ibid.* at 6.18); *Of Circe* (*ibid.*).

[1103] Cf. H. J. Ludlofs, *De Antisthenis studiis rhetoricis* (Amsterdam, 1900); A. Bachmann, *Ajax et Ulixes declamationes utrum iure tribuentur Antistheni necne* (Münster, 1911); F. Blass, *op. cit.* (2nd edit.) 2.337.

[1104] Cf. R. Höistad, *Cynic hero and Cynic king* 94–102; Xenophon, *Memor.* 1.2.59. In Dio Chrysostom, *Oratio* 2.3 ff., Alexander of Macedonia tells his father why he prefers Homer to all other poets: 'I look upon the poetry of Homer as alone truly noble and lofty and suited to a king . . . particularly if he expects to rule over all the peoples of the earth. . . .' Perhaps Alexander has in mind here also *Iliad* 2.188 ff. Hence 'many of Homer's lines would properly be sung to the sound of trumpets . . . [or] by a phalanx under arms.' *Ibid.* at 2.29. Cf. *ibid.* at 2.67–75 and *Oratio* 3.53.

[1105] Cf. notes 445, 446, 449, 453–457, 514–520 and 556–562, *supra*, and the text thereto.

[1106] This Cynic παιδεία ideal is discussed in Xenophon's *Cyropaedia* 2.1 and *ibid.* at 2.3; 3.3; 8.1–4; *Oeconomicus* 21.6–10. In *Oeconomicus* 14.9 ff. we are told that the noble person is always motivated by the

Notes to Chapter VI

φιλοτιμία (the love of honour), while a man of low mentality must be driven by force. *Ibid.* at 11.11. Cf. *The Old Oligarch* 1.9.

[1107] Cf. D.L. 6.10: 'He [*scil.*, Antisthenes] would prove ... that nobility belongs to none other than the virtuous.' Note 789, *supra*. D.L. 6.12: 'A good man deserves to be loved. Men of worth are friends.'

[1108] D.L. 6.4 and *ibid.* at 6.21; 6.30.

[1109] D.L. 6.32.

[1110] Dio Chrysostom, *Oratio* 3.62.

[1111] Dio Chrysostom, *Oratio* 3.85. Cf. *ibid.* at 4.24–25. The Homeric 'shepherd king' was for Antisthenes the ideal form of kingship, which he probably expressed in his *Cyrus, or On kingship* (D.L. 6.16) and *Archelaus* (D.L. 6.18). Cf. *Antisth. frag.* 3 and *ibid.* at 16; 18; 24; K. Joël, *op. cit.* at 1.387–390.

[1112] *Schol. ad Arist.* (edit. Brandis) 23.

[1113] *Antisth. frag.* 61. Cf. the four *Discourses on kingship* by Dio Chrysostom.

[1114] Cf. *ibid.* at 20.14 ff. and notes 424–431 and 521–532, *supra*; Xenophon, *Memor.* 1.2.63.

[1115] D.L. 7.121.

[1116] Zeno was a pupil of Crates the Cynic. D.L. 6.105 and *ibid.* at 7.2–4.

[1117] Cf. Plutarch, *Lycurgus* 31.

[1118] Stobaeus, *Florilegium* 29.92.

[1119] D.L. 6.73.

[1120] Cf. note 531, *supra*.

[1121] Listed in D.L. 6.16.

[1122] Cf. Xenophon, *Memor.* 3.1.6 and *ibid.* at 4.2.15–16, who enumerates the ability to steal from the enemy or to defraud him among the chief virtues of a good general; or *Cyropaedia* 1.6.27, where the same 'qualifications' are demanded of a good and successful general. *Memor.* 3.1.6 and 4.2.15–16, as well as *Cyropaedia* 1.6.27, are definitely under the influence of Antisthenian teachings.

[1123] Cf. K. Joël, *op. cit.* at 1.398–403; dialogue *Clitophon* 410AB.

[1124] Xenophon, *Cyropaedia* 1.6.31 and *ibid.* at 7.5.73. Cf. *Memor.* 4.2.15, which is likewise influenced by Antisthenian teachings, and *ibid.* at 2.1.13. This Antisthenian 'morality' is exploited by Callicles in Plato, *Gorgias* 484A ff.

[1125] *Antisth. frag.* 24 ff.; *Antisth. frag.* (Mullach) 27 ff., where Odysseus' deception of Calypso is justified with the remark that lovers may use deception. Antisthenes apparently approved of the saying that 'all's fair in love and war'. Compare Antisthenes' (?) *Odysseus* (F. Blass, *Antiphontis orationes et fragmenta*, 2d edit. (1892) 177–182), and the praise of the crafty and lying Odysseus in Plato, *Hippias Minor* 364C and *ibid.* at 365B; 369C; 369E; 370E; 371AB. This praise, aside from containing *Plato's* ridicule of the Antisthenian *Homerica*, has an elenctic purpose for Plato and, hence, must not be taken seriously.

Notes to Chapter VII

[1126] *Antisth. frag.* 43 ff.

[1127] *Antisth. frag.* 41.

[1128] D.L. 6.73. Plato (*Republic* 344A ff. and *Hippias Minor* 364B ff.) chides Antisthenes for having advocated a dual morality as regards friends and enemies. The notions expressed here by Socrates, like the statements found in Xenophon's *Memor.* 4.2.14–17 and *ibid.* at 4.2.20, impress us as being under the influence of Antisthenes' admiration for the wily Odysseus. See Xenophon, *Cyropaedia* 1.6.31–34, and the anonymous Περὶ τοῦ βίου καὶ τῆς ποιήσεως Ὁμήρου, 218 (edit. D. Wyttenbach 10.1246).

[1129] D.L. 6.15.

[1130] D.L. 6.17.

[1131] D.L. 6.18.

[1132] F. Blass, *op. cit.* at 175–177.

[1133] Isocrates (*Busiris* 44–48) states that Polycrates, in order to create sensation, had a definite penchant for defending and extolling what actually did not admit of any defence. Cf. Demetrius, Περὶ ἑρμηνείας 120; Athenaeus, *Deipnosophistae* 8.335; Pausanias 6.17.9; Dionysius, *Isaeus* 20.

[1134] The *Crito* could very well be Plato's rebuttal of Polycrates' allegation that Socrates was a 'despiser of the laws'. In this case it would have to be 'post-Polycratean'.

NOTES TO CHAPTER VII—PAGES 164–197

[1135] Cf. Xenophon, *Memor.* 1.2.59 and notes 289–290, 351, 432–434, 443–445, 448, 453–460, 507–508, 515 and 1097–1113, *supra*.

[1136] Libanius chaps. 93–95 (33.1; 34.14; 38.11; 40.15; 41.2; 41.7; 42.6; 43.1; 43.18; 45.3, Foerster); Xenophon, *Memor.* 1.2.9 and *ibid.* at 1.2.59, where Polycrates had charged Socrates with explaining a passage from Homer 'as if the poet recommended that lowly and poor people should be beaten'. See notes 350–352, 514, 518, 808–826, and 938–991, *supra*. In both instances, we can notice, Xenophon's rebuttal of the Polycratean allegations strikes us as being rather ineffective. *Memor.* 1.2.59: 'Socrates, however, said no such thing [that lowly and poor people should be beaten], but . . . that those who did not benefit others . . . should be curbed in every way. . . .' Also *ibid.* at 1.2.63: '[Socrates] was never the cause . . . of any sedition or treason.'

[1137] The Platonic *Gorgias* is no longer considered a strictly 'Socratic' dialogue.

[1138] Xenophon had the tastes, aspirations, and views of a well-to-do country squire, and a pronounced sympathy for the Spartan way of life.

Notes to Chapter VII

[1139] Xenophon, however, makes Socrates look rather 'democratic' when the latter reprimands his followers for despising certain kinds of labour commonly performed by slaves. Cf. *Memor.* 2.7–8, where Xenophon makes Socrates speak like the Cynics, who made a virtue out of the lowliest labours.

[1140] Socrates' admitted failure to participate in public affairs, to be sure, was detrimental to his cause. This might also explain why, according to Plato, he should justify at great length his withdrawal from all public activity. A man who persistently refrained from public service was called ἀπράγμων, an epithet that carried a reproach which few men were willing to incur. Cf. Thucydides 2.40. See also the nasty twist which Polycrates gives to Socrates' abstention from public service. Libanius, chaps. 127 ff. and note 541, *supra*. Hence it was really public opinion which played an important role in inducing the Athenian citizen actively to share in the business of the city, nay, frequently to turn into a vociferous and obnoxious busybody.

[1141] The siege of Potidaea in 432–430 (Plato, *Symposium* 219E; *Charmides* 153A); the battle of Delium in 424 (Plato, *Symposium* 221A; *Laches* 181A); and the battle of Amphipolis in 422 (D.L. 2.22). See Plato, *Apology* 28E.

[1142] Cf. note 269, *supra*.

[1143] D.L. 2.23.

[1144] Xenophon, *Memor.* 1.2.24. Cf. *Hellenica* 2.3.36.

[1145] Cf. Libanius, chaps. 165–166 (109.5–110.11, Foerster) and *ibid.* at chap. 164 (109.2–5). The ultimate purpose of this particular tradition seems to have been an apologetic effort on the part of the Socratics to absolve Socrates from all suspicion of ever having sympathized with autocrats and autocratic or despotic ideas about government, or of having been an enemy of democracy or perhaps a partisan of the Thirty Tyrants.

[1146] D.L. 2.25. Cf. Seneca, *De beneficiis* 5.6.2 ff.

[1147] Aristotle, *Rhetoric* 1398 a 24 ff.

[1148] Stobaeus, *Eclogues* 4.33.28. The *First Epistle of Socrates* also mentions Socrates' rejection of Archelaus' presents and invitation.

[1149] See notes 1317–1322, *infra*, and the text thereto.

[1150] Thucydides 2.40.

[1151] Cf. Libanius, chap. 49 (41.7–8): 'But he himself [*scil.*, Socrates] had no desire for visible success and, therefore, pushed others forward.' D.L. 2.29: 'He [*scil.*, Socrates] encouraged Charmides, however, to enter politics because he had a talent for politics.'

[1152] See Libanius, chap. 144 (77.13 ff.) and notes 536–538, *supra*.

[1153] Cf. Libanius, chap. 133 (89.3): 'Socrates never was a public speaker.' Further along Libanius admits (89.6 ff) that Socrates prevented inexperienced young people (perhaps people of political convictions different from his own?) from addressing the assembly. Libanius,

Notes to Chapter VII

chap. 20 (24.17 ff.) and chap. 151 (101.2 ff.); Xenophon, *Memor.* 3.6.1–18; and some passages in *Alcibiades I* and the Platonic *Gorgias*.

[1154] Xenophon, *Memor.* 3.7.2–3. Cf. D.L. 2.29.

[1155] Xenophon, *Memor.* 3.7.4.

[1156] Xenophon, *Memor.* 3.7.5–7. Cf. Aelian, *Var. hist.* 2.1., a report which probably is based on some lost *Alcibiades* dialogue. Plato, *Protagoras* 319c; D.L. 2.34: 'Of the mass of men who do not count, he [*scil.*, Socrates] said that it was as if some one should object to a single tetradrachm as counterfeit and at the same time let a whole pile made up of just such pieces pass as genuine.' Polycrates' allegation that Socrates had only contempt for the common people is rebutted in *Memor.* 1.2.59.

[1157] Cf. Plato, *Gorgias* 515A ff.

[1158] Xenophon, *Memor.* 2.1.1–20.

[1159] Cf. D.L. 2.34–35.

[1160] Cf. Plato, *Apology* 31D–32A; *Republic* 496c ff. It might be mentioned here that Epicurus, in his rejection of all active participation in political life, was prompted by the same motive.

[1161] Socrates alludes here to a divine command to seek a truly wise man. This does not leave him any time for engaging in politics or even for attending to his own private affairs. Cf. Plato, *Apology* 31B.

[1162] Similar ideas can be found in Aristotle, *Pol. Athen.* 28.3–4; *The Old Oligarch* 1.13 and *ibid.* at 1.16 ff.; 2.20; 3.3; 3.13.

[1163] The metaphor of the gadfly or spur appears also in D.L. 4.6, who reports that Xenocrates 'was naturally slow and clumsy. Hence Plato, comparing him to Aristotle, said: "The one required a spur, the other a bridle." And again: "See what an ass I am training and what a horse"....' *Ibid.* at 5.65: 'He [*scil.*, Lycon, the successor of Strato in the Academic scholarchate] used to say that modesty and love of honour were as necessary an equipment for boys as the spur and bridle were necessary for horses.' Cf. Xenophon, *Symposium* 2.10, where Socrates points out that those who intend to become expert horsemen 'do not train with docile but rather with spirited horses'. The same story is retold by D.L. 2.37.

[1164] This is brought out in Xenophon, *Memor.* 1.2.15.

[1165] In his *Clouds*, Aristophanes seems to adopt this popular opinion. Cf. Xenophon, *Memor.* 1.2.31, where we are told about a 'common charge made by the people against philosophers'.

[1166] Cf. H. Dittmar, 'Aeschines von Sphettos', in *Philol. Unters.* 21 (1912) 10 ff.; D.L. 6.16 and *ibid.* at 6.18.

[1167] Perhaps in the *Protrepticus*, the full title of which is *On justice and courage, a hortative work* (D.L. 6.16); or in the *On law, or On a commonwealth* (*ibid.*); or in the *On law, or Of goodness and justice* (*ibid.*).

[1168] Cf. Plato, *Gorgias* 515c and *ibid.* at 519A ff.; *Protagoras* 319cD; Xenophon, *Memor.* 1.2.9.

Notes to Chapter VII

¹¹⁶⁹ Cf. Plato, *Crito* 52E; *Protagoras* 342A ff.; *Hippias Major* 283A ff.; Xenophon, *Memor.* 3.5.14–28.

¹¹⁷⁰ Cf. Xenophon, *Memor.* 3.5.20.

¹¹⁷¹ That Socrates was a partisan of the aristocratic-oligarchic party and, hence, primarily a political rather than a philosophical figure in the history of Athens, is considered in some of our conclusions at the end of the present chapter.

¹¹⁷² Cf. Aeschines, *Contra Timarchum* 173.

¹¹⁷³ *Memor.* 1.2.9. See notes cited in note 1135, *supra*.

¹¹⁷⁴ Xenophon, *Memor.* 1.2.12 ff. See notes 299–305, 474, 556–569, 577 and 996–1009, *supra*.

¹¹⁷⁵ Cf. Plato, *Apology* 30D ff.

¹¹⁷⁶ Cf. Dio Chrysostom, *Oratio* 13.14 and *ibid.* at 13.16; Xenophon, *Memor.* 1.1.10.

¹¹⁷⁷ This statement probably contains his critique of the social and economic system which had developed in maritime and commercial (and democratic) Athens during the fifth century. Cf. Plato, *Gorgias* 519A ff.; *The Old Oligarch* 1.14–20 and *ibid.* at 2.1–20.

¹¹⁷⁸ Plato, *Apology* 36C. Cf. *ibid.* at 20B, where the Socratic παιδεία is defined as a 'combination of personal and political (or civic) virtue'. *Cleitophon* 407DE.

¹¹⁷⁹ Essentially the same idea can be found in Xenophon, *Memor.* 1.1.16: 'He [*scil.*, Socrates] would discuss . . . the nature of the city . . . the character of government . . . and the qualifications of a person skilled in the art of governing men.' Cf. *ibid.* at 4.6.13–14.

¹¹⁸⁰ Xenophon, *Memor.* 1.2.17. Cf. *ibid.* at 1.2.15.

¹¹⁸¹ Cf. Xenophon, *Memor.* 1.2.12 and *ibid.* at 1.2.58–59; Libanius 47.7 and *ibid.* at 34.14; 38.11; 41.2; 33.1; 40.15; 41.7; 42.6; 43.1; 43.18; 43.5. See notes cited in note 1135, *supra, et passim*.

¹¹⁸² This would dispose of the possible contention that Plato in his *Apology* purposely suppresses all references to political charges in order to avoid any self-incrimination.

¹¹⁸³ By 393/2, the year the κατηγορία Σωκράτους probably was published, the political amnesty law of 403 had probably fallen into disuse. In any event, since the pamphlet of Polycrates was a private document, unlike the official prosecution of Socrates in 399, it did not have to abide by the terms of this amnesty law.

¹¹⁸⁴ Cf. Xenophon, *Defence* 29 and *ibid.* at 31; Plato, *Meno* 95A; D.L. 6.9–10; *Scholia ad Platon. Apolog.* 18B; Aristotle, *Pol. Athen.* 27.5. Libanius, chap. 10; Dio Chrysostom, *Oratio* 55.22. See notes 805 and 936, *supra*.

¹¹⁸⁵ The restored democracy of 403 displayed exceptional leniency towards those people who had held public office during the reign of the Thirty Tyrants. Cf. Plato, *Epist.* 7.325B. Anytus, in particular, seems to have distinguished himself by his spirit of magnanimity. He set a

splendid example when he renounced all claims for compensation for the loss of a considerable estate that had been taken from him during the regime of the Thirty Tyrants. Isocrates, *Oratio* 18 (*Adversus Callimachum*) 23: '. . . Thrasybulus and Anytus, two men of the greatest influence in the city, although they had been robbed of large sums of money . . . are . . . not bringing suit . . . [nor do they] vent old grudges. . . . In matters covered by the Act of Oblivion they . . . put themselves on terms of equality with all other citizens.'

[1186] A. E. Taylor, *Plato, The man and his work*, 6th edit. (London, 1949) 158.

[1187] Cf. Plato, *Apology* 36A: 'I think that I escaped Meletus.'

[1188] Cf. Plato, *Apology* 36AB: 'Without the assistance of Anytus . . . anyone can see that he [*scil.*, Meletus] would not have had one fifth of the votes. . . .'

[1189] Cf. Plato, *Apology* 31A: 'You might easily strike me dead, as Anytus bids you to do. . . .' *Ibid.* at 30B: 'I say to you, do as Anytus bids or not as Anytus bids you to do. . . .' *Ibid.* at 29C.

[1190] Cf. Plato, *Apology* 29C: 'If . . . you are not convinced by Anytus, who said that since proceedings against me have been instituted I must be put to death, or if not put to death, that I never ought to have been prosecuted at all; and that if I should escape now, your sons will be utterly ruined by listening to me. . . .'

[1191] Cf. notes 62–65, *supra*, and the text thereto.

[1192] This incident is also referred to in Xenophon, *Memor.* 4.4.3; *Hellenica* 2.3.39; Andocides, *De mysteriis* 94. Cf. D.L. 2.24, where both the incident of Leon of Salamis and that of the generals of the Arginusae are quoted as proofs for Socrates' 'attachment to democracy'. *Epist. Socrat.* 7.1–2; Themistius, *Orat.* 2.32; [Plato], *Epist.* 7.324E–325A.

[1193] Cf. *Apology* 32B.

[1194] Cf. Plato, *Republic* 496C ff.; notes 1202 and 1317, *infra*, and the text thereto. Andocides (*De mysteriis* 101–102) tells us what happened to people who defied the Thirty Tyrants.

[1195] It is apparently the design of the Socratic apologists always to cite some sordid or absurd reason for the behaviour of Socrates' prosecutors and enemies. Cf. D.L. 2.38; Xenophon, *Defence* 29; Plato, *Apology* 20C; etc. The incident told by Xenophon does not really fit Critias, who seemed to have been an austere man. Hence it might be tempting to surmise that Antisthenes and not Xenophon originated this story. Maximus of Tyre (pp. 251 and 257, edit. Hob.) also refers to this incident, but instead of Critias he mentions Critobolus, the son of Critias. See Xenophon, *Memor.* 1.3.8–16; Athenaeus, *Deipnosophistae* 5.220; D.L. 2.49, who confounds Xenophon and Critobolus. This is due to the source he used: *On ancient luxury* by Aristippus.

[1196] The historicity of this law is very doubtful.

[1197] Cf. D.L. 2.19–20; Xenophon, *Memor.* 4.4–3.

Notes to Chapter VII

[1198] This probably refers to the charge, already mentioned in Aristophanes' *Clouds* 225 ff., that Socrates had made the worse cause appear to be the better.

[1199] Xenophon, *Memor*. 1.2.31 ff. Socrates' alleged clashes with Critias may be based on the popular assumption that Socrates was really a sophist, and as such did fall under the ban issued by Critias. The assumption that Socrates was a sophist seems to have been shared by Polycrates. Cf. Libanius 102.13 ff. and notes 579–582, *supra*.

[1200] Cf. *ibid*. at 3.2.1. The comparison of the king or political leader with a herdsman must be credited to Antisthenes who seems to follow Homer, *Iliad* 2.243.

[1201] It might be surmised, therefore, that Xenophon is here under the influence of some older text which can no longer be identified.

[1202] Cf. notes 1192–1194, *supra*, and the text thereto; note 1317, *infra*.

[1203] Libanius, chaps. 136 ff. and *ibid*. at 33.9; 90.15. It has already been pointed out that the Polycratean charge of Socrates' alleged association with Alcibiades, but not that of his keeping company with Critias, probably goes back to some Antisthenian source. Socrates' association with Critias, we may assume, was a matter of common knowledge at Athens. Cf. note 1000, *supra*.

[1204] Cf. *ibid*. at 94.10; 95.8.

[1205] Libanius 99.5, who mentions that Critias had suspended the freedom of speech. This is also intimated by Xenophon, *Memor*. 1.2.31.

[1206] Cf. Aeschines, *frags*. 1–4 (edit. Krauss); *Axiochus*, in Athenaeus, *Deipnosophistae* 5.220. See H. Dittmar, 'Aischines von Sphettos', in *Philol. Untersuch.* 21 (1912) 68 ff.; 97 ff.

[1207] *Antisth. frag*. 17 and *ibid*. at 51. Cf. H. Dittmar, *loc. cit*.

[1208] Cf. Plato, *Gorgias* 481D and *ibid*. at 519AB. This is the probable meaning of Plato, *Apology* 19DE and *ibid*. at 33A–33C, where Socrates denies that he had ever been the teacher of anyone.

[1209] The relationship of the Platonic *Symposium* to the Xenophontean *Symposium* should make an interesting study if carried out in the light of the impact which the publication of the Polycratean κατηγορία Σωκράτους had on the Socratic apologist.

[1210] Plato, *Gorgias* 518E ff. Cf. *ibid*. at 516A ff.

[1211] Cf. Pseudo-Platonic *Alcibiades I* 105B; Plato, *Gorgias* 482AB: '[Alcibiades] says one thing today and another thing tomorrow. . . .'

[1212] *Alcibiades II* relies heavily on *Alcibiades I* and the *Alcibiades* of Aeschines. Persius, in his *Fourth Satire*, seems to use the *Alcibiades I*.

[1213] This idea can still be found in Xenophon, *Memor*. 1.2.13 ff.

[1214] D.L. 6.18 and *ibid*. at 2.61.

[1215] D.L. 2.61, where we are also told that Aeschines made use of the *Alcibiades* of Antisthenes. Cf. H. Dittmar, 'Aischines von Sphettos' 97 ff. Eleven fragments of the *Alcibiades* of Aeschines have been preserved in the works of Demetrius (Περὶ ἑρμηνείας), Priscianus, Athenaeus,

Notes to Chapter VII

Maximus of Tyre, and Aelius Aristides. Cf. H. Dittmar, *op. cit.* at 266-274. Brief indications of the outline of the Aeschinean *Alcibiades* can also be found in Aelius Aristides, *Oratio* 2.292 ff. (edit. Dindorf); Cicero, *Tuscul. disp.* 3.77; and St. Augustine, *De civitate Dei* 14.8.

[1216] D.L. 2.108; Suidas, art. *Eucleides*. Of this dialogue only the title is preserved. Panaetius doubts the authenticity of the Eucleidean *Alcibiades*. D.L. 2.64. Phaedo of Elis is said to have also written a dialogue entitled *Zophyrus*, in which Alcibiades is one of the chief actors. D.L. 2.105; Cicero, *De fato* 10. Suidas, art. *Alcibiades*, claims that Phaedo also wrote a dialogue entitled *Alcibiades*. Panaetius likewise doubts the authenticity of this dialogue. Cf. D.L. 2.64. Herodicus the Cratetean, in his Πρὸς τὸν Φιλοσωκράτην, quotes an anonymous anti-Socratic poem, according to which Socrates had inquired of Aspasia how he could win the affection of Alcibiades. Cf. Athenaeus, *op. cit.* 2.219. This poem seems to reverse the relationship of Socrates and Alcibiades as stated by Plato, *Symposium* 217A ff. and *ibid.* at 219C.

[1217] Cf. Fr. Leo, *Griechisch-Römische Biographie nach ihrer literarischen Form* (1901) 118 ff., 124.

[1218] H. Dittmar, *op. cit.* at 68 ff. Cf. D.L. 6.16.

[1219] Cf. Satyrus (Athenaeus, *op. cit*, at 12.534 ff.); *Schol. ad Lucian. Jupp. conf.* 16; Bion of Borysthenes (D.L. 4.49); Olympiodorus, *op. cit.* (edit. Creuzer) 173; Arsenius, *Ionia* (edit. Walz) 507; Athenaeus, *op. cit.* 13.574.

[1220] The realization that the Alcibiades theme in the writings of Antisthenes is a form of Socratic apology necessitated by the publication of Polycrates' pamphlet, enables us also to date the Antisthenian *Alcibiades* about 392-390.

[1221] The fragments of this dialogue are collected by H. Dittmar, *op. cit.*, K. F. Hermann, *De Aischinis Socratici reliquiis* (1850), and H. Krauss, *Aischinis Socratici reliquiae* (1911). Two fragments, nos. 1 and 4, of the *Oxyrhynchus papyri* (edit. Greenfell and Hunt, London, 1919) part 13, pp. 88-94 (papyrus 1608), modify some of the reconstructions suggested by H. Dittmar. Cf. E. G. Berry, 'The Oxyrhynchus fragments of Aeschines of Sphettus', in *Transactions and Proceedings of the American Philological Association* 81 (1950) 1-8; G. C. Field, *Plato and his contemporaries* (London, 1930) 146-152 and *ibid.* at 156.

[1222] Cf. H. Dittmar, *op. cit.* at 144.

[1223] In Xenophon, *Memor.* 4.2.2-39 (4.2.2-10), Euthydemus takes the place of Alcibiades. Cf. H. Dittmar, *op. cit.* at 97 ff. and note 1240, *infra*.

[1224] Aelius Aristides, ῾Υπὲρ τῶν τεττάρων (edit. Dindorf) 2.292-294 and *ibid.* at 2.369.

[1225] Cf. E. G. Berry, *The history and development of the concept of* θεία μοῖρα *and* θεία τύχη *down to and including Plato* (Chicago, 1940). For the θεία μοῖρα of Aeschines, see *frag.* 3 (Krauss) and E. G. Berry, *op. cit.* at 43-44. Aeschines also touches on the Alcibiades theme in his dialogue *Axiochus* (D.L. 2.61). According to Herodicus the Cratetean (Athenaeus, *Deipnosophistae* 5.220), 'in his *Axiochus*, he [*scil.*, Aeschines] bitterly attacks Alcibiades as a drunken sot and an eager pursuer of other men's wives'. The *Axiochus* of Aeschines is not identical with the *Axiochus* which has been incorporated—though erroneously—into the *corpus Platonicum*. Two more fragments of the *Axiochus* of Aeschines can be found in Priscianus 18.296 (edit. Hertz 2.368; cf. H. Krauss, *op. cit.* no. 7, and *ibid.* at pp. 66 ff.) as well as in Pollux, *Onom.* Z 135 (cf. H. Krauss, *op. cit.* no. V). Lysias likewise is said to have written a *Contra Alcibiadem* of which two rather insignificant fragments survive in Athenaeus (*op. cit.* 12.534) and *Lexic. Patm.* 153. Cf. L. Gernet and M. Bizos, *Lysias* (1926) 2.270–271.

[1226] Cf. A. E. Taylor, *Philosophical studies* (London, 1934) 1–27. On page 14, Taylor disagrees with the view held by the present author that the *Alcibiades* of Aeschines is primarily apologetic. The Ἀλκιβιάδου λοιδορία of Antiphon, which is in all likelihood related to the political situation that existed at Athens in the year 418, has no connection with the particular Alcibiades literature which was called forth by the controversy over Socrates and the Polycratean attacks upon Socrates. See F. Blass, *op. cit.* 1.106; Plutarch, *Alcibiades* 3; Athenaeus, *Deipnosophistae* 12.525.

[1227] Cf. Xenophon, *Memor.* 4.2.2–39 and *ibid.* at 1.2.12–48, which seem to contain references to Themistocles and, therefore, are probably under the influence of the *Alcibiades* of Aeschines.

[1228] While Plato openly denounces Themistocles (*Gorgias* 519A and *ibid.* at 516A ff.), Aeschines apparently considers him a good statesman. Plato's negative attitude seems to have been prompted by the fact that Polycrates had praised Themistocles. Since the *Gorgias* is Plato's rejoinder to the κατηγορία of Polycrates who had extolled Themistocles, it is not altogether surprising that Plato should deprecate Themistocles and all those men whom Polycrates had called persons of excellence.

[1229] *Oxyrh. papyr.* part 13, no. 1608; *frag.* 4 (Krauss). Cf. the Pseudo-Platonic *Alcibiades I* 105A ff.; Aelius Aristides, Ὑπὲρ τῶν τεττάρων (edit. Dindorf) 2.292–304 and *ibid.* at 2.369.

[1230] Xenophon, *Memor.* 1.2.24, likewise seems to be under the influence of Aeschines' *Alcibiades*.

[1231] The same idea seems to be at the basis of an *Alcibiades* dialogue (no longer extant), where Socrates, according to the account preserved by Aelian (*Var. hist.* 2.1), reminds Alcibiades that compared with the expanse of the world all his many earthly possessions were insignificant.

[1232] Cf. Xenophon, *Memor.* 1.2.47. This idea can also be found in Plato, *Symposium* 216BC.

[1233] The discourse of Alcibiades in Plato's *Symposium* 215E ff. might also have been occasioned by the Polycratean allegation. Cf. Th. Gomperz, *Griechische Denker* 2 (3d edit.) 318.

Notes to Chapter VII

[1234] Cf., however, E. Dupréel, *La légende Socratique et les sources de Platon* (Brussels, 1922) 277 ff.

[1235] Isocrates implies here that, since Alcibiades was the most remarkable man of his day, it must be an honour to be called his teacher.

[1236] *Memor.* 1.2.12–48.

[1237] *Memor.* 3.7.4 is taken from a source which was also used by the author of *Alcibiades I* 114B; *Memor.* 3.7.6 is taken from a text which has survived in Aelian, *Var. hist.* 2.1; and *Memor.* 3.7.9 is based on a source which also underlies *Alcibiades I* 119B–124B. The *Alcibiades* of Aeschines is the probable source of the Pseudo-Platonic *Alcibiades I*, and the *Alcibiades* of Aeschines, in turn, might be under the influence of the *Alcibiades* of Antisthenes.

[1238] Xenophon (*Memor.* 3.11.1) reports about a visit of Socrates to Theodete: 'A person being present (τῶν παρόντων τινὸς) mentioned her name.' This 'person present' might have been Alcibiades, the lover of Theodete. Cf. F. Dümmler, *Kleine Schriften* 1.229 ff.; K. Joël, *op. cit.* at 2.720. Joël (*op. cit.* at 2.721 ff.) also maintains that in the Xenophontean *Symposium* Antisthenes substitutes for Alcibiades.

[1239] Charmides and Euthydemus also are mentioned together in Plato, *Symposium* 222B. It is perhaps from the Platonic *Symposium* that Xenophon derived the idea of using these two names in place of that of Alcibiades.

[1240] The problem of this man Euthydemus in itself is rather baffling. Aside from those instances where he is merely a 'straw man' for some other person, the Socratic literature refers to no less than five distinct men answering to that name: the 'lover' of Critias (Xenophon, *Memor.* 1.2.29); the disciple of Socrates (*Memor.* 4.2.1–40 and *ibid.* at 4.3.2–18; 4.5.2–12; 4.6.2–14); the 'dialectician' mentioned in Plato's *Cratylus* and *Euthydemus*; the brother of Polemarchus and Lysias (Plato, *Republic* 328A ff.); and the son of Diocles and 'lover' of Socrates (Plato, *Symposium* 222B). Athenaeus, *Deipnosophistae* 3.116, mentions a minor Athenian poet of the name Euthydemus.

[1241] In *Memor.* 4.2.11 reference is made to Euthydemus' 'kingly ambition', and in *Memor.* 4.2.1 this Euthydemus is called 'the beautiful'—two characterizations which traditionally are connected with the person of Alcibiades. Unlike Plato, Xenophon refers to this Euthydemus in a sympathetic manner. Cf. *Memor.* 4.2.40.

[1242] Cf. *ibid.* at 1.2.47.

[1243] Xenophon, *Memor.* 1.2.24, a passage which is probably under the influence of Aeschines' *Alcibiades.* Cf. note 1230, *supra.*

[1244] Cf. Athenaeus, *Deipnosophistae* 12.543C; 'Even Antisthenes ... affirms that he [*scil.*, Alcibiades] was ... manly ... and beautiful. ...'

[1245] Cf. Aeschines, *frag.* 4 (edit. Krauss).

[1246] Cf. F. Blass, *Attische Beredsamkeit* 1.336 ff.; R. C. Jebb, *The Attic orators* (London, 1876) 1.134 ff.; A. E. Raubitschek, 'The case

Notes to Chapter VII

against Alcibiades (Andocides IV)', in *Transactions and Proceedings of the American Philological Association* 79 (1948) 191 ff.

[1247] Thucydides 6.9–32.

[1248] There is no reason to surmise that the author of the *Contra Alcibiadem* had read Thucydides, or that Thucydides knew of the *Contra Alcibiadem*.

[1249] This may be gathered from *Contra Alcibiadem* 1 and *ibid.* at 2, where the author refers to himself and to his audience as ἀγαθός.

[1250] This passage probably refers to Alcibiades' implication in the profanation of the Mysteries and the mutilation of the *Hermae*.

[1251] A. E. Raubitschek, *op. cit.* at 206.

[1252] Cf. *ibid.* at 36AB; 30B; 31A.

[1253] We know of only one instance of this 'Socratic irony' in Xenophon's *Socratica: Memor.* 1.2.33–37. Cf. note 1201, *supra*.

[1254] The delay of Socrates' trial is explained in [Plato] *Epist.* 7. 325B: '... as chance would have it. ...' Plato, or whoever is the author of the seventh *Epistle*, seems to have been unable to give a definite reason for this delay.

[1255] Cf. P. Cloché, *La restauration democratique à Athènes en 403* (Paris, 1915); A. P. Dorjahn, *Political forgiveness in old Athens: The amnesty of 403 B.C.* (Evanston, 1946).

[1256] Cf. Plato, *Menexenus* 244A, where the Athenians are told to forget the battle of Munichia and live according to the terms of the Act of Oblivion. The battle of Munichia in 403, in which Critias fell (Xenophon, *Hellenica* 2.4.19), ended the reign of the Thirty Tyrants.

[1257] Cf. Andocides, *De mysteriis* (edit. Blass) 91; Aristotle, *Pol. Athen.* 39.6 and *ibid.* at 40.3.

[1258] Andocides, *op. cit.* at 91. Cf. Xenophon, *Hellenica* 2.4.43; Aristotle, *Pol. Athen.* 40.2; M. Fränkel, 'Der attische Heliasteneid', in *Hermes* 13 (1878) 452–466.

[1259] Cf. Isocrates, *Oratio* 18 (*Adv. Callimachum*), especially 1–4; Lysias, *Oratio* 6; 12; 13; 16; 18; 19; 25; 26; 31; 32 (*Oratio* 6 is probably not by Lysias, but by some unknown contemporary); Pausanias 3.9.2. For a general account of the internal affairs of Athens between the years of 403 and 399, cf. G. Grote, *History of Greece* (1879) 8.290–305; R. C. Jebb, *The Attic orators*, I (on Lysias). This brings up the question whether the trial of Socrates was not in violation of the law of Archinus in that the prosecution made allusions to matters anterior to the archonship of Eucleides. Cf. Plato, *Apology* 18A–19D. We must assume, however, that these allusions were made in the way of merely attesting to the character of Socrates.

[1260] Cf. Andocides, *De mysteriis* 81 ff.

[1261] Cf. Andocides, *op. cit.* 87.

[1262] Cf. Andocides, *op. cit.* 87; Demosthenes, *Contra Timocratem* 15.

[1263] Aristotle, *Pol. Athen.* 40.2. Cf. also Andocides, *De mysteriis* 81 ff.

Notes to Chapter VII

[1264] Cf. [Plato] *Epist.* 7.325BC, where we are told that Socrates 'was brought to trial by some powerful persons'. These powerful persons could very well have been the leaders of the restored Athenian democracy.

[1265] R. Hackforth, *The composition of Plato's Apology* (1933) 73-76, denies any and all political implications of the trial.

[1266] Cf. Josephus, *Contra Apionem* 2.264: '. . . a further charge was brought against him [*scil.*, Socrates], namely of . . . inducing youths to hold in contempt the existing constitution and the laws of their city'.

[1267] It would be interesting to speculate on whether Plutarch (or Cato) was familiar with the 'Polycratean version' of the Socratic controversy.

[1268] For a more detailed examination of these problems, see A.-H. Chroust, 'Treason and patriotism in ancient Greece', in *Journal of the History of Ideas* 15 (1954) 280-288.

[1269] Despite the constitutional reforms of Cleisthenes which dealt a severe blow to the institution of the *phratria*, the latter continued to play an important role in the political and social life of Athens. This may be gathered from the fact that among their members they continued to maintain jealously guarded special cults, feasts, and celebrations.

[1270] Aristophanes' *Ecclesiazusae* heaps ridicule upon the proposal that family ties should be abolished. Plato's *Crito* and *Republic*, on the other hand, stress patriotism above all other group considerations. Cf. N. M. Pusey, 'Alcibiades and τὸ φιλόπολι', in *Harvard Studies in Classical Philology* 51 (1940) 217 ff.; B. Haussoulier, *La vie municipale en Attique* (Paris, 1884) 196 ff.

[1271] Aside from kin attachment, friendship probably constituted the strongest tie among men known to the Greeks.

[1272] Cf. G. M. Calhoun, *Athenian clubs* (Austin, 1913) 27 ff. and *ibid.* at 39 ff.

[1273] This is clearly indicated by the fact that the Greeks severely censured any betrayal of one's friends. Plato, *Republic* 443A: 'Will a just man ever be guilty of sacrilege, or theft, or betrayal of his friends or of the city?—Never.' Apparently Plato places betrayal of one's friends, 'treason', and sacrilege in the same category.

[1274] It would be erroneous to assume—and this despite Plato's *Crito*—that the attachment of the Athenian to his city was something like the sum total of all these lesser attachments, or perhaps a 'larger loyalty' to a more comprehensive organization which comprised all these lesser groups.

[1275] This was the case in the year 411 and again in 404.

[1276] Cf. Aristotle, *Pol. Athen.* 20.1.

[1277] Cf. Plato, *Republic* 422E: '. . . not one of them is a true city, but really many cities. . . . For any city, however small, in fact is divided

Notes to Chapter VII

into two cities: the city of the poor and the city of the rich. And these two cities are at war with one another.'

[1278] Cf. Thucydides 8.54; Plato, *Theaetetus* 173D.

[1279] Cf. Polybius 20.6.5–6: 'People who had no children, instead of leaving their estate to relatives ... spent it on banquets and drinking parties, or bestowed it on their friends as common property [*scil.*, 'club property']. Many of those who had children, reserved the larger part of their estate for such convivial festivities. ...'

[1280] G. M. Calhoun, *op. cit.* at 7 ff., has pointed out that during the 'revolt' of the year 411, the members of the aristocratic clubs, who together with others engineered the overthrow of the democratic constitution of Cleisthenes, were identified with the oligarchs.

[1281] Cf. Thucydides 6.92: 'My patriotism I keep not at a time when I am being wronged, but only while I enjoyed my civil rights in security. Nor do I regard myself as one who is going against his own country, but rather as one who is recovering that country which is mine no more. The patriot, in the true sense, is not that man who, when he has unjustly lost his country, abstains from aggression against it, but he who, because of his longing for it, tries by all means to regain it.' These were the words attributed to Alcibiades when he offered his services to the Lacedaemonians against Athens, his native city. Cf. also Andocides (?), *Contra Alcibiadem* 27, where we are told that Alcibiades had considered Athenian democracy 'to be a sham'.

[1282] Cf. G. M. Calhoun, *op. cit.* at 141 ff.; N. M. Pusey, *op. cit.* at 221.

[1283] Thucydides 4.86.

[1284] If we can put any reliance in the accounts of Thucydides, Aristotle, and Xenophon, then we must assume that during the latter part of the fifth century it was far more normal to be extreme and even fanatical in one's political conduct than moderate and intelligent.

[1285] Cf. Herodotus 5.73.

[1286] Cf. Lysias, *Oratio* 12.55 ff.

[1287] Xenophon, *Hellenica* 1.7.2 and *ibid.* at 1.7.2; Lysias *Oratio* 25.25 ff.; Andocides, *De mysteriis* 96 ff.

[1288] Cf. N. M. Pusey, *op. cit.* at 230 ff.

[1289] Cf. Plato, *Apology* 36B, where Socrates emphatically denies that he was ever a member of a political 'club' or 'party'.

[1290] Xenophon, *Hellenica* 1.7.2 and *ibid.* at 1.7.8 ff.; Aristotle, *Pol. Athen.* 34.1.

[1291] Xenophon seems to allude to Socrates' membership in a 'club'. *Memor.* 3.14.1, where Xenophon apparently speaks of a 'dining club'. H. Diels, *Philosophische Aufsätze Edward Zeller gewidmet* (1887) 257–258, shows that Aristoxenus' remark (D.L. 2.20) about Socrates collecting money ($\chi\varrho\eta\mu\alpha\tau\iota\sigma\alpha\sigma\theta\alpha\iota$) refers to the collection of 'club membership dues'. See *Memor.* 1.2.18, where we are told that Critias and Alcibiades acted intelligently, 'not from fear lest they be fined or

Notes to Chapter VII

beaten. . . .' This remark may contain a reference to a club membership. As the members of a club, Critias and Alcibiades could be disciplined for having violated some club rule, either by being fined or beaten.

[1292] Cf. Xenophon, *Hellenica* 1.7.15; *Memor.* 1.1.18 and *ibid.* at 4.4.2; Plato, *Apology* 32B.

[1293] Somehow Socrates managed to escape prosecution in 406. But any reference to this incident would probably have been more damaging to Socrates than helpful.

[1294] Cf. A. E. Taylor, *Varia Socratica*, First series (1911) 30: 'I suggest, then, that one of the chief reasons for the prosecution of Socrates was that he was suspected of having been the centre of an anti-democratic ἑταιρία,' a suspicion which was strengthened by the popular belief that he was addicted to the 'foreign' cult by the Pythagoreans. Taylor's attempt to link Socrates' anti-democratic convictions with his religious convictions, in the opinion of the present author, is not convincing, unless Taylor would concede that the Pythagorean cult is here tantamount to a (political) 'club cult'. See also what A. S. Ferguson, 'The impiety of Socrates', in *Classical Quarterly* 7 (1913) 157-175, has to say about the theory advanced by Taylor.

[1295] H. Gomperz, "Sokrates' Haltung vor seinen Richtern', in *Wiener Studien* 54 (1936) 32-43; W. A. Oldfather, 'Socrates in court', in *Classical Weekly* 31, no. 21 (1938) 203-211.

[1296] This might be back of Socrates' refusal to arouse the sympathy or compassion of the judges by bringing into court his weeping wife and wailing children. Cf. notes 83-86 and 89-97 *supra*, and the text thereto. It may also explain the fact that Socrates seems to have expected that he would be condemned to death, a resignation which Xenophon (*Defence* 3 ff.) interprets as 'willingness to die'.

[1297] Cf. *ibid.* at 523E ff.; 526E-527A; *Theaetetus* 172C-175D, where the helplessness of a philosopher on trial is dramatically portrayed. The *Theaetetus* (174C) uses the expressions 'not knowing what to say' and 'become dazed'.

[1298] *Theaetetus* 172C-175D seems to be dependent on the *Gorgias*.

[1299] Maximus of Tyre, *Oratio* 3, p. 38, lines 5-18 (edit. Hobein).

[1300] Cf. here the interesting episode, recorded by Justus of Tiberias: 'In the course of the trial Plato mounted the platform [to address the judges], whereupon the judges shouted: "Get down! Get down!" ' D.L. 2.41. Apparently an effort in behalf of Socrates was actually made by some of his friends, and was 'shouted down'.

[1301] Cf. Proclus, *In Plat. Timaeum* 65, lines 22 ff. (edit. Diehl).

[1302] Plato possibly lends some support to this view. Cf. *Apology* 33A-33C, where Socrates insists that he had never been a (private) teacher (of philosophy?); that his activities had been always concerned with public matters (political issues?); and that he had never taught or professed a (philosophical?) doctrine.

Notes to Chapter VII

[1303] In Plato, *Gorgias* 473D ff., Socrates claims that he has no faith in numbers, implying thereby that he does not believe that truth can be decided 'democratically' by taking a vote. This statement could be interpreted as an 'anti-democratic' utterance. *Ibid.* at 490A: '... one wise man may often be superior to ten thousand fools, and he ought to rule them....' *Ibid.* at 513C: 'I do not share the love for the people (δήμου ἔρως),' Socrates says to Callicles. *Ibid.* at 481C–482C.

[1304] According to Xenophon, *Memor.* 3.7.1–9, Socrates persuaded Charmides, the uncle of Plato and a leading figure among the Thirty Tyrants in 404/3, to take an active part in Athenian politics. The account of Xenophon might indicate that Socrates was something like a 'political adviser' to the oligarchs. There exists a tradition, however, that not only Socrates himself, but also his 'real' disciples or followers (with the infamous exception of Critias and Alcibiades, who, after all, were not 'real' pupils of Socrates) preferred to live a private life rather than actively enter public life. This tradition is reflected in Xenophon, *Memor.* 1.2.48.

[1305] Neither Plato nor Aristotle had a favourable opinion of Athenian democracy. Cf., among others, Plato, *Gorgias* 515E; *Statesman* 303A; *Epist.* 7.326B; Aristotle, *Pol. Athen.* 25.1–3 and *ibid.* at 26.1; 27.1; 28.1 ff.; 29.1–32.3; *Politics* 1274 a 12–15. The passages from *Pol. Athen.* may be under the influence of *The Old Oligarch*, especially 1.2–9 and *ibid.* at 1.12–13.

[1306] Although Antisthenes and his social teachings had little in common with the general outlook on life held by the 'aristocrats', he fully concurred with the latter in his dislike of Athenian democracy. Antisthenes objected to democracy because it admitted to public office people who, in the opinion of the Cynic, lacked proper philosophical training.

[1307] This also holds true as regards Plato's *Apology*. Aside from dealing with the historical trial in a somewhat inaccurate and confusing manner, the Platonic *Apology* is primarily a literary testimony of Socrates' excellence of character and virtue. Cf. Xenophon, *Memor.* 4.8.11; Plato, *Phaedo* 118A.

[1308] Cf. H. Gomperz, 'Die sokratische Frage als geschichtliches Problem', in *Historische Zeitschrift* 129 (1924) 395–418.

[1309] Cf. Plato, *Apology* 19B.

[1310] K. Joël, *op. cit.* at 2.832, thinks of Archelaus who, in the opinion of F. Dümmler (*Akademika* 232 ff.), had a strong influence on Cynic teachings.

[1311] K. Joël, *op. cit.* at 2.808–895, maintains that the *Clouds* contains a large amount of Antisthenian elements. Joël (*op. cit.*) at 2.827 ff. insists that the Socrates of Aristophanes is actually Antisthenes. See K. Joël, *Geschichte der antiken Philosophie* 1.750, note 3. Joël's argument, which found little acceptance among scholars, seems to have much to recommend it.

Notes to Chapter VII

[1312] Demosthenes 54.39.

[1313] Lysias, *frag.* 53.2.

[1314] Isocrates 16.6; Plutarch, *Alcibiades* 22; Andocides, *De mysteriis* 1.12; Thucydides 6.28.

[1315] Cf. G. M. Calhoun, *Athenian clubs in politics and litigation* (1913) 36 ff.

[1316] Cf. Thucydides 6.27, where we are told that the mutilation of the *Hermae*, perpetrated by the club of Alcibiades, was considered part of 'a conspiracy to bring about a revolution and abolish democracy'.

[1317] Xenophon, *Memor.* 1.2.39. Cf. also notes 916, 918 and 1141–1148, *supra*, and the text thereto.

[1318] Plato, *Apology* 31c–32a.

[1319] Plato, *Republic* 496c–496e.

[1320] Cf. *Epist.* 5.322b, where the author explains the reason for Plato's abstention from taking an active part in Athenian political life: 'Plato ... found the democratic regime ... accustomed ... to many forms of action quite different from what he would advise. For nothing would have pleased him more than to have offered advice to the people ... if he had not realized that he would have been running useless risks where there was no prospect of doing any good.'

[1321] Cf. *ibid.* at 4.5.1–2.

[1322] Libanius, 77.13 and *ibid.* at 33.20. See notes 536–539, *supra*. Polycrates seems to have implied that Socrates was very active politically from his 'private station'.

[1323] After the death of Pericles in 429 the inner-political situation at Athens had entered a state of constant strain and turmoil, aggravated by the changing fortunes of the Peloponnesian War and the many unfortunate diplomatic, political, and military blunders of the democratic leaders. The realization that the last quarter of the fifth century above all was a period of intense political strife at Athens in which Socrates probably played an important role, might be of some help in understanding the historical Socrates.

[1324] H. Maier, *Sokrates, sein Werk und seine geschichtliche Bedeutung* (Tübingen, 1913) 294–295. Cf. *ibid.* note 1: 'I wish to stress still another point: the historians who have tried to turn Socrates into a "philosopher" and who have essayed to discover his philosophical doctrine, have too readily ignored the fact that he never wrote anything.'

[1325] Cf. A.-H. Chroust, 'Philosophy: its essence and meaning in the ancient world', in *Philosophical Review* 56, no. 1 (1947) 19 ff.

[1326] Cf. Xenophon, *Memor.* 1.2.31, where we are told that Critias levelled against Socrates 'charges that had been imputed to all philosophers by the masses'. These 'popular charges' were also used by Aristophanes.

Notes to Chapter VIII

NOTES TO CHAPTER VIII—PAGES 198–226

[1327] Some of these Late, or Rhetorical, Sophists were Antiphon, Thrasymachus of Chalcedon, Critias, Theodorus of Byzantium, Andocides, Anaximenes, Zoilus, and Isaeus. F. Blass, *Attische Beredsamkeit* 2.91.203 and *ibid.* at 2.244–399.

[1328] Cf. notes 1397–1398, *infra*, and the text thereto.

[1329] Cf. Xenophon, *Memor.* 1.2.31; D.L. 2.19–20.

[1330] Cf. I. Bruns, *Das literarische Porträt der Griechen* (1896) 194–196.

[1331] K. Joël, *Der echte und der xenophontische Sokrates* 2.705, claims that the κατηγορία Σωκράτους of Polycrates was directed against Antisthenes and not against Socrates.

[1332] Cf. Isocrates, *Busiris* 4–5.

[1333] In itself the Polycratean pamphlet does not seem to have been a work of great literary importance. Cf. Isocrates, *Busiris* 4.5.

[1334] Cf. J. Geffken, 'Studien zu Platons Gorgias', in *Hermes* 65 (1930) 20 and *ibid.* at 22.

[1335] The enmity between Plato and Antisthenes is the subject of many anecdotes. Plato, *Sophist* 251B; *et passim*; D.L. 3.35: 'Thereupon he [*scil.*, Antisthenes] wrote a dialogue against Plato and entitled it *Sathon.*' In this dialogue he probably claimed, among other things, that Plato was a conceited and showy person. Cf. D.L. 6.7 and *ibid.* at 6.16. Sathon (Σάθων), which is actually a pun on the name of Plato (Πλάτων), means the *membrum virile*. See Athenaeus, *Deipnosophistae* 5.220.

[1336] It is not likely that the *Crito* constitutes Plato's reply to the Polycratean κατηγορία, as Christ-Schmid assumes (*Geschichte der griechischen Literatur*, 6th edit., 1.676 ff.). The *Crito* is much too restrained for such a task. Cf. T. Gomperz, *Griechische Denker* (3d edit.) 2.289; H. Maier, *Sokrates* 132; Christ-Schmid, *op. cit.* 1.682; A.-H. Chroust, 'Socrates—a source problem', in *The New Scholasticism* 29, no. 1 (1945) 50, note 21.

[1337] Isocrates, *Busiris* 4–5 and *ibid.* at 48.

[1338] Cf. *ibid.* at 463B; 465B; 501A.

[1339] *Ibid.* at 521E.

[1340] Cf. Plato, *Gorgias* 448A ff. and *ibid.* at 461CD.

[1341] F. Blass, *op. cit.* 2.82–85.

[1342] The Socratics must have taken the κατηγορία Σωκράτους of Polycrates very seriously. This may be gathered from the many apologies answering the Polycratean pamphlet, such as the *Defence* and *Memor.* 1.1.1–1.2.64 of Xenophon, the *Gorgias* of Plato, the *Apology* of Lysias, the *Apology* of Theodectes, etc. As to the *Apology* of Theodectes, cf. F. Blass, *Attische Beredsamkeit* 2.447 and note 390, *supra*.

[1343] Cf. notes 805 and 935–936, *supra*.

Notes to Chapter VIII

[1344] This interpretation of Plato, *Meno* 95A ff., is contradicted by M. Schanz (*Apologia* 91) and F. Dümmler (*Akademika* 28), but supported by R. Hirzel, 'Polykrates' Anklage und Lysias' Verteidigung des Sokrates', in *Rheinisches Museum* 42 (1887) 249 ff.

[1345] The lenient treatment which Anytus receives from the hands of Plato would also lend some support to our theory that originally the whole controversy over Socrates was primarily a political debate.

[1346] K. Joël, *Der echte und der xenophontische Sokrates* 2.1121 ff.

[1347] This might also be one of the reasons why Plato, perhaps prompted by jealousy, disliked Antisthenes so intensely. Cf. note 1335, *supra*, and the text thereto.

[1348] Cf. Libanius 20.14 ff. and *ibid.* at 30.2; 38.1; 78.15; 36.13; 3.18 ff. See notes 289–291, 425–426, 432–433, 443–449, 451–461, 519–520, 808–819, 938 and 939, *supra*.

[1349] Cf. Aristotle, *Rhetoric* 1393 b 3–8, which is based either on the κατηγορία of Polycrates, or *Memor.* 1.2.29, or on some Antisthenian source.

[1350] *Memor.* 1.2.10–11. See notes 432–434 and 455, *supra*.

[1351] Cf. D.L. 6.5 and *ibid.* at 6.6; 6.8; Plato, *Phaedrus* 260C and notes 940–984, *supra*; Aristotle, *Rhetoric* 1284 a 15–17, where Aristotle discusses political equality and the privileged status of men of preeminent virtue: 'Anyone would be ridiculous who should attempt to make laws for them. They would probably reply what, in the fable of Antisthenes, the lions said to the hares, when in the assembly of the animals the latter began haranguing and demanding equality for all.' The story told by Aristotle probably is based on some Antisthenian source. Cf. *The Old Oligarch* 1.2 and *ibid.* at 1.6–9.

[1352] Cf. Plato, *Protagoras* 319B ff. and the whole tenor of the *Gorgias* and *Euthyphro* 4A ff. It appears also, on the other hand, that Socrates objected to the abuses which went hand in hand with the Athenian territorial and economic expansion after the Persian Wars. See also *The Old Oligarch* 1.14–20 and *ibid.* at 2.10–16; Plato, *Apology* 29DE: 'Are you not ashamed of hoarding the greatest of wealth. . . .' *Ibid.* at 30AB: '. . . do not think too much about . . . your property and possessions. . . .' *Ibid.* at 41E; *Cleitophon* 407B ff.

[1353] Xenophon, *Memor.* 1.2.56–61. Cf. Libanius 48.12 and *ibid.* at 61.14; 62.7; 63.4; 67.17; 72.2; 72.8 ff.; 73.7; 73.10 and notes 348–353, 492–520, 864–869, and 1040–1067, *supra*.

[1354] Cf. D.L. 6.15–18.

[1355] The diatribe (διατριβή) was originally synonymous with the dialogue (διάλογος). Cf. Plato, *Apology* 37D, where Socrates maintains that the Athenians are condemning him because they cannot bear τὰς ἐμὰς διατριβὰς καὶ τοὺς λόγους. D.L. 2.48 reports that Aristippus wrote six diatribes. The diatribe is a 'popularized' form of dialogue which makes much use of anecdotes and quotations, frequently

Notes to Chapter VIII

fictitious. Xenophon, *Memor.* 1.6.14. Unlike the Platonic dialogue, the diatribe as well as the χρεία, is never a 'heuristic' or 'zetetic' (ζητητικός, D.L. 3.49) argument, but rather a simple exposition.

[1356] Cf. D.L. 6.15–18, who mentions the following Antisthenian works dealing with Homer and the Homeric poems: *Ajax or, The speech of Ajax; Odysseus or, Concerning Odysseus; On Homer; On Chalcas; On the Odyssey; Athena or, Of Telemachus; Of Helen and Penelope; Cyclops or, Of Odysseus; Of the use of wine or, Of intoxication or, Of the Cyclops; Of Odysseus; Of Odysseus, Penelope and the dog.*

[1357] Some scholars have conjectured that the collection of verses which has come down under the name of Theognis includes many Cynic additions.

[1358] This is suggested by Xenophon, *Memor.* 1.2.56–58, where he uses a quotation from Hesiod's *Works and Days* 309. Cf. notes 348, 503–505, and 1043–1044, *supra*. Although D.L. (6.15–18) does not mention a specific Antisthenian title referring to Hesiod, we may surmise that Antisthenes wrote on, as well as interpreted, Hesiod. Plato's *Charmides* (163B) contains the same Hesiodic quotation which is cited in connection with a passage where Critias defends the Antisthenian definition of wisdom (σωφροσύνη). According to Antisthenes, wisdom signifies τὰ ἑαυτοῦ πράττειν (doing one's own business). Cf. Plato, *Symposium* 204E; *Charmides* 161B; E. Zeller, *Philosophie der Griechen* 2 (4th edit.) part 1, 304, note 1. Hence we may assume that this particular Hesiodic passage was quoted and discussed in one of Antisthenes' writings.

[1359] Xenophon, *Memor.* 1.2.56.

[1360] Cf. notes 702–704, *supra*.

[1361] Cf. Plato, *Charmides* 163C: 'Things nobly and usefully made he [*scil.*, Hesiod] called works (ἔργα), and such things he styled workings (πράξεις) and deeds (ποιήσεις). And he must be supposed to have called such things only the proper business of man (πράξεις τὰς τοιαύτας ποιήσεις), and what is harmful not the proper business of man (τὰ δὲ βλαβερὰ πάντα ἀλλότρια).'

[1362] Cf. Libanius 61.17.

[1363] Contrary to the views held by Critias in *Charmides* 163B.

[1364] *Charmides* 163A. Πράττειν τὰ τῶν ἄλλων is not ποιεῖν τὰ τῶν ἄλλων. The latter signifies the senseless minding of someone else's business. Πράττειν τὰ τῶν ἄλλων on the other hand, means doing some useful work for others.

[1365] Cf. D.L. 6.12: 'To the wise man nothing is foreign or impractical.' —E. Zeller, *loc. cit.*, has pointed out that the Hesiodic statement is a 'corollary' to the Antisthenian τὰ ἑαυτοῦ πράττειν. The derogatory remarks of Critias about tradesmen in the *Charmides* 163B, however, is his own personal contribution. Critias seems to utter here a general and apparently deeply rooted prejudice harboured by the Athenian gentry against certain forms of manual labour.

Notes to Chapter VIII

[1366] Cf. Plato, *Euthydemus* 281B; note 973, *supra*, and the text thereto; note 809, *supra*.

[1367] Cf. Plato, *Euthyphro* 7A.

[1368] If we concede that *Memor.* 3.9.14 and *ibid.* at 3.9.15 belong together, then we must also admit that there exists a close connection between *Memor.* 3.9.14–15 and *ibid.* at 1.2.56–57.

[1369] See Plato, *Republic* 434D: 'The power of each individual ... is to do his own work.' *Ibid.* at 433D: 'Justice is ... the quality of every one performing his own business.' Cf. *ibid.* at 434A ff.; 397E ff.; 351A ff.; *Gorgias* 470B ff.; *Laws* 716A ff. Plato's idea, which could very well be of Antisthenian origin, is that every man within a harmonious society must be assigned to the task for which he is best fitted. Once assigned to this task, he must perform it to the best of his ability. A.-H. Chroust, 'The function of law and justice in the ancient world and the middle ages', in *Journal of the History of Ideas* 7, no. 3 (1946) 298–320, especially 299 ff.

[1370] Cf. D.L. 6.46. Gambling, according to the Cynics, is no 'work' in that it does not measure up to their concept of a noble and useful activity. See notes 1052–1056, *supra*.

[1371] Cf. Plato (?), *Alcibiades I* 127AB.

[1372] Plato, *Charmides* 163C; *Republic* 433E: 'Justice is the having and doing what is in accord with one's own [or, one's nature]. . . .'

[1373] Cf., however, notes 702–713, *supra*.

[1374] Cf. D.L. 6.36: '[Diogenes] gave some one a piece of cheese to carry, worth half an obol. When the other declined to do this, he remarked: "The friendship between you and me is broken by a little cheese costing half an obol." ' D.L. 6.12: 'Diocles records the following sayings [of Antisthenes]: "To the wise man nothing is foreign or impracticable (ἄπορον)." '

[1375] Libanius 61.17 and notes 541–542, *supra*.

[1376] Plato, *Apology* 29DE; D.L. 6.27–28.

[1377] Cf. Xenophon, *Defence* 19.

[1378] Aside from the generally 'anti-social' teachings of Antisthenes and his disciples, see Plato, *Apology* 29DE and *ibid.* at 23C; 31C–32A; 30B; 36B; 41E; *Gorgias* 521D and *ibid.* at 515D; *Cleitophon* 407A ff. Of the works of Antisthenes, Polycrates probably consulted the political pamphlet which, although no longer extant, seems to have left its imprint on the *Cleitophon* and *Oratio* 13 of Dio Chrysostom. The comic poets of the late fifth century (the *Clouds* of Aristophanes, the *Konnos* of Ameipsias, and the *Flatterers* of Eupolis) already had charged Socrates with 'loafing'.

[1379] Cf. *ibid.* at 1.2.49–50; *Defence* 20 and notes 175, 335–347, 479–484, 490, 793–806, 883–887 and 1010–1035, *supra*.

[1380] Cf. D.L. 6.12: 'A good man deserves our affection. Men of worth are friends. Make friends and allies of men who are both brave and just. . . . Treasure an honest man above a kinsman.' *Ibid.* at 6.105: 'The wise man deserves to be loved . . . [he is] a friend of his kind.' *Ibid.* at 6.6: 'If brothers are of one mind (ὁμονοοῦντες) no fortress is as strong as their common life.' What Antisthenes stresses here is not 'brotherly affection' (φιλία) based on the ties of kinship, but rather the ὁμόνοια. And ὁμόνοια, according to the *Cleitophon* (409DE), is the foundation of all true friendship and as such is always subordinated to the idea of moral improvement. Similar ideas can be found in Aristotle, *Nicomachean Ethics* 1156 b 6 ff. See, however, D.L. 6.65; notes 793–806, 883–887 and 1010–1035, *supra*.

[1381] Similar ideas can be detected in Plato's *Lysis* 210B ff. and the *Cleitophon* 409D.

[1382] Cf. note 1355, *supra*.

[1383] Cf. D.L. 6.1 and *ibid.* at 6.3; 6.11; 6.30; 6.34; 6.71; 6.72–73; 6.88; *Antisth. frag.* 47 and *ibid.* at 55; 59.

[1384] D.L. 6.72 and *ibid.* at 6.86; 6.95. Epictetus, *Diss.* 3.24.68.

[1385] D.L. 6.26 and *ibid.* at 6.104.

[1386] D.L. 6.8 and *ibid.* at 6.28; 6.29; 6.93.

[1387] D.L. 6.72.

[1388] D.L. 6.11 and *ibid.* at 6.72.

[1389] D.L. 6.12 and *ibid.* at 6.29; 6.38; 6.63; 6.72; 6.93; *Antisth. frag.* 59; Epictetus, *Diss.* 3.24.66.

[1390] D.L. 6.11 and *ibid.* at 6.27–28; 6.73; 6.103–104.

[1391] D.L. 6.11.

[1392] D.L. 6.26 and *ibid.* at 6.32; 6.73; 6.79.

[1393] D.L. 6.11 and *ibid.* at 6.32; 6.37; 6.46; 6.53; 6.69; 6.88–89; 6.96.

[1394] D.L. 6.24 and *ibid.* at 6.29; 6.73; *Antisth. frag.* 24 (Mullach).

[1395] The case of Anytus and his son would be in point. Cf. Plato, *Apology* 33D–34D; Xenophon, *Defence* 29, and notes 804–805, *supra*.

[1396] Xenophon, *Memor.* 1.2.52. Cf. *ibid.* at 1.2.49; Libanius 70.17, where we are told that Socrates cast such a magic spell over his followers that they thought more of him than of their own fathers or older brothers. Cf. notes 175, 335–347, 479–484, 490, 793–806, 1010–1035 and 1379–1380, *supra*.

[1397] This theory finds support in the fact that around the year 390, that is, about two years after the publication of the Polycratean κατηγορία Σωκράτους, Lysias composed a Ὑπὲρ Σωκράτους πρὸς Πολυκράτην. Cf. Isocrates, *Busiris* 4; *Scholia ad Aristidem* (edit. Dindorf) 1133.16; note 88, *supra*, and the text thereto.

[1398] Cf. *ibid.* at 2.58 (Plato and Xenophon 'were jealous of each other') and 3.34: 'And although both [*scil.*, Xenophon and Plato) make mention of Socrates, neither of the two refers to the other, except that Xenophon mentions Plato in the third book of his *Memorabilia*.' The passage to which Diogenes Laertius refers here can be found in *Memor.* 3.6.1. Plato, *Menexenus* 244B, praises those who assisted the Persian

King (Artaxerxes). This remark may contain a slap at Xenophon who had joined Cyrus in his futile attempt at dethroning Artaxerxes. Herodicus (Athenaeus, *Deipnosophistae* 11.504E ff.), Marcellinus (*Vita Thucyd.* 27), and Gellius (*Attic nights* 14.3) likewise report that Plato and Xenophon were 'rivals' and jealous of each other.

[1399] Xenophon, *Defence* 1.

[1400] Cf. H. Maier, *Sokrates* 44.

[1401] Despite the attitude which Xenophon displays in *Memor.* 1.4.1, he himself frequently characterizes Socrates' activities as protreptics. Cf. *Memor.* 1.2.64 and *ibid.* at 1.7.1; 2.1.1; 2.5.1; 4.3.1 ff.; 4.8.11; *et passim*.

[1402] Since Plato's *Euthydemus* makes a caricature of Antisthenes and his eristic dialectics or protreptics, it is not impossible that Xenophon might be here under the influence of the *Euthydemus*, as may be gathered from *Memor.* 1.4.1. This, then, would also explain why Xenophon should maintain that the τινές had insisted that Socrates ἐρωτῶν ἤλεγχεν.

[1403] Cf. *Memor.* 4.3.2: 'That such was the tenor of his [*scil.*, Socrates'] conversation may be gathered from the current accounts written down [or recorded] by others (ἄλλοι). . . .' *Ibid.* at 1.4.1: 'A belief is current among certain people (τινές), in accordance with views advanced by some (ἔνιοι) about Socrates both orally and in writing. . . .' Here, too, we encounter the story that some people 'wrote down' the sayings of Socrates. Naturally, these 'others' are Antisthenes and his followers. According to *Memor.* 4.3.2 and *ibid.* at 1.4.1, Antisthenes and his followers would be the authors of the first λόγοι Σωκρατικοί.

[1404] This idea, which is also found in the Platonic *Euthydemus*, has been taken up by Plutarch, *Moralia* 798B, and Cicero, *De oratore* 1.47.204.

[1405] Cf. K. Joël, *op. cit.* 1.51 ff. and *ibid.* at 1.547 ff.

[1406] Cf. *Memor.* 4.3.2, quoted in note 1403, *supra*.

[1407] Cf. notes 1398–1400, *supra*, and the text thereto.

[1408] In *Memor.* 1.2.19 Xenophon refers to 'some self-styled philosophers' who maintained that 'a just man can never become unjust'. Judging from D.L. 6.12 ('Virtue is a weapon that cannot be taken away'), or *ibid.* at 6.105 ('They [the Cynics] hold that virtue . . . once acquired cannot be lost'), it can be assumed that these 'self-styled philosophers' are Antisthenes and his followers. Cf. Plato, *Protagoras* 340D and *ibid.* at 344D. In *Symposium* 4.56 ff. and *ibid.* at 4.61 ff., Xenophon refers to Antisthenes in a very unflattering manner by calling him a 'go-between' or 'procurer'.

[1409] It is surmised here that Plato's *Apology* was written after 393/2, that is, after the publication of the κατηγορία Σωκράτους of Polycrates. Cf. R. Hackforth, *The Composition of Plato's Apology* (Cambridge, 1933) 8–46. If this assumption should prove correct, then it may also

Notes to Chapter VIII

be maintained that the Platonic *Apology* was motivated by the publication of the κατηγορία, even though Plato makes a studied effort to ignore the particular content of the Polycratean pamphlet. It has been maintained (*see* chap. VI, at the beginning) that certain passages in Plato's *Apology* (33C ff. and *ibid.* at 29B) may possibly reflect the influence of the Polycratean κατηγορία.

[1410] Cf. the interesting story recorded by D.L. (3.35): 'They say that, on hearing Plato read the *Lysis*, Socrates exclaimed, "By Heracles, what a pack of lies this young man is telling about me." For he has included in his dialogue much that Socrates never said.' This passage, if we can attach to it any credence, poses a number of problems. The exclamation, 'By Heracles', is definitely Cynic. Cf. Plato, *Euthyphro* 4A. This would suggest that Diogenes Laertius (or his source) may have confounded here Socrates and Antisthenes. It is also very unlikely that Plato should have written the *Lysis* during the lifetime of Socrates. This, too, would lend support not only to our contention that Diogenes Laertius confounds here Socrates and Antisthenes, but would also confirm our suspicion that many of the statements and deeds attributed to Socrates were actually Antisthenes'.

[1411] Cf. notes 1474 and 1475, *infra*.

[1412] Cf. notes 1323–1324, *supra*.

[1413] Cf. Xenophon, *Defence* 26; Plato, *Apology* 41B.

[1414] Diels-Kranz, *Die Fragmente der Vorsokratiker*, 5th edit. (Berlin, 1935) 82 B 11a; F. Blass, *Antiphontis orationes et fragmenta*, 2d edit. (1892) 159–174.

[1415] Cf. note 207, *supra*.

[1416] Cf. Plato, *Apology* 28B ff. and *ibid.* at 35A; 38D.

[1417] Cf. Plato, *Apology* 28B and *ibid.* at 30CD; 32A; 38A; 39A; 41CD; Xenophon, *Defence* 3. See Plato, *Crito* 43BC; *Gorgias* 526D.

[1418] Cf. Plato, *Apology*, 28A and *ibid.* at 29BC; 30B.

[1419] Cf. Plato, *Apology* 24C.

[1420] Cf. Plato, *Apology* 18D and *ibid.* at 19AB; 23E–24A; 24B; 28AB.

[1421] Cf. Plato, *Apology* 17B and *ibid.* at 19DE; Xenophon, *Memor.* 1.2.1–2; *Defence* 24–25.

[1422] Cf. Plato, *Apology* 31C and *ibid.* at 33D–34A; Xenophon, *Defence* 19; *Memor.* 1.2.56–57.

[1423] Cf. Plato, *Apology* 19C–19D and *ibid.* at 31C; 33AB; Xenophon, *Defence* 16 and *ibid.* at 18; 26; *Memor.* 1.2.1 and *ibid.* at 1.2.6–7.— Compare the wording of *Palamedes* 15: τούτων δε ἐμοὶ πρόσεστιν οὐδέν, ὡς δ' ἀληθῆ λέγω, μάρτυρα πιστὸν παρέξομαι τὸν παροιχόμενον βίον; and Plato, *Apology* 19C: ἀλλὰ γὰρ ἐμοὶ τούτων . . . οὐδὲν μέτεστιν, as well as *ibid.* at 31C: ἱκανὸν γάρ, οἶμαι, ἐγὼ παρέχομαι τὸν μάρτυρα, ὡς ἀληθῆ λέγω, τὴν πενίαν.

[1424] Cf. Plato, *Apology* 18B and *ibid.* at 26B; 39C; 38A; Xenophon, *Defence* 24–25; *Memor.* 1.1.2 and *ibid.* at 1.1.17.

Notes to Chapter VIII

1425 Cf. Plato, *Apology* 26A–28A; Xenophon, *Defence* 19. Compare the wording in *Palamedes* 26: οὐ σοφός εἰμι. ὥστε δι'ἀμφότερα ἂν εἴης ψευδής; and Plato, *Apology* 26A: ἄκων, ὥστε σύ γε κατ' ἀμφότερα ψεύδει.

1426 Cf. Plato, *Apology* 36B–37A and *ibid.* at 37BC; Xenophon, *Defence* 21.

1427 Cf. Plato, *Apology* 30CD. See also *Apology* 18A and *ibid.* at 20D; 21A; 21B; 31E, where Socrates asks his judges not to resent his statements.

1428 Plato, *Apology* 17A ff. and *ibid.* at 19AB; 37A; Xenophon, *Defence* 1 and *ibid.* at 9; 14.

1429 Cf. Xenophon, *Defence* 11 and *ibid.* at 16; *Memor.* 1.1.10–11.

1430 Cf. Plato, *Apology* 29DE and *ibid.* at 30AB; 36D; Xenophon, *Memor.* 1.1.11 and *ibid.* at 1.2.60–61; 1.2.7. See especially Plato, *Apology* 36C: ἐπὶ δὲ τὸ ἰδίᾳ ἕκαστον ἰὼν εὐεργετεῖν τὴν μεγίστην εὐεργεσίαν.

1431 Cf. Plato, *Apology* 25A ff. and *ibid.* at 31AB; 37B; 37E–38A; Xenophon, *Memor.* 1.1.18 and *ibid.* at 1.1.20; 1.2.1–3.

1432 Cf. Xenophon, *Defence* 23; Plato, *Apology* 36B ff.

1433 Cf. Plato, *Apology* 19AB and *ibid.* at 23C; 24B; 28D ff.; 32A ff.; 33A ff.; 37A; Xenophon, *Memor.* 1.1.16 and *ibid.* at 1.2.1–11; 1.2.18; 1.2.63; *Defence* 9 and *ibid* at 16. The contrast of 'the old' and 'the new' also appears in Plato, *Apology* 33A and *ibid* at 33D ff.; 37D; and the opposition of 'the rich' (εὐτυχοῦντες) and 'the distressed' (δυστυχοῦντες) is reflected in Plato, *Apology* 33B.

1434 Cf. Plato, *Apology* 34CD and *ibid.* at 35BC; 35D; 37A ff.; 38DE; Xenophon, *Defence* 4. See *Memor.* 4.4.4.

1435 Cf. Plato, *Apology* 17A ff. and *ibid.* at 18A ff.; 19B–19D; 34A; 35CD; Xenophon, *Memor.* 1.1.17; *Defence* 18.

1436 Cf. Plato, *Apology* 32A and *ibid.* at 35D; 38C; 39C.

1437 Cf. Plato, *Apology* 38D. See note 1431, *supra*.

1438 Cf. Plato, *Apology* 29DE and *ibid.* at 30AB; 37A; 39CD; Xenophon, *Memor.* 1.1.17; *Defence* 26.

1439 Cf. J. Geffken, *Griechische Literaturgeschichte* 2 (1934) 20 and note 51; E. Wolff, 'Plato's Apologie', in *Neue philologische Abhandlungen* 6 (1929) 67; H. Gomperz, *Sophistik und Rhetorik* (1912) 9–11; J. Morr, *Die Entstehung der platonischen Apologie* (Reichenberg, 1929) 29 ff.

1440 Frag. 470 (anonym.). Cf. frag. 96.

1441 Aeschylus, *Prometheus Bound* 436 ff.

1442 Cf. Dio Chrysostom, *Oratio* 13.21.

1443 F. Dümmler, 'Zum Herakles des Antisthenes', in *Philologus* 50 (1891) 295–296. Xenophon (*Cynegeticus* 1.1) later maintained that it was not Odysseus (whom he admired) who, as it is commonly believed, had brought about the death of Palamedes, but some evil people who are not further identified. In *Memor.* 4.2.33, however, he had insisted that Palamedes was killed by Odysseus.

Notes to Chapter VIII

[1444] O. Frick, *Xenophontis quae fertur Apologia Socratis num genuina putanda est* (Halle, 1909) 159.

[1445] Cf. Xenophon, *Symposium* 1.5 and *ibid.* at 2.26; *Anabasis* 2.6.16.

[1446] Cf. Gorgias, *Defence of Palamedes* 25.

[1447] Cf. F. Blass, *op. cit.* 1.77, note 3: 'The tragedy of Euripides is not the model used [by Gorgias in his *Palamedes*].' L. Radermacher, 'Über den Cynegeticus des Xenophon', in *Rheinisches Museum* 52 (1897) 24, note 2.

[1448] The 'Palamedes myth' has also been treated by Alcidamas (?), *Odysseus or, Concerning the betrayal of Palamedes*, in F. Blass, *Antiphontis orationes et fragmenta*, 2d edit. (1892) 183-193.

[1449] Cf. C. Müller, *Fragmenta Historicorum Graecorum* 3.163, frag. 14.

[1450] Cf. Plutarch, *Pericles* 6.

[1451] Plato, *Apology* 26D.

[1452] D.L. 2.14. Cf. *frag.* 9 (Hill.).

[1453] Xenophon, *Defence* 8. Cf. *ibid.* at 6-7.

[1454] C. Müller, *Fragmenta Historicorum Graecorum* 3.43, *frag.* 31.

[1455] Cf. notes 299-334, *supra*.

[1456] C. Müller, *Fragmenta Historicorum Graecorum* 3.70, *frag.* 90. Cf. also Diels-Kranz, *op. cit.* 59 A 17; Plutarch, *Pericles* 49.

[1457] Cf. Philodemus, *Rhetoric* 2.180 (edit. Sudhaus), *frag.* 7.

[1458] Aristotle, *Rhetoric* 1398 b 15.

[1459] The same story is also told of Pericles. Cf. Diels-Kranz, *op. cit.* 80 B 90; D.L. 2.35.

[1460] D.L. 2.6-7. Cf. Plutarch, *Pericles* 28.

[1461] D.L. 2.7.

[1462] D.L. 2.10. An interesting parallel to this story would be Plato, *Theaetetus* 173E, where we are told that the philosopher's mind, 'disdaining the pettiness ... of human affairs, flies all about ... measuring earth and the heavens. ... But it does not condescend to anything which is within reach.'

[1463] Aristotle, *Nicomachean Ethics* 1179 a 13.

[1464] Cf. Plato, *Apology* 21A.

[1465] As to the sources for the life of Antiphon, cf. Thucydides 8.68; Pseudo-Plutarch, *Vit. decem. orat.*; Philostratus, *Vita Apollonii* 1.15; Photius, *Cod.* 259. Philostratus and Photius derived their information from Pseudo-Plutarch, *Vit. decem. orat.*, while the author of the *Vit. decem. orat.* relied on Caecilius of Calacte who wrote during the time of Emperor Augustus. Cf. J. S. Morrison, 'Xenophon, *Memorabilia* 1.6.: The encounters of Socrates and Antiphon', in *The Classical Journal* 3 (1953) 3-6. Morrison maintains that this Antiphon could very well be Antiphon of Rhamnus.

[1466] Cf. A.-H. Chroust, 'Socrates—a source problem', in *The New Scholasticism* 19, no. 1 (1945) 48-72.

[1467] Cf. W. Fite, *The Platonic Legend* (1934) 102.

Notes to Chapter VIII

[1468] Cf. K. Joël, *Der echte und der xenophontische Sokrates* 1.257–258.

[1469] This would also explain Socrates' contention that 'concerning these matters [*scil.*, philosophical speculations] I do not pretend to know much or little. . . . I have nothing to do with physical speculation . . . and many of those present here are witnesses to the truth of what I am saying. . . .' Plato, *Apology* 19CD. Cf. *ibid.* at 19DE; Xenophon, *Memor.* 1.1.11–15, where Socrates denies that he was ever interested in physical speculations. See A.-H. Chroust, 'Socrates and pre-Socratic Philosophy', in *The Modern Schoolman* 29, no. 2 (1952) 119 ff. It may be interesting to conjecture that the famous Socratic dictum, 'I know that I know nothing' (cf. *Laches* 200E; *Charmides* 175A ff.; *Hippias Minor* 372E ff. and *ibid.* at 372E; 376C; *Meno* 80B; *Apology* 21D and 23B), is Socrates' way of professing that he was not a philosopher.

[1470] Cf. note 791, *supra*.

[1471] Cf. A.-H. Chroust, 'Socrates in the light of Aristotle's testimony', in *The New Scholasticism* 26, no. 3 (1952) 327–365; Th. Deman, *Le temoignage d'Aristote sur Socrate, Collection d'études anciennes, publiée sous le patronage de l'Association Budé* (Paris 1942).

[1472] Cf. H. Gomperz, 'Die sokratische Frage als geschichtliches Problem', in *Historische Zeitschrift* 129 (1924) 419: 'Of all the Socratics it is Antisthenes to whom Socrates is closest.' It would perhaps have been better if Gomperz had said: 'Of all the Socratic legends it was probably the legend created by Antisthenes which became the most influential and sensational.'

[1473] Cf. notes 921–929, *supra*, and the text thereto.

[1474] Aristotle, *Poetics* 1447 b 9 ff. Cf. *Rhetoric* 1417 a 20 and *frag.* 61 (1485 b 38 ff.); L. Robin, 'Les mémorables de Xenophon et nôtre connaissance de la philosophie de Socrate', in *L'année philosophique* (1911) 26; K. Joël, 'Der λόγος Σωκρατικός', in *Archiv für Geschichte der Philosophie* 8 (1894) 466 ff.

[1475] Plato, *Symposium* 215D. The italics are supplied. Cf. H. Maier, *Sokrates* (1913) 106, note 1: 'No one would contest the fact that, like all Platonic dialogues, the *Apology* [of Plato] is nothing other than fictitious λόγοι Σωκρατικοί. *Ibid.* note 2: '. . . no one would deny the fictitious nature of the λόγοι Σωκρατικοί'. *Ibid.* at 38, note 1: '. . . the unhistorical nature of the λόγοι cannot be denied'. See notes 921–929, *supra*, and the text thereto. Note 1410, *supra*.

[1476] O. Gigon, *Sokrates* (1947) 315.

Index

(*Plain number refers to page,* n *before number refers to footnote*)

Achilles, 159, n870
Acumenus, 29
Adeimantus (brother of Plato), 34, 168
Aeantodorus, 34
Aelian, 69, 94, 102, 166, n589, n644, n677, n736, n745, n836, n1032, n1156, n1231, n1237
Aelius Aristides, 176, n217, n518, n1215, n1224, n1229
Aeschines the Orator, 58, 95, 136, n328, n1000, n1172
Aeschines of Sphettus, 1, 8, 59, 97, 102, 106, 137, 138, 174, 175, 176, 177, 178, 191, 211, n115, n174, n1166, n1206, n1215, n1225, n1226, n1227, n1228, n1230, n1231, n1243, n1245; his *Alcibiades*, 175 ff., n1212, n1215, n1221, n1230, n1237, n1243; his *Alcibiades* occasioned by the κατηγορία Σωκράτους 176, n1226
Aeschylus, 218, n190, n887, n1441
Aesop, n791
Aetius, n589
Agamemnon, 129, 139, 219
Agatharchus (painter), 59
Agathon, 158
Agesilaus (king), 4, 13, 46, n918
Ajax, 159, 160
Alcibiades (*see also* Critias), *passim*; aims at tyranny, 180; his anti-democratic sentiments, 59, 180, n458, n1281; deserts Socrates, 61, 136; distrusted by the people, 180; good person while under the influence of Socrates, 174 ff., 176, 177, 178, 179; inflicts many evils on the city, 58, 95, 97, 135, 147, 174, 176, 180, n170, n474; his insolence, 60, 174, n566; not a true pupil of Socrates, 59, 62, 95, 136, 147, 178, n997; seeks the company of Socrates, 179; his treason, 60, 96, n565, n1281
Alcibiades literature, is apologetic, 181; its origin, 59, 136, 174 ff., 181
Alcidamas, 221, n1448
Alexamenus, n924
Alexander, n382
Alexander of Macedon, 147, n692, n752, n1104

Allegiance in antiquity, 185 ff.
Ameipsias, 79, 192, 197, n1378
Amnesty (Act of Oblivion) of 403, 73, 74, 78, 136, 170, 171, 181, 182, 184, n1183, n1185
Anacharsis, 124
Anaxagoras, 24, 27, 28, 50, 54, 59, 66, 97, 98, 159, 192, 219, 220, 221, n586, n902
Anaximenes (orator), 70, n1327
Andocides (and pseudo-Andocides), 29, 171, 180, n90, n130, n458, n562, n578, n997, n1192, n1194, n1257, n1258, n1260, n1261, n1262, n1263, n1281, n1287, n1314, n1327
Antipater, n136
Antiphon, 11, 34, 55, 65, 106, 109, 111, 115, 195, 196, n89, n746, n1327
Antiphon of Rhamnus, 70, 129, 222, n1226, n1465
Anti-Socrates and anti-Socratic tracts, 210 ff.
Anti-Socratica, 137
Anti-Socratic sentiments in Athens, 167
Antisthenes (and Antisthenian, *see also* Cynics and Diogenes of Sinope), *passim*; his admiration for Sparta, 122, 126, 132, n904, n984; his advice to refrain from engaging in politics, 110; advocates removal of everything worthless, 152; his *Alcibiades*, 148 ff., 175 ff., n1220, n1237; his treatment of the 'Alcibiades theme', 148 ff.; his asceticism, 117, n766; objection to busybodies, 155; rejects change (τύχη), 121, 144 ff., 154, 206; condones crimes, 161 ff.; contempt for earthly goods, 115 ff., 159, 207, n680, n760, n878, n1088; his contempt for established institutions, 110, 120, 121, 141, 142, 143 ff., 148, 155 ff., 158, n676, n806, n984, n1378; his contempt for democratic practices and institutions, 109 ff., 121, 122, 141, 144 ff., 148, 158, 168, 203, n313, n598, n1306; contempt for politicians, 110 ff., 121, 122, 127, 148, n692, n824, n961; credits Socrates with the authorship of diatribes and apophthegms, 208; death is

325

Index

no evil, 23, 107, n639; denounces pleasure, 108 *et passim*; deplores decadence of the city, 134, 143, 148; his disapproval of the manner in which fathers brought up their sons, 150 ff.; discusses laws and political institutions, 143; his doctrine of 'intellectual and moral aristocracy', 203; his 'enmity' with Anytus, 37, 139 ff.; equates ignorance and insanity, 150; his concept of ἔργον, 205 ff.; his advice to 'esteem an honest man above a kinsman', 120, 151; an example to his pupils, 56; his reliance on strong expressions, 114, 134, 141, 152; extols virtue, 113 *et passim*; fanatic of abstract justice, 149 ff., n887; his frugality, 114 ff., 207, n760; holds that only good men can be true friends, 151, n1380; quotes approvingly Hesiod, 153, 204 ff., n1358; favours Homer, 159, n1356; his concept of idleness, 154 ff., n1052, n1370; contempt for the indolent and incompetent, 160 ff.; invents the association of Socrates and Alcibiades, 147 ff.; knowledge (virtue) is the sole true possession, 116 ff., 132; his praise of leisure, 155; his λόγοι Σωκρατικοί, 204, 208; his λόγοι Σωκρατικοί a collection of Socratic χρεία, 204; his concept of 'man's own', 116, 204 ff.; mastery of reason over passion, 147 ff.; only what is 'by nature' is 'universally valid', 155; holds that nobility belongs only to the virtuous, 119, n1107; his notion of ὁμόνοια, n1380; opposed to violence, 145; his notion of φιλανθρωπία, 141 ff.; his φιλοπονία, 111 ff., 125, 126, 153, n712; his intellectual pleasures, 34, 114; cites Pindar, 115 ff., 158; rejects some of the ancient poets, 153; his political philosophy, 143; his concept of πόνος, 111 ff., 113 ff., 125, 126, 153, n711; supplies Polycrates with his materials, 162 ff., 204; his *Protrepticus*, 148; the senseless or unintelligent is worthless, 127, 128, 129 ff.; his *Socratica* attract attention, 163; considers suicide an 'escape', 106 ff., n644; turns Socrates into a Cynic, 204; possibly a reliable Socratic witness, 162 ff.; his concept of skilfulness, 121; the sources for his teachings, 103 ff.; teaches contempt for friends, 151 ff.; teaches contempt for parents, 151; teaches contempt for relatives, 151 ff.; refers to Theognis, 158 ff.; threatens the unity of the Socratic tradition, 199; his views on justice and filial piety reflected in Plato's *Euthyphro*, 129, 149; reduces man's wants to a minimum, 156

Antisthenes of Rhodes, 102

Anytus, *passim*; promotes amnesty of 403, 73, 181; his 'belated patriotism', 75, n460; has no case against Socrates, 80, n460; 'grain inspector' (σιτοφύλαξ), 17; motivated by patriotism, 75, 77; his offer to withdraw complaint, 77, n182; his spirit of restraint, 96; a sycophant, 80

Apelt, O., n597

Apollodorus (brother of Aeantodorus), 34

Ἀπομνημονεύματα, their nature, 106

Apuleius of Madaura, n136

Archedemus, 188, 189

Archelaus, 50, n1310

Archelaus of Thessaly (tyrant), 165, n520, n1148

Archinus, 182

Ariarathes (satrap), 156

Aristarchus, 11, 94, 95

Aristides (the 'Just'), 98

Aristides, n174

Aristippus, 1, 8, 11, 102, 112, 113, 166, 199, 216, n28, n37, n558, n1195

Aristocratic - democratic struggles in Athens, 184 ff.

Aristodemus, 11

Ariston, 34

Aristophanes, 26, 28, 37, 50, 59, 79, 97, 118, 167, 192, 193, 194, 197, n93, n95, n121, n129, n132, n241, n262, n336, n459, n466, n589, n591, n646, n836, n887, n1014, n1165, n1198, n1270, n1311, n1326, n1378; calls Socrates a Melian, 26; did not find a single philosophical statement attributable to Socrates, 193

Aristoteles (one of the Thirty Tyrants), 59

Aristotle, *passim*; his views on athleticism, 126 ff.; his views on the τέχνη πολιτική, 145 ff.; his Socratic testimony, 1, 224, n1471

Aristoxenus, n1291

Arnim, H. v., 18, 19, n73, n227, n243, n744, n947

Arsenius, n1219

Artaxerxes, 12, n1398

Asceticism, road to virtue, 118

Aspasia, n1216

Athenaeus, 70, 98, 102, 147, 148, 150, 175, n144, n187, n190, n597, n693, n791, n822, n823, n944, n960, n961, n1133, n1195, n1206, n1215, n1216, n1219, n1225, n1226, n1240, n1244, n1335, n1398

Athenian παιδόνομος, 126, n845

Athens, its reputation for liberalism, 24

Augustine, St., n1215

Augustus (emperor), n1465

Autolycus (son of Lycon), 36

Axiochus, 108

Axiochus, a *consolatio mortis*, 107

Babelon, E., n1072

Bachmann, A., n1103

Index

Baiter-Orelli-Winckelmann, n529
Baiter-Sauppe, n383
Bdelycleon (*Wasps*), n459
Bentley, A., n389
Berry, E. G., n1221, n1225
Betrayal of the city, 185, 187 ff., 191
Beyschlag, F., n479
Βιαιῶν τὸ δικαιότατον, 89, n507
Bias, 99, n214
Bion of Borysthenes, 103, 107, 131, n646, n647, n677, n1026, n1219
Bizos, M., n1225
Bizoukides, P. K., Pref. xiv
Blass, F., n88, n300, n301, n374, n382, n399, n932, n1103, n1125, n1132, n1226, n1246, n1327, n1341, n1342, n1414, n1447, n1448
Body without soul is worthless, 128
Bonner, R. J., n205
Brasidas, 187
Breitenbach, L., n269, n378
Brémond, É. (G. Mathieu), n120, n207, n374, n401
Bruns, I., n217, n1330
Büchler, F., n738
Busiris, 139
Busiris (of Isocrates), rejoinder to the κατηγορία Σωκράτους, 69
Busse, A., 89, n73, n507
Bywater, I., n1075

Caecilius of Calacte, n1465
Calhoun, G. M., n1272, n1280, n1282, n1315
Callias (brother-in-law of Alcibiades), 59
Callicles (or Charicles), 10, 21, 173, 190, n170, n173, n174, n582, n1124, n1303
Callicrates, 168, 191
Callimachus, 220, n151
Callixenus, 188, 189
Calypso, n1125
Canthos of Boeotia (king), 92
Capital crimes, n192
Cato, n1267
Chaerecrates, 9, 11
Chaerephon (or Chairephon), 11, 30, 31, 33, 36, 221
Charicles (or Callicles), 173, 174, n174, n582; substitutes for Critias, 173
Charmides, 11, 77, 165, 168, 178, 179, n1151, n1239, n1304
Chevalier, J., n646
Chilon, n214
Chiron (tutor of Heracles), 104
Χρεία, its nature, 106
Christ-Schmid, n225, n291, n378, n636, n1336
Chroust, A.-H., n1, n4, n16, n29, n90, n93, n159, n260, n325, n377, n396, n597, n635, n677, n888, n903, n1268, n1325, n1336, n1369, n1466, n1469, n1471

Cicero, 20, 71, 104, n11, n136, n155, n190, n589, n640, n728, n870, n885, n1215, n1216, n1404
Cimon, 98, 174, n961
Cineas, 194
Circe, 115, n872
Cleaenetus (father of Cleon), 168
Clearchus, 4
Cleigenes (Cleisthenes), 188
Cleisthenes, 188, 191, n1269, n1280
Cleitophon, 213
Clement of Alexandria, n686, n688, n698, n745
Cleomenes, 103
Cleon, 168, 191, 221
Cleophon, 168, 191
Cloché, P., n1255
Clouds, a Socratic testimony, 192 ff.
Clubs engaged in political action, 185 ff., 186, 188, 194, 210, n1280
Clytemnestra, 129, 139
Cobet, C. G., n378, n400, n597
Comedians, The, do not contradict contention that Socrates was a political figure, 192 ff.
Conon, 71, 72, 73, 75, 96
Consolatio mortis, a Cynic theme, 107 ff.
Contra Alcibiadem, omits reference to the relationship of Socrates and Alcibiades, 180
Controversy over Socrates, an incident in the inner-political struggles of Athens, 198
Cornford, F. M., n247
Craterus, n692
Crates of Thebes, 102, 121, 124, 142, 144, n629, n651, n752, n840, n844, n906, n987, n1116
Critias (and Alcibiades), *passim*; deserts Socrates, 61, 62; the 'greatest thief', 75, 174; inflicts many evils on the city, 58, 95, 96, 97, 135, 147, 174, n170, n474; instigator of many atrocities, 60, 96; μισοδημότατος, 95, 174, n457; not a true pupil of Socrates, 59, 95, 173; sacrilegious person, 75, n562; suppresses freedom of speech, 96, n1205; head of the Thirty Tyrants, 75
Crito, 11, 34, 151, 165, n27
Critobolus (son of Critias), 11, 34, n1195
Crönert, W., n609, n610, n611
Ctesias, 113
Cynics (Cynic, *see also* Antisthenes and Diogenes of Sinope), ἄσκησις, 125, 126, 132, n857, n859; have no attachments, 146, n676; general characterization, 144; condemnation of athleticism, 124, 155, n840, n863; condone crimes, 161 ff.; contempt for wealth, 146, 154, 159, n680, n906; cosmopolitanism, 141 ff., n950, n951, n970; unceremonial disposal

of dead bodies, 128; 'educational programme', 124 ff.; emphasis on εὐπραξία, 145, n809, n1370; notion of freedom, 109, n676; 'freespokenness', 144; search for 'ideal father', 120; ignorant people be kept in bondage, 150; integration of physical and mental training, 125 ff., n855; integration of πόνος and σοφία, 125; ideal παιδεία 124, 126, 160 ff., n835, n1106; φιλόπονος and φιλόσοφος, 125, n858; quote and interpret the ancient poets, 127, 153, n869; recommend the removal of useless things, 127 ff., 129, 150; recommend sensible physical exercise, 124, 125; oppose theorizing, 130 ff., n891, n899, n901; refuse to speculate about nature, 130 ff.; training of body and soul, 124, 125; utopia, 144; put virtue above theory, 130; virtue sufficient to happiness, 159

Cyrus the Elder (king), 112, 113, 128, 148, 162, n719; the Cynic 'ideal', 112 ff., n717

Cyrus the Younger, 4, 12, 13, n636, n1398

Damonides (or Damon) of Oa, 192

Defence (of Xenophon), critique of Plato's *Apology*, 39; dependent on Plato's *Apology*, 39, n77, n209; general nature, 17 ff., 44 ff.; corrects and supplements other authors, 17 ff., n74, n203, n209; expansion of *Memorabilia* 4.8.1–11, 17; genuineness, 17; motivated by the κατηγορία, Σωκράτους, 19, 45, 200, 215, 224, n1342; probable date, 17, 19, 45, n226; *Defence*, 20; summary of *Memorabilia* 1.2.49–55, 17, 45, n335

Delphic god (Apollo), 30 ff.

Deman, Th., n1, n1471

Demetrius, 70, 142, n382, n956, n1133, n1215

Demetrius Magnes, 17

Demetrius of Phaleron, 69

Demophanes (Demophantus), 188

Demophantus, 188, n578

Demosthenes, 111, n89, n90, n547, n692, n1262, n1312

Dercylidas, 13

Diagoras of Melos, 26, 27, 50, 97, 98, n586, n589, n591

Diehl, E., n791, n963

Diels, H., n153, n160, n190, n242, n288, n529, n906, n1291

Diels-Kranz, n562, n1414, n1456, n1459

Dindorf, L., n223, n378, n597

Dinos, 50

Diocles of Magnesia, 102, 156, n601, n1374

Diocles (father of Euthydemus), n1240

Dio Chrysostom, *passim*

Diodorus, 11

Diodorus Siculus, 4, 37, 39, 101, n27, n590

Diogenes Laertius, *passim*

Diogenes of Apollonia, 50, 193, 223

Diogenes of Sinope (*see also* Antisthenes and Cynics), *passim*; a 'debaser of currency', 156 ff.; denounces existing laws, 143 ff.; the founder of Cynicism, 101 ff.; his hardihood, 123, n745, n839; keeps his pupils in good physical condition, 123; recommends physical hardihood, 124; his political philosophy, 143 ff.; the sources of his teachings, 102 ff., 104 ff.; the 'successor' of Antisthenes, 101 ff.

Dionysius of Halicarnassus, 70, n223, n224, n1133

Diopeithes (seer), 49, 221

Δικαιῶν τὸ βιαιότατον, 89, n507

Discretionary crimes, 65 ff.

Disposal of worthless things, 64

Dittmar, H., 175, n38, n634, n1166, n1206, n1207, n1215, n1218, n1221, n1222, n1223

'Doing one's own' signifies 'doing something good', 204 ff.

Domitian (emperor), n677

Döring, A., n12

Dorjahn, A. P., n1255

Dracon, 182, n576

Dudley, D. R., 156, n602, n603, n621

Dümmler, F., 69, 219, n6, n7, n259, n375, n692, n729, n813, n847, n955, n957, n1018, n1041, n1238, n1310, n1343, n1344

Dupréel, E., n1234

Düring, H., n139

Τὸ ἑαυτόν, a good, 116

Τὰ ἑαυτοῦ πράττειν, 154 ff., 204 ff., 206, n1361, n1364, n1365, n1369

'Εγκράτεια, of the Cynics, 108 ff., 113 ff., n658, n835; of Socrates, 108, 113 ff., n728

Elter, A., n791

Empedocles, 159, n869

Ephialtes, 191

Ephorus, 220

Epicharmus, 29, n757

Epictetus, 102, 107, 115, 116, 120, n664, n676, n678, n684, n685, n689, n698, n706, n748, n878, n883, n941, n949, n951, n952, n986, n1026, n1092, n1095, n1384, n1389

Epicurus, n1160

Epigenes, 188

Epiphanius, n688, n972, n1096

'Εργάζεσθαι, constructive work, 154

Eryximachus, 29

Eryxis, 59

Eubulides, 40, 104, 156, n627

Eubulus, 103, n627

Euclides (archon), 182

Euclides of Megara, 1, 59, 102, 137, 175, 176, 191, 211, n1216; his *Alcibiades*, 175 ff., n1216

Index

Eucrates, 168, 191
Eupolis, 79, 192, 197, n1378
Euripides, 28, 105, 218, 219, n207, n868, n887, n1075; his *Palamedes* an allusion to Socrates, n207
Eurylochus of Larissa (tyrant), 165, n520
Eusebius, n698, n723
Eutherus, 11
Euthydemus, 7, 11, 179, n27, n1223, n1239, n1240, n1241
Euthydemus (poet), n1240
Euthyphro, 24, 27, 49, 149
Everything excellent a matter of practice (or exercise), 61
Experimental sciences need no divination, 51, 53

Favorinus, 47, 71, 73, n400, n601
Ferguson, A. S., n117, n128
Field, G. C., n1221
Fite, W., n1467
Foerster, R., *passim*
Frank, E., n597
Fränkel, M., n1258
Freedom of speech, n498
Frick, O., 219, n73, n1444
Fritz, K. v., n73, n620, n621, n962

Geffken, J., 93, n369, n378, n507, n510, n512, n595, n597, n1334, n1439
Geiger, W., n606
Geissler, A., n205
Gellius, n698, n1398
Generals of the Arginusae battle, The, Pref. xii, 10, 21, 55, 165, 172, n269, n1192
Gercke, A., n378, n536, n597
Gerhard, G. A., n620
Gernet, L., n1225
Gigon, O., n160, n187, n221, n222, n1476
Gildemeister, J., n738
Glaucon, n677
Glotz, G., n94
Gomperz, Heinrich, n73, n92, n209, n1308, n1439, n1472
Gomperz, Theodor, 15, n66, n378, n597, n604, n1233, n1336
Gorgias, 70, 72, 158, 159, 216, 218, 219, n207, n381, n399, n1080, n1446, n1447
Γραφὴ ἀργίας, 94
Grote, G., n70, n1259

Hackforth, R., n77, n209, n216, n227, n243, n400, n1265, n1409
Hartman, J., n30, n70, n233
Haussoulier, B., n1270
Hector, n870
Helen, n666
Hense, O., n646, n954
Hephaestion, n562
Heracleides Lembos, n601

Heracleides of Pontus, 62
Heracles, 104, 105, 112, 113, 124, 129, 139, 149, n634, n666, n723; idol of the Cynics, 104 ff., 124, n634, n721, n722
Heraclitus of Ephesus, 29, 32, 48, 114
Hercher, R., n791
Hermann, K. F., n597, n757, n1221
Hermippus, 59, 70, 73, 220, n386, n400
Hermodorus, 191
Hermogenes, 20, 25, n21, n85, n737
Herodicus the Cratetean, 175, n1216, n1225, n1398
Herodorus, 105
Herodotus, 113, n150, n507, n520, n719, n903, n1285
Herondas, n549
Hesiod, 64, 86, 88, 89, 90, 112, 153, 160, 204, 205, n348, n493, n502, n713, n1043, n1358, n1361
Heuer, E., n596
Hieronymus of Rhodes, 220
Hikesias (father of Diogenes of Sinope), 156, 157, n1072
Hipparete (wife of Callias), 59
Hippias, 11, 117, 155, 158, n27, n40, n174; his πολυτροπία, 117
Hippocrates, 51; his empirical method, 51 ff.
Hirzel, R., 69, 72, n88, n375, n388, n390, n396, n397, n597, n1344
Höistad, R., n606, n631, n634, n716, n848, n857, n860, n1072, n1104
Homer, 64, 86, 88, 89, 90, 91, 109, 127, 159, 160, 204, n350, n394, n493, n502, n528, n533, n745, n872, n1042, n1100, n1104, n1136, n1200, n1356
Humbert, T., 75, n376, n378, n383, n510, n597
Hyperbolus, 168, 191

Idleness, sister of freedom, 94
'I know that I know nothing', Pref. xi
Immisch, O., n73, n646
Intellectual possessions the sole possessions, 110
Ion of Chios, 98
Isaeus, n89, n90, n1327
Isagoras, 191
Isocrates, 20, 56, 59, 64, 69, 70, 72, 84, 95, 112, 136, 147, 178, 201, n82, n307, n382, n413, n431, n541, n571, n931, n981, n1133, n1185, n1235, n1259, n1314, n1332, n1333, n1337, n1397

Jacoby, F., n632
Jamblichus, n155
Jason of Pherae, 70
Jebb, R. C., n88, n374, n382, n1246, n1259
Joël, K., Pref. xi, 55, 107, 124, 132, 138, 223, n6, n18, n33, n45, n52, n96, n201, n260, n341, n405, n559, n606, n658,

n716, n835, n847, n858, n861, n885, n887, n903, n907, n920, n921, n924, n928, n934, n955, n1018, n1057, n1111, n1123, n1238, n1310, n1311, n1331, n1346, n1405, n1468, n1474
John, St., n672
Josephus, 55, n121, n122, n197, n275, n591, n1266
Julian (the 'Apostate'), 102, n625, n686, n690, n723
Justus of Tiberias, 36, n1300

Kaibel, G., n847
Κατηγορία Σωκράτους, bristles with political charges, 182 ff.; gave birth to Socratic legend, 211; part of the 'counter-attack' launched by the Late Sophists, 198 ff.; delivered through Anytus, 46, 47, 73; directed against Antisthenes, 73 ff., 139 ff., 203, 214; a forensic speech, 72, 73; its probable date, 69, 72; its relation to Socrates' trial, 71, 73, 135, 137, n384; stimulated Socratic apologies, 71, 217, n597, n1342; transition from 'political' anti-*Socratica* to 'personal' anti-Socrates tracts, 210 ff.; ushered in third stage of Socratic controversy, 211
Κατήγορος, is Polycrates, 63, 67 ff., 69, 71, 72, 73, n228, n378
Kirchhoff, A., n992
'Know thyself', 32, 33
Knowledge, confers nobility, 113 ff.; once acquired can be lost, 60
Krauss, H., n1221, n1225
Krohn, A., n6

Laches, 165
Lactantius, n121
Lamprocles, 9, n93
Late Sophists, spokesmen of Athenian democracy, 198; started anti-Socratic literature, 191 ff.
Legal reforms at Athens in 403, 181 ff.
Leisure (philosophical), n555
Leo, Fr., n34, n1217
Leon of Salamis, 10, 172, n1192
Libanius, *passim*; acquainted with the κατηγορία Σωκράτους, 72; *Apologia Socratis*, basis for reconstructing the κατηγορία, 74
Lincke, K., n6, n45
Literary Socrates, mostly legend, Pref. xi
Λόγοι Σωκρατικοί, 5, 7, 8, 137 ff., 199, 209 ff., 225, n924, n929; as μίμησις, 138 ff., 225; of Aeschines, 8, 137; of Antisthenes, 8, 137, 204; apologetic or post-Polycratean, 211; of Aristippus, 8; of Euclides, 137; of Phaedo of Elis, 137; panegyric or pre-Polycratean, 211; of Plato, 8; their use by Xenophon, 15

Lucian (and pseudo-Lucian), 102, 124, n121, n723, n746, n760, n948, n953, n1026, n1096
Ludlofs, H. J., n1103
Lycon (the Academic), n1163
Lycon (one of Socrates' prosecutors), 36, 68, 71, 183
Lycurgus ('law giver'), 4, n712
Lycurgus, n562
Lysanias, 34
Lysias, 19, 20, 59, 69, 71, 171, n72, n88, n90, n130, n184, n390, n519, n528, n541, n571, n926, n1225, n1259, n1286, n1287, n1313, n1342, n1397; his '*Defence*', 20, n88, n1397
Lysias (brother of Euthydemus), n1240

Madmen to be confined, 63
Madness related to ignorance, 63, 150
Magalhâes-Vilhena, V. de, Pref. xiv
Mahaffey, J. P., n11
Maier, Heinrich, 8, 10, 198, n11, n35, n51, n69, n378, n597, n1324, n1336, n1400, n1475
Maintenance in the Prytaneum, 37, 40, 67, n177, n190, n356, n365
Marcellinus, n1398
Markowski, H., 76, 93, n378, n383, n396
Mathieu, G. (É. Brémond), n120, n207, n374, n401
Mattingly, J. A. H., n1072
Maximus of Tyre, 102, 190, n92, n136, n1195, n1215, n1299
Medea, 161
Megabazus, 13
Μεγαληγορία (of Socrates), 10, 18, 19
Meier-Schoemann-Lipsius, n548
Meinecke, M., n129
Meiser, K., n378
Melanthus, 92
Meleagros of Gadara, 102
Melesias (father of Thucydides), 220
Meletus, *passim*; the prosecutor of Andocides, 171
Memorabilia, a collection of λόγοι Σωκρατικοί, 5; determined by the κατηγορία Σωκράτους, 6, 224; as encomia, 10, 12, n223; general nature, 5 ff.; a rejoinder to Polycrates, 6, 44, 45, 46, 200
Memorabilia 4.8.1–11, excerpt from *Defence*, 17, 45
Memorabilia 1.1.1–1.2.64, consist of three parts, 45 ff.; different from other works of Xenophon, 47; originally an independent work, 5, 44, n222; probable date, 44, n225; a rejoinder to the κατηγορία Σωκράτους, 69, 215, n335, n1342; a Socratic apology, 44; unoriginal, 67
Memorabilia 1.2.9–61, basis for reconstructing the κατηγορία Σωκράτους, 74

Index

Memorabilia 1.3.1–4.8.11, probable date, 45
Menander, n137, n1100
Menexenus (son of Socrates), n93
Menon, 4
Melissus, 99
Menippus, 103, 107, n644
Mesk, J., 86, n71, n378, n396, n435, n478, n491, n534, n597
Metrocles of Maroneia, 103, 107, n629, n644, n680
Metrodorus, 159
Meyer, E., n215
Midas, n666
Milesian tripod, The, 32
Military campaigns of Socrates, Pref. xii, 165
Milne, J. G., n1075
Miltiades, 98, n594
Μισοδημία, in *The Old Oligarch*, 147, 183
Monimus, n852
Moral autarchy, 117; of the Cynics, 108 ff.; of Socrates, 109
Morr, J., n190, n1439
Morrison, J. S., n1465
Müller, C., n305, n332, n596, n1449, n1454, n1456
Myson, 32

Nauck, A., n207
Neocles (father of Themistocles), 177
Neon, 4
Neoptolemus, 160
Nestle, W., n144, n716
Nicias, 165, 180, n174
Nicostratus, 34
Νόμισμα and νόμος, 157
Non-discretionary crimes, 65 ff.

Odysseus, 72, 91, 92, 115, 135, 159, 160, 162, 219, n207, n872, n891, n1125, n1128, n1443; 'hero' with the Cynics, 159 ff.; his labours (πόνοι), 160
Old age, burdensome, 107
Oldfather, W. A., n92, n209
Old Oligarch, critical of democratic practices, 147, 165
Oligarchs, started pro-Socratic literature, 191 ff.
Olympiodorus, 175, n1219
Orestes, 31, 129, 139
Ovid, n208

Palamedes, 41, 148, 216, 218, 219, n207, n208, n209, n1443, n1448
'Palamedes theme', The, 216 ff., 219 ff.
Panaetius, n925, n1216
Pandaron, n533
Paralus (son of Pericles), 34, 151
Παραχάραξις, 156 ff., 158, n1075
Parmenides, 159, n869

Party loyalty and 'patriotism', 187 ff.
Patroclus, n870
Paul, St., n712
Pauly-Wissowa, n85, n185, n379, n528, n632
Pausanias, 12, 70, n381, n398, n1133, n1259
Peisander, 191
Penelope, n666
Perdiccas, n692
Pericles the Elder, 59, 62, 98, 122, 126, 150, 165, 168, 174, 191, 192, 195, 220, 221, n824, n1323
Pericles the Younger, 11, 45, n32
Persius, n1212
Phaedo of Elis, 59, 137, 211, n1216
Phaedrus, 29
Phaenarete, Pref. xii
Phaidon, 188
Pheidippides, n887, n1014
Philenis, 70
Philip of Macedonia, n692
Phillipson, C., n247
Philo of Alexandria, n869
Philochorus, n207
Philodemus, 102, 141, n962, n1026, n1457
Philodemus (disciple of Anaxagoras), 59
Philoponus, n755, n966
Philostratus, n677, n1465
Photius, n1465
Φρόνησιν ἀσκεῖν, 145
Φροντιστέριον, a parody on Athenian club life, 193 ff.
Phrynichus, n562
Pieper, J., n467, n555
Pindar (Pindaric), 86, 88, 89, 90, 105, 158, 204, n493, n502, n506, n507, n597, n1042, n1064, n1082
Pisistratus, 94, 164, 180
Pittacus, 149
Pitthos (father of Meletus), 47
Plato, *passim*; absolves Alcibiades from causing evils to Athens, 174; his treatment of the Alcibiades episode, 179; addresses court, 36; avoids stereotype apology, 43; his *Apology* under the influence of the κατηγορία Σωκράτους, n1409; his *Apology* influenced by Gorgias' *Defence of Palamedes*, 216 ff.; his views on athleticism, 127; his *Charmides*, quotes Antisthenes, 204 ff.; his *Charmides*, quotes Hesiod, 204; his *Crito*, motivated by the κατηγορία Σωκράτους, n830, n1134, n1336; his attitude towards democracy, 140 ff., n1305; his earliest dialogues unimportant as Socratic sources, 163; his *Gorgias*, critical of democratic Athens, 164; his *Gorgias*, occasioned by the κατηγορία Σωκράτους, 69, 98, 202, n291, n597, n1228; his *Gorgias*, a reckoning with the Late Sophists, 200 ff.; ignores the κατηγορία

Index

Σωκράτους, 214 ff.; his *Meno*, exonerates Anytus, 202 ff.; his *Meno*, presupposes the κατηγορία Σωκράτους, 69; denies the political implications of Socrates' trial, 183 ff.; denies that Socrates was a politician, 195; his concept of πόνος, 112; his *Protagoras*, critical of democratic Athens, 164; his reason for Socrates' condemnation, 41 ff.; his *Symposium*, part of the 'Alcibiades literature', 175, n1233; his *Symposium*, presupposes the κατηγορία Σωκράτους, 69; his aversion to teach philosophy to the morally unfit, 60
Plutarch, 20, 49, 71, 102, 175, 184, n87, n88, n136, n139, n158, n303, n439, n456, n549, n562, n612, n739, n745, n869, n951, n1117, n1226, n1267, n1314, n1404, n1450, n1456, n1460
Pohlenz, M., n40, n378, n404, n597
Ποιεῖν ἀλλότριον, 154 ff.
Ποιεῖν and πράττειν, 153 ff.
Polemarchus (brother of Eythydemus), n1240
Polus, 201
Polux, n1225
Polybius, n1279
Polycrates, *passim*; considers Antisthenes a true Socratic, 162 ff., 204; his reliance on Antisthenes, chap. 6, 139, 148 ff., 162 ff., 183, 204, 205 ff., 208, n559, n670; author of the κατηγορία Σωκράτους, 57; calls Socratics 'despoilers of Athenian democracy', 199; his career, 70 ff.; his charges against Socrates (general), 74 ff.; compels Socratics to reply in the form of Socratic apologies, 19 ff., 210 ff.; his praise of Conon and Thrasybulus, 73, 75; denounces Critias and Alcibiades, 75, 135; his 'enmity' with Antisthenes, 139 ff.; possibly relies on *The Old Oligarch*, 147; relies on λόγοι Σωκρατικοί, 204; partisan of radical democracy, 70, 74; has no personal quarrel with Socrates, 77, 198; embarrasses Socratics, 199; his sources, 137 ff., 139, 162 ff., 204
Polyeuctus, 73
Πόνος, its cathartic meaning, 153, n1048; remedy against ἡδονή, 153, n1047
Popper, K. A., n939
Praechter, K., n378, n597
Preuner, E., n190
Priscianus, n1215, n1225
Proclus, 175, n1301
Prodicus, 105, 112, 154, 159
Prometheus, 218
Proper worship, 49
Protagoras, 24, 27, 50, 62, 66, 97, 98, 159, 192, 193, 223, n586, n855, n869
Proxenus, 4
Pusey, N. M., n1270, n1280, n1288
Pythagoras, 32, 99

Quintilian, 69, 71, n87, n384, n886, n932

Radermacher, L., n1447
Raeder, H., n378, n597
Raubitschek, A. E., n1246, n1251
'*Refutation*' of Lysias, a rebuttal of the κατηγορία Σωκράτους, 71, 72
Reinach, Th., n1072
Richter, E., 7, n7, n8, n9, n10, n11, n21, n23, n24, n26, n42, n47, n71, n227, n229
Ritter, C., n106, n198, n376, n378
Robin, L., n11, n1474
Robinson, D. M., n1072
Robinson, E. S. G., n1072
Rogge, K., n406
Roquette, H., n30
Ryssel, V., n791

Sabinus, T. Flavius, n677
Satyrus, 102, 143, 175, 219, 220, n1219
Sauppe, G., n31, n88, n378, n536, n597
Sayre, F., n620
Schanz, M., 74, 86, n73, n76, n209, n219, n378, n389, n396, n410, n528, n530, n546, n597, n919, n1342
Scheel, E., n383
Schleiermacher, F., 2, n2, n597
Schmitz, L., n70
Schöll, R., n190
Scopas of Crannon (tyrant), 165, n520
Seltmann, C. T., 156, 157, n1072
Seneca, n644, n744, n902, n1146
Sextus Empiricus, n11, n589, n698, n970
Simplicius, n903
Sittl, K., n13, n14, n53
Socher, J., n597
Socrates, *passim*; abuses ancient poets, 83 ff., 86 ff., 99; acts from inner compulsion, 42; always acts in public, 79; acts like a Cynic, 146; admirer of Sparta (and Crete), 168; the nature of his personal contacts with Alcibiades, 178; not associated with Alcibiades, 176, 178, 180 ff., n309, n997, n1203; 'all philosophies to all philosophers', 196, 223; discusses 'anthropomorphic' problems, 54; his anti-democratic sentiments, 75, 78, 91, 135, 159, 160, 171, n1303; attacks all traditions, 86; believes in omens (or divination), 29, 48, 50, 51, 52 ff., 55, 123, n254; his asceticism, 118; considers himself benefactor of Athens, 169; benefits others, 38, 50; the best time for him to die, 23, 37, 42, 107; not to be blamed for Alcibiades and Critias, 61; casts a spell over his disciples, 83, 85; cause of disunity, defection and treason, 99; cause of Athens' downfall and of abolishment of democracy, 211; never the cause of sedition or treachery (treason), 38, 55, 66, 78, n197, n412; never the cause of war,

Index

38, 66; censures Alcibiades, 178; the charges against him, 26, 47 ff., 181; cites the ancient poets, 64 ff., 75, 85, 86, 127, 153, 204, n413, n1040; cites ancient poets to make his pupils tyrannical (evil-doers), 64, 75, 83, 153, 204, n1040; cites approvingly Hesiod, 64, 88, 89, 90, 153, 204, n1042; cites Homer, 64 ff., 88, 91 ff., 159, n1042; cites Pindar, 88 ff., 89, 155, n1042, n1082; cites Theognis, 88, 158, n1042; committed no crime (no capital crime), 38, 65, 66, 92, 181; compared to a Cynic (by Antiphon), 111; compared to Diagoras of Melos, 26, 97; compared to Protagoras, 97; his concept of religious piety, 27 ff.; confounded with Anaxagoras, 28, 50, 97, n121; a conservative, 134, 168; his contempt for accepted standards, 206 ff.; his contempt for democracy, 91, 122, 134, 146, 159, 165, 166, 169, 176, 189, 203; his contempt for the little man, 64 ff., 72, 81, 90, 91 ff., 100, 165; his contempt for politicians, 26, 57, 78, 122, n114; his contempt for the popular assembly, 166, n1156, n1303; controls his passions, 108, 111, n161; corrupts youths, 26, 34, 35, 38, 39, 46 ff., 55, 56, 66, 75, 77, 78, 99, 135, n172, n173; counsels others (to consult auguries), 51; association with Critias, 58, 168, 169, 174, n1000, n1203; his criticism of Critias, 62, 136, 172 ff.; his criticism of existing legal and political institutions, 81, 141, 146, 168, 204, n444, n1177; entitled to criticize political institutions, 85, 87; his daemon, 22 ff., 27, 29 ff., 48, 52, 55, n96; advocates unceremonial disposal of dead bodies, 128; death not to be feared, 23 ff., 107; never defended himself, 190, n92; deity his personal monitor, 50, 55, n134, n135; Delphic god (oracle), 30, 39, 40; denounces ancient poets, n493, n1040; never denounced Athenian democracy, 176; denounces pleasure, 113; deserves death, 97, 99, 100, 181, 210; did not deserve death, n578, n586; his 'desire of death', 10, 24 ff., 42, 107, n108, n639; desires and brings about downfall of Athenian democracy, 203; despoiler of Athens, 78, 182; his disdain of death, 18, 26, 37; disposes people to acts of violence, 57, 58, 122, 140, 145, 146, n472; disseminates the principle of virtue, 119; his 'divine mission', 42, n1160; meaning of the 'divine sign' (or 'voice'), 48 ff.; his contempt for earthly goods (*see also* frugality), 115 ff.; educates Alcibiades and Critias, 83, 95 ff., 97, 147 ff.; disastrous effects of his teachings, 84, 95 ff., 97; doomed after restoration of 403, 184; encourages people to enter politics, 166 ff., n1151; his ἐγκράτεια, 108, 132; ἐγκρατέστατος, 132 ff., n728; his enmity with Anytus, 37; his enmity with Lycon, 36; his enmity with Meletus, 36; his refusal to enter politics, 166 ff., n1151; does not equate ignorance and insanity (madness), 150, n1017; escapes the ills of old age, 24, 107, 108; excels in the instruction of youths, 35, 38, 119; an example to his pupils, 55 ff., 60, 119, 170, n783; exempted from all obligations towards the city, 194; expects condemnation, 25, 190; expected to go into exile, 24; extols virtue, 113; his faith in the gods, 51; not an ideal 'family man', n883; forbids friends to name counter-penalty, 40; favoured (warned, compelled) by a daemon, 23, 29, 30; favours tyranny, 80, 81, n445; his forensic inexperience, 20 ff.; a 'free' man, 110, 111; friend of the common people, 65, 81, 91, n449; his notions as to friends, 120, n1029, n1037, n1038; his friends 'advocates of tyranny', 82; his friends (and associates) aristocratic-oligarchic partisans, 167, 168, 171 ff., 189; his friends contemptuous of democracy, 82, 207; his friends 'despisers of civic equality', 82; his friends plead (testified) for him, 36, n1300; his friends preferred not to enter politics, n1304; his oligarchic friends blamed for Athens' defeat in the Peloponnesian War, 172; a frugal person, 79, 93, 115, n283, n658, n659, n747, n765, n836; gods oppose his escape, 24; does not make his pupils greedy, 56; advocates honest work, 94; brought honour to Athens, 65; ideal Cynic, 109, 111; absolved from impiety, 54; incites people to commit crimes, 75, 77, 92, 100, 161 ff.; incurs the displeasure of the 'democrats', 189; his official indictment only token charges, 171, 181; never induced people to commit crimes, 77, 92, n523; never induced people to disdain the laws, 77; inflicts many evils on the city, 82; his general conduct inimical to Athenian democracy, 170; inimitable idol of the Socratics, 199; intellectual leader of oligarchs, 74, 77, 210, n1304; his intellectual pleasures, 33 ff., 114; induces his disciples to 'sabotage' city, 82 ff., 93; never rendered people intemperate, profligate, incontinent or effeminate, 118; introduces new gods, 26 ff., 29 ff., 47 ff., 49, 52, n133; inured to hardships, 93, 118, 123; inures his disciples to hardships and toils, 132, n660; his καλοκαγαθία, 10; a κοσμοπολίτης, 143; a law-abiding citizen, 122, n1082; to lead a better life, 24; his praise of leisure, n1058; his liberal and kind disposition, 65; cannot live under

Index

any form of government, 143, 165, 173, 194; his suggestion that lowly people be beaten, 64 ff., 72, 160, n1136; a 'martyr', 40, 222 ff.; called a Melian, 26, n589; member of a club, n1289, n1291, n1294; his military campaigns, Pref. xii, 164; a μισόδημος, 74, 78, 80, 81, 140, 160, 165, 189, n445, n560, n1145; victim of misunderstanding, 79; a model for others to emulate, 55; a despiser of manual labour, 95; chided for not accepting money, 65; not neglectful of the body, 56, 123; plans (or participates in) overthrow of Athenian democracy, 74 ff., 77 ff., 82, 97, 140, 168 ff., 181, 184, n452, n675; never planned the overthrow of democracy, 77, 80; associated with oligarchs, 77, 165, 167, 171 ff., 191, n1171; one of the oligarchic-aristocratic leaders, 77, 184, n1304; his oligarchic leanings, 99, 165, 168, 189, n1145; averse to ostentatiousness, 56, n748; paragon of virtue, 134; did not participate in revolution⟩of 411 or 404, 78, 80, n448; his participation in the campaign of Potidaea, 164 ff., n1141; people seek his company, n577; persuades Athenians of the errors of democracy, 193; persuades Charmides to enter politics, n1304; persuades his disciples that he was the wisest, 63, 119, 120; not a philosopher, 177, 191, 192 ff., 196, 223, n1171, n1302, n1324, n1469; recommends physical exercise, 56, 123, n835; his physical prowess, 118, 123, 126, n836, n837; his φιλοπονία, 111; the paucity of reports on his political activities, 164, 166; stresses political expertness, 58; a political figure, 191, 192, 223, n1171; his political views, 54, 195; never engages in politics, 93, 164, 165, 195 ff., n1140, n1151, n1161, n1304; his private| views on politics, 54; his practical philosophy only incidental to his political discussions, 193; prefers death, 18, 23, 24, 42, 108; prophesies, 40 ff.; had no pupils, 34, 56, 177, 179 ff., n167; rebukes people who deprecated lowly work, 206 ff., n1139; recruits young men for his political programme, 209; refers to cobblers and tanners, etc., 36 ff., 77, 94, 166, n327, n444, n805; his efforts to reform Athens, 169; reforms evil people, 66; dissuades unqualified people from entering politics, n465, n677, n1153; his refusal to accept the 'Defence' of Lysias, 20; his refusal to name penalty (or counter-penalty), 40, n190, n205; his refusal to prepare for trial, 20, 42; his refusal to use forensic language or methods, 19, 21 ff., 25 ff., 30, 37, n1296; rejects ἡδονή, 132; rejects τύχη, 121; related to Euripides, 28; related to the scandal of the *Hermae*, 28; his religious convictions, 52 ff., 66; asks for no remuneration, 56 ff., 65; has the proper religious sentiments, 55; not responsible for the deeds of Critias and Alcibiades, 174 ff.; a sacrilegious person, 78; his 'secret crimes', 75, 93; sentenced unjustly, 25, 38, 65; a sinister political influence operating in the background, 166; no slave of sensual desires, 33, 55, 108, 109, 111; a dangerous sophist, 75, 97, 100, 167, n438, n479, n1199; seeks to free men from superstition, 26; does not speculate about nature, 36, 50, 53, 79, 130, 192, n261, n888, n1469; the story of his trial and death similar to the trial and death of Anaxagoras, 220 ff.; the story of his trial and death similar to the trial and death of Antiphon of Rhamnus, 222; suspected of being atheistic, 26, 28, 37, n119; suspected of being anti-religious, 26; swears strange oaths, 55, n121; the teacher of Critias and Alcibiades, 58 ff., 72, 75, 83, 95 ff., 97, 98, 133, 135, 147, 174, 181, n996; the best teacher, n174; not a teacher, 177, n167, n174, n1208; teaches contempt for the laws and political institutions, 57, 74, 75, 76, 85, 99, 121 ff., 122, 135, 140, 146, 165, 203, n175, n670, n1266; teaches contempt for friends, 35, 63 ff., 99, 119, 207; teaches contempt for parents, 35, 63 ff., 75, 78, 83, 84 ff., 99, 119, 127, 135, 149, 207, 208 ff., n175, n793, n1010; teaches contempt for relatives, 35, 63 ff., 99, 119, 207; teaches idleness and anti-social conduct, 75, 77, 78, 82, 99 ff., 100, 154, 207, n407, n543; teaches neglect of the gods, 75; never teaches anything in private, 34 ff., n1302; his teachings endanger democratic institutions, 75, 99, 100, n456; his teachings endanger the foundations of human society, 99, 120; people who testified in his behalf, n181; absolved from associating with the Thirty Tyrants, 172 ff.; his association with the Thirty Tyrants, 62, 136, 172, n1145; clashes with the Thirty Tyrants (or, with Critias), 61, 143, 164, 165, 166, 172 ff., 174, n582, n1198, n1326; his time one of intense inner-political struggles, 188, n1323; a 'traitor', 184 ff., 191; his trial a 'partisan affair', 189 ff.; his trial a political trial, 170 ff., 181 ff., 183 ff., 189; his trial a political incident, 183, 189, n1264, n1265; the delay of his trial, 181 ff., n1254; his deportment during the trial of the generals of the Arginusae, 165, 172, 189, n1192, n1293; tried by 'little boys', 25 ff., 201; tries to restore oligarchy, 209; intends to turn people into virtuous people, 169 ff., n164, n171; makes his disciples 'tyrannical', 83, 84, 88 ff., 90, 99, 145, 153, n459, n1040; his contempt for the tyrants of Thessaly, 166, n520, n1142, n1148; makes his disciples unprincipled, 83, 84, 88, 90, 153, n1049; undermines the political and social institutions of Athens, 55, 57, 77 ff., 80, 81 ff., 93, 99, 100, 146, n442, n546; his courageous uprightness, 55; his suggestion that useless and insolent people be restrained, 65, 91, 150, 160, n1010; advocates removal of useless things, 127, 150 ff.; only virtuous men should enter politics, 169 ff.; his vocation to philosophy, 31 ff.; will have attestation of time to come, 38, 39; generally unfavourable views (opinions) about him, 78 ff., 192 ff., n1165, n1326; holds that virtuous parents have noble children, 119; opposed to violence, 58, 145; his willingness to die, 23 ff., 108; wisest (most just, freest) man, 30, 32, 33, 40, 42, 149, 209, n140, n1396; does not worship the gods which the city worships, 26 ff., 47 ff., 52, 75; always worships properly, 27, 48, 52, 53, 55; his worship of birds or dogs, animals and stones, 27; wrong conclusions about him, 54, 196, n193; calls work honourable, n701; worthy of great honour, 65, 66; never wrote anything, 162, 223, 224, n791, n1324

Socratic apologies, of two types, 200; those which take issue with the trial of Socrates, 200; those which take issue with the Anti-Socratic literature (Polycrates), 200; connected with defence of oligarchy, 198; considered a threat to democracy, 198

Socratic apologists, acted as character witnesses, 192; of the fourth stage, 211 ff.; of the third stage, 211; turned the politician Socrates into the philosopher Socrates, 192

Socratic issue a political issue, 198

Socratic legends, primarily of an apologetic nature, 211

Socratic reporters, Pref. xiv

Socratica, in general, 137 ff.; of Xenophon under the influence of Cynic teachings, n6; intentional legends, Pref. xii and xiii, 216; part of a literary campaign, 191 ff.; their subdivisions (or stages), 209 ff.

Socratics, caused consternation by their apologetic fervour, 198; oligarchic partisans, 191; turned the political Socrates into a philosophical legend, 196; unable to refute political charges against Socrates, 192

Solon, 32, 94, 97, 123, 124, 182, n576, n578

Sophaenetus, 4

Sophocles, 160, n100

Sophroniscus (father of Socrates), Pref. xii, 47

Sophroniscus (son of Socrates), n93

Sosicrates of Rhodes, 102, 143, n601

Sotion of Alexandria, 102, 143, 221, n601

Spartan παιδόνομος, 126

Spengel, L., n382

Stenzel, J., n4, n597

Stesimbrotus, 98

Stilpon, 66, n762

Stobaeus, 102, 131, 141, 149, n88, n604, n646, n650, n688, n690, n699, n813, n821, n852, n872, n891, n899, n900, n972, n1032, n1092, n1093, n1094, n1095, n1118, n1148

Stoic cosmopolitanism, 141 ff.

Strato, n1163

Strepsiades, n887, n1014

Stuart, D. R., n17, n597

Suetonius, n677

Suidas, 69, 70, n1216

Σωφροσύνη is τὰ ἑαυτοῦ πράττειν (an Antisthenian-Cynic statement), 204 ff.

Taureas (*choregos*), 59

Taylor, A. E., 48, 77, n117, n128, n422, n470, n507, n1013, n1186, n1226, n1294

Telecleides, 28

Teles, 142

Tertullian, n121

Thales, 32, 99, 131, n902

Themistius, 69, 70, 71, 114, 116, 146, n72, n751, n752, n753, n754, n757, n759, n761, n762, n776, n800, n809, n843, n844, n949, n964, n985, n988, n989, n990, n991, n1029, n1192

Themistocles, 59, 92, 98, 152, 174, 176, 177, n1227, n1228

Theodectes, 69, n1342

Theodete, n1238

Theodorus, 66, n679, n698

Theodorus of Byzantium, 70, n1327

Theodotus, 34

Theognis, 32, 86, 88, 89, 90, 91, 158, 159, 204, n317, n493, n502, n516, n1042, n1084, n1087, n1357

Theophilus, n121

Theophrastus, 66, 101, 104, n626

Theramenes, n457, n576

Theseus, 97, n578

Thibron, 13

Things without intelligence are without value, 128

Thrasybulus, 73, 75, 96, 182, n573, n1185

Thrasymachus of Chalcedon, 70, n1327

Thucydides, 15, 126, 180, 184, 186, 187, 188, n116, n302, n330, n458, n529, n562, n565, n566, n862, n1140, n1150, n1247, n1248, n1278, n1281, n1283, n1284, n1314, n1316, n1465

Index

Thucydides (son of Melesias), 220
Thyestes, 92, n528
Tisamenus, 182
Toil (πόνος) a good thing, 113, n699; preferable to pleasure, 111 ff.
'Treason' in ancient Greece, 185

Ueberweg-Heinze, n378, n597

Valerius Maximus, n87, n150
Virtue, once acquired can be lost, 60 ff., n757; once acquired cannot be lost, 60, n757, n1408; a matter of exercise, 60 ff.
Voss, O., n333

Waddington, W. H., n1072, n1073
Wegehaupt, J., n259
Wendland, P., n41
Wilamowitz-Moellendorff, U. v., n11, n38, n72, n80, n119, n184, n207, n209, n507, n511, n597, n858, n886, n955
Wilhelm, A., n31
Winckelmann, A. W., n85, n624
Winspear, A. D., n92
Wolff, E., n1439
Wyttenbach, D., n1128

Xanthippe, 151
Xanthippus (son of Pericles), 151
Xeniades, 151, n1016, n1075
Xenocrates, n1163
Xenophanes, n190, n869
Xenophon, *passim*; his absence from Athens, 3, 136, n918; acquainted with the κατηγορία Σωκράτους, 72, 136 ff.; his adaptability, 15; admirer of the Cynic ἐγκράτεια, 132; admirer of Sparta, 132; seems to admit the charges of Polycrates against Socrates, 192, 208 ff., n1136; does not name Alcibiades in *Memorabilia* 1.3.1–4.8.11, 178 ff.; his anachronisms, 8; considers Antisthenian λόγοι Σωκρατικοὶ depository of Socratic teachings, 119, 203, 212, 213, n838; the 'apologist', 12; no friend of Aristippus, n28; his banishment from Athens, 12 ff., 46, n62, n65; his bias, 3, 15, n1138; his characterization of Socrates, 4, 10, 41, 47, 67, 111, 132 ff., 134, 153, n1401; his characterization of persons participating in Socratic conversations, 9, n48; substitutes Charmides for Alcibiades, 11, 178 ff., n 1239; consults λόγοι Σωκρατικοὶ, 137 ff., 212; denies that Socrates suggested maintenance in the Prytaneum, 40, 67; his dependence on Antisthenes, 106, 131, 137 ff., 161, 183, 203, 204, 205 ff., 208, 215, n318; dramatizing witness, 3; his eclecticism, 134, 215, n913; his effort to improve on earlier *Socratica*, 7, 14; his encomia of Socrates, 10, 12, n7, n15; substitutes Euthydemus for Alcibiades, 11, 179, n1223, n1239, n1240, n1241; his Homeric quotations are of Antisthenian (Cynic) origin, n872; his (intentional) fictions, 8, 12, 14, 15; an impostor, 14; invention or substitution of persons with whom Socrates converses, 10 ff.; his lack of historical objectivity, 4, 5, 6, 8, 14, 215, n14; his lack of first-hand information, 3, 6, 7, 8, 14, 16, 131 ff., 136 ff.; his lack of literary skill, 3, 5; his low intellectual level, 4, 6, 11 ff., 15, n44; his literary rivalry with Plato, 212; his 'method', 6; his narrow outlook, 3, 5, 15; not mentioned by Polycrates, 12; used 'Palamedes theme', 219; his participation in Socratic discussions, 7, 9, 14; his 'portraiture' of Socrates, 11 ff., 41; the 'practical man', 8, 11, 51, 54; his reason for Socrates' condemnation, 41 ff.; reduces Socrates to his own level, 12; not regarded as a Socratic, 12, 14; his scanty acquaintance with Socrates, 10, 12, 13 ff., 15, 106, n60, n69, n636; his self-revelatory tendencies, 3, 4, 6, 8, 11, 14 ff., 54, 139; his 'sources', 7, 9, 14, 15, 106, 133 ff.; transforms Socrates into a Cynic, 112, 115, 131 ff.; his 'treason', 12 ff., 45; turns Socrates into an Antisthenian Cynic, 132 ff.; his instability of character, 15; his vanity, 9, 15; his own verdict about his historical objectivity, 15 ff.; his views on friendship, 152, 208; his 'working methods', 106

Zeller, E., n3, n12, n924, n1358, n1365
Zeno of Elea, 59
Zeno the Stoic, 131, 159, n970, n1024, n1116
Zoilus, 70, n1327
Zurborg, A., n31

For Product Safety Concerns and Information please contact our EU
representative GPSR@taylorandfrancis.com
Taylor & Francis Verlag GmbH, Kaufingerstraße 24, 80331 München, Germany

www.ingramcontent.com/pod-product-compliance
Lightning Source LLC
Chambersburg PA
CBHW071758300426
44116CB00009B/1131